# The Navy and German Power Politics, 1862–1914

# The Navy and German Power Politics, 1862–1914

Ivo Nikolai Lambi
*University of Saskatchewan*

Boston

## ALLEN & UNWIN

London                Sydney

**Allen & Unwin, Inc.,**
**Fifty Cross Street, Winchester, Mass. 01890, USA**

George Allen & Unwin (Publishers) Ltd,
40 Museum Street, London WC1A 1LU, UK

George Allen & Unwin (Publishers) Ltd,
Park Lane, Hemel Hempstead, Herts HP2 4TE, UK

George Allen & Unwin Australia Pty Ltd,
8 Napier Street, North Sydney, NSW 2060, Australia


First published in 1984

---

**Library of Congress Cataloging in Publication Data**

Lambi, Ivo Nikolai.
  The navy and German power politics, 1862–1914.
Bibliography: p.
Includes index.
1. Germany. Reichsmarine—History—19th century.   2. Germany.
Reichsmarine—History—20th century.   3. Germany—Military
policy.   4. Germany—Foreign relations—1848–1870.   5. Germany—
Foreign relations—1871–1888.   6. Germany—Foreign relations—1888–
1918.
I. Title.
VA513.L27   1984      359′.00943      84–11071
ISBN 0–04–943035–1 (alk. paper)

---

**British Library Cataloguing in Publication Data**

Lambi, Ivo Nikolai
  The navy and German power politics
1862–1914.
1. Germany. *Kriegsmarine*—History
359′.00943      VA513
ISBN 0–04–943035–1

---

Set in 10 on 11 point Times by Phoenix Photosetting, Chatham
and printed in Great Britain by Mackays of Chatham

# Contents

*To my five children*

*Jon Nikolai Lambi, d.1979*
*Eric Robert Lambi*
*Peter Alexander Lambi, d.1981*
*Katherine Jean Lambi*
*Shauna Elizabeth Lambi*

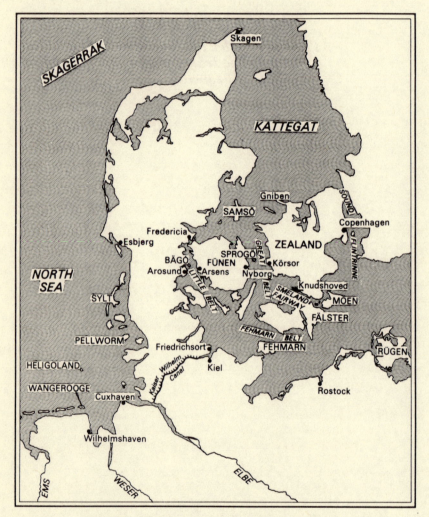

The German North Sea coast and Danish waters

# Preface

This book is a story of power: the attempt in the years 1862–1914 to use the German navy in various ways. At first it was expected to show the flag, to engage in minor skirmishes in world seas and to protect the German coast, particularly against the French. At the beginning of this period the navy was small and its contribution to the Bismarckian wars was negligible in comparison to the achievements of the army. Supporting army operations remained one of its tasks throughout this period. Subsequently its expansion was decided upon. There was debate about how it should occur. From 1900 to 1911–12 it was given priority over the army and it was assigned the additional grandiose task of being the instrument of German *Weltpolitik*, particularly against Britain, and served as a sort of national dream of German imperialism and internal consolidation. But it was never completed for the fulfillment of its functions; it remained incapable of taking on Britain and the Triple Entente militarily; the diplomatic assumptions for its success proved inaccurate; it contributed more than any factor to the deterioration of Anglo-German relations and the "encirclement" of Germany; and in the form that it was conceived, i.e. in terms of battleships, it failed to assist substantially the German war effort in 1914–18.

The story is also one of an armaments race, of the allocation of internal priorities for the needs of defense, and of national defense planning (or lack thereof).

The book was conceived in the spring of 1969 when I visited the Bundesarchiv-Militärarchiv in Freiburg to use the naval materials to write a few chapters on naval operations in my then projected work on German foreign and armaments policy from 1871 to 1914. The introduction to the enormous holdings of naval materials soon convinced me that there was room for a separate study of the operational planning of the German navy before 1914, partly because of the light it would shed on the renewed debate on German responsibility for the outbreak of World War I, partly as a case-study for operational planning in general, and partly because of the information it would provide for the war plans of the Prusso-German army, whose archives were largely destroyed in World War II.

It soon became apparent that naval operations and contacts with the army could not be studied in isolation of other developments. They do, however, constitute the central theme of the book. The concern is chiefly with operations plans against France and Russia, against Britain, and against the United States of America. The plans for ships located abroad are treated only in so far as they involved operations against the European powers, the United States, and Japan. But these plans had to be placed in the context of the strategic building program of the German navy, which would only have impact over a long period of time: the plans of Albrecht von Stosch, Leo von Caprivi, and, above all, Alfred von Tirpitz. Until the navy was ready for its aims (as it was not in 1914), its operational planning and war preparedness would be based on inadequate power. It almost became a joke among German political and army leaders before 1914 that the navy would never be ready for war. I also had to examine the tension between different naval agencies after 1889 when the Admiralty was broken up and even more so after 1899 when Tirpitz managed to split the High Command of the Navy. Not the least issue in this debate involved the contradictions of Tirpitz's long-term building program and the greater need to use the navy immediately which the long-term building made a matter of greater urgency. While Tirpitz played a secondary role in naval operational planning after he was appointed Secretary of State in 1897, his role as the dominating figure in the navy, although chiefly involving building, continued to influence immediate defensive needs, operational planning, diplomacy, and the competence of other naval agencies.

What is more, the operational planning of the Imperial Navy and the Prusso-Imperial Army had to be placed in the framework of international power politics. I have attempted this difficult task. War plans were sometimes prepared for their own sake, lacking relationship to political reality; more often they more or less corresponded to diplomatic conditions or the way they were perceived either by the leaders of the navy, army, or diplomacy. I have made extensive use of German diplomatic records.

I have almost entirely ignored the significance of the Tirpitz Plan for internal German politics, the role of the navy's propaganda, its appeal to industry, the political parties, and the public. These subjects have been well covered by other recent publications; their inclusion in this book would have involved me in rather pedantic debate with excellent if sometimes controversial scholars (whose contribution is acknowledged in the notes and discussed in the bibliographical essay). In terms of the navy in relation to German power politics, this is the most complete study as yet undertaken.

I am indebted to many individuals and agencies. I should first acknowledge the help of the late Dr Gert Sandhofer of the Bundesarchiv-Militärarchiv; Dr Fleischer of the same agency recently helped me to identify an important naval officer whose signature I was unable to decipher. I have been greatly assisted by the rest of the staff of the Bundesarchiv-Militärarchiv, the staffs of the Foreign Office Archives in Bonn, the Bundesarchiv in Koblenz, particularly its former president Dr Wolfgang A. Mommsen, of the Baden, Bavarian and Württemberg state archives, the Bismarck-Archiv in Friedrichsruh, and, during my brief stay in Vienna, the staff of the Austrian War Archives. I owe deep gratitude to Professor Paul M. Kennedy, Professor J. Michael Hayden, and my brother-in-law Dr David M. McConnaughey, who read all of the manuscript, and to Professor Hubert C. Johnson, who read much of it, for their time, effort, and many valuable suggestions. My wife Jackie, who read all of the text, criticized it, and was scolded in return, put up with me as did my five children. Mmes Janice Falk-MacNeill, Jean Horosko, Margaret MacVean, and Miss Suzan Piot typed many of my notes and earlier versions of the manuscript. Mrs Jean Horosko, assisted by Miss Suzan Piot and Mrs Jeanne Marken, typed the final version on a word processor under the supervision of Mrs Jackie Fraser. While in Germany, I enjoyed the hospitality and help of many people, particularly my close friends Herr Peter and Frau Renate Bopp, my *Betreuer* for the Alexander von Humboldt-Stiftung Professor Dr Karl Erich Born, my stepfather's brother and his wife Herr Fritz and Frau Anne-Maria Deutsch, and the late Prince Otto von Bismarck. My close friend and former teacher Professor John B. Wolf and my adviser, the late Professor Lawrence D. Steefel, have been sources of inspiration and encouragement.

The research and writing of what eventually took the form of this book were supported by the Canada Council in 1967–68 through a Senior Fellowship, in the summer of 1973 through a Research Grant, its successor The Social Sciences and Humanities Research Council of Canada in 1982–83 through a Leave Fellowship, the Alexander von Humboldt-Stiftung through a *Dozenten-Stipendium* from 1967 to 1969, an interim grant in the summer of 1974, and excellent accommodation and other assistance in the first part of 1983, and the University of Saskatchewan through sabbatical leaves in 1975–76 and 1982–83, several research grants, secretarial help, and general encouragement. Mr Keith M. Ashfield of Allen & Unwin was very encouraging and helpful. I alone am responsible for any of the shortcomings of this book.

Bad Godesberg (Bonn 2),                                              I. N. LAMBI
Federal Republic of Germany,
June 1983.

# 1 Beginnings of Construction, 1862–88

Apart from memories of the Hanse, the traditions of the Imperial German Navy go back no further than to the middle of the nineteenth century—to the naval enthusiasm of 1848 and the slow development of a Prussian navy under the leadership of Prince Adalbert. In 1867 the Prussian navy became an institution of the North German Confederation and in 1871 of the German Empire. During the Bismarckian wars the navy played only a modest part. Comprehensive plans for construction, however, had already been proposed during the Prussian constitutional struggle. They were not accepted by the Prussian House of Representatives and hence their importance is confined to their reflection of current Prussian naval thinking and to their anticipation of subsequent plans. A project submitted by Albrecht von Roon in his capacity as Minister of the Navy to the House of Representatives in July 1862 proposed an eight-year plan which was to provide for the construction of two naval bases, one on the Jade in the North Sea, where territory had been acquired from Oldenburg in 1853, and the other on the island of Rügen in the Baltic, and of a number of ships.[1] Coastal defense, involving possible offensive activity, and protection of Prusso-Zollverein interests overseas were the twin responsibilities of the Prussian navy.[2]

Roon's more ambitious project of 1865 followed the inconclusive joint Austro-Prussian naval activity against the superior naval power of tiny Denmark[3] and took account of the Prussian acquisition of Kiel, a highly favorable site for a naval base. Bismarck had gained Wilhelm's consent for the transfer of the Baltic Sea naval station from Danzig to Kiel before Prussia had acquired that city from Austria at Gastein. He had also been converted by Prince Adalbert to the idea of connecting the North Sea and the Baltic with a canal and even considered extending the canal from the Elbe to the Weser and from there through the Jade to the Ems. This would have provided an interior communication system for the North Sea. The Minister-President supported Roon's plan and was to challenge its critic, the pathologist Rudolf Virchow, to a duel. A bill of 1865 provided for an immediate appropriation for the construction of a naval base in the Kiel Bay serving the Baltic Sea, for the completion of the future Wilhelmshaven in the Jade Bight, and for the acquisition of two armored frigates and the improvement of the armament of available ships.[4] A twelve-year plan, drafted by Roon in cooperation with the Admiralty Council, identified Prussian maritime interests with those of the rest of Germany. The tasks of the fleet were to consist of:

(1) defense and representation of the emerging shipping of Prussia and Germany on all seas and the extension of their rights and relations;

(2) defense of the coasts and harbors of the Fatherland in the Baltic and North Seas;

(3) development of an offensive capacity not only for the disturbance of enemy shipping but also for attacks on hostile fleets, coasts and harbors.[5]

It was maintained that limited finances and a relatively small seafaring population precluded the building of a navy which could fulfill all its tasks if confronted by a naval power of the first rank. The Prussian navy was restricted to second-class status. It was to consist of three basic types of ship: (*a*) armored frigates which were to maintain the high seas against the enemy, do battle in the open sea, and, if necessary, force the passage between the Baltic and North Seas through Danish waters; (*b*) armored batteries and smaller units such as gunboats which were to defend the coast but also be able to assist the frigates on the high seas; and (*c*) ships which were to protect indigenous and damage enemy trade on the high seas. In addition came dispatch-boats, transport-ships for landing troops on enemy coasts, and school and artillery units.

The fleet was to be composed of ten armored frigates, ten larger coastal-defense units, and fourteen ships for the protection and damaging of trade. Armored frigates "as the core of the battle fleet"[6] were given priority. "The implementation of the fleet plan in its full extent will have to be governed by the availability of the necessary funds. None the less . . . the speediest possible establishment of a respectable Prussian naval power is absolutely necessary in the interest of trade and power relationships."

Modest in scope, aspiring only to second-class naval strength, the plans of 1862 and 1865 none the less emancipated the fleet from the coast, represented the battle fleet as the core of naval power, and provided for a long-term building schedule without, however, requiring the Prussian legislature to commit itself in advance to the expenditure.

The tasks of the navy as defined by Roon and the Admiralty Council in 1865 were restated in the construction plan presented to the Reichstag of the North German Federation in October 1867.[7] To fulfill all three tasks, "a navy . . . must be of such a strength and structure as to be able with one part to protect trade in the far seas, with the second to defend the coasts of its country, and with the most important and strongest part to attack the main force of the enemy in the high seas, throw it back into its harbors, and blockade it there." The number of ships necessary for the attainment of all three tasks could not yet be determined. To achieve a fleet in an orderly and economical fashion, however, long-term planning was essential. "For the first stage of development a period of ten years has been taken, because within it the construction of the harbors can be completed and, further, a fleet can be built which provides the necessary defense and representation for maritime trade and fulfills the defensive part of the above-stated tasks, finally because in this period the training of the personnel . . . can be promoted which according to calculations is necessary for the fleet that is to be constructed."

In ten years the fleet was to consist of sixteen armored ships and vehicles, twenty corvettes, eight dispatch-boats, three transport-ships, twenty-two steam-driven gunboats, two artillery-training ships, and five school ships. Nine large and eight small ships were to be commissioned for service at five overseas stations, and a training squadron of six armored and four other ships in European waters was to be ready for action in case of war or for the relief of ships abroad.

In the first stage of development, in contrast to previous plans, the offensive capability in European waters was played down. In the words of Kontre-Admiral Eduard Karl Emanuel Jachmann in October 1867, priority was to be given to the construction of those ships "which are suitable for the commercial-political tasks of the navy or for coastal defense," that is, smaller units.[8] Only after the completion of the first stage could the third task, the offensive purpose of the navy, be realized through a more rapid construction of ships. The plan was accepted by the Reichstag with objections expressed only to the fiscal arrangements. Since, contrary to his Reichstag statement, Jachmann was an adherent of large battleships, he succeeded under the vague category of "sixteen armored ships and vehicles" to commission in 1869–71 the construction of five such ships, three in Germany, and two in England,[9] and to purchase three others abroad.[10] Three of these ships were larger than any other built in Germany before the accession of Wilhelm II.

In spite of the completion of Wilhelmshaven on the Jade as a naval base and the availability of the three large ships that were purchased, the North German navy, in stark contrast to the army, played an undistinguished role in the Franco-Prussian War. Probably in recognition of the weakness of its navy, the Presidency of the North German Confederation declared at Bismarck's insistence, shortly after the declaration of war, that there would be no action against French commercial shipping. Commerce warfare was only reluctantly undertaken later in the war.[11] As Albrecht von Stosch remarked, "It will certainly not be advantageous for the development of the navy that it had no importance whatsoever in this war . . . But thereby it is not damned for all eternity . . . we may eventually be in great need of it."[12] In 1870–71, Bismarck categorically refused to accept French ships in place of annexations on the grounds that there were no officers or ratings to man them.

In the new Empire "From 1871 to 1888 the navy worked under land generals." Roon and Prince Adalbert were both ailing; the former was incapable of retaining responsibility for the navy and the latter of assuming it. As no naval officer appeared suitable for or willing to take on the position, Stosch, a highly competent general, was to be the Chief of the newly established Imperial Admiralty from 1872 to 1883. Not lacking in political ambition, friend of the Crown Prince and Princess, Stosch was to appear to Bismarck as a potential rival and head of a "Gladstone ministry."[13] His tenure of the Admiralty involved him in many conflicts with Bismarck,[14] which did not advance the interests of the navy. Bismarck, however, did not discourage forceful representation of Germany's interests overseas by her naval forces as long as such action served his aims. Stosch presented a plan of naval construction to the Reichstag in 1873 which was viewed as the guide for German naval development until 1897 when Tirpitz tried to link his first navy law to it.

Soon after being appointed Chief of the Imperial Admiralty, Stosch reported to Bismarck about the progress made in implementing the plan of 1867.[15] He mentioned the impossibility of completing the plan by 1877 and the increase in costs. He concluded by stressing the need for a canal between the Baltic and North Seas which would augment the strength of the Imperial Navy, facilitate what was called "offensive coastal defense," and make it necessary for the enemy either to concentrate much superior naval forces for action in either sea or to refrain from attacking the German coasts. The plan that Bismarck in 1873[16] forwarded to the Reichstag revised the requirements of 1867. Increasing German trade, greater national consciousness among Germans living abroad, and more attention paid by established naval powers to German naval development were viewed as enhancing the tasks of German ships overseas. Their number was to be increased substantially to a total of six armored frigates (those that were also included in the defense of the North Sea), eighteen corvettes and six gunboats. There were to be two overseas stations, the Far Eastern and West Indian, an overseas squadron, and a substantial reserve.

Coastal defense was closely linked to the development of offensive capacity—both of which were established as tasks of the navy according to construction plans of 1865 and 1867. ". . . [It] is beyond question that the most effective defense in wartime lies in a firm attack on the enemy." But, as Stosch stated both as a general and as a realist, in a major war Germany's offensive strength lay with her army.

On 3 December 1871 he had written to his friend Gustav Freytag: "We need ships which are suitable to secure the merchant marine through offensive action, and the squadrons which we station on remote shores must also comprise such ships. But I consider large battleships still to be erroneous and superfluous for our conditions, since we cannot for a long time be called to fight a naval battle."[17] To the Reichstag he stated: "For one point cannot be forgotten in the comparison of land and sea war: every hostile place which is occupied becomes an actual success, a seized ship only becomes important when the sum total of a war is computed. A captured fortress secures a province. The capture of a whole fleet at the most provides the means to begin a conquest." As for the offensive capacity of the fleet: "It does not, according to the now envisaged plan, have the task to proceed offensively against the great European states, but it should extend our power only where we have to represent lesser interests and where we cannot otherwise bring to bear the actual power of our state, our power on land . . . The question how we will protect our merchant marine in case of a European war is not answered, because the German navy would not be capable of doing this in a war with the great naval powers. This can only be done indirectly by our land forces. The German navy will only contribute to the outcome."

The defense of the North Sea and of the Baltic Sea had to be viewed separately as long as there was no canal serving as an internal line of communication between the two theatres of operation. Since hostile land operations were difficult because of the nature of the German coast, it sufficed to concentrate coastal defense forces in the form of batteries and torpedo-boats and gunboats at particularly vulnerable points. The defense of the North Sea was regarded as being easier than that of the Baltic since in it the vulnerable area was limited to the Elbe, Weser, and Jade estuaries into each of which the defending fleet could withdraw. The enemy, however, had the advantage of using British-owned Heligoland as a base. In order to prevent a permanent blockade "our defensive means must be at least approximately as strong as his offensive means." Germany would therefore need eight large armored frigates, of which six could be also detached abroad. The defense of the longer and therefore more vulnerable Baltic coast was regarded as more difficult. It must be conducted independently from Kiel and from another base in the east. "If the German navy in the Baltic Sea were to be restricted to the single harbor of Kiel it would never dare to wage a battle in the east, for it cannot count on returning to Kiel with a damaged ship." For the Baltic Sea, therefore, the plan envisaged beside the completion of the base at Kiel the construction of a dockyard in Danzig and the presence of six smaller battleships described as armored corvettes whose smaller size would be more suitable for its shallower waters. Twenty-eight torpedo-boats, two floating batteries, seven dispatch-boats and some gunboats were to be distributed among the Baltic coastal ports for local defense.

The eight armored frigates required for service overseas or for the defense of the North Sea coast which were either available or in construction, together with the six armored corvettes in the Baltic, formed a force of fourteen ships described as battleships. The composition of the fleet is set out in Table 1.1.[18]

Stosch's plan was a setback in Prussian–German naval planning in so far as the offensive tasks of the navy in European waters were moved further into the background and coastal defense forces were fragmented. Greater emphasis was placed on overseas service, and the armored frigates required for this purpose were also to serve for the defense of the North Sea.

Table 1.1

| | Total strength | Ready | In construction | To be built |
|---|---|---|---|---|
| Armored frigates | 8 | 3 | 5 | – |
| Armored corvettes | 6 | – | 1 | 5 |
| Armored monitors | 7 | 2 | – | 5 |
| Armored floating batteries | 2 | – | – | 2 |
| Corvettes | 20 | 10 | 2 | 8 |
| Dispatch-boats | 6 | 2 | – | 4 |
| Gunboats | 18 | 18 | – | – |
| Torpedo-vehicles | 28 | 6 | – | 22 |

None the less, Stosch occupies a significant place in German naval history. He increased the number of naval personnel, improved their training and discipline, regularly built and replaced ships according to plan,[19] and cultivated relations with the press, industry, and members of the Reichstag. Toward the end of his career Stosch may have realized the importance of emancipating the navy from the coast and using it for gaining mastery of the seas and for the defense of German world interests.[20] By 1884 most of the goals set by the plan of 1873 had been met. Only one of the twenty corvettes required for overseas service had remained unbuilt, although those that had been constructed were antiquated by the time they entered service. As for the naval forces to be used in home waters, of the six armored corvettes that were to be constructed, five had been built, four ships of the Saxony class, launched between 1877 and 1880, and *Oldenburg,* launched in 1884. These were ships of limited range, seaworthiness, and fighting value. Most of the required torpedo-boats were not yet available and some modifications were made in the plan. It had been decided not to build the two armored floating batteries because of their vulnerability to torpedoes, and to build, instead of the five dispatch-boats, thirteen armored gunboats, each armed with a single short-barrelled 30·5 cm gun. These were cheaper, could be more effectively distributed along the coast and could, together with torpedo-boats, attack superior hostile forces from coastal waters.[21]

Naval construction fared considerably worse under another very gifted general, the later Chancellor, Leo von Caprivi, who headed the Admiralty from 1883 to 1888. Unlike Stosch, Caprivi never felt at ease in his naval position and was widely disliked.[22] He later described his attitude toward the navy as having consistently been that it "must be kept within narrow limits, as narrow as our conditions permit," that it was to be assigned lower priority than the army, and was to be relegated to the defensive.[23] Tirpitz, however, claims that under him the navy obtained a strategic aim which it had lacked under Stosch, namely "to prepare a strong coastal defense for the next war against Russia and France."[24]

In consultation with the Admiralty Council, Caprivi made the basic decision at the beginning of his tenure to reject the primacy of cruiser war and to continue to build armored ships while emphasizing the new torpedo weapon. Bismarck tried to establish a better relationship with Caprivi than he had had with Stosch. He estimated naval strength in a Continental war as superior to the Danish, equal to the Russian, and, if the Baltic–North Sea canal were completed, able to defend the German coast against both France and Russia. In the face of Caprivi's objections, which coincided with those of his predecessor Stosch, and Moltke, he continued to emphasize the need for the canal.[25] Otherwise he supported Caprivi's plans, which were summarized in the "Memorandum concerning the further development of the Imperial Navy" submitted to the Reichstag on 11 March 1884.[26]

The memorandum reflected the prevailing uncertainties about naval construction. Considering the tasks set by Stosch's plan of 1873 as solved, Caprivi refused to propose another long-term plan for naval development and instead looked at aims that could be reached within the next three or four years. Any long-range projections would be too theoretical and might either have to be modified considerably or become dogma that would thwart further development. The existing naval strength was described as a minimum for peacetime or wartime tasks. But whether the promotion of one or another branch of the navy should be given higher priority "would depend either on military–political considerations or on technology." None the less, Caprivi admitted that the navy could not live from hand to mouth. He paid lip-service to the need for replacing out-of-date ships at a regular pace, partly to enable dockyards to maintain a permanent labor force.

Apart from those used for training, ships were classified into three groups: (*a*) ships used for political service, including unarmored corvettes, gunboats and dispatch-boats, (*b*) battleships, and (*c*) ships for coastal defense, primarily the requested torpedo-boats.

The twenty unarmored corvettes, ten gunboats and a few dispatch-boats located overseas were considered relatively useless in case of a European war. Contrary to the *jeune école,* Caprivi considered commerce raiding as an anachronism: ". . . the development of steam shipping has reached a point where cruiser warfare against merchantmen and passenger-boats becomes progressively less favorable. The manifold requirements that the builder of warships has to meet do not allow him to build almost exclusively for high speed, as is now the case with many passenger and other boats."[27]

Armored battleships were described as the core of a fleet. Without them ships used for political service abroad would lack support, Germany would be valueless as an ally in a war against navally superior powers, and be unable to fight even the weakest of the European naval powers or to attack any coastal place. ". . . [W]herever there is struggle for control of a part of a sea, one cannot dispense with armored ships and heavy artillery. Every European fleet must have in mind such a struggle and must prepare a part of its forces accordingly if it wants to remain a fleet at all. A navy which concentrates on the land or on the coast no longer deserves its name."[28] Except for referring to control of the sea in relative rather than in absolute terms, these words are worthy of a Tirpitz. But then came serious qualifications: a battle at sea is less decisive than one on land and, as trials may determine, many small armored ships such as corvettes and gunboats may be preferable to a few gigantic ones. Caprivi was by no means alone in lacking faith in large ships. "The enormously destructive power of the torpedo and the apparent impossibility for even battleships to withstand its attack led many to believe that the heavily armored and armed warship was doomed and that in the future only small fast ships, armed with light guns and strongly fortified bows for ramming, should be constructed."[29] While during the next three or four years a waiting stance was to be taken in the construction of armored ships and ships for service abroad, certainty concerning the development of the torpedo weapon and pressing urgency for coastal defense justified the demand for the immediate construction of seventy torpedo-boats. "The torpedo-boats are a weapon that is of particular value for a power that is weaker on the high seas"[30] and, if well employed, would make a close blockade of a coast very difficult. Since 1878 the development of the torpedo had been greatly advanced in Germany by Alfred von Tirpitz. In 1886 the Torpedo Inspection had been established under his headship. He, however, concluded that the purpose of torpedo-boats was the support of the battle fleet rather than coastal defense, as Caprivi had thought in 1884. The cheap torpedo-boats "were considered by many naval officers as a type of panacea for the supremacy in numbers of foreign battle fleets."[31]

By the end of May 1886, Caprivi informed Bismarck that increased Russian shipbuilding could make the Russian Baltic Sea fleet superior to the entire German navy, and asked whether any countermeasures were being contemplated. In a marginal comment to this letter Bismarck remarked that Germany would have to consider combined Franco-Russian naval power—which it would never be able to match—rather than just Russian naval power, since it was certain that France would join Russia in any conflict with Germany. He subsequently stated that he was prepared to increase the size of the navy to the extent that Germany's manpower and finances allowed and asked if it could reach a strength surpassed only by Britain or France.[32]

Bismarck's encouraging reply did not affect Caprivi. In a secret memorandum, probably drafted in June 1886,[33] Caprivi maintained that, while naval power was important because of world trade, definite limits were imposed on Germany's naval development by her inability to train many additional recruits and by competition for funds with the army, on which the most important military decisions depended. "Only after another victorious struggle for Germany's existence has taken place will consideration for overseas relations of the Reich assume full significance. Until then additional requests for money and men will have to be kept within modest limits in so far as the navy is concerned."

Ideas of the *jeune école* were again rejected. Germany was viewed as being in an unfavorable position for raiding enemy commerce, since the nearby Baltic and North Seas offered poor prospects for it and in remoter waters German raiders lacked the support of bases and coaling stations. For the raiding that would have to be done as a matter of honor or for the representation of German interests abroad in peacetime small unarmored cruisers would be adequate. In so far as battleships were concerned, Caprivi had by now also decided in favor of smaller units. In view of her limited means, Germany should avoid competing with other powers in the size, armor, and armament of battleships, particularly since many small ships could be as effective as a few large ships and since the loss of one of many small ships was less serious than that of one of a few large ships. But "Even concerning those ships used in home waters, we have to see to it that they are of such size as not to be confined to river estuaries and harbors, but capable of attacking in the open sea. We should not build a single ship or vehicle that is not capable of doing battle before Copenhagen or Kronstadt and which cannot fight by Heligoland." Caprivi was obviously also thinking about more offensive operations.

Caprivi then elaborated on his earlier-expressed doubts about the value of naval battles. Important as a successful battle would be for the morale of a young navy which coexisted with a glorious army, the outcome of a battle at sea was less predictable than that of a land battle and the German navy would probably have to face superior opponents. Unlike those on land, sea battles were decisive not in themselves, but only in their results, such as landings or blockades. Nor would a naval battle guarantee the victor control of the sea, but only of parts of the sea such as the Baltic, the Mediterranean, or the English Channel. While battle was therefore not the aim of German naval construction, Germany was not to refrain from constructing battleships which remained necessary for use in coastal waters. And there were always exceptions to the rule of avoiding naval battle: in the case of a war against Russia alone Germany might want to seek such a decision as soon as possible.

To deliver offensive blows, one needed armored ships and armored vehicles "which should be at the same time capable of moving freely in the North Sea and, if necessary, participating in the long-distance expeditions." Caprivi concluded that the construction of such armored vehicles was to be the next task of German naval development. These were the Siegfried-class armored ships which he requested in the budget of 1887–88.[34] Ten such ships, now described as armored gunboats, each 3,000 tons in displacement and equipped with two 24 cm guns, were to be built in approximately a decade. The memorandum enclosed with the 1887–88 budget repeated many arguments of the June 1886 memorandum, some of them verbatim, but, in sharp contrast to it, took a favorable view of commerce raiding, according to Hallmann for the sole reason that faster cruisers had recently been constructed.[35] "Against naval powers with considerable sea trade, after the advances made in the technology of ship and machine construction, cruiser war, even if slow in its effects, can none the less become decisive."[36] The *jeune école* thus affected the planning of the German naval leadership. It was to confuse its building program until 1897.

At Bismarck's insistence Caprivi's objections to the construction of the canal between the Baltic and the North Seas were overcome and the project was approved by the Reichstag in February 1886 and completed in 1895. Extending from the Bay of Kiel into the Elbe estuary, sufficiently wide and deep to enable passage of even the largest men-of-war, the canal was to make it possible for the German naval forces, whether located in the North Sea or in the Baltic, to operate jointly or separately in either sea by using an internal line of communication and without risking the dangerous passage through potentially or actually hostile Danish straits. A completed canal would also strengthen the offensive capacity of the German navy. As the then Chief of Staff of the Admiralty, Kapitän-zur-See Friedrich Hollmann, explained to the Reichstag committee examining the canal bill, "With coastal vehicles and torpedo-boats one can defend the coast; against a blockade only an offensive fleet can protect us," which with the help of the canal could be emancipated from tasks of coastal defense. It would be no exaggeration, he claimed, to say that the canal would double the strength of the fleet.[37]

Caprivi also encouraged the study of tactics. In the "Twelve tactical questions" which he posed on 30 January 1888 to a committee of naval officers as well as to several naval agencies, he did explore the operations of a fleet of twelve armored ships in the open seas against a hostile line. He inquired into questions such as what would be the appropriate battle formation, at what distance was gunfire to open, how the opposite battle line was to be broken through or surrounded, and what was the role of close-up battle or the mêlée. The questions were those of a sailor, not of a soldier concentrating on coastal defense.[38] Caprivi's preliminary conclusion drawn from the replies was that "There is no doubt that any final decision in a naval battle will occur in a totally lawless and leaderless confusion, the mêlée." In such a mêlée more depended on voluntary cooperation, morale, and the officer corps than on *matériel* or the personality of the commander, who could not oversee the chaotic fighting. "Rules for a mêlée are few and simple. For every ship sunk a hostile ship must be incapacitated. No ship should leave the mêlée as long as it can use any of its weapons. Torpedo-boats are not to leave the mêlée when they have used up their torpedoes, but are to hinder hostile torpedo-boats . . . the purpose of the mêlée is not the capture but the destruction of the enemy's fleet."[39] As will be seen in the next chapter, he also developed the operations plans which effectively freed the German fleet from the coast.

## Notes: Chapter 1

1   Prussia, Landtag, *Haus der Abgeordneten, 1862. Anlagen,* Anlage I zu Aktenstück No. 153, "Leitende Grundgedanken für die Entwickelung unserer Kriegsmarine," p. 1621.
2   ibid.
3   Reinhold Gadow, *Geschichte der deutschen Marine* (Frankfurt, 1943), pp. 32–4.
4   A brief treatment of Roon's activity as Minister of the Navy is Elmar Dinter, "Albrecht von Roon: Seine Stellung und sein Wirken als Marineminister in Preussen, im Norddeutschen Bund und im Deutschen Reich," *Marine-Rundschau,* vol. 68, No. 8 (1971) pp. 467–78. Also see Prussia, Landtag, *Haus der Abgeordneten, 1865. Anlagen,* Aktenstück No. 111, "Entwurf eines Gesetzes betreffend den ausserordentlichen Geldbedarf der Marineverwaltung," p. 909. For Bismarck, see Hans-Otto Steinmetz, *Bismarck und die Deutsche Marine* (Herford, 1974), pp. 20, 22–3.
5   Militärgeschichtliches Forschungsamt, *Handbuch zur deutschen Militärgeschichte, 1648–1939.* 7. Lieferung. VIII. *Deutsche Marinegeschichte der Neuzeit* (Munich, 1977), p. 83. For the activity of the German navy abroad, see Wolfgang Petter, "Die überseeische Stützpunktpolitik der preussisch-deutschen Kriegsmarine 1859–1881," University of Freiburg doctoral dissertation, 1975, and Willi A. Boelcke, *So kam das Meer zu uns: Die preussisch-deutsche Kriegsmarine in Übersee 1822 bis 1914* (Frankfurt, 1981).
6   Prussia, Landtag, 1865, Aktenstück No. 111, p. 912. Different figures appear in *Deutsche Marinegeschichte der Neuzeit,* p. 83.
7   *Stenographische Berichte der Verhandlungen des Nord-Deutschen Reichstags,* Session 1867, Legis. I, Vol. 4, Anlagen, Aktenstück No. 106, "Entwurf des Gesetzes Betreffend den ausserordentlichen Geldbedarf des Nord-deutschen Bundes zum Zwecke der Erweiterung der Bundes-Kriegsmarine und der Herstellung der Küstenverteidigung, nebst Motive."
8   ibid., Legis. I, Vol. 26, Sitzung, 22 Oktober 1867. Jachmann was Director of the Naval Department in the Naval Ministry.
9   *Grosser Kurfürst,* 6,779 tons and 5,400 HP, and her sister ships *Friedrich der Grosse* and *Preussen* were to be built in Germany, and *Kaiser,* 7,676 tons and 8,000 HP, and her

sister ship *Deutschland* were to be built in England. See Hans Hallmann, *Der Weg zum deutschen Schlachtflottenbau* (Stuttgart, 1933), pp. 6–7.

10  *Kronprinz*, 5,600 tons, in England; *König Wilhelm*, 9,800 tons, in England; and *Prinz Friedrich Karl*, 6,800 tons, in France. Gadow, *Geschichte*, p. 36.

11  Steinmetz, *Bismarck*, pp. 26–8. *Denkwürdigkeiten des Generals und Admirals Albrecht von Stosch, ersten Chef der Admiralität, Briefe und Tagebuchblätter*, ed. Ulrich von Stosch (Stuttgart, 1904), entry for 4 January 1871, p. 220.

12  Steinmetz, *Bismarck*, pp. 30–1.

13  Alfred von Tirpitz, *Erinnerungen* (Leipzig, 1919), p. 11; Steinmetz, *Bismarck*, pp. 32, 35–7; 51, 66. Frederick B. M. Hollyday, *Bismarck's Rival: A Political Biography of General and Admiral Albrecht von Stosch* (Durham, NC, 1960), pp. 136–251 passim.

14  Steinmetz, *Bismarck*, pp. 38 ff.; *Deutsche Marinegeschichte der Neuzeit*, pp. 103–8.

15  Bundesarchiv-Militärarchiv, Freiburg (henceforth abbreviated as BA-MA) F 2030/PG 66012, Stosch to Bismarck, 8 March 1872, enclosing "Denkschrift betreffend eine Darlegung wie weit der in den Motiven von Anleihegesetz vom 9 November 1867 enhaltene Plan für die Entwickelung der Kaiserlichen Marine—der sogenannte Flotten-Gründungs-Plan bereits zur Ausführung gelangt und welche Mittel noch erforderlich sind zu seiner Durchführung."

16  *Stenographische Berichte über die Verhandlungen des Deutschen Reichstags*, I Legislatur-Periode, IV Session, 1873, Vol. 3, Anlagen, No. 50, Bismarck to Simpson, 21 April 1873, enclosing "Denkschrift betreffend die Entwickelung der Kaiserlichen Marine und die sich daraus ergebenden materiellen und finanziellen Forderungen," pp. 236 ff.

17  Quoted in Ulrich von Hassell, *Tirpitz: Sein Leben und Wirken mit Berücksichtigung seiner Beziehungen zu Albrecht von Stosch* (Stuttgart, 1920), pp. 24–5.

18  See Hallman, *Der Weg*, p. 14.

19  See particularly Hollyday, *Bismarck's Rival*, pp. 99–136; Hassell, *Tirpitz*, pp. 23–47.

20  He expressed these views in an article, "Die deutsche Marine und die Kolonisation," which he wrote in September and November 1884, unsuccessfully tried to publish in the *Kölnische Zeitung,* and subsequently sent as a memorandum to his successor Leo von Caprivi. See Hollyday, *Bismarck's Rival*, pp. 243–54.

21  See *Stenographische Berichte über die Verhandlungen des Deutschen Reichstags*, V Legislatur-Periode, IV Session, 1884, Vol. 3, Anlagen, "Denkschrift betreffend die Ausführung des Flottengründungsplans von 1873," submitted by Boetticher to the Reichstag on 6 March 1884, pp. 101–70. *Deutsche Marinegeschichte der Neuzeit*, pp. 127–8.

22  Tirpitz, *Erinnerungen*, p. 23–4; *Denkwürdigkeiten des General-Feldmarschalls Alfred Grafen von Waldersee*, ed. Heinrich-Otto Meisner, 3 vols (Stuttgart, 1922), diary entry of 8 November 1887, Vol. 1, p. 332. For Caprivi's appointment, see Steinmetz, *Bismarck*, pp. 68–9. *Deutsche Marinegeschichte der Neuzeit*, pp. 129–30.

23  Schulthess, *Europäischer Geschichtskalendar 1893* (Munich, 1894), pp. 20–1.

24  Tirpitz, *Erinnerungen*, p. 24; Hallmann, *Der Weg*, p. 25. Senden-Bibran's assessment of Caprivi is more negative. He considers Caprivi to have achieved most in mobilization arrangements, transferring effectively to the navy his rich army experiences. BA-MA N 160/11 "Erlebnisse als Chef des Marine Kabinetts, Notizen und Auf Zeichnungen."

25  Steinmetz, *Bismarck*, pp. 70–1.

26  *Stenographische Berichte über die Verhandlungen des Deutschen Reichstags*, V Legislatur-Periode, IV Session, 1884, Vol. 3, Anlagen, No. 26, "Entwurf eines Gesetzes betreffend die Bewilligung von Mitteln zu Zwecken der Marineverwaltung," submitted by Boetticher to the Reichstag on 11 March 1884, enclosing the "Denkschrift betreffend die weitere Entwickelung der Kaiserlichen Marine," pp. 430 ff.

27  ibid., "Denkschrift," p. 434.

28  ibid., p. 435.

29  Arthur J. Marder, *The Anatomy of British Sea Power* (London, 1940), p. 124.

30  "Denkschrift," p. 437.

31  Hassell, *Tirpitz*, p. 51; *Deutsche Marinegeschichte der Neuzeit*, p. 133.

32  Steinmetz, *Bismarck*, p. 72.

33  BA-MA, F 3187, Adhib. 18, III, 1.–1., Vol. 1, "Über die weitere Entwickelung der Marine." At first glance this memorandum appears to be dated 14 June 1882. But on that date Caprivi had as yet nothing to do with the navy and the file concerned opens in March

1883 and has no closing date. Upon closer examination the figure 2 may be a carelessly executed 6 or 4. Moreover, the request made in this memorandum for small armored ships for coastal defense suggests a date close to 1887 when such ships were requested from the Reichstag. I therefore suggest 14 June 1886 as the date for the document.

34  Hallmann, *Der Weg*, p. 35.
35  ibid.
36  Quoted from Volker R. Berghahn, *Der Tirpitz-Plan: Genesis und Verfall einer innenpolitischen Krisenstrategie unter Wilhelm II* (Düsseldorf, 1971), p. 55.
37  A summary of Hollmann's comments appears in *Stenographische Berichte,* pp. 678–9, Anlagen, No. 149, "Bericht der XI Kommission über den derselben zur Vorberathung überwiesenen Gesetzentwurf, betreffend die Herstellung des Nord-Ostseekanals."
38  BA-MA, N 253(Nachlass Tirpitz)/35, Caprivi, "Zwölf taktische Fragen."
39  ibid., Caprivi to Knorr, Chef der Manöverflotte, 1 April 1888, "Nur zur vertraulichen Kenntniss für die Herrn Offiziere."

# 2 Operations Plans under Stosch and Caprivi, 1877–88

Tirpitz was to claim that "Stosch hardly had to reckon with a direct enemy." In the first years of Stosch's tenure of office the navy held an insignificant position beside the victorious army on which, of course, fell the burden of operations in a continental war against France, or, as generally anticipated by Moltke after 1879, against both France and Russia.[1] In such a war the Imperial Navy had as its main bases the Baltic Sea station in Kiel and the North Sea station in Wilhelmshaven. Another important harbor in the Baltic Sea was Danzig. Naval operations had to take account of the geography of the German coasts. Denmark divided German naval operations into two theaters of war. Her probable hostility to Germany because of the legacy of Schleswig-Holstein would create serious difficulties for the movement of German warships through the Danish Belts and the Sound in wartime. Danish territory could also serve as a base of operations of other powers against Germany. The two theaters of war would be united through the construction of a canal linking the Kiel Bay with the Elbe; its construction was started only in 1887 and it was finally opened in 1895.

Several North Sea islands, among them Borkum, Sylt, Pellworm, and above all Heligoland (in British possession until 1890), were important for German naval operations. These islands, if unfortified, could be seized by a stronger naval power and used as bases for the blockade of the German North Sea coast. But, if strongly fortified, they would serve as an effective deterrent and defense against a close blockade. Ships in the North Sea naval station in Wilhelmshaven, in the Jade Bight toward the west of the German North Sea coast, were exposed to the danger of being cut off from the rest of the German fleet by a strong naval power at the beginning of war. The German Baltic Sea coast was longer and less defensible than that of the North Sea. Until the completion of the Kaiser Wilhelm Canal a powerful enemy in control of Danish waters could threaten to enclose the German Baltic Sea forces in their major base in Kiel. Ships at the Danzig base could be cut off by energetic Russian action. The eastern location of the fortress of Königsberg, which served as the base for the First Army Corps, exposed it to the danger of being cut off by Russian land forces. This eventuality posed the problem of Königsberg having to be supplied and reinforced by sea. This possible task, as well as naval action against the Russian coast for the support of the operations of the army, raised in the eastern war theater more acutely than in the west the need of army–navy cooperation.

If Germany's naval forces were divided by geography, so were those of her potential continental enemies. The Russian European naval forces were after 1871 concentrated in the Baltic and the Black Seas. The latter were legally confined by the closure of the Turkish straits. If the former were deployed in the Russian naval base of Kronstadt or in the ports of the Gulf of Finland, they could be bottled up there by energetic German action. French naval forces were also divided between the Mediterranean, the Atlantic, and the English Channel, with Toulon, Brest, and Cherbourg respectively serving as the main bases. In a war with France, Germany would at first have to contend with the French northern fleet. After the conclusion of the Triple Alliance in 1882, French Mediterranean forces might be tied down by the Italians and Austrians; in any case it would take time before they could arrive in the north. With a Denmark friendly or allied to France and Russia it would not be difficult for the French northern and the Russian Baltic forces to unite for common action against Germany; until the completion of the Kaiser Wilhelm Canal it was easier for them than for the German North Sea and Baltic Sea fleets to unite. It was not impossible for the Russian Black Sea forces to join the French Mediterranean forces, if the Russian forces were able, contrary to international law, to force the Bosporus and the Dardanelles, for common action against Austria-Hungary and Italy in the Mediterranean or even eventually for action against Germany in the north. On the other hand, common Austro-Italian action in the Mediterranean was hampered by mutual suspicion that continued to exist in spite of the conclusion of the Triple Alliance and, except for the most unusual circumstances, common action between the German and the Austro-Italian fleets could be ruled out altogether. In a war between the Triple Alliance and France or France allied with Russia, all that the German navy could do was to encourage its allies by its own energetic action.

The army at first did not seriously count on the navy in a continental war. In 1873, Moltke expected the powerful French navy to take offensive action which might involve a landing on the German coast at the beginning of war. To counter it a sufficient number of German land troops were to be kept back. "An army and navy so formed operate at first entirely independently of one another; reciprocal direct support cannot take place. Until the moment that a landing actually occurs the fleet at first has the offensive and the army the passive waiting."[2] Moltke subsequently played down the danger of a landing, claiming that "in a civilized, densely populated country covered by roads and railways a catastrophe can be predicted for an invading enemy,"[3] but considered the German North Sea coast, especially Hamburg, Bremen, and Wilhelmshaven, vulnerable to destruction either by enemy ships or by landing parties. In 1879 the Admiralty concluded that the defense of the home waters was to have priority over the use of ships abroad. After a war game, Stosch considered an offensive against the French northern coast which was to include mine-laying.[4]

The first fairly well documented naval operations plan originated in March 1882. At that time, in spite of the Three Emperors' Alliance concluded in the previous year, there was considerable concern in the German military and political leadership about the possibility of a war with France and Russia, chiefly because of General Skobelev's visit to Paris where he was well received and because of his anti-German statements in Warsaw.[5] Count Alfred von Waldersee, Quartermaster-General in the Great General Staff, remarked on 1 March: "Conditions in Russia, the evidently weak and timorous Emperor Alexander, and in addition the uprising in Herzegovina are grave matters which now make it necessary for me to devote particular attention to our deployment [*Aufmarsch*] on our eastern border."[6] Although Bismarck did not at this time expect a war with Russia to be imminent, Moltke shared Waldersee's concern.[7] The Great General Staff intended to wage a two-front war by launching an opening offensive against Russia,[8] expecting that a decision could more easily be reached in the wider expanses of the east than against the well-fortified French positions in the west. Moltke did not hope for a repetition of the rapid and total military decision of 1870–71. Bismarck disagreed with the General Staff also in respect to the choice of the direction of the offensive, "for in Russia there exist no objects whose seizure could end the war."[9]

It is therefore most probable that the initiative for the preparation of the naval operations plan of 1882 came from the army. In the Admiralty, tasks such as war preparation, mobilization, the keeping of ships in service, and coastal defense were handled by sections (Dezernate) 1–3 of the "A" or Military Department, which was headed by the Chief of Staff. On 12 March the incumbent of that office, Eduard von Knorr, instructed the officers of the "A" department to make preparations for a war with Russia in July.[10] From these preparations emerged two memoranda, both initialed by Kapitän-zur-See Karl Eduard Heusner, who was later to be Commander of the Far Eastern Squadron and Secretary of State of the Imperial Naval Office, the first dated 3 June[11] and the second 4 August. The documents are very similar, except that the earlier one also deals with the waging of war with Russia outside the Baltic Sea and is specifically concerned with a war in July, citing a timetable for that month, whereas the later one is confined to operations in the Baltic and avoids specific dates. There are differences in wording and statistics.

Heusner had at his disposal some detailed information about the Russian navy. He concluded that in armored ships and vehicles the Russian navy was considerably inferior to the German and would therefore probably take a defensive stance in a war against Germany; the German navy, however, if proceeding to the offensive, would face the threat of considerable damage from Russian mines and torpedoes. In view of its superiority the German navy should none the less take offensive action in the Baltic as soon as possible. This was the first of many detailed proposals made by the planners of the Imperial German Navy for offensive operations in European waters.

The deployment of the German naval forces, drawn from both Kiel and Wilhelmshaven, was to occur on the fourteenth mobilization day in Danzig or Memel. These forces would, according to the memorandum of 4 August, consist of seven armored frigates, two armored corvettes, four covered corvettes, four smooth-deck corvettes, five dispatch-boats, one armored vehicle, eleven armored gunboats, one torpedo-vehicle, ten torpedo-boats, and a train. The strongest ships were to constitute an attack squadron. The first task of these forces was the elimination of the Russian fleet, best accomplished through a battle. The Russian fleet would, however, because of its inferiority probably avoid battle and withdraw behind the fortifications of its bases, the most important of which was Kronstadt. If so, the German fleet was to avoid battle with the powerful coastal fortifications but was to try to blockade the Russian navy with its light forces and the laying down of mine-booms, or to draw it out to battle. To achieve the latter aim, weakly defended Russian coastal cities were to be shelled. For its offensive operations the bulk of the German fleet was to station itself at the entrance to the Gulf of Finland. No mention was made of the establishment of a suitable base there. The naval operations in the Baltic were considered to be supportive of the German war effort on land: the elimination of the Russian fleet would deprive Russian land forces of its support and, more directly, the German navy would disturb the Russian mobilization and troop-transports and cause the Russians to withhold troops from the front for the defense of the coast.

Bold offensive action on the part of the fleet in European waters—without as yet taking adequate consideration of logistic factors or making provision for necessary bases—so as to support the war effort on land, which was viewed as decisive, had thus emerged in the operational thinking of the German navy, although it was directed against an inferior enemy.[12] Stosch approved the memorandum two days later, on 6 August, expressing his gratitude "for the industrious and fast work. I think it will be a good basis for the actual situation."[13]

In a memorandum drafted by Otto von Diederichs a few months later the possibility of a war against both France and Russia was considered.[14] In such a war the task of the German navy was to ward off enemy attacks against the German coast, secure shipping, and prevent hostile landing operations. Offensive action was again recommended against the Russian navy in the Baltic, whereas in the North Sea a "sortie fleet" was to be deployed in Wilhelmshaven for action against a French blockade. Diederichs also envisaged the disturbance and damaging of the blockading forces in the west through constant sorties and skirmishes in which the new torpedo-boat arm was to play a considerable part.[15] The concentration of a fleet for sorties against a blockading enemy was, as Volker Berghahn correctly observes, "a typical idea for the future, even if one recognizes that the term 'sortie' [*Ausfall*] was borrowed from land warfare."[16]

Tirpitz claimed that Caprivi, by introducing Admiralty staff voyages for the study of specific tasks in a war against France and Russia, which he viewed as imminent, departed from his own ideas of coastal defense and gradually "reached the request for a High Seas Fleet. Caprivi's activity culminated in his working out our first operations plan, which he did in person, after studying the matter for himself; then he sought me out for comment [*Korrevision*]."[17] Tirpitz is not entirely correct, for while—as will be shown—Caprivi's strategic thinking as related to operations gradually became more offensive, except for cruiser warfare, it—as has been shown—became more defensive as it related to construction.

On 29 April 1883, Caprivi asked a series of precise questions about the operations plan against Russia.[18] He remarked in the margin of the memorandum of 3 June 1882: "Not the Russians but only we can in my opinion have an interest in keeping the war so close to the coast that the fleet would have direct effect. And only with respect to supplies; the Russians can use their railways for this purpose; for us the sea can be most suitable." Fearing that the Admiralty may not have worked as realistically as Stosch had concluded, he queried whether contact had been established with other agencies, presumably the Great General Staff. Except for later stages of war, he considered that the most effective support that the navy could give the army, which, he assumed, would be advancing toward St Petersburg along the Baltic coast, was to maintain its supply-lines. He questioned how the German fleet could disturb the mobilization of the Russian army, doubted what effect attacks against the Russian-controlled coastal cities on the Baltic Sea would have on actions of the Russian fleet because of their being chiefly inhabited by Germans for whom the Russians would have no sympathy, queried how the fleet that was located at the entrance of the Gulf of Finland could be supplied with coal, and showed interest in a landing near St Petersburg in case of a defeat of the Russian fleet, and in the seizure of Riga as a base for the advance of the army. He also questioned to what extent the Russian war effort depended on imports through the Baltic Sea.

These queries indicate a professional concern for working out the operations more specifically and for subordinating the activities of the navy more closely to the operations of the army. The answers to them provided by the Chief of Staff, Knorr,[19] revealed considerable modifications of the original plan. He stated that communications had been established with the General Staff, which welcomed collaboration with the navy. The navy could accomplish much by moving in provisions for an advancing army, using successively the major harbors on the Russian Baltic coast as field-bases. The mobilization of the Russian army could be disturbed by cutting off its troop-transports from Helsingfors, Wiborg, Reval and Riga. Knorr admitted that attacks by the fleet on the largely German-inhabited cities on the Baltic coast would have no military effect. He asserted that the German fleet, when located at the entrance of the Gulf of Finland by the island of Ösel, could be supplied with coal from the German Baltic Sea ports or from England! He suggested Narva as a landing-place close to St Petersburg if there existed sufficient protection against attacks by Russian ships and torpedo-boats, otherwise Reval or Baltischport, and agreed about the suitability of Riga as a base. As for the significance of the Baltic trade for the Russian military effort, he briefly stated that if Russia could fully utilize her own means she would be dependent only on imported coal, but past experience had shown that in wartime she drew heavily on foreign industry. This was a rather cavalier disposal of the possible effects of the blockade.

Knorr arranged that Caprivi's questions and his replies would serve as the basis for a revised operations plan against Russia on which Dezernat 3 was to begin work no later than 1 January 1884.[20] This plan is not in the German naval files. By the end of May 1886, however, Caprivi had become aware that the relative decline of Germany as a naval power was affecting her position toward Russia. The impending superiority of the Russian Baltic Sea fleet over the entire German navy would constitute a direct economic threat to the German coast and a military threat to Königsberg and Danzig if the German land forces suffered reverses.[21]

In spite of his doubts about the future, his public admission that Germany had declined to a position of a third-class naval power, his preference for coastal defense and, most recently, commerce raiding, Caprivi proceeded in the fall of 1887 to prepare elaborate operations plans for all probable cases of war. This was at a time when, notwithstanding the recent conclusion of the Reinsurance Treaty with Russia (18 June 1887), the renewal of the Triple Alliance (20 February 1887), and the conclusion of the First Mediterranean Agreement (February–May 1887), the tensions produced by the Bulgarian crisis and the Boulanger affair in France continued. There existed particular concern about the Russian attitude,[22] especially in view of pan-Slav agitation and the movement of troops on the Austrian border.

On 6 December 1887, Count Philipp von und zu Eulenburg reported that he had to relate "some interesting but unpleasant news" about his recent visit to Berlin.

> First is the growing concern about Russia. St Petersburg views a colossal and hardly controllable financial confusion and calamity and growing nihilist disturbances as springs for war preparations into which to flee if internal difficulties become too great. The concentrations of troops on the Austrian border are assuming a very threatening character. In addition we are worried because of Austria which in its incompetence does nothing.
>
> In France the conviction gains more ground that . . . [the French army] possesses a better rifle than we, and this is not incorrect . . .
>
> If Russia attacks Austria, then the *casus foederis* is present and France cannot be held back.
>
> In Italy nothing is done for the army . . . Only Salisbury has become energetic and can possibly be used . . . So are things now, and the Chancellor is rather nervous.[23]

Waldersee, now the most influential man in the General Staff, was most alarmed about the Russian intentions and proposed to counter the increasing Russian troop concentrations in the west with a preventive attack. He had managed to win the ear of the aged Moltke, and his views were shared by some diplomats, among them Friedrich von Holstein. Thus, on 8 October, Waldersee reported to Bismarck that he considered the transfer of another Russian cavalry division to the Austrian border a measure "of considerable significance"[24] but remarked to Herbert Bismarck that during the next six months the French would be entirely helpless before Germany.[25] On 16 November, Waldersee reported to

Moltke, convincing him that Russia intended to start a war in the spring which Germany should prevent by an attack in the winter.[26] On 30 November, Moltke wrote to Bismarck, stating that:

> The general impression of the preparations made in the Russian army produces the conclusion that Russia is directly arming for war . . . Only if we, together with Austria-Hungary, attack Russia early would—as conditions are—favorable chances exist for us. . .
>
> If we want to counter this danger in order not to obviate war under less favorable circumstances, then we must not tolerate the Russian preparations for war, whether they are directed against Austria-Hungary alone or against us. Winter does not present an obstacle to an offensive war against Russia . . .[27]

Attached to the letter was an undated memorandum of the General Staff which on the basis of extensive data reached the conclusion "that Russia directly arms for war and through gradually advancing mobilization or by fits and starts prepares the deployment [*Aufmarsch*] of its army."[28]

Holstein remarked on 18 November that "the outlook in foreign affairs is gradually becoming really serious. War fever is increasing in the French army . . . And the Russians judge that the time is ripe for a war with Austria . . .".[29] On the same day the young Bülow reported from St Petersburg "that many things . . . recently indicate that Russia expects war in the near future, and is making preparations for it"[30] and three weeks later indicated that, although Russia had calmed down, she was not to be trusted, proposing a scheme for her break-up.[31]

Bismarck was certainly getting nervous. At the end of October he was beginning to doubt the pacific nature and firmness of Alexander III, remarking that he was too susceptible to public opinion, overestimated himself, and believed that the Germans feared him.[32] A month later he suspected that Russia was doing everything possible to provoke an Austrian attack.[33] At the beginning of December he informally counseled the Austrian government to strengthen the forces in Galicia "since in case of war we will undoubtedly have the whole French army on our neck and therefore can give little or nothing to support the Austrians."[34] Moltke's letter of 30 November caused him to make inquiries about the security of the horse depots in East Prussia.[35] But his marginal comments on Moltke's letter rejected the fighting of an offensive war against Russia[36] and those on Bülow's dispatch dismissed the scheme for the partition of Russia as fantastic.[37] He, however, underlined parts of the General Staff memorandum and, according to Eulenburg, "was to a certain extent receptive to it."[38]

Caprivi's operations plans were thus drafted at a time of considerable tension of which he was certainly aware because of his position. Although he was not close to Waldersee or Moltke,[39] as a high-ranking officer and in the opinion of some Moltke's obvious successor, he must have been aware of the thinking and phobias of the General Staff.[40] There appeared four lengthy memoranda that were written by him personally: "Coastal war in the North Sea," 20 October;[41] "Our waging of war at sea against France," October;[42] "The waging of war in the Baltic Sea," 5 November;[43] and "Report concerning the prospects of the waging of war at sea between Germany, Austria, and Italy on the one side and France and Russia on the other side," signed by Caprivi on 15 November 1887 and dispatched by him on the same day to Bismarck and Wilhelm I.[44] The memorandum "Coastal war in the North Sea" was reported on in matters of detail by the future Chief of the Naval Cabinet, Gustav von Senden, read by the future Secretary of State of the Imperial Naval Office, Friedrich Hollmann, and sent at Caprivi's request to the Command of the North Sea Station in Wilhelmshaven. The memorandum "Our waging of war at sea against France" received further attention from a committee consisting of Hollmann, Senden, Rudolf Siegel, and Geissler. The others do not seem to have been further examined within the Admiralty. Only the memorandum concerning warfare between the Triple Alliance and France and Russia, which appears to have been prepared upon request, was communicated outside the naval leadership to Bismarck and Wilhelm I. In addition there exists an undated memorandum by Siegel, entitled "Thoughts about a waging of war against France."[45]

The memorandum "Coastal war in the North Sea" does not identify the enemy. The stronger western naval power is obviously France. As the title of the document indicates, the German navy was assigned a defensive task. Because of its limited strength, its operations would be confined to the Jade, Weser, and Elbe estuaries. A successful naval battle was viewed as the best means of coastal defense, but, if there was no prospect of success because of enemy superiority, that superiority would have to be eroded through constant harassment by German forces. "We can with certainty assume that the energy of the enemy will be tested more than ours and that a long coastal war will burden him more than us. We can with equal certainty expect that his ships will suffer more than ours." Proximity to its resources, familiarity with coastal waters, and support of coastal fortifications would provide the defending German navy with definite advantages. While the destruction of the enemy was to be the final aim of the German fleet, its more immediate tasks were: (1) keeping the Jade, Weser, and Elbe estuaries open to German shipping; (2) observation of the North Sea; (3) offensive action when the enemy was located in the North Sea or proceeding from there to the Baltic; and (4) cooperation in the defense of coastal fortifications.

Specific German measures, which were to be considered at leisure in peacetime, but which were not to bind the fleet commander in wartime, depended on enemy action, in its more energetic form involving attack on coastal fortifications, possibly assisted by landings, and in its less decisive form the blockade of German river estuaries with sunken ships or mines. A superior enemy would be most tempted to attack the naval base of Wilhelmshaven—but for this a force of at least twenty armored ships would be necessary, i.e. the combined strength of the French Mediterranean and northern fleets. To counter this action, the German navy was to leave limited forces in the Elbe and Weser estuaries, and offer battle to the main enemy force in front of Wilhelmshaven, supported by its fortifications. "A defeat of our enemy outside the Jade is the most secure means for the defense of Wilhelmshaven, and whatever would thereafter remain of our naval forces would have complete freedom of action." While the plan was a defensive one, naval battle was still considered important, and the fleet was advised against being too dependent on the coast. Blockade measures were held to be relatively ineffective against the blockaded party and costly to the blockading party. A powerful enemy was accorded an almost natural instinct to seek out the most challenging objective. Given these assumptions, a defensive war in the North Sea was not a hopeless prospect for a weak naval power such as Germany.[46] Similar ideas were to reappear subsequently in German naval thinking and to prevail in the Admiralty Staff concerning operations against England when Germany entered the war against her in 1914.

At approximately the same time appeared Siegel's brief memorandum "Thoughts about a waging of war against France." According to it, France with both her Mediterranean and northern fleets would enjoy so great a superiority that Germany, with her Baltic and North Sea bases separated by Denmark, would be unable to defend them both against her. She was thus compelled to concentrate her strength in one base. She might do so in Wilhelmshaven, as Caprivi proposed, were it not that Denmark—no friend of Germany since 1864—and Russia—a potential aggressor in the opinion of the General Staff—might join France. In such a case, a French fleet could advance to Kiel and the pursuing German Wilhelmshaven force could fare badly in the narrow Danish waters at the hands of her superior enemies. For defensive purposes, therefore, Kiel was a much safer base. From there, the flank of the French forces operating in the North Sea could be threatened and the French forces operating in the Baltic could be more easily worn down because of their great distance from home. So their defeat was a possibility.

Siegel also raised the question of an offensive advance against the French northern fleet at the beginning of the war, before the arrival of reinforcements from the Mediterranean. Except for a torpedo-boat attack, he dismissed the notion, for ships lost in the expedition would be indispensable for the later defense of Kiel. The question of a surprise torpedo-boat attack against the French naval base of Cherbourg was to be studied more closely, for it promised great material success and would in any case weaken French morale.[47] While it cannot be definitely claimed that the idea of an offensive advance against the French coast which was to be advocated in more bold terms by Caprivi originated with Siegel, for it cannot be proven that his undated memorandum antedated Caprivi's, it is interesting that Siegel's proposal to concentrate in the Baltic Sea against a superior western enemy was later seriously entertained in the preparation of operations against England.

In his memorandum "Our waging of war at sea against France," which he drafted in October, Caprivi considered in general terms various types of naval warfare against that superior naval power: coastal defense, activity outside of European waters, and offensive action against the French coast.

Coastal war received short shrift, undoubtedly because it had already been discussed in another memorandum. Two types of activity outside European waters were discussed: commerce raiding and action against the French fishing fleets near Newfoundland and Iceland. Both were dismissed, however, on grounds of being ineffective. France's war effort could not be undermined by cutting off foodstuffs, which she did not need, or war materials, which she could import through neutral neighboring countries or in faster ships. Nor did Germany possess adequate numbers of cruisers or adequate resources for the launching of auxiliary cruisers even if military honor and consideration for possible allies required the German fleet to wage cruiser war against the enemy.

Caprivi seriously advocated major offensive naval action against the French northern coast. This was to consist not only of a surprise attack of torpedo-boats against the naval base of Cherbourg immediately after the outbreak of war, as proposed by Siegel, and of possible mining of French ports, but also of an offensive thrust of the German navy against the French northern fleet before it was joined by the Mediterranean fleet from Toulon. Better preparation for war and quicker mobilization, as well as the shorter distance from both Wilhelmshaven and Kiel than from Toulon to the French northern coast, would enable the united German fleet to arrive there before the French Mediterranean forces. Between the ninth and eleventh mobilization days the German fleet was to bombard Calais with the purpose of rousing a public outcry which would force the French naval leadership to commit the inferior French northern fleet to an immediate battle. Caprivi was aware of the difficulties of the operation: its dependence on British goodwill that would be shaken by the German action in the Channel, inadequate facilities for obtaining coal and ammunition, imperfect intelligence about French fortifications, the possibility that the operation would be either condemned to futility by the refusal of the French northern fleet to come to battle or culminate in disaster if the Mediterranean fleet arrived too soon. Caprivi coolly remarked that one could well accept the loss of the eight or nine armored ships which would participate in the expedition if an equal number of French ships were put out of action for the duration of the campaign. A defensive war on the German coast could be fought without them. Caprivi explicitly refused to consider the use of army troops in the advance, pointing out that they could be better employed elsewhere.

If Germany were to have strong naval allies in Italy or England—not an unrealistic assumption at the time—then Caprivi was willing to extend the operations of the German fleet further to the west, bombard Le Havre and Cherbourg, and attempt a blockade of the entire French northern coast for the purpose of relieving the allies.[48] Caprivi, whose building program was mostly directed toward coastal defense, thus made one of the boldest proposals for action against a clearly superior enemy, relying on a chance of success arising from the division of his forces. Unlike the earlier operations plan against Russia in which naval action was coordinated with offensive military activity, the navy was now to operate independently with a battle as an aim. The battle lacked decisiveness, however, for even if the

French northern fleet were defeated the Mediterranean fleet could still carry operations into German coastal waters, although it would on its own probably be unable to attack either Wilhelmshaven or Kiel.

Caprivi's memorandum was worked through by the Commission für die Bearbeitung taktischer Aufgaben, consisting of Hollmann, Senden, Geissler, and Siegel, who produced an eighty-two-page document. The committee had been instructed to examine which measures were to be taken to secure the success of the operations proposed by Caprivi and how the operations might be changed in the interest of speed and practicability. Its report went into considerable detail, particularly in respect to the bombardment of Calais and Le Havre. It also expressed strong reservations, pointing out that until May or June the crews lacked adequate training for the attack to succeed. For the attack on Le Havre, which Caprivi was prepared to undertake only if Germany had allies, the committee also stipulated the additional requirement of Russian neutrality. For the bombardment of Calais it emphasized the need of an element of surprise, of thorough training of the crews, and of the highest degree of war preparedness,[49] which were lacking. In some respects the French were better prepared for war than the Germans. Some remedies were then suggested which led to Caprivi's comment, dated 18 December 1887: "If our conditions were as unfavorable for quick action as described here, then these insignificant improvements would change little. I have a higher faith in us, above all in our officer corps, and think less of the battle readiness of the French."[50] A deadlock seems to have resulted between Caprivi and his officers in respect to projected action against France.

Before getting this discouraging reaction from his subordinates, Caprivi had, in his memorandum "The waging of war in the Baltic Sea" of 5 November 1887, for the first time fully considered German naval actions in various possible combinations: Germany against Russia, against Russia and Denmark, against France and Denmark, or Germany, Austria, and Italy against France and Russia with Denmark neutral. The title of the document is somewhat misleading, for, although concentrating on the waging of war in the Baltic, the memorandum also deals with the waging of war elsewhere and constitutes the first full exposition of Germany's naval strategy against her possible enemies and of the power relationship between Germany and her allies and their enemies. The displacement tonnage of the battleships and seaworthy coastal armored ships of the major powers concerned was estimated as set out in Table 2.1.[51]

Caprivi boldly assumed that both the German and Russian fleets wanted to seek victory in battle. "Nothing protects a coast better . . . The German fleet needs a battle in order to remain viable [*lebensfähig*]." In line with the sentiments expressed in his criticisms of Heusner's operations plan against Russia, but in stark contrast to the operations he envisaged against France,[52] Caprivi now recommended that the German navy, deploying in the strong base of Kiel for protection against surprise torpedo-boat attacks—such as planned by himself against Cherbourg—should await a Russian attack rather than advance into Russian waters immediately after the outbreak of war. Although weaker than the German, the Russian fleet

Table 2.1

| | | |
|---|---:|---:|
| France | | |
|    Toulon | 104,000 | |
|    Brest | 69,000 | |
|    Cherbourg | 69,000 | |
| Russia in the Baltic Sea | 53,000 | |
| | | |
| France and Russia combined | | 295,000 |
| | | |
| Germany | 103,000 | |
| Italy | 98,000 | |
| Austria-Hungary | 48,000 | |
| | | |
| Triple Alliance combined | | 249,000 |

was expected to attack because of the Russian offensive mentality. Caprivi's assumption that the General Staff also expected Russian aggression was corrected by someone in the margin by the remark "Until now the Russians have none the less steadily and successfully chosen the defensive." Once ready for action, the German fleet was to advance to Danzig, and await a Russian advance which might be prompted by the blockade of relatively close Russian harbors, such as those of Libau, Windau, and Riga. But an advance into the Gulf of Finland before the defeat of the Russian navy was definitely rejected: coastal conditions would make a fleet operating there most vulnerable to torpedo-boats and mines (*Kleinkrieg*), and the setting up of a base would require army support which was not available. If the Russians refused to do battle despite attacks on ports close to Germany, they would decline battle if the German fleet advanced into the Gulf of Finland. While Caprivi's caution about an advance was warranted, his expectation that an inferior fleet would voluntarily offer battle was certainly not. After the defeat of the Russian fleet a blockade of the bays of Bothnia and Riga and the Gulf of Finland and support of German land operations could be undertaken.

A potentially hostile Denmark constituted a threat in the rear of the German naval forces advancing toward the east. Caprivi, however, rejected the possibility of a preventive attack on the Danish fleet because the battle with the fortifications of Copenhagen which would be involved could entail disproportionately heavy losses. If Denmark did enter the war, the German fleet was to remain in Kiel, with the objective of preventing the Danish navy from uniting with the Russian and trying to defeat them separately.

In a war between Germany and France, Denmark was expected to join France if operations were extended to the Baltic. The possibility of a German attack against a French port was briefly mentioned as preferable to an attack on Copenhagen—an indication that Caprivi had not definitely committed himself to the notion of an offensive thrust into the Channel.

Like Siegel's undated memorandum, the document concerned itself with the taking of a defensive position in Kiel where the bulk of German forces in the North Sea were to repair. The uncertainty in Caprivi's thinking was also shown by his current assumption that the French Toulon forces would remain in the Mediterranean instead of proceeding north as expected in the October memorandum.

Finally Caprivi examined the situation in the event of a war of the powers of the Triple Alliance against France and Russia, with Denmark neutral. In such a war he assumed that the French would choose the Mediterranean as their more important theater of war because of their North African possessions and interests in the Levant and in the Suez Canal. To obtain the superiority over Austria and Italy necessary for a decisive success[53] they were expected at the very least to send their Brest forces to the Mediterranean. Subsequently, the focus of the examination shifted from the Baltic to the Mediterranean. It was claimed that the Triple Alliance should attempt to defeat the French Mediterranean forces before they were reinforced by the Brest squadron. For this purpose speedy union of the Austrian and Italian navies was necessary, although close cooperation between the two navies was considered to be difficult to attain. On the other hand, the French might boldly attempt to defeat the Italian navy before its union with the Austrian. An allied naval victory over the French was a prerequisite to further actions such as a blockade, an attack on Toulon, operations against the French coast or against Algeria or Tunis, or even for an energetic Italian war effort against the French on land.

It therefore lay in German interests to encourage allied activity in the Mediterranean through action in the north. Caprivi recommended a thrust against the French forces in Cherbourg before the third mobilization week when the Russians were expected to be capable of appearing before Wilhelmshaven. German naval strategy in case of a general war was then to be defensive in the east and offensive in the west with the aim of encouraging Italy to undertake offensive action on land.[54] Caprivi's "Report concerning the prospects of the waging of war at sea between Germany, Austria, and Italy on the one side and France and Russia on the other side" of 15 November added little to the above considerations except for expressing pessimism about the strategic situation in the Mediterranean. "If we can with some confidence look ahead to the war as it would be shaped in the north, then the conditions in the Mediterranean present fewer prospects for success. The joining of the Central Powers by England would considerably improve the chances of the war in the home waters and of cruiser war. But the Austro-Italian fleet would have a definite advantage from this alliance only if assistance in the form of the English Mediterranean squadron would be provided immediately upon mobilization and thereby its union with the Italians and Austrians would be guaranteed."[55]

Actually the Admiralty had some realistic reservations about the effectiveness of the British navy. According to the German naval attaché in London, Kapitän-zur-See Schröder, it was deficient in cruisers and its personnel was no better than that of other navies.[56] Caprivi concurred with

Schröder's observations, maintaining that while the Royal Navy consisted of a large number of excellent ships no new constructions had been added to it since 1881. In making this statement he was wrong. In all, nine British battleships had been launched from 1882 to 1888. In order to avoid a partial blockade of the English coast by the French, the Royal Navy had to offer battle immediately after the outbreak of war—something for which its peacetime preparations were inadequate. It was simply not prepared for a sudden outbreak of war because of its weak leadership. Moreover, if the French carried out their plan to concentrate their whole fleet in Toulon, they could defeat the British Mediterranean and Channel squadrons separately.[57] Bismarck did not challenge any of the statements made by Schröder and Caprivi and ordered on 1 January 1888 that they be forwarded to the Emperor and the Crown Prince.[58]

Caprivi's audacity waned. According to his supplementary comments of 21 November 1887, the thrust against Cherbourg was only possible if Russia was neutral or if her fleet was frozen in.[59] True, by that time he had learned from Bismarck that "we will not necessarily have to expect a Russian attack in the near future."[60] To a man supposedly obsessed with the notion of a two-front war, this statement did not provide a guarantee that Russia would not become involved in a Franco-German war or mean that Germany could keep out of a war resulting from a Russian attack on Austria. Caprivi therefore did not intend to go along with the advance against Cherbourg on the safe assumption of Russian neutrality: he stated the conditions under which the thrust would be possible.

Caprivi's considerations were related to attempts to negotiate a military convention between Germany and Italy. Plans for coordinated actions between Italian and German forces had been worked on by Italian military authorities since 1882.[61] Early in October 1887, the Italian Prime Minister, Francisco Crispi, suggested to Bismarck that conversations take place between German and Italian army and navy officers concerning common operations. Bismarck, wishing to cement the bonds of the Triple Alliance in a period of tension, welcomed the conversations, acquired Wilhelm's approval for them, and established contact—sometime after 15 October—with the General Staff and the Admiralty.[62]

Bismarck complimented Caprivi on his memorandum of 15 November and requested that its substance be communicated to Rome.[63] He considered the naval power relationship to be unfavorable for bold action and instructed: "Thereby on the basis of the data supplied by Herr von Caprivi it is in particular to be pointed out how desirable it would be if Italy would not enter a naval war with France without England. If Germany and Italy alone would have to fight off a French attack at sea, then we would in all cases be equal to the Cherbourg squadron in the offensive, [but] against the united Cherbourg and Brest squadrons our fleet would have to limit itself to the defensive."[64] Italy was to be restrained from aggressive action against France, just as Austria was to be held back from attacking Russia, unless sure of British support. Bismarck therefore discouraged the conclusion of military conventions, both between Germany and Austria as well as between Germany and Italy, for he feared that they would provide defensive alliances with an offensive edge. Accordingly he refused to forward to Rome the war plans which Moltke had provided upon Crispi's request with Wilhelm's approval, pointing out that they were as yet premature and that mere military discussions would suffice.[65] The three memoranda prepared by Moltke, which at Bismarck's request were successively made more general, stipulated an offensive war on the part of Germany on land, just as Caprivi had planned at sea, expecting "great and decisive battles" aimed at the destruction of the French army,[66] which would relieve the Italians of French pressure, enable them to invade southern France, and dispatch troops to the German–French front.

Moltke agreed with many of Caprivi's operational notions. "Although the German fleet is capable of pinning down [*auf sich zu ziehen*] a substantial part of the French fleet, the latter alone would none the less remain superior to the Italian fleet alone in the Mediterranean. It can make difficult the use of coastal roads, trouble individual harbors, but otherwise not greatly influence decisive land operations."[67] In the memorandum which he submitted to Bismarck on 26 November, Moltke pointed to the possibility of the cooperation of the Austrian and Italian navies (prompting Bismarck's marginal comment that "the French navy is still stronger than both"), which would lead to their command of the Mediterranean. It could lead to attacks on all French Mediterranean ports, Tunis and Corsica, and the calling off of French troop-transports from Algeria.[68] It was, however, inconsistent on the part of Moltke to have considered offensive waging of war on the part of Germany in the west at the same time that he, in agreement with Waldersee, recommended a preventive war against Russia.[69]

The military discussions held in Berlin did lead to an agreement in January 1888 according to which in the event of a war of the Triple Alliance against both France and Russia the Italian General Staff was bound to take an offensive against France through the Alps and to transfer six corps and six cavalry divisions to Germany to operate jointly with German forces on the Rhine.[70] The sending of Italian troops to Germany depended on their passage through Austrian territory. The government of Austria-Hungary reserved for itself the right to refuse passage if the war was localized to the west. It subsequently also turned down Italian suggestions for a naval convention, involving cooperation of the two navies along lines as indicated by Caprivi.[71]

The German and Italian navies were thus not bound to any common course of action. What did result were agreements between Germany and Italy to exchange naval attachés and information, and closer cooperation between the British and Italian navies. It is most unlikely, however, that the British promised naval support for Italy as Crispi thought they had.[72] German diplomacy continued through 1888 to promote Anglo-Italian naval cooperation and to encourage Britain to strengthen her navy. "If England is not only pacific but also strong, then she would not lack friends in Europe; as long as she is pacific and counts on exploiting foreign strengths and on preserving her own financially, she will only be able to count on allies according to their convenience."[73]

## Notes: Chapter 2

1   Tirpitz, *Erinnerungen*, p. 23; Graf [Helmuth von] Moltke, *Die deutschen Aufmarsch-pläne 1871–1890, Heft 7 der Quellen und Darstellungen aus dem Reichsarchiv*, ed. Ferdinand von Schmerfeld (Berlin, 1929), pp. 77 ff.
2   ibid., Moltke to Stosch, 22 February 1873 (Über die geringe Gefahr feindlicher Landungen), p. 32.
3   ibid.
4   Walther Hubatsch, *Der Admiralstab und die obersten Marinebehörden in Deutschland, 1848–1945* (Frankfurt, 1958), pp. 41–2.
5   William L. Langer, *European Alliances and Alignments, 1871–1890*, 2nd edn (New York, 1952), pp. 240–2, and Wolfgang Windelband, *Bismarck und die europäischen Grossmächte, 1879–1885* (Essen, 1942), pp. 310–15. For a recent treatment, see Horst Müller-Link, *Industrialisierung und Aussenpolitik* (Göttingen, 1977), pp. 240 ff.
6   *Waldersee*, Vol. 1, p. 219.
7   ibid., diary entries of 11 and 15 March 1882. See also Konrad Canis, *Bismarck und Waldersee* (Berlin, 1980), pp. 81 ff.
8   Gerhard Ritter, *Der Schlieffen-Plan: Kritik eines Mythos* (Munich, 1956), pp. 14–15; Moltke, *Die deutschen*, especially "Denkschrift vom April 1879: Zweifrontenkrieg gegen Russland-Frankreich," pp. 77–81.
9   *Denkwürdigkeiten des Botschafters General von Schweinitz*, Vol. 2 (Berlin, 1927), p. 174. For French military weakness in the 1870s and 1880s, see in particular Allan Mitchell, "'A situation of inferiority': French military reorganization after the defeat of 1870," *American Historical Review*, vol. 86, no. 1 (February 1981), pp. 49–62.
10  BA-MA, F 5593, III, 2.–2., Vol. 1. According to Knorr's "Verfügung" of 12 March 1882, Dezernat 1 was to make provisions concerning all naval forces to be used, Dezernat 2 was to look after the mobilization arrangements and personnel requirements, and Dezernat 3 was to collect information about the Russian fleet and to draft an operations plan. Once the work of the three departments had progressed sufficiently, Knorr wanted them to confer. Then, following a meeting with or a report to the Chief of the Admiralty, further work was to be undertaken.
11  ibid., "Die Verwendung der Flotte im Krieg gegen Russland."
12  ibid., "Allgemeiner Kriegsplan. Zur Übersendung an die Kommandos der Marine-stationen und an die Geschwaderchefs, 4 August 1882."
13  ibid., Stosch's comment on Heusner's covering letter of 5 August 1882 to the memo-randum of 4 August.
14  "Betrachtungen über die Verteidigung der deutschen Küsten gegen Seemächte welche gleichzeitig vor Ostsee und Nordsee auftreten," 9 November 1882. Cited by Berghahn, *Tirpitz-Plan*, p. 51, from BA-MA, F 7599 (alt). We do not know whether this document had any official status other than being drafted by an officer in the Admiralty.
15  "Lage für die Herbstmanöver der Flotte am 10–11. 9. 1882," September 1882, cited in ibid.
16  Berghahn, *Tirpitz-Plan*, p. 51.
17  Tirpitz, *Erinnerungen*, p. 25.
18  BA-MA, F 5593, III, 2.–2., Vol. 1.
19  ibid., undated sixteen-page memorandum of "A."
20  ibid., notation of Knorr, 16 June 1883.
21  BA-MA, F 2050, PG 66104, Caprivi to Bismarck, 24 May 1886.
22  Steinmetz, *Bismarck*, p. 72.
23  *Philipp Eulenburgs Politische Korrespondenz*, ed. John C. G. Röhl, Vol. 1, *Von der Reichsgründung bis zum neuen Kurs, 1866–1891* (Boppard, 1976), p. 254.
24  Politisches Archiv des Auswärtigen Amts, Bonn (henceforth abbreviated as PAAA), Russland 72, Geh., Bd 2, Waldersee to Bismarck, 8 October 1887. Also see Canis, *Bismarck und Waldersee*, pp. 207 ff.
25  Bismarck Archiv, Friedrichsruh (henceforth abbreviated as Bism. Ar.), D 27, Herbert Bismarck to Kuno Rantzau, 9 October 1887.
26  *Waldersee*, Vol. 1, entry for 17 November 1887, p. 334.
27  PAAA, Deutschland 121, Geh. No. 12a, Bd 1.

28 ibid., "Die Entwickelung der Wehrkraft Russlands seit 1878 unter besonderer Berücksichtigung seiner Rüstungen im laufenden Jahre 1887." Waldersee claims authorship for this document: *Waldersee*, Vol. 1, entry for 4 December 1887, p. 339.

29 *The Holstein Papers: The Memoirs, Diaries, and Correspondence of Freidrich von Holstein, 1873–1909*, ed. Norman Rich and M. H. Fischer, Vol. 2, *Diaries* (Cambridge, 1957), p. 359.

30 PAAA, Russland 72, Vol. 18, Bülow to Bismarck, 18 November 1887.

31 *Holstein Papers*, Vol. 3, *Correspondence* (Cambridge, 1961), Bülow to Holstein, 10 December 1887, pp. 236–40. Peter Winzen, in *Bülows Weltmachtkonzept: Untersuchungen zur Frühphase Seiner Aussenpolitik, 1897–1901* (Boppard, 1977), pp. 43–4 interprets this dispatch as an attempt to make clear to the anti-Russian Holstein the futility of a war with Russia in support of Bismarck's policy of avoiding war with Russia.

32 Bism. Ar., B 27, Bismarck's marginal comment on Bülow to Herbert Bismarck, 18 October 1887.

33 *Die Grosse Politik der Europäischen Kabinette: Sammlung der Diplomatischen Akten des Auswärtigen Amtes*, ed. Johannes Lepsius, Albrecht Mendelssohn-Bartholdy, Friedrich Thimme, 40 vols in 54 (Berlin, 1924–27) (henceforth abbreviated as GP), Vol. 6, p. 12.

34 Bism. Ar., F 4, Rantzau, Friedrichsruh, to Herbert Bismarck, 11 December 1887.

35 PAAA, Deutschland 121, Geh. No. 12a, Bd 1, "Aufzeichnung Rantzau," 5 December 1887.

36 "Dazu werden wir weder den Rtag noch Oestreich überreden können."

37 Fritz Fischer, in his *Krieg der Illusionen* (Düsseldorf, 1969), pp. 87–9, completely perverts the meaning of Bismarck's and his son's comments by taking them to refer to the whole document rather than to specific passages. For a mild criticism of this incident, see Fritz T. Epstein, "Der Komplex 'Die russische Gefahr' und sein Einfluss auf die deutsch-russischen Beziehungen im 19. Jahrhundert," in *Deutschland in der Weltpolitik des 19. und 20. Jahrhunderts: Fritz Fischer zum 65. Geburtstag*, ed. I. Geiss and B. J. Wendt, in cooperation with P. C. Witt (Düsseldorf, 1973), esp. pp. 158–9.

38 Bundesarchiv Koblenz (henceforth abbreviated as BA), Eulenburg Correspondenz, Vol. 2, Notizen, 27 December 1887.

39 *Waldersee*, Vol. 1, p. 332, entry for 8 November 1887; Eberhard Kessell, *Moltke* (Stuttgart, 1957), pp. 701–2.

40 Including Prince Heinrich. See *Das Tagebuch der Baronin von Spitzenberg, geb. Freiin v. Varnbüler: Aufzeichnungen aus der Hofgesellschaft des Hohenzollernreiches*, ed. Rudolf Vierhaus (Göttingen, 1961), p. 487, diary entry for 10 September 1908.

41 BA-MA, F 5598, Nebenakten zu O.K.d.M., III, 3.–1., Vol. 1, "Kriegführung in der Ostsee."

42 ibid., "Unsere Kriegführung zur See gegen Frankreich."

43 BA-MA, F 5244, III, 2.–7., Vol. 1, "Kriegführung in der Ostsee."

44 BA-MA, F 5598, Nebenakten zu O.K.d.M., III, 3.–1., Vol. 1, "Bericht über die Aussichten der Kriegführung zur See zwischen Deutschland, Oesterreich und Italien einerseits und Frankreich und Russland andererseits."

45 ibid., undated document on which there is written "Caprivi?!" and subsequently "Siegel!" It is in Siegel's handwriting. It is entitled "Gedanken über einer Kriegsführung [sic] gegen Frankreich."

46 ibid., "Küstenkrieg in der Nordsee."

47 ibid., "Gedanken über einer Kriegsführung [sic] gegen Frankreich."

48 ibid., "Unsere Kriegführung zur See gegen Frankreich," October 1887.

49 This statement produced Caprivi's marginal comment that the expectation was too high: "Das lässt sich im Kriege nie fordern, man muss immer zufrieden sein, wenn das Mittelmässige erreicht wird." That led to the anonymous rejoinder in the margin: "Für den beabsichtigten Gewaltstreich muss aber mehr als 'Mittelmässige' gefordert werden" (ibid.).

50 ibid., n.d., but commented on by Caprivi on 18 December 1887, "Ausarbeitung der in der Denkschrift Seiner Exzellenz des Hern Chef der Admiralität vom Oktober 1887 betreffend den Kriegsfall mit Frankreich gegebenen Direktiven seitens der 'Kommission für Bearbeitung takischen Aufgaben!'"

51 Slightly different figures are given by someone in pencil in the margin of the document. The major difference lies in the tonnage of the Russian Baltic Sea fleet being estimated at 75,000.

52   See above, pp. 17; 22 ff.
53   See Table 2.1 on p. 24.
54   BA-MA, F 5244, III, 2.–7., Vol. 1, "Kriegführung in der Ostsee," 5 November 1887.
55   BA-MA, F 5598, Nebenakten zu O.K.d.M., III. 3.–1., Vol. 1, Caprivi, 15 November 1887, "Bericht über die Aussichten der Kriegführung zur See zwischen Deutschland, Oesterreich u. Italien einerseits und Frankreich und Russland andererseits."
56   PAAA, England 71b, Vol. 1, Schröder's report of 20 December 1886.
57   ibid., Caprivi to Bismarck, 31 December 1886, in response to Berchem's request on Bismarck's behalf for a reaction to Schröder's report of 20 December 1886. For British constructions, see Marder, *Anatomy*, app. 1, p. 547.
58   PAAA, England 71b, Vol. 1, Bismarck's instruction of 1 January 1888.
59   ibid., Deutschland 143, Geh., Bd 1, memorandum dated 21 November 1887, initialed H(olstein), entitled "Ergänzende Bemerkungen des Generals von Caprivi."
60   BA-MA, F 5598, Nebenakten zu O.K.d.M., III, 3.–1., Vol. 1, Herbert Bismarck to Caprivi, 18 November 1887.
61   GP, VI, No. 1290, report of Major von Engelbrecht, military attaché in Rome, pp. 225–8.
62   PAAA, Deutschland 143, Geh., Bd 1, Herbert Bismarck to Wilhelm I, 3 October 1887. The most important part of the communication is reprinted in GP, VI, No. 1291, pp. 228–9; also see GP, VI, No. 1292, Herbert Bismarck to Count zu Solms-Sonnenwalde, ambassador in Rome, 15 October 1887, pp. 229–30, in which there is a statement that Herbert Bismarck will get in touch with the Chiefs of the General Staff and the Admiralty.
63   BA-MA, F 5598, Nebenakten zu O.K.d.M., III, 3.–1., Vol. 1, Herbert Bismarck to Caprivi, 18 November 1887. Caprivi initially agreed: ibid., Caprivi to Herbert Bismarck, draft, 18 November 1887; later, however, he expressed the wish that the Italians should not be informed of the advantages that faster mobilization provided for Germany, for any leakage of this information to the French would enable them to remedy the situation. PAAA, Deutschland 143, Geh., Bd 1, "Ergänzende Bemerkungen . . .", 21 November 1887.
64   PAAA, Deutschland 143, Geh., Bd 1, Rottenburg's notation, 17 November 1887. A truncated version of Caprivi's memorandum of 15 November was forwarded to Solms by Herbert Bismarck on 23 November 1887: ibid.
65   GP, VI, No. 1296, Bismarck to Foreign Office, 24 November 1887, p. 234; also PAAA, "Deutschland 143, Geh., Bd 1, marginal comment on "Denkschrift betreffend militärische Vorbesprechungen für einen von Deutschland und Italien gegen Frankreich zu führenden Krieg," submitted by Moltke to Bismarck on 26 November 1887.
66   GP, VI, No. 1295, "Vorläufige Darlegung des Generalfeldmarschalls Grafen von Moltke über eine eventuelle militärische Kooperation Deutschlands und Italiens gegen Frankreich," November 1887, p. 232.
67   ibid., p. 233.
68   PAAA, Deutschland 143, Geh., Bd 1, "Denkschrift. . .", submitted by Moltke to Bismarck on 26 November 1887.
69   ibid., Deutschland 121, Geh. No. 12a, Bd 1, Moltke to Bismarck, 30 November 1887. See also Canis, *Bismarck und Waldersee*, pp. 220 ff.
70   GP, VI, No. 1307, Moltke to Bismarck, 23 January 1888, and enclosure, pp. 247–9.
71   ibid., VI, No. 1323, Solms to Bismarck, 22 July 1889, pp. 265–6, and No. 1324, Solms to Bismarck, 23 July, pp. 266–7.
72   Langer, *European Alliances*, pp. 479–81; Marder, *Anatomy*, pp. 129, n. 18; 141–3.
73   PAAA, England 71b, Vol. 5, notation of Rantzau, Friedrichsruh, 20 August 1888, instructing the Foreign Office at Bismarck's request to inform Hatzfeldt; also Holstein to the ambassadors in Rome and Vienna, 7 February 1888; and Herbert Bismarck to the ambassador in London, 28 April 1888. See also Paul M. Kennedy, *The Rise of the Anglo-German Antagonism, 1860–1914* (London, 1980), p. 197.

# 3 Wilhelm's Naval Dreams

The accession of Wilhelm II on 15 June 1888 marks the end of the decline of the German navy, relative to that of the major Continental powers against which Caprivi had considered its ambitious if rather desperate use. This decline had been accompanied by confusion about the strategic purposes of the navy and about corresponding ship construction.

Wilhelm II undoubtedly provided significant stimulus for German naval construction. Hallmann has entitled a chapter "The naval passion of the young Kaiser,"[1] and sees him as dominating "the construction policy of the naval administration until the first fleet law."[2] On the other hand, Eckart Kehr scathingly remarks: "The fleet preference of Wilhelm II reflected no insight into either the political or economic necessities of overseas power politics, but was mere games-playing. He handled the fleet question from the viewpoint of a lieutenant."[3] His childhood interest in ships and naval matters had been encouraged by his parents. During his visits to England he had visited English dockyards and inspected Nelson's flagship, *Victory*. English naval power greatly fascinated him and he was extremely proud when, in 1889, his grandmother Queen Victoria named him admiral of the British fleet, an appointment which he considered more than honorary. A former Director of British Naval Construction, Sir Edward Reed, once questioned whether any other admiral in the British navy was as "well informed concerning the most trivial detail of a ship or its machinery as the head of the German navy."[4] In his youth Wilhelm read naval history, particularly the six-volume naval history of Great Britain by William James. He was to remain an enthusiastic ship-designer, although it is alleged that one of the ships he designed would have sunk immediately if launched.[5] A close personal link with the German navy was forged when with his parents' approval his brother Heinrich entered it. At the time of his accession to the throne Wilhelm announced: "The Navy knows that it has not only filled me with great joy to belong to it through an external bond, but since my earliest youth in full agreement with my dear brother, Prince Heinrich of Prussia, I have a warm and vital interest in it."[6] In his memoirs Wilhelm remarks that it was when he briefly served in the Foreign Office in 1886 and was instructed about commercial policy and colonies that he "became aware of our dependence on England because we lacked a fleet and Heligoland was in English hands."[7]

Upon ascending to the throne, claims Wilhelm, he "immediately took in hand the building and reform, yes, one can say building anew, of the

German fleet on the basis of preliminary studies in England and at home. That did not suit the competent but somewhat obstinate general [Caprivi] who was not entirely free of vanity."[8] Caprivi's departure was the first sign of Wilhelm's active naval interest. As Caprivi wrote to Tirpitz: "It was clear to me that I would not be adequate to the young Kaiser with his sailor-like passion."[9] And Tirpitz maintained: "The basic reason for Caprivi's departure was that the Kaiser wanted to split up the powers of the Admiralty so that he might better be able to interfere personally."[10] Bismarck approved, for he had found the Admiralty too powerful.[11] Caprivi was succeeded by an admiral, Count Anton Monts, whose task was to preside over the dissolution of his office. A special committee recommended a division of the powers of the Admiralty between the High Command of the Navy (Oberkommando der Marine) and the Imperial Naval Office (Reichs-Marine-Amt). Accordingly Wilhelm ordered on 30 March 1889:

(1)   The High Command of the Navy will as of 1 April of this year be separated from the administration thereof and will be directed by the commanding admiral named by me according to my instructions. His duties and rights correspond to those of a commanding general of the army.
(2)   The administration of the navy will be directed under the responsibility of the Imperial Chancellor by the Secretary of State of the Imperial Naval Office with the powers of a higher imperial agency.[12]

Two days earlier Wilhelm had decreed that "for 1 April of the current year a special Cabinet for naval matters be set up for me and report to me in the future in these matters to the same extent as until now has been done by the Chief of my Military Cabinet."[13]

The obvious parallel was the organization of the army. The High Command, which comprised the total of the *Kommandogewalt* of the Emperor, including operational planning, was stronger than the Great General Staff or the Imperial Naval Office. It was deliberately broken up in 1899 at Tirpitz's behest, who wanted to make his agency, the Imperial Naval Office, which after 1889 was limited to "administrative tasks and parliamentary representation of naval needs,"[14] the dominant naval institution. The Naval Cabinet was in charge of personnel issues. Its chief, by virtue of his office, was in close contact with the Emperor and often played a decisive role, particularly when the other two agencies disagreed.

Bernhardt von Bülow was to maintain: "What Wilhelm I accomplished for the army, he [Wilhelm II] wanted to achieve for the navy. While Wilhelm I succeeded in the unification of Germany, Wilhelm II wanted to found German naval importance [*Seegeltung*] and thereby German world position."[15] Wilhelm admired his grandfather greatly, suggested that in the Middle Ages he might have been canonized, and tried to emulate him. When encountering parliamentary obstacles to his naval ambitions in the 1890s, it is natural that he thought of comparisons between his own situation and that of his grandfather during his struggle with the Prussian parliament over the military increase and reform. "Build now and present the bill to the Reichstag later"—just as Bismarck and Wilhelm I had done—he told Hohenlohe in March 1897.[16] A *Staatsstreich* was an imminent possibility and "the eighteen army corps he had would soon settle accounts with the south Germans."[17] His duty was "to fight out the conflict over the navy, as his grandfather had fought out the conflict over the army."[18] In talking to Hohenlohe on 30 March, he countered the Chancellor's moderating comments by saying "that nothing can be gained without struggle, that he was obligated to secure Germany's defensive strength and that he was then prepared for a life-or-death struggle."[19] And on 29 November 1899 he cabled the Foreign Office that the naval question is one of "To be or not to be. In the face of this question there is for me no more of a retreat than for my most blessed grandfather in the question of army reorganization."[20] It is, however, somewhat far-fetched to deduce from it as Berghahn has done that Wilhelm copied the army reorganization of his grandfather so as to limit the possible increase of parliamentary influence over the navy to the Imperial Navy Office.[21]

The establishment of a tripartite naval leadership in 1889 and the further elimination of the powerful High Command in 1899 created a situation in which the frictions within the leadership could only be solved by Wilhelm II. Even an extremely competent individual like Tirpitz could not establish his domination within the navy: he merely managed to make himself the most influential naval figure. And Wilhelm II was not able to eliminate the conflicts and coordinate the activities between the leading agencies of the naval leadership any more than he could in the case of any other military, naval and civilian powers.

In the case of the navy it would have helped if Wilhelm had known exactly what he wanted. He did very much want a large fleet, but he did not really know why he wanted it and whether it should primarily consist of large ships of the line or cruisers. Count Alfred von Waldersee, Chief of the General Staff, noted in his diary in the fall of 1888: "The naval passion of the Kaiser expresses itself strongly; more strongly than is good for us . . . The Kaiser is now also determined to make great monetary demands for the navy, in order again to build greater ships than Caprivi considered necessary."[22] He had just managed to start the construction of four battleships. In 1894 the Empress Frederick described her son's plans to her mother as follows: "William's one idea is to have a Navy which shall be larger and stronger than the British Navy."[23] In February 1895 he reported to the Prussian Royal Military Academy about the general inadequacy of the navy[24] and in November 1895 he wired to Hohenlohe "about the conditions of our navy which are screaming to high Heaven and about its total inadequacy."[25] Along with his naval advisers he was certainly prepared to provoke a crisis with Britain over Transvaal in January 1896 to generate popular support for at least filling some major gaps in the navy.[26] About a year later Hohenlohe regarded Wilhelm's aim as being a "gigantic fleet plan."[27] The more excitable "Grey Eminence" Friedrich von Holstein claimed "that today the value of a person for H[is] M[ajesty] depends on his willingness or usefulness to cooperate directly or indirectly in increasing our supply of ships." Holstein saw Wilhelm's aim as a gigantic fleet for which he was "willing to stake the peace and one might even say the existence of the Reich."[28] To his friend Count Paul von Hatzfeldt, ambassador in London, he confided: "With the Kaiser the navy question now takes precedence over everything . . . The Kaiser wants a fleet like England's—with twenty-eight first-class battleships—and wants to direct his entire domestic policy to that end, i.e. to fight."[29] Hohenlohe maintained that "Wilhelm stands under the influence of people who make him believe that he can undertake a great period of conflict, change the Imperial Constitution, and build countless cruisers."[30]

Why did Wilhelm think that Germany needed a navy? Above all, to be a world power, to protect her trade, and to assert her power abroad. In 1894 he boasted that he was "not reading, but devouring Captain Mahan's book; and I am trying to learn it by heart." It is doubtful, however, whether he ever understood the message of the author of *The Influence of Sea Power upon History, 1660–1783*.[31] In his speech to the Royal Military Academy on 8 February 1895, Wilhelm pointed out that the extent of a nation's maritime commerce ought to be the measuring-stick for the size of her navy. In Germany's case, whose commercial shipping in general ranked fourth and whose steamshipping ranked second in the world, the navy failed to measure up altogether. While Germany's interests might bring her into collision with maritime powers, particularly the United States and Japan, she would be totally incapable of dealing with them. Germany would also be unable to participate actively in any complications in the Far East arising out of the Sino-Japanese War. Within European waters the German navy was no longer a match for the French and Russian fleets, which would be capable of blockading the German coast, destroying German trade, undertaking landings, and, above all, cutting off essential food-imports. To offset the French threat the German fleet, according to Wilhelm—and the German operations plans—would have to carry the offensive into the English Channel. But without a substantial increase the German navy would by 1899 be incapable of leaving port in the face of growing Russo-French strength. Wilhelm pointed out that the events of the Sino-Japanese War—which he discussed at inordinate length—had demonstrated the importance of navies for land war. "Only he who dominates the sea can effectively reach his enemy and maintain, undisturbed by him, the freedom of military operations . . . Naval strength in European waters is chiefly measured in terms of first-class armored ships."[32]

Wilhelm's views as expressed in this speech were influenced by the thought of Kapitän-zur-See Tirpitz, Chief of Staff in the High Command,[33] and fell in line with the renewed emphasis on the importance of battleships. Wilhelm also stressed to Hohenlohe in March 1897 the importance of a strong fleet against France when he said that "we must have an armored fleet in order to protect our trade and to supply ourselves . . . our fleet must be strong enough to prevent the French fleet from cutting off the necessary foodstuffs."[34] But the concept of a fleet for the execution of world policy did not fade from Wilhelm's mind, even when he switched his interest to cruisers and viewed England as the opponent. In October 1896, Wilhelm saw in the reports of a possible British fleet demonstration in the Persian Gulf a warning that some day "*à la* Transvaal England would take away our colonies, which we are entirely incapable of preventing." In desperation Wilhelm suggested an agreement with France and Russia—something he had already recommended to Hohenlohe in April 1895[35]—to guarantee each other's colonial possessions.

It now again becomes evident how foolish it was ten years ago to launch a colonial policy without possessing a fleet, and to develop this policy without keeping equal pace in the development of the fleet. We now have the liability of a large colonial possession which has become the Achilles' heel of Germany . . .[36]

In March 1897, Wilhelm attributed Germany's failure to exercise sufficient pressure on Greece during the Cretan affair to her naval weakness at sea. Had a cruiser squadron instead of a single ship been used, Athens could have been blockaded and other powers would have been compelled to cooperate. But nothing was done because England did not want anything done. And she prevailed "*Because she had the strongest fleet!* Thereby our 1,000,000 grenadiers are of *no* avail."[37] Wilhelm also viewed Germany as unable to advance her commercial interests in China because of inadequate naval strength.[38]

Soon after Tirpitz's appointment Wilhelm saw in the termination of the commercial treaty between Britain and Germany the beginning of a ruthless war waged by Albion for the destruction of German industry which would meet with success unless met by speedy German fleet construction. He did not think that Britain would have dared to terminate the treaty if Germany had possessed a respectable fleet.[39]

At the beginning of November 1897, Wilhelm was more specific about the use of naval power against British economic "egotism," which he deplored at length. Then he added:

In the face of such egotism finally nothing avails but the actual might that stands behind one's claims. All skill of diplomacy is of no avail if it cannot threaten and induce fright through this threatening. And this automatically [*von selbst*] leads to the *ceterum censeo* of the strengthening of the German fleet—not only for the direct protection of German transoceanic trade—although it is also essential for that—but also much more effectively for the concentrated action of an armored battle fleet which, protected by the North–Baltic Sea canal and leaning on Heligoland—whose strategic value is still not recognized—can any moment break out of this strong position against the English Channel and threaten the English coastal cities, when the English naval power was occupied in the Mediterranean against the French or in the East Asian waters against the Russian fleet, perhaps simultaneously. [This] probable case is not overlooked in Britain for whom the keeping back of an adequate reserve for the control of the Channel and for the protection of the coast is already made prohibitive by the shortage of competent crews whose acquisition already now creates the greatest difficulty because of voluntary enlistment. Only if the armored fist is thus held before his face will the British Lion hide his tail as he recently did in face of American threats.[40]

These comments are highly significant. They coincide chronologically with the launching of the Tirpitz plan for a fleet against England[41] and are very specific in terms of an offensive use of the fleet against her, reflecting some of the operational thinking of the naval High Command,[42] as well as in terms of the German advantages over Britain because of expected British shortages of manpower and naval commitments elsewhere, anticipating points which were later stressed by both Tirpitz and Wilhelm as giving the German navy a fighting chance against Britain. In the mention of a fleet as a frightening threat there appears some of that negation of diplomacy in favor of force which, when appearing in the Pan-German League and the Navy League, is seen by Eckart Kehr "as a concept of clear and basic materialism . . . in international relations."[43]

As Wilhelm was to admit later, he was at this time "highly doubtful, whether . . . the intended increase of the fleet during the Septenannate [originally intended time-period for the duration of the Navy Law] would be able to keep pace with the so rapid growth of Germany into an industrial state of the first rank, with her correspondingly increased need for the protection of her overseas trade in the competition for overseas markets with superior naval powers, and with the entire development of international politics in general whose centre of gravity shifted more and more out of continental boundaries to a world power position with naval power for its protection."[44] Wilhelm's comments, like similar ones by Tirpitz when justifying to contemporaries and posterity increases going beyond the original Navy Law, may to a certain extent be taken with a grain of salt, but are on the whole plausible in view of the fact that the fleet proposed in 1897 was unable to perform the tasks both Wilhelm and Tirpitz expected from it.

By 1897, and even more by 1899, Wilhelm's naval thinking had come under the influence of Tirpitz, who had at the beginning of June 1897 taken over the duties of the Secretary of State of the Imperial Naval Office. Tirpitz, as is well known, had imparted his opinions to Wilhelm earlier.[45] But prior to Tirpitz's appointment the main influence on Wilhelm in naval matters was the Chief of the Imperial Naval Cabinet from 1889 to 1906, Admiral Gustav Freiherr von Senden-Bibran. A bachelor of narrow interests, tactless, anglophobic, and totally dedicated to his duty, "he was enthusiastic to the highest degree about the development of our navy. This went so far that he sincerely demanded from our political leadership . . . that it must according to the growing strength of our fleet provide it with smaller or greater political conflicts as opportunities for activity."[46] From 1889 to 1899 he had the difficult task of mediating between the conflicting policies and personalities of the Imperial Naval Office and the naval High

Command and was closer to the Kaiser than either. Hohenlohe noted in his journal—although his source was Admiral Hollmann, Secretary of State of the Imperial Naval Office—in December 1896: "The importance of Senden for His Majesty lies in the fact His Majesty only has superficial knowledge of the navy, but since he wants to issue orders himself he cannot ask questions or request instruction. If he now has a plan for the navy, or a wish or idea, then Senden must put it in proper form for him. With him the Kaiser feels at home; he asks him questions and allows himself to be instructed by him."[47] Senden was consistent in his adherence to a battleship program,[48] sided with the High Command against the Secretary of State Hollmann, and, although by no means uncritical of him, in the interests of the navy advanced Tirpitz into the position of Secretary of State of the Imperial Naval Office.[49] It was he who impressed on Wilhelm the need to undertake a large-scale campaign to create interest and enthusiasm among the population for the navy,[50] something that Tirpitz was to do later with such skill and success.

Although Wilhelm was to maintain his interest in the navy until the end of his reign, he did not fully agree with Tirpitz even during the period of peace. He found his Secretary of State somewhat of a bore, his program a bit of a straitjacket, and the principle that it was necessary to have quantity before one could afford quality potentially dangerous. Deist maintains that "there exists no doubt that he was a supporter of cruiser warfare at least until the taking over of the Imperial Naval Office by Tirpitz in 1897. And even thereafter the Imperial dilettante shipbuilder retained his preference for the cruiser type much to the dismay of his State Secretary."[51] Subsequent chapters will provide the details.

## Notes: Chapter 3

1 Hallmann, *Der Weg*, pp. 48–101.
2 ibid., p. 56.
3 Eckart Kehr, *Schlachtflottenbau und Parteipolitik, 1894–1901: Versuch eines Querschnitts durch die innenpolitischen, sozialen und ideologischen Voraussetzungen des deutschen Imperialismus* (Berlin, 1930), p. 177.
4 Quoted in Jonathan Steinberg, *Yesterday's Deterrent: Tirpitz and the Birth of the German Battlefleet* (London, 1965), p. 62.
5 Bernhardt Fürst von Bülow, *Denkwürdigkeiten*, Bd I, *Vom Staatssekretariat bis zur Marokko-Krise* (Berlin, 1930), p. 69.
6 Quoted in Hallmann, *Der Weg*, p. 52.
7 Wilhelm II, *Ereignisse und Gestalten, 1878–1918* (Leipzig, 1922), p. 10.
8 ibid., p. 43.
9 Hassell, *Tirpitz*, Caprivi to Tirpitz, 26 June 1888, p. 53.
10 Tirpitz, *Erinnerungen*, p. 38.
11 ibid.; also Steinberg, *Yesterday's Deterrent*, pp. 62–3.
12 Wilhelm II to Bismarck, 30 March 1889, quoted in Hubatsch, *Der Admiralstab*, p. 236.
13 Wilhelm II to the Chief of the Admiralty, 28 March 1889, quoted in ibid.
14 ibid., pp. 52–3; Berghahn, *Tirpitz-Plan*, pp. 30–9.
15 Bülow, *Denkwürdigkeiten*, Bd I, p. 173.
16 Fürst Chlodwig zu Hohenlohe-Schillingsfürst, *Denkwürdigkeiten aus der Reichskanzlerzeit*, Bd III, ed. Karl Alexander von Müller (Stuttgart/Berlin, 1931), journal entry for 7 March 1897, p. 311.

17  ibid.
18  BA, Bülow, *Nachlass* No. 90, Holstein to Bülow, 24 March 1897.
19  Hohenlohe, *Denkwürdigkeiten*, Bd III, journal entry for 30 March 1897, p. 327.
20  PAAA, Deutschland 138, Bd 16, Wilhelm to the Foreign Office, 29 November 1899.
21  See Berghahn, *Tirpitz-Plan,* esp. pp. 28–9.
22  *Waldersee,* Vol. 2, p. 4, diary entry for 9 October 1888.
23  Quoted from William L. Langer, *The Diplomacy of Imperialism,* 2nd edn (New York, 1960), p. 428.
24  BA-MA, N. 160(Nachlass von Senden-Bibran)/13, "Vortrag Seiner Majestät des Kaisers und Königs in der Königlichen Kriegs-Akademie am 8. Februar 1895."
25  PAAA, Deutschland 138, Bd 7, Wilhelm II to Hohenlohe, telegram, 23 November 1895.
26  See John C. G. Röhl, *Germany without Bismarck: The Crisis of Government in the Second Reich, 1890–1900* (Berkeley, Calif., 1967), pp. 166–7; and particularly Hohenlohe, *Denkwürdigkeiten*, Bd III, Wilhelm to Hohenlohe, 8 January 1896, pp. 153–4.
27  Hohenlohe, *Denkwürdigkeiten*, Bd III, Hohenlohe to Eulenburg, 4 February 1897, pp. 297–8.
28  *Holstein Papers,* Vol. 4, *Correspondence, 1897–1909* (Cambridge, 1963), Holstein to Bülow, 17 February 1897, p. 19; and Holstein to Eulenburg, 1897, p. 11.
29  ibid., Holstein to Hatzfeldt, 14 April 1897, pp. 27–8.
30  Hohenlohe, *Denkwürdigkeiten*, Bd III, journal entry for 20 March 1897, p. 327.
31  See Thomas Baecker, "Mahan über Deutschland," *Marine-Rundschau,* Vol. 73, No. 1 (1976), p. 14. Also Wilhelm Deist, *Flottenpolitik und Flottenpropaganda Das Nachrichten Büreau des Reichmarineamtes, 1897–1914* (Stuttgart, 1976), pp. 43–4.
32  BA-MA, N. 160/13, "Vortrag Seiner Majestät . . . am 8 Februar 1895."
33  See below, pp. 62–5; 68–79. I have not found an *Immediatvortrag* apparently used by Hallmann (*Der Weg,* p. 129), prepared by Tirpitz, dated 4 February 1895, which concludes with the words: "If one considers the development of the Russian and French fleets in the near future, then, unless no increase in battleships occurs on our side, the still existing chance to create for us some breathing-space through a battle at the beginning of the war would cease to exist, even if we were victorious in that battle." Hubatsch claims to have used this memorandum as well: *Der Admiralstab,* p. 63.
34  Hohenlohe, *Denkwürdigkeiten*, Bd III, journal entry for 2 March 1897, p. 311. On 3 February 1897, Wilhelm told Hohenlohe that "we must have half of the total number of Russian and French ships. Otherwise we are lost" (ibid., journal entry for 3 February, p. 295).
35  ibid., journal entry for 11 April 1895, p. 58.
36  GP, XIII, No. 3396, Wilhelm to Hohenlohe, telegram, 25 October 1896, p. 4.
37  ibid., XII, ii, No. 3215, Wilhelm's final comment on Plessen, minister in Athens, to Hohenlohe, 28 March 1897, p. 396.
38  PAAA, Deutschland 138, Vol. 1, "S.E. geh. vorgelegt, Ki," 17 March 1897.
39  GP, XIII, No. 3413, Wilhelm's final comment on Monts, Prussian minister in Munich, to Hohenlohe, 31 July 1897, p. 34; and No. 3414, Wilhelm to Hohenlohe, 1 August 1897, pp. 34–5.
40  Hauptstaatsarchiv Stuttgart (henceforth abbreviated as H St Ar St) E 73/73a, 12e, Verz. 61, Axel von Varnbüler, Württemberg minister in Berlin, to Mittnacht, 5 November 1897, reporting a conversation with Wilhelm during a hunting party at Liebenberg.
41  See below, pp. 138–51.
42  See below, pp. 118 ff.
43  Kehr, *Schlachtflottenbau,* p. 407.
44  H St Ar St, E 73/73a, 12e, Verz. 61, Varnbüler to Mittnacht, 2 November 1899, reporting Wilhelm's conversation with Varnbüler, 31 October 1899.
45  See below, pp. 64–5; 71–3; 83; 86; 115–16.
46  Walter Görlitz (ed.), *Der Kaiser . . . Aufzeichnungen des Chefs des Marinekabinetts Admiral Georg Alexander v. Müller über die Ära Wilhelms II* (Göttingen, 1965), p. 26. For a favorable view of him, see Hallmann, *Der Weg,* pp. 54–6.
47  Hohenlohe, *Denkwürdigkeiten*, Bd III, journal entry for 12 December 1896, pp. 288–9.
48  Steinberg, *Yesterday's Deterrent,* pp. 101–2.
49  ibid., pp. 93–4; Bernhardt von Bülow maintains that Senden hated Tirpitz, Bülow,

*Denkwürdigkeiten*, Bd I, p. 68. The full text of Senden's opinion of Tirpitz—of which Steinberg gives the essence on p. 69—appears in BA-MA, N. 160/11. "Erlebnisse als Chef des Marine-Kabinetts: Notizen und Aufzeichnungen." The full text also refers to Tirpitz as "rabid" and brings out more clearly Tirpitz's fluctuations between euphoria and depression.

50  Steinberg, *Yesterday's Deterrent*, pp. 99–100.
51  Deist, *Flottenpolitik*, p. 44.

# 4 Foreign Policy and Naval Operations, 1888–89

In the face of increasing expectations of war in the first years of Wilhelm's reign, the navy had to face the prospect of fighting a war without as yet enjoying the advantages of a completed canal at a time of deteriorating power relationships. Naval operations were now planned in the High Command, headed from 1889 to 1895 by Vize-Admiral Max von der Goltz and from then until its dissolution by Admiral Knorr. From January 1892 to 1895 the Chief of Staff Kapitän-zur-See Alfred Tirpitz and his collaborators from the Torpedo Inspection (Inspektion des Torpedowesens) brought to the High Command new energy and clearer views concerning strategy, tactics, and ship construction.

On 16 October 1889, Goltz presented to Wilhelm a 144-page "Memorandum concerning the waging of war by the navy against France, against Russia, and against France and Russia together."[1]

The cases of war under consideration were the obvious ones. War was still imminent in the opinion of many. In March 1888, Holstein had commented: "Bismarck wants to put off making war while he remains at the helm. The generals, regardless of their views on other matters—Waldersee, Bronsart, Verdy, Loë, Caprivi—think that time is running *against* us, that 1889 will be a particularly unfavorable year and that we ought not to allow certain military preparations along our frontier or the Galician frontier."[2] And Moltke feared in April that the very concentration of Russian troops on the German border would force the outbreak of "the dreadful [*heillose*] war."[3] He warned Bismarck that information about Russian military preparations and troop movements to the west indicated "that Russia wanted to be ready for war by the end of the year."[4]

At the beginning of November 1888, Wilhelm II conceded to Waldersee that "this general political situation points to a war in the course of the next year. Against the enormous power of Russia and France the assistance of Austria and Italy should not be given too high an estimate."[5] In the spring of 1889, Waldersee, the Minister of War Verdy du Vernois, and Wilhelm were in agreement that a preventive war should be fought against Russia in the near future, as soon as German armaments were complete, and that Bismarck should be dropped if he refused to agree. According to Waldersee, Germany would be ready on 1 April 1890; according to Verdy, in the fall of 1890.[6] Since "we should have nothing before our eyes but preparing ourselves for the impending struggle with France–Russia," Waldersee advised Wilhelm to avoid serious involvement in the Samoa crisis.[7] In the fall of 1889, a few days before Goltz presented his memorandum to Wilhelm, Waldersee, when reporting on the deployment and mobilization arrangements for 1890–91, declared "that the war for which we are preparing will be the most violent one ever waged and that we risk everything."[8]

And, just one day before the report of Goltz, Waldersee stated in respect to Czar Alexander III's visit, which Bismarck considered a success:[9] "Whatever the course of the visit the Russians continue to arm and will, when they are ready, face us and Austria in the most threatening position."[10] It is very probable that the memorandum of the naval High Command was drafted as a specific response to this expectation of and wish for a two-front war.

Not only the impressionable young Kaiser but also the shrewd and experienced Geheimrat Holstein fell under Waldersee's spell. Holstein had for some time been very critical of Bismarck's policy, particularly his alleged neglect of Austria and his—or, rather, his son's—preference for Russia.[11]

Holstein had certainly been right in stating that Bismarck did not want a war. None the less, as he told Baroness von Spitzenberg in early January 1888, war was possible if not probable.[12] At that time Herbert Bismarck maintained that according to the available information France did not want war and Russia did not consider herself equal to the coalition facing her.[13] But soon there was increased concern about France. In February, Herbert was worried about rising germanophobia in that country,[14] and in March the Chancellor considered it possible that "France sought to pick a quarrel with Italy and make a *German* war resulting from it appear as an attack on France."[15] By May he was both more pessimistic about the maintenance of peace and more belligerent, stating in the Prussian Ministry of State: "If the worst came to the worst . . . war with France would not be a disaster. Russia was not yet ready, and certainly needed time to become so. France's attitude showed that war could not be avoided in the long run."[16] But by November Bismarck had calmed down, thinking that the outbreak of a two-front war in the next few years was improbable.[17] He emphatically rejected a preventive war and the premiss for its justification: namely that the Russians were planning an attack against the Central Powers. He considered the Russian troop movements to the west not as a deployment for war against Austria and Germany but as preparations for the seizure of Constantinople.[18] He encouraged Austria-Hungary, whose internal weakness alarmed him to the point of doubting her value as an ally,[19] to strengthen her armed forces and counter the Russian preparations, while restraining her from taking an aggressive line against Russia unless she was sure of British support. He closely observed the Bulgarian conflict, however, expecting that a Russo-Austrian war resulting from it would plunge Germany into a war with both Russia and France.[20] In his recent book, Paul Kennedy states that Bismarck made his famous alliance offer of January 1889 to Britain because of indications "that a two-front war was perhaps unavoidable."[21] His confidence in Russia's friendship was shaken. In the summer of 1889, Joseph Maria von Radowitz summarized the Chancellor's view of the German relations with Russia as follows: "We can no longer as before count on Russian friendship and must allow for this in our foreign policy . . . [Therefore] we must at once or in the near future do battle with the Russians. As before he saw his task as avoiding conflict with Russia, not seeking it."[22] He again regarded Alexander III as a guarantee of peace with Russia.[23]

In April 1889 the Württemberg minister in Berlin remarked: "We are following with great attention the endeavors of England to improve her navy, because its cooperation is being counted on in a European war."[24] In the summer of 1889 there also appeared a possibility of war between France and Italy, which raised the question of naval operations. Crispi, the Italian Premier, now feared a French surprise attack by land or sea. He raised the question of naval cooperation between the powers of the Triple Alliance, suggesting that the best course of action would be for the three fleets to unite for common action in the Mediterranean. When the German ambassador in Rome, Count zu Solms, retorted that the German fleet would have to take on the Russian and French navies, Crispi, seeming to ignore the Russian navy altogether, remarked that if Germany "could prevent the French Channel fleet from going to the Mediterranean, Italy's and Austria's fleets would be strong enough to battle with the French Mediterranean fleet."[25]

Solms had encouraged Crispi to try to conclude a naval convention between Italy and Austria. As in 1887 and in 1888, Bismarck, however, suggested that Italy should, above all, seek a naval understanding with England, for "the Austrian fleet does not assure supremacy, even if we take on the [French] Channel fleet and the Russians wait."[26] On 23 July, Bismarck told the Italian delegate Francesco Cucci that jointly the English, Italian and German fleets could paralyze the French navy. When Cucci inquired why he did not include the Austrian navy, he remarked "that it had good personnel but poor *matériel*."[27] Wilhelm agreed with Bismarck's position. He told Herbert: "Even if France would do the unlikely and would remove her ships from the north and west, then our fleet would still have the task of protecting the very active German trade passing through the Channel against French cruisers and undertaking an attack against Cherbourg."[28] Goltz, too, was opposed to making specific promises to the Italians, preferring to retain free scope for the German fleet,[29] but wanting to encourage Austro-Italian discussions.[30]

According to Goltz's memorandum of 16 October 1889, in the case of war against France, Russia, or both, the navy was given as tasks: (1) the protection of the German coast, (2) destruction of hostile trade, (3) cooperation with land forces, and (4) direct attack against enemy coasts.

"The first task will always and best be solved through the defeat of hostile naval forces on the high seas; control of the sea then involves the security of the coast. But if the enemy is too superior and attack on the high sea is hopeless, or if he does not consider himself strong enough to meet our forces, one must have recourse to other means; in the first case the strategic offensive will have to be selected." The plan thus placed strong emphasis on the offensive waging of war with the naval battle as the key to the achievement of the all-important control of the sea.

The second task, destruction of enemy commerce, was assigned relatively low priority, and left to the ships stationed abroad in peacetime. Cruiser war against Continental powers could not be decisive because the important communications were by land and the merchant marines of both France and Russia did not offer a sufficiently significant object of attack. Moreover, German cruisers abroad would be in a difficult position for commerce raiding because of a lack of bases. None the less, since "through a ruthless and energetic cruiser war a young navy can gain glory," preparations were to be made to enable ships abroad to engage in commerce raiding. A network of locations for the equipment and supply of cruisers was to be established to make up for the absence of bases, reliable agents were to be recruited, and ship commanders instructed in the arrangements made and given sufficient information to decide at the outbreak of war whether they were to return home, exchange an old ship for a faster auxiliary cruiser, proceed individually to damage the enemy, or try to join other ships for common action. Damaging the enemy was to take precedence over defending German colonies. Goltz thus took cruiser war more seriously than did Caprivi in his operations plans of 1887. We shall see how the basic guidelines established here were fairly consistently followed after 1896 once regular operations directives were provided for ships abroad and preparations were made for their activity there.

Cooperation with the army, the third task assigned to the navy, was expected to occur only in the later course of war, after the first decisive battles had been fought, and was to include the protection of troop-transports and communications at sea, support of the attacks on and defense of fortifications, and the pinning down of enemy land forces by attacks against his coast. In the initial stages of war the navy was thus freed from supporting army operations—an emancipation that had been anticipated in Caprivi's plans of 1887.

The fourth naval task, attacking the enemy coast, was viewed from the vantage-points of both strength and weakness: "If the mobile forces of the enemy have been beaten and our own coasts are secure from the enemy, we carry the war into his territory and damage him in all ways through incendiary action, destruction, and disturbance, and prepare him for subjection through the violence of war; but if nothing can be achieved in any other way, be it because the enemy is too strong for us to attack on the high seas, or because he is not strong enough for an offensive on his part, it can become necessary to turn to this sort of waging of war in order to achieve anything at all." Like Caprivi, Goltz argued that an energetic offensive on the part of the navy in the next war was necessary if it was to become an equal and respected partner of the army.

The detailed discussion of operations was confined to the summer period, for only then were most of the ships in service or capable of being put in service and the exercise squadron was at home. Because Denmark occupied a highly strategic position in a naval war before the completion of the Baltic–North Sea canal, her attitudes and role were considered in some detail—unlike in Caprivi's plans. As in Caprivi's plans, the value of Austria and Italy as allies was taken into consideration. The possibility of an alliance with England was not considered, and it was admitted that because of her enormous naval strength her involvement would provide the war with an entirely different character.[31]

The more simple cases of war against France alone and against Russia alone were discussed first with the hope that from these would emerge principles for action that could be applied in more complicated cases. Then the case of a war of Germany, Austria, and Italy against France and Russia was considered, and subsequently came the examination of how German waging of war at sea would be affected by the participation of Denmark. The systematically prepared document reflected a detailed knowledge of the naval forces and fortifications of European powers.[32]

In dealing with a war against France alone the document pointed out that if the French decided to confront Germany with their united fleet their force of twenty-seven seagoing armored ships and ten armored-deck cruisers, as opposed to eleven armored high-seas ships and two armored-deck cruisers on the German side, would prevent the German force from coming to battle at the beginning of the war. It would first have to try to wear down the French fleet through constant attacks by light forces. If the French were to attack, they would probably do so in the Baltic where they could more easily find bases and where Kiel offered a more tempting object of attack than did Wilhelmshaven in the west.

Neither Kiel, nor the Elbe estuary, nor Wilhelmshaven could in the long run withstand the attack of the united French fleet. The best defensive strategy would be to avoid dividing the German fleet since it was impossible to defend both Kiel and Wilhelmshaven, and to concentrate the united fleet before Wilhelmshaven from where it would threaten the rear communications of the French if they proceeded to the Baltic and thus compel them to do battle there or to divide their forces by leaving behind an observation force at least the size of the German fleet. The strategy proposed here is similar to that recommended by Caprivi in his memorandum "Coastal war in the North Sea."[33] But the author of the memorandum of 1889 was also influenced by Caprivi's proposal of an offensive thrust against the French coast.[34] Like Caprivi he recommended that this attack occur in the first days of the war when the French Mediterranean forces had not yet arrived in the north, although he was more aware of the risks involved. But he considered seriously only an attack of torpedo-boats, followed by that of the armored fleet, against Cherbourg, to make its docks inoperable. No mention was made of the possibility of drawing inferior French naval forces to battle through the bombardment of less important coastal places, such as Calais, as proposed by Caprivi. After the attack, the fleet was to concentrate in Wilhelmshaven.

In a war against Russia, the German navy would enjoy superiority, since the Russian Baltic Sea fleet possessed only six armored ships capable of taking the offensive and only one full-strength armored battleship. Caprivi's prediction that the Russian navy would soon surpass the German had not yet come true. It was considered unlikely that the Russian fleet would take the offensive if the German fleet was in the Baltic, but it could still play a fairly effective defensive role, which best suited the Russian national character. Also the Russians might try to send out a few cruisers into the Atlantic to prey on German shipping. The German naval tasks would consist of preventing the exit of the Russian cruisers, blockading the southwest coast of Finland, the Gulf of Finland, and the coasts of Livonia and Courland, and, if necessary, supporting the land forces. The German navy was to be concentrated in the Baltic Sea and proceed to an offensive. Libau and Windau were to be destroyed. Then various alternative courses were discussed and the difficulties involved carefully considered. Finally the author, more specifically than either Heusner or Caprivi, recommended setting up with army support a base in the Moon Sound, off the Estonian west coast. He estimated that a 15,000-man force would be necessary for the capture and defense of this base and claimed that the General Staff would provide it, since such a diversion would assist land operations. There is no evidence, however, that he had consulted with the General Staff. This base would support the blockade of the Gulf of Finland and possible operations within it. The navy was to refrain from engaging in battle with the powerful Kronstadt fortifications until Estonia and Ingermanland had been occupied by German troops.[35]

A war of the Triple Alliance against both France and Russia would greatly complicate matters. The Russian navy would probably take the offensive but the French would take the defensive in the north and engage the bulk of their forces in the Mediterranean. This was the course that Caprivi had also expected France to take. The German navy would thus have the choice of either fighting Russia under circumstances similar to those in a war between Germany and Russia or taking the offensive against France, as Caprivi had proposed, to provide relief for Austria and Italy. Like Caprivi, the author of this memorandum considered the French fleet stronger than the Austro-Italian forces. He, as well as Huene, the military attaché in Paris, expected France to launch an offensive against Italy. Huene thought that after the outbreak of war the French would immediately attack the Italians through the Alps, attempting to occupy Turin and Milan, and use their naval superiority to blockade the Italian coast and cut off the Italian fleet from the Austrian. Thus Italy was to be forced out of the war "before Germany could have any advantage from the Italian participation in war."[36] According to an earlier report of the German naval attaché in London, Kapitän-zur-See Schröder, France would remain on the defensive against Italy on land but take the offensive at sea.[37] The German naval attachés in London and Rome viewed the Austrian fleet as small but capable, but considered the larger Italian fleet as weak in terms of leadership, training, personnel, and confidence.[38] Like Caprivi, the author of the 1889 operations plan realized the difficulties standing in the way of effective Italo-Austrian cooperation, but considered it in the German interest that the two navies unite themselves, for only thus could more energetic action against the French be expected. He maintained that "It is completely out of the question that we should send a force to the Mediterranean"—a statement repeating the objection raised by Goltz to Crispi's invitation.[39] "On the other hand, we could show our allies our good faith by attacking the French northern coast so as to influence the French to strengthen their forces there. This would mean that we would have to give up the control of the Baltic Sea and turn ourselves with our whole strength against the northern coast of France." It is this course of action which was then chosen. The major attack was to be directed against Cherbourg and Le Havre; Boulogne, Calais, Dieppe and Dunkirk were to be shelled. The author then proceeded to contradict his statement about sending the whole fleet against France by suggesting that limited forces were to be kept in Danzig to hold the Russians in check and, if necessary, to prevent the Danish naval forces from uniting with the Russian.

As for Denmark, it was not assumed that she would join Germany's enemies at the very outbreak of war. Rather, she was expected to do so later under pressure from them, particularly if Germany had suffered setbacks, and only if France was engaged against Germany. For Russia alone would not be able to offer necessary support to the Danes. Therefore, at the beginning of war the German navy could without hindrance from Denmark deploy in either Kiel or Wilhelmshaven. But if it chose Wilhelmshaven, and Denmark declared war on Germany, then the return of the fleet to Kiel would become progressively more difficult depending upon whether Denmark alone was the belligerent or was joined by Russia. Should the French fleet also appear in Danish waters a return would be impossible. Therefore, except in the case of the war against France alone, the preferable deployment of the fleet should be in Kiel. Thus the author appeared to negate his recommendation of a large-scale action against the French northern coast in the event of a war of the Triple Alliance against France and Russia. Nor was it entirely clear why deployment in Kiel was unnecessary in the event of war against France if it was the French fleet that would be the greatest obstacle to the return of the German fleet. And later he went on to say, "If Denmark later takes France's side, which it will probably do as soon as the French fleet arrives in the Baltic Sea, then nothing is changed for our waging of war, whether we have deployed in Kiel or Wilhelmshaven," whereas in discussing the case of war against France he had advocated deployment in Wilhelmshaven! The author was evidently unable to resolve the puzzle presented to the German naval planning by Denmark's controlling and yet ambiguous position. Later he discussed landing operations in Denmark, claiming to have heard the Chief of the General Staff declare himself in favor of such action. It is amazing, however, that he did not follow up this hearsay with official consultation. He concluded that the effect of Denmark declaring herself on the side of Germany's enemies, particularly at the outbreak of war, would require further examination.

The final part of the memorandum dealt with waging war in the winter. The freezing in of the northern part of the Baltic Sea from the beginning of December to the middle of May made most naval operations by or against Russia impossible. The French would not be expected to blockade the North Sea coast or to enter the Baltic, and the German forces should be deployed in Wilhelmshaven and await further developments. But the most complicated factor lay in the presence of the active fleet in the form of the exercise squadron in the Mediterranean. It was to be decided whether in the case of the outbreak of war the squadron should attempt a return home or should remain in the Mediterranean. The latter course would be very unfavorable if Germany had no allies. Were she allied with Austria and Italy, arrangements were to be made for the cooperation of the German force with their navies.

Although more systematically developed than Caprivi's plans and emphasizing more strongly the need for offensive action and the value of a naval battle, the High Command's plan of 1889 essentially followed Caprivi's notions. Except in a war against Russia alone, an offensive was to be undertaken in the west. This, however, was not entirely consistent with army planning. Waldersee proposed waging an offensive preventive war against the Russians, and Moltke's memoranda of February and March 1888 advocated a two-pronged offensive on the part of the German and Austrian armies against Russia. In the event of a war between Germany and France, Russia was expected to be hostile but not necessarily belligerent. The entire German army could not be deployed against France. It was to concentrate in Lorraine, but its offensive capacity was limited.[40]

On 16 October when the High Command memorandum was presented to Wilhelm, he substantially modified it by rejecting its most aggressive operation: the use of the armored fleet against the French northern coast and Cherbourg—an action which he had envisaged a few months earlier. The caution which had appeared in the Admiralty in response to Caprivi's similar proposal now reasserted itself in Wilhelm's mind. Most probably Wilhelm was influenced by his new Chief of the Naval Cabinet, Senden-Bibran, who had been one of the critics of Caprivi's proposals.[41] Only in the case of war against France alone, which he considered improbable, did Wilhelm consent to the deployment of the fleet in Wilhelmshaven. In insisting that it otherwise deploy in Kiel, Wilhelm appears to have gone along with the author's concern about the danger a hostile Denmark could constitute to a western deployment and to have adjusted the plan to the eastern emphasis of the operational work of the General Staff. In accordance with the eastern emphasis he ordered preliminary studies about establishing a base in the entrance of the Gulf of Finland.[42] Unfortunately there is no evidence about the immediate reaction of Goltz or the operational department of the High Command to Wilhelm's orders. Cryptic as these orders were, they rejected along with the advance of the navy into the English Channel the only way the navy could contribute to the common war effort of the Triple Alliance, encourage more aggressive Austro-Italian action, and relieve Italy of French pressure. By ordering deployment in Kiel—except in the improbable case of a war against France alone—they brought about a decision in favor of concentration in the Baltic Sea.

In short, the use of the fleet in wartime was substantially changed. In this switch Waldersee's influence may well have played a role, although there is no evidence that he was consulted. But even Bismarck had not placed any particular importance on the encouragement of Austro-Italian naval cooperation, which he considered both premature and unimportant.[43] In view of what was then basically the rejection of Goltz's operational notions —close as they were to those of Caprivi—it is significant that they were in 1892 essentially taken up again by Tirpitz and developed in a period of further deterioration of Germany's naval power relationship to the Continental powers, of her political relationship to Britain, and of her power position in Europe in the course of the 1890s.

## Notes: Chapter 4

1  BA-MA, F 5596, III, 3.–1, Vol. 1, "Promemoria betreffend die Kriegführung der Marine gegen Frankreich, gegen Russland und gegen Frankreich und Russland Zusammen." The document is a calligraphic masterpiece in a clerk's hand. It is not specifically dated. In someone's hand there is a comment: "Jahr? 1890? . . . Nach dem Inhaltsverzeichniss 1889." Internal evidence also points to 1889 as the year of its preparation. The document is unsigned and it is impossible to determine its authorship. By presenting it to Wilhelm, Goltz none the less took responsibility for it.
2  *Holstein Papers*, Vol. 2, diary entry for 27 March 1888, p. 366; Canis, *Bismarck und Waldersee*, pp. 241 ff.; Müller-Link, *Industrialisierung und Aussenpolitik*, pp. 338–53.
3  BA-MA, Nachlass Feldmarschall Moltke, Stück No. 13, Helmuth von Moltke to Wilhelm von Moltke and his family, 2 April 1888.
4  PAAA, Russland 72, Geh., Bd 3, Moltke to Bismarck, 8 May 1888.
5  *Waldersee*, Vol. 2, entry for 3 November 1888, p. 14.
6  ibid., entry for 15 April 1889, p. 48; Joseph Maria von Radowitz, *Aufzeichnungen und Erinnerungen aus dem Leben des Botschafters Joseph Maria von Radowitz*, ed. Hajo Holborn (Stuttgart, 1925) Bd II, p. 297; also Norman Rich, *Friedrich von Holstein: Politics and Diplomacy in the Era of Bismarck and Wilhelm II* (Cambridge, 1965), Vol. 1, pp. 251–2.
7  *Waldersee*, Vol. 2, entry for 5 April 1889, p. 48.
8  ibid., entry for 10 October 1889, p. 69.
9  GP, VI, No. 1358, Bismarck to Solms, 15 October 1889, pp. 359–61; and No. 1359, Bismarck to Heinrich VII Reuss, 15 October 1889, p. 362.
10  *Waldersee*, Vol. 2, entry for 15 October 1889, p. 72.
11  Above all, Rich, *Holstein*, Vol. 1, pp. 174–283 passim.
12  *Spitzenberg*, diary entry for 4 January 1888, p. 238.
13  PAAA, Frankreich 102, Bd 8, Herbert Bismarck's circular to the Prussian ministers in Munich, Dresden, Stuttgart, and Weimar, 13 January 1888.
14  ibid., 2 February 1888.
15  PAAA, Italien 88, Bd 2, Bismarck's comment at the head of a dispatch of Solms to himself, 20 March 1888.
16  *Holstein Papers*, Vol. 2, diary entry for 13 May 1888, p. 375.
17  PAAA, Frankreich 95, Bd 26, dictation of Bismarck, 4 November 1888.
18  PAAA, Russland 72, Geh., Bd 4, Bismarck's marginal comment on the report of the German military attaché in St Petersburg, Count York von Wartenburg, of 17 November 1888, and dispatch to Herbert Bismarck, 2 December 1888.
19  On 18 October 1888 he told Schweinitz "that it is all the same to me whether German or Slavonic is spoken in Carinthia or Crain, but it is important to us that the Austro-Hungarian army remains unitary; if it is loosened by national differences, then the value of our ally lessens and it must be considered whether or not the renewal of our alliance is advisable": *Denkwürdigkeiten des Botschafters General von Schweinitz*, Bd II (Berlin, 1927), p. 370.
20  PAAA, Deutschland 137, Bd 1, Bismarck to Dönhoff, Prussian minister in Dresden, 12 February 1888.
21  Kennedy, *Antagonism*, p. 90.

22  Radowitz, *Aufzeichnungen*, Bd II, p. 296.

23  *Spitzenberg*, diary entry for 5 December 1889, p. 265.

24  H St Ar Stuttgart, E 73/73a, 12c, Verz. 61, Zeppelin to Mittnacht, 12 April 1889.

25  PAAA, Italien 88, Bd 5, Solms to Bismarck, 15 July 1889.

26  GP, VI, No. 1323, Solms to Bismarck, 22 July 1889, pp. 264–5.

27  ibid., No. 1324, Bismarck's remark at the head of Solms to Bismarck, 23 July 1889, p. 267.

28  Otto von Bismarck, *Die gesammelten Werke*, 2nd edn, Bd VIII, ed. Willy Andreas (Berlin, n.d.), p. 663.

29  PAAA, Deutschland 143, No. 1, Vol. 1, Herbert Bismarck to Berchem, 28 July 1889. The attack against Cherbourg, which Goltz was to propose in his operations plan, becomes an attack against the French northern coast in Berchem to Solms, 30 July 1889, GP, VI, No. 1326, p. 269.

30  PAAA, Deutschland 143, No. 1, Bd 1, Goltz to the Foreign Office, 2 August 1889.

31  A document entitled "Zusammenstellung der Stärkeverhältnisse der Flotten von Deutschland, England, Italien, Oesterreich einerseits und Frankreich, Russland und Dänemark andererseits," n.d., no signature, probably dating from 1889 since it lists all ships and vehicles launched by the powers concerned until that year, leads to the conclusion that if Britain were on the German side the situation would become extremely favorable to Germany. France would be entirely involved in the north with Britain, and the German fleet would be equal to the Russian Baltic Sea fleet. The number of ships given in the tables of this document differs, however, from those listed in the operations plan, suggesting different authorship. The document was forwarded to the Foreign Office and is located in PAAA, Deutschland 138, Bd 1.

32  On 3 February and 13 August 1889, the German military attaché in Paris, Captain Hoiningen, "genannt Huene," provided extensive detailed and technical information about the defenses of the French coast from Dunkirk to Cherbourg.

33  See above, pp. 20–1.

34  See above, pp. 22 ff.

35  Colonel Klopsch reported from St Petersburg on 14 October 1889 that at the start of war the Russian Baltic fleet would proceed immediately to Copenhagen so as to join with the Danish fleet: PAAA, Russland 72, Geh., Bd 6. By this time Germany was represented abroad only by two naval attachés: since 1882 one was accredited to London and since 1886 another to St Petersburg. Before 1898 naval attachés had been accredited to Washington only on a temporary basis. See Klaus-Volker Giessler, *Die Institution des Marineattachés im Kaiserreich* (Boppard, 1976), pp. 32–3; 308–14.

36  PAAA, Frankreich 95, Bd 32. Military reports of Hoiningen, 13 July and 23 August 1889. According to the latter, the French had a very low opinion of the Italian navy.

37  ibid., Italien 72a, Bd 1, report of Schröder, 23 March 1888.

38  ibid., report of Schröder, 20 February 1888; also report of the military attaché in Rome, Engelbrecht, 22 March 1888, ibid., Bd 3, report of Engelbrecht, 5 June 1889.

39  See above, p. 42.

40  See Gerhard Ritter, *Der Schlieffen-Plan*, pp. 16–18; and Moltke, *Aufmarschpläne*, No. 34, "Denkschrift vom Februar 1888 über den Feldzug gegen Russland bei gleich-zeitigem Krieg mit Frankreich," pp. 150–6, and No. 35, "Denkschrift betreffend Krieg gegen Frankreich," March 1888, pp. 156–62; Canis, *Bismarck und Waldersee*, pp. 241–79.

41  See above, p. 23.

42  Comment at the head of a memorandum signed by Goltz on 17 October (1889).

43  See above, p. 27.

# 5 Coordination of the Army and Navy for Coastal Defense, 1889–95

In the meantime attempts were made to strengthen Germany's maritime–strategic position. Consideration was given to the defense of Heligoland, acquired in 1890, and of the Baltic–North Sea canal, scheduled for completion in 1895, which involved general discussions of coastal defense, cooperation between various navy and army agencies, and examination of the role of the navy in the overall defense effort.

As stated above,[1] much had been expected for the navy from the Baltic–North Sea canal. In spite of Tirpitz's denial that Heligoland had been acquired because of its military value,[2] Wilhelm II, the Secretary of State at the Foreign Office Adolf Hermann Marschall von Bieberstein, and Caprivi asserted at the time of the negotiations for its acquisition or soon thereafter that it had great strategic importance. In June 1889, Wilhelm was reported as saying "Militarily Heligoland was of the greatest importance for us; in case of war the French would establish a foothold there and provision themselves; if Germany occupied this island the Elbe and the Jade Bight were easy to defend."[3] Marschall maintained: "The possession of Heligoland is militarily of the greatest importance for us because of the North–Baltic Sea canal."[4] Caprivi, now Chancellor, told the Badenese minister Brauer that the acquisition of the island had given the North–Baltic Sea canal its true significance, for the German Baltic Sea fleet would have had to fight the enemy by the island, were it not in German hands, before being able to unite with the German North Sea fleet. With the island in German hands, the unification of the German naval forces was assured and a blockade of the German North Sea coast was made much more difficult.[5] It appears that it was Wilhelm who was most insistent on the acquisition of Heligoland.[6]

In one of the few attempts to coordinate Germany's overall defense effort Wilhelm in 1889 established the Land Defense Committee (Landesvertheidigungskommission), which met first under the chairmanship of Moltke and, after his death on 24 April 1891, of Prince Albrecht of Prussia.[7] In respect to questions pertaining to coastal defense, the Committee made its preliminary recommendations in the spring of 1889,[8] asked that the Prussian Ministry of War and the High Command of the Navy discuss these recommendations, circulated submissions from its members, and held meetings on 25 June and 24 November 1891. On the basis of its deliberations Wilhelm issued orders on 17 December 1891 and 6 February 1893.

In the communications between the Ministry of War and the High Command of the Navy the former showed some reluctance to assume responsibility for the costs involved in building fortifications for the canal,[9] whereas the naval authorities argued that since the canal would serve military and economic as well as naval interests its defense costs should not be charged to the naval budget.[10] At the same time an exchange of views occurred between the General Staff of the Army and the High Command of the Navy. Saying that he had to consider measures to be taken during the next mobilization year against hostile landings on the German coast, Waldersee told Goltz that, while an enemy landing on the flat coast of the North Sea could be disregarded altogether and a landing on the coast of Prussia, Pomerania or Mecklenburg could soon be checked by swift German troop movements, a possible landing on the Schleswig-Holstein coast would be a more serious matter, if the enemy had a fleet that was too powerful to be defeated by the German navy and enjoyed the support of Denmark. Waldersee therefore wanted to know whether the army would be pinned down in the face of such a landing by the need to defend Kiel.[11] Goltz replied with some delay, pointing out that contrary to Waldersee's assumption a hostile landing on the German North Sea coast was not entirely out of the question, particularly if the navy was tied down in the Baltic Sea at the time of the landing. Goltz agreed, though, that a landing on the southern coast of the Baltic Sea, while easier to execute than on the North Sea coast, did not offer the enemy a good opportunity to advance inland. The success of a landing on the coast of Schleswig-Holstein—with the aim of seizing or destroying Kiel—would depend on two factors: the defeat or absence of the German fleet and Danish support. The elimination of either would doom the landing or cause the landed forces to be tied down. The defense of Kiel against an enemy operating from the land, Goltz pointed out in full agreement with his staff, was the task of the army. The fortifications of Kiel had been constructed primarily against an attack from the sea and the Kiel garrison was too weak to undertake a successful defense against a large land force.[12]

In their correspondence with the Ministry of War and in their submissions to and statements in the Land Defense Committee the naval leaders successfully argued that the defenses of the North–Baltic Sea canal and of Heligoland must be capable of holding out against the enemy without the cooperation of the fleet. The fleet must retain its full freedom of movement, and be able to debouch from or withdraw into either end of the canal without the danger of serious interference from the enemy. This would require strong fortifications at either end of the canal. In the words of Knorr: "The North–Baltic Sea canal is significant only if the navy is not tied down to local tasks. If the navy would have to undertake the strengthening of local fortifications, at the expense of its mobility, then I would see in it no advantage but rather a disadvantage for the security of the North–Baltic Sea canal."[13] Goltz maintained:

The German navy has to expect to encounter superior enemy forces in open sea. It is all the more important for it to seize every opportunity and to remain in its disposition as free as possible in war and battle situations imposed by the enemy. In a war with superior naval powers the chances of our fleet rest on the independence of its movements and use. The greater the number of vulnerable spots in our coastal land defenses and the more mobile forces must be used for direct coastal defense, the less favorable will become the prospects of engaging the whole strength of our fleet in the decisive battle on the high seas which will remain the most actual and the most important task within the framework of our coastal defense. Accordingly the securing of the island of Heligoland through its own defense measures is an indisputable requirement for our waging of war at sea.[14]

The naval point of view was generally accepted by the Land Defense Committee. The aged chairman Moltke, shortly before his death, conceded that "The navy correctly requests that its activity on the sea not be restricted by keeping back the greater part of its fighting strength for the defense of the canal and therefore requests its strengthening through fortifications and artillery." Moltke, however, was not much more sympathetic to the North–Baltic Sea canal than he had been in 1873,[15] stating that:

the navy alone has use from the canal while the army finds a great difficulty in the guarding of the fourteen-mile-long ditch. If one considers that under the most favorable circumstances the fleet can never decide a campaign, that this decision lies on the battlefields of the mainland, and that we must appear there in full strength, then from the general standpoint of the Land Defense Committee a compromise between the demands of the army and navy must be recommended. The financial means which can be made available for military purposes are to be divided proportionately between both land and sea forces . . .[16]

Count Alfred von Schlieffen, Waldersee's successor as Chief of the General Staff, expressed himself in favor of the navy:

Through the North–Baltic Sea canal the fleet can be helped and . . . enabled to unite as needed in the Baltic or North Sea or to switch quickly the theater of war from one to the other . . . If one, however, wants to use the canal in wartime, then it should not be exposed along its whole length to hostile attacks. Ships which sail on it must not only be protected against the final blocking of their exit by hostile forces but they must also possess a protected place by the canal estuary where they can deploy before entering the sea . . .[17]

This was full acceptance of the naval view of the use of the canal.

Toward the end of May 1891, the Commanding Admiral Goltz attempted to state the specific advantages that would accrue to the Imperial Navy from the canal.[18] He maintained that the tasks that the navy had to perform in a war justified the expenditure of 156 million marks on the canal construction. In particular, in the event of a war against Russia and Denmark control over the Baltic Sea would be of great importance and the navy would play the major role in the capture of Copenhagen. In a war against France, which could present the German navy simultaneously with superior forces in both the Baltic and North Seas, or in a war against Russia, which would in all probability also involve France, the success of the navy depended on its chance to seize a suitable opportunity. Thus the fleet must be able to operate in unison and its exits from both ends of the canal must be well secured.

The basic position-paper about the importance of Heligoland and its fortifications was prepared by the General-Inspector of the Foot Artillery, Lieutenant-General von der Golz.[19] Golz maintained that the island was an important position for the observation of the Elbe, Weser and Jade estuaries, that its lighthouses and seamarks played an important role in the navigation in the German Bight, that its southern part could serve as a base for torpedo-boats, and that heavy guns placed on the island would severely limit the maneuverability of enemy attacking the North Sea river estuaries. Golz had thus realized that an adequately defended Heligoland would hinder enemy action against the German coast. He also stressed that a German-controlled Heligoland would deprive a blockading enemy of a potential base. The High Command of the Navy essentially concurred with Golz's views about the importance of Heligoland.[20]

Schlieffen and Moltke, however, attributed greater importance to the island. Schlieffen came close to maintaining that a fortified Heligoland would make hostile landings on and bombardments of the North Sea coast almost impossible and render a close blockade of the German coast extremely difficult.[21] Moltke considered "the securing of our possession of Heligoland to be more urgent than other measures that have been mentioned in respect to the canal," because of the significant role of the island in the defense of the Elbe estuary.[22] This recognition of the importance of Heligoland induced Prince Albrecht to recommend to Wilhelm on behalf of the Land Defense Committee on 15 May 1891: "the significance of the island of Heligoland is so great that the fortification of the island is urgent and should be carried out in so far as possible in this year."[23] Fearful that the emphasis on Heligoland would lead to the neglect of the fortifications on the Elbe, Goltz warned the members of the committee that "we should not overestimate the value of the island. Fleet operations usually occur during a good season; then a hostile fleet will easily remain outside the range of Heligoland and thus be at any moment ready for an attack on the Elbe. If, however, Heligoland has been captured, then it offers the enemy very great advantages. But if Heligoland is built up as a place for artillery and is fortified I do not want the Elbe position correspondingly weakened."[24]

For the main armament of Heligoland, Golz had recommended four 21 cm L35 cannon and eight 29 cm howitzers, located centrally, which could threaten hostile ships within a ten-kilometer radius and prevent effective bombardment of the island[25]—a recommendation supported by most members of the committee and approved by Wilhelm II. These guns and a small garrison equipped with light quick-firing cannon were expected to make the island impregnable. The building of a harbor for torpedo-boats was unanimously considered to be desirable but not urgent.[26]

There was general agreement among the members of the committee that the defenses of the eastern and western entrances of the canal were inadequate and had to be improved. Disagreement occurred mainly on specific measures. It was recognized that the fortifications of Kiel required strengthening through several batteries of heavy guns and either a dam or underwater defenses which would block the entrance of hostile torpedo-boats and ships into the harbor.[27] On the basis of the original recommendation of Moltke[28] the committee concluded that eighteen Landwehr battalions, three cavalry squadrons, six batteries of artillery, and one Landwehr pioneer company should be involved in protecting the canal against hostile landings. No special fortifications were to be provided against enemy landings, which were to be immediately attacked by land troops.[29] On the other hand, there was disagreement about how to protect the western entrance of the canal. On 31 August 1891, after much debate, the committee recommended to Wilhelm that the position by Cuxhaven be substantially strengthened, and opposed the establishment of a defensive line further upstream or by Klotzenloch.[30]

Wilhelm, however, leaning on the dissenting opinion of the commander of the Third Army Corps, Lieutenant-General von Versen, who favored giving up the fortifications by Cuxhaven altogether since they did not control the passage through the Klotzenloch fairway,[31] opposed the strengthening of the Cuxhaven defenses and proposed, along with Versen, the building up of the Brunsbüttel–Groden position. He also blamed the committee for not considering the defense of the canal against a possible Danish attack from Jutland. The committee met on 24 November to deal with Wilhelm's objections. Prince Albrecht explained Wilhelm's position, reiterated the reasons for the committee's recommendations, and invited Versen to elaborate on his views. Subsequently he asked the representatives of the navy to speak. Kontre-Admiral von Hollen, director of the Marinedepartment of the Imperial Naval Office, stated that the giving up of the fortifications of Cuxhaven would considerably damage the navy by making it possible for the enemy to establish a base in the very estuary of the Elbe. The fortifications of Heligoland, undertaken primarily to prevent the enemy from establishing a base in the North Sea, would thus be in vain. A second defensive line on the Elbe could not be established because of limited financial means. He also challenged the claim that the Cuxhaven fortifications could not control the Klotzenloch fairway. Goltz seconded Hollen's stand. While conceding that the guns of the Cuxhaven fortifications did not entirely command the Klotzenloch passage, he asserted that the navy needed the Cuxhaven fortifications for its deployment. Lieutenant-General Golz added that fortifications at the opening of the Elbe estuary, as provided by Cuxhaven, were also necessary to offer adequate protection for a retreating fleet. With the exception of Versen, the committee upheld its original stand in favor of maintaining the

Cuxhaven position.[32] On 9 December, Prince Albrecht informed Wilhelm that the committee adhered to its previous stand[33] and, on 6 February 1893, Wilhelm ordered that first priority be given to the strengthening of the Cuxhaven fortifications.[34] The navy had thus managed to prevail in securing support for its strategic aims as well as its specific demands.

In order to prevent the establishment of an enemy base in the German Bight which would facilitate a close blockade of the German North Sea coast it soon appeared necessary to garrison and fortify the most suitable islands in the area. In 1894 the defense of the Frisian islands, particularly Borkum, Pellworm, and Sylt, and of the entire North Sea coast had been made the responsibility of the naval High Command, to whom the troops necessary for the defense of the islands were to be subordinated. Army garrisons were to be quartered on Borkum, Norderney, and Sylt; field- and emplacement guns were to be located on Borkum, Sylt, and Pellworm; army objections to these arrangements had to be overruled by Wilhelm personally, and it was eventually agreed to provide two Landwehr infantry battalions, and one regular artillery battalion, to be replaced at the time of mobilization by Landwehr units, and one Landsturm field-artillery battery for Borkum, and half a Landwehr infantry battalion and a Landsturm field-artillery battalion for Sylt.

## Notes: Chapter 5

1  p. 9.
2  Tirpitz, *Erinnerungen*, p. 59.
3  GP, IV, No. 951, Berchem to Bismarck, 21 June 1889, p. 414; for Wilhelm's later interest, see Rich, *Holstein*, Vol. 1, p. 327.
4  GP, VIII, Nos 1680 and 1681, Marschall to Hatzfeldt, 25 May 1890 and 29 May 1890, pp. 16–19.
5  Generallandesarchiv, Karlsruhe (henceforth abbreviated as GLA), 233 (Staatsministerium), 34799, Brauer to Turban, 18 June 1890.
6  Botschafter Paul Graf von Hatzfeldt, *Nachgelassene Papiere, 1838–1901*, ed. Gerhard Ebel and Michael Behnnen, 2 vols (Boppard, 1976), Vol. 2, No. 464, Holstein to Hatzfeldt, 29 May 1890. "Aber für uns ist Helgoland Hauptsache S. M. Wegen," p. 778. See also Kennedy, *Antagonism*, pp. 205–6.
7  During the discussion of naval defenses the naval representatives were the Commanding Admiral Max von der Goltz and the Director of the Marine Department Kontre-Admiral von Hollen. The army was represented by the Inspector-General of Fortresses, Lieutenant-General Golz, General of Infantry Kessler, the Commanding General of the Guard Corps, General of Infantry Freiherr von Meerscheidt-Hüllessem, Colonel-General of Infantry von Pape, Chief of the General Staff General Alfred von Schlieffen, Commanding General of the Third Army Corps Lieutenant General von Versen, and Director of the General War Department Lieutenant-General Vogel von Falkenstein. The secretary of the committee was Colonel von Paulus, department head in the Ministry of War.
8  The details of these recommendations can only be elicited from later correspondence dealing with them, for the first volume of the Landesverteidigungskommission is not available. Volumes 2 and 3 are located in BA-MA, F 7618, Handakten betreffend Landesverteidigung.
9  ibid., Vol. 2, Verdy to Goltz, 24 June 1890.
10 ibid., Goltz to Verdy, 11 October 1890, enclosing a ninety-seven-page report by Knorr, Commander of the Marinestation Ostsee, entitled "Vorschläge für die Sicherung des

Nordostseekanals," 20 July 1890. The above points were made in Knorr's report and were not reiterated by Goltz personally.

11   BA-MA, F 5598, Nebenakten zu O.K.d.M. III, 3.–1., Vol. 1, Waldersee to Goltz, 30 October 1890.

12   ibid., Goltz to Waldersee, 25 November 1890. There were, however, comments made within the High Command by a number of officers between 4 and 8 November, as Waldersee's letter circulated internally, unanimously expressing the view that the navy was responsible only for the defense of Kiel toward the sea.

13   BA-MA, F 7618, Handakten betreffend Landesverteidigung, Vol. 2, Knorr, "Vorschläge für die Sicherung des Nordostseekanals," 20 July 1890.

14   ibid., Goltz, n.d., *Ganz Geheim*. On the first page of the document there is the statement in pencil (initial illegible), "Dem Herrn Chef des Stabes zu s. geh. Kentnisse vorgelegt 4/5."

15   See above, p. 6.

16   ibid., "Votum des Vorsitzenden," Moltke, 18 April 1891.

17   ibid., "Votum, Chef des Generalstabs," Schlieffen, 22 May 1891.

18   ibid., Goltz, "Referat über diejenigen Massnahmen, welche entsprechend der Bedeutung des Nord-Ostsee-Kanals für die Kriegführung der Marine und unter der Annahme einer ausreichenden Befestigung der Insel Helgoland zum Schutze des Kanals für erforderlich erachtet werden," 20 May 1891.

19   ibid., Golz's *Immediatbericht*, 13 December 1890, enclosing "Gutachten über die Benutzung Helgolands im Kriegsfalle und ihre Vorbereitung."

20   ibid., "Promemoria zur Befestigungsfrage," initialed "R" for Chief of Staff, 11 March 1891; and Goltz, n.d., *Ganz Geheim*, "Dem Herrn Chef des Stabes zu s. geh Kentnisse vorgelegt 4/5."

21   ibid., statement by Schlieffen, 6 April 1891. The marginal comments of Heeringen express disagreement with Schlieffen's expectation that a fortified Heligoland would make a close blockade difficult.

22   ibid., "Votum des Vorsitzenden," Moltke, 18 April 1891.

23   ibid., Albrecht to Wilhelm, 15 May 1891.

24   ibid., Landesvertheidigungskommission, Verhandelt, 25 June 1891, Paulus, Proto-kollführer.

25   ibid., Golz, "Die militärische Bedeutung von Helgoland und die für die Insel notwendigen militärischen Einrichtungen," 27 February 1891.

26   ibid., Prince Albrecht, "Bericht über die Verhandlungen der Landes-Vertheidigungs-Commission betreffend die Sicherung der Insel Helgoland," May 1891.

27   ibid., Paulus to Goltz, 17 June 1891, listing the votes in favor of the various measures; "Bericht vom 31 August 1891;" and "Ordre-Entwurf an den Reichskanzler," made on the basis of the meeting of 31 August.

28   ibid., "Votum des Vorsitzenden," Moltke, 18 April 1891.

29   ibid., "Bericht vom 31 August 1891."

30   ibid., Landesvertheidigungskommission, Verhandelt, 25 June 1891, Paulus, Proto-kollführer; "Bericht vom 31 August 1891."

31   ibid., copy, "Votum" of 22 July 1891.

32   ibid., Landesvertheidigungskommission, Verhandelt, 24 November 1891.

33   ibid., Prince Albrecht to Wilhelm, 9 December 1891.

34   ibid., Vol. 3, Wilhelm, countersigned by Caprivi, to the Chancellor, 6 February 1893.

# 6

# The New Era and the Rise of Tirpitz, 1890–95

## (1) Caprivi and the Threats of War

The accession of Wilhelm II had provided the navy with "all-highest" patronage and the departure of Caprivi from the Admiralty had freed it from the leadership of generals. The preparations made for the defense of Heligoland and the much-sought Baltic–North Sea canal would by 1895 very much improve its strategic position and free it from the concerns voiced in the plans of 1887 and 1889 about the role of Denmark in a war against Russia and France.

As Chancellor from March 1890 to October 1894, Caprivi did not give naval development the highest priority. Although he substantially altered the principles of Bismarckian foreign policy by refusing to renew the Reinsurance Treaty with Russia,[1] like Bismarck, he, together with Marschall and Holstein, thought in terms of continental, not world policy. Substantial colonial gain, as Caprivi noted on 19 September 1892, would result from the success of German arms on land. "If it should come to a war on the Rhine, then its success would be decisive for the colonies; if we win, we will have the choice; if we are defeated, our colonial policy is over entirely."[2] They soon became aware that Russia and France were drawing together. With the wire to St Petersburg cut, Germany became more dependent on her allies Italy and Austria. In May 1891 the Triple Alliance was renewed, with Germany promising to support Italy in North Africa. Caprivi and his advisers, however, continued the Bismarckian policies of restraining Austria from taking steps that might precipitate a war with Russia and of encouraging close relations between Britain and the Triple Alliance. The British navy was viewed as a potentially friendly force, necessary for assisting Italy against France in the Mediterranean, and the British government was encouraged to strengthen it.[3] Caprivi also attempted to improve Germany's position in central Europe through the conclusion of commercial treaties with Italy and Austria-Hungary.[4] Although Russian military preparations and troop concentrations continued throughout Caprivi's tenure of office, the discharge of Waldersee from the position of Chief of the General Staff in February 1891 removed from the German leadership the foremost alarmist and advocate of preventive war against Russia. There is no evidence that his successor Schlieffen at this time agitated for a preventive war. He was, moreover, beginning to realize the difficulty of gaining a speedy decision against Russia. Already in August 1892 he expressed himself in favor of trying to gain first a decisive victory against the more dangerous French enemy.[5]

The possibility of a two-front Continental war against formidable French and Russian strength loomed large in Caprivi's thinking. This prospect and the decline of the military might of Austria and Italy[6] persuaded Caprivi that a substantial increase of German armed forces was necessary. On 19 October 1891 he told the Württemberg minister Moser that "there existed the intention to approach this question seriously in the winter of 1892–93 . . . Indeed, we had allies, but matters were such that we would essentially have to wage war by ourselves."[7] As he told Moser on 3 April 1892: "Even if the momentary political situation gives no cause for any particular concern, it must none the less always be kept in mind that . . . [the situation] can quickly change and naturally in the case of all measures directed toward our military preparedness consideration must also be given to a more remote future." The Austrian army, he said on both occasions, was high in quality but much too low in numbers, and the Italian army was hardly capable of engaging a French army of 100,000–150,000 men. "Since the total fighting force of the Triple Alliance was at least 1,200,000 men below that of Russia and France, Germany could not avoid the strengthening of her forces."[8] He was not yet sure how it was to be done. At the same time he mentioned an increase of 77,500 men;[9] and generals, such as the former Minister of War, General Julius von Verdy du Vernois, and Schlieffen, held that "All men capable of service must be trained."[10] Schlieffen doubted whether operations against France and Russia could be carried out with the available forces.[11]

Caprivi's most detailed expositions on the connections between the diplomatic situation and the defense needs were made in the confidential statements to the Bundesrat on 20 October 1892 and the Reichstag Military Committee on 11 January 1893. On both occasions he admitted that for the time being there existed no imminent danger of war, but that latent threats were present. He told the Bundesrat that France entertained notions of revanche and that Russia had taken an ambivalent attitude toward Germany since 1871, with her generals and press hostile and her Czar "perhaps the only honest friend." But it was doubtful if the Czar could in the future direct Russian policy according to his own intentions. He informed the Reichstag Military Committee three months later that there existed a tendency to establish a dictatorship in France. Only the right man was missing. Were he to appear, he would probably plunge the country into a war to escape the filth of the Panama affair. Russia, who according to some observers was diplomatically allied to France but was generally viewed as linked to her by military agreements, had a public that was hostile to Germany. Denmark would undoubtedly join the anti-German forces. At both times Caprivi expressed doubts about the value of the Triple Alliance. In both Austria-Hungary and Italy were forces hostile to the continuation of the alliance, Italy could be bought by France through concessions in North Africa, the political views of the Austro-Hungarian heir-apparent were unknown, national strife could get the better of Austria-Hungary, and austrophobia could force Italy out of the alliance. Sounding more pessimistic on 11 January 1893 than on 20 October 1892, Caprivi concluded: "Our political situation is thus such as to make us envisage for the future a war on two fronts and the dissolution of the Triple Alliance." At both times Caprivi pointed to the formidable military might of France and Russia.[12] And he complained later: "We—I mean the army—lack a firm and clear understanding of what a future war will require of us. We fare almost like the navy."[13]

On 11 January 1893, Caprivi, contrary to Schlieffen's change of thinking about operations, pointed out that Germany's 1,000-kilometer eastern border could be defended only by making offensive thrusts into enemy territory. Moreover, the political situation required initial successes from German arms: only so could hesitant allies be carried along. Germany needed "a short and decisive war. France and Russia can endure longer wars; the former because she is richer; the latter because she is poorer and more insensitive." While doubtless overstating the case to gain approval for the army increase, Caprivi's statements on these two occasions generally accord with the diplomatic and military reporting of the time. His pessimistic view of the situation agreed with that of Schlieffen and Verdy. His emphasis on the need for speedy decisions had already appeared in his memoranda of 1887 dealing with naval operations.

Caprivi sought to increase the army, not the navy. None the less, he did not forget the navy. On 7 April 1890 he had told Count Carl von Wedel that "there hovered before him in the maritime direction an alliance with Denmark and Holland, for if both of these countries with their extensive seafaring populations could be won over, then it would be possible to establish and maintain a powerful and mighty navy for which Germany alone did not possess the human *matériel*."[14] His concern about financial and economic preparations for war, including the supply of the country with the essential foodstuffs and raw materials, also led him as Chancellor to question the naval contribution to the war effort. On 31 May 1891 he queried in the Prussian Staatsministerium whether, in view of Russian enmity and the lack of an exportable surplus of grain in Austria-Hungary, Italy, Serbia, or Romania, anything could be imported by sea, except by blockade-runners. Perhaps grain would not be declared a contraband? The most favorable situation would arise from a continuous import of food materials through a neutral Holland—a consideration in the navy's opposition to the violation of Dutch neutrality later.[15] In response to Caprivi's question, the Secretary of State of the Imperial Naval Office, Hollmann, stated that he hoped that an enemy would not be able to blockade the entire coast of the North Sea and that Britain would not tolerate grain being declared contraband.[16] Caprivi also showed personal concern for the provisions made by the navy for war.[17]

In March 1893, Caprivi intervened in the Reichstag debate concerning naval appropriations. He pointed out that in order to protect commerce at sea it was necessary both to prevent a blockade and to protect ships against enemy cruisers. The former was the task of armored ships and torpedo-boats, the latter that of cruisers.

What we must import and what comes across the Atlantic Ocean must either come through the Channel or circumnavigate England. A hostile fleet that was superior in cruisers would not find it difficult to observe the route around the northern tip of Scotland so as to make the passage of our ships more difficult. We must therefore always depend first on protecting our coast through armored ships and torpedo-boats in order to keep the entrance into harbors open for our ships when they approach our coast from the Channel or around Scotland. We do not need the armored ships to conduct adventures, but to secure our existence during a land war; for if during a war we can no longer count on imports our existence can be seriously threatened.[18]

The speech reflects Caprivi's emphasis on coastal defense and his late appreciation of the need for cruisers. Obviously the navy was still important to him, but mostly to keep supplies coming in during a land war.

Did the German leadership want a war in the period between the dismissal of Waldersee and the resignation of Caprivi? The Foreign Secretary Marschall was ready to join England in a war with France and Russia over Siam. As he told Holstein, "if England goes to war, we, too, will enter it; for if England is broken the Triple Alliance is also broken, since Italy would defect."[19] Wilhelm, however, on 30 July 1893 during his visit to Cowes panicked since "England's fleet was weaker than the fleets of France and Russia together . . . Our army was *not yet strong enough* to fight simultaneously against France and Russia . . ."[20] When reporting this incident to Berlin, Paul von Hatzfeldt, the German ambassador in London, asked several precise questions. Was a European conflict, which would necessarily involve Germany, suitable for her at this time on political or military grounds? If the answer to this question was affirmative, should an agreement between England and Italy be encouraged, with Germany remaining in the background? Or should Germany respond to a British request for participation with the demand that Britain join the Triple Alliance? Hatzfeldt thought that she should make this demand and that Italy should immediately become involved on Britain's side.[21]

Caprivi's marginal comments indicate a calm acceptance of the possibility of war: "From the standpoint of internal politics a war would not be undesirable if it were in a very popular cause. Militarily it was as good for us now as later"—the results of the army increase surprisingly did not appear to matter very much to Caprivi at this time. What was important to him, as it had been to Bismarck, was "that the first shot be fired from a British ship. We are then sure of being able to extend the Triple Alliance into a Quadruple Alliance. We must avoid sending Italy forward alone. She would suffer blows and it would be worse for us later. Thus: first England must be irrevocably involved, but then—whether or not Russia plays along—let all Triple Alliance powers or Italy and Germany go into action. This is what is correct from the military standpoint, and diplomacy must act accordingly."[22] Following the views of the Imperial Naval Office, Caprivi took a dim view of the naval power relationship of Britain vis-à-vis France and Russia. The arrival of a

Russian squadron in the Mediterranean would tip the balance there from the Anglo-Italian to the Russo-French naval forces. Such an event would threaten Britain's position in India and Turkey and also intimidate Turkey. Moreover, a defeat of the British fleet by the French northern fleet might enable the French to encourage an insurrection in Ireland or effect an invasion of Britain.[23] Marschall's response, drafted by Holstein, stated that a reduction of British power by France and Russia was contrary to the interests of Germany and the Triple Alliance, but that great caution would have to be observed concerning British loyalty before undertaking any commitment to her. The "first cannon shot theory" was thus restated with greater suspicion, typical of Holstein.[24] Two days later, in another dispatch drafted by Holstein, Marschall instructed Hatzfeldt that "the possibility of a treatyless support can never be expressed in your discussions with English statesmen."[25] But the crisis subsided. There was neither war nor closer rapprochement with Britain.

## (2) Hollmann and Naval Construction under Caprivi

What was the navy able or willing to do during the chancellorship of its former chief? Tirpitz maintains: "the Imperial Naval Office under Hollmann continued to work toward cruiser warfare, pushed the Kaiser in this direction, and represented this view in the Reichstag, although unsystematically, so that as before the Reichstag could not see in which direction the navy wanted to go."[26]

In June 1890 the High Command prepared a memorandum which examined how the navy could with its prescribed strength wage war against Russia, France, or both. Coastal defense was best to be accomplished through energetic action of the battle fleet and through the scattering of most of the torpedo-boat divisions along the Baltic Sea coast. After the completion of the four Brandenburg-class armored ships, whose construction had been insisted on by Wilhelm II, it would be possible to maintain control over the Baltic Sea, but limited means would preclude the certainty of gaining a victory over the French fleet.[27] Vague as the memorandum was about the tasks assigned to the navy and its strategic purpose, it was one of the first statements pointing out that the navy would soon be unable to perform a specific task. On 20 May 1891, Kapitän-zur-See Wilhelm Büchsel, head of the Military Department of the Imperial Naval Office, completed a position-paper stating that, in contrast to the fourteen high-seas armored ships stipulated by Stosch's plan in 1873, by 1895 only the four ships of the Brandenburg class would match the quality of foreign vessels. Five of the older armored ships had to be replaced before the end of the century. It would be best to require their replacement in the budget of 1893–94. The Saxony-class ships and *Oldenburg*, launched between 1879 and 1883, would have to be rebuilt.[28] He requested that the Reichstag be given a clear picture of the situation.

Hollmann, however, failed to make a comprehensive statement about the needs of the navy and to present a definite plan. Instead he confined himself to piecemeal requests, mostly for cruisers, torpedo-boats, dispatch-boats, and coastal armored ships. In all there had been approved in the period 1888–94 five armored ships, seven coastal armored ships, one cruiser corvette, five station cruisers, and two dispatch-boats. By the summer of 1894 the High Command had concluded that the previous fleet increases were inadequate and openly proceeded to do battle with the Imperial Naval Office.[29]

## (3)  The Emergence of the Ship-of-the-Line School

While Caprivi concerned himself with the increase of the army and Hollmann was content with a hand-to-mouth existence for the navy, the High Command of the Navy came under the influence of Tirpitz, who was appointed Chief of Staff in January 1892. He had been born in 1849 into an educated middle-class family. A poor student, he established a reputation for fighting urchins, and his family was delighted to go along with his request and enroll him at the age of 16 as a sea cadet. In the navy the youngster appears to have found the sense of purpose which he previously lacked and he excelled in it from his admission examinations onward.

It is interesting that Tirpitz had already arrived at some of his later guiding principles as a 22-year-old *Unterleutnant*. On 11 September 1871 he sent his father a review of a recently published pamphlet. In it he developed at some length his own thoughts. He viewed the notion that private property might be respected at sea as Utopian for the next hundred years: "[The] prevention of a blockade, can only be achieved with a fleet, and namely a battle fleet."[30] He also thought that "The North–Baltic Sea canal is of incalculable value . . . We must have Heligoland, and indeed as soon as possible."

In 1877, Tirpitz was appointed by Stosch to work in the torpedo section of the navy and in the next year he was put in charge of it. Tirpitz claims that work in this new area encouraged precision which soon also appeared in tactical trials. First, the previously unexamined battle situations between individual ships as well as the maneuvers of single ships were studied. Along with these the common operations of several units were worked on.[31] At the very beginning of his appointment to the torpedo section Tirpitz stated in a memorandum to Stosch that in a naval battle the aim was the destruction of the enemy fleet. "At sea success lies only in destruction."[32] In answering Caprivi's "Twelve tactical questions" in the spring of 1888, he stressed the energetic use of the fleet in formation rather than of ships individually, avoidance of dividing the fleet, and the need to defeat the enemy.[33] Tirpitz's ninety-page memorandum of 18 April 1889, entitled "Über die Entwickelung des Torpedobootswesens,"[34] "could be viewed as a résumé and justification of his work in the torpedo department."[35] But it also contains significant observations concerning principles of strategy and ship construction. The document strongly suggests that the torpedo department was the original workshop for future German naval development as guided by Tirpitz, first as Chief of Staff in the Naval High

Command and later as Secretary of State of the Imperial Naval Office, implying the principle of limiting ship types for the performance of general rather than excessively specialized tasks.

Equally important for Tirpitz's later activity as Chief of Staff in the High Command, if not as Secretary of State of the Imperial Naval Office, was the stimulus provided by the new torpedo weapon for experimentation.

> . . . what we have determined is that methodical procedures can substantially clarify questions pertaining to naval tactics. This has been done in such a way that a solution has been sought for only one tactical question, worked at for weeks and months in maneuvers relating to this specific question. Our findings that in such a way one could come much closer to actual war situations, that all experiences can be reduced to simple rules, that we learned clearly what demands we could make on the *matériel*—in this case the ship type—but above all that mutual confidence among commanders would be greatly increased led us to recognize without doubt the correctness of the road we had taken.

In a memorandum dating from March 1888 he maintained: "The question of type determination of the individual ship broadens itself through the working out of tactics finally into the general question of the composition of our fleet and how it will have to be constituted for maximum achievement of our purposes with the given personnel and means."[36]

In late 1888, Tirpitz resigned from the Torpedo Inspection, commanded successively two battleships, and in September 1890 was appointed Chief of Staff of the Baltic Sea naval station at Kiel where he assumed his duties in January 1891.[37] His superior was his later rival Knorr. It was there that he composed two key documents: "Reasons which speak for the retention of a High Command with great powers," dated according to Berghahn 1 February 1891,[38] and "Our further maritime–military development," dated April 1891.[39] Berghahn claims that the first document is the early version of the second. It related Tirpitz's strategic–tactical concepts specifically to the organization of the naval leadership, was more critical of the navy than the second, was commented on and basically approved by Knorr, and reached Senden.[40] The April memorandum focused on the main task confronting the navy: its use in a European war. Peacetime representation abroad and coastal defense were deliberately excluded from consideration as distractions. "For a number of years our strength must be concentrated on the development of our navy for a European war." And the war he considered was that previously examined by both Caprivi and Goltz: Germany against France and/or Russia. Unlike the army, the navy

> lacked, at least from its own viewpoint, the concept of large fleet operations with all that entailed. Not only was our navy too small for such tasks, but other tasks were assigned to it during its period of development. We therefore know these matters essentially from our mobilization work and from theoretical considerations. We have indeed

undertaken short peacetime marches of our maneuver fleet without its appendages; but we do not know what it means and which auxiliary forces will become necessary for our fleet to move longer distances and to maintain itself in the [English] Channel for 8–14 days or to hold positions on the Russian coast. We do not know whether we are strategically able, in German waters, to prevent the Russian fleet from reaching Copenhagen.

In short, Tirpitz showed awareness of the problems facing the German naval operations in European waters and condemned the plans that had been drawn up as theoretical or outright amateurish. As we shall see, however, the plan that he was to draw up in February 1892 for a war in European waters was to differ little from those of his predecessors.[41]

Tirpitz further deplored German ignorance in areas where strategy and tactics met, such as reconnaissance and outposts. He conceded that it had been agreed that the main task of the navy was to defeat the enemy in battle, but maintained that differences continued to exist about the meaning of the battle and how it was to be brought about. However, all ships capable of fighting must be concentrated for use in this battle. The strategic aim of winning a naval battle should set quite specific tactical tasks for peacetime. Tactical exercises should start at the bottom, first involving individual ships, then squadrons, flotillas, and finally the entire fleet. A number of specific questions required solution. At what range should firing open for guns of different caliber? What battle formations should be used? Various phases of battle had to be worked through, and the use of torpedo-boats with the fleet required study. From the details of tactical and strategic study and exercise would emerge answers to long-term questions pertaining to ship types and the composition of the fleet. Tirpitz thus connected in a masterly manner questions of naval construction and operations with tactics and strategy.

His views aroused much opposition among the older officers but won the approval of his immediate superior Knorr, who complained that the maintenance of a maneuver fleet of six battleships required an increase of personnel and *matériel*.[42] They were also accepted by Tirpitz's old crew-comrade Büchsel, who was doing some hard thinking about naval building in the Imperial Naval Office. He wholeheartedly concurred with Tirpitz's view that the tactical and organizational developments of a navy should be subordinated to its strategic purpose. In so far as tactical development was concerned, he accepted Tirpitz's judgment implicitly because of his excellent achievements in torpedo-boat tactics.[43] Büchsel thus reinforced Tirpitz's later claim that at the time of his appointment as Chief of Staff in the High Command in January 1892 "I had the most thorough tactical–strategic apprenticeship of all officers of the navy."[44] Senden-Bibran, who had read his memorandum of 1 February, at least in general approved his ideas and encouraged him on 6 April 1891 to express them to Wilhelm at a dinner party in Kiel Castle. Wilhelm, who had already gained a good opinion of Tirpitz,[45] was impressed by the man who could say more about the improvement of the navy than "die Schweinerei muss aufhören," which was the refrain of the naval officers during the dinner.[46] Caprivi, who had gained an extremely high opinion of Tirpitz, now as Chancellor advanced the cause of his former head of the torpedo department with the Emperor. On 28 March 1891, Caprivi reported to Tirpitz that Wilhelm "considers you the future leader [*Träger*] of the navy and thinks that you must concern yourself with its tactical and strategic training."[47]

Hallmann maintains that the decisive influence for Tirpitz's appointment to the position of Chief of Staff in the High Command was the impact of the "Memorandum concerning the reorganization of the armored fleet"[48] which he composed toward the end of 1891 as a reply to a proposal of Hollmann to introduce the so-called "doubling system." According to Hollmann, all ships should be organized in pairs, one with a full crew and the other unmanned. In case of mobilization one ship would transfer half of its crew to the other and reservists would bring both up to full strength. The disadvantage of this system would have been that at the time of mobilization not a single ship would be ready for service. Needless to say, any operations envisaged at the beginning of war, such as the advance proposed by Tirpitz, Caprivi, and Goltz into the English Channel or against the Russian coast, would thus become impossible. On the first pages of his memorandum Tirpitz restated the principles of the importance of naval battle:

> Strategic considerations led us some time ago to the realization that the decision for our navy must be sought in an open-sea battle. We must keep this future naval battle before our eyes as the steady aim in our tactics, in our training of personnel, and in our organization.

Already in peacetime an *ordre de bataille* must therefore provide for an organization wherein one part of the navy would always be manned with active personnel and the rest would be capable of mobilization, if necessary as mere reserve divisions. This organization would provide at the very beginning of a war two armored divisions of full strength and battle readiness, "create in the active divisions stability, tradition, and squadron pride," improve battle tactics and naval capability, enable the reserve formations to attach themselves to the active divisions, and impress on the armored fleet "that our aim is the open naval battle." The views expressed here by Tirpitz appear again to have won the approval of Knorr, who forwarded the memorandum to the High Command. Subsequently Tirpitz had several interviews with Wilhelm and was appointed by him, on 20 January 1892, Chief of Staff in the High Command.

By the time of his appointment Tirpitz had thus worked out the broad outlines of his strategic and tactical thinking. In his memoirs he remarks that one of his next challenges was to develop line tactics. "While we found out these things empirically in the small exercise area before the Kiel Bay, the American Admiral [sic] Mahan simultaneously developed them theoretically from history."[49] Captain Alfred Thayer Mahan's books, *The Influence of Sea Power upon History, 1660–1783* (1890) and *The Influence of Sea Power upon the French Revolution and Empire, 1793–1812* (1892), were immensely influential. The first of them was translated into German by Vice-Admiral Karl Ferdinand Batsch at the request of Tirpitz and Knorr. It had a first printing of 8,000 copies, of which at least 2,000 were distributed by the Imperial Naval Office during the campaign for the first fleet law.[50] Mahan's views were very similar to those of the British Admiral Philip H. Colomb, first stated in his essays in the *Illustrated Naval and Military Magazine* and published in book form in 1891 under the title *Naval War: Its Ruling Principles and Practice Historically Treated.*[51] As Marder points out, Mahan's first, more influential book and Colomb's volume "contained the same arguments and lessons, but, in a sense, they complemented each other. While Mahan aptly defined his subject as the 'influence of sea power,' Colomb gathered facts to show what sea power was, how it acted, and how it must be used in order to exercise this influence."[52]

Mahan showed the immense role that sea power had played in the course of war and in the rise and fall of states and empires. Referring to the growth of British sea power, Mahan, for instance, notes: "It can scarcely be denied that England's uncontrolled dominion of the seas, during almost the whole period chosen for our one subject [1660–1783] was by long odds the chief among the military factors that determined the final issue."[53]

And when Napoleon was preparing for the invasion of England it was the fleet that saved her. "The world has never seen a more impressive demonstration of the influence of sea power upon its history. Those far-distant, storm-beaten ships, upon which the Grand Army never looked, stood between it and the domination of the world."[54]

Mahan postulated a direct connection between sea power and national wealth. "The due use and control of the sea is but one link in the chain of exchange by which wealth accumulates; but it is the central link, which lays under contribution other nations for the benefit of the one holding it, and which, history seems to assert, most surely of all gathers to itself riches."[55] From the events of war between England and Holland in 1667, Mahan deduced a general principle which was to have devastating effect on the as yet current theories of *jeune école*: what was disastrous for Britain was

> maintaining a sea-war mainly by preying upon the enemy's commerce. This plan, which involves only the maintenance of a few swift cruisers . . . possesses the specious attractions which economy always presents. The great injury done to the wealth and prosperity of the enemy is also undeniable . . . Such a war, however, cannot stand alone; it must be *supported* . . . unsubstantial and evanescent in itself, it cannot reach far from its base. That base must be either home ports, or else some solid outpost of the national power, on the shore or the sea; a distant dependency or a powerful fleet. Failing such support, the cruiser can only dash out hurriedly a short distance from home, and its blows, though painful, cannot be fatal.[56]

The relevance of this principle for Germany was obvious: both Caprivi and the author of the High Command memorandum of 1889 had referred to Germany's lack of bases abroad. So did Tirpitz later. Its acceptance meant that Germany required a powerful battle fleet as the essential support for cruiser warfare.

After referring briefly to the subsequent naval warfare, including the War of the Spanish Succession, the Seven Years War, the War of American Independence, the War of 1812, and the American Civil War, Mahan reached the conclusion toward which Tirpitz was groping:

> It is not the taking of individual ships or convoys, be they few or many, that strikes down the money power of a nation; it is the possession of that overbearing power on the sea which drives the enemy's flag from it, or allows it to appear only as a fugitive; and which, by controlling the great common, closes the highways by which commerce moves to and from the enemy's shores. This overbearing power can only be exercised by great navies . . .[57]

As he states in *The Influence of Sea Power upon the French Revolution and Empire, 1793–1812,* "The best coast defense is the navy; not because fortifications are not absolutely necessary, but because beating the enemy's fleet is the best of all defenses."[58]

A major lesson drawn by Mahan from the War of American Independence is the mistake of dividing a navy, as Britain did, between different theaters of war, rather than concentrating it close to home for use against hostile ports "by either shutting up or forcing battle upon the hostile navy, recognizing that it is the key of the situation, when the sea at once unites and separates the different parts of the theatre of war."[59] As for ships, few larger ones are preferable to many smaller ones.

It should also be pointed out that a number of German naval writers were developing views similar to those of Tirpitz and Mahan. "At the turn from the eighties to the nineties the specialist writers began increasingly to attribute to a battleworthy high-seas fleet a decisive significance for the stability of the Reich and to demand for their branch of service [*Waffe*] a position of equality beside the army."[60] The chief of them were Vize-Admiral Batsch, Kapitän-zur-See Alfred Stenzel, Kontre-Admiral Bartholomäus von Werner, Kapitän-Leutnant Georg Wislicenus. They showed the significance of sea power in different wars, stressed the importance of control of the seas, claimed that naval battles were more decisive than land battles, and pointed to the significant role of navies in cutting off the supply-lines and seizing the colonies of weaker sea powers. Wislicenus went so far as to argue that an offensive fleet was more important for Germany than an army capable of mounting an offensive.[61] And Werner maintained that "in given circumstances our fleet can be of greater use to our fatherland than a whole army of soldiers."[62] The fear of a two-front war against France and Russia re-emphasized the relief that the navy would provide for the army by assuming the responsibilities of coastal defense, be it against landings or incendiary action as advocated by the French admiral, Hyacynthe Aube.[63] Werner, Wislicenus, as well as the military historian Hans Delbrück, expressed in public the concern they shared with Caprivi that Germany would in wartime be deprived of necessary food-supplies.[64]

Batsch, Stenzel, and an author in the *Neue Militärische Blätter* maintained that the navy would only fulfill its purpose through taking the offensive against the enemy, seeking him out, and challenging him to a decisive battle.[65] The naval writers further stressed the importance of maritime power for Germany's position as an exporting industrial state and as a colonial power and in the struggles that would arise in the partition of the world.

As Reinhardt concludes: "Tirpitz did not stand in isolation when he, departing in the middle of the decade from the naval–political course of Caprivi, drew attention to the importance of the fleet for the development of the Reich as a world and naval power, and attributed to it its own sphere of action, independent of that of the army."[66]

## (4)  Tirpitz, Operational Planning, and the Construction Program of the High Command

Tirpitz himself claims that the years during which he served as Chief of Staff in the High Command "comprise my best achievement, the filling of the fleet with military content."[67] He brought with him to the High Command a group of like-minded individuals who had learned to work with him and on whom he could depend, his former subordinates in the torpedo section. Members of this so-called "Torpedo Gang" who played a particularly important role in the High Command were the Chief of the Command Department Hunold von Ahlefeld, head of the Third Section of the Admiralty Staff Department (A3) August von Heeringen, and head of the Fourth Section (A4) Otto Braun.[68] On the one hand, Tirpitz's work in the High Command helped clarify his own thinking about the strategic purpose and composition of the German navy, as expressed in the Dienstschrift No. IX "General experiences drawn from the maneuvers of the autumn exercise fleet" ("Allgemeine Erfahrungen aus den Manövern der Herbstübungs-Flotte"), of which the Fleet Law of 1898 is the intellectual descendant and which thus relates to his future building program. On the other hand, his activity vitalized the tactics and strategy of the German navy and defined its immediate military tasks.

One of the first duties that Tirpitz performed was to submit a new operations plan. He was probably requested to do so in view of the expectations of war, since drawing up a plan so soon after assuming office was contrary to his methodical habits of work. His appointment was on 20 January and his "Memorandum concerning the waging of war in European waters in 1893"[69] was dated February and presented to Wilhelm on 9 March.

Berghahn correctly points out that it cannot be demonstrated with certainty that Tirpitz personally drafted the memorandum but concludes on the basis of a comparison of the offensive aims of the plan and those which according to the "Our further maritime–military development" of April 1891 were described as requiring further examination[70] that "the influence of his ideas is none the less unmistakable."[71] Berghahn, however, had not studied the earlier operations plans. Hubatsch, who looked at Caprivi's "Memorandum concerning the waging of war against France," stated that Tirpitz's memorandum "is still entirely rooted in Caprivi's train of thought."[72] Actually, however, Tirpitz's memorandum, while bearing some resemblance to Caprivi's, which is not surprising since he himself claims to have corrected Caprivi's plan for war against France,[73] resembles most closely the High Command memorandum of 1889.[74] It is possible that when ordered at short notice to prepare a new operations plan he simply used the most recent and systematic document as a model. Wilhelm's order of 25 August 1891 for a presentation by the High Command of a comparison of the German, Russian and French naval forces by March 1892, according to Goltz, by necessity led to the revision of the operations plan of 1889—apparently by the time that the comparison was due.[75] Upon being appointed Chief of Staff, Tirpitz thus appears to have faced a deadline for the completion of an important task. According to Tirpitz's later testimony, there did not at the time exist a single department in the High Command which engaged in Admiralty Staff activity.[76] It is also possible that he had a hand in the preparation of the 1889 memorandum. Certainly, his observations in "Our further maritime–military development" indicate that he was well acquainted with German operational thinking. This acquaintance may of course date from his activity as Chief of Staff in Kiel. While he served in this capacity, the maneuvers of autumn 1891 involved essentially defensive stances on the part of Germany against hypothetical eastern and western powers—presumably France and Russia—and against two Baltic Sea powers—presumably Russia and Denmark. In the former, the German fleet was deployed in the Baltic Sea and had as its task the prevention of the unification of French and Russian fleets in Danish waters for the purpose of forcing Denmark to join them. In another maneuver against the same powers there were to be examined the operations of German light forces proceeding from Wilhelmshaven to Kiel upon finding out that a French fleet had arrived there ahead of them. In the case of war against Russia and Denmark, the German forces in Danzig were to try to block the Russian fleet which was proceeding into Danish waters at the time that other German forces were blockading Denmark. The final maneuver dealt with an offensive in narrow waters, presumably the Danish, involving action against mine blockings, torpedo-boats, coastal fortifications, and coastal armored ships.[77] The presence of the description of the maneuvers in the Tirpitz papers indicates his awareness of and probable participation in them. On 23 December 1891, Goltz, moreover, wrote to the Baltic Sea naval station about the position of Denmark in a war between Germany and France and/or Russia. Assuming that Denmark would declare her neutrality at the beginning of such a war to enable her to complete preparations for war and enter the war if a suitable opportunity arose later, he wanted the Baltic Sea base to make arrangements for securing intelligence about Danish preparations in such an eventuality and for a possible surprise attack on Denmark which could be delegated to the Baltic Command.[78] Tirpitz must surely have had to start dealing with some of the issues raised by this communication. His close involvement in the preparation of the memorandum of February 1892 is demonstrated by the preparation in his hand of the notes for the report on the plan to Wilhelm II on 11 April 1892[79] which reveal an intimate understanding of the document.

Unlike the memorandum of 1889, that of February 1892 reduced the main tasks of the navy to (1) the defense of the German coast and waters against hostile attack and (2) indirect influence on land warfare. Tirpitz reported to Wilhelm that cruiser war was to be handled separately.[80] The two tasks of the navy could best be solved through gaining control over the sea, which was only attainable through the defeat of hostile naval forces. This reasoning was almost identical to that of the 1889 memorandum. So was the reference to naval forces as an entirely offensive weapon. The term "Seeherrschaft" (control or domination of the sea) was broken down into either complete or spatially and chronologically limited control. The navy could only effectively participate in coastal war or support the land forces "when the struggle for the control of the sea had ended and one or the other of the hostile fleets has been definitely defeated." Tirpitz was thus elaborately using the general principle of control over the seas to buttress the arguments in favor of the initial strike against the French northern coast which had been advocated by Caprivi in 1887 and Goltz in 1899, but which was in the first case discouraged by the Committee for the Working Through of Tactical Questions and in the second case vetoed by Wilhelm II.

Then Tirpitz, confining himself to the waging of war in the summer only—unlike the 1889 memorandum—proceeded to discuss the cases of war (1) against France, (2) against Russia, and (3) against France and Russia, with or without the support of Austria and Italy; he also considered (4) the joining of France and Russia by Denmark, and (5) the joining of the powers of the Triple Alliance by England. The document is supported by statistics concerning the power relationship between the possible belligerents. German naval strength was given as fifteen armored ships, five protected cruisers, five dispatch-boats, six armored gunboats and sixty-two torpedo-boats. Until 1894 the German fleet would be superior to either the French northern fleet or the Russian Baltic Sea fleet. It was considerably inferior to the united French northern and Mediterranean fleets, which possessed twenty-eight armored ships. It was also inferior to the united Russian Baltic Sea and French northern fleets, which had twenty-six armored ships, augmented to thirty-one ships by a Danish alliance. Unlike Goltz, Tirpitz reserved specific matters, such as the location and details of an advance against the French northern coast or the Gulf of Finland, for further detailed study. Certain courses of action were contingent upon an agreement with the General Staff.

In a war against France alone, which Tirpitz considered improbable,[81] Germany could expect a strategic offensive once the two French fleets were united. In this case the German navy would have no hope of maintaining full control over both the Baltic and North Seas as long as the canal between the two seas was not open. It would have to deploy in the North Sea, for in the Baltic it would risk being enclosed in Kiel and the French would gain control over the North Sea. Concentration in the North Sea would offer the German navy greater advantages against a superior enemy. Were he to advance into the Baltic, or convey troops there for a possible landing, he would expose his flank and supply-routes, relinquish the domination of the North Sea to the German navy, and enable it to threaten French shipping and ports. The enemy was thus unlikely to make the strategic mistake of proceeding to the Baltic with the bulk of his forces if the German fleet deployed in the North Sea. He would have to seek out the German fleet with superior forces. Tirpitz had thus adhered to the view, earlier expressed by Goltz, that an inferior navy possessed a good defensive chance in the North Sea against an opponent lacking nearby bases—a view which was to relate to his later assumption that Germany could with an inferior fleet be a match for England.

But Tirpitz also adhered to Caprivi's and Goltz's proposals for a thrust against the French northern coast at the beginning of the war with the hope of engaging the French northern fleet in battle before the arrival of the Mediterranean forces. During the first ten days of mobilization "we can at the most count on superiority, or at the least equality, in the strength of naval forces" for a successful sea battle. In his notes for the report to Wilhelm, Tirpitz admitted that such action had the character of a coup (*Handstreich*).

As for a war against Russia, the German fleet, during the next two or three years, would enjoy naval superiority and, using Danzig as its base, could thus seek control over the Baltic Sea. This control could only be attained through either the defeat of the Russian fleet or the blockade of the Gulf of Finland. Since it was unlikely that the inferior Russian fleet would offer battle, only the latter course was feasible. And for its successful execution the establishment of a base at the mouth of the Gulf of Finland was necessary within the first two weeks of war. Tirpitz was optimistic about securing army support for the seizure of the base since this action would tie down substantial numbers of Russian troops. Close cooperation with the army had to be arranged. Naval domination in the Baltic would mean the cutting off of one-third of the total of Russian imports and the interruption of Russian troop-transports. Again, the plan does not substantially differ from that of 1889.

According to his notes for the report to Wilhelm, Tirpitz considered the two-front war against both France and Russia the most probable. If Germany alone was at war with these powers, she could not be expected "to maintain control over even one of our seas." Only the North Sea would "offer natural chances for offensive advances of the fleet and for the development of a cruiser war which was to be carried out directly from the home ports." This was the only mention of cruiser war in this memorandum. None the less, Tirpitz correctly assumed that in such a war Italy and Austria-Hungary would be Germany's allies and therefore France would be unable to move her Mediterranean fleet to the north. In such a case, Tirpitz, following both Caprivi and Goltz, recommended that the German fleet be used for offensive purposes against the entire French northern coast, so as to relieve Italy's fleet and provide her with an example of energetic action which she might emulate. Tirpitz added that, unlike the advance in the case of war against France alone, this action was not just a coup, required reinforcements, and was to extend as far as Bordeaux. He also considered and eventually dismissed alternative courses of action. One course would be an offensive strike against Russia: but unlike the French the more defense-minded Russian fleet could not be forced to fight and any blockade of the Gulf of Finland would have to be given up if the French fleet were to appear in the Kattegat. Another alternative would be the deployment of the German fleet in the Kattegat, but the French could not be compelled to do battle in this location and the position would become precarious if Denmark were to join the Franco-Russian alliance. Tirpitz saw that the major objection to the advance against the west would lie in the exposure of the German Baltic Sea coast to Russian depredation. He thought, however, that it would be a serious mistake on the part of the Russians to engage their whole fleet in the bombardment of German cities before being assured of domination over the Baltic. To protect Danzig against attack by individual ships or smaller squadrons, ships and vehicles not participating in the expedition against the French coast should be concentrated there. In general, a temporary giving up of the control of the Baltic Sea should not deter the German fleet from undertaking an advance to the west.

If Denmark were to join the Franco-Russian alliance at the beginning of a war, she could not be adequately assisted by her allies and would be extremely vulnerable to German naval action—even more so if German land forces could be used against her. In his notes for the report to Wilhelm, Tirpitz advocated the immediate occupation of Denmark if she were to join Russia and France but, knowing now from Schlieffen that large numbers of troops would not be available for this action, recommended detailed study to determine if it could be achieved with limited forces. Knowledge of her vulnerability would incline her to remain neutral, unless it were in the German interest to force her to show her colors at once. If she were to join France and Russia later, this would cost Germany control of the sea. But Tirpitz did not think that Denmark would join Germany's enemies if the French northern fleet were defeated. Tirpitz thus shared the concern of the author of the 1889 memorandum about Denmark's role as a possible ally of France and Russia, but was more optimistic about her remaining neutral.

If England was allied with the Triple Alliance—something that was not impossible in the political climate of the time—the German naval leadership "need only concentrate on Russia as an enemy in the European waters." Whether the bombardment of the French Channel coast in the first weeks of war by the German fleet would particularly incline England toward the Triple Alliance was left out of consideration by the future architect of a fleet that was to be used against her.

Tirpitz pointed out to Wilhelm that the execution of the proposed operations in the summer of 1893 required detailed working through of the plans, preparation of orders, and energetic work on tactics and battle leadership. He used the opportunity to oppose the requests of the Imperial Naval Office to become involved in the development of strategy and tactics, pointing out that they must be "left in the hands of the agency which has the command power and carries for it direct responsibility in wartime."[82] Thus he continued his feud with the Imperial Naval Office.

The operations proposed by Tirpitz thus affected the relations between the High Command and the Imperial Naval Office and put pressure on the mobilization arrangements, tactical and strategic training, war preparedness, organization, and size of the navy. Once the operations plan was approved, the High Command proceeded to use it against the Imperial Naval Office in the areas of immediate discord: the claim of the Imperial Naval Office to participate in maneuvers, which the High Command viewed as an infringement on its authority, and the introduction of the "doubling system," which would greatly weaken the war preparedness of the navy and had already been attacked by Tirpitz.[83]

Büchsel admitted on behalf of the Imperial Naval Office on 13 August that adequately trained personnel was unavailable for the execution of the proposed operations plan. In March Goltz had requested the General Staff to express its reaction to the operations plan. This was the first recorded attempt at coordinating the operations of the army and the navy. The approach also had the ulterior purpose of strengthening the case of the High Command before the Emperor.[84] Schlieffen replied almost immediately, pointing out that in the present political climate the only possible war was that of the Triple Alliance against France and Russia. In such a war an advance of the navy against the French northern coast would be "the most effective of all possible operations at sea." Indeed, the proposal of the thrust against the French coast fitted into the change of thinking of the Great General Staff, for we know that by August 1892 Schlieffen had come out in favor of seeking an initial victory over France rather than Russia.[85] For a while there was thus established a general coordination between the operational planning of the army and the navy. Schlieffen maintained that such an offensive would give Germany control of her most important waters, the North Sea, discourage Denmark from joining the anti-German league, damage the French, prevent them from attacking the German coast, and assist the war effort on land by tying down enemy troops. Schlieffen, however, expressed reservations about the availability of troops for any action against Denmark since they would be needed against Germany's major enemies. This was the first recorded expression of the reluctance on the part of the General Staff to support naval operations with land troops—subsequently a recurring theme in German army–navy relations. Somewhat half-heartedly Schlieffen assured Knorr on 16 March of his "willingness to support from my office the operations plans of the navy in so far as the interests of the army leadership would be served" and agreed to have an army officer participate in the common planning of operations.[86] On 24 April 1892, Goltz informed

Schlieffen that he had brought his statement of 12 March to Wilhelm's attention and that he would communicate to him the results of the preparations undertaken for the operations plans in so far as they related to the interests of the army.[87]

In the subsequent years of Tirpitz's tenure of the position of Chief of Staff, maneuvers were used to test the proposed operations. It does not appear that they caused considerable changes in the operational planning. They did, however, further expose the lack of preparedness of the navy for war, something that Tirpitz feverishly attempted to remedy. The maneuvers and the preparation of operations combined to reinforce Tirpitz's conviction that Germany's naval future lay in the development of a battle fleet. This conviction further embroiled the High Command in its fight with the Imperial Naval Office about the definition of the areas of competence of the two agencies—a fight that had broken out before Tirpitz's appointment to the High Command, but in which he was to engage vigorously.

Until 1892, German autumn maneuvers had been short and had involved but a few ships beside the maneuver squadron and torpedo-boat flotillas. "Only since 1892 has the principle been put into effect that, except for ships located in foreign stations, all ships, etc., in service would be formed into the autumn maneuver fleet and drawn into the autumn maneuvers. The latter as a result turned out to be considerably more instructive and could every year serve a considerably larger part of the officer corps." Gradually strategic exercises came to assume a more important role than the tactical ones which had prevailed earlier.[88]

The maneuvers had in the fall of 1892 dealt with the case of war between Germany and a naval power of the first rank blockading both Kiel and Wilhelmshaven. Everything possible was to be done on the German side to prevent the enemy from proceeding to the eastern part of the Baltic Sea where Memel harbored five older German armored ships. In a second variation of the same military situation the enemy tried to entice the German armored squadron to come to battle by attacking the German coast. The third maneuver dealt with war against an eastern power which tried to send its fleet to the western Baltic Sea to enclose the German ships in the Kiel Bay. The German navy was to take a position in the middle of the Baltic, weaken the Russian fleet through attacks by light forces, but only engage it in battle in the Kiel Bay.[89] A maneuver in the fall of 1893 dealt with an attempt by a superior enemy fleet to bring the German fleet in Wilhelmshaven to battle by demonstrative bombardment of the German coastal locations. The German fleet was to avoid battle and to try to weaken the enemy through continuous disturbances by day and attacks by night through its light forces.[90] Another maneuver concerned the situation after the German fleet had been defeated and was blockaded in Wilhelmshaven by a superior western naval power, which could therefore detach substantial forces to blockade Kiel, devastate the German Baltic Sea coast and attempt to destroy the German naval forces based in Danzig. The German forces of the Baltic were to do maximum damage to the enemy through the use of light forces. Both maneuvers of 1893 were to gather experience for the most effective use of light forces in offensive and defensive situations. The second maneuver was also to examine how a navy forced on the defensive could best utilize coastal fortifications and harbors and how a navy taking the offensive could most effectively bombard coastal places.[91] Goltz's comments about the maneuvers— according to Trotha they were drafted by Tirpitz[92]—were scathing. Lack of coordination among participating units, poor tactical and strategic training of the officer corps, and, in a later document, unpreparedness of German artillery for any tactical tasks, and the lack of uniformity of armament of the artillery were criticized.[93]

While continuing with maneuvers and the preparation of operations, Tirpitz was able on 16 June 1894 to issue over Goltz's signature his famous Dienstschrift No. IX, "General experiences drawn from the maneuvers of the autumn exercise fleet."[94] This document drew explicitly on the experiences gathered by Tirpitz as Chief of Staff and somewhat more implicitly on naval history, including the writings of Mahan. On 28 May 1894 a communication of the High Command to the Imperial Naval Office in response to its query of 19 April about ship types basically represented the standpoint that was fully developed in Dienstschrift No. IX less than three weeks later, thus constituting Tirpitz's first positive input into the German naval construction program.[95]

In Dienstschrift No. IX the fleet was viewed as an instrument for strategic offensive. In the course of history, the gaining of control over the sea had become the first task of the navy. Only after it was attained did the means for forcing the enemy to conclude peace become available, among them landings in cooperation with the army, blockade of the hostile coast, hindrance of the enemy's imports, the damaging of his transoceanic interests, and the devastation of his coasts. Offensive, claimed Tirpitz, was much more significant for war at sea than for war on land, for one could never choose the location of a battle with the enemy if one remained on the defensive behind coastal fortifications.

Subsequently Tirpitz related naval power to world power. "A state which has sea interests or—what is equivalent—world interests must be able to represent them and to make its power felt beyond territorial waters. National world trade, world industry, and to a certain extent high-seas fisheries, world transportation, and colonies are impossible without a fleet capable of taking the offensive." Germany and Holland had declined along with their sea power and the rising American sea interests were seeking to build as protection an offensive fleet. Moreover, "only an offensive fleet forms a desirable alliance value" and exerts influence on neutral powers.

"The entire endeavor of the strategic fleet offensive will . . . in principle be aimed at coming to battle as soon as possible." Since the enemy can refuse battle and hide out in ports, naval offensive requires superior strength, which at the time of sailing ships was measured at a one-third supremacy over the enemy. Pointing out that "the history of all previous naval wars irrefutably shows [that] squadron war is the most effective type of fleet offensive and . . . that its major decision lies in battle," and rejecting the claims of the *jeune école* that the difficulties resulting from the coaling of steamships and the threat to ships of the line presented by torpedo-boats rendered squadron warfare obsolete, Tirpitz concluded "that no event in modern history [*Erscheinung der Neuzeit*] justified the assumption that offensive with big squadrons will present greater difficulties than in bygone times. But since it is the best, and in many cases indeed the only, means of naval warfare which is capable of having a positive effect on the enemy, it will also in the future be as correct and necessary as naval warfare itself."

Tirpitz conceded that the exclusive waging of cruiser war could be correct under certain conditions.

But even this cruiser war would be fought under the most unfavorable circumstances at those places where hostile squadrons rule the sea, as earlier naval wars have proven. Then the squadrons form the firm bases on which anti-cruiser warfare and one's own commerce lean. But since exclusive cruiser war from the beginning renounces the strongest means which naval war offers it can gain validity only in specific cases and cannot therefore be the purposeful [*planmässige*] major aim for the development of a great naval power. It is, rather, the last and only means of the vanquished or originally impotent power at sea. But if cruiser warfare forms only one part of naval war, then every won battle, apart from its direct results, allows the opportunities of cruiser war to increase on the one or the other side.

However one may plan in the specific case of waging war at sea, strategically offensively or defensively, by limitation to squadron war or through the addition of cruiser war, the struggle for control of the sea is decisive and its major outcome will be achieved today as always through battle.

The conclusion which Tirpitz thus reached was that the peacetime development of the navy must be toward its preparation for battle. Enclosure 1 dealt with the ships required for the purpose. Since maneuvers had demonstrated that the present-day ship of the line continued to represent the core of fleet power and that the battle line was the best formation for the effective use of artillery, the ship of the line must be a large ship no less than 8,000 tons and because of expense and German coastal conditions no larger than 15,000 tons. For ships of the line Tirpitz did not consider speed of particular importance for actual battle, but wanted a cruising range of 3,400 sea-miles. The ships were to be equipped with heavy artillery of no less than 20 cm, middle artillery of 20 to 10 cm, and light artillery of less than 10 cm. Heavy artillery was to be used at a close range against the vital parts of enemy ships and at all ranges against particular enemy ship types, rapid-firing middle artillery was to play the major role in most battle situations, and light artillery was to be used against enemy torpedo-boats. In addition ships of the line were to be armed with torpedoes and a ram.

Defensively, the ships should be secured through internal watertight partitions against the effect of torpedoes. Above the water-line protection should be provided against the armor-piercing shells of the middle caliber and against the grenades of the heavy caliber. Also the heavy and middle artillery should be protected against enemy middle-artillery fire.

Of the light forces, torpedo-boats were viewed as most important for battle. Their strength lay in numbers, their small size, and speed which was to exceed considerably that of battleships. They should be sufficiently seaworthy to participate in strategic offensives against the enemy coast and sufficiently armed to fight enemy torpedo-boats. One should not expect a single torpedo to sink an enemy ship. "For the continuation of the torpedo-boat it will be adequate if the injury from an accurate shot will be serious, just as one must be satisfied with a similar effect from a shot from the heaviest gun into the vital parts of a ship."

Tirpitz limited cruisers to two types: the heavy cruiser of more than 6,000 tons and the light cruiser of 2,000–3,000 tons, which corresponded to the existing cruisers of the first and the third class. Both were to possess a cruising range of 5,000 sea-miles. The large cruiser should have a speed that would enable it to escape from or catch a battleship and to pursue torpedo-boats. Although the task of heavy cruisers was not the fighting of ships of the line—a consideration to which Tirpitz later adhered in the face of the Kaiser's pressure for larger cruisers—two large cruisers should be capable of fighting successfully one ship of the line. Therefore the light and middle artillery, ram, and torpedo weapons of a heavy cruiser should be equal to those of a battleship, whereas the heavy artillery and armor were to be lighter, so as to reduce the weight and size of the armored cruiser in comparison to the battleship.

The small cruiser was to be provided with the speed to elude a ship of the line and to give chase to torpedo-boats and the strength to resist hostile reconnaissance-ships of equal size and to enable several small cruisers to fight successfully a large cruiser. It was to have sufficient protection to remain afloat while most of its guns were still active. The main tasks of cruisers comprised security, reconnaissance and outpost duty. For their fulfillment they had to operate in groups. It was deplored, however, that the experiences gained about the use of cruisers were limited. Some uncertainty also existed about the use of the train.

As a rule, the fleet should at the outbreak of war concentrate in the harbor closest to the coast from which an offensive was expected or against which one's own attack was to be directed. Thus Tirpitz again spoke out in favor of deployment in the North Sea rather than in the Baltic. This was consistent with the operations plans of both Caprivi and Goltz as well as with his later opposition to Admiral Henning von Holtzendorff's proposals in favor of deployment in the Baltic Sea against England.[96] Strong emphasis was placed on offensive action against the enemy at the very beginning of a war, for then the morale of the attacker was the highest. "The quest for immediate success cannot, however, extend so far that the main aim, which consists of defeating or decisively weakening the enemy fleet, would be lost sight of." Tirpitz quoted Clausewitz to explain the main requirement for any offensive: the concentration of strength at the decisive point, which is particularly important in naval warfare, "as the defender, particularly when he has a larger number of accessible ports, is more quickly and easily in the position of throwing himself on individual parts of the hostile force than is possible in land warfare, especially as by means of his coastal signal stations he is as a rule better informed about the location and strength of the enemy than the latter."

To have a naval strength of the second class, Germany was to possess two squadrons of ships of the line plus a flagship for the commanding admiral, in all seventeen ships of the line, six torpedo-boat flotillas, six cruisers of the first class, twelve cruisers of the third class and an as yet unspecified number of train, auxiliary cruisers and special ships.

The communication of the High Command to the Imperial Naval Office of 28 May 1894 linked the recommended fleet size, which was identical with that required in Dienstschrift No. IX, to the fleet foundation plan of 1873, stating that it only slightly exceeded the size of the then stipulated armored fleet of fourteen ships. But contrary to Dienstschrift No. IX, which justified the fleet requirements in terms of world policy, the letter of 28 May regarded the limit of the requested increase as realistic only "as long as Germany maintains her present standpoint in regard to her world policy, as long as she refuses to view the development of her entire sea interest as her main task, and as long as she limits herself in wartime to the preservation of her existing sea interests only in her home waters or in her neighboring waters." Thus the requested fleet strength would not be adequate to fulfill the requirements of Dienstschrift No. IX. The letter further pointed out that in the coming autumn only the four ships of the Brandenburg class would be fully capable of ranged battle. While it would be unrealistic to demand an immediate replacement of the remaining armored ships, at least the active maneuver squadron and the flagship of the commanding admiral should consist of first-rate ships. Thus *Preussen* and the four single-screw ships would have to be replaced in the near future. Still more urgent was the need for cruisers. Even if inferior substitutes for required cruiser types were acceptable, there was need for the speedy construction of four cruisers of the first class and seven cruisers of the third class. Otherwise, if any cruisers were to be diverted overseas, operations of the battle fleet in the high seas would be almost impossible. Only the number of torpedo-boats came close to being adequate. Except for them "Our need for useful ships of all three types is so great at this time that it is necessary that the construction of all three be started if the strength and capacity of our navy does not in the near future sink from year to year."[97] Six weeks later the High Command[98] rejected a proposed request of the Imperial Naval Office for a coastal armored ship, pointing out that the type no longer suited the German shipbuilding program. The demands of the Imperial Naval Office for the budget of 1895–96, however, almost completely disregarded the wishes of the High Command, placing the emphasis on the construction of cruisers.

In 1893 doubts arose in the High Command about the future execution of the operations plans in the Baltic Sea because of the development of Libau into a first-class Russian naval base. In the spring Tirpitz pointed out that, although the construction of the fortifications at Libau would take ten years, once the base was rebuilt it would entirely change German offensive and defensive strategy in the Baltic Sea. The best German counter-measures would consist of the quantitative and qualitative improvement of the German fleet and the perfection of its mobilization.[99] In October, Tirpitz maintained that a reconstructed Libau would give Russia an ice-free port at the periphery of its waters. It would prevent the German navy from establishing a base at the entrance of the Gulf of Finland for the support of its operations, thereby threatening its rearward communications; as a base it would also enable the Russian fleet to attack the German Baltic Sea coast much sooner and would compel the German navy to direct an offensive against it from Danzig—without, however, having converted that city into a first-rate naval base. For Germany's major bases would remain at either end of the Baltic–North Sea canal and her most vital naval concern would lie in the North Sea and the Danish waters rather than in the eastern Baltic. Tirpitz had thus, in spite of the expected strengthening of the Russian position, remained true to his conviction that the major German naval interests were located in the west.[100] His representation was approved by both Goltz and Wilhelm.[101] It was subsequently agreed to station those naval forces not needed in the advance against the French northern coast in Danzig to protect this port against a Russian attack.

While the position vis-à-vis Russia was being re-examined, Heeringen, head of the department of the High Command dealing with France (A3), drafted a memorandum concerning the operations against France which was explicitly based on Tirpitz's operations directives of February 1892.[102] The memorandum discussed the possibilities of war between Germany and France, Germany against France and Russia, and the Triple Alliance joined by England against France and Russia. Even if Italy remained neutral, France was expected to retain at least nine armored ships in the Mediterranean. The balance between French and German armored ships in the north is set out in Table 6.1.

Table 6.1

| Day of mobilization | France | Germany |
|---|---|---|
| 5 | 11 | 14 |
| 11 | 18 | 20 |
| 17 | 21 | 20 |
| 25 | 24 | 22 |

The advantages thus lay at first on the German side. The thrust on the part of the German fleet against the French northern coast at the beginning of war was described "as perhaps the best chance for a victory which the fleet would find in perhaps a hundred years in the war concerned. A victory in the [English] Channel creates for us after a successful war the right to become a fleet of the first rank, as required by Germany's world mission and world position." If the French Mediterranean fleet remained in the south—for even a victorious German force would not be able to take it on there—the result of such a victory would be control of the home waters and the English Channel and security of imports. If Russia were allied to France, the advance against the French northern coast was also the correct course of action; but, in contrast to Tirpitz, Heeringen proposed that, after defeating the French, the German navy must turn against the Russians rather than remain in the Channel. If the French were not defeated and the Russians were advancing to the west, the German fleet was still to try to defeat either of the two navies separately, but was not to delay too long the decision to sail against the Russians. If the English were on the German side, then Heeringen, like Tirpitz, advised that the German fleet turn at once against Russia.

For the first time there is evidence of systematic preparation of operations by the different sections of the Admiralty Staff Department of the High Command. In the fall of 1895 the High Command consisted of the K (Command) Department, the P (Personnel) Department, and the A (Admiralty Staff) Department. The last, a creature of Tirpitz, concerned itself with operations plans, tactics, maneuvers, and intelligence. It consisted of five sections (A1–A5). A1 dealt with all non-European matters, particularly the use of German ships abroad; A2 with eastern Europe, Russia and Scandinavia; A3 with western Europe, the Mediterranean states, specifically France, Holland, Belgium, Spain, and the Orient; A4 with Britain and the British Empire; and A5 with the development of tactics. By 12 October 1897 there had occurred some change in organization. In the A Department, A1 still dealt with non-European matters; in addition to Russia and Scandinavia, A2 was now specifically involved with Austria-Hungary and the Balkans; A3 handled France, Spain, Portugal, and Italy; A4 Britain, Holland and Belgium; and A7 intelligence. The C (Central) Department had two sections involved in the preparation of operations plans: A5a mobilization; and A5b current annual mobilization arrangements. The K (Command) Department was also sometimes involved in the preparation of operations through sections K1 and K2, organization, K3, artillery, K4, tactics, and K5, torpedoes and mines.[103]

On 24 April 1894, Heeringen forwarded his memorandum to sections A1, A2, A4 and A5 of the Admiralty Staff Department for examination and comment. Most critical were the comments of Siegel, in charge of section A1, who had already criticized the advance into the English Channel when advocated by Caprivi.[104] He wanted a more specific examination of the case of war of Germany alone against France alone, for it would provide a definite basis for the general strategic situation. If the Italians joined Germany, her situation would improve but, if Italy and Austria were on the German side, Russia would be on the French side. Therefore he suggested that the cooperation between France and Russia be examined separately. He also considered the involvement of England on the side of the Triple Alliance to be unlikely. Further, he raised the question whether the French Mediterranean fleet might arrive in the north by the time the German fleet reached the Channel and pointed out that a victory over the French fleet would not give the German navy control over the English Channel if there were unblockaded French naval units in

Cherbourg or if the French Mediterranean forces arrived there. A2, Winkler, agreed with many of Siegel's criticisms, suspected that Heeringen may have viewed the power relationship as being too favorable to Germany, and expressed fear that the Russians might take the offensive against the German coast at the time that the German fleet was in the English Channel.[105] A4 and A5, however, were in general agreement with Heeringen's plan.

Heeringen presented his memorandum to Tirpitz at the beginning of 1895,[106] suggesting that it be submitted to Wilhelm, whose approval of current operations plans was now required before the actual preparations of the operations could be undertaken. In line with Tirpitz's struggle against the Imperial Naval Office, Heeringen remarked "that the whole situation of the High Command can be promoted if the demands of the operations plan will come up for recognition." He then indicated which preparations were still necessary for the execution of the thrust into the Channel. His most important point was that it was not practicable to undertake the thrust without the support of the reserve squadron. The expedition would therefore be launched only on the fifth rather than the third mobilization day, whereby "our chances are somewhat reduced." He stated that the plan could be put into effect at any time, except for the months when the ships were frozen in. He made suggestions about the distribution of work between different departments and advised that contact be established with the Great General Staff, "which would have the final say in the defeat of our eastern and western enemies." It appears that this communication led to the submission of the operations plan by Goltz for Wilhelm's approval on 19 February 1895.[107]

Certain comments from the High Command about Heeringen's proposals dating January 1895 led to a separate presentation to Wilhelm from Goltz. K2, Ahlefeld, expressed his agreement with A4's position in favor of the fleet remaining longer in the Channel and with his realistic concern for Britain's attitude toward the activity of the German fleet in the English Channel. He recommended closer contact with the army so as to correlate operations. Were the army to choose the western theater of war for its offensive operations, the navy must be able to support it even if it meant the loss of Danzig in the east. In case of alternative plans by the army a more defensive course of action against the French must be examined.[108] A2, Winkler, produced a document pointing out that the thrust against the French northern coast would mean that the Russians

> can then seize the whole Baltic Sea, destroy our trade totally, blockade our harbors, burn the open places, bind a part of our army through landing demonstrations. They can also bombard coastal fortifications and with their superior guns remain outside their range. The Russians can also with their whole force appear by Copenhagen and influence Denmark to join our enemies . . . The Russians could then also send some of their forces into the North Sea and force the Channel fleet to return.

Winkler concluded that it was extremely uncertain whether the strike against the French northern coast would succeed, for it might have to be interrupted because of "the screams for help which will arise on the Baltic coast." The German forces left in the Baltic Sea were insufficient to confront steadily growing Russian strength during the next years: five armored ships at the time, seven in 1896, ten in 1897, twelve in 1898 and thirteen in 1899. This unfavorable situation could be remedied by securing an additional squadron of armored ships which could take a defensive position in the Fehmarn Belt where it would protect both Kiel and the rear of the fleet operating in the Channel and whence it could proceed for the relief of Danzig.[109] In his minutes and his submission of 28 January 1895, Heeringen concurred with the glum view taken by Winkler. He stated that Germany must have a fleet which after a successful battle in the English Channel and a loss of 30 percent of its strength would still be capable of taking on a united Russo-Danish fleet. If one counted two Siegfried ships for one ship of the line, Germany would in 1897 possess eighteen such ships, thus twelve ships after the expected loss of 30 percent of the force, or six ships, in the Channel. These twelve ships would be confronted by twenty-two Russian and Danish ships. To be superior to them at least thirteen additional ships of the line would be necessary for the German fleet. In view of the critical nature of the situation Heeringen proposed that the High Command analyze it in an enclosure to the report to Wilhelm concerning the operations plan in the west and demand accelerated construction on the part of the Imperial Naval Office, which did not even suspect that what was at stake here was the existence of Germany. Winkler was somewhat more skeptical about such drastic action, remarking that the response of the Imperial Naval Office would be to "tell us with a smile: 'You thus realize that your offensive plans are adventurous and we must limit ourselves through them to having the enemy come to us, for an increase of the fleet by ten ships is out of the question.'"[110]

The High Command of the Navy prepared a memorandum dated 28 January 1895 for Wilhelm which, in view of the increase of the northern fleets of France and Russia, recommended that the size of the German navy be enlarged to twenty-five ships of the line.[111] Two memoranda, both written by Tirpitz, date 14 February 1895. One was addressed to the Imperial Naval Office[112] as a response to its inquiries and request for cruisers.[113] In it Tirpitz repeated his previous arguments in favor of a battle fleet for offensive action in European waters, pointing out that they had been reinforced by the work on the operations plans, by tactical exercises, by the experiences of the Sino-Japanese War and by the development of other navies. He expressed satisfaction that the days of concentrating on coastal defense had passed, but warned that defense of German overseas interests should not be

> carried out through the use of the *matériel* and personnel of the navy for the construction and sending out of a relatively large number of cruisers before one has in a battle fleet a support which is in the final analysis alone capable of putting the necessary pressure behind the demands of our diplomatic representatives.

Although it might be tempting to possess both a strong fleet in the home waters and strong units abroad, only Britain had the resources for this. Germany must remain content with detaching ships from her home fleet for overseas service when European conditions permitted it. Tirpitz then said that the continued construction of cruisers instead of battleships was sapping German naval power and demanded the immediate replacement of the four oldest ships of the line and the modernization of remaining single-screw ships "so that we could, including the four ships of the Saxony class, soon come to the total of seventeen ships of the line, having recognized that the ships of the Siegfried class have proven themselves less and less capable of being put in the battle line." Including the eight Siegfried ships, Tirpitz was thus aiming for a battle fleet of twenty-five armored ships. He cut down the requests for cruisers, and wanted their size to conform to the types proposed in Dienstschrift No. IX. In view of the rapid building of ships of the line by France and Russia, and the stagnation of the German building program,

> if the national representation once more rejects the increases for the navy, the High Command will not be able after a few years to undertake the task set for it by His Majesty and the strength of the navy will then not even be adequate to protect the German coast and harbors from blockade, burning, and shelling.

The memorandum prepared for Naval Cabinet[114] more specifically related the deteriorating power relationship between Germany and her prospective European enemies to the operations envisaged by the High Command. It pointed out that the inferiority of the German fleet in the face of France alone or France allied with Russia and Denmark made it necessary for it to try with its concentrated strength to defeat separately the dispersed enemy forces. The German offensive would be directed to the west. Whether the first battle would occur in the English Channel, or on the Dogger Bank, or in the Skagerrak, the principle involved in choosing its time and place was that there existed a fair tactical chance of victory. The increase of enemy strength during the next years, however, would reduce these chances substantially. In 1901, France would have in the north fifteen ships of the line, and Denmark would possess four or five armored ships. Russia would, moreover, have thirteen armored cruisers of which seven would be in the Baltic. These forty-one or forty-two ships could be countered by twenty-five German armored ships if the oldest were included. Germany would only have five modern ships to confront their ten Russian and nine French equivalents. Moreover, France would have twenty-seven armored ships in the Mediterranean and Russia eight large modern warships in the Black Sea which could also proceed to the north. The disastrous results of the action of such overwhelming strength could be prevented only through a substantial strengthening of the German battle fleet.

Finally, on the very day that Heeringen's operations plan was presented to Wilhelm for approval, Tirpitz handed him a polemical letter that he had originally addressed to Goltz.[115] In it he stated that the operations plan required from the navy great war preparedness which could only be achieved if the navy were directed in a coherent manner in peacetime. For this the High Command had to have sole jurisdiction over the preparation and execution of operations plans.

On 28 November 1895, just before the introduction of the naval budget to the Reichstag, Knorr, who had succeeded Goltz as Commanding Admiral, launched a major attack on Hollmann which included a presentation to Wilhelm of a document entitled "Draft of a plan for the renewal or respectively the supplement of fleet *matériel*" ("Entwurf eines Planes für die Erneuerung bzw. Ergänzung des Flotten-materials").[116] By this time Tirpitz had left the High Command. Hallmann attributes the authorship of the memorandum addressed to Wilhelm to Tirpitz's "pupil and younger friend" Braun and maintains that "With it begins the immediate prehistory of the fleet law."[117] He views it as "the last and most ripe fruit of the work of Kontre-Admiral Tirpitz, executed in detail by younger officers, who had gone through his school."[118] Steinberg views the memorandum as "a remarkable document. In it the first outlines of the future naval laws can be seen."[119] It stated that Germany's naval strength had, particularly since the beginning of the 1890s, fallen considerably behind that of her potential enemies. Already now the rebuilding of some ships and the increase of naval forces in east Asia had imposed serious limits on the activity of the fleet in home waters. A comparison of the German fleet with its probable opponents, the French northern fleet and the Russian Baltic Sea fleet, in 1896 and in 1901—a date by which the Sachsen ships would be rebuilt and all approved German constructions completed—showed the deteriorating power relationship (Table 6.2).

The document proceeded to express the concern of the High Command about the development of Libau after the next three or four years into a first-class naval base capable of sheltering twenty large battleships and a corresponding number of cruisers, claiming that this project indicated that a considerable increase of the Russian Baltic Sea fleet was intended. Subsequently the change of the power relationship was more specifically than in Tirpitz's previous remonstrances linked to German naval strategy. Accurately reflecting the operational planning of the High Command, the memorandum pointed out that as long as the German fleet was superior to either the French northern fleet or the Russian Baltic Sea fleet its task consisted of deploying as soon as possible against one of its opponents and defeating it. Such a victory provided a chance to defend the German seas against the other opponent. But conditions changed to Germany's disadvantage from year to year, and in 1901, as indicated in Table 6.2, each of her Continental opponents would have twice her strength in armored ships and two or three times her strength in cruisers. The German fleet would no longer have the slightest chance of defeating either of its opponents or preventing their unification. The just-completed Baltic–North Sea canal would lose its military value and the considerable investment made in it would have been in vain.

Table 6.2

| | Power relationship in the spring of 1896 | | | | |
|---|---|---|---|---|---|
| | High-seas armored ships | | Smaller coastal-defense armored ships | Armored cruisers | Protected cruisers |
| | New | Old | | | |
| French northern fleet | 8 | 8 | 2 | 2 | 9 |
| Russian Baltic Sea fleet | 5 | 1 | 8 | 9 | 2 |
| German fleet | 4 | 10 | 8 | 0 | 4 |

| | Power relationship in 1901 | | | | |
|---|---|---|---|---|---|
| | High-seas armored ships | | Smaller coastal-defense armored ships | Armored cruisers | Protected cruisers |
| | New | Old | | | |
| French northern fleet | 9–10 | 10 | 0 | 4 | 18 |
| Russian Baltic Sea fleet | 10 | 1 | 7 | 12 | 8 |
| German fleet | 5 | 10 | 8 | 1 | 7 |

The fleet would within a few years be incapable of covering the rear [*Rückendeckung*] of the army, of securing the imports which Germany requires for the execution of the land war, or even of adequate defense of the coast and harbors, and the question would have to be asked whether, in spite of its importance, such a none the less relatively expensive fleet has any justification for its existence.

Nor would the fleet then be able to fulfill any better its task of protecting German transoceanic interests.

Somewhat modestly describing the strategy of the fleet in home waters as defensive in spite of its planning of an offensive thrust, the memorandum proceeded to establish a flexible formula for the strength of the German fleet: in view of the uncertain position of Denmark in a war between Germany with Russia and France, and Germany's inability to prevent her fleet from joining forces with one of the other powers, the German navy must possess a 30 percent superiority over the stronger of its two major opponents, the Russian Baltic Sea fleet or the French northern fleet.[120] It was assumed that adherence to this formula would make it possible in the event of conflict with non-European naval powers to detach ships of the line for transoceanic service from the home fleet without seriously weakening it.

The enclosed "Draft of a plan for the renewal or respectively the supplement of fleet *matériel*" proceeded to point out that, on the basis of the information available about the French and Russian building programs, the formula for the size of the German fleet would call for a strength of twenty-five armored ships in 1901. In effect, the German fleet would then consist of twenty-three ships—but only five of them would be modern. To replace the antiquated vessels, the plan provided for the first systematic ship-replacement schedule since 1873. As stipulated by Tirpitz's Dienstschrift No. IX, the armored fleet was to be supported by six reconnaissance groups, each consisting of one armored cruiser of 7,000–7,500 tons, and three protected cruisers of the third class. Ships were also required for transoceanic service.

When asked by Senden to comment on the High Command memorandum, Tirpitz requested nineteen—the same as in the first fleet law—instead of the original seventeen battleships, three additional armored cruisers and two fewer first-class cruisers.[121] As his correspondence with Stosch showed more clearly,[122] his thoughts were now, unlike when composing Dienstschrift No. IX, also directed toward the use of the fleet against England. What appeared in Tirpitz's response was an early version of the "risk theory." "Even the greatest sea power of Europe would be more conciliatory toward us if we were able to throw two or three effective and highly trained squadrons into the scales of politics and correspondingly into those of conflict. We shall never achieve that through overseas cruisers."[123] Also the fleet was linked closely in a Social Darwinistic sense to Tirpitz's view of Germany as a world power: "The danger is represented in the world situation that our Empire will in the next century decline from its position as a great power if our total naval interests are not pushed ahead energetically, without any delay, and systematically!" The navy also appeared to Tirpitz as the best cure for Social Democracy. These were thoughts that Tirpitz had not yet expressed in respect to the specific recommendations of Dienstschrift No. IX and which were to form an integral part of his later thinking and the hindsight of his critics. The fact is, however, that Tirpitz's thinking had moved ahead of that of the leading naval agencies. Anglophobia, of course, became endemic in Germany and entered German naval prejudices on the same day as Tirpitz's position-paper was presented to Wilhelm, who, along with Hollmann, Senden, and Knorr, as well as Marschall, decided on the dispatch of the Kruger telegram. Shortly thereafter the first operations plan against England was prepared.

By the beginning of 1896 the High Command, largely as the result of the work of Tirpitz, had developed systematic operational planning against the Dual Alliance and a rational fleet-building program to make these operations plans feasible. In doing so it had also become involved in bitter in-fighting with the Imperial Naval Office. Tirpitz's thinking was also beginning to concern itself with the use of the fleet against Britain, its importance for German imperialism, and its potential against Social Democracy.

# Notes: Chapter 6

1 Above all, Rich, *Holstein*, Vol. 1, pp. 307–24.
2 GP, VII, No. 1589, "Aufzeichnung . . . Caprivi," 19 September 1892, p. 329.
3 Especially PAAA, England 92, No. 3, Bd 3, Marschall to Hatzfeldt, 24 November 1893.
4 See in particular J. Alden Nichols, *Germany after Bismarck: The Caprivi Era, 1890–1894* (Cambridge, Mass., 1958), esp. p. 140. Fritz Fischer states: "Behind Caprivi's commercial policy stood the idea of a close customs union of *Mitteleuropa* against the British World Empire, against Russia, and above all against the United States," *Krieg*, p. 24.
5 Ritter, *Der Schlieffen-Plan*, pp. 19–35; see also, Dennis E. Showalter, "The eastern front and German military planning, 1871–1914—some observations," *East European Quarterly*, vol. 15, no. 2 (June 1981), pp. 163–76.
6 See Theodore A. Bayer, *England und der Neue Kurs* (Tübingen, 1955), pp. 31–3. See in particular PAAA, Oesterreich 73, Vol. 26, Schlieffen to Marschall, 7 May 1892, and enclosure concerning the Austro-Hungarian military budget for 1887–92, provoking Schlieffen to remark: "dieselbe dürfte erkennen lassen wie sehr die Aufwendungen Oesterreichs für die Erhaltung und Vermehrung seiner Wehrhaftigkeit hinter den Opfern zurückstehen, welche Deutschland für die gemeinsame Sache bringt."
7 H St Ar, Stuttgart, E 73/73a, 12c, Verz. 61, Moser to Mittnacht, 20 October 1891.
8 ibid., Moser to Mittnacht, 3 April 1892.
9 Gordon Craig, *The Politics of the Prussian Army, 1640–1945* (New York, 1956), p. 244.
10 ibid., p. 243; also Nichols, *Germany after Bismarck*, pp. 204–5; further Generalfeldmarschall Graf Alfred Schlieffen, *Briefe*, ed. Eberhard Kessel (Göttingen, 1956), to his sister Marie, 13 November 1892, pp. 295–7.
11 ibid., Verdy to Waldersee, 24 May 1891; H St Ar, Stuttgart, E 73/73a, 12c, Verz. 61, von Neidhardte (?) to Mittnacht, 25 August 1892; and Schlieffen to his sister, 13 November 1892, in Reichsarchiv, *Der Weltkrieg 1914 bis 1918, Kriegsrüstung und Kriegswirtschaft*, Bd I (Berlin, 1930), p. 43.
12 BA-MA, No. 253/219, Caprivi to Tirpitz, 2 July 1889. See Mitchell, "Situation of inferiority," for French military weakness in the 1870s and 1880s.
13 BA-MA, N 253/40, Caprivi to Tirpitz, 19 December 1889.
14 *Zwischen Kaiser und Kanzler: Aufzeichnungen des Generaladjutanten Grafen Carl von Wedel*, ed. Count Erhardt von Wedel (Leipzig, 1943), p. 79.
15 PAAA, Deutschland 121, No. 12, Bd 8, Sitzung des königlichen Staatsministeriums (Abschrift), 31 May 1891.
16 ibid.
17 PAAA, Deutschland 127, No. 12, Bd 5, Caprivi to Kontre-Admiral Koester, 6 April 1890; also ibid., Deutschland 121, No. 11, Bd 1, Foreign Office to Imperial Naval Office and to various consuls, 10 June 1891, stressing the need for preparations for the appointment of agents and for making provisions for the support of the activity of German cruisers abroad.
18 Caprivi, 8 March 1893, *Stenographische Berichte*, VIII, Session 2, Vol. 3, p. 1499, summarized and partly quoted in Hallmann, *Der Weg*, pp. 89–90.
19 Hatzfeldt, *Nachgelassene Papiere*, Vol. 2, No. 568, Holstein to Hatzfeldt, 25 July 1893, p. 927.
20 BA, Eulenburg Correspondenz, 25, Politische Notiz *für mich* gemacht, 30 July 1893, pp. 326–7.
21 GP, VIII, No. 1753, Hatzfeldt to the Foreign Office, 31 July 1893, pp. 109–10.
22 ibid., p. 110.
23 These comments are not reprinted in GP, VIII, No. 1753. They appear in Hatzfeldt, *Nachgelassene Papiere*, Vol. 2, No. 571, Holstein to Hatzfeldt, 2 August 1893, n. 5, pp. 931–2, and are available as "Aufzeichnung . . . Caprivi," 1 August 1893, PAAA, England 92, No. 3, Bd 2.
24 GP, VIII, No. 1756, Marschall to Hatzfeldt, 2 August 1893, pp. 113–15.
25 ibid., No. 1757, Marschall to Hatzfeldt, 4 August 1893, p. 115.
26 Tirpitz, *Erinnerungen*, p. 49.
27 Hallmann, *Der Weg*, p. 81.

28  ibid., pp. 82–3.
29  ibid., pp. 83–96.
30  Hassell, *Tirpitz*, p. 88.
31  Tirpitz, *Erinnerungen*, p. 42.
32  Hassell, *Tirpitz*, pp. 94–5; Berghahn, *Tirpitz-Plan*, p. 60.
33  BA-MA, N 253/35, "Beantwortung der 12 taktischen Fragen," n.d.
34  BA-MA, F 2050, PG 66104.
35  Berghahn, *Tirpitz-Plan*, p. 63.
36  BA-MA, N 253/228, Tirpitz to Senden, 20 January 1889; ibid., N 253/35, "Denkschrift Tirpitz," March 1888, also cited in Berghahn, *Tirpitz-Plan*, pp. 64–5; Hallmann, *Der Weg*, pp. 109–10.
37  See Michael Salewski, *Tirpitz: Aufstieg-Macht-Scheitern* (Göttingen, 1979), p. 24.
38  ibid., N 253/39, "Gründe welche für die Beibehaltung eines Oberkommandos mit kräftigen Befugnissen sprechen," n.d.; also in Berghahn, *Tirpitz-Plan*, p. 68.
39  BA-MA, F 2050, PG 66104, "Unsere Maritim-Militärische Fortentwickelung," April 1891.
40  Berghahn, *Tirpitz-Plan*, pp. 68–9; Salewski attributes great tactical and psychological skill to these memoranda; *Tirpitz*, p. 33.
41  See below, pp. 68 ff.
42  BA-MA, N 253/3, Knorr's "Notiz" of 29 May 1891. For the opposition, see Salewski, *Tirpitz*, p. 34.
43  BA-MA, F 2050, PG 66104, Comment to "Unsere Maritim-Militärische Fortentwickelung."
44  Tirpitz, *Erinnerungen*, p. 41.
45  Hallmann, *Der Weg*, pp. 115–16.
46  Tirpitz, *Erinnerungen*, p. 40; Hallmann, *Der Weg*, p. 116; Steinberg, *Yesterday's Deterrent*, p. 68; Berghahn, *Tirpitz-Plan*, p. 70.
47  Hassell, *Tirpitz*, p. 65.
48  "Denkschrift über die Neuorganisation unserer Panzerflotte," Hallmann, *Der Weg*, pp. 117–19.
49  Tirpitz, *Erinnerungen*, p. 47.
50  Berghahn, *Tirpitz-Plan*, p. 179.
51  Langer, *Diplomacy of Imperialism*, p. 418.
52  Marder, *Anatomy*, p. 47.
53  A. T. Mahan, *The Influence of Sea Power upon History, 1660–1783* (London, 1965), pp. 63–4.
54  A. T. Mahan, *The Influence of Sea Power upon the French Revolution and Empire, 1793–1812*, 2 vols. (London, 1892), Vol. 2, p. 118.
55  Mahan, *Influence of Sea Power upon History*, pp. 225–6.
56  ibid., p. 132.
57  ibid., p. 138.
58  Mahan, *Influence of Sea Power upon the French Revolution and Empire*, Vol. 1, p. 321.
59  Mahan, *Influence of Sea Power upon History*, p. 534.
60  H. D. Reinhardt, *Tirpitz und der deutsche Flottengedanke in den Jahren 1892–1898* (University of Marburg dissertation, 1964), p. 27. The following section draws on ch. 2, "Die Flotte im Schrifttum von Militär-Fachschriftstellern," pp. 27–67.
61  ibid., p. 38.
62  loc. cit.
63  ibid., pp. 42–6.
64  ibid., pp. 46–9; see also Lothar Burchardt, *Friedenswirtschaft und Kriegsvorsorge: Deutschlands wirtschaftliche Rüstungsbestrebungen vor 1914* (Boppard, 1968), esp. pp. 53–4.
65  Reinhardt, *Tirpitz*, pp. 55–7.
66  ibid., p. 61. See also Deist, *Flottenpolitik*, pp. 30–1.
67  Tirpitz, *Erinnerungen*, p. 47.
68  Hallmann, *Der Weg*, p. 154.
69  BA-MA, F 5596, III, 3.–1., Vol. 1, "Denkschrift über Kriegführung Deutschlands in den Europäischen Gewässern im Jahre 1893;" summarized in Hubatsch, *Der Admiralstab*, pp. 61–3, and Berghahn, *Tirpitz-Plan*, pp. 71–2.

70  See above, pp. 63–4.
71  Berghahn, *Tirpitz-Plan*, p. 72.
72  Hubatsch, *Der Admiralstab*, p. 63.
73  Tirpitz, *Erinnerungen*, p. 25.
74  See above, pp. 42–8.
75  BA-MA, F 5598, Nebenakten zu O.K.d.M. III, 3.–1., Vol. 1, Goltz to Wilhelm, 8 March 1892.
76  BA-MA, N 253/20, "Vortrag Sr. Exz. gehalten in Hamburg," 13 February 1901.
77  ibid., 36, Goltz, 9 November 1891, "Relation über die Herbstmanöver der Marine im Jahre 1891."
78  BA-MA, F 5244, O.K.d.M, III, 2.–7., Vol. 1, Goltz to the Imperial Command of the Baltic Sea Naval Station, 23 December 1891.
79  BA-MA, F 5596, III, 3.–1., Vol. 1, "Stichworte zum gehaltenen Vortrag am 11. 4. 1892."
80  ibid.
81  See below, p. 71.
82  BA-MA, F 5596, III, 3.–1., Vol. 1, "Stichworte zum gehaltenen Vortrag am 11. 4. 1892."
83  See above, p. 65.
84  BA-MA, F 5598, Nebenakten zu O.K.d.M., III, 3.–1., Vol. 1, Goltz to Schlieffen, 10 March 1892, enclosing a copy of the February memorandum.
85  ibid., Schlieffen to Goltz, 12 March 1892; see also Friedrich-Christian Stahl, "Armee und Marine im kaiserlichen Deutschland," in *Die Entwicklung des Flottenkommandos* (Bd IV, Beiträge zur Wehrforschung, Darmstadt, 1964), pp. 38–9.
86  BA-MA, F 5598, Nebenakten zu O.K.d.M., III. 3.–1., Vol. 1, Schlieffen to Goltz, 16 March 1892.
87  ibid., Goltz to Schlieffen, 24 April 1892.
88  BA-MA, N 253/2, Goltz to Hollmann, 17 May 1894, copy.
89  ibid., N 253/37, "Herbstmanöver 1892."
90  ibid., N 253/34, Taktische und strategische Dienstschriften der Marine vom 1. Oktober 1893 bis zum 30. September 1894, "Befehle . . . für die Herbstübungsflotte, 1893, Bestimmungen für das I. Manöver."
91  ibid., "Relation über das zweite Manöver, 1893," 18 December 1893.
92  A. von Trotha, *Grossadmiral von Tirpitz* (Breslau, 1933), p. 46.
93  BA-MA, N 253/34, Taktische und strategische Dienstschriften des Oberkommandos der Marine, Nr. VIII, "Erfahrungen aus dem Sommer 1893 über Verwendung der Schiffsartillerie und Aufgaben für 1894," 14 March 1894. Nr. VI, "Taktische Flottenübung im Jahre 1893," 15 February 1894.
94  ibid., "Dienstschrift Nr. IX., Allgemeine Erfahrungen aus den Manövern der Herbstübungsflotte," Berlin, 16 June 1894.
95  BA-MA, F 2043, PG 66069a, O.K.d.M. to Imperial Naval Office, 28 May 1894.
96  See below, pp. 351 ff; 391 ff.
97  BA-MA, F 2043, PG 66069a, O.K.d.M. to Imperial Naval Office, 28 May 1894.
98  BA-MA, F 2042, PG 66065, O.K.d.M. to Imperial Naval Office, 12 July 1894.
99  ibid., F 5593, III. 2.–2., Vol. 2, Tirpitz's *Promemoria*, 10 March 1893. On its first page appears Goltz's comment of 13 March to the effect that Wilhelm for the time being decided to postpone a report on the matter.
100 ibid., Tirpitz's *Promemoria*, 16 October 1893.
101 ibid., Hollmann to the Commanding Admiral, 22 December 1893; and "A2," Winkler, "Denkschrift über die zu treffende Organisation des Danziger Panzerkanonenboots und evtl. auch Torpedoboots-Division," 28 April 1894, presented to the Chief of Staff with a request for a decision.
102 ibid., F 5596, III, 3.–1., Vol. 1, "Denkschrift betr. den Operationsplan gegen Frankreich bearbeitet im Frühjahr 1894."
103 See Admiral A. Hopmann, *Das Logbuch eines deutschen Seeoffiziers* (Berlin, 1924), pp. 216–17.
104 BA-MA, F 5596, III, 3.–1., Vol. 1, A1, Siegel, to A2, 4 May 1894.
105 ibid., A2 to A4, 7 May 1894.
106 ibid., "Von Hand zu Hand," 5 January 1895.

107   ibid., Goltz to Wilhelm, 19 February 1895.
108   ibid., "Bemerkungen vom K 2 zum Kriegsplan IV Abschnitt," 13 January 1895. He favored variant strategies against France: (*a*) the major plan, involving an advance against Le Havre and a battle in the English Channel; (*b*) the forward plan, involving a blockade of the entire French coast and a battle before Ouessant; and (*c*) the backward plan, involving a battle by Terschelling if the French and German fleets were to leave port simultaneously or by Heligoland if the departure of the German fleet was delayed.
109   ibid., Winkler, "Betrachtungen über die Verhältnisse in der Ostsee bei einem Offensiv-Vorstoss unserer Flotte nach Westen," 26 January 1895, submitted on the same day to the Chief of Staff.
110   ibid., statement of A3, Heeringen, 28 January 1895.
111   BA-MA, F 3303, PG 66707, Wilhelm to the Chancellor, Imperial Naval Office, 16 February 1895.
112   BA-MA, F 2043, PG 66069a, O.K.d.M. to Imperial Naval Office, 14 February 1895; Berghahn, *Tirpitz-Plan*, pp. 85–6.
113   See above, p. 78.
114   The draft is in BA-MA, F 5596, III, 3.–1., Vol. 1, and is initialed for the Commanding Admiral by Tirpitz. It is initialed by A2 and A4 on 13 February and by A3 on 12 February. The finished copy is in BA-MA, F 3301, PG 66700, signed by Tirpitz and dated 14 February 1895. See also Berghahn, *Tirpitz-Plan*, pp. 86–7.
115   BA-MA, N 253/3, Tirpitz to the Commanding Admiral, 19 February 1895, copy. On the first page there is a comment dated 20 February 1895 to the effect that this letter was presented by him to Wilhelm along with the operations plan.
116   BA-MA, F 2031, PG 66016, Knorr to Hollmann, 28 November 1895; F 3303, PG 66707, Knorr to Wilhelm, 28 November 1895; also see Hallmann, *Der Weg*, pp. 158–62; Steinberg, *Yesterday's Deterrent*,, pp. 77–81.
117   Hallmann, *Der Weg*, p. 158.
118   ibid., p. 162.
119   Steinberg, *Yesterday's Deterrent*, p. 77.
120   ibid., p. 79.
121   BA-MA, F 3303, PG 66707, "Stellungnahme Tirpitz zu Knorrs Denkschrift vom 28. 11. 1895," 3 January 1896.
122   See below, pp. 118–19.
123   Also see Hallmann, *Der Weg*, p. 175; Steinberg, *Yesterday's Deterrent*, pp. 83–4.

# 7 Incompetent Naval Planning for an Improbable Continental War, 1895–99

**I**

Having proclaimed to Wilhelm that the execution of the approved operations plans was becoming from year to year more difficult, the High Command continued to work on them. What is more, responding to the new hostilities arising out of attempts to pursue *Weltpolitik*, it proceeded to prepare contingency plans for war against the leading naval power of the world, Great Britain, as well as against the United States of America. In so far as the Continent was concerned, the High Command occupied itself chiefly with the operations against Russia, which were the primary responsibility of section A2, headed by Korvettenkapitän Winkler. Albert Hopmann, who was commandeered to work in that section at the end of July 1895, later remarked that he often chuckled over the work on the operations plan "for the unlikely case that we come to war with Russia alone."[1]

The period 1895–99 saw no desire or serious fear of a Continental war on the part of the German political leadership. In October 1894, Holstein wrote to Eulenburg that "[t]here is little prospect now of a defensive war . . . because no one wants to do anything to us."[2] The fire-eater Waldersee, now demoted to being the oldest commanding general in the Prussian army, remarked a year later: "Since I cannot believe in a war in the near future, I must again think of my resignation."[3] In July 1895, Holstein, who was at the height of his influence in the first years of the Hohenlohe chancellorship, for the first time hinted at the policy of the free hand: "In my opinion our position is a good one; it has improved thanks to the fact that we can now count on an energetic policy on the part of the English. We will go along with the Triple Alliance and preserve a free hand with regard to the rest of the world. The Russians will need us before we will need them. So for the time being we will sit quietly and wait."[4] Germany's hand became freer still as colonial conflicts between Britain on the one hand and Russia and France on the other increased. In April 1896, Holstein observed that "the Franco-Russian war against Germany has been put off; indeed, it seems further away today than it did a year ago because of the aggravated state of Anglo-Russian relations."[5] Bülow, who became acting Secretary of State of the Foreign Office in June 1897, had already in August 1895 taken Holstein's hint.[6] Upon taking charge of German foreign policy, he resolved to play the free hand until the navy was sufficiently strong to enable Germany to take the side of Russia at a convenient time in an inevitable Russo-British war.[7]

Except for Germany's seizure of Kiao-chow late in 1897, the Far Eastern problems lessened the danger of war between Germany and either France or Russia or both. Russia's attention was diverted from the Balkans, and new areas of tension appeared between her and Britain. Peter Winzen maintains that the cooperation of France, Russia and Germany against Japan in the spring of 1895 showed that there no longer existed a direct threat of a Continental war for Germany.[8] On the other hand, the alleged proposal of Salisbury in the summer of 1895 to partition the Ottoman Empire led the German political leadership, particularly Holstein, to suspect for the next year and a half that the British intended to foment a war among the Continental powers so as to divert Franco-Russian hostility from themselves.[9] Balkan questions had for a while to be treated with particular care.

In spite of the conclusion of the Franco-Russian alliance in January 1894, the danger of a Franco-German conflict faded into the background. From 1894 onward German policymakers actually believed that the relationship between the two allies was cooling, that French attitudes toward Germany were improving and revanchist sentiments were disappearing, while French bitterness toward Britain was increasing. This was the thrust of German reporting from Paris, particularly on the part of the ambassador, Prince Georg Münster von Derneburg.[10] Only in October 1896 did the military attaché, Lieutenant-Colonel Maximilian von Schwarzkoppen, report that he thought that revanchist tendencies in France had been strengthened by the Russian alliance;[11] but then, just a month later, Münster still adhered to his view that the Franco-Russian agreement was no more than an entente.[12] Subsequently Holstein wrote to Bülow that "[t]he Franco-Russian honeymoon is over, even if the divorce is still distant,"[13] but balked at Wilhelm's rash conclusion that Germany must establish a closer relationship with France, who "like [Gabriel] Hanotaux [the French Foreign Minister] now will still sooner or later realize that Russia has the better of it and the *Reichslande* [Alsace-Lorraine] are lost. If it then wakes up it will be furious and *then we must step in and* represent to it its task as main pillar of European culture against barbaric supremacy from the east; also in the Mediterranean. The Gauls are vain and will go along with it." According to Holstein, France, not Germany, should take the initiative for such cooperation.[14]

When, in August 1897, the existence of a Franco-Russian alliance was announced by the Czar's toast to the "nations amies et alliées," Münster did not think that the situation was in any way changed.[15]

Holstein thought that the German response should be a firm warning to the Russians that the alliance with France increased the possibility of war. The result of such a statement might be "that the Russian government would not knowingly allow matters to drive to war and will not stir up anything that can bring it about. A firm decisiveness on our part to counter any inclination for the revision of the Peace of Frankfurt with arms in hand is the only certain means to suppress at the very outset such inclination on the Russian side."[16] In his opinion the public acknowledgment of the existence of the Franco-Russian alliance should also caution Germany to avoid any Russian suggestions of cooperation against Britain. Wilhelm remarked that nothing had been changed by the Czar's toast: the French had to accept Russo-German cooperation and to forget Alsace-Lorraine.[17]

When in the summer of 1898 Théophile Delcassé replaced Hanotaux as French Foreign Minister, Münster reported: "In so far as we are concerned, we gain nothing from this ministerial change, for the Russo-French relations *do not become any worse* [Wilhelm's marginal comment: Let us wait (*abwarten*)]; on the contrary France will at first pursue a policy that is more dependent on Russia than previously."[18] He considered Delcassé to be one of the most eager supporters of the Franco-Russian alliance.[19] In October, however, he reported that the prospects of a Franco-German war had receded into the background. The country was shaken by labor unrest and the Dreyfus case, which had undermined the authority of the government, the judiciary, and the military. Germany appeared as too dangerous an opponent, no one counted on Russian help, there existed other diplomatic problems, and the Fashoda incident had destroyed amicable relations with Britain.[20] He did not share Bülow's concern about the possibility of a coup d'état or revolution in France.[21]

The deterioration of Anglo-French relations, which had for some time been the subject of German diplomatic reporting, culminated in the Fashoda incident in September 1898. The unyielding and belligerent line taken by Britain during the crisis was reported by the German embassy in London.[22] In view of the expected British endeavor to push France, who was only weakly supported by Russia, to the wall, Bülow recommended that Germany take a neutral stance.[23] As Britain continued her military preparations against France, Wilhelm, on the one hand, offered to Nicholas "to conform my politics [sic] as far as possible to yours"[24] and, on the other, proposed to take the side of Britain "with his entire military strength [*Streitmacht*] if in the ensuing war Russia came to France's help, thus raising the specter of an entirely different type of war than envisaged in the long run by Bülow." As late as January 1899 he considered French fears of a war with Britain, as reported by Münster, to be justified.[25]

Although as of 1897 Russia appeared in Bülow's grand scheme as an eventual partner of German *Weltpolitik*, she posed more of an enigma to German policymakers than did France. They were unwilling to risk friction with her in the Near East. Suspicious of alleged British attempts to cause European complications by furthering the disintegration of the Ottoman Empire, and concerned lest an aggressive Austrian Balkan policy involve Germany in a war with Russia, they were reluctant to oppose her ambitions in the Straits.[26] On the other hand, in the spring of 1895 they cooperated with her and France in the Far East in compelling Japan to restrict her territorial gains from the war with China, fearful lest their extent make China a Japanese protectorate, threaten China's continued existence, encourage a scramble for concessions in the Celestial Empire, and raise the specter of a general war.[27] Cooperation with Russia was considered as bringing France closer to Germany as well.[28] In encouraging Nicholas to become more deeply involved in the Far East, Wilhelm went so far as to promise to protect his rear and to subordinate to him the German Far Eastern naval forces.[29]

An element of suspicion of Russia was voiced by Holstein in June 1895 concerning the joint arrival of French and Russian naval units in Kiel to celebrate the opening of the Kaiser Wilhelm Canal: "If the Russians will really conclude the alliance [with France], then they will also want to strike soon. But things have not yet come so far. None the less, even the demonstrations are unwelcome."[30] At the same time Hatzfeldt thought that it was immaterial whether a Franco-Russian alliance existed: in any conflict between France and Germany, Russia would be on the side of the former. He doubted whether Russia wanted war, but feared that her sense of power or French pressure might cause her to take a stance hostile to Germany.[31] And the German ambassador in St Petersburg, Prince Hugo von Radolin, reported extensive hostility toward Germany at the imperial court, and among the educated Russian public.[32] At the beginning of October 1895, Wilhelm jumped to the conclusion: "The Russians have an entente with France and arm against us. They will forbid the French to proceed against us as long as it suits them. In a given moment the permission will be granted. The Emperor Nicholas has no idea how things are . . . I know what I have to guard myself against from Russia."[33] But Wilhelm's alarm about the future threat from Russia and France did not last long. When, on 8 October 1895, Münster reported from Paris that "[t]he tip of the Russo-French combination is directed entirely against England," he noted "well possible."[34] Still Russia was by no means to be trusted. At the very time Hohenlohe suspected that the Russian Foreign Minister, Prince A. B. Lobanov-Rostovsky, attempted to alienate Germany from Britain and to split up the Triple Alliance without in turn cutting the French connection.[35] Somewhat later Holstein and Marschall attributed to the Russian Foreign Minister the sinister design of first using France and the Austrian elements dissatisfied with the outcome of the war of 1866 to defeat Germany and later utilizing a weakened Germany as a buffer against France.[36] Hohenlohe and Holstein expressed reservations about supporting Russia in either the Near or the Far East if this would mean supporting the Franco-Russian bloc and would tilt the balance of power in its favor.[37] Nor did Holstein think that Germany could afford to jeopardize relations with other powers for the sake of Russia.[38] Wilhelm's indiscreet interview with the British military attaché Colonel Swaine, during which he suggested that Britain, instead of proposing to establish an Anglo-Russian condominium over Constantinople, should have forced the Straits since Germany would have assured her of her own and Italian support, caused Holstein to fear war with Russia and France. For, if British Prime Minister Salisbury communicated the conversation to St Petersburg, Lobanov would advise the Czar to make use of French enthusiasm for Russia for a settlement of accounts with Germany.[39]

Yet, in February 1896, Holstein, being faced with British hostility as a result of the Kruger telegram, recommended cooperation with Russia. Were the English to use force against the Transvaal, "we would inevitably be forced to the Russian side, for alone we cannot do anything against England at sea."[40] And, were Britain to draw close to France, Germany was to go so far as to seek a treaty with Russia![41] In May, Hohenlohe concluded that a repetition of the cooperation of Germany with France and Russia in East Asia was not in Germany's interest because experience had since shown that France used any estrangement between Germany and Britain toward the eventual revision of the Treaty of Frankfurt,[42] and in January 1897 he saw French chauvinism as an obstacle to any Franco-German cooperation.[43] In April 1897, Wilhelm expressed his disappointment that Russia, in spite of all German encouragement, had not yet shifted her attention from the Balkans to Asia, and his fear that the concentration of her forces on and the construction of her strategic railways toward the German border were a prelude to Russia's aggression toward the west![44]

The Austro-Russian agreement of 5 May 1897,[45] which in effect "put the Near East 'on ice' for the next ten years,"[46] loosened the two alliance systems and made it less necessary for Britain to seek the support of the Central Powers,[47] was welcomed by Wilhelm, although Marschall, about to trade the Foreign Office for the embassy in Constantinople, thought that it "was valueless for the preservation of European peace in the immediate future" since it made no provision for the eventual disposition of Constantinople and the Straits.[48] Prince Karl Lichnowsky, the chargé d'affaires in Vienna, expressed some concern lest the agreement weaken the Austro-Hungarian ties to Germany and Italy because of supporting the Slavo-clerical elements within the Dual Monarchy.[49] Bülow quite rightly reported from Rome that Italy's exclusion from the Balkans and the establishment of closer relations between Austria-Hungary and Russia through the agreement may have been contrary to the terms of the Triple Alliance.[50] While sharing all these concerns, Holstein concluded that none the less the advantage of the treaty was "the high probability that during the next years Russia would want peace in Europe."[51] Upon visiting St Petersburg in August in his new capacity as Secretary of State of the Foreign Office, Bülow concluded that Russo-German relations had become cordial.[52]

However, Germany's seizure of Kiao-chow at the end of 1897 conjured up a threat of a war with Russia, the very power whom Bülow viewed as his future ally against Great Britain! Although Czar Nicholas II had initially stated that he "cannot approve nor disapprove" the sending of German ships to Kiao-chow,[53] the Russian Foreign Ministry subsequently expressed its opposition to the permanent German occupation of the site. This opposition led the Deputy Secretary of State of the German Foreign Office to expect "a break with Russia,"[54] and caused Tirpitz to issue the warning that "martial complications must be counted on."[55] Tirpitz, however, appears to have been most concerned about a war with China.[56]

Holstein, who directed the Kiao-chow operation diplomatically, at first discounted the danger of war, although he later convinced the General Staff of the need to check whether the railway network was ready for an immediate mobilization.[57] Neither Wilhelm[58] nor Hohenlohe[59] nor

Bülow[60] thought that the Russians were prepared to go to war for Kiao-chow, and only relatively late did Bülow think of a war with Japan.[61] They were none the less worried. When in December the Russian Foreign Minister suggested that Germany and Russia go "hand in hand in the Far East,"[62] thereby implicitly dropping the objections to the seizure of Kiao-chow in return for German support for the Russian seizure of Port Arthur,[63] both Bülow and his patron Philipp zu Eulenburg were relieved.[64] Radolin, however, expected Nicholas to continue bearing a grudge against Germany in spite of all protestations of friendship.[65]

## II

On 2 March 1895, Tirpitz had on behalf of the Commanding Admiral arranged for an Admiralty Staff journey to play a war game on the basis of a war of the Triple Alliance with France and Russia during which weak German forces were to face an attack against the German Baltic Sea coast by some Russian ships and prevent the major Russian force from proceeding to the North Sea to join the French northern fleet. On the basis of the game two memoranda were to be drawn up, one to answer questions such as whether the German forces in the Baltic should be scattered or concentrated, where and how a defensive position should be selected, and the other to deal specifically with the defense of the German Baltic Sea harbors.[66] The memoranda were either not prepared or have not been preserved. In June 1895, however, Winkler produced a 197-page document entitled "General considerations concerning our operations plan against Russia and the more precise preparation of Operations Plan I."[67] The document was very detailed, providing for a day-by-day account of operations and a full listing of the German and Russian forces, and indicating a good knowledge of the geography of the Russian Baltic coast. There were admissions of shortcomings in preparations, such as both the German army and navy lacking agents in Russia. The plan rightly assumed Russian naval inferiority to Germany, both in quantity and quality. It was unorthodox in allowing the German fleet to divide its forces during the attack.

The military–political assumption of the plan was questionable. Discussing first the most probable case of war—that of the Triple Alliance against France and Russia—Winkler pointed out that Tirpitz had in his plan of 1892 left the question open whether, after a defeat of the French fleet, the German navy was to continue its operations against the French coast. or turn against the Russian fleet in the Baltic. He stated that in preparing the operations plan against Russia the second alternative was chosen, admitting, however, that calculations for action by a fleet that had not fought a battle were of necessity uncertain. Therefore Winkler proceeded to examine the case of war between Germany and Russia, both unallied, which he originally considered improbable (the reference was subsequently put in brackets and a comment in the margin reads: "Why so improbable?"), but which, if well worked out, he regarded as providing a good basis for other cases of war. The proposed course of action in this improbable case of war did not substantially differ from the operations proposed in similar cases by Goltz in 1889 and by Tirpitz in 1892, except for attention to detail and rigidity of prescription. The aim of the operations was the achievement of full control of the Baltic Sea, including the Gulfs of Finland and Bothnia, so as to protect the German trade and coast, interrupt Russian trade and entirely cut off the imports which were so important to Russia, tie down the Finnish army as well as substantial Russian troop units for the defense of the coast, and make any Russian troop-transports by sea impossible.

This memorandum was subjected to serious criticism by the heads of the other sections of the Admiralty Staff Department. Most severe and detailed was that of A3, Heeringen, author of the operations plan against France.[68] Heeringen's major objection was that the extent of the proposed operations exceeded German strength. In the opinion of the head of section A5, the assumptions on which the plan was based—that the Russian fleet would not be able to offer battle and that the German fleet could launch an offensive toward the north while Denmark did not pose a threat—were not valid because Denmark would have to be closely watched in that very period. For the plan to have general validity one would either have to estimate Russia's naval strength as existing after the completion of her mobilization or subtract those units that would be needed against Denmark from the German forces to be used against Russia. He also had doubts about the splitting up of the German forces in the course of operations and emphasized the need of contact with the General Staff.[69]

On 15 February, Winkler's successor as head of section A2, Scheder, presented Winkler's memorandum to the Chief of Staff, Diederichs, requesting the clarification of a number of questions, among them whether the army had any interest in the naval operations, whether those could be adjusted to the wishes of the army, whether the General Staff was willing to provide troops for the occupation of the base, whether in the opinion of the army the number of troops required by Winkler was adequate, and which troops the Russian leadership intended to leave for coastal defense in case of a war with Germany. Diederichs ordered Scheder to establish contact with the General Staff. Between 15 and 24 February, Scheder had interviews with Hauptmann Schrotter (responsible for coastal fortifications), Oberstleutnant Gronan (in charge of intelligence about Russia) and Oberstleutnant von Wittgen (specializing in operations against Russia). He was informed that the General Staff was working on only one operations plan, against both France and Russia, regarding war against only one of those powers as improbable, and that there existed no operations plan against Denmark, who was not expected to enter the war at the outset; if she was to take the side of Germany's enemies later, troops necessary for dealing with her could always be detached from other theaters of war. In view of the superiority of numbers that the Russian army enjoyed over the German, not a single man could be provided by the army to support naval operations at the beginning of war. While a naval action in the Gulf of Finland was thus out of the question at the beginning of war, its execution later on was not precluded by the General Staff. Reserve formations for the establishment and defense of a base in the

Moon Sound might then be provided.[70] Obviously the General Staff, which had by now definitely decided to launch an offensive against France and to keep forces in the east at a minimum, was unwilling to commit troops for the support of naval operations in the Baltic.[71]

On 25 February, Scheder reported the results of his inquiries to Diederichs, who ruled:

> The intended operation in the Moon Sound in my opinion exceeds the strength of the navy. The whole blockade of the Finnish islets and inlets [*Schären*] is in all cases a very risky undertaking in which the effort is probably not in proportion to the achievement. The decision of His Excellency [Knorr] is to be sought as to whether the view of the General Staff concerning the support of the army should be officially requested; whether in his opinion the undertaking in the Moon Sound promises any success and whether another operations plan should be prepared. In the latter case a decision of His Majesty should be obtained.[72]

Both Schröder and Scheder concurred with the proposal to pin the General Staff down officially. One would thus be able either to document the army's lack of interest in cooperation with the navy and secure a change in Wilhelm's decision of April 1892 that the establishment of a base in the Baltic with army support was necessary[73] or establish firm collaboration of the two services in their operational planning.

Knorr, therefore, on 11 March proceeded to write to Schlieffen, forwarding to him Winkler's plan and arguing that the operations it envisaged would support the war effort of the army by making Russian landings on the German coast impossible and thus freeing German army units from the task of coastal defense, by pinning down Russian troops for the defense of the Russian coast, and by undermining Russian morale through the total disruption of maritime trade.[74] Schlieffen replied on 19 March, admitting that through the proposed operations the navy would "effectively and desirably support the operations of the land army" but that, as he had already informed the High Command in 1892,[75] in the current political situation the case of war "Germany against Russia alone" was so improbable as to be no longer considered in the mobilization preparations of the army. But, if a change in the political situation would require consideration of this case of war, the army would participate in the setting up of a base in the Moon Sound. Upon receiving this polite but negative response, Knorr decided to drop the consideration of the case of war "Germany against Russia alone" as well.[76]

By the time that Scheder had established contact with the General Staff, his section had also prepared a memorandum concerning the use of mines in support of the operations proposed by Winkler as well as in two cases of war in the Baltic for which no operations plans as yet existed: (1) the Triple Alliance at war with France and Russia, with Germany on the defensive in the Baltic until the return of her fleet from the advance into the English Channel, and (2) the same case of war with Denmark on the side of France and Russia.[77] In the war of Germany against Russia alone it stipulated that mines be used for the defense of the proposed base in the Moon Sound, as well as for the closing of a number of bays and coves in the Gulf of Finland. The memorandum strongly reflected the earlier concern about the strengthening of the Russian naval power through the construction of new ships and of a major base at Libau by stating that in 1899 that base would be able to support the major part of the Russian Baltic Sea fleet. The only possible offensive action open for Germany would then be to throw back the Russian fleet, blockade it in Libau, and try to destroy it there. It remained to be examined whether mines could be used in this blockade, as well as how the bombardment of the base could be carried out.

In case of a defensive German stance in the Baltic during a war between the Triple Alliance and France and Russia, little hope was placed in the use of the mines against a Russian fleet advancing against the German coast. Mines were to be used, however, for the defense of individual German Baltic Sea ports and for the hindrance of the passage of the Russian fleet through the Danish Belts on its way to join the French navy. With Denmark hostile, the German forces would also have to establish control over the Belts to prevent the Russian fleet from reaching Copenhagen. This would involve extensive use of mines and the destruction of several Danish ports and of as many ships and ferries as possible to impede Danish mobilization. In discussing mine warfare Scheder, in criticism of the Admiralty Staff, deplored the absence of operations plans for the Baltic in cases of war other than that of "Germany against Russia alone."

Following his discussions with the General Staff Officers, Scheder established contact with section A3 regarding the preparation of an operations plan in a war of Germany with France and/or Russia in which Denmark was also her enemy—a case which according to him had been handled in general terms in Tirpitz's memorandum of February 1892 but on which no subsequent work had been done. He proposed that in such a case the German naval forces should at first attack Denmark before she could obtain any assistance. The objective of the operations was the destruction of the Danish fleet, the establishment of control over the Danish waters, and the hindrance of the mobilization of the Danish army. The best course of action would be the now time-honored thrust into the English Channel, for it would prevent the French fleet from uniting with the Danish. None the less, operations against a combined Danish–Russian fleet also had to be considered, and for those army support would be necessary. Schröder's hopes for army support were definitely quashed by Scheder, who informed him of the official refusal of the General Staff to cooperate. Scheder did not dismiss the suggestion of an advance into the Channel, however, and inquired about the naval forces available for use against Russia and Denmark during the time when the bulk of the fleet was engaged in the English Channel.[78] Schröder replied that they would be negligible.[79]

On 17 May 1896, Scheder informed the sections of the Admiralty Staff Department that since the Commanding Admiral had decided that the operations plan in case of "Germany in a war with Russia in the near future" be dropped the most urgent task was the preparation of an "operations plan in the Baltic Sea for the war of Germany with Russia and France in the period during which the fleet directs the intended blow to the west."[80] He stated that since some operations against Denmark might become necessary in spite of them not being planned by the General Staff he and A3 had agreed on a division of forces as stated in their previous correspondence. Scheder proposed the following guidelines for the plan:

(1)  The Station Chief in Kiel undertakes the direction of operations which the navy has to carry out in the area of the Baltic Sea.
(2)  The tasks of the Station Chief are: (a) defense of Kiel, (b) preventing the breaking through of the Russian naval forces into the North Sea, (c) protection of German coastal places in the Baltic Sea. The relative importance of these tasks is indicated by their listing above. Tasks (b) and (c) are only to be approached more closely once task (a) has been solved. The possibility of the participation of Denmark in the war must not be ignored.

The other sections were requested to react to the guidelines as soon as possible.

Heeringen, who had in 1894 prepared the operations plan against France and was now in charge of section A1, was the first to reply. He, needless to say, had a somewhat vested interest in the thrust into the English Channel for which he now invoked Tirpitz's authority, and must have been horrified by Scheder's proposal to deliver the first blow against Denmark. But, above all, he appears to have considered it necessary to reassert basic strategic principles. In a war against France, Russia, and Denmark it was of particular importance to keep the fleet concentrated. It was wrong to turn it against Denmark. There the fleet would be engaged in a debilitating battle with the fortifications of Copenhagen which promised no prospect of strategic success. A Danish invasion of Germany, moreover, was primarily a concern of the army, not of the navy. Since an offensive against Russia would hardly produce decisive results, it was necessary to adhere to the plan for an advance against the French.

> If the navy is engaged in such a difficult task, then we must involve the last man at the place where the decision will be made on which the whole favorable development in the northern naval war will depend . . . I consider it out of the question and incorrect that we deliver a blow to the west and at the same time prevent the union of the Danes and the Russians and also attempt to defend the Baltic Sea ports. If we set such tasks, then we will direct our leaders to incorrect measures. Our task will be: "Attack the French and hold Kiel."[81]

Plans were to be made for action by the fleet upon its return from the Channel, but these must be based on the premiss that "our main task is to keep open the Elbe and hang on to Kiel and Wilhelmshaven." If this task was fulfilled, offensive action against the Russians could be considered. Also, if the army decided to take an offensive against Denmark, it was to be supported by the navy. The telegraph communications of Denmark with the rest of Europe were to be cut and mines laid in Danish waters as soon after the outbreak of war as possible. Lastly Heeringen suggested the examination in war games and other exercises of a number of specific questions relating to warfare in the Baltic, including the following:

(a)  What importance do Fehmarn, Fälster, Rügen have as the operation base for a greater landing, and in which way can the fleet participate in attacking and defending [them]?

(b)  Could we, i.e. the navy, in case of an ill-fated campaign of our army in Poland through which our left wing in Königsberg would be cut off, bring these troops back to Pomerania, and how should we act in this case?

(c)  How can we support the campaign against Denmark if she takes either an offensive or a defensive stance against us?

(d)  What does the fleet do if our army besieges Copenhagen?

(e)  Can and may the fleet alone proceed against Copenhagen?

(f)  What do we do against Russia if the military situation requires action against the Russian Baltic Sea ports?

Heeringen's case for the deployment of the entire fleet in the west did not pass unchallenged by Schröder[82] and by A6a, who questioned altogether the wisdom of building the operations around the projected strike against the French northern coast. Even with Austria and Italy on the German side, France could by assuming a defensive stance move a considerable part of her Mediterranean fleet to the north. If Austria and Italy were neutral—and A6a was aware that the Triple Alliance was due to expire in 1903—it was doubtful whether even by defeating the French northern fleet the German forces could, in the face of the advancing French Mediterranean fleet, turn against the Russians and Danes without exposing the entire North Sea coast to the French.[83] A4, A5, and A6b, on the other hand, gave Heeringen their unqualified support, agreeing with his contention that his proposals were in line with the plan of Tirpitz in 1892. They were willing to depart from the plan for a western offensive only in response to special needs of the army.[84]

On 1 August, Scheder presented an outline for the waging of war in four different cases to the Chief of Staff and obtained his approval for it.[85] In case "A", during the execution of the strike to the west, the defense of the Baltic was to be conducted by the Chief of the Baltic Sea Station with limited forces. Attempts were to be made to lay mines in front of the most important Russian Baltic Sea harbors, although not much was expected from such action. In case "B", when the fleet had returned from the west, and a sizeable force was available for action in the Baltic at a time that an attack from the west was not expected, the German aim was to seek control of the Baltic Sea either through defeating the Russian fleet or through enclosing it. Scheder did not think it very likely that the Russian fleet would offer battle or that it could be enticed to do so through the destruction of the Russian coastal cities—doubts expressed in earlier operations plans against Russia. In case "C", if the Danish fleet joined Germany's enemies, sufficient forces were to be kept back to counter the Danish fleet and disturb the communications between the Danish islands. If the rest was strong enough, it could turn against Russia and first of all attack Libau. Copenhagen was to be bombarded either if it was politically desirable or if army help was available. In the unlikely case "D", war against Russia alone, Scheder, like Winkler, proposed a strong offensive, involving the blocking of Kronstadt with mines, the blockade of the Gulf of Finland and the Bay of Riga, and the destruction of Libau.

By 18 December 1896, Scheder circulated among the other sections of the Admiralty Staff Department a sixty-page document entitled "Operations plans for the Baltic Sea theater,"[86] which he regarded as a statement of guidelines on which he sought agreement before preparing a more detailed plan. The memorandum was confined to deployment of forces and operations at the beginning of war, for it was maintained that later circumstances arising from the enemy operations would invalidate peacetime assumptions. It was stipulated that any plan should not be binding on the commanding admiral. It was further stated that, although certain operations involving cooperation between the army and the navy, such as the landing of army troops in Zealand or the establishment of a base in the Gulf of Finland, could be worked on in peacetime, they should not be made an integral part of the plan. Devastation of the coast was to be carried out only as it could contribute to the attainment of naval domination, and battles with coastal fortifications were to be generally avoided as not being worth the risk.

Four different cases of war were discussed: (A) Germany in a war with France and Russia; (B) Germany in a war with Russia; (C) Germany in a war against Russia and Denmark; and (D) Germany in a war with France, Russia, and Denmark. In case "A" it was proposed to provide the Chief of the Kiel Station with orders for the defense of the base and the Baltic Sea. Operations against Russia after the return of the forces from the English Channel were not even mentioned. It is curious that case "B" was discussed at great length in spite of the earlier decision that it should not be considered and of Scheder's own admission in the outline he presented to the Chief of Staff on 1 August that it was improbable. Possibly case "B" was included to serve as the basis for action against Russia after the victorious return of the expedition to the English Channel discussed as case "B" in the outline which Scheder had presented to the Chief of Staff on 1 August.[87] Beside providing additional detail, Scheder now proposed that, in the likely case that the Russian fleet would not come out from behind the Kronstadt fortifications, a blockade line of light forces should be established where the Gulf of Finland was narrowest—along the line from Nargö to Rönneskar—whereas the bulk of the fleet would stand further to the west, supported by a modest base. Possible locations of the base would be the Fögle Fjörd in the Aaland Islands, the Utö island group, or Worms in the Moon Sound. The details of setting up and defending such a base, including the difficult question where the troops were to come from, were not discussed. In case "C" the uncertainty of Denmark's position was deplored and the German aim defined as the gaining and maintaining control of the Baltic Sea and of Danish waters. Slight preference was given to the concentration against Russia since decisive operations against the Danish fleet were also expected to involve action against the powerful fortifications of Copenhagen. But political circumstances, such as forcing Denmark to take a stand, or favorable military conditions, such as those presented if German war preparations were considerably ahead of the Danish or if the Russian fleet were blockaded or so weak as to be unable to attack the German coast, might still justify an attack on Denmark. Certain circumstances might even justify the splitting up of the German forces, for example a Russian attack on the German coast at the time that the German navy was attacking Denmark. Forces would then have to be detached to attack the Russians. The basic assumption was that the German fleet would be strong enough to deal with the Danes and the Russians, even when dividing its forces.

If army support were assured—as it was not—in case "D"—which was considered improbable—it would be preferable to attack Denmark first, just as Winkler had proposed. Without army support the prime consideration in case "D" was that naval strength should not be divided and that current military and political factors should be taken into account in deciding whether it should be directed against France or Denmark.

The heads of the other sections of the Admiralty Staff were in general agreement with Scheder's guidelines for operations in cases "A" and "B." Heeringen, from whom most criticism might have been expected, had by December 1896 left section A1 where he had been succeeded by Jauntze, who only feared that the blockade of the Russian coast would be impossible without the establishment of a base.[88] In respect to case "C," section A5a raised doubts about proceedings against Russia along the lines proposed in case "B" as long as Denmark had not been knocked out of the war and stressed the need of defeating the Danes and the Russians separately. A7 doubted whether in a war against Russia it was adequate to control the Baltic Sea and advised that domination over the North Sea be sought as well to protect German shipping, particularly the grain imports, against Russian cruisers located abroad or Russian Black Sea forces.[89] The new Chief of Staff, Carl Barandon, minuted that the fleet should not be used at all against Russian fortifications but should be concentrated for maintaining control of the sea and thus securing the German imports. He did, however, quite inconsistently then insist that the Russian base of Libau be destroyed before the German navy proceeded into the Gulf of Finland. Also he had doubts about Denmark declaring war on Germany and therefore thought that the German forces, in a war not involving France, could be first directed against Russia. If Germany was none the less engaged in a war with both Russia and Denmark, he naïvely sought a solution in close cooperation with the army. The course of action to be taken in a war involving both France and Russia was outlined by Barandon in a submission to Knorr on 5 February 1897.[90] Following Scheder's earlier proposal,[91] he recommended that the German fleet should be turned against Denmark immediately with the purpose of occupying her or forcing her to side with Germany. Thus the unification of the French and Russian fleets and any landing of hostile forces in Denmark would in effect be prevented and the German fleet would enjoy full freedom of action. The implementation of this plan would have rendered impossible the execution of the initial strike against France, which, as will be seen below, Barandon opposed, and have called for a revision of German naval operations in case of a two-front war. It is most astounding, however, that Barandon was expecting to force Denmark to join Germany or to occupy her without army support, which, as he must have known, was unavailable. Knorr, however, at his leisure turned down Barandon's recommendation not because he explicitly rejected action against Denmark, but because he was unwilling to give up the initial attack against France.[92]

On 9 March 1897 a conference was held about Scheder's memorandum between the heads of sections A1, A2, A5 and A7. It was agreed not to consider the long-range effect of Russian operations in the North Sea against German commerce and to use the mobilization preparations as existing for the western case of war as the basis for the eastern theater of war. In case of war "B" the main purpose of the blockade of the coast of Courland and the Bay of Riga was seen as prevention of the exit of hostile Russian forces, rather than damage to Russian trade. In case of a blockade the dangers resulting from a division of the forces was to be avoided and arrangements were to be made for the relief of parts of the fleet. What is more important, the establishment of a base immediately after the beginning of operations was not viewed as essential and was left for the Chief of the Fleet to decide. The conference took a more serious view of the position of Denmark than had the Chief of Staff. If there was any doubt about Danish neutrality, the fleet was to refrain from proceeding *in toto* to the Gulf of Finland, but was to take a position in the center of the Baltic in order to prevent the Danish and Russian fleets from uniting. Scheder was persuaded that it was unwise to divide the fleet if Denmark sided with Russia, but that the navy should in such a case attack Denmark, just as he had proposed a year earlier. An attack on Copenhagen, however, could only be undertaken if the army participated in it. A2 was further instructed to examine two cases of war in the east: (1) that of Germany against Russia alone with Danish neutrality certain, and (2) that of Germany against Russia with Denmark on the side of Russia or with her neutrality doubtful. He was also to make plans for the bombardment of Danish and Russian coastal places and for the seizure of a base in the Gulf of Finland.[93] In case of war (2) Scheder proposed to examine two possibilities: (*a*) when the conditions of the Russian fleet enabled immediate action against Denmark, or (*b*) when the state of the Russian fleet led to the expectation of its appearance in the western part of the Baltic Sea and made it necessary for the German fleet to assume a waiting stance.[94]

Until its dissolution in 1899 the High Command continued work only on the improbable and most simple case of war (1). Scheder provided the first draft for circulation between the various sections by the latter part of November 1897.[95] The operations that were proposed did not basically differ from those suggested by him in the memorandum circulated on 18 December for the case of war "B," Germany in a war with Russia. Contrary to the view expressed at the conference of 9 March, a base to support the operations in the Gulf of Finland was regarded as essential. For its location the Utö island group or the islands by Fögle Fjörd were to be considered. The base was to be set up without help from the army. The destruction of the base of Libau was considered desirable, but not essential as Barandon had stipulated. Departments A3a, A3b, and A5a made minor suggestions about this document.[96] By 4 December, Scheder had prepared a new version of the plan, which came under fire from Barandon, who had neither seen the previous version nor had been present at the meeting of 9 March.[97] On 12 January 1897 he minuted that the proposals that were made in it were not yet specific enough. He criticized the mention of several locations for a base, ambiguity about action against Libau, which he had stressed, and against Kronstadt. Also he censured Scheder for neglecting possible action by Russian ships in the Black Sea and the Mediterranean which could either be directed against German commercial shipping or toward the Baltic.

Scheder obligingly revised his memorandum and at the request of the Chief of Staff sent it to sections A1, A3, and A5 for comment.[98] In case of a war against Russia, a fleet command was to be formed with the Chief of the Fleet to be assigned the task "permanently to exercise domination in the Baltic Sea." This task was to be best achieved through the destruction of the Russian fleet or, if this was not possible, through its enclosure in the eastern part of the Gulf of Finland. Before the German forces proceeded to the north: ". . . It is desirable to make the harbor of Libau useless to the point that it can no longer serve the Russian fleet." Barandon prevailed in so far as Utö was chosen as the base for the fleet operating in the Gulf of Finland, as special orders were required for action against Kronstadt, and as it was stated that action against coastal fortifications was to be avoided. While the fleet might be divided during its operations, each of its units was to be equal to the enemy forces it was expected to confront. The enemy was to be damaged by blockade, the destruction of ports, particularly Hangö, Baltischport and Reval, of ships, and of communications, but these actions were to be subordinated to the main task of destroying or cutting off the enemy's fleet. A detailed description of the German forces to be used and their movements was provided. Six reconnaissance groups of four ships each and a total of nineteen armored ships, organized into three squadrons, were to be involved. The ratings of both the German and Russian ships in terms of strength were then provided. The plan did not substantially depart from the one that Winkler had provided except for not counting on army support and selecting a base which could be seized and maintained exclusively by the naval forces. It was presented to Barandon on 20 February 1898, and received the approval of Knorr on 28 June 1898. Certain enclosures dealing with special operations were as yet incomplete, among them those dealing with supplies, the attack on Libau, the regulation of communications, the establishment of a base in Utö, the closing of navigable waters in the Aaland Islands and the Finnish inlets, the organization of the blockade, and the blocking of Russian imports and exports. By 6 August 1898, Winkler, who appears to have replaced Scheder in charge of his old section A2, completed the appendix dealing with the details of securing supplies for the fleet advancing into and operating in the Baltic Sea.[99] By 18 October 1898, Winkler proposed two substantial changes in the approved operations.[100] The improvement of the fortifications of Libau, which had been anticipated for some time, in his opinion now required action by the whole of the German fleet before it proceeded north, rather than by a detachment as originally planned. On the basis of further study he also recommended that the island of Worms at the northern entrance of the Moon Sound rather than Utö or Fögle Fjörd be selected as the base for the German fleet's operations in the Gulf of Finland. For neither Utö nor the Fögle Fjörd provided adequate anchoring-places, entry or exit, and they were exposed to enemy attack. In all these respects Worms was more suitable.[101] Sections A3 and A4 speedily approved the changes proposed by Winkler.[102] On 17 February 1899 they gained the approval of the new Chief of Staff, Kontre-Admiral Felix Bendemann. On 14 March 1899, when the High Command was dissolved, the operations plan against Russia was still incomplete.[103]

Although the High Command did not at this time appear to concern itself with the future Russian naval development and the way it would affect the naval balance of power in the Baltic, the German naval attaché in St Petersburg, Eugen Kalau vom Hofe, took an optimistic view of the future. He had reported on 22 March 1898 that Russian naval increases were occurring in the Far East and were primarily directed against Japan. They would affect European affairs only in so far as they would tie the naval forces of the other powers down in the Far East.[104]

Like the naval High Command, Kalau vom Hofe thought in terms of Germany against Russia. The conveniences that the concentration of the Russian fleet in Libau would present to Germany in such a war would become a serious handicap if Germany was engaged in a war with France and/or Denmark as well.

An examination of the work of the High Command on the operations plan in the Baltic Sea shows considerable weakness. Although a decision had been made in the spring of 1896, when the General Staff announced that it considered a war between Germany and Russia alone improbable and did not plan for it, to suspend work on an operations plan against Russia, the officers in charge of planning disregarded it and kept working on the plan. In their work they frequently came back to other previously disregarded proposals. Denmark was a particularly perplexing problem. Although it had been decided in March 1897 to examine the changes in the strategic conditions in the Baltic resulting from the attitude of Denmark, nothing was done in this respect. Barandon appears to have provided little effective leadership, and his successor Bendemann rightly gave the war plans against Russia lower priority than those against the Dual Alliance and England.[105] It is a sad reflection about the quality of the High Command, however, that it was unable to complete the work on the operations plan against the one major power in the face of which the German navy still enjoyed a superiority.

In so far as operations in the west were concerned, the dire warnings uttered in the High Command's memorandum of 28 November 1895 about impending impotence were materializing. Doubts about the feasibility of the strike against the French northern coast at the beginning of war had already arisen in the preparation of operations in the Baltic Sea.[106] When he departed from section A3 in the fall of 1895, Heeringen provided an extensive list of tasks to be performed by his successor in preparing the offensive against France.[107] He himself had obviously been unable to do much detailed work on the plan. It is not clear how much work was done by his successor Schröder, who still adhered to the notion of an advance into the English Channel. In a presentation to Knorr on 5 February 1897, however, Barandon spoke out against it.[108] He did so in part because he, as shown above, rather unrealistically wanted to take action against Denmark in case of a two-front war, but in part because he quite realistically assessed the changes that had occurred in the political climate and in the naval power relationship. The Kruger telegram more than a year ago had brought about a serious deterioration in Anglo-German relations, and the High Command had been working on an operations plan against Britain. Barandon correctly stated that the successful execution of the advance into the English Channel depended on the benevolent neutrality of Britain since German ships would have to take on coal under the protection of the British coast and enter British harbors for repairs. But the days of British benevolence were gone as Britain regarded Germany as her worst commercial rival and entertained close economic relations with and sympathy for France. She would simply disarm the German ships entering her waters. Confronted by British hostility, lacking a base, and suffering from a shortage of reconnaissance ships and an inadequate communication service, the German navy was not strong enough to undertake the advance against the French coast. It was unlikely that the French northern fleet would undertake a "death ride" against the Germans; if, on the other hand, it confronted them with respectable forces while they bombarded Le Havre, they could not accept the challenge under the guns of the enemy base. The Germans would therefore have to suspend the action against Le Havre while the French forces would withdraw to Cherbourg. Finally Barandon suspected that the advance into the English Channel as projected in 1895 was less of a serious operations plan than a brilliant ploy through which the High Command sought to enhance its own power and discredit the Imperial Naval Office.

Almost three months later, on 22 April 1897, Knorr reacted in writing.[109] He rejected Barandon's arguments and claimed that the thrust against the French northern coast was the obvious course of action for the German fleet. It was "so simple and self-evident" that the French in fact expected it! Even if nothing was gained and the French northern fleet remained undefeated, nothing would be lost, either. Knorr made no comment at this point about how the British attitude would affect the German operations. On 13 June, however, he instructed section A3 to include in the draft of the new operations plan against France an undertaking against Dunkirk.[110] The plan was completed on 14 June,

presented to Wilhelm on 15 June, and approved by him on 1 July.[111]
Pointing out that the strategic considerations that served as the basis for
the operations plan presented by Tirpitz in 1892 still retained their validity,
and using the old arguments in favor of the advance, Knorr conceded that
if the advance against the French northern coast were to succeed a friendly
attitude on the part of Britain and "a certain forbearance in the application
[*Handhabung*] of English neutrality towards us" was necessary. "How far
the latter could be attained was beyond prediction and would for instance
be improbable today. From the above points there arises the necessity to
provide for a further plan . . ." The alternative plan was to attack Dunkirk
instead of Le Havre. This action would be less dramatic but also less risky
and would promise success even against strengthened French naval forces.
But, on 15 December 1897, Knorr was compelled to report to Wilhelm that
weakening of the German naval forces in Europe, with the First Squadron
being limited to six ships of the line, through the dispatch of the force to
East Asia for the acquisition of Kiao-chow—which the new Secretary of
State of the Imperial Naval Office, Tirpitz, opposed—rendered offensive
naval operations on the part of the German fleet in the west impossible,
except in the most opportune circumstances, until the putting into service
of the new ships of the Kaiser Friedrich III class.[112] The construction of
the three ships of that class had started in 1894, 1896, and 1897. All three
of them would not be in service before 1900.

The predictions of the High Command of 1895 had thus materialized: by
the end of 1897 the operations plans in the west could no longer be
followed and the plan against Russia had not even been completed. The
latter, however, was owing less to the change in the power relationship
than to the incompetence of the officers of the High Command responsible
for operational planning.

## Notes: Chapter 7

1   Hopmann, *Das Logbuch*, p. 217.
2   Rich, *Holstein*, Vol. 2, p. 488.
3   *Waldersee*, Vol. 2, entry for 28 October 1895, p. 361.
4   *Holstein Papers*, Vol. 3, No. 474, Holstein to Radolin, 2 July 1895, p. 528; Winzen,
    *Bülows Weltmachtkonzept*, p. 53.
5   *Holstein Papers*, Vol. 3, No. 541, Holstein to Bülow, 22 April 1896, p. 605; ibid., No.
    550, Holstein to Radolin, 21 May 1896, p. 616.
6   BA, Eulenburg Correspondenz, 37, Bülow to Eulenburg, 25 August 1895; also
    Winzen, *Bülows Weltmachtkonzept*, pp. 53–4.
7   ibid., p. 81.
8   ibid., p. 53.
9   For Hatzfeldt's misrepresentation of Salisbury's proposals, see J. A. S. Grenville, *Lord
    Salisbury and Foreign Policy at the Close of the Nineteenth Century* (London, 1964), pp.
    31–7. The most recent standard interpretation of the incident appears in Rich, *Holstein*,
    Vol. 2, pp. 453 ff.
10  PAAA, Frankreich 87, Bd 71, Münster to Hohenlohe, 31 October 1894; ibid.,
    Russland 91, Bd 22, Münster to Hohenlohe, 27 November 1894; ibid., Frankreich 87,
    Bd 72, Münster to Hohenlohe, 3 March 1895, 17 May 1895, 16 July 1895; ibid.,
    Russland 91, Bd 25, Münster to Hohenlohe, 3 July 1896; ibid., Bd 27, Münster to

Hohenlohe, 3 December 1896; GP, XIII, No. 3430, Münster to Hohenlohe, 3 February 1897, p. 66; PAAA, Frankreich 87, Bd 74, Münster to Hohenlohe, 7 April 1897, reproduced in part in GP, XIII, No. 3432, pp. 67–9; GP, XIII, No. 3434, Münster to Hohenlohe, 3 July 1897, p. 71; ibid., No. 3469, Münster to Hohenlohe, 11 December 1897, pp. 108–9; ibid., No. 3611, Münster to Foreign Office, 10 October 1898, p. 309.

11  GP, XI, No. 2874, "Bericht . . . Schwarzkoppen," 30 October 1896, pp. 377–8.

12  PAAA, Russland 91, Bd 27, Münster to Hohenlohe, 23 November 1896.

13  BA, Bülow, *Nachlass*, No. 92, Holstein to Bülow, 3 February 1897; also see GP, XI, No. 2846, Holstein to Saurma, 15 April 1896, p. 339, and No. 2848, Holstein to Münster, 23 April 1896, p. 344, for similar views.

14  GP, XII, i, No. 3104, Hatzfeldt to Hohenlohe, 20 January 1897; Wilhelm's marginal and final comment, p. 263; Holstein's complaints in *Holstein Papers*, Vol. 4, No. 599, Holstein to Eulenburg, 3 February 1897, p. 10, and BA Bülow, *Nachlass*, No. 90, Holstein to Bülow, 4 February 1897.

15  Hohenlohe, *Denkwürdigkeiten*, Bd III, Münster to Hohenlohe, 19 October 1897, p. 395.

16  ibid., "Aufzeichnung . . . Holstein," 18 October 1897, pp. 393–4.

17  GP, XIII, No. 3446, Wilhelm's final comment on Müller to Hohenlohe, 27 August 1897, p. 84.

18  PAAA, Frankreich 87, Bd 75, Münster to Hohenlohe, 9 July 1898.

19  ibid., Frankreich 105, No. 1, Bd 13, Münster to Hohenlohe, 13 July 1898.

20  ibid., Frankreich 87, Bd 76, Münster to Foreign Office, telegram, 10 October 1898; Münster to Hohenlohe, 17 October 1898.

21  ibid., Bülow, Jerusalem, to Foreign Office, telegram, 29 October 1898; Münster to Foreign Office, telegram, 30 October 1898.

22  GP, XIV, ii, No. 3895, Castell-Rüdenhausen to Hohenlohe, 22 October 1898, pp. 378–9; No. 3904, 3 November 1898, p. 385; No. 3906, 3 November 1898, p. 386; No. 3909, 8 November 1898, pp. 389–91; No. 3898, report of naval attaché Coerper in London, 25 October 1898, pp. 380–1.

23  ibid., No. 3920, Bülow, Malta, to General-Consul in Cairo von Müller, 15 November 1898, p. 399; No. 3941, "Aufzeichnung . . . Bülow," 14 March 1899, pp. 421–2.

24  GP, XIV, ii, No. 3916, Bülow to Foreign Office, 13 November 1896, p. 397; see L. Bittner, "Neue Beiträge zur Haltung Kaiser Wilhelms II in der Faschodafrage," *Historische Zeitschrift*, no. 162 (1940), pp. 540–50, esp. 543; Paul M. Kennedy, *The Samoan Tangle: A Study in Anglo-German-American Relations, 1878–1900* (New York, 1974), p. 157; *Antagonism*, p. 237.

25  GP, XIV, ii, No. 3927, Münster to Hohenlohe, 6 January 1899, and Wilhelm's marginal comments, pp. 409–11.

26  PAAA, Bulgaria 20, Vol. 110, Hohenlohe to ambassador, Vienna, 19 August 1895; Hohenlohe, *Denkwürdigkeiten*, Bd III, Eulenburg to Hohenlohe, 20 August 1895, pp. 88–90; Hohenlohe to Eulenburg, 23 August 1895, p. 91.

27  GP, IX, No. 2232, Marschall to Tschirschky, 4 April 1895, p. 261; No. 2235, Marschall to Hatzfeldt, 6 April 1895, pp. 263–4.

28  Rich, *Holstein*, Vol. 2, p. 439.

29  BA, Eulenburg Correspondenz, 37, Notizen, 5 July 1895, 28 July 1895.

30  BA, Eulenburg Correspondenz, 36, 1895 III, Holstein to Eulenburg, 17 June 1895.

31  GP, IX, No. 2315, Hatzfeldt to Holstein, 18 June 1895, pp. 353–4.

32  ibid., No. 2317, Radolin to Hohenlohe, 14 July 1895, pp. 357–8.

33  ibid., No. 2321, "Aufzeichnung . . . Eulenburg," October 1895, p. 369.

34  PAAA, Russland 91, Bd 24, Münster to Hohenlohe, 8 October 1895.

35  Hohenlohe, *Denkwürdigkeiten*, Bd III, "Aufzeichnung," n.d. (between 9 and 21 October 1895), p. 113.

36  PAAA, Orientalia Generalia 5, Geh., Bd 4, Marschall to Bülow, 15 November 1895, draft by Holstein; also in GP, IX, No. 2328, pp. 379–82.

37  GP, X, No. 2495, Hohenlohe to Eulenburg, 5 November 1895, draft by Holstein, pp. 155–6; BA, Eulenburg Correspondenz, 38, 1895 V, Holstein to Eulenburg, 2 November 1895.

38  BA, Hohenlohe, *Nachlass*, Rep. 100 XXII A6, Holstein's memorandum, 12 November 1895.

39  *Holstein Papers*, Vol. 3, No. 515, Holstein to Eulenburg, 21 December 1895, p. 576; Hatzfeldt, *Nachgelassene Papiere*, Vol. 2, No. 664, Holstein to Hatzfeldt, 21 December 1895, pp. 1063–4; Röhl, *Germany without Bismarck*, pp. 160–1.
40  Hatzfeldt, *Nachgelassene Papiere*, Vol. 2, No. 671, Holstein to Hatzfeldt, 15 February 1896, p. 1073.
41  GP, XI, No. 2637, "Aufzeichnung . . . Holstein," 20 February 1896, p. 57.
42  ibid., No. 2735, Hohenlohe to Radolin, 20 May 1896, pp. 188–9.
43  Hohenlohe, *Denkwürdigkeiten,* Bd III, Hohenlohe to Wilhelm, January 1897, draft, pp. 296–7.
44  GP, XII, i, No. 2941, Wilhelm's marginal comments on Tschirschky to Hohenlohe, 4 April 1897, pp. 82–3.
45  See A. F. Pribram, *The Secret Treaties of Austria–Hungary, 1879–1914*, Vol. 2 (Cambridge, Mass., 1920), pp. 185–95.
46  A. J. P. Taylor, *Struggle for Mastery in Europe, 1848–1918* (London, 1954), p. 370.
47  Langer, *Diplomacy*, pp. 378–9; Kennedy, *Antagonism*, p. 230.
48  GP, XII, i, No. 3127, Marschall to Hatzfeldt, 7 May 1897, p. 298.
49  ibid., No. 3128, Lichnowsky to Hohenlohe, 7 May 1897, p. 299.
50  ibid., No. 3129, Bülow to Hohenlohe, 25 May 1897, pp. 301–2.
51  ibid., No. 3130, "Aufzeichnung . . . Holstein," 13 July 1897, pp. 302–3.
52  Taylor, *Struggle*, p. 370.
53  GP, XIV, i, No. 3689, Wilhelm to Hohenlohe, 7 November 1897, p. 69; and No. 3690, Wilhelm to Bülow, 7 November 1897, pp. 69–70.
54  ibid., No. 3693, Rotenhan to Wilhelm, 10 November 1897, pp. 73–4; and No. 3694, Rotenhan to Bülow, 9 November 1897, pp. 75–6.
55  Hohenlohe, *Denkwürdigkeiten*, Bd III, Tirpitz to Hohenlohe, 10 November 1897, p. 412.
56  *Holstein Papers*, Vol. 4, No. 630, Holstein to Hatzfeldt, 13 November 1897, p. 51.
57  ibid., 52; Röhl, *Germany without Bismarck*, pp. 252–3.
58  GP, XIV, i, No. 3695, Rotenhan to Bülow, 11 November 1897, p. 78.
59  ibid., No. 3702, Hohenlohe to Hatzfeldt, 16 November 1897, p. 86; Hohenlohe, *Denkwürdigkeiten*, Bd III, Hohenlohe to Rotenhan, 10 November 1897, p. 412; Hohenlohe to Wilhelm, 15 November 1897, p. 414. Also BA, Hohenlohe, *Nachlass*, Rep. 100, XXII, A12, Hohenlohe to Wilhelm, telegram, 11 November 1897.
60  *Holstein Papers*, Vol. 4, No. 636, Bülow to Hatzfeldt, 2 December 1897, p. 57.
61  Winzen, *Bülows Weltmachtkonzept*, pp. 134–6.
62  GP, XIV, i, No. 3733, Muraviev to Osten-Sacken, 2/14 December 1897, p. 121.
63  Winzen, *Bülows Weltmachtkonzept*, p. 136.
64  ibid., Bernhard Fürst von Bülow, *Denkwürdigkeiten*, Vol. I (Berlin, 1930), p. 203.
65  *Holstein Papers*, Vol. 4, No. 639, extract from a very confidential private letter from Hugo von Radolin, 28 December 1897, p. 60.
66  BA-MA, F 5593, III, 2.–2., Vol. 2, Commanding Admiral, initialed by Tirpitz, to Kapitän-zur-See Fritze, Chief of Staff of the Command of the Baltic Sea Station, 2 March 1895.
67  BA-MA, F 5592, III, 2.–1., Vol. 1, "Allgemeine Gedanken über unseren Operationsplan gegen Russland und nähere Ausarbeitung des Operationsplans I," June 1895.
68  ibid., "Votum von A III zu der Denkschrift betreffend den russischen Operationsplan," 26 June 1895.
69  ibid., "Bemerkungen von A V zum russischen Operationsplan," 11 February 1896.
70  ibid., "Aktennotiz zu der Arbeit des Korvetten-Kapitäns Winkler 'Allgemeine Gedanken über unsere Operationspläne gegen Russland und nähere Ausarbeitung des Operationsplans No. I,'" 25 February 1896.
71  Ritter, *Der Schlieffen-Plan*, pp. 27–8; 36.
72  BA-MA, F 5592, III, 2.–1., Vol. 1, "Aktennotiz zu der Arbeit des Korvetten-Kapitäns Winkler . . ." 25 February 1896.
73  ibid., Vol. 2, Statement of A2, Scheder, 28 February 1896.
74  ibid., Knorr to Schlieffen, 11 March 1896.
75  See above, p. 73.
76  BA-MA, F 5592, III, 2.–1., Vol. 2, Schlieffen to Knorr, 19 March 1896, and Knorr's undated marginal comment on the first page of the letter. For Schlieffen's contempt for

naval planning, see Jehuda A. Wallach, *Das Dogma der Vernichtungsschlacht: Die Lehren von Clausewitz und Schlieffen und ihre Wirkung in zwei Weltkriegen* (Munich, 1970), p. 217.

77  BA-MA, F 5593, III, 2.–2., Vol. 2, A2; "Denkschrift betreffend den Streuminenkrieg auf den östlichen Kriegstheater," 15 February 1896.
78  ibid., F 5592, III, 2.–1., Vol. 2, Scheder to A3, n.d.
79  ibid., Schröder to A2, 29 April 1896.
80  ibid., A2, Scheder, to A1–7, 17 May 1896.
81  ibid., A1 to A3, 29 May 1896.
82  ibid., A3, Schröder, to A5, 4 June 1896.
83  ibid., A6a to A7, 5 June 1896.
84  ibid., joint statement of A5, A4, A6b, forwarded to A6a, 5 June 1896.
85  ibid., F 5593, III, 2.–2., Vol. 2, "Notizen zum Vortrage beim Chef des Stabes betreffend Kriegführung in der Ostsee," n.d. In the margin of the document is Scheder's comment that the Chief of Staff declared himself to be in agreement, dated 1 August 1896.
86  ibid., F 5592, III, 2.–1., Vol. 2, A2, Scheder, to A1, A3, A4, A5, A7, 18 December 1896, enclosing "Operationspläne für den Ostsee-Kriegsschauplatz."
87  See above, p. 106.
88  BA-MA, F 5592, III, 2.–1., Vol. 2, A1 to A3, 29 January 1897.
89  ibid., A7 to A2, 3 March 1897.
90  ibid., F 5596, III, 3.–1., Vol. 2, "Seiner Exzellenz vorzulegen. Votum des Chefs des Stabes zum Operationsplan gegen Frankreich," 5 February 1897.
91  See above, p. 99.
92  BA-MA, F 5596, III, 3.–1., Vol. 2, Knorr, "Kriegsplan gegen Frankreich," 22 April 1897.
93  ibid., notation of Scheder, 9 March 1897.
94  ibid., A2, Scheder, to A3,5,7,1, 16 March 1897.
95  ibid., "Erstes Koncept. Entwurf zum Operationsplan gegen Russland," n.d. Circulated by A2 to A5,1,7, K4.
96  ibid., A3a, Schröder, 20 November 1897; A3b, Capelle (?), 22 November 1897; and A5a, 26 November 1897.
97  ibid., A2, Scheder, "Denkschrift zu dem Operationsplan: Krieg zwischen Deutschland und Russland," 4 December 1897.
98  ibid., Scheder to A3, A1, A5, enclosing "Reinkonzept . . . Operationsplan für den Fall: Krieg Deutschlands gegen Russland."
99  ibid., A2, Winkler, 6 August 1898.
100  ibid., A2, Winkler, to A3 and to A4, to be passed on to A, 18 October 1898.
101  ibid., A2, "Anlage A, Utö als Stützpunkt."
102  ibid., A3 to A4, 26 October 1898; A4, 27 October 1898.
103  ibid., F 2015, PG 65956, Chief of the Admiralty Staff, "Denkschrift zum Immediatbericht," 26 February 1900.
104  PAAA, Russland 72b, Vol. 12, report of Kalau vom Hofe, 22 March 1898.
105  BA-MA, F 2015, PG 65956, Chief of the Admiralty Staff, "Denkschrift zum Immediatbericht," 26 February 1900.
106  See above, p. 84.
107  BA-MA, F 5596, III, 3.–1., Vol. 2, Heeringen, "Arbeiten welche A III noch auszuführen hat," 18 September 1895. The tasks included:

(1)  securing direct communications with naval attachés;
(2)  a short plan for distribution to commanders at the time of the outbreak of the war;
(3)  the first operations order to be issued;
(4)  plan for the bombardment of Le Havre;
(5)  plan for the bombardment of Cherbourg;
(6)  plan for the bombardment of Calais;
(7)  plan for the bombardment of Dunkirk;
(8)  the blockade declaration;
(9)  determination of war contraband;

(10)  arrangements concerning the train and matters such as coaling, cable steamers, security in the English Channel, reconnaissance on the French coast, preparations for the burning of Le Havre, destruction of all French cables, the study of the French maneuvers of 1895, and the defense of the German coast. The last topic was to be studied during the Admiralty Staff voyages of 1896 and 1897.

108  BA-MA, F 5596, III, 3.–1., Vol. 2, "Seiner Exzellenz vorzulegen. Votum des Chefs des Stabes zum Operationsplan gegen Frankreich," 5 February 1897.
109  BA-MA, F 5596, III, 3.–1., Vol. 2, statement of Knorr in response to the "Votum" of the Chief of Staff of 5 February, 1897, 22 April 1897.
110  ibid., Knorr to A3, 13 June 1897.
111  ibid., Knorr, "Denkschrift zum Vortrag bei Seiner Majestät, Operationsplan gegen Frankreich," 14 June 1897.
112  ibid., Knorr to Wilhelm, 15 December 1897.

# 8 The Navy and World Power, I: Transoceanic Tension and Operational Planning against Great Britain and in Non-European Waters, 1895–99

## I

The years 1895–97, during which the navy was proved incapable of carrying out operations against Germany's Continental opponents, were marked by an increasing desire to use it as an instrument of *Weltpolitik*. Colonial enthusiasm increased in Germany as it did elsewhere, and attempts to make colonial gains generated friction between her and overseas powers, including Britain and the United States of America.

Britain had since 1887 been viewed by the German leadership as a potential ally of the Triplice powers in the Mediterranean. The constructions and operational planning of the British Admiralty were directed primarily against Russia and France.[1] The German High Command of the Navy had even counted on British naval support against France. But as of 1893 German attempts to draw closer to Britain and to get her to provide stronger backing to Austria and Italy in the Mediterranean failed and the German leadership came to view her increasingly as a fomentor of strife among the Continental powers. At the very same time she seemed everywhere to be blocking Germany's attempts to make colonial gains, particularly in Africa and Samoa, or to spread her influence, as in Turkey. To the British leadership and public German actions appeared as bullying and threatening. The change in the official relations between the two countries was accompanied by hostile press utterances and by commercial competition.[2] By 1897 "The previous Anglo-German friendship had been replaced by coolness, the cooperation by working alone, and the confidence by suspicion."[3] The incident contributing most to the deterioration of Anglo-German relations was the decision of Wilhelm II and his advisers at a meeting in the Chancellor's palace on 3 January 1896 to send a telegram to President Paul Kruger of the Transvaal, congratulating him on repelling the Jameson raid. "Probably no single act in the years before 1914," remarks Norman Rich, "did more to inflame British and German public opinion against each other."[4] Present at the meeting were Wilhelm, the three leading admirals Hollmann, Knorr, and Senden, the last of whom was soon to earn the reputation of an inveterate anglophobe, Hohenlohe, and Marschall. According to the Secretary of

State of the Foreign Office: "HM developed some weird and wonderful plans . . . Finally, at my suggestion, His Majesty sends a congratulatory telegram to President Krüger."[5] Overriding the objections of his adviser Holstein, who was waiting in the antechamber together with the head of the Colonial Department of the Foreign Office, Paul Kayser, who drafted the telegram, Marschall appears to have been "so carried away by the chauvinistic tidal wave which was sweeping German public opinion that he totally misjudged the effect the telegram would have on British opinion." He does not seem to have regretted sending the telegram before 11 January when *The Times* was writing of an alliance of England, France and Russia against Germany.[6] Hohenlohe laconically concluded that the Schele Mission, of which he disapproved along with Marschall, Holstein, and Kayser, would be handled in a dilatory manner.[7] It is safe to agree with Röhl that most probably the navy was behind Wilhelm's "weird and wonderful plans." As Holstein wrote to Hatzfeldt on 22 January, "HM has at the moment only one interest: to bring through an enormous additional request for the fleet as a result of the political scuffle with England."[8] As for the High Command, both Knorr and Heeringen had on 31 December 1895 agreed with Marschall on landing troops to protect German citizens in Pretoria.[9] The naval leaders may have hoped that the threat of war between Germany and the greatest maritime power of the world could rally the government and people behind the naval increases to such an extent as to ensure their passage through the Reichstag—as proposed by the High Command memorandum of 28 November 1895.[10] But now Senden and Wilhelm also proposed that in addition to the long-term building plan short-run arrangements be made to improve Germany's representation abroad—a task rendered more urgent by the Transvaal issue "where it has been shown most clearly that the continuously shrinking navy possessed no adequate number of ships in order in any way to do justice to the position of the Reich as a world power." A loan of a few hundred million marks was to be raised with the approval of the Reichstag for the purpose of immediately purchasing some cruisers abroad and starting the construction of others at home.[11] Tirpitz would have been horrified about the demand for cruisers—a demand which was, indeed, to influence the naval building program until his appointment as Secretary of State.

   Although he would probably have been unable at the time to distinguish between the relative significance of a battle fleet and cruisers, even the aged Hohenlohe was infected by the naval fever, concluding that "The fleet needs 300–400 million to attain the level of parity with other naval powers." For it a fleet foundation plan was necessary, which, however, would not be ready for another two or three months. He thought of the navy in terms of world politics:

   The development of German trade will excite the jealousy of other commercial nations. Now, we have previously succeeded in maintaining the most peaceful relations with all powers. But this can change and it cannot be denied that a deterioration of these relations can set in. Unless we are prepared to yield at all times and to give up the role of a world power, then we must be respected. Even the most friendly word makes no impression in international relations if it is not supported by adequate material strength. Therefore a fleet is necessary in face of other naval powers.[12]

Hollmann, however, remained pessimistic about a long-term building program,[13] and Hohenlohe concurred with him.[14]

Wilhelm and Senden were most indignant about being stalled. The Chief of the Naval Cabinet advised a complete change of system. As

the King and Emperor had no majority either in the Government, in the Bundesrat, or in the Reichstag . . . I recommended a change in personnel. We must completely rebuild the government on a different basis and behind one program . . . We must rule with one party . . . The whole country is ignorant about the purpose and tasks of the navy. The Reichstag must be enlightened and propaganda must be made in the entire country. This is not attainable at once. It requires time. An energetic man with a broad vision as State Secretary must bring about change, perhaps Tirpitz.[15]

Soon thereafter, Senden was speaking of the establishment of an absolute monarchy in which maritime and commercial interests would be mobilized for the support of the navy and the army would be used to put down any possible revolution.[16]

On 28 January, Tirpitz had an interview with Wilhelm concerning his appointment to the position of Secretary of State of the Imperial Naval Office.[17] Tirpitz's terms under which he would take on the job were high and escalated as Wilhelm assented to them. The Emperor himself and the whole government, particularly the Chancellor and the Minister of Finance, must stand behind the naval construction program. The Minister of Finance "must directly state that the re-establishment of the fleet was a necessity for the economic future of Germany." He, Tirpitz, must be allowed to explain honestly the purpose of the fleet.

The political motivation finds its final basis in the effect that a fleet has in war; only from this result [*Ausgang*] will its significance as alliance strength, in diplomatic negotiations, in foreign conflicts [and] as the actual basis of colonies become intelligible. In view of the ignorance of the effect of the fleet as real power, the Secretary of State of the Navy must carry the major share of the political or strategic explanations, the Secretary of State of the Foreign Office must second him [*mehr secondieren*].

During the campaign for the fleet program, other naval officers were to be strictly subordinated to the Imperial Naval Office and requests of other naval agencies were to be relegated to the background. But the re-establishment of the fleet would by no means be easy.

Possibly persons in high places must be replaced, public opinion was
unprepared and unfavorable. The tree would not be felled with one
strike of the axe and probably the first bill would not achieve victory . . .
I consider a dissolution of the Reichstag over the naval question only
then correct if one is certain of a considerable increase in votes . . . A
rational re-establishment of the fleet is only possible if the perennial fight
for the approval of individual ships would cease. If necessary, pressure
must be exercised through the rejection of partial approvals.

It was very important that the first presentation have an element of
surprise and that a suspicious nation be convinced that the Secretary of
State acted out of his own inner conviction and did not merely follow
Imperial orders. "Everything must be done so that the nation would gain
personal confidence in the person of the Secretary of State, otherwise, as
things lay, nothing would ever be approved . . ." This was a plea for
personal independence as well as an obvious attempt to discredit the
incumbent, Hollmann. Subsequently Tirpitz proceeded to demand the
reorganization of the naval agencies.[18] Wilhelm consented to the transfer
of a number of departments concerning maritime matters, including the
Imperial Commissariat for Emigration, from other government agencies to
the Imperial Naval Office but was significantly silent when Tirpitz also
asked for the colonies. None the less, according to Tirpitz, the Kaiser
ended the interview by approving everything and expressing his full
confidence in him.

Tirpitz, however, had to wait almost a year and a half before he assumed
the duties of Secretary of State of the Imperial Naval Office. Partly this was
because Hollmann strengthened his position with Wilhelm and the
Reichstag by managing to get three cruisers and one ship of the line
approved in March;[19] partly, as Berghahn suggests, because the suggestion
of a super-agency for the navy was hardly welcome to Wilhelm,[20] who in
order to increase his personal control over the navy had dissolved the
Admiralty; partly, no doubt, because the possibility of Tirpitz as another
Colbert did not appeal to the monarch, who had dismissed Bismarck so as
to be able to rule personally; and partly because Tirpitz could promise no
instant cures for Germany's naval impotence.

British hostility, however, remained a matter of immediate concern. On
15 February, Holstein expressed his surprise at the vehement British
reaction to the Kruger telegram.[21] At the beginning of March 1896,
Holstein, Marschall, and Hohenlohe were concerned about poor
Anglo-German relations. The first two claimed that Germany could not
ask any favors from the British—as the Kaiser did, in requesting them to
help the Italians after the defeat of Adowa—and blamed the Kaiser for
British hostility. The Chancellor, however, attributed British hostility to
"our colonial policy and the flourishing of our industry and the competition thereby created in world trade. Finally our policy in South Africa
which has been pursued for years and has been crowned by the telegram of
the Kaiser has embittered the English."[22] At the end of April, Holstein
wrote about "The aggressive and swaggering attitude which England has

adopted since the New Year—unfortunately in the first instance against ourselves . . ."[23] A month later, however, Hatzfeldt reported a change in British opinion.

> If one goes to the Foreign Office or meets English statesmen elsewhere, one gets the impression that Europe is living in a state of profound peace and that there is not a cloud on the horizon out of which a thunderstorm could develop within the next fifty years. Even interest in the Transvaal, although it is still being stirred up by some newspapers, is beginning to evaporate.

He further thought that the Prime Minister, the Marquess of Salisbury, and other Cabinet members "undoubtedly have a secret desire . . . to seek our friendship."[24] When learning in October 1896 of a British demonstration in the Persian Gulf, Wilhelm, recognizing Germany's inability to prevent Britain from seizing her colonies, advocated negotiations for an alliance with Russia and France for the mutual defense of their colonies.[25] Holstein and Hatzfeldt welcomed conflict between Britain and the powers of the Dual Alliance, claiming that this would deflect British attention from German colonies.[26] At the end of December, Hatzfeldt reported that "our relations with England have in the recent past not exactly improved,"[27] but that Salisbury's personal annoyance with Germany, which originated with the Kruger telegram, should not lead to the conclusion "that he wanted to destroy all bridges between us."[28] Still, in April 1897, Holstein complained about the limitations imposed on German freedom of action by the British hostility caused by the Kruger telegram and suggested a way out through a settlement of colonial disputes with Britain on the basis of giving her a free hand in South Africa in return for compensation in China. He played down the role of commercial rivalry in the deterioration of Anglo-German relations and astutely observed that it was possible that the Kaiser "will be afraid that his plans for the fleet will lose in urgency the moment our relations with England are again somewhat better." Marschall agreed with Holstein in principle.[29] So did Hatzfeldt, who warned that if Britain were to undertake aggressive action against the Transvaal

> no protest on our part and no dispatch of auxiliary troops from our colony would prevent it from being carried out. The sole result of such steps would be a conflict between England and ourselves, in which we could do absolutely nothing against the English; whereas they could take Heligoland away from us again and perhaps bombard Hamburg.[30]

In a conflict with Germany, Britain would not hesitate to use her fleet to inflict serious damage on her opponent. British public opinion

> now as before holds Germany responsible for Krüger showing no inclination until now to yield to English bidding. The irritation which because of it prevails among the public towards Germany is also evident today on every occasion, and particularly in press statements which concern themselves with this question.[31]

Wilhelm agreed with Hatzfeldt's assessment[32] and by 4 May was prepared to accept a rapprochement along the lines originally proposed by Holstein.[33] Holstein also thought that another provocative act on the part of Germany in South Africa would lead to war with Britain—and possibly with France.[34] Salisbury, however, was unwilling to accept a *quid pro quo* arrangement[35] leading Hatzfeldt to conclude: "In other words, he doesn't love us and hasn't forgiven us for the Krüger telegram, but he would nevertheless like to see relations improved for political reasons if it doesn't cost anything." He recommended that Germany try to soften up Britain by taking at every occasion the side of her enemies.[36] Wilhelm remarked that he had predicted the outcome: "We get nothing voluntarily that we do not seize ourselves with an armored fist."[37] By 20 May, according to Hatzfeldt, more than Salisbury's reluctance stood in the way of a colonial agreement with Germany: "The feeling here against us, as you will have seen from the cuttings from the English press, is again very strong."[38] Less than a month later Tirpitz, appointed Secretary of State of the Imperial Naval Office on 31 March, arrived in Berlin to take on his new duties the chief of which was to construct a navy against Britain.

In December 1897, Bülow was impelled to ask Metternich, who was regarded as an expert on Britain, whether he expected a British attack against Germany over the seizure of Kiao-chow. Metternich replied: "Because of East Asia, no. Also because of trade envy, no. But in case of the sharpening of the South African question—yes."[39] During the following year anglophobia continued. On 31 May 1898, Holstein wrote to Hatzfeldt: "The Kaiser has been afraid for some time that the English might suddenly attack us one day. Tirpitz shares this fear . . . ."[40] And, on 29 January 1899, Waldersee noted in his diary:

> I adhere to the view that England is and will remain our most in-commodious [*unbequemester*] enemy. Our striving industry, our industrious merchants, finally our navy which is gaining in importance disturb it.[41]

## II

Operations against Britain began to be discussed in German naval circles soon after the Kruger telegram. Tirpitz developed his views in response to an inquiry from his former chief Stosch of 12 February 1896: "how do we with any success fight a naval war against England?"[42] In his lengthy reply on the next day Tirpitz proceeded, in view of the great British superiority of cruisers and the total absence of German overseas bases, to reject commerce raiding and cruiser warfare. "There remains the actual battle fleet which is to be concentrated in the North Sea, [and] which, as long as it exists, protects the Baltic Sea and paralyzes English trade there." If the British underestimated German naval power, particularly its strongest component, the torpedo weapon, they might launch a rash offensive with inadequate forces and the Germans might conceivably defeat them by

Heligoland. That could encourage Russia to attack Britain as well. But in any case the German navy would be unable to withstand a second British attack. If, on the other hand, the British acted correctly, they would mobilize their entire home fleet, attack with an overwhelming supremacy, seize Borkum and establish it as a base, blockade both the North and Baltic Seas, destroy German trade wherever possible, and damage the German coast as much as they could. Except for the unlikely case of France joining her, Germany would lie prostrate before such an onslaught. But there was one ray of hope: correct British action, requiring the mobilization of the entire home fleet, would take more time than the mobilization of the German fleet.

. . . There would arise the question whether we should not with everything that can crawl proceed into the Thames. There our many ships built for harbor and river war would also play a part. We could with one strike seize a considerable part of the English merchant shipping and threaten parts of London with shelling. The question is whether this success of short duration is great enough to bring about a compromise peace acceptable to both parties.

Your Excellency sees that it would be a question of a *coup désespoir*, but perhaps also of the only chance for also in case of strategically defensive conduct our opportunity lies only in gaining time and in finding allies.[43]

When Stosch suggested that the German fleet concentrate in Danzig in the Baltic rather than in the North Sea so as to compel the British to scatter their forces along the entire German coast,[44] Tirpitz almost immediately rejected the proposal, pointing out the advantages of deployment in the Elbe:

The Elbe provides us with the auxiliary sources of Hamburg and Kiel simultaneously, and *the strategic significance of the North–Baltic Sea canal is added to it.* The last becomes effective as soon as the English go into the Baltic. Also then we have a chance, and indeed a better one, to defeat individual parts of the English fleet.[45]

In a war against Britain the Elbe, moreover, offered the best opportunities for the exit of cruisers and mine-laying ships. While the British would be able to use their older vessels against the German forces in the Baltic, in the North Sea they would be compelled to use their most seaworthy ships, whereas the Germans could use against them their inferior ships built for coastal defense.

Three weeks after Tirpitz suggested a desperate advance into the Thames estuary, while the British fleet was mobilizing, his disciple Heeringen proposed the same action in the first official German operations plan against Britain. Although direct evidence is lacking, it can be assumed that Heeringen prepared the plan at the instruction of his superiors who were responsible for provoking the crisis with Britain and consulted his former chief Tirpitz. By 5 March, Heeringen, now in charge of section A1, prepared a document entitled "Points of view for an operations plan of the home forces in case of a war Germany alone against England alone."[46] Estimating the British naval strength in northern waters at thirty-one armored ships, thirteen armored cruisers, and thirty-seven cruisers, with an additional ten armored ships, one armored cruiser, and eight cruisers in the Mediterranean, Heeringen maintained that it was out of the question that Germany could gain from the British a favorable peace settlement. But since it took Britain longer than Germany to mobilize her fleet the German navy should seize the initiative and steam against Britain no later than the third mobilization day. On the fourth and fifth mobilization days the British would have eleven armored ships and two armored cruisers ready for action, and to this force the German navy would be superior if it were accompanied by its reserve formations. The purpose of the advance was to seek battle with the British forces before the Thames estuary by attacking British shipping entering the river. Unlike Tirpitz, Heeringen doubted if after a victory the German fleet could enter the Thames estuary and shell London; instead he envisaged that the fleet would at the most remain before the Thames for one or two days or throw mines into the estuary. Beside offering the German fleet its best, although inconclusive, chance of victory, such an advance would delay the British offensive against the German coast by ten to fourteen days and thus enable the Germans to prepare their coastal defenses, complete their mobilization, and send out their auxiliary cruisers. In addition to the thrust into the Thames estuary, mines were to be laid before various British harbors. In the event of a British naval offensive against Germany either in the North Sea or in the Baltic, Heeringen saw little advantage in postponing battle until the enemy was worn down by time and weakened through mines and torpedo-boat attacks (*durch kleinen Krieg*), but advised that he should be attacked immediately by the united German forces.

It is not surprising that Tirpitz, who in his operations directives of 1892 had recommended a coup-like advance against the French northern coast so as to utilize the more rapid German mobilization for the defeat of unprepared and divided enemy forces, and his disciple Heeringen, who in 1894–95 had worked it out in detail and subsequently defended it against criticism, should have proposed a similar, even if more desperate, action against the greatest naval power of the world. Those who had little to lose could afford to take risks. Later, when they had more to lose, both men were to become cautious to the point of risking inactivity.

The heads of the other sections were requested to respond to Heeringen's memorandum. A4 (Lans), A5a, A5b, and A7 agreed in principle with the proposal of an offensive against the Thames estuary. A4 referred to the political advantages of a German success at the beginning of war but stated that the proposed advance could only be carried out if the first battle line was capable of it. This, however, would not be the case for some time. Heeringen's proposal was thus valid only for the future and not for the present, and then only from 1 May to 1 October.[47] A5a and A5b also pointed out that the necessary prerequisites for the execution of the plan would not exist before 1900. They thought that the German political leadership would never consider a disastrous war of Germany alone against Britain, but rather that of Germany allied with other powers against Britain. In such a case "an offensive blow can even under the present circumstances appear possible and advisable."[48] Schröder, who as head of section A3 still favored an advance against the French northern coast, along with A6a, rejected Heeringen's plan as not corresponding to military–political realities, for "England will never declare war before she has collected a fleet of overwhelming superiority in the Channel or before the Thames."[49] A6a, however, turned to an even bolder course of action: "The transport of land troops to England must be counted on; I see no other means of avoiding an otherwise inevitable defeat . . . If one renounces the latent strength of the army, then this appears to me tantamount to forswearing the prospects of the war."[50] Thus the issue of cooperation with the army, which had been raised previously as a remedy for the navy's weakness in the fulfillment of its more ambitious plans, such as the establishment of a naval base in the Moon Sound or the occupation of Denmark, re-emerged as the only possible way of achieving a victory over Britain.

On 23 April the Chief of Staff, Diederichs, formulated his position. He described "the driving of Germany without allies into a war with England" on the part of German diplomacy as a "blunder bordering on a crime." None the less, even in this case the German war aim should remain, in Clausewitzian terms, as "subjecting the enemy's will to ours." He rejected fighting a naval battle for prestige and glory and approved it only for the purpose of gaining an honorable peace. The weaker side, as naval history showed, was also able to gain success through a tough defensive strategy. The British, true to their traditions, would attempt as soon as possible to annihilate the German fleet, blockade the harbors, and destroy maritime installations. Aware of the advantages presented to the German fleet by the completion of the Baltic–North Sea canal, Diederichs pointed out that, by using either exit of the canal, it could prevent the British fleet from attacking the coastal fortifications. He then declared: "That our naval forces, in so far as possible, be engaged in open naval battle remains also in the defensive the highest principle"—even against a many times superior enemy. Hence Diederichs again drew closer to Heeringen's position. Like Heeringen, he also favored mine-laying operations against the English coast but unlike him expected more from the use of auxiliary cruisers. He hoped that these forms of activity would prepare the British public for peace. One is then taken by surprise when Diederichs maintains:

> If we should succeed in perfecting our war preparedness to the extent that we can at the beginning of a war assemble forces before the Thames to which England cannot so soon oppose [forces] of equal strength then I too hold the offensive advance to be the best . . .

The reasons that Diederichs gave for his advocacy of the advance were the time that it would provide for mine undertakings, for the sending out of auxiliary cruisers and for the preparation of coastal fortifications, and the damage it would cause British morale.[51] The impression remains that he attempted to hunt with the hounds of offensive and run with the hares of defensive strategy. Perhaps he was reluctant to oppose outright the authority of Tirpitz and Heeringen. In any case Diederichs did not appear to view the preparation of the operations plan as urgent, deciding not to present it to Knorr before the end of the maneuvers in September.

In the meantime, on 27 July, Friedrich von Ingenohl, who appears to have been temporarily in charge of section A7, made proposals for the distribution of the work that had to be done on the operations plan between the different sections.[52] His proposals were based on the assumption that until 1900 the German strategy against Britain would be defensive but that from then on the plan for the offensive thrust before the Thames would have to be operative. The various defensive measures, involving chiefly mobilization of the coastal defenses, provision of security against hostile *coups de main,* the defense of coastal waters, and the gathering of intelligence about the movements of the British navy, were to be the responsibility of section A7. Smaller offensive endeavors which were to be combined with a defensive strategy were also to be prepared. Section A1, with the possible cooperation of A7, was to deal with cruiser war. A3 was to examine mine warfare, for which a study had been prepared by Kapitänleutnant Otto Wurmbach.[53] The mining of enemy ports and river estuaries would be undertaken by auxiliary mine-ships relying on surprise and superior speed. Eight such ships leaving port on the night between the seventh and eighth mobilization days would lay 920 mines at thirteen different locations, while 580 mines would be reserved for defensive purposes in the North Sea. Ingenohl further suggested that A3 examine the possibility of torpedo-boat attacks against British ships and ports and be responsible for the offensive plan which was to be ready by 1900. He pointed out that the preparation of all offensive undertakings against Britain required additional information about her coast, coastal fortifications, and harbors.

Winkler, who was in charge of section A7, essentially agreed with his deputy. He thought, however, that section A4 should be specifically placed in charge of operations against Britain, along with sections A3 and A7. "I consider it more correct to prepare for the war against England than against France; it is more probable, more difficult and the navy plays a more decisive part in it."[54] In a submission of 25 January 1897 to the Chief of Staff[55] he extravagantly maintained that an Anglo-German war was inevitable because of the tough competition of both powers for world markets, that Britain had occasion (*Anlass*) for it, had been preparing for it for ten years and "must also use a war of Germany against another country to render her harmless at sea." He saw only one way for Germany to escape disaster in a war with Britain: to become involved in a war of another power against Britain. In other words, Winkler was suggesting a pre-emptive strike on the part of Germany against Britain if she happened to be at war with France and/or Russia—not an unlikely event. He suggested the preparation of a plan for the defensive and another for the offensive. The former, he maintained, was already being worked on and required only some cooperation on his part. He was prepared to assume temporary responsibility for the latter, but hoped that it would be put in the hands of an independent section by the fall. This section was to cooperate closely with the German naval attaché in London and to undertake a reconnaissance journey to England. He took a decisive step beyond the operations guidelines of Heeringen by agreeing with A6a's suggestion of 24 March that a landing of troops in Britain be considered, for only through it could Britain be brought to her knees. Moreover, rumors about the assembly of invasion troops in German ports at the beginning of war would induce the British to attack immediately with inferior or divided naval forces, thus exposing themselves to defeat. He therefore recommended that contact be established with the General Staff. Winkler appears to have had two mutually contradictory expectations from military cooperation: a German invasion of Britain and a British attack on Germany which, however premature, could be fatal to the German force while being embarked or being at sea.

On 23 February 1897, Diederichs' successor Barandon completed a report to Knorr about the operations plan against Britain.[56] He gave the operations a new twist. Agreeing with the various section heads that the German fleet was incapable of defeating the British fleet on the British coast for the next few years, he came out strongly in favor of a defensive position in the German Bight which with the support of Heligoland and with careful preparation could be held open against any enemy, including the British. But then he picked up A7's and A6a's proposal that an expeditionary force be prepared, but less for the invasion of Britain than as a threat of an invasion. Such a threat would bring the British navy immediately after the outbreak of war to blockade the German Bight and the German Baltic ports or the exits from the Baltic Sea. Such unprepared and divided forces could be defeated by the German fleet. The army was to be consulted and a study made whether in case of a British naval defeat an invasion of Britain was possible. Barandon was more realistic than many of his fellow-officers in considering a landing in Britain impossible as long as a permanent supply-route could not be maintained.

In a memorandum dated 20 May,[57] Winkler, who had persuaded himself that war with Britain was impending,[58] took a position that was diametrically opposed to Barandon's. Going back to Heeringen's initial position, he considered a German defensive strategy as entirely hopeless once the British forces were mobilized and enjoyed a tenfold supremacy over the Germans. Winkler therefore came out strongly in favor of the offensive strike which Heeringen had recommended. He maintained that the existing power relationship "cannot lead us to consider an offensive procedure as something that would be rash. The wager will become smaller the more carefully we prepare and train our forces in a deliberate manner." It appears that Winkler held offensive action possible in the near future, rather than for 1900, as had been concluded from the discussion a year earlier. The objective of the advance was to be the defeat of the British fleet before the Thames. A successful battle would be followed by action against shipping and harbors in the Thames estuary and against the British forces mobilizing in Chatham, Portsmouth, and Plymouth, and by a possible landing of troops, in respect to which Winkler remained vague. The operations were to be based on the Schelde estuary, which would also be a very convenient place for a defeated German fleet to withdraw into. "The Dutch government must be induced into an alliance by our political leadership, and if this does not succeed, then we establish ourselves there by force." To the man who more than two years earlier had drafted a bold offensive plan against Russia, the offensive against Britain was becoming more than an act of desperation.

It is significant, however, that the other section heads went along with Winkler's proposals, with reservations expressed only by Schröder, head of A3, and Ruppel, head of A5. Schröder pointed out that the advance was only feasible if war broke out suddenly, not if Britain had had the opportunity to make preparations during a period of tension. He stressed the need for close discussions with the General Staff which must determine the nature of operations and stated that the operations against Britain would be greatly facilitated if Germany had France as an ally or an enemy: in the latter case the decisive operations would be on land and the defeat of France would provide Germany with a sure compensation for any damages caused by Britain. He was thus the first to express what later came to be the "hostage theory."[59] Ruppel shared Schröder's doubts about the feasibility of an offensive strike, since he did not think that a sudden outbreak of war was possible in a case other than a German attack, "a hardly possible case," but suggested that

A landing in England must in my opinion be seriously considered in a solid connection with the offensive blow. It has certainly something adventurous about it, but not more than the offensive blow alone. But the double adventure has in its favor that I achieve through its success probably a permanent and decisive victory; the success of the offensive blow merely achieves for me a partial success which will be soon evened out in the course of war.[60]

Winkler's plan was accepted by Knorr with the modifications of giving greater prominence to the landing of troops and eliminating the action against Chatham, Plymouth, and Portsmouth after a successful naval battle on the grounds that the fleet would be too much weakened for the purpose. Knorr also ruled that the question of naval bases on the Dutch and Belgian coast required further, more detailed, consideration. Knorr obtained Wilhelm's approval on 31 May, a few days before Tirpitz arrived in Berlin to assume his new duties as Secretary of State.[61] Wilhelm ordered that further specified preparations be worked on, that contact be established with the General Staff, and that the choice of the ports of embarkation for the troops be governed by the location selected for their landing in Britain.

On 2 June 1897, Knorr requested Schlieffen's cooperation. He wanted to know which would be the best landing-areas and embarkation ports, which troops would be available and which transportation facilities would be required, and finally admitted that the navy would probably be unable to keep open the supply-lines to the expeditionary forces.[62] Knorr suggested to Schlieffen that in a war against Britain Germany would probably have allies; Schröder had remarked on the draft of the document submitted by Knorr to Wilhelm on 31 May that, unless Germany had France as an ally, a *sine qua non* for success in a war against Britain was the occupation of both Holland and Belgium. He now had orders to study how this could be done.[63]

Jonathan Steinberg describes the memorandum that Schröder prepared as "worthy of Jules Verne." He assumed that both Holland and Belgium would remain neutral in a war between Britain and Germany. The great strategic advantage that Germany gained from the control of the coast of Holland and Belgium in a war with Britain in which "our national wealth, the welfare of the German people, yes, perhaps, our very existence as a state were at stake" would justify the violation of the neutrality of both states. Offensive operations and an invasion could be more easily undertaken from the Dutch and Belgian coast but the mere possession of it by the Germans would compel the British to detach forces to attack and blockade it and weaken the blockade of the German North Sea and Baltic coasts. Although Knorr had initially subordinated the planning against Holland and Belgium to the broader scheme of offensive operations against Britain, Schröder thus pointed out its significance for a defensive war against Britain as well. He also

cast a glance at the operation against Antwerp in the event of a war between the Triple Alliance and the Dual Alliance. The operation under those circumstances seems to be even more promising, assuming England remains neutral at first . . . As long as we lay within the mouth of the Schelde with a portion of our naval strength, it would be impossible for the French to maintain a serious blockade of the North Sea, even if the powerful Mediterranean squadron was transferred to the operation.

The conclusion that the possession of Antwerp and the mouth of the Schelde would be enormously valuable for the German naval operations, whether in a war against England or against France or against both together, seems, therefore, to be entirely justified.

Schröder's operational notions thus dovetailed with those of the army. Schlieffen had already in 1891 considered the violation of Belgian neutrality for the purpose of bypassing the French fortifications,[64] but the idea did not gain firm form before August 1897 when he remarked that an offensive "which wants to bypass Verdun cannot shrink from violating the neutrality of Luxemburg as well as that of Belgium."[65] Schlieffen was therefore, as will be seen, more interested in cooperating with the navy in the operations against Belgium and Holland than in the invasion of Britain. The work on the operations against Belgium and Holland also continued after the plan for the offensive against Britain to which it was initially subordinated had in effect been dropped.

Schröder envisaged the operations against Belgium and Holland as requiring extensive cooperation between the army and the navy and depending on an element of surprise. Neither the countries about to be raped nor Britain could be alerted. In the dark of night seven steamers carrying nine battalions of infantry and some artillery and pioneer units, in all 11,000 men, with a modest escort consisting chiefly of the eight Siegfried-class ships, would slip out of the German North Sea ports. Twenty-four hours later the convoy would enter the Schelde. At the break of day a simultaneous landing and attack would be launched against the forts of Antwerp and the Schelde estuary. Since, however, the troops involved were inadequate for the occupation and defense of the position, at the time of the departure of the convoy from German ports the Seventh and Eighth Army Corps in the Rhineland would start moving toward the Belgian and Dutch borders. They would cross the borders at the same time as the landing operation would commence and swiftly advance toward Breda and Antwerp. "There is no reason to expect serious resistance."

While none of the department heads to whom Schröder's plan was circulated objected to it on moral grounds, there was general opposition to its adventurous and impractical nature. The German navy had just recently gone through one of its few practical tests in preparing the expedition for the seizure of Kiao-chow which had shown how much time it would take to embark a sizeable force. Nevertheless, Schröder persisted. Information was sought about the Belgian coast, particularly coastal defense; and, by 21 February 1898, Knorr was able to present a more specific plan to Wilhelm. The general outlines of the plan did not, however, significantly differ from that of Schröder. Knorr's request for permission to establish contact with Schlieffen about the implementation of the plan was approved. He wrote to Schlieffen on 4 March, leaving the question open whether subsequent consultations occur in writing or orally in a committee.[66] Knorr's approach to Schlieffen occurred after the latter had in December for all practical purposes ruled that the plan to invade Britain was ludicrous. With some delay Schlieffen replied on 17 June, agreeing to establish a committee consisting of the representatives of the navy, the Ministry of War, and the General Staff, whom he named, to make preparations which in the case of the army involved a plan for attack on fortresses and arrangements for the embarkation and landing of troops.[67] Following a letter from Knorr to Schlieffen of July 1898, the file including the material on the operations against Belgium and Holland closes. The subsequent file on the same topic does not open until May 1905. Thus, as Steinberg points out, "the ultimate fate of the plan is unknown."[68] What the discussion between the High Command of the Navy and the General Staff does reveal, however, is a unique willingness on the part of the army and navy to cooperate in the preparation of operations. Whether Schröder had any inkling of the General Staff's intentions to violate Belgian neutrality remains unknown, but the very fact that he and the General Staff seriously started to contemplate the identical violation of international law which could serve the same operation, i.e. war against the Dual Alliance, led to Schlieffen's willingness to cooperate.

On 14 December 1897, Schlieffen had provided a different type of reply to Knorr's inquiry about a possible landing in Britain. It was a masterly analysis of the situation, showing "that he also had a clear view of questions of naval power."[69]

England's might rests in her fleet. To defeat it or to seize it must be the task of every power that fights with the island state.

Germany in a war against England unfortunately has no fleet which is strong enough to carry out the battle of destruction against the hostile fleet. Her ships, ready earlier, better prepared for battle, and commanded more skillfully, can only hope to defeat one part of the overwhelmingly superior might of the enemy and to drive it back. The sea cannot be held against the later emerging mass of English naval power by the small number of German ships. After the extensive losses which even the victor will have suffered in the initial stage of war, he must flee to a protecting harbor.

The rest of the task of the war will fall to the German army. It is to use the hoped-for partial victory of the navy for a landing on the hostile coast. However great victories it might win over the hostile army, it cannot do anything to the English fleet, the real enemy. Only indirectly can it get at it. Through our army, Englishmen's life and their continued existence on their island must be made impossible. The German must kneel on the chest of his prostrate enemy until he begs for mercy, for peace at any price. This price can only consist in the handing over of the English fleet . . . If we wanted to set ourselves a more limited aim than the capitulation of the English fleet, then it cannot be imagined how we, even as victors, can again return home. As long as the English fleet exists and the island state rules the surrounding seas, the victorious German army is the prisoner in the conquered state. It finds itself in a similar situation as the garrison of an invested fortress. It will be gradually starved, not through it being cut off from its food-supplies—it will find food as long as the English have anything to eat—but through the cutting off of any replacement of personnel and *matériel,* but particularly munitions. When the last cartridge has burned out the victor must lay down his gun.[70]

Having thus admitted that an invasion of Britain was impossible as long as the navy would be unable to guarantee the army's rearward communications, Schlieffen pointed out that in spite of the operations against Belgium and Holland at the beginning of the war it would be impossible to use the coastline of these countries for the embarkation of invasion troops to Britain after a speedy naval victory. The invasion forces would thus have to embark from German ports. Ships should be provided for the transportation of as many troops as the capacity of the railways would allow to enter the ports in time for the launching of the invasion. (A marginal comment suggested preliminary arrangements for two army corps.)

Knorr and Winkler were both sobered by Schlieffen's reply. The former remarked that he shared Schlieffen's opinion. The latter commented that his views about the war with Britain "under the present circumstances and those in the next ten years were confirmed." Both, however, favored the continuation of the preparation of offensive operations against Britain.[71]

Such, however, was the state of affairs in the High Command that, along with the topics selected by Knorr for further study, work continued on many aspects of the offensive operations plan against Britain which involved correspondence with the General Staff, whereas nothing appears to have been done about preparing the required defensive operations plan. On 12 September 1898, Knorr initialed a document which had circulated among A1, A2, A3, and A4, the last of whom was now in charge of the operations against Britain.[72] It pointed out that the studies that were undertaken revealed that in case of sudden mobilization in the spring of 1898 there would be available 145 steamships, sufficient for the transportation of two and a half army corps to Britain. This force was not adequate for the General Staff, which stipulated for an invasion army of six to eight corps. It was stated that the merchant marine was capable of transporting the considerably larger force, but that the preparations could not be kept secret and that the embarkation could not occur at the very beginning of the war. Thus there was further confirmation that Germany alone could not undertake a successful invasion of Britain. The document pointed out, however, that under special circumstances Britain could be injured by an invasion of Egypt and India. Proceeding to discuss different cases of war, it showed that the support of Germany by her allies Italy and Austria would be of little advantage. The British navy would soon force Italy to defect—a realistic assumption. But if Germany were allied with Russia an offensive war by both was possible against India and, if the two could press Turkey to enter the war, against Egypt as well. Were France on the side of Germany and Russia, it would also be possible to consider realistically an invasion of Britain. As the allied fleets would establish mastery in the North Sea, the French could land on the south coast of Britain and their current German allies undertake a landing on the east coast. These findings justified the conclusion that Germany should make peacetime preparations for the organization of a large transport fleet. This plan would have struck Tirpitz as fantastic, for he saw no advantage in an alliance with Russia, who would not be able to launch an attack on India and would have her hands full with the defense of her Far Eastern possessions, and no possibility of an alliance with France because of Alsace-Lorraine. Bülow, however, had since 1897 entertained an eventual alliance with Russia against Britain.[73]

On 28 October 1898, Knorr reported to Wilhelm about the preparations for a landing in Britain, admitting, however, that they had only theoretical significance for the time being.[74] On 10 January 1899, Knorr belatedly informed Schlieffen what he undoubtedly suspected and what had been known to the High Command and Wilhelm since December 1897: that without allies even a temporary achievement of mastery of the North Sea was impossible and that temporarily the idea of defeating Britain on her own soil had to be given up.[75] Although the proposal of an offensive thrust against Britain probably originated with Tirpitz at a time that he did not hold a responsible position, on 23 October 1898 he expressed his agreement with Schlieffen's position of 14 December: "An invasion of England is nonsense. Even if we should succeed in landing two army corps in England, that would be of no avail, for these corps would not be strong enough to maintain their position without support from home."[76] Approximately a year later he gave as one of his objections to the publication of Kapitän-zur-See Kurt Freiherr von Maltzahn's work his statement that in 1805 Napoleon needed mastery of the English Channel for only a few days in order to invade Britain: "This was Napoleon's error. If he had really succeeded in getting across, then he and his army would have been lost as in Egypt, where only flight and an early conclusion of peace saved him from total defeat."[77] And Tirpitz, in contrast to the naval High Command, now as again at the end of 1904,[78] did not consider Russia—or France—as an ally for Germany. "The Russians cannot come over the mountains to India, they have enough to do to maintain their Far Eastern possessions."[79]

## III

The adventurous spirit of the German navy in the realm of *Weltpolitik* was also reflected in the thoughts some of its officers were devoting to operations against the United States of America. At the beginning of 1889, when Germany and the United States clashed over Samoa,[80] Goltz had requested a memorandum from the Chief of Staff, Guido Karcher, about the waging of war against the United States. He was informed that in view of its weaknesses the activity of the German fleet against the United States would have to be chiefly confined to cruiser war, with possible raids against the American east coast.[81] The operational proposal that was to serve as the basis for the planning of the newly created Admiralty Staff as of March 1899 first appeared in the *Winterarbeit* of the later Admiral, as yet Leutnant-zur-See, Eberhardt von Mantey.[82] Indeed, the first five topics of the *Winterarbeiten* of 1897–98, probably selected by the Inspekteur des Bildungswesens, Kontre-Admiral Iwan Oldekop, related to America: Cuba, the Philippines, the Monroe Doctrine, Central America, and the United States as concerns for the German navy.[83] Although German–American relations were not yet as tense as they were to become during the Spanish–American War, by the spring of 1897 the German leadership had become concerned about the American economic threat to Europe and had initiated discussions with Russia and Austria-Hungary for cooperation against it. The preparations for the American annexation of Hawaii had caused considerable excitement in German imperialist circles and provided even Hohenlohe with incentive to settle the Samoan situation. Furthermore, the Cuban crisis of September 1897 impelled Wilhelm to think of rallying the Continental powers to Spain's defense.[84]

Mantey did not see how Germany could impose her will on the United States through a blockade. Instead it would have to be defeated on the American mainland. Holding an extremely low opinion of the American navy, army, and militia, he suggested a bold amphibious operation, involving both the army and the navy, as did current High Command proposals for action against Britain, Holland, and Belgium, leading to the "occupation of Norfolk, Hampton Roads, and Newport News (later on also Gloucester, Massachusetts), to be followed by operations up to the Chesapeake Bay in the direction of Washington and Baltimore." He devoted little attention to the problem of supplying such an expeditionary force. Admiral Hans von Koester, Chief of the Baltic naval station, agreed with Mantey's proposals, and stated that his survey of the American coast was "particularly interesting at the given moment," indicating that at least some of the higher German naval officers considered war with the United States possible. In his *Winterarbeit* of 1898–99, probably ordered by Koester or Oldekop, Mantey became even more daring. He now selected New York as the target of attack. Success depended on speed and surprise. Troops and *matériel* were to be assembled in German ports in peacetime so that the armada could proceed against the United States immediately after the declaration of war, when American mine-blockings would not yet be set up and coastal fortifications would be unprepared, and seize Norfolk as the base for its operations. Subsequently the German fleet would be divided into two units: a blockade fleet at the exit of Long Island Sound and the main force which would undertake the attack on New York on the very day of arrival. Estimating the American naval strength at seven ships of the line, fourteen cruisers, and fourteen coastal armored ships, Mantey required for Germany the strength of seventeen ships of the line, thirty-three cruisers, and four auxiliary cruisers; forty to sixty freighters would be needed to transport the necessary coal. The problem of supplying this force from the homeland during its operations was not discussed.

By the time that Mantey's work was presented to his superiors it had become even more "relevant." The German attitude toward the United States during the Spanish–American War was unfriendly, with the press largely condemning American imperialism.[85] In the spring and summer of 1898 there were extensive demands for compensation for American aggrandizement, with Tirpitz, who had earlier coveted Manila,[86] wanting the Danish West Indies, Knorr being particularly interested in the Caribbean, Prince Heinrich asking "Will we have chances for the Philippines and Samoa?", Wilhelm wanting Samoa, the Carolines, Borneo, and an island in the Philippines "if possible," and even Hatzfeldt proposing the seizure of the Sulus and the Carolines. The Foreign Office also wished compensations, but did not want to risk war with the United States.[87] On New Year's Day 1898 the German ambassador in Washington, Theodor von Holleben, stated in his annual report that because of economic rivalry most Americans viewed Germany as "the most hated land," a statement with which Wilhelm concurred, concluding that what she needed was a large battle fleet.[88] On 15 June 1898 the Admiralty Staff Department of the High Command of the Navy decided to start work on operations plans against the United States. In July, Diederichs and George Dewey confronted each other in Manila. The Samoan crisis, erupting anew in January 1899, continued the mutual suspicions of the Germans and Americans.[89]

Vice-Admiral August Thomsen, Chief of the First Battle Squadron, to whom Mantey's second *Winterarbeit* was submitted, rejected the proposed attack on New York: it could not be undertaken before the American fleet had been defeated and, even if it had been destroyed, the German fleet would have been weakened too much to launch an attack on the fortifications. He suggested the establishment of a base in Puerto Rico rather than in Norfolk, since its seizure would present less difficulty for the Germans and its distance from the United States coast would present greater difficulties for the American fleet if it came to engage the German fleet there. From it none the less the German fleet could at its convenience conduct operations against the American mainland. He was, however, not certain if the United States would be forced to conclude peace if New York, Washington, Baltimore, and Philadelphia were seized by the Germans, but acknowledged that "much would none the less be achieved if the east of North America would be seized and in our hands." Finally he welcomed Mantey's work "since at the moment every German naval officer capable of making judgments concerns himself with the consequences of a military conflict between Germany and the United States of America . . ."[90]

As yet, however, we need not attribute more significance to Mantey's work and its favorable reception by Koester and Thomsen than it being another expression of the naval officers' adventurous and unrealistic attitude, which had already appeared in previous operational studies by responsible officers in the High Command, particularly Schröder's plan for the occupation of Belgium and Holland, and the thrust against the Thames estuary, followed by the invasion of Britain, and of a naïve zeal to respond to the immediate challenges presented by *Weltpolitik*. Other than considering the possibility of war with the United States, the High Command had little to do with the studies involving offensive operations against the United States, which were in fact inconsistent with its and the Emperor's previous decisions.

## IV

The desire of the navy to establish naval bases, particularly in China, culminating in the seizure of Kiao-chow in November 1897, was another obvious sign of its greater involvement in *Weltpolitik*. Bases overseas were made more necessary because of the need to refuel steamships which had replaced sailing ships.[91] It must be kept in mind, however, that Tirpitz was opposed to the seizure of Kiao-chow because it was "unfavorable to the naval bill and objectionable in its form, since as a result of this type of action one must count on war-like developments."[92] He was fearful of Russian hostility at a time that the agitation for the First Navy Bill could arouse British enmity. Moreover, it was the sending of the additional ships to Kiao-chow that compelled the High Command to decide that offensive operations against France and Britain were impossible for the time being.

Starting with late 1896 the High Command proceeded to issue new operational orders to ships abroad for various probable cases of war, taking into account the current power relationship. The last instructions, issued in 1885, were no longer considered valid since conditions had changed through the replacement of sails by steam and the consequent dependence on coal. In his report of 8 December 1896, which was approved by Wilhelm without change on 12 December 1896,[93] Knorr provided guidelines for the operation of the ships abroad in the following cases of war: (*a*) Germany against France: (*b*) Germany against France and Russia; (*c*) Germany against Britain; (*d*) Germany allied with Russia against Britain. A final set of orders to the Chief of the Cruiser Division and the commanders of ships in the East African and Australian stations of 22 January 1897, which was approved by Wilhelm on 15 February 1897,[94] added case (*e*) Germany against the United States of America. In case (*a*) the Cruiser Division was viewed as at least equal to French forces in East Asia whereas the power relationships in other areas overseas would be less favorable. The Cruiser Division was therefore to attack the French forces as soon as possible and was to be joined by the ships of the East African and Australian stations. In case (*b*) the power relationship in East Asia was unfavorable to Germany. Therefore the Cruiser Division was to leave that area and seek out more suitable places for its operations, observing the principle that hostile ships were to be attacked whenever prospects for success existed. The ships of the East African and Australian stations were again to join the Cruiser Division and were to be subordinated to its chief. In both cases (*a*) and (*b*) the ships of the West African station were not to participate in the action. In case (*c*) in view of the extent of British shipping all German ships abroad were to engage in destroying commerce. In case (*d*) the Cruiser Division was to unite itself with the Russian forces so as to bring the British to battle, and all other ships abroad were to engage in commerce raiding. In case (*e*), depending on circumstances, special orders were to be issued. The Chief of the Cruiser Division and the senior officers of the individual stations were invited to make representations if the orders no longer corresponded to actual conditions, particularly the power relationship.

Additional regulations were provided for the acquisition of money, coal, ammunition, and of auxiliary ships, and for meetings of ships of the Cruiser Division and the individual stations. Contact was established with the Imperial Naval Office, particularly about the provision of the necessary funds.[95] The High Command also made it clear that the navy could not in case of war contribute to the defense of the colonies.[96]

After the acquisition of Kiao-chow, war against Japan also entered the thinking of the High Command. At an audience with Wilhelm on 20 December 1897, Knorr stated that Kiao-chow could not be held against the Japanese. The Chief of the Cruiser Squadron, Diederichs, was therefore instructed to report about the actions he proposed to undertake between the outbreak of hostilities and the arrival of reinforcements from home and where he proposed to meet these reinforcements. On 4 February 1898, Diederichs proposed that the rendezvous be in the very remote Bay of Sumbawa, in the Dutch East Indies. He rejected Manila as unsuitable because Japanese residents there would inform the Japanese fleet of the German presence. Knorr proposed on 11 February that the garrison of Kiao-chow leave with the Cruiser Squadron and reoccupy it when the reinforcements arrived. Wilhelm approved of the departure of the Squadron, but insisted that the Kiao-chow garrison remain to defend the base against the Japanese and that the construction of the fortifications of the base start at the same time as work on the harbor.[97] Kiao-chow was never, however, expected by the German naval authorities to serve as a base that could support the Cruiser Squadron against a powerful naval opponent.

## Notes: Chapter 8

1   Marder, *Anatomy*, pp. 120–273, passim.
2   There is a great deal of literature concerning Anglo-German relations in this period. See in particular Kennedy, *Antagonism*, pp. 205–50, and *Samoan Tangle*, pp. 114–22. Also Rich, *Holstein*, Vol. 1, pp. 356–74; Vol. 2, pp. 433–65; R. J. Sontag, *Germany and England: Background of Conflict, 1848–1894* (New York, 1964), pp. 266–342; Langer, *Diplomacy of Imperialism*, pp. 101–254; Oron J. Hale, *Publicity and Diplomacy, with Special Reference to England and Germany, 1890–1914* (Gloucester, Mass., 1964), pp. 181–237; and Ross J. S. Hoffmann, *Great Britain and the German Trade Rivalry, 1875–1914* (New York, 1964), esp. pp. 225–72, dealing with the alarm of the British public in 1896 about German commercial competition. For British policy, consult in particular Grenville, *Salisbury*, pp. 3–53; 94–107. See also C. J. Lowe, *The Reluctant Imperialists: British Foreign Policy, 1878–1902*, Vol. 1 (London, 1967), pp. 166–218.
3   Kennedy, *Samoan Tangle*, p. 122.
4   Rich, *Holstein*, Vol. 2, p. 469; see also Kennedy, *Antagonism*, 220–2.
5   Röhl, *Germany without Bismarck*, p. 165, quoting Marschall's diary, entry for 3 January 1896.
6   ibid., p. 166.
7   Hohenlohe, *Denkwürdigkeiten*, Bd III, p. 151, journal entry for 3 January 1896.
8   Hatzfeldt, *Nachgelassene Papiere*, Vol. 2, No. 668, Holstein to Hatzfeldt, 22 January 1896, p. 1070. See also Deist, *Flottenpolitik*, p. 28, referring to Wilhelm's wish in October 1895 to use conflict with Britain to gain support for naval increases.
9   Röhl, *Germany without Bismarck*, p. 164.
10  See above, p. 84. Particularly rabid was Senden. Hatzfeldt, *Nachgelassene Papiere*, Vol. 2, No. 668, Holstein to Hatzfeldt, 22 January 1896, p. 1070.
11  See "Niederschrift des Chefs des Marinekabinetts Kontreadmiral Freiherrn v. Senden-Bibran," 7 January 1896, in Hans Hallmann, *Krügerdepesche und Flottenfrage: Aktenmässiges zur Vorgeschichte des deutschen Schlachtflottenbaus* (Stuttgart, 1927), p. 77, which appears to be the early version of the more detailed letter of Wilhelm to Hohenlohe, 8 January 1896: Hohenlohe, *Denkwürdigkeiten*, Bd III, pp. 153–4.
12  "Aufzeichnung," n.d., presumably for the *Immediatvortrag* on 5 January 1896: ibid., pp. 151–2.
13  ibid., entry, n.d., p. 152.
14  Hohenlohe to Wilhelm, 7 January 1896; Wilhelm to Hohenlohe, 8 January 1896, ibid., pp. 152–4.
15  Kehr, *Schlachtflottenbau*, app. IV, Senden's diary entry for 14 January 1896.
16  Steinberg, *Yesterday's Deterrent*, p. 91.
17  BA-MA, N. 253/3, Tirpitz's notes of the "Vortrag am 28. I. 1896." These notes have been edited by Hallmann, who has omitted some detail, and improved the grammar and syntax, in *Der Weg*, 183–7. See also Berghahn, *Tirpitz-Plan*, p. 93. My quotations are from the original text.
18  BA-MA, F 3303, PG 66707, "Stellungnahme Tirpitz zu Knorrs Denkschrift vom 28. 11. 1895," dispatched on 3 January 1896.

19  BA-MA, N 160/5, Senden to Tirpitz, 31 March 1896; also Steinberg, *Yesterday's Deterrent*, p. 95; Kehr, *Schlachtflottenbau*, pp. 60–2; Hallmann, *Der Weg*, pp. 200–1.
20  Berghahn, *Tirpitz-Plan*, pp. 93–4.
21  Hatzfeldt, *Nachgelassene Papiere*, Vol. 2, No. 671, Holstein to Hatzfeldt, 15 February 1896, p. 1073.
22  Hohenlohe, *Denkwürdigkeiten*, Bd III, journal entry for 7 March 1896, pp. 191–2.
23  *Holstein Papers*, Vol. 3, No. 541, Holstein to Bülow, 22 April 1896, pp. 604–5.
24  ibid., No. 551, Hatzfeldt to Holstein, 22 May 1896, pp. 616–17.
25  GP, XIII, No. 3396, Wilhelm to Hohenlohe, telegram, 25 October 1896, pp. 3–4.
26  Hatzfeldt, *Nachgelassene Papiere*, Vol. 2, No. 690, Holstein to Hatzfeldt, 26 October 1896, p. 1095.
27  ibid., No. 695, Hatzfeldt to Marschall von Bieberstein, 28 December 1896, p. 1107.
28  ibid., p. 1109.
29  *Holstein Papers*, Vol. 4, No. 608, Holstein to Hatzfeldt, 12 April 1897, pp. 21–5.
30  ibid., No. 612, Hatzfeldt to Holstein, 22 April 1897, p. 29.
31  GP, XIII, No. 3404, Hatzfeldt to Hohenlohe, 22 April 1897, p. 18. Hatzfeldt forwarded this report upon Holstein's request to Marschall.
32  ibid., No. 3405, Hohenlohe to Hatzfeldt, 2 May 1897, p. 21.
33  *Holstein Papers*, Vol. 4, No. 616, Holstein to Hatzfeldt, 4 May 1897, p. 35.
34  Hohenlohe, *Denkwürdigkeiten*, Bd III, Holstein to Hohenlohe, n.d., p. 328.
35  GP, XIII, No. 3407, Hatzfeldt to Hohenlohe, 12 May 1897, pp. 23–7.
36  *Holstein Papers*, Vol. 4, No. 617, Hatzfeldt to Holstein, 12 May 1897, p. 36.
37  GP, XIII, No. 3407, Wilhelm's final comment on Hatzfeldt to Hohenlohe, 12 May 1897, p. 27.
38  *Holstein Papers*, Vol. 4, No. 618, Hatzfeldt to Holstein, 20 May 1897, p. 37.
39  Winzen, *Bülows Weltmachtkonzept*, p. 209.
40  *Holstein Papers*, Vol. 4, No. 656, pp. 81–2.
41  *Waldersee*, Vol. 2, p. 426.
42  Tirpitz, *Erinnerungen*, pp. 53–4; Hassell, *Tirpitz*, pp. 105–6, misdating Stosch's letter to 2 February.
43  ibid., p. 108.
44  ibid., Stosch to Tirpitz, 17 February 1896, pp. 109–10.
45  ibid., Tirpitz to Stosch, 18 February 1896, p. 111.
46  BA-MA, F 5587, III, 1.–10., Vol. 1, "Gesichtspunkte für einen Operationsplan der heimischen Streitkräfte bei einem Kriege Deutschland allein gegen England allein," 5 March 1896. An excellent discussion of the German operations plans against England is Paul M. Kennedy's, "The development of German naval operations plans against England, 1896–1914," *English Historical Review*, vol. 89, no. 350 (January 1974). Kennedy errs, however, in attributing the authorship of the document of 5 March to the Chief of Staff Diederichs. Hubatsch admits that the first considerations about operations against England dated back to 1896: *Der Admiralstab*, p. 65. Carl-Axel Gemzell in his *Organization, Conflict, and Innovation: A Study of German Naval Strategic Planning, 1888–1940* (Lund, 1973), still dates the operations plan against England 1897 (p. 68).
47  BA-MA, F 5587, III, 1.–10., Vol. 1, A4 to A2, 10 March 1896.
48  ibid., A5a and A5b to A2, 19 and 20 March 1896.
49  ibid., A3, 11 March 1896.
50  ibid., A6a to A2, 24 March 1896.
51  ibid., Diederichs, "Seiner Exzellenz gehorsamst vorzulegen," 23 April 1896.
52  ibid., A7, *i. V.*, Ingenohl, 27 July 1896.
53  ibid., "Betrachtungen über die Verwendung der Minen C/A in einem Kriege gegen England," July 1896.
54  ibid., Winkler's marginal comment on A7, *i. V.*, Ingenohl, 27 July 1896.
55  ibid., A7, "Dem Ch. d. St. gehorsamst vorzulegen," 25 January 1897.
56  ibid., Barandon, "Sr. Exzellenz gehorsamst vorzulegen. Krieg gegen England," 23 February 1897.
57  ibid., "Grundzüge für einen Operationsplan Deutschlands gegen England Allein." In my paper "Die Operationspläne der Kaiserlichen Marine bis zur Auflösung des Oberkommandos in europäischen Gewässern im Jahre 1899," in *Tradition und*

*Neubeginn: Internationale Forschungen zur deutschen Geschichte im 20. Jahrhundert. Referate und Diskussionen eines Symposiums der Alexander von Humboldt-Stiftung, Bonn-Bad Godesberg, veranstaltet vom 10. bis 15. September 1974 in Bad Brückenau,* ed. D. Papenfuss and others (Cologne, 1975), p. 43, I mistakenly dated this document May 1896. On top of it there is written in someone's hand "1895 oder 1896?", and the location of the document in the file between Wurmbach's memorandum concerning mine warfare of July 1896 and Heeringen's memorandum of 5 March likewise suggested 1896 as the year. Upon closer scrutiny, however, I noticed Jauschke's signature in his capacity as A1, a position he held in 1897 and not in 1896, and a diminutive 1897 written behind 20 V under the initial of A7.

58 BA-MA, F 5587, III, 1.–10., Vol. I, Winkler's remark of 21 May in the margin of the document of 20 May in response to Jauschke's (A1) comment to the effect that he did not view war with England as being imminent.

59 ibid., "Votum von A III," 24 May 1897.

60 ibid., statement of A5, 25 May 1897.

61 ibid., "Zur Denkschrift zum Immediat-Vortrag betreffend Grundzüge für einen Operationsplan Deutschlands allein gegen England allein," 31 May 1897, with the *Grundzüge* being enclosed.

62 ibid., Knorr to Schlieffen, 2 June 1896; Kennedy, "Development of German naval operations plans," p. 52.

63 Schröder's office changed to A3a, with A3b being split off and placed in charge of Grapow to deal specifically with the operations against England. His memorandum "Denkschrift: Operationsplan gegen Antwerpen und Wester-Schelden" appears in BA-MA, F 5600, III, 3.–18., Vol. 1. See also Jonathan Steinberg, "A German plan for the invasion of Holland and Belgium, 1897," *Historical Journal*, vol. 6, no. 1 (1963), pp. 107–19, reproducing extensive excerpts from the memorandum. Following Schröder's error, he misdates the audience with Wilhelm to 3 May.

64 Ritter, *Der Schlieffen-Plan*, p. 20.

65 ibid., pp. 39, 81.

66 Steinberg, "German plan," pp. 108–9; BA-MA, F 5600, III, 3.–18., Vol. 1, Knorr to Schlieffen, 4 March 1898, enclosing Knorr's "Zum Immediatvortrag" of 21 February and his "Aktenvermerk" of 21 February concerning Wilhelm's decision.

67 Steinberg, "German plan," p. 110; BA-MA, F 5600, III, 3.–18., Vol. 1, Schlieffen to Knorr, 17 June 1898.

68 Steinberg, "German plan," p. 110, n. 17.

69 Stahl, "Armee und Marine," p. 41.

70 BA-MA, F 5587, III, 1.–10., Vol. 1, Schlieffen to Knorr, 14 December 1897. For army objections to the invasion of Britain, see Wallach, *Das Dogma*, pp. 214–16.

71 BA-MA, F 5587, III, 1.–10., Vol. 1, Knorr's remark dated 20 December appears at the head of the document and Winkler's comment at the bottom, n.d.

72 ibid., "Kriegführung gegen England," 12 September 1898; Kennedy, "Development of German naval operations plans," p. 54.

73 Hallmann, *Der Weg*, p. 291; Winzen, *Bülows Weltmachtkonzept*, p. 81.

74 BA-MA, F 5587, III, 1.–10., Vol. 1, Knorr, "Zum Immediatvortrag," 25 October 1898; the audience was held on 28 November.

75 ibid., Knorr to Schlieffen, 10 January 1899.

76 Hohenlohe, *Denkwürdigkeiten*, Bd III, journal entry for 24 October 1898, p. 464; Kennedy, "Development of German naval operations plans," p. 55.

77 BA-MA, F 2044, PG 66075, "Auszug aus der Schrift Maltzahn," with marginal comments in Tirpitz's hand. Kennedy, "Development of German naval operations plans," p. 55, is using a copy from the Tirpitz Papers.

78 See below, p. 264.

79 Hohenlohe, *Denkwürdigkeiten*, Bd III, p. 464; Kennedy, "Development of German naval operations plans," p. 55.

80 See Kennedy, *Samoan Tangle*, esp. pp. 73–97.

81 See Holger H. Herwig and David S. Trask, "Naval operations plans between Germany and the United States of America, 1898–1913: a study of strategic planning in the Age of Imperialism," *Militärgeschichtliche Mitteilungen*, no. 2 (1970), p. 6. Also Holger H. Herwig, *Politics of Frustration: The United States in German Naval Planning, 1889–1914*

(Boston, Mass., 1976), p. 17; the article is reprinted in *The War Plans of the Great Powers, 1880–1914*, ed. Paul M. Kennedy (London, 1979), pp. 39–74.

82    Friedrich Forstmeier, "Deutsche Invasionspläne gegen die USA um 1900," *Marine-Rundschau*, vol. 68, no. 6 (June 1971), p. 346.

83    Herwig and Trask, "Naval operations plans," p. 9; Herwig, *Frustration*, pp. 43–4; Alfred Vagts, *Deutschland und die Vereinigten Staaten in der Weltpolitik*, 2 vols (New York, 1935). In October 1897 the German naval attaché in Washington was instructed by the Imperial Naval Office to collect information about the American navy: for this purpose he engaged a press-clipping service: ibid., Vol. 2, p. 1272, n. 4.

84    Herwig, *Frustration*, pp. 18–21; Kennedy, *Samoan Tangle*, p. 136; GP, XIII, No. 3409, Hohenlohe to Hatzfeldt, 18 July 1897, p. 28; Vagts, *Deutschland*, Vol. 1, pp. 301, 792–3; Vol. 2, p. 1278.

85    E. Malcolm Carroll, *Germany and the Great Powers, 1866–1914: A Study in Public Opinion and Foreign Policy* (Handey, Conn., 1966), p. 412; Vagts, *Deutschland*, Vol. 2, pp. 1331–2.

86    BA-MA, N 253/153, 83, Notiz, 110: Vagts, *Deutschland*, Vol. 2, p. 1325; 1423.

87    See in particular, Kennedy, *Samoan Tangle*, pp. 137–44.

88    Herwig, *Frustration*, p. 22.

89    Kennedy, *Samoan Tangle*, pp. 139, 164–5, 169–72.

90    Herwig and Trask, "Naval operations plans," p. 12; Herwig, *Frustration*, pp. 47–8.

91    A. Harding Ganz, "Colonial policy and the Imperial German Navy," *Militär-geschichtliche Mitteilungen*, vol. 21, no. 1 (1977), pp. 39–40; also Baldur Kaulisch, "Zur überseeischen Stützpunktpolitik der kaiserlichen deutschen Marine am Ende des 19. Jahrhunderts," *Militärgeschichte*, vol. 19, no. 5 (1980), pp. 585–98.

92    Hohenlohe, *Denkwürdigkeiten*, Bd III, Tirpitz to Hohenlohe, telegram, 10 November 1897, p. 412.

93    BA-MA, F 5161, III, 1.–3b., Vol. 3, Knorr, "Denkschrift zum Immediatvortrag betr. Operationspläne für Auslandschiffe," 8 December 1896.

94    ibid., F 7639, Vol. 3, Knorr to the Chief of the Cruiser Division and the Commanders of HM Ships at the East African and Australian Stations, 22 January 1897.

95    ibid., F 2528, XVII, 1, 1.–24a., Vol. 1, Knorr to Tirpitz, 9 December 1897.

96    ibid., F 5161, III, 1.–3b, Vol. 3, Knorr to the Foreign Office, 12 May 1897; Richthofen to Knorr, 27 June 1897.

97    ibid., F 2024, PG, 65990b, Knorr, "Denkschrift zum Immediatvortrag," 11 February 1898.

# 9 The Navy and World Power, II: Tirpitz and the First and Second Navy Laws, 1897–1900

On 31 March 1896, Tirpitz was informed of Wilhelm's decision to keep Hollmann and soon thereafter left for the Far East to take on the command of the Cruiser Squadron. Hollmann remained in office with the support of Hohenlohe. Although both the "Z" Commission, established by Hollmann on 18 December 1895, and the Military Department of the Imperial Naval Office proceeded to prepare long-term fleet-construction plans on the basis of Wilhelm's order of 16 December,[1] Hollmann himself, while in favor of enlarging the fleet, "is at the same time a decided opponent of the fleet plan and rather wants to reach the same aim with individual requests from year to year."[2] As Holstein told Württemberg's minister, Axel von Varnbüler:

> His [Hollmann's] office was indeed one of the most difficult in Imperial service [im Reichsdienste], between the Kaiser's love for the navy and his endeavor to make Germany a naval power of the first rank on the one hand and the limited inclination and willingness to sacrifice for it among the German taxpayers.[3]

In addition, Hollmann was engaged in a running battle with Knorr on a number of matters such as cruiser types, with Knorr adhering to Tirpitz's proposals to limit cruisers to two types and the Imperial Naval Office insisting on three types,[4] the caliber of artillery for ships of the line,[5] and the division of labor between their bureaus. He was also under steady attack from the most fanatical supporter of the big navy, Senden.[6] The Kaiser's brother, Prince Heinrich, used every opportunity to point out that only Tirpitz was the right man to head the Imperial Naval Office.[7]

In the report of the "Z" Commission, presented by its chairman, Büchsel, to Hollmann on 23 May 1896,[8] the requests of the High Command of 18 November 1895 were generally accepted. In an interview Hollmann, however, dissuaded Wilhelm in the face of Senden's objections from presenting a long-term plan to the Reichstag.[9] In November 1896 a piecemeal budget went to the Reichstag which led Tirpitz to write to Senden from the Far East:

> The presentation [Vorlage] of the [Imperial Naval Office] has filled me with pain. It may be advantageous for a one-time or this year's Reichstag session, but the chances for the future are extraordinarily damaged

through the type of presentation. We could not and should not hold back the truth, we must clearly and without glossing over announce the need, purpose, aim, and limit of the fleet on the basis of the political situations into which Germany can come and now is . . .[10]

Hollmann's defense of the estimates was anything but skillful. By the end of March his failure to avoid serious cuts in them by the Reichstag, continuous friction with Knorr and Senden, and consequently mounting dissatisfaction on the part of Wilhelm led to Hollmann's fall, in spite of efforts on the part of Hohenlohe and Holstein to retain him. The circumstances surrounding his fall raised serious questions concerning the Imperial Constitution, the Emperor's personal rule, the Chancellor's powers, the relationship between Chancellor and Emperor,[11] and the possibility of a coup d'état on the part of Wilhelm.[12] This resignation was the first of the several personnel changes of 1897, leading to the establishment of Wilhelm's alleged *persönliches Regiment*.

Tirpitz was summoned back from East Asia on 31 March 1897 to take over the Imperial Naval Office. At first he hesitated in taking on his new responsibilities; then he returned at his leisure, not arriving in Berlin before June 1897.[13] During this period Büchsel served as acting Secretary of State. Wilhelm, however, wanted to benefit from Hollmann's departure immediately and prepare a long-term building program. On 6 April, Senden opened discussions about such a program with Knorr and Büchsel and issued written instructions to them on the following day to prepare memoranda by 12 April about the tasks of the navy in war and peace. But Wilhelm seems to have anticipated them, probably with the help of Senden. On 9 April he had a long talk with Hohenlohe during which "the principle was settled that the German fleet must be half as strong as the combined Franco-Russian fleets, that is, it must be *unconditionally* superior in the Baltic Sea to the entire Russian Baltic fleet, and in the North Sea be able to oppose successfully the French northern fleet or Channel fleet which may be used for action in the North Sea."[14] "This principle," Steinberg correctly remarks, "marked a return to the fixed naval programme of the High Command Memorandum of November 28, 1895"—involving, however, a larger ratio in Germany's favor.[15]

The Imperial Naval Office proceeded under the direction of Büchsel to reduce the demands of the High Command to the level of its requirements as stated in the memorandum of 28 November 1895.[16] In 1910 the fleet was to consist of twenty-five ships of the line, including those of the Siegfried class, eight cruisers of the first class, thirty cruisers of the second class, and sixteen cruisers of the fourth class, five gunboats, fourteen torpedo division boats and ninety-six torpedo-boats. But it was to be stipulated that the Siegfried ships as well as the older armored ships were to be replaced by armored ships of the first class.[17]

Upon his return, Tirpitz dismissed this plan as "not useful." The number of armored ships was indeed identical with his figure in Dienstschrift No. IX, but the number and tonnage of cruisers was greater.[18] The strategic purpose of the navy was thus obscured. Nor could such a request obtain the approval of a recalcitrant Reichstag. He therefore refused Wilhelm's suggestion that he merely approve the plan and persuaded Büchsel and Knorr to drop it. On 15 June he presented his own proposals to Wilhelm.

Consistent in Tirpitz's thought was the linking of naval power to economic power and the equation of economic power with political power. This thinking was underpinned by vague Social Darwinist terminology: there was constant competition and the alternative to political expansion was decline. He had written to Stosch at the end of December 1895: "Germany sinks in the next century quickly from her position as great power, unless she now systematically and without waste of time advances [her] general sea interests."[19] He expressed similar views in his correspondence concerning the First Navy Bill,[20] and expounded them more elaborately in one of his reports over the Second Navy Bill to Wilhelm:

> The statement of Salisbury: great states become greater and stronger and small states become smaller and weaker, [is] also my view. Corresponding to modern development, trust system. Since Germany has remained particularly backward in respect to sea power, it is a vital question for Germany as a world power and *Kulturstaat* to catch up with what has been missed. Both because a sea power has to be established in the narrowest sense (fleet) and preserved as such and because power is important in itself, Germany must keep her population German and develop herself further as an industrial and commercial world power. In the latter lies at present the strongest means for keeping the surplus population German. The development of Germany into an industrial and commercial power is irresistible like a law of nature. If one wanted to dam Germany in, the development would none the less continue [*so würde die Entwickelung hinweggehen*] . . . In the case of such commercial and industrial development, points of contact and conflict with other nations increase. Naval power is essential if Germany does not want to go under.[21]

And as he put it more crisply in his memoirs: "But if we did not want to build a fleet and had from the nineties on taken the road of renunciation, we should also voluntarily have wound back our trade and industry, set afoot our emigration, and allowed our interests abroad to wither away."[22] For if a nation is saturated it goes under. As his close aide Eduard Capelle noted: "Germany . . . cannot stand aside in the solution of the great questions and problems which the coming century will bring in the area of world policy." In the words of Paul Kennedy, he "was bitterly opposed to the liberal, cosmopolitan doctrines of the Manchester school with its advocacy of materialistic individualism, denial of state power, and lack of fervent patriotism."[23]

On 15 June 1897, as in his interview of 28 January 1896, Tirpitz insisted that the entire government stand behind the fleet construction. For himself he demanded the power to select subordinates, organize his agency, establish contact with other branches of government, and direct the entire campaign for fleet construction. He asked that dissenting views in the navy be repressed and that during the campaign no additional financial requests be made for the army. For the first time, the aim of the fleet was to be clearly stated. As in Knorr's and Büchsel's plan, a long-term financial arrangement for fleet construction was to be made: as we shall see, it was an integral part of Tirpitz's program. Then, in stark contrast to the plans prepared in his absence, he announced that the aim of his plan was "the strengthening of our political might [and] [u.] importance against England." As could be expected from the author of Dienstschrift No. IX, the emphasis was placed on ships of the line: "Since true success in cruiser war and transoceanic war against England is absolutely out of the question because of [our] lack of bases abroad and the geographic position of Germany, and since English naval officers, admiralty, etc., fully know this, then even politically it comes to a battleship war [Schlachtkrieg] between Heligoland and the Thames." The fleet was to consist of twenty-one ships of the line, eight coastal armored ships and cruisers which in accordance with Dienstschrift No. IX were restricted to two types: sixteen large cruisers of approximately 8,000 tons and thirty small cruisers of approximately 3,000 tons. Much to Tirpitz's surprise, Wilhelm approved everything that he proposed.[24] The momentous decision to marshal the German government behind Tirpitz to build a battle fleet against England had been made.

Following his audience with Wilhelm, Tirpitz's deputy Büchsel issued on his behalf an order[25] requesting various sections of the Imperial Naval Office to work out the details of the naval estimates for the budget of 1898–99 in accordance with the size of the fleet proposed to Wilhelm. The date for the completion of the fleet was 1910, as in Büchsel's earlier plan.[26] In less than a week Büchsel wanted in his hands a schedule of new and replacement constructions until 1910, the number of personnel necessary at that time, and the rates for the costs, construction and personnel accretion for individual years. A special budget committee headed by Capelle, who was henceforth to be the key figure in Tirpitz's financial calculations, was to work out the details of the budget. Shortly thereafter Heeringen was placed in charge of the newly established Section for News and General Parliamentary Affairs, whose activities were to establish Tirpitz's reputation as "the first propaganda minister of modern stamp."[27]

By 2 July 1897, Büchsel, most probably in consultation with his chief, had made a significant decision: that the target date be moved to 1905 when the fleet was to consist of seventeen ships of the line, eight coastal armored ships, twelve large cruisers, twenty-seven small cruisers, twelve torpedo-boat divisions, three individual division boats and four gunboats. The reduction in battleships and large cruisers would still make it possible to launch two squadrons of battleships, but the moving of the target date from 1910 to 1905 would greatly accelerate construction. It is also an early indication of Tirpitz's intention to go beyond the First Fleet Law as soon as possible.[28] His memorandum "General considerations on the constitution of our fleet according to ship classes and types," completed at the beginning of July,[29] somewhat modified the strength of the fleet required for 1905. It was to consist of: nineteen ships of the line (two in *matériel* reserve); eight coastal armored ships; twelve large cruisers (three in *matériel* reserve for abroad); thirty small cruisers (three in *matériel* reserve for abroad); twelve torpedo-boat divisions. The cost was considerably lower than that of Büchsel's original plan.[30] The memorandum also elaborated on the strategic principles enunciated by Tirpitz to Wilhelm on 15 June: "For Germany at the present time the most dangerous enemy at sea is England. It is also the enemy against which we most urgently require a certain measure of naval force as a political power factor." The battle fleet that was to bring its strength to bear between Heligoland and the Thames was also expected to fulfill the requirements of war against France and Russia and to extend its operations "as far as Brest or Cherbourg and . . . as far as Kronstadt"—in short, carry out the offensive thrusts considered in their planning for Continental war by the officers of the High Command. The higher priority given to the waging of war against Britain than against France and Russia fell in line with the current diplomatic situation since risks of a Continental war had diminished and relations with Britain had deteriorated. It corresponded to the view of Tirpitz, Bülow and others of a future repartition of the non-European world in which Germany was to play an active part. Using Britain as the measuring-stick would also enable the German navy to match the inferior naval power of the Dual Alliance. There was no suggestion, however, that the German fleet might have to be used against both Britain and the Dual Alliance. Rather, Tirpitz, like Bülow, thought of the German fleet as a factor in increasing Germany's value as an ally of other powers. He entertained no illusions about the fleet projected for 1905 being adequate against Britain:

> *The military situation against Britain requires ships of the line in as great a number as possible* [my italics]. According to our power of development, which is limited by the capacity of our shipbuilding, armor, and armament industry, by the expansion of our naval stations and dockyards, by the possibility of training the necessary personnel and raising the necessary funds, as well as by our organization which has been developed and tested in the last few years, we cannot create in the near future, i.e. roughly by 1905, more than two full squadrons of eight ships of the line each.

He explained the technical obstacles to more rapid expansion somewhat more fully to his friend Karl von Eisendecher, Prussian minister in Baden:

> . . . we cannot proceed more rapidly than we do; too much has been missed earlier and there has been too little system in our procedure. The latter is particularly bad. There is a lack of officers and continuous-service men. Almost worse is the absence of technical personnel . . . There is a lack of shipyards and docks. There is a lack of industries for the creation and direction [*bahnen*] of the fleet. The strength of our fleet

stands in a definite relationship to the German shipbuilding and iron industry. The latter as a branch of industry is of primary significance. In it lies also the basis for the technical supply in wartime. Before we take the next forward step [*Etappe*] with our feet, these wide gaps must be filled.[31]

Moreover, it was necessary to make the Navy Bill appear moderate in order to secure its passage, obtain the Reichstag's commitment to the principle of a long-term building program, and avoid undue alarm in Britain.

But what could a fleet with a core of nineteen ships of the line do? While aiming to construct by 1905 a fleet of thirty-one armored ships of more than 6,000 tons displacement (nineteen ships of the line and twelve large cruisers), the Imperial Naval Office was according to its own estimates faced by the existing strength of other fleets as set out in Table 9.1.[32]

Table 9.1    *Armored ships of over 6,000 tons under construction or available on 1 February 1898*

|  | Number | Displacement |
|---|---|---|
| England | 74 | 796,000 |
| France | 52 | 479,000 |
| Russia | 31 | 280,000 |
| Italy | 17 | 181,000 |
| United States | 13 | 130,000 |
| Japan | 9 | 102,000 |

According to *Brassey's Naval Annual,* in 1898 Germany had seven ships of the line of the first class and two large cruisers, compared to Britain's thirty-eight ships of the line of the first class and thirty-four large cruisers.[33] As Tirpitz wrote to the Prussian Minister of Finance, Johannes von Miquel:

> if the bill passes . . . then I do not doubt that in the year 1905 we will have a fleet which represents a true power factor among the world powers. That we thereby have a fleet which could stand as equal beside the French or could even compete with the English fleet is naturally an absurdity . . .
>
> But we will have a fleet whose plus or minus will also fall into the scale against England. In the eyes of expert Englishmen we will not be, as now, a mere plucking object.[34]

He held a struggle with Britain inevitable in the long run. As he remarked to the Saxon military attaché in December 1899, "we must undoubtedly in the next century get into a conflict with England at some point on the globe, be it from economic rivalry or as a result of colonial friction."[35] In his remarks to the Bavarian minister, Tirpitz attributed to Britain the intention to crush Germany as a commercial rival:

The German navy had to have at least enough strength that its neutrality would have weight in a struggle between other sea powers. He thought for example of a war of France and Russia against England. In such a case, if Germany's fleet was of no importance, England could prefer Germany's hostility to her neutrality in order to damage its most dangerous commercial rival. But if Germany would throw a fleet of the envisaged strength into the scales, then the question would be posed differently to England.[36]

In his notes prepared for reporting to Wilhelm in Wilhelmshöhe on 29 August 1897, Tirpitz minimized the importance of the Navy Bill, obviously with the public agitation and Reichstag in mind: "The whole represents the implementation of the intention approved by the Reichstag in 1867 and of the plan approved generally in 1873. It is not a battle fleet which makes possible a policy of a world power but a sortie fleet." The two sentences were interrupted by the following comment by Tirpitz in pencil: "For the agitation, yes, but in fact a power factor which works politically also against England."[37] Accordingly, the final version of the bill which was presented to the Bundesrat and Reichstag omitted any reference to the fleet being built against England and represented it as a mere sortie fleet.[38]

Although admittedly more than a sortie fleet since it served as a deterrent against England and raised Germany's value as an ally in the eyes of other powers, the projected two squadrons could in a case of war of "Germany alone against England alone" do no more than undertake a death ride into the Thames. And at the outset of hostilities, which had in 1896 been considered by Tirpitz himself as the only suitable time for such a thrust, only the one active squadron could be considered for action. For Tirpitz rejected both any invasion of Britain and, according to Hallmann, a strategic defensive. On 15 June he reported to Wilhelm about the presentation of the High Command of 2 May:

> The operations plan of the High Command bases itself on the strategic defensive in the Baltic and North Seas. One wants to await the enemy and to defeat him here. The purpose is to keep open our imports. But I believe now that the enemy will not come at once and that we will then wait with our large fleet while France without much loss cuts off two-thirds to three-quarters of our imports in the Channel and North of England. But this is not my business."[39]

This was certainly becoming Tirpitz's business, particularly as the same course of action could be expected from the British. Tirpitz had thus placed his finger on the most vulnerable point in the operational planning against Britain before World War I and on the futility of his own program.

According to an estimate of the Admiralty Staff of January 1900, prepared by Grapow who was in charge of operations against Britain (A4), the strength of the German navy provided by the First Navy Law would not suffice to break a British blockade of the German coast if it were obligingly undertaken. Although the British would be unable to enclose the German fleet if it concentrated in the Kiel–Elbe position behind the defenses of Heligoland and utilized the Kaiser Wilhelm Canal, they could blockade the German Baltic Sea ports and raid the German North Sea coast with the possible support of a base established on Borkum, Sylt, or the Lister Tief in the German Bight. They were expected to confront the German strength of seventeen ships of the line and four heavy cruisers with a force of twenty-eight ships of the line and eight heavy cruisers. While the inferior German forces could attack divided enemy strength with some hope of victory, the extent of such a victory was limited since Britain could easily replenish her losses from her extensive reserves. The blockade of the German coast would thus continue regardless of any German successes.[40] Nor would German strength be adequate for effective action against the United States of America through the blockade of its eastern seaboard.[41]

But, as Tirpitz stated in his memoirs, "It was always clear to me . . . that the First Navy Law did not create the ultimate fleet."[42] While the First Navy Bill was being prepared he wrote to Senden: "If it is possible to get the bill passed, then in the year 1905 very good ground will have been gained to undertake the further rounding out of the navy."[43] In his "General considerations on the constitution of our fleet according to ship classes and types," he had pointed out that "ships of the line in as large a number as possible" were militarily necessary against Britain,[44] and Hohenlohe had noted him as remarking in October 1898 that all hostility to Britain would have to be avoided "until we have as large a navy as the English."[45] Less than a year later his marginal comments to Captain Curt von Malzahn's manuscript *Seelehre* emphasized the importance of a successful battle in a naval war between Germany and Britain, and his subordinates were soon to envisage the construction of a third double squadron which would provide Germany with fifty-seven ships of the line.[46] According to Anton Count von Monts as early as November 1897, when Tirpitz visited the Prince-Regent of Bavaria and spoke of "giving the German fleet a strength which would enable it to fight the strongest of other navies, namely the British," his rejoinder to the objection that Britain would never give up the rule of the sea and would always maintain a lead over Germany was that since Britain did not and would never have universal military service, "However many ships she built, crews for them would be absent. We, on the other hand, could with the annual draft of 20,000 recruits into the navy build up a strong reserve in trained crews and finally man the same number of ships as the English."[47] Significantly this is the same argument as used by both the Imperial Naval Office and Wilhelm until 1901 about Britain being unable to match the increases of the Second Navy Law. But what was Tirpitz's evidence? It appears that this alleged British weakness had been drawn to his attention by the report of the German naval attaché in London of 19 August 1897,[48] and that he made no attempt to verify it before December 1899 when he wanted ammunition for the defense of the Second Navy Law in the Reichstag.

By that time the Admiralty Staff also reported that the British fleet maneuvers of 1899 showed that, while at the time of mobilization there were enough sailors, there would be shortages of technical personnel, particularly of stokers.[49] In his notes concerning naval organizational changes, probably made in the summer of 1898, Tirpitz remarked: "After the expiry of the sexannate [the six-year period to which the Navy Law was eventually limited], or if practicable even earlier, a naval–political and parliamentary situation must be created from which the increase of the navy—with the retention of the freedom that the fleet law gives His Majesty the Emperor—can safely be brought about,"[50] with a view of providing Germany as soon as possible with a fleet of the first rank.

Certainly in the summer of 1898 Tirpitz considered the possibility of further increasing the fleet "if technically or organizationally possible" before the expiration of the law in 1905. In the fall of the same year he envisaged after the expiry of the six-year period two subsequent six-year terms for the construction of two further squadrons. And Wilhelm told the Württemberg minister in Berlin, Axel von Varnbüler, at the time of the decision to introduce the Second Navy Bill, that

he was already extremely doubtful at the time of the last fleet bill whether the increase of the fleet therein envisaged could even for the duration of the septenannate [sic] keep up with the rapid growth of Germany as an industrial state of the first rank, her correspondingly increased need for the protection of her overseas trade in competition with superior naval powers for overseas markets, [and] in general with the entire development of international politics whose centre of gravity shifts itself more and more out of Continental boundaries into a world power position and its defense through naval power.[51]

Contrary to his memoirs, according to which he was still determined to adhere to the First Navy Bill in the winter of 1898–99,[52] Tirpitz already on 28 November 1898 proposed to Wilhelm a new fleet increase to be undertaken in 1902.[53] He pointed out that the First Navy Law offered several opportunities for further increases, such as a demand for overseas cruisers or the replacement of the inferior Siegfried ships with ships of the line. He rejected these opportunities, the latter because the Siegfried ships were not due for replacement until 1910, and chose instead the construction of an additional squadron of ships of the line. This course was approved by Wilhelm. On 7 February 1899, Tirpitz stipulated that the new bill provide for the construction of nine new ships of the line, three replacement ships of the line, four large and six small cruisers.[54] In 1897, Tirpitz had been chided by Felix Bendemann for including the worthless Siegfried ships in the fleet strength; now their inclusion was beginning to pay off.[55]

On 28 September 1899, Tirpitz reported to Wilhelm on the preparations made by his office for the introduction of a new fleet bill in 1901 or 1902. Its aim was to provide forty-five ships of the line, forty for the home fleet and five for Asia, eight large cruisers for the home fleet, one for Asia, and two or three for America, twenty-four small cruisers and ninety-six torpedo-boats for the home fleet, and an assorted number of small ships for abroad. The aim was to be reached in two stages: the first was the construction of the new ships of the line and of the ships for abroad and the modernization of some of the old *matériel*, and the second was the replacement of the Siegfried ships with full-fledged ships of the line.

> As soon as the aim is reached, Your Majesty has an effective strength of forty-five ships of the line along with complete accessories—so powerful . . . that only England [will be] superior. But also against England we undoubtedly have good chances through geographical position, military system, torpedo-boats, tactical training, planned organizational development, and leadership united by the monarch.
>
> Apart from our by no means hopeless conditions of fighting, England will have lost [any] political or economic . . . inclination to attack us and will as a result concede to your Majesty sufficient naval presence [*Seegeltung*] . . . for the conduct of a grand policy overseas [*eine grosse überseeische Politik zu führen.*].[56]

The desired naval strength would have been achieved by 1920, with the keels of the last three ships laid down in 1916.

Indeed, according to an estimate of the Imperial Naval Office of November, the current naval strength of other powers was as set out in Table 9.2.[57]

Table 9.2

| Ship Type | England | France | Russia | USA | Italy |
|---|---|---|---|---|---|
| Ships of the line | 53 | 32 | 23 | 16 | 15 |
| Armored cruisers | 23 | 14 | 8 | 5 | 4 |
| Large cruisers of over 5,600 tons | 37 | 5 | 7 | 3 | 0 |
| Total of large ships | 113 | 51 | 38 | 24 | 19 |
| Total of small cruisers | 146 | 53 | 20 | 38 | 36 |

Although Tirpitz had to satisfy himself with fewer ships than he originally proposed to build, the Second Navy Law would none the less have provided him with a formidable force. In this third handwritten draft he modified his demand to one fleet flagship, two squadrons of eight ships of the line each, two large and eight small cruisers for the home fleet, five ships of the line *or* large cruisers and four small cruisers for service abroad, and a further two ships of the line, one large cruiser and two small cruisers as *matériel* reserve. In his final draft of 15 January 1900 he asked only for six large cruisers rather than ships of the line for abroad. Those were struck by the Reichstag with his consent. The Second Navy Law of 14 June 1900 provided for (1) a battle fleet of two fleet flagships, four squadrons of eight ships of the line each, eight large cruisers and twenty-four small cruisers; (2) an overseas fleet of three large cruisers and ten small cruisers; and (3) a *matériel* reserve of four ships of the line, three large cruisers, and four small cruisers.

The preamble of the Second Navy Bill elaborated on the chances of the completed fleet against Britain:

. . . it is not necessary that the battle fleet at home is equal to that of the greatest naval power. In general this naval power would not be in a position to concentrate its entire naval forces against us. Even if it succeeds in encountering us with a superior force, the destruction of the German fleet would so much damage the enemy that his own position as a world power would be brought into question.

Tirpitz thus assumed that Britain's imperial interests would continue to require her to scatter her ships of the line around the globe and give her leaders grounds to fear that other powers, presumably Russia and France, would permanently remain sufficiently hostile to take advantage of the weakening of her naval power at the hands of the Germans.

It is indicative of both the rigidity of Tirpitz's planning—his adherence to an *idée fixe*—and his meticulous short-term preparations that he asked only the naval attaché in London, Karl Coerper, whether Britain could by 1916 maintain the existing proportion between her naval strength and Germany's (sixty to nineteen ships of the line) after the essentials of the fleet increase were decided. On 4 December 1899 he thus inquired whether Britain, like Germany, could double the size of her fleet. Including replacement constructions, could British dockyards by that date construct eighty or a hundred ships of the line? Would necessary manpower, including technical personnel and officers, be found?[58] These were key questions for the success of the German navy against Britain. Coerper replied on 3 January 1900 that British dockyards would without any doubt be able to sustain the doubling of the British navy by 1916, which would, inclusive of replacement constructions, involve the building of no less than ninety ships of the line, forty-five large cruisers, and 120 small cruisers. There might be some difficulty in acquiring armor and armaments, but it could be overcome through adequate planning; and 86,000 additional men could also be found if the Admiralty did not shy away from the expense. More serious was the problem of finding technical personnel and officers and of raising the money for the doubling of the fleet. The latter was only possible "through a permanent increase of the income tax which no government would venture to undertake and which would mean a breach with the principles of free trade."[59] Tirpitz's assistant, Max Fischel, used Coerper's estimates in a report intended for Wilhelm.[60] However, in a memorandum prepared for the discussion of the naval bill in the Reichstag committee, Tirpitz's other assistant, Capelle, continued to emphasize the British personnel difficulties even if the money could be found to sustain the construction rate for the doubling of the fleet: "such a fleet strengthening by the English would founder from lack of personnel, for it is known that the English are barely able to man their existing fleet; according to our information, personnel is not even available for the fifth squadron which is being constructed."[61] For several years Wilhelm was to comment on the limits that lack of manpower imposed on British naval construction.[62]

In the Admiralty Staff, Grapow also doubted whether by 1920 the British could raise the funds and personnel needed to increase their fleet in proportion to the German. But even if they could, then:

The history of naval warfare proves that the effectiveness of the greater fleet ceases at a certain level . . . with the growing number of ships the situation of the weaker becomes more favorable. The greater the number of the ships, the greater the obstacles to efficiency. The English fleet maneuvers of recent years give us numerous examples of this. Keeping a large fleet together always led to difficulties which offered the weaker opponent a chance to bring a superior force to bear here or there.[63]

The assessment by the German naval leadership of Germany's chances against Britain once the terms of the Second Fleet Law had been carried out was thus rather uncertain. But how much more vulnerable was the German fleet before it had reached the strength stipulated by the Second Navy Bill if Britain were to recognize it as her enemy! A Copenhagen-style preventive strike was the nightmare of the German naval and civilian leaders alike throughout the years before 1914. The perpetual unreadiness of the navy became a standard joke for many.

None the less, the construction rate of three large ships per year from 1898 to 1900 was having some effect. It appeared to be the maximum rate of construction in view of the current capacity of industry and the adsorption capacity of the fleet. Continuation of this building rate beyond 1900, when it would have dropped according to the terms of the First Navy Law, was one of Tirpitz's aims in promulgating a new naval law. As Volker Berghahn has so convincingly demonstrated, the perpetuation of a construction rate of three large ships per year was one of Tirpitz's major aims.

According to Tirpitz himself, the building program of the first years of his tenure of office was already influencing Germany's political position in 1902–03. In respect to the battle fleet he noted for his report to Wilhelm on 20 February 1899: "Significance of 1902: Already considerable improvement of the political position of Germany."[64] And half a year later he wrote to Büchsel: "It is all-important to possess something in 1903 that has some weight, namely two squadrons (I Kaiser class, II Brandenburg class and Saxony class beside the Siegfried class)."[65] Tirpitz's notes were rather cryptic. Since the Kaiser class consisted only of five ships, some of the more recently built Wittelsbach-class ships would also have had to be ranged in the first squadron.

None of these ships, however, was of the best quality. The Siegfrieds were notoriously useless; the Saxony class consisted of the four sortie corvettes constructed by Stosch in the late 1870s, displacing only 7,400 tons; the four Brandenburg ships launched in 1891–92, although armed with six 28 cm guns, eight 10·5 cm guns, and eight 8·8 cm guns, were described by a British critic as "the most unsatisfactory battleships to be found in any navy in the world." The Kaiser-class ships launched between 1896 and 1900 carried as heavy armament only 24 cm guns, and the Wittelsbachs, Tirpitz's first series, only 25 cm guns.[66] This low caliber was a serious shortcoming as ships of other navies built at this time were equipped with 30·5 cm guns.[67] In the British navy the Royal Sovereign class, launched in

1891–92, was equipped with a 13·5 inch (34·5 cm) and the Majestic class, launched in 1894–96, and its successors with a 12 inch (30·5 cm) primary armament.[68] British ships of the line of the same vintage were also considerably larger. Although Tirpitz, drawing on the practices of other navies and the experiences of the Spanish–American War, increased the caliber of the heavy guns to 28 cm and the size of the ships to 13,000 tons, for the Braunschweig and Deutschland classes, German ships of the line both before and after the "dreadnought leap" of 1905 remained behind the British both in size and caliber of primary armament.[69] This was actually Tirpitz's deliberate intention. Already in his "General considerations on the constitution of our fleet according to ship classes and types" he had stated: "Because of the cost and also because of the depth of our home waters we shall be prudent if we go no further in displacement than required for a 'good' capacity for action."[70]

According to the terms of the Second Navy Law, the construction of three large ships per year would continue until 1906: of those fifteen ships ten were to be ships of the line. With these ships completed the Imperial Naval Office expected in 1908 to place into service two full squadrons of newer battleships.[71]

In Bülow's words:[72]

The first fleet law switched the naval policy to an entirely new track. Previously new constructions had been ordered from time to time and in part approved, but the navy had lacked the firm foundation that the army possessed in the required strength [*Sollbestand*] of its formations. Only by determining the useful life of ships and its effective strength in serviceable ships did the navy become a firm part of our national fighting forces.

Volker Berghahn has effectively argued that Tirpitz was building his navy both against Britain and against the Reichstag: against the latter in so far as he sought to cut its power substantially by removing the fleet from its fiscal purview.[73] As Hallmann has conceded, in the First Navy Law "The Reichstag was to bind itself for all time to build a certain minimum number of ships according to a regular schedule."[74] Militarily, this arrangement undoubtedly was a prerequisite for regular fleet construction; politically, it restricted the power of the Reichstag and enhanced that of the Emperor; economically, it appealed to shipbuilding firms and related industries; and it also undoubtedly helped stabilize the existing regime. But it is questionable if it was coherently planned. Moreover, the First Navy Law merely stated a principle; Tirpitz found its provisions inadequate and had to come back to the Reichstag for many more ships. Following Büchsel's earlier draft, which Tirpitz had otherwise rejected, it provided for only a twenty-five-year lifespan for ships of the line, a twenty-year lifespan for large cruisers, and a fifteen-year lifespan for small cruisers. Tirpitz apparently considered the construction of three large ships per year to be the desirable building rate, but the First Navy Law gave him this rate only until 1901. Although Capelle's tables for the second draft of the Second

Navy Bill, which had as an aim sixty large ships, had provided for a construction rate of three large ships per year until 1916,[75] the Second Navy Law provided this rate only until 1906. Hence both the First and Second Navy Laws made further presentation to the Reichstag necessary. Only the navy law of 1908 opened the door to a permanently stabilized construction rate of three large ships per year and a fleet of sixty large ships by reducing the life duration of ships of the line to twenty years. But neither the navy law of 1908 nor that of 1912 succeeded in stabilizing the construction rate at three large ships per year. Until this was done—and as long as the German fleet lacked adequate strength against Britain—Tirpitz continued to depend on the Reichstag. Of course, as Berghahn rightly argues, it was obvious to him from the outset that he could not present the Reichstag with a bill providing for an annual construction of an equal number of ships and for their replacement after a certain period. This sort of "iron budget," similar to what the army had sought before 1874, would have been unacceptable to it.[76] But he consistently based his presentations to the Reichstag on the principle of the legal determination of the strength of the fleet, avoiding all extraordinary grants for additional naval construction.

The First Navy Law had a definite cost limitation which bound both the Imperial Naval Office and the Reichstag. The Second Navy Law, however, although binding the Reichstag to a building schedule and the established principle of replacing ships at the stipulated age, left the financial appropriations to the Reichstag's annual approval. As Tirpitz himself admitted:

> The Reichstag's right of annual approval was fiscally an open hand. But the Reichstag bound itself morally much more strongly than through any financial limitation. For it had through law bound itself to a certain building program. If now the ships became bigger and costlier, then the Reichstag, which by virtue of the law *had to* approve the ships, could . . . never assume the responsibility for making the legally stipulated ships come out small and bad because of inadequate appropriations. Through the *lex imperfecta* which the second fleet law represented . . . the Reichstag indeed renounced the opportunity to refuse money for the types that were increasing in size and cost if it did not want to expose itself to the charge of building inferior ships.[77]

The financial issue, however, was a coin with two sides: if the Reichstag found it difficult to refuse appropriations for the more expensive ships, Tirpitz found it more difficult because of greater cost to request ships necessary for his final aim that were not provided by the valid fleet laws. He therefore also continued to economize in requesting smaller ships with lighter guns, in avoiding innovations, and thus exposing himself to the charge from his contemporary and future critics of inadequately preparing for the showdown with Britain.

Even before the Second Fleet Bill had become a law, Tirpitz allegedly told the mayor of Bremen "that the *Novelle* was still inadequate."[78] This was obvious, for neither the desired strength of sixty large ships nor the desired permanent building rate of three large ships per year, which had been the stated goal of the Imperial Naval Office, would be reached through it. But it is more surprising that at about the same time the Budget Department of the Imperial Naval Office undertook calculations for the construction of a *third* double squadron of nineteen ships of the line, four large cruisers, twelve small cruisers, and twelve torpedo-boat divisions.[79] Such a further increase would have given Germany fifty-seven ships of the line and twelve large cruisers in European waters—a fleet which in ships of the line would surpass the current British total of fifty-three. It is unlikely that such calculations would have been undertaken in the department of Tirpitz's trusted colleague Capelle without his cognizance. Considered again in 1903, such an increase lends credence to Tirpitz's other statements that he was seeking to match Britain's naval strength. Tirpitz, when reporting to Wilhelm on 7 May 1900 about the proposal of the Centre Party in the Reichstag budget committee to drop from the bill the six large cruisers requested for service abroad, stated that he felt honor-bound to request these ships in 1905 (as the building rate fell to two large ships per year in 1906) and that probably in view of arming against Japan and the United States or responding to further armaments of Britain "We would request more than the number of ships requested now."[80] In order to bring the increase of German naval strength more effectively to bear on Britain along the lines of Schröder's proposals, Tirpitz according to Hohenlohe's journal entry of 1 May 1899 considered that Holland be closely tied to Germany through a customs union and military and naval convention.[81] The construction program established by the Second Navy Law would not be completed before 1920, however.

## Notes: Chapter 9

1　BA-MA, F 3188, III, 1, 5.–1a., Vol. 1, Wilhelm to Chancellor (Imperial Naval Office), 16 December 1895, certified copy; Steinberg, *Yesterday's Deterrent*, p. 81; Hallmann, *Der Weg*, p. 168.
2　GLA, Karlsruhe, 233/34802, Jagemann to Brauer, 1 June 1896.
3　H St Ar Stuttgart, E 73/73a, 12d., Verz. 61, Varnbüler to Mittnacht, 2 April 1896.
4　BA-MA, F 2031, PG 66017, Knorr to Hollmann, 28 January 1896, copy; N 253/3, A, Fischel, "Denkschrift zum Immediatvortrag . . . ," 1 February 1896, copy; F 2031, PG 66017, Knorr to Wilhelm, 1 March 1896, copy; Steinberg, *Yesterday's Deterrent*, p. 93.
5　Hallmann, *Der Weg*, pp. 211–12.
6　Steinberg, *Yesterday's Deterrent*, pp. 107–8.
7　Hallmann, *Der Weg*, p. 216.
8　BA-MA, F 2043, PG 66070, Büchsel, "Dem Herrn Staatssekretär vorzulegen," 23 May 1896, "Promemoria für den Immediatvortrag betreffend den Ausbau der Flotte u. Marineanlagen bis 1908."
9　Hohenlohe, *Denkwürdigkeiten*, Bd III, journal entry for 2 July 1896, pp. 240–1.
10　BA-MA, N 160/5, Tirpitz to Senden, 20 January 1897.
11　Hallmann, *Der Weg*, pp. 213–37; Steinberg, *Yesterday's Deterrent*, pp. 106–16; Röhl, *Germany without Bismarck*, pp. 210–17.
12　ibid., 217–22.
13　Tirpitz, *Erinnerungen*, p. 79; Steinberg, *Yesterday's Deterrent*, pp. 116, 123–5.

14    BA-MA, F 3304, PG 66712, Wilhelm to Senden, 9 April 1897; Senden to Knorr and
      Senden to Büchsel, 9 April 1897; Hallmann, *Der Weg*, p. 239; Steinberg, *Yesterday's
      Deterrent*, p. 117; Berghahn, *Tirpitz-Plan*, p. 103; P. J. Kelly, "The naval policy of
      Imperial Germany, 1900–1914," PhD thesis, Georgetown University, 1970, fo. 52.
15    Steinberg, *Yesterday's Deterrent*, p. 117.
16    BA-MA, F 3304, PG 66712, "Immediatvortrag des Oberkommandos der Marine," 10
      May 1897.
17    ibid., F 2031, PG 66017, Büchsel's memorandum, 20 May 1897; Hallmann, *Der Weg*,
      pp. 241 ff.; Steinberg, *Yesterday's Deterrent*, p. 122; Berghahn, *Tirpitz-Plan*, p. 105.
18    Tirpitz, *Erinnerungen*, p. 79.
19    Hassell, *Tirpitz*, Tirpitz to Stosch, 21 December 1895, p. 103.
20    BA-MA, N 253/4, especially Tirpitz to Thielmann, 8 August 1897.
21    ibid., F 2044, PG 66074, "Vortrag, Rominten, 28 September 1899." A corrected version
      appears in Tirpitz, *Erinnerungen*, p. 107.
22    ibid., pp. 57–8.
23    BA-MA, F 2034, PG 66028, "Dispositionen für die Begründung," D. Akten, E.
      Capelle, 8 February 1900. Paul M. Kennedy, "Fisher and Tirpitz: political admirals in
      the Age of Imperialism," in *Naval Warfare in the Twentieth Century: Essays in Honour of
      Arthur Marder*, ed. Gerald Jordan (London, 1977), pp. 56–7. See also Tirpitz's letter to
      his daughter Blanca of 18 July 1897 cited in Salewski, *Tirpitz*, p. 52.
24    BA-MA, N 253/4, "Immed. Vortrag" 15, June, 1897; see also Hallmann, *Der Weg*, pp.
      248–9; Berghahn, *Tirpitz-Plan*, pp. 108–9.
25    BA-MA, F 2031, PG 66017, Order No. 2335, Büchsel, 19 June 1897; Steinberg
      incorrectly attributes it to Tirpitz personally; *Yesterday's Deterrent*, p. 130.
26    See above, p. 138.
27    See J. Meyer, *Die Propaganda der deutschen Flottenbewegung, 1897–1900* (Bern, 1967),
      p. 25; also Deist, *Flottenpolitik*, pp. 72 ff., 81. According to Geoff Eley, *Reshaping the
      German Right: Radical Nationalism and Political Change after Bismarck* (New Haven,
      Conn., 1980), esp. p. 208, this is an exaggeration.
28    BA-MA, N 253/3, Order No. 4186, Büchsel, 2 July 1897.
29    Reprinted in Steinberg, *Yesterday's Deterrent*, pp. 208 ff. Berghahn has pointed out
      Steinberg's erroneous statement that the memorandum was presented to Wilhelm on 15
      June: *Tirpitz-Plan*, p. 109, n. 7; Steinberg, *Yesterday's Deterrent*, p. 126.
30    See ibid., pp. 220–1.
31    American Historical Association, Project II, 8, *Nachlass* Eisendecher, Tirpitz to
      Eisendecher, 31 August 1897.
32    BA-MA, F 2033, PG 66024, "Schiffbauprogramm von England, Frankreich, Russland,
      Italien, Japan und Vereinigten Staaten von Amerika," 1 February 1898.
33    Paul M. Kennedy, "Maritime Strategieprobleme der deutsch-englishen Flotten-
      rivalität," *Marine und Marinepolitik im kaiserlichen Deutschland, 1871–1914*, ed. H.
      Schottelius and W. Deist (Düsseldorf, 1972), pp. 180–1.
34    BA-MA, N 253/4, Tirpitz, St Blasien, to Miquel, n.d.; quoted partly in Hallmann, *Der
      Weg*, p. 266; the same arguments are used by Tirpitz to Thielmann, 8 August 1897; ibid.
35    Volker R. Berghahn, "Zu den Zielen des deutschen Flottenbaus unter Wilhelm II,"
      *Historische Zeitschrift*, vol. 210, no. 1 (1970), p. 68.
36    Bay Geh St Ar, Abt Geh St Ar, Bay Ges Berlin, 1068, Report of 3 October 1897.
      Berghahn dates it 30 October (*Tirpitz-Plan*, pp. 115, n 29; 116, n. 32); the finished
      version is, as Berghahn correctly states, also dated 3 October 1897 (p. 116, n. 32).
37    BA-MA, N 253/4, "Vortrag in Wilhelmshöhe," 29 September 1897.
38    ibid., F 2031, PG 66018, "Gesetzentwurf betreffend die deutsche Flotte," approved by
      Wilhelm on 11 October 1897.
39    Hallmann, *Der Weg*, pp. 240–1; P. M. Kennedy, "Tirpitz, England and the Second Navy
      Law of 1900: a strategical critique," *Militär-Geschichtliche Mitteilungen*, no. 2 (1979), p.
      47; Kelly leaves out the crucial words "But this is not my business."
40    Tirpitz requested the estimate of the Admiralty Staff for the purpose of obtaining
      support from the Reichstag for the Second Navy Bill. Tirpitz to the Chief of the
      Admiralty Staff, 3 December 1899, draft. Diederichs replied on 22 January 1900,
      enclosing Grapow's (A4) sixty-three-page memorandum "Betrachtungen über die
      Kriegführung Deutschland zur See gegen England in den Jahren 1904 und 1920." While

Tirpitz requested that the estimate "should convincingly demonstrate how extraordinarily unfavorable our position would be in such a war," Grapow's memorandum was by no means unrealistic. See BA-MA, F 2036, PG 66040. Diederichs also forwarded the document to Wilhelm, Hohenlohe, and Schlieffen, and described it as representing "the actual relationship on the basis of assembled material." Diederichs to Wilhelm, 24 January 1900, BA-MA, F 5656, VI, 1.–3., Vol. 1.

41  BA-MA, F 5656, VI, 1.–3., Vol. 1, Grapow's notation, 20 January 1900 for *Immediatvortrag* of 23 January 1900.

42  Tirpitz, *Erinnerungen*, p. 101.

43  BA-MA, N 253/4, Tirpitz to Senden, 11 August 1897.

44  See above, p. 141.

45  Hohenlohe, *Denkwürdigkeiten*, Bd III, journal entry for 24 October, 1898, p. 464, Hallmann, *Der Weg*, p. 290, and J. Steinberg, "The Copenhagen complex," *Journal of Contemporary History*, vol. I. no. 3 (1966), p. 28, think that the aged Chancellor may have misunderstood Tirpitz, who, they claim, never sought such a fleet. Berghahn takes the statement at its face value: *Tirpitz-Plan*, p. 191. I have found no evidence for Steinberg's claim that the occasion for Tirpitz's statement was a meeting with him at Hohenlohe's request to discuss the seizure of Antwerp.

46  See below, pp. 151; 165–6.

47  K. F. Nowak and F. Thimme, *Erinnerungen und Gedanken des Botschafters Anton Graf Monts* (Berlin, 1932), p. 194.

48  See BA-MA, F 2340, PG 94545, Tirpitz to naval attaché, London, 4 December 1899. Wilhelm referred to the British shortage of crews in a discussion reported by the Württemberg minister to Berlin, Varnbüler, on 5 November 1897, Kennedy, *Antagonism*, p. 224.

49  BA-MA, F 2015, PG 65955, Bendemann's "Denkschrift zum Immediatvortrag," 18 December 1899.

50  BA-MA, N 253/39, "Motive für die Organisationsänderung," n.d., in Tirpitz's hand; also Berghahn, *Tirpitz-Plan*, pp. 159–60.

51  H St Ar Stuttgart, E 73/73a, 12e Verz. 61, Varnbüler to Mittnacht, 2 November 1899.

52  Tirpitz, *Erinnerungen*, p. 101.

53  BA-MA, F 2044, PG 66075, "Notizen zu einer Denkschrift des Staatssekretärs des RMA für Seine Majestät den Kaiser. Vorgetragen . . . am 28. November, 1898;" also "Notizen für vorstehenden Immediatvortrag von 28. November, 1898," in pencil, in Tirpitz's hand; ibid., N 253/4.

54  ibid., F 2046, PG 66084, "Protokoll der Plenarsitzung von 7. 2. 1899;" Berghahn, *Tirpitz-Plan*, pp. 163–4.

55  BA-MA, N 253/40, Bendemann to Tirpitz, 6 October 1897.

56  ibid., F 2044, PG 66074, "Vortrag, Rominten," 28 September 1899. In his memoirs Tirpitz states that he only requested thirty-eight ships of the line, the number that the Second Navy Law provided: *Erinnerungen*, p. 107.

57  BA-MA, F 2034, PG 66034, comment of A to E, 14 November 1899.

58  BA-MA, F 2340, PG 94545, Tirpitz to naval attaché, London, 4 December 1899.

59  ibid., Coerper to Tirpitz, 3 January 1900.

60  ibid., F 2034, PG 66034, Fischel, "A," "Denkschrift zum Immediatvortrag . . .," 31 January 1900, copy.

61  ibid., N 253/19, n.d., no signature, Capelle's handwriting. Für Kommissionsberathung der Novelle: "Stärkevergleich zwischen England und Deutschland." See also Berghahn, *Tirpitz-Plan*, p. 193, referring to a memorandum of February 1900 which also emphasized British personnel difficulties.

62  BA-MA, F 2235, PG 94006, Wilhelm's comments on an excerpt from *The Times*, 30 October 1899; ibid., PG 64007, Wilhelm's comment on an article in the *Naval and Military Record*, 4 July 1901, the *Army and Navy Gazette*, 6 July 1901, and an article in the *Naval and Military Record*, 16 December 1901.

63  BA-MA, F 2036, PG 66040, "Betrachtungen über die Kriegführung Deutschlands zur See gegen England in den Jahren 1904 und 1920."

64  ibid., N 253/4, 20 February 1899, "Notizen zum Immediatvortrag."

65  ibid., N 253/16, Tirpitz to Büchsel, 23 August 1899.

66  J. E. Sutton, "The Imperial Navy, 1910–1914," PhD thesis, Indiana University, 1953, fos

222–4. Holger H. Herwig, *"Luxury" Fleet: The Imperial German Navy, 1888–1918* (London, 1980), pp. 42–4, table 2.

67  Hallmann, *Der Weg*, p. 204.
68  Marder, *Anatomy*, p. 5.
69  Sutton, "Imperial Navy," fo. 224, Herwig, *"Luxury Fleet,"* pp. 42–4, table 6.
70  Steinberg, *Yesterday's Deterrent*, pp. 210–11.
71  BA-MA, F 2035, PG 66035, "Seiner Exzellenz vorzulegen. Schiffsliste und Indienst-haltungspläne für den 1. Oktober 1908," 5 May 1900, initialed by Capelle and Dähnhardt.
72  Bernhard Fürst von Bülow, *Deutsche Politik* (Berlin, 1916), pp. 21–2; quoted by Berghahn, *Tirpitz-Plan*, p. 128.
73  "Denkschrift Tirpitz," November 1905, quoted in ibid., p. 111. I have used the copy in BA-MA, F 2031, PG 66019.
74  Hallmann, *Der Weg*, p. 301.
75  BA-MA, F 2034, PG 66028, "Zweiter Entwurf v. 14. 11. [18]99. Tabelle 2. Einstel-lungsjahr der ersten Raten für Neue und Ersatzbauten in den Etat." Also a prior version declared "Ungültig."
76  Berghahn, *Tirpitz-Plan*, p. 112.
77  Tirpitz, *Erinnerungen*, pp. 108–9.
78  GLA Karlsruhe, 233/3480, Jagemann to Brauer, 19 February 1900.
79  BA-MA, F 2034, PG 66029, "Berechnung der Kosten eines Dritten Doppelgesch-waders," initialed by several individuals on 9 February 1900 and cosigned by Dähnhardt "Zu den Akten," on 12 February.
80  ibid., BA-MA, N 253/5, "Notizen zur Immediatvortrag. Erledigt 7.5 [1900]."
81  Hohenlohe, *Denkwürdigkeiten*, Bd III, journal entry for 1 May 1899, p. 498.

# 10 The Acceptance of the Tirpitz Plan, 1897–1905

**I**

Whether or not the German leadership deliberately built the fleet as a solution for the allegedly permanent internal crisis of the Empire will not be examined in detail. Obviously Bülow, the Prussian Minister of Finance Johannes Miquel, Tirpitz, Wilhelm, and a number of politicians and publicists at one time or another spoke of marshaling the property-holding classes behind the fleet, enhancing the profits of industry, reconciling the working classes to the existing regime, and thus using the navy as a means of easing or resolving internal difficulties. But can these statements be represented as constituting a program? Only in Bülow's case can it be stated with certainty that imperialism was a deliberate means of eliminating internal dissension and consolidating national unity. According to him, it was a national cause to reconcile Social Democracy to the state.[1]

Wilhelm, as stated above, wanted ships for their own sake and as an essential prerequisite for the successful conduct of an imperialist policy. He appears never to have become fully converted to Tirpitz's battleship doctrine and continued to promote schemes such as that of the fast ship of the line. But he was one of the few German leaders outside the navy who at least occasionally realized that the navy would not for a long time begin to play a significant role against Britain. In a conversation with the French ambassador, the Marquis de Noailles, on 28 October 1899, his response to the query about what could be done to block British expansion in Africa was that without an adequate fleet Germany could do nothing: "After twenty years when it is ready, I will speak another language." This statement is corroborated by the Austro-Hungarian ambassador Szögyenyi, who reported on 5 February 1900 that because of the weaknesses of the navy "Kaiser Wilhelm nourishes the smallest illusion at all" about falling heir to the British Empire, "for he has repeatedly hinted that he personally will not survive to see the realization of these ambitious plans, although he regards it as his duty to prepare his country in the best way for these expected events."[2]

On 12 November 1902, Wilhelm warned Bülow that great caution would have to be observed toward the British, who "have thirty-five armored ships in service and we eight, and in the year 1905 England will have ready for service 196 new armored ships, cruisers, and armored deck cruisers against our forty-six."[3] At the end of 1904, at the height of the Anglo-German war scare arising from the Dogger Bank incident, he stated that Germany would have needed two more years to be able to face Britain.[4] In February 1906, however, Wilhelm admitted that the German navy could never face the British with any prospect of success.[5] Hence war with Britain should be avoided well beyond 1905. Earlier, however, he had expected quicker results. Thus on 5 May 1898 he had expressed the opinion that in terms of naval power "in one year we will already be stronger, in three years considerably stronger," and that peace with Britain was only essential until 1901.[6]

Upon assuming the chancellorship in 1894, Hohenlohe had agreed to seek "complete cooperation of the navy."[7] In December of that year he stated in the Reichstag that in view of disturbances overseas it was necessary "to increase our navy at least to such an extent as to make it capable of providing for our overseas interests the protection without which commerce and shipping cannot exist."[8] His specific reference was to the shortage of cruisers. By January 1896 he had accepted Tirpitz's view that the navy had become a necessity because of Germany's industrialization and the consequent increase of her overseas trade which had aroused the envy of others.[9] Moreover, like Tirpitz, Hohenlohe viewed a strong fleet as a guarantee for peace. He none the less defended his incompetent colleague Admiral Hollmann, opposed any *Staatsstreich* over naval increases, and considered their approval by the Reichstag to be indispensable. He hoped that in time "the conviction that a strong fleet is necessary will break more and more ground."

But there is no evidence that Hohenlohe had given much thought to naval strategy. In November 1897 he seems to have thought purely of a sortie fleet for breaking a close blockade of the German ports. After the promulgation of the First Navy Law he spoke with unusual enthusiasm of Tirpitz as "truly a mighty [*gewaltiger*] man."[10] He registered no reaction to Tirpitz's statement in October 1898 that he sought "as large a navy as England."[11] In January 1900 he was interested in securing the passage of the Second Navy Bill, which he had opposed in 1899 on grounds of unfavorable circumstances. He now thought that the new bill was necessary since "we cannot subject ourselves to the danger of experiencing at the hands of England the fate of Spain at the hands of North America, and it is clear that the English only wait to jump on us."[12] Hohenlohe was thus obviously impressed by the events of recent years, the tension between Britain and Germany, and the downfall of the Spanish Empire. The aged Chancellor's anglophobia is also evident from a statement at the end of October 1899 that the reason for introducing the Navy Bill at this time was that Britain could not create difficulties because of her involvement in the Transvaal. He further appears to have realized dimly that the establishment of a strong fleet would increase Germany's value as an ally in expecting that "the powers hostile to England, France and Russia, will greet the *Novelle* with joy."[13]

On the other hand, the navy played a central role in Bernhard von Bülow's policies as Secretary of State of the Foreign Office and as Chancellor. His appointment as Secretary of State was linked to the construction of the fleet. In his memoirs, written after the collapse of the

Empire when many viewed the German naval program as a fateful folly, he states:

> The task set for me when I was called from Rome to Berlin was to make possible the strengthening of the fleet which had become a question of our very existence, without, however, allowing its construction to lead to a war with England.[14]

In his *Deutsche Politik,* written for the twenty-fifth jubilee of Wilhelm's coronation, he attributed even greater importance to the navy:

> To make possible the construction of an adequate fleet was the next great task [*nächstliegende und grosse Aufgabe*] of post-Bismarckian German policy, a task with which I saw myself primarily confronted as I was on 28 June 1897 in Kiel, aboard *Hohenzollern,* entrusted with the direction of foreign policy.[15]

In his memoirs Bülow maintained that he "supported Tirpitz personally and politically from the first to the last day of my tenure of office."[16] But did Bülow understand the implications of the naval policy? In his memoirs he speaks of the detailed discussions of the First Navy Bill between Wilhelm, Tirpitz, and himself: "It was temporarily only a project, but a plan which opened great, very great and wide horizons. In these horizons . . . lay the greatness, but also the political danger of Tirpitz's naval bill."[17] These words are temptingly suggestive, particularly to suspicious historians of Imperial Germany. Naval construction certainly fitted his scheme of eliminating internal dissension through a national policy. As he wrote to his then friend and patron Philipp Eulenburg soon after becoming Secretary of State: "Only a successful foreign policy can help to reconcile, pacify, rally, unite."[18] Even Holstein realized that.[19] In Bülow's opinion imperialism and navalism would accomplish the same: in the passage of the First Navy Bill he saw a great boost to Wilhelm's prestige. On numerous occasions he, like Tirpitz and Hohenlohe, described the fleet as essential for *Weltpolitik,* which Germany had to pursue because of her industrialization. In his memoirs the fleet construction appears as a "necessity because of our elemental economic development."[20] He reports as having told Wilhelm already in August 1897 that the fleet was essential since "we had to protect the value of billions which we had gradually entrusted to the sea, our shipping, our commerce, and our mightily developing industry."[21] And in 1906 he stated that the navy was necessary because of Germany's involvement in *Weltpolitik* as the result of "the rapid increase of our population, the mighty rise of our industry, the courage and enterprise of our merchants, the economic proficiency of our people."[22] He also accepted Mahan's view that "at all times the flourishing and thriving [*Blüte und Gedeihen*] of great states stands in closest connection to the development of their naval forces."[23] And, like Tirpitz, he accepted Britain, the European great power which he understood least, as the main opponent of German economic and imperial development. In the *Deutsche Politik* he maintained that the construction of the fleet was necessary to provide Germany with the same independence in world affairs as she possessed in European affairs.[24] Without a major fleet she might as well forget about her shipping and about any competition with Britain in international trade.[25] In his memoirs he claimed that Germany had to beware of dependence on Britain, "for if we bound ourselves entirely to England she would not allow us to protect our economic development, which has already very much alarmed the British cousin."[26] He was fully aware of the limitations that naval weakness imposed on German policy in the Philippines and the Portuguese colonies in 1898, in Samoa in 1899, and in 1900 in China.[27]

In the semi-confidential deliberations of the Reichstag Budget Committee Bülow remarked in March 1900 that Britain was currently the only power capable of attacking Germany with impunity. For Germany was incapable of defending herself at sea against Britain or of finding allies against her. Anglo-German relations had, moreover, reached a critical stage because of the growth of British imperialist sentiment and economic jealousy of Germany. Crises like those over Samoa and the confiscation of German mail steamers at the outset of the Boer War could not always be solved diplomatically. In order to be able to participate in a peaceful competition with her, Germany must, "in facing England, at least be capable of taking the defensive."[28] Bülow thus entirely accepted Tirpitz's views of Britain's envy of Germany as a commercial rival and of the increase of Germany's value as an ally to other continental powers because of her growing naval strength. He also accepted the risk theory: according to the *Deutsche Politik*, the aim of naval construction was to build a fleet "the attack on which would for every enemy be connected with an excessive risk."[29]

In spite of this extensive agreement between Bülow's and Tirpitz's thinking, George Alexander von Müller remarks "that Bülow was very poorly informed about naval matters," citing the example of Bülow inquiring in the winter of 1908–09 whether the German fleet would be able to defeat the British in the spring.[30] Müller may have had in mind Bülow's letter to Tirpitz of 30 November 1908, in which he proposed the reduction of the German building rate in face of the British naval panic and asked Tirpitz "if Germany and the German people could with calm and confidence look forward to a British attack."[31] Bülow's question was thus somewhat different from the one attributed to him by Müller and was probably more the result of tactical considerations to slow down the Anglo-German naval race than of sheer ignorance. None the less, there is no evidence that Bülow, like Tirpitz or occasionally even Wilhelm, expected the completion of the navy to require twenty or thirty years. In his memoirs he remarks that in the first years of his chancellorship, in response to his question when the navy would be strong enough to deter a British attack, Tirpitz replied

that in 1904 or 1905 we would reach the most critical phase of our relations with England. At this time our navy's strength would provoke in England envy and great alarm. After this foreseeably most critical moment the danger of an English attack would decrease further and further. The

English would then realize that action against us would also expose them to excessive risk.[32]

In the *Deutsche Politik* he discusses the "danger zone of the first rank" as lasting "for the first decade after the introduction of the navy bill of 1897."[33] It may therefore indeed be that Bülow expected the navy to be in a stronger position vis-à-vis Britain in 1908. Earlier he appears to have expected speedy results from naval construction. On 16 May 1898 he accepted as his own Klehmet's view that the Spanish–American War had come too early: "He would have preferred it after we had had the opportunity through the acceptance of our naval bill to participate actively."[34] It is strange to have the promulgation of a law to build a navy being viewed as tantamount to having a navy! Nor did Bülow express any doubts about Wilhelm's remark of 5 May 1898 that the navy would be ready for action in 1901. Instead he saw fit to record the comment in a private note.[35] Bülow's mind cleared somewhat by December 1904, the height of the war scare resulting from the Dogger Bank incident, when he informed Holstein: ". . . the assumption that we would be 'ready' with our fleet in two years is incorrect. The disproportion between us and England at sea will be much the same as today in two, four, six years."[36]

It appears that Bülow may not have understood Tirpitz's battleship doctrine or North Sea strategy. While admitting on 27 March 1900 in the Reichstag Budget Committee that "above all we need a battle fleet," he at the same time stated the need for increasing the number of cruisers.[37] In his memoirs he asserts that in the Wilhelmshöhe discussions of 1897 between Wilhelm, Tirpitz and himself over the First Navy Bill he was censured by Wilhelm for remarking: "The political situation would be very much facilitated for me if in our new constructions the large ships would not be given so much prominence and the emphasis would be placed on cruisers, also on torpedoes and on coastal fortifications."[38] He further maintains that he retained his doubts concerning the construction of battleships and preferred cruisers and torpedo-boats and later on submarines and airplanes.[39] Bülow's memoirs are not corroborated by other sources, however.

Bülow's initial patron Philipp Eulenburg appears to have given very little thought to the fleet, although Johannes Haller remarks that he was an opponent of the naval program since he feared that it would lead to rivalry with Britain and since he lacked confidence in Senden.[40] Bülow's other confidant and adviser, Holstein, disapproved of the navy partly from lack of confidence in Wilhelm. In February 1897 he complained to Bülow that "it was a sad truth . . . that today the value of a person to the Kaiser depends on whether he is willing and able to contribute directly or indirectly to the increase of ship *matériel*."[41] Soon he realized that the new naval policy jeopardized his efforts to improve relations with Britain. Bad relations with Britain, however, would limit Germany's diplomatic freedom of action.[42] His antipathy to the navy increased further because of the insistence of its leaders on the seizure of Kiao-chow, which raised in his mind the specter of war with Russia.[43]

According to Bülow, Holstein viewed the construction of the navy without a collision with Britain as squaring the circle.[44] Norman Rich regards it as one of Bülow's most remarkable accomplishments "that he avoided a rupture with Holstein over the fleet issue, and that he so successfully disguised his own attitude that Holstein kept until his death the illusion that Bülow could be persuaded to take a strong stand against the fleet programme."[45] Paul Kennedy remarks that both Holstein and his friend Hatzfeld "did not perhaps realize that German policy towards Britain was undergoing a decisive change."[46] This appears to be the case, although the two men were among the ablest diplomats of Wilhelmian Germany. Holstein had realized as early as November 1897 the limitation on German freedom of action by the naval agitation against Britain: Germany had thereby lost her "really valuable trump against Russia," a rapprochement with Britain.[47] There is one faint indication, however, that Holstein may have understood and accepted the diplomatic aim of the fleet policy. When, on 16 May 1899, he expressed his disgust over Salisbury's uncooperative attitude over Samoa to Hatzfeld, Holstein stated: "I told myself that since such behavior would have to be restricted [*gekappt sein muss*], the present occasion would be very appropriate. By "restriction" I do not mean naval battles *for which on our side prerequisites are still lacking*."[48] At the end of 1899, when Holstein charged Bülow with launching "an irresponsible and aggressive anti-English policy as soon as we were a little stronger at sea than we are today," Bülow came close to disclosing his policy to his adviser. After falsely protesting that he had done all he could to improve relations with Britain, he stated that what he had meant by the statement on which Holstein based his charge was "only that right now we should pursue a doubly cautious policy toward England, for . . . we are not even strong enough to deal with England defensively and would be at England's mercy like butter under a knife."[49] If Holstein did not fully comprehend the diplomatic implications of Bülow's policy, he did not delude himself about the German navy being able to confront Britain in the near future. More than a year and a half before being told by Bülow that the Anglo-German power relationship would not change "in two, four, six years," Holstein had written to his chief that he saw no chance of Germany, if allied with Russia, defeating Britain and the United States at sea "even if we build ships for years with the utmost effort."[50]

"Although clear proof is lacking," states Volker Berghahn, "there is every indication that at the turn of the year 1899–1900 the final decision was reached to make the army the main victim of financial pressure,"[51] in short, to give the navy priority over the army. This had, indeed, been Tirpitz's demand of 15 June 1897, but apparently only for the duration of the campaign for the First Navy Law. The Prussian Ministers of War Heinrich von Gossler (1896–1903) and Karl von Einem (1903–09) were not interested in substantially increasing the army. In his memoirs Einem remarks that Gossler had "already in 1900 by necessity . . . to renounce supplementary additions to the army budget in view of naval construction . . ." Even earlier, on 8 June 1899, Gossler had informed Schlieffen that "The German army has in its war formation now gained an extent which has exceeded its limits and in my opinion contains serious dangers."[52] A decline in military quality had taken place, he claimed, particularly as in the field-army regular units were being mixed with reserve and Landwehr units. The presence of these inferior troops thus undermined the efficiency of the entire field-army. Gossler therefore proposed to strengthen the quality of the field-army by reducing its strength from 899 to 755 battalions through the removal from it of the Landwehr units as well as some of the reserves.[53] Since the decisive battles of the Bismarckian wars had been won by active troops, Gossler believed

> that we would do well in the future also to count essentially on the solid fighting strength of our active army corps for the decisive battles that were to be expected soon after the outbreak of war, and in so far as these were not sufficient to use for the first line reserve troops that had been attached to or included in formation with troops of the line.[54]

Gossler, moreover, appears to have opposed the increase of the army lest the inclusion of socially undesirable and politically unreliable elements, particularly into the officer corps, weaken it as a pillar of the established order. This was, according to Berndt-Felix Schulte, the view of the traditionalist–statist–aristocratic leadership of the army. Expressions of this tradition were Waldersee's advocacy in 1877 of a small professional army to shoot the *canaille* in the struggle between the propertied and the property-less,[55] Wilhelm's address to the recruits in 1891 to the effect that in case of socialist disturbances they would have to obey orders to shoot down their brothers and sisters, and repeated consideration of the use of troops against workers in the 1890s.[56] The army could thus not be increased substantially if it was to function effectively in a civil war.

While Einem later deplored the priority given to the navy over the army, he, too, opposed any substantial army increases. He justified his reticence by claiming that any proposed increases would have been rejected because of Germany's favorable diplomatic position before the Morocco crisis, financial shortage, and Reichstag opposition.[57] On 19 April 1904, Einem expressed his agreement with the views of his predecessor when he wrote to Schlieffen:

> The development of the army in the direction of the establishment of new formations and the setting up of new troop units can for the time being be regarded as essentially completed.
>
> The question whether the number of our cadres is adequate for war needs is in my opinion on the whole to be answered in the affirmative, as is the further question whether the effective numbers [*Präsenzziffer*] are adequate for the appropriate strength [*angemessene Etatsstärke*] of the existing cadres and for the training of the adequate number of men in order to set up the reserve and Landwehr formations required in the event of war.[58]

Einem had, indeed, gained the approval of Wilhelm, Bülow, and the Chief of the Military Cabinet for his position.

The General Staff, however, strongly disagreed with the policies of the Ministry of War. Schlieffen had supported Caprivi's army increase of 1893 because of his conviction that the German forces were incapable of meeting the needs of a two-front war.[59] Thereafter he agreed with Gossler that the quality of the army was important, that the active army was most capable of carrying out offensive operations, but he did not want to dispense with those regular troops that exceeded the existing corps formations and wanted to combine them with reserve troops to set up additional corps of the field-army. While insisting on quality, i.e. the use of the standing army in the opening operations, he realized that it had to be reconciled with quantity. Regarding the participation of Germany's allies in a war as illusory, and refusing to consider a war on two fronts since "the war against France alone is sufficient to strain all [our] strength,"[60] Schlieffen subsequently reasoned on 10 November 1899:

> In a war against France we will do well to take the offensive. Under certain conditions we will have no other choice than to attack France immediately.
>
> But an offensive against the numerous French army which can lean on mighty fortresses and take a stand behind strongly defended lines must be carefully prepared and executed by involving all available forces. In order to overcome such an opponent, we require superiority.
>
> In active infantry battalions France is superior to us, but we can count on a few more batteries. I propose to utilize this situation by . . . uniting superfluous third divisions and fifth brigades in case of mobilization into four new corps . . .[61]

This would have raised the number of German corps from twenty-three to twenty-seven. No increase in manpower would be involved beyond the establishment of the new field-batteries and the setting up of peacetime staffs of the corps and divisions, and thus Schlieffen hoped "to counter the unwieldy French corps which were well supplied with infantry with a larger number of smaller corps which were better equipped with artillery."[62] He saw no alternative to an offensive strategy, for a defensive was only possible behind fortified lines and wide rivers which were not available for the number of troops Germany possessed. "The modern defensive is counterattack; but for it no less than for the offensive we require numerous troops and good weapons."[63]

Schlieffen's hopes were not realized in the army budget of 1900, and Gossler's successor Einem did not even consult him about the budget of 1905 before reaching an agreement on it with Wilhelm, Bülow, and the Chief of the Military Cabinet. He did not share Einem's view as expressed on 19 April 1904 that the army had reached an adequate size. He stated his disagreement on 4 November 1905, approximately a month before he drafted his final operations plan against France, the famous December Memorandum. Realizing that the army could not be increased, he argued on the basis of the experiences drawn from the Russo-Japanese War that no troops could be detached from the advancing field-army for occupation duties and the maintenance of rearward communications, and therefore requested that better preparations be made in peacetime for the use of Landwehr units for this purpose.

Thus the military agencies were far from unanimous in accepting the higher priority assigned to the navy. The differences between the General Staff and the Ministry of War were not resolved until after the Agadir crisis of 1911.[64] Tirpitz could therefore not have been entirely incorrect when he claimed to have evidence of army hostility toward naval development. On 28 October 1899 he reported to Hohenlohe that some military considered the navy to be a threat to them.[65] At the end of August 1900 he wrote to Senden that "the army, etc., likewise works in a new direction and therefore against the navy with an increased vigor."[66]

At the meeting of the Prussian State Ministry of 20 January 1900, in which Tirpitz requested the approval of the Second Navy Bill, Gossler expressed certain reservations concerning the effect that the doubling of the naval strength would have on the army. According to the protocol of the meeting:

> The . . . Minister of War remarked that since in its greater need for crews the navy will have to draw on the population of the interior, a considerable increase for the army was for the time being out of the question. Also the requirements for the condition of replacements would have to be somewhat lowered. It was therefore advisable to consider whether lower requirements might not also be set for the physical condition of naval personnel . . . In view of the great financial requirements of the navy, the army administration would have to be as frugal as possible and in particular avoid in the next years loans for its aims.[67]

He therefore hoped to have the support of the Imperial Treasury for the inclusion of a number of items in the current budget so as to avoid future extraordinary expenditure. Also, he was willing to desist the next year from requesting the 7,000 men due for the strengthening of infantry and instead concentrate on building up the foot artillery, which was still lacking in three army corps, and the pioneer units. And then he made a statement suggesting a total revision of army strategy:

> The fortresses in the west would in 1902 be entirely capable of defense; this aim was also to be sought from the point of view of our foreign policy, which assumed more and more of the character of *Weltpolitik* and according to which it was above all desirable to strengthen the defensive in such a way as to secure the boundaries without having to invade hostile territory.

Bülow was not present to comment on this statement from the point of view of the Foreign Office. Hohenlohe and the Foreign Office representative, Körner, who were present, are not recorded as having said anything. It is not known whether the General Staff had been consulted before this statement was made. The reference to a defensive strategy on the European continent, particularly in the west, seems to indicate that there existed serious doubts about the feasibility of the western offensive that was central to Schlieffen's operational thinking. This is corroborated by Count Hutten-Czapski, confidant of Hohenlohe, whom Schlieffen told in May 1900 that "after long dutiful considerations he had reached the conclusion that in the event of a two-front war in certain circumstances success would depend on Germany not allowing her operational measures to be narrowed by her existing international agreements"—a statement that was taken to mean the violation of Belgian neutrality.[68] Hesitations about such a breach of international obligations may have caused the Great General Staff to have second thoughts about offensive strategy. A defensive strategy was not entirely discarded. For we do know that as late as 1905 a war game in which Schlieffen himself participated was played in the General Staff in which Germany was on the defensive in a two-front war against Russia, France and Britain, and from which she emerged victorious![69]

Or was it that the Ministry of War and the General Staff, which disagreed about the size of the army, also disagreed about strategy? The latter would have logically resulted from the former. And disagreements between leading agencies, naval, military, or civilian, were symptomatic of Imperial Germany.

Should concern about the feasibility of offensive strategy not have given cause to the General Staff to press more strongly for increased numerical strength in spite of the doubts of the Ministry of War and to oppose the increase of the fleet? But, since this was not done, perhaps the violation of Belgian neutrality was chosen as the cheap price to be paid both for the maintenance of the political reliability of the army and for the construction of an allegedly first-class navy?

Instead there were only grumbles from the army about naval construction, as from the retired Waldersee in January 1904 to the effect that "the army was coming off badly" because of the navy.[70]

## II

In his memoirs Tirpitz maintains that the legal determination of the size of the navy and the ship types was also necessary to secure its systematic development against the interventions of Wilhelm II and against different opinions within the navy itself.[71] According to him, Wilhelm was notoriously susceptible to other influences, Bülow did not appear a reliable supporter,[72] and even Senden was suspect. Wilhelm was indeed known to have leanings toward the *jeune école* in which he was supported by other naval officers. As for the navy, Tirpitz remarks: "Where it came to specialized knowledge, there was noisy disagreement. When I took over as Secretary of State, the German Navy was a collection of different models, even if not such a motley one as the Russian [fleet] under Nicholas II . . . . If a German is presented with a system, he has more faith in it."[73] Uniformity of opinion among naval officers was also essential to secure the support of the Reichstag and of the public for the Tirpitz Plan. Tirpitz also had to ensure that limited financial resources would be directed to the battle fleet and that the fleet law not be jeopardized in favor of the demands of other naval agencies or of the Kaiser himself.

As the chief protagonist of the battleship school Tirpitz had, as Chief of Staff in the High Command, developed great skill in the in-fighting between the supreme naval agencies. The butt of his attacks had been the confused, generally pro-*jeune école* Imperial Naval Office. With his appointment as Secretary of State of the Imperial Naval Office, the battleship school had come to dominate that agency. His old cronies from the "Torpedo Gang" and the staff of the High Command came along with him as loyal and efficient supporters. Tirpitz had felt it necessary to request of Wilhelm in June 1897, when stating his terms for the appointment, that dissenting naval opinions be repressed,[74] and complained in August 1897 that "older active naval officers were reluctant to concede the necessary power to the Secretary of State."[75] Somewhat later he stated that "at the time of the bringing in of the first fleet law, not one of the seven admirals I consulted agreed with it."[76]

Most dangerous was the continuation of the *jeune école* heresy. In 1899, Kapitän-zur-See Curt Maltzahn attempted to publish a book entitled *Seekriegslehre* at about the same time that a retired Vize-Admiral, Victor Valois, had published a pamphlet entitled *Seemacht, Seegeltung, Seeherrschaft* (*Naval Power, Naval Presence, Naval Domination*). Tirpitz knew both men well. Maltzahn had referred to him as "Du" when crossing swords with him in 1895. In what appears to be a half-hearted attempt at reconciliation an otherwise unrepentant Maltzahn despaired of the success of a personal talk, since "we could not have convinced each other . . ." He denied, however, that he was a supporter of the *jeune école* and conceded that the battle fleet was of decisive importance in wartime. But cruisers were still important in peacetime. He told Tirpitz that he resented the orthodoxy introduced into the High Command by the Dienstschrift No. IX: ". . . I cannot deny that when I hear people speak of the offensive and naval domination—in short of the Dienstschrift No. IX.—anger often forces a pen into my hand." That service manual—Tirpitz's highest theoretical achievement—said little that was new to justify its arrogant tone and the assumption that all earlier naval leaders had been wrong. Strategically, the naval strength stipulated by the manual was inadequate for the stress placed on the ruthless offensive.[77] Maltzahn, enjoying the prestige of a successful teacher at the Naval Academy, requested permission to publish his book at the very time that Tirpitz was formulating the provisions of the Second Navy Bill on the basis of battleship strength. Among the statements in Maltzahn's book that appeared most objectionable to Tirpitz were: his championship of a geographically and chronologically limited mastery of the sea such as sought by Napoleon in 1805 for the invasion of England; his justification of ships of the line for cruiser warfare if there existed no viable opportunity to break the naval domination of the stronger enemy; the capability of a weaker sea power to damage England through attacks on her shipping, trade centers, and overseas possessions; the avoidance of sea battle against overwhelming odds; the refusal to give priority to the battle fleet to the point of making cruiser warfare impossible, allowing cruiser warfare to accompany or follow squadron warfare; and admitting the viability of cruisers as a weapon of the power that was weaker at sea.[78]

Whereas Maltzahn pleaded for the coexistence of cruiser and squadron warfare, which in Tirpitz's opinion was a dangerous division of Germany's scarce resources and a repetition of the error of Büchsel's plan of May 1897, Valois, who had previously been forbidden to publish his work, rejected squadron warfare for Germany altogether. While granting that the battleship school was theoretically correct in so far as success in a naval battle was the only way of obtaining domination of the sea, such a success would be denied to Germany in a war against Britain because of her weakness. Instead of seeking naval domination in a war with Britain, Germany would have to remain content with maintaining her naval presence (*Seegeltung*) by hitting her opponent's weakest spot: the extended and inadequately defended shipping throughout the high seas. This type of action would in Valois' opinion inflict such losses on Britain as to force her to conclude peace. Valois thus proposed that Germany build cruisers rather than ships of the line: this was the exact opposite of Tirpitz's position that Germany could never compete with the British in cruisers because of their enormous lead in them and because of her lack in overseas bases which were so important under conditions of modern cruiser warfare. The Secretary of State challenged the views of the retired admiral on the ground that he had failed to provide any proof for the effectiveness of cruiser warfare under modern conditions. Instead Tirpitz claimed that cruiser warfare presented fewer chances of success in the age of steam, which reduced the duration of the voyage of merchantmen, increased their speed in relation to that of warships, and tied commerce raiders to their coaling stations.

On 28 September 1899, Tirpitz did secure Wilhelm's order prohibiting the publication of Maltzahn's book[79] and subsequently obtained a statement from Bülow that Maltzahn's concentration on England as the enemy would produce an unfavorable reaction in that country—a statement which he communicated to the various naval agencies, probably to inhibit discussion of Maltzahn's views. In the fall of 1899, Tirpitz succeeded in effectively muzzling the German naval officer corps by securing from Wilhelm firm regulations about their public utterances.[80]

On the other hand, the battleship school was consolidated through the sale at low cost of Mahan's work and its distribution in the schools and officer corps through the assistance of the Prussian Kultusministerium, the Great General Staff, and the Prussian, Bavarian, Saxon and Württemberg ministries of war. Thereby the fleet agitation was provided with additional arguments and the work was given an official stamp of approval. "The distribution of Mahan's writings was thus also an instrument for disciplining the officer corps."[81]

Then there was the chronic problem of rivalry between the higher naval agencies, the Imperial Naval Office and the High Command. It had existed since the break-up of the Admiralty in 1889 and required resolution on the part of Wilhelm and the Chief of his Naval Cabinet. As Chief of Staff in the High Command, Tirpitz had eagerly supported his superior, the

Commanding Admiral Knorr, against the Imperial Naval Office. The battle continued after his departure from the High Command. Upon his appointment Tirpitz concluded peace with Knorr on the basis of the *status quo* and both men requested that a reorganization not take place.[82] The armistice did not last long, however. Already, when interviewed by Wilhelm for the position of Secretary of State in January 1896, Tirpitz had requested extensive powers for the Imperial Naval Office. In 1927 he was to remark that the only correct organization for the navy would have been the Admiralty, but that it could not have been re-established in 1898–99.[83] He certainly wanted more power for his agency. But whether it was he who broke the armistice is another matter. The jurisdictional dispute between Tirpitz and Knorr, starting in January 1898, culminated in the "all-highest" order of 14 March 1899 dissolving the High Command. Its functions as the Admiralty Staff Section and as the military–political supervisor of ships abroad were turned over to the Admiralty Staff, whose chief was provided with direct access to the Emperor. The chiefs of the two naval stations, Kiel and Wilhelmshaven, the chief of the old Fleet Command, and the chief of the Cruiser Squadron essentially retained the powers that they had possessed earlier but were now directly subordinated to Wilhelm. So were independent ship commands overseas.[84]

Wilhelm was now personally commander-in-chief of his navy as well as his army. Directly subordinated to him were: the Secretary of State of the Imperial Naval Office, the Chief of the Naval Cabinet, the Chief of the Admiralty Staff, the Chief of the Educational and Training System, the Chief of the First Squadron, the Chief of the Baltic Sea Station Command, the Chief of the North Sea Station Command, the Chief of the Cruiser Squadron, and all independent ship commands abroad. He was further assisted by the General Inspector of the Navy. With minor modifications, this form of organization was to last until World War I.[85] A single erratic man had in his hands the final decisions of the Prussian and Imperial government, of the administration and command of both the army and the navy, and the coordination of this highly complex and unwieldy machinery. In his personal command of the navy the coordination of eight independent agencies and the settlement of frequent disputes between them required considerable technical expertise, administrative skill, and tact. In this activity Wilhelm was by necessity dependent on the Chief of his Naval Cabinet, until 1906 Senden and thereafter Georg Alexander von Müller.

During Müller's tenure, the Chief of the Admiralty Staff reported to the Emperor on Tuesday mornings and the Secretary of State and Chief of the Naval Cabinet on Saturday mornings. While the Chief of the Naval Cabinet and the Commander of the Headquarters were present during the reports of the Secretary of State, as were the Chief of the Admiralty Staff, and presumably the other directly subordinated officers, partly as witnesses and partly as experts on the personnel questions, the Chief of the Naval Cabinet had the privilege of reporting privately.[86] His powers probably increased after the break-up of the High Command as the Emperor required assistance in the handling of more numerous as well as more trivial issues. He had to arbitrate more issues of dispute between Tirpitz and other directly subordinated naval agencies. Tirpitz's relations with Senden were to deteriorate further and Müller, although often protecting the Secretary of State against Wilhelm's often justified ire, also soon came to be seen by the former as more of a foe than a friend.

Although the break-up of the High Command of the Navy did not improve the efficiency of the naval organization, and overtaxed the Emperor and the Chief of the Naval Cabinet, the Imperial Naval Office became the strongest naval agency. No longer facing the rest of the navy united in the High Command, Tirpitz, if not dominating the navy, was assured of his position as *primus inter pares*.

Another consistent disagreement between Tirpitz, who held that it would take a generation to build an effective fleet, and those officers of the "Front" who would have to do the fighting if war broke out sooner was over the issue of quantity versus quality. According to Tirpitz, it was not possible to have both, i.e. build many ships and maintain a high fighting efficiency at the same time. Quantity, i.e. shipbuilding, had to take precedence over quality, i.e. fighting efficiency.[87] At the beginning of the planning of the Second Navy Law, when he proposed to Wilhelm the building of the Third Squadron, Tirpitz stated that as a result of the increased construction "a number of wishes and requests of the Front and perhaps of Your Majesty would have to be dropped," referring in particular to the construction of coastal fortifications.[88] Nor would the training of officers and men, the building of dockyards and harbors, and the acquisition of various accessories and supplies be able to keep pace with the building of ships. In short, the war preparedness of the fleet would suffer. This problem had been obvious to some of the senior naval officers such as Admiral Hans Koester and Felix Bendemann[89] when the First Navy Law was being prepared.

To some extent the misgivings of the "Front" arising from this situation were allayed by the fact that Tirpitz had at last got naval construction going and had contributed to the enormous increase of the naval establishment and the growing prestige of the naval executive officer corps.[90] As Senden wrote in March 1898: "We now stand under the sun of the approved fleet law. Who would have only half a year ago held possible such a glorious achievement?"[91] These obvious assets were offset, however, by liabilities: the navy was not entirely battleworthy, German *matériel* remained inferior to the British, and Tirpitz irritated many. Ambitious, oversensitive, and suspicious,[92] he was "Held by his comrades and colleagues to be insufferable,"[93] and "got into fights and controversies with many a former colleague."[94]

Provision had been made at the beginning of Wilhelm II's reign for the defenses of the Kaiser Wilhelm Canal, including Cuxhaven, and of Heligoland[95] and the Frisian islands. On 5 December 1898, Wilhelm had ordered at Tirpitz's request that in the following years greater expenditure for coastal defences be avoided and that those defense measures made necessary by the increase of the fleet be assigned higher priority than others.[96] In January 1901 the Chief of the Admiralty Staff, Otto von Diederichs, reported that these provisions were no longer adequate,[97] since the offensive against the German coast was no longer expected from the

Franco-Russian alliance but from Britain. In this case the army was expected to have fuller resources at its disposal for the defense of the German coast. On 14 January, Wilhelm authorized consultations between the involved agencies. On 10 February, Diederichs approached Tirpitz about the need to strengthen coastal defenses in the entire area where the German fleet would deploy.[98] His concern was, first, with the strengthening of the fortifications at the entrance into Kiel and in the Elbe estuary and, second, in protecting the fairway into Wilhelmshaven. Diederichs' requests were also supported from the army by the General Inspector of the Engineer and Pioneer Corps, von der Goltz.[99] In his opinion the fortifications of the river estuaries were antiquated and no longer capable of fighting modern ship artillery. He therefore proposed as a general principle that each cluster of coastal fortifications be equipped with at least one modern long-range battery. Tirpitz managed to reduce these requests and to oppose similar ones from Koester, Chief of the First Squadron. Relatively little was done about the construction of coastal fortifications until the fall of 1904 when the Dogger Bank incident raised the specter of war between Britain and Germany.[100]

Another issue of contention between Tirpitz and the other naval agencies was the keeping of ships in service. In this area he encountered steady pressure from Koester, his successor, Prince Heinrich, the successive chiefs of the Admiralty Staff and of the naval stations of Kiel and Wilhelms-haven—in short, the "Front," who often managed to enlist the support of the Chief of the Naval Cabinet and of the Kaiser himself. They pressed for the best *matériel,* sufficient numbers of cruisers in which Germany fell far behind Britain, better arrangements for mobilization, keeping more ships in service throughout the year, and more personnel. All these demands placed additional stress on the scarce financial resources of the navy and threatened the achievement of quantity at the expense of quality. Behind some lay the interest of individual agencies to extend their jurisdiction, which threatened the predominant position of Tirpitz and the Imperial Naval Office. In the face of all of them Tirpitz insisted that other naval agencies lacked adequate information and saw only their special needs, and that the Imperial Naval Office alone was able to oversee the entire German naval development.

Tirpitz's comments on a memorandum of Prince Heinrich of May 1903 are particularly significant. They indicate, above all, that questions of war preparedness and operational planning did not concern him:

> None the less, perfection is only in order when the size of the fleet has so grown that the political importance of the fleet begins to become reality. This it is not with one squadron. Was Scharnhorst right after 1807 as he brought in the *Krümper* system or would it have been correct according to the above principle to turn the 42,000 men that were allowed Prussia into an elite force? Besides, the entire struggle of the Secretary of State aims at concentrating all resources on the battle fleet. Therefore I am against coastal fortifications, against the fortification and coastal defense of Heligoland, against numerous officer clubs, squadron festivities, the Kiel week, the *rage de perfection* of the first mobilization days, against the

setting up of the geodesic system, against participation in Borkum [?], against the [royal] yacht squadron, etc., etc.[101]

Tirpitz's building program led to the beginning of the creation of a second active squadron in 1903. The development of the third squadron would commence in 1908. The establishment of new squadrons would raise questions of organization and tactics. How would one operate with more than one squadron? What would be the powers of the individual squadron leaders and of the Chief of the Fleet? Where would the latter take his position? In an attempt to answer these questions it was decided to establish after the autumn exercises of 1903 a second squadron from the core ships of the reserve squadron and to appoint the Chief of the First Squadron as Chief of the Active Battle Fleet.[102] In September 1903 the Imperial Naval Office held a meeting about the subsequent organization of the remaining reserve formations. It was proposed that in the mobilization of the reserve one-quarter of the crews of every ship consist of fully trained personnel, one-quarter of oriented active personnel from the artillery and torpedo inspections, and the remainder of reservists. It was recognized that the level of the training of these crews would be lower than that of the existing reserve and that the reserve would not be ready for action for eight to fourteen days after mobilization.[103] Tirpitz's insistence on quantity at the expense of quality was seriously challenged by the threat of war in 1904–05.

## Notes: Chapter 10

1  Winzen, *Bülows Weltmachtkonzept*, p. 73; Berghahn, *Tirpitz-Plan*, pp. 16, 148–9. The views of Berghahn, Kehr, and Deist have been recently disputed by Salewski, *Tirpitz*, pp. 63–6.
2  GP, XV, No. 4394, Wilhelm to Bülow, 29 October 1899, p. 408. Szögyinyi is quoted from Paul M. Kennedy, "The Kaiser and German *Weltpolitik*: reflections on Wilhelm II's place in the making of German foreign policy," in *Kaiser Wilhelm II: New Interpretations*, ed. J. C. G. Röhl and Nicolaus Sombart (Cambridge, 1982), p. 158.
3  BA, Bülow, *Nachlass*, p. 112. Also cited in GP, XVII, No. 5031, Wilhelm to Bülow, 12 November 1902, p. 117.
4  GP, XIX, ii, No. 6149, Wilhelm's marginal comments to Coerper's report, 18 November 1904, p. 353.
5  GP, XXI, i, No. 7024, Wilhelm's marginal comment to Stumm to Bülow, 20 February 1906, p. 191.
6  Winzen, *Bülows Weltmachtkonzept*, p. 89. Winzen maintains that Tirpitz deliberately concealed the long construction period from Bülow and Wilhelm.
7  Röhl, *Germany without Bismarck*, p. 127.
8  For Hohenlohe's Reichstag speech of 11 December 1894, see Schulthess, *Europäischer Geschichtskalender*, 1894, p. 168.
9  Hohenlohe, *Denkwürdigkeiten*, Bd III, memorandum apparently intended for a report to Wilhelm on 5 January 1896, p. 151.
10  ibid., p. 437.
11  ibid., journal entry for 24 October 1898, p. 464.
12  ibid., Hohenlohe to Alexander Hohenlohe, 7 January 1900, p. 554.
13  ibid., journal entry for 26 October 1899, p. 534.
14  Bülow, *Denkwürdigkeiten*, Bd I, pp. 412–13.
15  Bülow, *Deutsche Politik* (Berlin, 1916), pp. 20–1.
16  Bülow, *Denkwürdigkeiten*, Bd I, p. 111.

17  ibid., p. 115.
18  Röhl, *Germany without Bismarck*, p. 252; Kennedy, *Antagonism*, pp. 226–7.
19  Röhl, *Germany without Bismarck*, p. 127.
20  Bülow, *Denkwürdigkeiten*, Bd I, p. 412.
21  ibid., p. 58.
22  Quoted in Berghahn, *Tirpitz-Plan*, p. 174.
23  PAAA, Deutschland 138, Bd 14, Bülow to Krupp, 22 May 1898; also quoted in Berghahn, *Tirpitz-Plan*, p. 145.
24  Bülow, *Deutsche Politik*, p. 29.
25  ibid., p. 31.
26  Bülow, *Denkwürdigkeiten*, Bd I, p. 115.
27  Winzen, *Bülows Weltmachtkonzept*, pp. 87–96.
28  BA, Bülow, *Nachlass*, No. 24, Sitzung der Kommission für den Reichshaushalt am 27 März, 1900; Budgetkommission, 29 März 1900.
29  Bülow, *Deutsche Politik*, p. 57.
30  G. A. von Müller, "Fürst Bülow und die Marinefragen," *Front wider Bülow*, p. 186; *Der Kaiser . . .*, p. 78.
31  Tirpitz, *Der Aufbau der deutschen Weltmacht* (Stuttgart, 1924), pp. 94–6; GP, XXVIII, No. 10235, Bülow to Tirpitz, 30 November 1908, pp. 21–3.
32  Bülow, *Denkwürdigkeiten*, Bd I, p. 413.
33  Bülow, *Deutsche Politik*, p. 129; also p. 40.
34  BA, Bülow, *Nachlass*, No. 22, *G. A. Bülow*, 16 March 1898, signed Klehmet.
35  Winzen, *Bülows Weltmachtkonzept*, p. 89.
36  PAAA, England 78, Secr. Bülow to Holstein and Richtofen, 3 December 1904.
37  BA, Bülow, *Nachlass*, No. 24, "Sitzung der Kommission für den Reichshaushalt am 27 März. 1900;" Winzen, *Bülows Weltmachtkonzept*, p. 75.
38  Bülow, *Denkwürdigkeiten*, Bd I, p. 116.
39  ibid., Bd III, p. 17; p. 182.
40  Johannes Haller, *Aus dem Leben des Fürsten Philipp zu Eulenburg* (Berlin, 1924), p. 249.
41  BA, Bülow, *Nachlass*, No. 90, Holstein to Bülow, 17 February 1897.
42  *Holstein Papers*, Vol. 4, No. 630, Holstein to Hatzfeldt, 13 November 1897; esp. p. 50; BA, Bülow, *Nachlass*, No. 91, Holstein to Bülow, 25 July 1898.
43  Rich, *Holstein*, Vol. 2, pp. 562–3.
44  Bülow, *Denkwürdigkeiten*, Bd I, p. 431.
45  Rich, *Holstein*, Vol. 2, p. 613.
46  Paul M. Kennedy, "German world policy and the alliance negotiations with England, 1897–1900," *Journal of Modern History,* vol. 45, no. 4 (December 1973), p. 611; also *Antagonism*, pp. 245–9.
47  *Holstein Papers*, Vol. 4, No. 630, Holstein to Hatzfeldt, 13 November 1897, p. 50; Kennedy, *Antagonism*, p. 233.
48  Hatzfeldt, *Nachgelassene Papiere*, Vol. 2, No. 759, Holstein to Hatzfeldt, 16 May 1899, p. 1228 (my italics).
49  *Holstein Papers*, Vol. 4, No. 720, Bülow to Holstein, 28 November 1899, telegram, pp. 167–8. Also BA, Bülow, *Nachlass*, No. 91. Holstein's letter and Bülow's statement have not been found.
50  GP, XVIII, i, No. 5421, Holstein to Bülow, 16 April 1903, p. 69.
51  Berghahn, *Tirpitz-Plan*, p. 250.
52  Reichsarchiv, *Kriegsrüstung und Kriegswirtschaft* (Berlin, 1930), Vol. I, p. 58; *Anlage-Band*, No. 16, Gossler to Schlieffen, 8 June 1899, p. 57.
53  ibid., Vol. I, *Anlage-Band*, p. 59.
54  ibid., No. 18, Gossler to Schlieffen, 19 October 1899, p. 68.
55  Waldersee to Erwin Manteuffel, 8 February 1877, quoted in B.-F. Schulte, *Die deutsche Armee 1900–1914: Zwischen Beharren und Verändern* (Düsseldorf, 1977), p. 258.
56  ibid., pp. 265–97.
57  Einem, *Erinnerungen*, pp. 61–2, 82–3; *Front wider Bülow*, pp. 161, 166; Reichsarchiv, *Kriegsrüstung*, Vol. I, *Anlage-Band*, No. 22, Einem to Bülow, 3 June 1903, pp. 84–5; No. 23, Aufzeichnung Einem, Autumn 1903, pp. 85–7; No. 24, Einem to Schlieffen, 26 February 1904, p. 87.

58  ibid., Vol. I, *Anlage-Band*, No. 26, Einem to Schlieffen, 19 April 1904, p. 90.
59  See above, p. 58; also Reichsarchiv, *Kriegsrüstung,* Vol. I, pp. 31, 43–5.
60  ibid., *Anlage-Band*, Schlieffen's marginal comments "e" and "f" to No. 19, Oberhoffer to Gossler, 30 October 1899, p. 76.
61  ibid., No. 20, Schlieffen to Gossler, 10 November 1899, p. 77.
62  loc. cit.
63  ibid., p. 79.
64  Schulte, *Die deutsche Armee,* p. 392.
65  Hohenlohe, *Denkwürdigkeiten,* Bd III, Tirpitz to Hohenlohe, 28 October 1899, p. 536.
66  BA-MA, N 160/5, Tirpitz to Senden, 30 August 1900.
67  BA-MA, F 2044, PG 66074, "Protokoll der Staatsministerialsitzung vom 20. I. 1900," utilized by Berghahn, *Tirpitz-Plan,* p. 251, but not cited in detail.
68  Ritter, *Der Schlieffen-Plan,* p. 96.
69  Militärgeschichtliches Forschungsamt, Nachlass Schlieffen (Now BA-MA, N 43) Mappe II, Stück I/32. An den Chef des Generalstabes . . . Armeekorps. Signatur Grf. Schlieffen. Eurer Hockwohlgeborenen übersende ich anliegend die Schlussbesprechung des in November und Dezember d. Js. von mir geleiteten Kriegsspiels. Dez. 30. "*Chef des Generalstabes der Armee* J. Nr. 13088 Z. Schlussbesprechung. *Geheim* Berlin, den 23. Dez. 1905."
70  *Waldersee,* Vol. 3, entry for 10 January 1904, pp. 227–8.
71  Tirpitz, *Erinnerungen,* pp. 85–6.
72  BA-MA, N 253/4, Tirpitz's notes in pencil: Bülow on 19 August 1897 did not make a very good impression and on 21 August appeared as "somewhat patronizing."
73  Tirpitz, *Erinnerungen,* p. 86.
74  BA-MA, N 253/4, "Immed. Vortrag," 15 June 1897.
75  AHA, II, 8, Tirpitz to Eisendecher, 31 August 1897.
76  BA-MA, N 253/39, "Motive für die Organizationsänderung," n.d., in Tirpitz's hand.
77  ibid., N 253/235, Maltzahn to Tirpitz, 28 August 1895. According to *Deutsche Marinegeschichte der Neuzeit,* p. 143, Tirpitz decided to join the navy at the urging of Curt von Maltzahn. Salewski refers to a Carl von Maltzahn, however: *Tirpitz,* p. 11.
78  BA-MA, F 2044, PG 66075, "Auszüge aus der Schrift Maltzahns" with Tirpitz's marginal comments.
79  ibid., Wilhelm to Tirpitz, 28 September 1899.
80  ibid., Tirpitz to Bülow, 18 October 1899; Bülow to Tirpitz, 20 October 1899; Tirpitz to the Naval Cabinet, the Naval Station Commands Kiel and Wilhelmshaven, Inspectorate of the Educational and Training System, Command of the First Squadron, Chief of the Admiralty Staff, and Chief of the Cruiser Squadron, 22 October 1899; Berghahn, *Tirpitz-Plan,* p. 192; Deist, *Flottenpolitik,* pp. 88–92.
81  Deist, *Flottenpolitik,* p. 89.
82  BA-MA, N 160/11, "Erlebnisse als Chef des Marinekabinetts: Notizen und Aufzeichnungen. Zur Organisationfrage," 27 July 1897.
83  See above, pp. 115–16. Tirpitz's postscript appears at the bottom of his "Motive fur die Organisationsänderung," n.d., Summer 1898, BA-MA, N 253/39.
84  Hubatsch, *Der Admiralstab,* pp. 83; 237–9.
85  ibid., p. 239.
86  Walter Görlitz (ed.), *Der Kaiser . . . Aufzeichnungen des Chefs des Marinekabinetts Admiral Georg Alexander von Müller über die Ara Wilhelms II* (Göttingen, 1965), p. 51; Tirpitz, *Erinnerungen,* pp. 135–6.
87  BA-MA, N 253/4, "Notizen zum Immediatvortag-Indiensthaltungsplan bis 1903," 20 February 1899.
88  ibid., F 2044, PG 66075, "Notizen . . .," 28 November 1898.
89  ibid., N 255/8, Koester, Chief of the Baltic Sea Naval Station, to Diederichs, 20 December 1897; N 253/4, Bendemann, "Bemerkungen zum Gesetz," 15 August 1897; F 2044, PG 66075, Bendemann to Tirpitz, 6 October 1897.
90  See Holger H. Herwig, *The German Naval Officer Corps, 1890–1918: A Social and Political History* (London, 1973), esp. 98–101.
91  BA-MA, N 255/9, Senden to Diederichs, 30 March 1898.
92  Tirpitz, *Erinnerungen,* p. 204.
93  Bülow, *Denkwürdigkeiten,* Bd I, p. 109.

94   Hassell, *Tirpitz*, p. 171.
95   See above, pp. 50 ff.
96   BA-MA, N 253/20, A.K.O. signed by Wilhelm, countersigned by Tirpitz, 23 March 1901.
97   BA-MA, F 3302, PG 66704, Diederichs to Wilhelm, 11 January 1901.
98   ibid., N 253/20, Diederichs to Tirpitz, 10 February 1901.
99   ibid., "Niederschrift des Vortrages . . . von der Goltz, 19.3.1901 in Berlin," sent by von der Goltz to Tirpitz on 29 March 1901.
100  See below, pp. 252 ff.; 277 ff.
101  ibid., F 2044, PG 66075, Prince Heinrich to Tirpitz, 21 March 1903.
102  ibid., memorandum in Tirpitz's handwriting, n.d., and typescript memorandum corrected by Tirpitz, "Über die organizatorische Weiterorganization unserer aktiven Schlachtflotte in den Jahren," n.d.: also A.K.O. signed by Wilhelm, countersigned by Tirpitz, 29 June 1903.
103  ibid., F 2046, PG 66086, "Protokoll der Sitzung am 12 September 1903."

# 11 Diplomatic Background to Naval Operations, 1899–1904

Waldersee reports Bülow as stating toward the end of 1903 that "in foreign policy we had to avoid complications until the fleet was available in the strength required by the Emperor."[1] Although it is uncertain whether Bülow had a clear concept of the required strength of the navy or the time when this strength would be available, contemporary evidence abounds to the effect that his main task was to get the navy built and to avoid war until it was ready. Indeed, from 1899 to 1904 the international political situation was favorable to Germany. From October 1899 until 1902 the Boer War was a serious embarrassment to Britain. Her frictions with France and Russia gave Germany the opportunity to pursue the policy of the free hand. In December 1899, about half a year after the new Admiralty Staff picked up the threads of naval operational planning, Bülow reported to his friend Philipp Eulenburg that "our foreign position is brilliant."[2] Tirpitz was in full agreement with Bülow's policy. He, too, stressed that "The fleet construction required, in order to succeed, peace," and spoke of the "egg dance which German diplomacy has to perform before the naval armaments are completed." On 16 November 1899 he inquired from the naval attaché in London whether the British government planned any new naval increases as a response to the Second Navy Bill or considered Germany a naval opponent. He had opposed the acquisition of Kiao-chow and, although reluctant to give up the German rights in Samoa and the Tonga islands short of the risk of war, he warned that "the Samoa question was under no circumstances to lead to a war with England."[3] Nor did he like the expedition to suppress the Boxer uprising, which involved the removal from European waters of an entire division of ships of the line, and agreed to it only when Bülow was willing to guarantee that in the near future there existed no danger of war with Britain and little danger of war with France.[4] Holstein, however, was either less aware of or less concerned about the need to avoid diplomatic crises while the fleet was incapable of facing Britain, and charged Tirpitz with loss of nerve during a number of risky situations.[5]

Behind the concern to avoid international complications lay the fear of a British attack on the German navy before it was capable of defending itself: the Copenhagen complex. It affected Tirpitz, many other naval officers, Bülow,[6] and a man as calm as Friedrich, Grand Duke of Baden, who thought in January 1900, at the time of the British seizure of *Bundesrath*, that there existed elements in Britain who on account of military failures in South Africa "now wished to create a diversion at sea to show the importance of English might and also to deliver a destructive blow to our blooming and competitive trade."[7] Thus caution was in order. The German fleet was not to appear conspicuous to the British.[8] Diplomatic entanglements were to be avoided. As Bülow later noted: "In 1900 and 1901 England (. . . Chamberlain) wanted to engage us as a mercenary on the Continent. England wanted to push us forward against Russia and France and they wanted to push us forward against England."[9]

In his memoirs Bülow frankly admitted: "We could neither provoke England nor bind ourselves to England . . . If we bound ourselves by treaty to England we would more or less renounce the implementation of our fleet plans, for they were hardly compatible with an entirely honest and trustworthy Anglo-German alliance."[10] Recent research has supported Bülow's admission. Peter Winzen has gone further and pointed out that an Anglo-German alliance would have made impossible the execution of the final stage of Bülow's master-plan: a German offensive alliance with Russia against Britain at a suitable occasion during an eventually inevitable Anglo-Russian war. Winzen convincingly demonstrates how Bülow blocked the alliance negotiations, sabotaged any real improvement in Anglo-German relations, and promoted the growth of anti-British sentiment in Germany as a means of national solidarity.[11] He regards Bülow's dispatch of 15 January 1901 to Eckhardtstein as the clearest revelation of his deliberately concealed final aim:

> The progressive influence of so-called imperialism on the behavior of the British government abroad has hitherto not been damaging to us and can in certain circumstances be useful, namely when it is directed even more strongly and decisively than before against Russia and escalates the existing Anglo-Russian differences to armed conflicts.[12]

Bülow had reflected on the opportunities presented by a strong German fleet in case of conflicts between Britain and other powers earlier. On 6 December 1899 he remarked during a dinner at which both Wilhelm and Hohenlohe were present that, in case of a British attack on a France deserted by Russia, Germany would have to remain neutral. "If we had a respectable fleet, we could have gone with France, but this is not possible now."[13] His interest in a partition of the British Empire is shown in his comment to Hatzfeldt's observation of 16 December 1899.[14] On the whole, however— as Winzen correctly maintains—it was his policy not to weaken Britain so much that the partition of her empire would occur before Germany could through the possession of a strong navy get her share of the spoils.[15]

Neither Wilhelm II, the Foreign Office staff, nor the London embassy fully understood Bülow's policy toward Britain. Wilhelm's attitude toward his mother's homeland was a mixture of love and envy. He was certainly not consistently hostile toward Britain, and in 1898–1901 he favored the conclusion of a treaty with her on terms that were not disadvantageous to Germany. Nor is there evidence that he favored ganging up on her with Russia. At the end of 1901, however, he did envisage a German–American alliance against her.[16] Although speculating about a transoceanic alliance against Britain,[17] Wilhelm was genuinely indignant when he was informed of British suspicions "of having placed himself on Russia's side against England."[18] But from 1901 to 1903 he had promised to protect Russia's back toward Europe while she was involved in the Far East, and in 1903 he sought to establish closer relations with her.[19]

Although distrustful of Britain, Holstein sought improved relations and an eventual, truly reciprocal, alliance with her. Both he and his friend Hatzfeldt hoped that specific treaties over individual issues would pave the way to such an alliance.[20] With the exception of Bülow, the leading figures of the Foreign Office agreed with Holstein. Led by Klehmet, in the spring of 1901 they favored Britain's joining the Triple Alliance. None the less, Bülow's policy prevailed.[21]

Anglo-German relations deteriorated soon after the dissolution of the High Command. With the arrival in Berlin on 29 March 1899 of the news of Anglo-American military action against the German-supported Mata-afa faction in Samoa, German indignation erupted. Both Bülow and Wilhelm considered breaking off diplomatic relations with Britain, and Tirpitz allegedly feared that Britain and the United States intended to destroy the German fleet before it posed a threat to them.[22] The continuing Samoan crisis, the failure on the part of Britain to consult the German authorities over the Saxe-Coburg-Gotha succession issue, and Wilhelm's remonstrances over the bad British treatment of him and his country made Anglo-German relations tense until June.[23] Thus there existed diplomatic justification for the Admiralty Staff to become involved in operational planning against Britain. Nor was there cause to terminate the planning once it had been started. The Tirpitz fleet was built against Britain, and soon the preparations for the passage of the Second Navy Bill were to generate and utilize anglophobia. The anglophobia of the German press was encouraged by Bülow and fanned by the hostilities of the Boer War; the British press reciprocated.[24] Bülow's "hammer and anvil" speech of 11 December 1899 threw cold water on whatever improvement in Anglo-German relations had occurred.[25] Warmer Anglo-German relations established by Wilhelm's visit to his grandmother Victoria's deathbed in January 1901[26] cooled when Bülow stated in the Reichstag on 15 March 1901 that the Anglo-German China agreement did not extend to Manchuria.[27] The German Chancellor's deliberately strong "bite on granite" response in the Reichstag to Chamberlain's Edinburgh speech of 8 January 1902 provided an immense stimulus to germanophobia in Britain. By that time it was becoming obvious to Bülow and the rest of the German political leadership that Germany was increasingly viewed in Britain as the major foe.[28]

On 21 February 1902, Metternich, Hatzfeldt's successor in London, concluded a report to Bülow: "I wouldn't give twopence for Anglo-German relations."[29] On 2 August, Bülow instructed Metternich:

We must leave it to time to calm excited minds and above all we must take a stand against the insane and equally malicious view, which unfortunately seems to have adherents in England and is probably not sufficiently strongly opposed by Lascelles,[30] that we intend to attack England after having increased our fleet.[31]

The concern with British hostility continued. During his visit to Britain in November, Wilhelm himself warned Bülow about British irritation with Germany.[32] And on 19 January 1903, at the time of the Venezuela crisis, Metternich reported: "As long as I have known England, I have never observed such bitterness toward any other nation as now against us."[33] Bülow attributed this attitude to fears of the German navy and extravagant pan-German utterances—both his own doing.[34] While in the course of 1903 German leadership noted an abatement of British hostility, the reverse was the case in 1904, particularly after the Dogger Bank incident of 21 October.[35]

The operational planning of the Admiralty Staff against Britain continued to have its political justification. But what about the reasons for the planning against Germany's more traditional enemies, those of the Dual Alliance? One reason was that this planning was traditional, going back to the 1880s. Another was that it corroborated the planning of the Great General Staff. Actually, however, there appeared less justification for it in view of the German political estimates of the possibility of war with the two powers because of their decreased aggressiveness or in view of the disappearance after February 1901 of the traditional need to reinforce Italy's obligations as a member of the Triple Alliance.

Bülow himself observed in August 1899 that since Fashoda the French wanted to improve their relations with Germany.[36] In the course of the following year the Paris embassy reported the presence of strong anti-British feeling and waning revanchist sentiment among the French, predicting that Franco-German relations would improve further.[37] But Berlin remained cautious. On 13 June 1901, Holstein and Bülow advised the new ambassador in Paris, Prince Radolin, that "if the new French government decides that a rapprochement with Germany will not offend the instinct of the masses there will easily be found areas in which cooperation promises advantages for both sides. Nevertheless, any premature attempts of this type could result in mutual suspicion and shyness." They therefore advised that for the time being Franco-German cooperation be confined to the cultural and social spheres.[38] Shortly thereafter, when faced by French proposals for cooperation, they commented that "it will be difficult for Germany to take up new obligations as long as old ones continued undiminished, whose change could only be countenanced when both parties announced their intention to guarantee each other's possessions,"[39] which meant that France was to renounce Alsace-Lorraine. Throughout 1901 and 1902, Radolin's reports from Paris stressed the waning of French revanchism and the desire of the Waldeck-Rousseau's ministry to establish good relations with Germany.[40] None the less, Berlin remained cautious about collaboration with France. In August 1901, Holstein held a revanche-inspired French attack on Germany, supported by a Russia driven by the pan-Slav movement, to be possible[41] and in 1903 thought that France would because of revanchist considerations fight against Germany with any enemy of hers.[42]

Both Bülow and Holstein took for granted the hostility between Britain and the Dual Alliance. On 30 January, Metternich had reported that negotiations were under way between Chamberlain and the French ambassador concerning the settlement of all Anglo-French colonial differences.[43] Further information about an agreement chiefly involving Morocco reached the German Foreign Office at the end of September 1902.[44] But the feasibility of this agreement was rejected by both the German chargé d'affaires in London, Eckhardstein, and by Holstein.[45] Both men independently concluded that Britain would not freely yield Morocco to France. On 20 February 1903 Bülow and on 7 March the Secretary of State Oswald von Richthofen agreed that the concession of Morocco to France would be too great a sacrifice by Britain. Bülow further thought that it was not in France's interests to enter into an agreement with Britain since it would mean the end of the Russian alliance.[46] Nor did the view change upon the receipt of Eckhardstein's report of 10 May 1903, according to which a comprehensive Anglo-French colonial agreement was about to be concluded, which, instead of contributing to a break-up of the Franco-Russian alliance, as Bülow expected, would lead to a Russian–British–French alignment:

> The new triple alliance would be suitable to France because it would thus obtain financial relief, to Russia because it could easily take on new loans, and to England because it may yearn now, after the Boer War, even more for absolute peace than after the Crimean War.[47]

Bülow did seek the views of Metternich, the chargé d'affaires in London Bernstorff, the ambassador to France Radolin, the ambassador to Russia Alvensleben, and consulted Holstein.[48]

On the basis of their reactions Bülow informed Wilhelm on 20 May in a memorandum which he prepared in consultation with Holstein that Eckhardstein's fears were not shared by others and summarized the more optimistic views of the diplomats whom he had consulted. He represented the question of the possession of Tangier as the main stumbling-block to the solution of the Moroccan dispute between Britain and France, one which was not likely to be removed in the near future, and viewed the obstacles to an Anglo-Russian agreement as even greater.[49]

Nor did an Anglo-French rapprochement strike Bülow as altogether bad as long as there was no corresponding Anglo-Russian agreement. The latter struck him at different times as either improbable or undesirable. In refuting Eckhardstein's memorandum he described it as improbable; on 13 March 1902 he had informed Metternich that

> An agreement of England with Russia would always be tantamount to England's declaration of bankruptcy in Asia and Europe. Time runs for Russia, and any English paying court to Russia [*couressieren an Russland*] only accelerates the decline of English prestige in Asia and Europe.[50]

Improbable as this agreement was, he tried to prevent it since it would entirely wreck his policy. He therefore promoted—and welcomed—the conclusion of the Anglo-Japanese alliance, encouraged the outbreak of hostilities between Russia and Japan,[51] and opposed the replacement of the Russian ambassador in London by "a younger and more active personality."[52] Without an Anglo-Russian rapprochement Bülow expected an Anglo-French agreement to alienate Russia from France and to increase the chances of her entry into the German orbit.[53] Wilhelm, however, did not share his Chancellor's optimism and doubted whether an Anglo-French rapprochement was incompatible with good Franco-Russian relations.[54]

The publication of the Anglo-French colonial agreement of 8 April 1904 none the less produced a shock in Berlin. Baroness von Spitzenberg wrote of the deep discouragement of the Foreign Office.[55] Holstein, who had earlier realized that a rapprochement between Britain and France would weaken Italy's ties to Germany and Austria, was soon to speak of Germany's encirclement. He realized, moreover, that "no overseas policy is possible against England and France." According to him, German *Weltpolitik* was thus bankrupt.[56] Wilhelm considered the agreement as providing France with the predominant position in Morocco, possibly at the expense of German economic interests, and, by removing French enmity, making Britain less considerate towards Germany.[57] In a lengthy report Bernstorff argued from London, however, that the agreement was primarily an attempt on Britain's part to benefit from the weakening of Russia in Asia. The "entente cordiale" was only dangerous to Germany if Britain entertained hostile intentions toward her. But this was not the case in spite of the growth of British annoyance toward her since the outbreak of the Russo-Japanese War. And if the French "now believed that England would stand by them in a war of revenge against Germany they would be as disappointed as the Japanese are now. France could scarcely expect more from the British than a few benevolent newspaper articles."[58] Bülow was in strong agreement with Bernstorff[59] and forwarded his report to Wilhelm, conceding only that the agreement gave both France and Britain more diplomatic weight and freedom of movement and served as a magnet to Italy.[60] He also doubted whether Britain would take her obligation "to support France diplomatically in Morocco particularly seriously."[61] Metternich shared these doubts.[62] However briefly, Wilhelm, as his marginal comments indicate, was also impressed by Bernstorff's report.

Bülow, as stated before, saw Russia as an eventual ally against Britain. He was consistent in seeking her friendship so as to prepare the ground for alliance and granted her a number of favors.[63] It became German policy to encourage her to become more deeply involved in the Far East so as to relieve the tension between her and Austria and the pressure of the Dual Alliance on Germany. None the less, Russo-German relations were not consistently friendly. In the spring and summer of 1899 they deteriorated as the Russian government opposed Germany's penetration of Asia Minor and her perceived intentions of taking over the Dual Monarchy if it disintegrated. Annoyed also by Russia's Foreign Minister, Count M. N. Muraviev, Wilhelm minuted that her Napoleonic ambitions would bring her to an end similar to that of the Second Empire.[64] In the course of 1900 the Foreign Office entertained suspicions about Russian policy and misgivings about the anti-German utterances of the Russian press which appear to have increased toward the end of the year.[65] By then Wilhelm's hostility toward Russia had also grown, leading him to remark that the Russians were Asiatics and had to be treated as such.[66] In December 1900, Holstein recommended that in the face of Russia's threats and arrogance Germany avoid making any concessions or leaving any impression of being dependent on her.[67] Soon thereafter Lüttwitz, the military attaché in St Petersburg, reported the discussion of joint Franco-Russian deployment against the Triple Alliance during the visit to St Petersburg of the Chief of the French General Staff, General Pendezec,[68] and Schlieffen wrote to Bülow with some concern of unprecedented Russian trial mobilization measures along the entire German border. Bülow felt impelled to inform Wilhelm and to undertake inquiries in St Petersburg.[69] Operational planning against the Dual Alliance was not altogether out of order.

Some improvement of Russo-German relations set in with Nicholas II's visit to Danzig in September 1901, prompting Bülow to describe the diplomatic situation "as entirely peaceful and satisfactory;"[70] and the meeting of the two emperors in August 1902 in Reval struck him as a total success.[71]

While Bülow courted Russia, he suspected that her government was trying to embroil Germany in a conflict with Britain and Japan. Nor was he sure that she would restrain France from a revanchist policy toward Germany,[72] or that she might not reach an agreement with England after all. He welcomed the conclusion of the Anglo-Japanese alliance since it would make such an agreement entirely impossible, prompt Japan to block Russia's advance in the Far East, and increase the prospect of a war between them. Subsequently he encouraged Britain to take a strong stand in the Far East, instructing Metternich to inform the British government that in case of an Anglo-Russian war Germany would remain neutral and thus assure the neutrality of France.[73]

A Russo-Japanese war appeared imminent in May 1903, and from January 1904 Bülow and the Foreign Office did their best to promote its outbreak. Such a war appeared to provide Germany with several opportunities. It would definitely free her from the vise of the Dual Alliance, increase her freedom of action in Europe, make possible a preventive war against France, and make Russia more dependent on her, perhaps opening the door to an immediate or eventual Russo-German alliance. If Russia was victorious in the war against Japan, and if Britain joined her oriental ally, Germany might, given a favorable military and naval situation, join Russia and achieve the final aim that Bülow set for her. But Bülow and the Foreign Office would have to tread their ground carefully, averting any suspicion that Germany was trying to benefit from the situation and avoiding any alliance with Russia that would be disadvantageous to her.[74]

Holstein was particularly cautious about a Russian alliance. He expressed his reservations on 12 July 1902[75] and had become even more specific and pessimistic by April 1903. As he wrote to Bülow:

Russian reinsurance [*Rückendeckung*] was adequate for Germany as long as the latter only pursued a Middle European policy. In today's *Weltpolitik* a "rapprochement" of Russia with Germany—under which some sort of general or specific alliance is thought of—can be advantageous only to Russia. If Germany protects her back as coastguard in the Baltic Sea, Russia can on land occupy whatever territory she wants from Scutari to Korea while Germany is for her expansion relegated to the sea where, as Russia's assistant, she will be confronted with the concerted envy of England and America.[76]

At this time he saw no chance for the conclusion of a Continental League, for France would remain neutral and Austria-Hungary and Italy would not oppose Britain. Russia would be able to establish her hegemony over Asia whereas Germany's seaborne trade would be destroyed for at least a generation. German expansion was possible only through victories at sea, not on land, ". . . and I do not assume that our navy, even if we built ships with the utmost effort, hopes as an ally of Russia to defeat England and America."[77]

The impracticability of a Russo-German alliance came to be more widely recognized in November 1903 when Czar Nicholas II suggested to a receptive Wilhelm that their countries jointly guarantee Denmark's neutrality so as to prevent the British navy from entering the Baltic.[78] Such a guarantee could have involved joint Russo-German naval and military action in the Danish Sound and Belts and fitted into the current planning of the Admiralty Staff. Its Chief, Wilhelm Büchsel, however, objected to the guarantee because it would discourage the British navy from entering Danish waters and render its recent work futile.[79] By 12 November the Secretary of State, Richthofen, and soon thereafter Bülow had come to adhere to Holstein's objections. Thus already before the outbreak of the war between Russia and Japan one of Bülow's options—an alliance with Russia—was being eliminated.

If Bülow, who since the 1880s when he served in St Petersburg had overestimated Russian power, expected a Russian victory over Japan to lead to an Anglo-Russian war from which Germany might benefit, his expectation in a Russian victory was not shared by Wilhelm and the military. Already in March 1901 the Kaiser had observed that "Japan was undoubtedly as superior to the Russians at sea as on land."[80] In April 1903 the military attaché in St Petersburg reported that Russia would be at a disadvantage in East Asia as long as the Trans-Siberian Railway remained incomplete.[81] In January 1904 the Great General Staff informed the Foreign Office that it did not then consider the Russian army to be a match for the Japanese.[82] To what extent had Bülow taken Russian military weakness into his calculations? One suspects not very much. In July 1904, as Russia was suffering military reverses at the hands of Japan, Richthofen added to Holstein's old arguments against a Russo-German alliance that of Russian military weakness: "the strength of Russia as an ally has been decreased for one knows not how many years." Richthofen's memorandum had lines in the margin drawn by Bülow, indicating his agreement.[83] By December

1904, with the decrepit Russian Baltic fleet sailing to meet its end at the hands of the Japanese, Bülow had definitely realized that within the next six years the German fleet would not be ready to face Britain.[84]

From 1899 to 1905 the Triple Alliance, as Bülow was aware, was an insignificant factor in *Weltpolitik,* for it could be of no avail to Germany in conflicts with Britain and the United States of America. Moreover, German representatives reported that both Austria-Hungary and Italy would be alienated from Germany by growing tensions between her and Great Britain.[85] But in the area of Continental policy, in the face of France and Russia, the Triple Alliance still played a role. It is surprising, however, that the German leadership did not take into account how the pursuit of *Weltpolitik* would affect relations with Austria and Italy. Continental policy appears to have been isolated from world policy. It was not the pursuit of *Weltpolitik* alone, however, that undermined the reliability of Germany's traditional allies. Austria-Hungary was weakened internally by national strife in her non-Hungarian territories and, in Hungary, by the attacks of the Independence Party on the Compromise of 1867. Italy's reliability as an ally was becoming extremely questionable because of her rapprochement with France, growing hostility toward Austria, and indifference toward Germany.

Already, in March 1899, Bülow had expressed doubts about the solidarity of the Triple Alliance. While his doubts diminished toward the end of the year,[86] those of others did not. Thus Schlieffen was reported as saying at the beginning of January 1900 that he no longer believed that Austria-Hungary was capable of launching an offensive against Russia.[87] From 1899 to 1905, German representatives in the Dual Monarchy were telling a generally dire tale, complaining about instability and growing hostility toward Germany in the non-Hungarian parts of the Dual Monarchy and of Hungarian separatism. Wilhelm, perhaps, summed up the German attitude by remarking on a report from the ambassador to Vienna, Wedel: "thus the Triple Alliance seems to be gently lost in the rushes. Nice prospects."[88]

Italy's unreliability as member of the Triple Alliance increased with the accession of Victor Emmanuel III after the assassination of his father Humbert on 29 July 1900.[89] On 12 February 1900, Wedel had stressed that Italy was more sympathetic toward Britain. Referring to the fact that Italy imported more than 95 percent of her coal from Britain, he had stated that "Italy finds herself almost absolutely dependent on England not only economically but to a certain extent militarily."[90] This dependence was also stressed by Wedel almost two years later. Bülow then expressed his full agreement with the ambassador.[91] In view of Bülow's deliberate anti-British policy, the link between Italy and the Triple Alliance was weak indeed.

Although in September 1900 the Italian military had shown interest in naval cooperation between the powers of the Triple Alliance, by February 1901 the entire question of German–Italian military cooperation suffered a serious setback when Victor Emmanuel told the German military attaché in Rome, Major Oskar von Chelius, that he opposed arrangements that had been made for dispatching Italian troops to Germany to fight on the German southern flank against France, since this action would expose the Italian coast to French attack.[92] The German ambassador in Rome, Count Karl von Wedel, thereupon voiced his reservations about the value of the Italian alliance: "I still consider the Italian alliance useful and necessary, but not actively important unless the English fleet provides Italy with the assurances without which she can scarcely decide to weaken her already inadequate coastal defenses." He closed his dispatch by citing Bismarck's comment that the alliance with Italy merely assured "that she would not bite Austria's heels."[93] Schlieffen, responding to Chelius' and Wedel's reports, informed Bülow that the dispatch of troops to Germany was the only way in which the Italians could significantly contribute to a joint war effort against France. The only alternative, a landing on the southern coast of France, had as the prerequisite the destruction of the French fleet, for which "the Italians lack not so much a fleet of adequate strength as self-confidence and joyous courage to wage war at sea against a stronger enemy." Britain alone was capable of assisting Italy in undertaking such a landing. Some 240,000 troops were required to defend the Alpine boundary against France. Without a landing on the French coast or the transport of troops to Germany, 700,000 men would be left "to defend the peninsula against a landing not contemplated by the French as long as they wage war against Gemany, and to prevent the bombardment of a coastal city, e.g. Naples, which would be impossible since a field-army, however large, is impotent against a few armored ships located at a great distance."

Since it was in any case unlikely that the Italians would send the promised troops to Germany, Schlieffen recommended that they be freed from this obligation. The sole positive advantage that the Italian alliance gave Germany was in the 150,000 French troops who would be diverted from the German to the Italian front. The negative advantage of the alliance was that it prevented Italy from becoming Germany's and Austria's enemy and enhanced Austria's military effectiveness as an ally by enabling her to concentrate her entire strength against Russia.[94] Schlieffen thus saw the British and not the German navy as the guarantee of Italy's membership of the Triple Alliance. Political considerations regarding Italy were thus removed as a factor in German naval planning against France—something of which the German Admiralty Staff was not directly informed.

In January 1902, Bülow took a hard line about the conditions for the renewal of the Triple Alliance, wanting to make the renewal dependent on the clarification of the Franco-Italian relationship which had shown signs of becoming closer. He stressed that the international situation made the Italian alliance less necessary for Germany than it had been earlier.[95] Wedel did not fully concur, wanting the Triple Alliance to be renewed. Agreeing with German military opinion that not much help was to be expected from Italy militarily, he still thought that she would be of some help. "The positive service that we expect from her is that she does not bite Austria's heels and pins a certain part of the French army down on the Alpine border."[96] Were she freed from the bonds of the Triple Alliance, Italy's chauvinism, expansionism, radicalism, and republicanism would become rampant.

Bülow himself now admitted that he was not entirely indifferent to the continuation of the Triple Alliance when he termed "entirely true" a statement by the former Italian Foreign Minister Visconti Venosta to the effect that "the Triple Alliance paralyzed the irredentist and other turbulent Italian elements. Were the Triple Alliance to end, serious conflicts with Austria would probably arise at once. This point was in his opinion one of the most important ones in the entire Triple Alliance."[97] None the less, the German leadership adamantly refused to make any changes in the terms of the Triple Alliance to accommodate the Italians, viewing such changes as a French gain. On 28 June 1902 the Triple Alliance was renewed unchanged."[98]

Soon thereafter the Chief of the Italian General Staff, Lieutenant-General Saletta, left Schlieffen with the impression during a visit to Germany "as if nothing had changed in the arrangements of the Triple Alliance and as if in particular all the military arrangements were still in force" and spoke of the contingency measures to be taken if the passage of the Italian troops to Germany through Austrian territory were blocked.[99] Schlieffen qualified the impression by remarking that Saletta did not show his earlier friendship for the Triple Alliance. Wedel reported from Rome on 18 November that both Saletta and Victor Emmanuel were delighted by Italy's relief from her military obligations and that, although Italy's military leadership was proposing a conference to test the arrangements for the transport of Italian troops to Germany, he did not expect "material advantages from the renewed arrangements"—a conclusion with which Wilhelm concurred.[100]

The skepticism of the German leadership would have been more than justified if it had known that two days after the renewal of the Triple Alliance an agreement had been signed between the Italian Foreign Minister, Giulio Prinetti, and the French ambassador in Rome, Camille Barrère, according to which Prinetti in effect renounced Italy's obligations to her Triplice partners.[101]

In the latter part of 1903 the German leadership took cognizance of extensive anti-Austrian and anti-German agitation in Italy in the light of which Bülow threatened to dissolve the Triple Alliance.[102] The proposed visit of the King of Italy to Paris led Wedel's successor, Count Anton Monts, and his chargé d'affaires, Gottlieb von Jagow, to expect Franco-Italian relations to become more intimate.[103] They expected irredentism, which was also associated with anti-German sentiments, to grow and to influence any Italian government. Wilhelm concurred. On 18 December, Bülow summed up the Italian situation for Wilhelm's benefit to the effect that it "had very much changed to Germany's disadvantage, but that the position was far from lost in regard to France."[104] By that time both he and Schlieffen had concluded that Italian reinforcements were no longer to be expected in Alsace.[105]

On 3 March 1904, Holstein had observed that the rapprochement between Britain and France further undermined Italy's loyalty as a member of the Triple Alliance. He correctly suspected that there existed a Franco-Italian treaty which made her obligations to her partners regarding

France invalid. Yet Italy would not formally leave the alliance, for she would "as a member of the Triple Alliance be better treated and obtain better terms from France and all other enemies of the Triple Alliance than an isolated Italy. In this the dupes . . . would be Germany and Austria, and, indeed, not secretly, but before the eyes of the entire world." He advised that Italy be threatened with the re-establishment of the Three Emperors' League. Realizing the different pressures at work in world policy and Continental policy, he added "whatever effect the Three Emperors' League would have on Germany's overseas interests, nothing could withstand this group on the European continent."[106]

In spite of these massive doubts about Italian reliability, Bülow still recommended to Wilhelm on 5 March 1905 that it was not in German interests

> to reject the Italians entirely or, by offending their strongly developed national vanity, to drive them to the side of the enemy. For peacetime and for all international combinations it is in our interest to keep the Triple Alliance as intact as possible, if only because the Italians, as long as they are still in the Triple Alliance, are viewed by our enemies with distrust. In the event of complications we need have no illusions about active Italian cooperation. But it will still be useful if Italy remains neutral instead of going with France.[107]

Wilhelm, however, expressed himself as less than satisfied with Bülow's expectations from the Italian alliance.[108]

German–American relations were such as to induce the Admiralty Staff to continue the planning against the United States which had been started in the High Command.[109] German anger and frustration over being unable to benefit from the Spanish–American War and resentment over the Manila incident were aggravated by the reopening of the Samoan issue.[110] In June 1899 the German ambassador in Washington, Holleben, reported:

> Only once before, on the occasion of the first Samoan conflict, has there been serious talk of a war between Germany and the United States. Today the possibility of such a war lies much nearer, and it will be good to remember this possibility in any dealings with the United States.[111]

In 1900, Holleben further stated that if Germany wanted to be a world power a confrontation with the United States was inevitable. Wilhelm remained concerned about the American economic challenge and was to advocate the establishment of a Continental customs union as the appropriate response.[112] In 1901–03, German naval circles, particularly Tirpitz, were interested in acquiring bases in the Caribbean and on the Latin American coast. The German naval attaché in Washington, Kapitän-Leutnant Hubert von Rebeur-Paschwitz, argued that such bases were necessary in a future military collision between Germany and the United States.[113]

German–American friction continued over the British–German–Italian blockade of Venezuela, who had defaulted on the repayment of her foreign loans. There were American protests,[114] particularly after the German cruiser *Vineta* leveled Fort San Carlos.[115] As President Roosevelt told the German extraordinary legate to Washington, Speck von Sternburg, on 18 February 1903: "The German warships involved in the blockade had seen in the fleet of Admiral Dewey their future enemy; on the other hand, Dewey's people had seen in Germany's ships their next battle object."[116]

Germany's frictions with the United States more than those with other great powers, except Japan, directly involved naval forces, and any war between the two powers would initially have to be fought at sea. Thus it is not altogether surprising that the new Admiralty Staff continued to work on operations against the United States until 1906 in spite of their fantastic nature in the light of the international political constellation.

In view of Germany's poor relations with Japan since the Peace of Shimonoseki in 1894 and her pro-Russian and anti-Japanese policy during the Russo-Japanese War, it is understandable that war with Japan continued to be considered in the contingency plans provided for German ships abroad.

The diplomatic situation as perceived by German leaders from 1899 to 1905 justified naval planning against Great Britain, the United States, and Japan. The unreliability of Italy made naval operations against the French northern coast for the encouragement of better Italian cooperation futile. Planning against Russia was an increasingly academic exercise with her growing involvement in the Far East. Planning against France was less necessary and should have taken closer consideration of her increasing rapprochement with Britain, unless a preventive war against her was being considered. In such a case, however, the contingency plans should have dealt with operations against Britain as well if she were to support France. Very definitely the Anglo-French rapprochement and the military and naval reverses of Russia should have led to the re-examination of the premisses of the Tirpitz Plan: the one power that could still remotely come into consideration as a naval ally against Britain, the United States of America, was perceived as being hostile to Germany.

## Notes: Chapter 11

1   *Waldersee*, Vol. 3, entry of 8 December 1903, p. 222.
2   BA, Eulenburg Correspondenz, 54, 1899, Bülow to Eulenburg, 6 December 1899; also Winzen, *Bülows Weltmachtkonzept*, p. 224.
3   Tirpitz, *Erinnerungen*, p. 163; Kelly, "Naval policy," fo. 161; GP XIV, ii, No. 4107, Tirpitz to Bülow, 11 October 1899, pp. 660–2; Berghahn, *Tirpitz-Plan*, p. 384; BA-MA, N 160/5; Tirpitz to Senden, 15 July 1900; Bülow, *Denkwürdigkeiten*, Bd I, p. 461.
4   BA-MA, N 253/20, Tirpitz to Prince Heinrich, 14 July 1900.
5   *Holstein Papers*, Vol. 4, No. 792, diary entry of 11 January 1902, p. 245.
6   Bülow, *Denkwürdigkeiten*, Bd I, p. 115.
7   Hohenlohe, *Denkwürdigkeiten*, Bd III, Friedrich von Baden to Hohenlohe, 9 January 1900, p. 555.
8   Hence in February 1900 Bülow counseled against the visit of a German warship to Cherbourg: PAAA, Deutschland 138, Bd 17, Bülow to Wilhelm, 11 February 1900; Berghahn, *Tirpitz-Plan* , pp. 382–3.

9   BA, Bülow, *Nachlass*/153, 1900, II., 2; 199, II., 8.
10  Bülow, *Denkwürdigkeiten*, Bd I, pp. 115–16.
11  Kennedy, "German World Policy," pp. 605–25; Berghahn, *Tirpitz-Plan*, pp. 380–401; 411–15; Winzen, *Bülows Weltmachtkonzept*, pp. 17, 52–9, 156–75, 211–30, 321–5, 359–61; also Rich, *Holstein*, Vol. 2, p. 662.
12  Winzen, *Bülows Weltmachtkonzept*, p. 360. Bülow had welcomed the prospects of an Anglo-Russian war earlier in his diplomatic career: Kennedy, *Antagonism*, p. 226.
13  BA, Hohenlohe, *Nachlass*, Rep. 100, XXII, A 19, C. Hohenlohe to Alexander Hohenlohe, 6 December 1899.
14  BA, Bülow, *Nachlass*/23, Hatzfeldt to Bülow, 16 December 1899 (Bülow's italics).
15  Winzen, *Bülows Weltmachtkonzept*, p. 210.
16  PAAA, England 78, secr. Bd 5, Wilhelm's comment on Metternich to Foreign Office, 29 October 1901.
17  GP, XVIII, ii, No. 5840, Wilhelm's minute on Metternich to Foreign Office, 21 December 1901, p. 727.
18  PAAA, England 78, Bd 16, Richthofen to Wilhelm, 7 April 1901, copy. Wilhelm minuted: "Hölle und Teufel" and "Mir solches zuzutrauen."
19  ibid., Russland 131, Geh., Bd 9, Bülow, Sorrent, to Foreign Office, 15 April 1903, reporting Wilhelm's instructions that Russia's suspicions about Edward VII's visit to Paris should be cultivated so as to draw her closer to Germany.
20  See in particular Rich, *Holstein*, Vol. 2, pp. 571, 579, 583, 600, 611, 615, 626–7, 630, 635–42, 649, 662.
21  ibid., p. 668; Winzen, *Bülows Weltmachtkonzept*, pp. 321–5, 330, 341; Kennedy, *Antagonism*, pp. 245–6.
22  Kennedy, *Samoan Tangle*, esp. p. 167; Bülow, *Denkwürdigkeiten*, Bd I, p. 283; BA, Bülow, *Nachlass* 154, 1899.
23  Kennedy, *Samoan Tangle*, pp. 178–84.
24  Winzen, *Bülows Weltmachtkonzept*, pp. 229–30.
25  ibid., pp. 226–7.
26  ibid., pp. 304–5.
27  ibid., pp. 309–10.
28  ibid., pp. 363–7.
29  *Holstein Papers*, Vol. 4, No. 799, Metternich to Bülow, 21 February 1902, p. 254.
30  British ambassador in Berlin.
31  *Holstein Papers*, Vol. 4, No. 805, Bülow to Metternich, 2 August 1902, p. 261.
32  GP, XVII, No. 5031, Wilhelm to Bülow, 12 November 1902, pp. 116–17.
33  PAAA, England 78, secretissima, Bd 6, Metternich to Foreign Office, 19 January 1903; see Vagts, *Deutschland*, Vol. 2, pp. 1598–9.
34  PAAA, Frankreich 116, No. 1, Geh., Bd 1, Bülow to London embassy, 27 May 1903.
35  ibid., England 78, Bd 19, Coerper to Tirpitz, 3 March 1903; Bülow to Wilhelm, 11 June 1903; England 78, secr., Bd 7, Metternich to Bülow, 25 Ocober 1903; "Aufzeichnung . . . Bülow," 3 January 1904; England 78, Bd 21, Richthofen (initialed Holstein) to Metternich, 27 February 1904; Metternich to Bülow, 2 April 1904; Bernstorff to Bülow, 1 May 1904; Bd 22, Metternich to Bülow, 14 July 1904; Bernstorff to Bülow, 31 August 1904; England 78, secr., Bd 7, Bernstorff to Bülow, 6 September 1904; England 83, Bd 10, Bernstorff to Bülow, 14 September 1904.
36  ibid., Deutschland 137, Bd 3, "Aufzeichnung . . . Bülow," 15 August 1899.
37  ibid., Frankreich 87, Bd 79, Münster to Hohenlohe, 4 February and 3 March 1900; Bd 80, Schlözer to Hohenlohe, 26 July 1900; Münster to Hohenlohe, 10 October 1900.
38  ibid., Frankreich 102, Bd 23, Bülow to Radolin, draft Holstein, 13 June 1901.
39  ibid., Bülow to Radolin, draft Holstein, 19 June 1901.
40  ibid., Frankreich 116, Bd 9, Radolin to Bülow, 26 July 1901; Frankreich 102, Bd 24, Radolin to Bülow, 11 December 1901; Frankreich No. 116, Bd 9, Radolin to Bülow, 10 February 1902; Frankreich 87, Bd 82, Radolin to Bülow, 14 July, 8 October, and 19 December 1902.
41  ibid., Russland 131, Geh., Bd 8, "Aufzeichnung . . . Holstein," 10 August 1901.
42  GP, XIX, i, No. 5967, "Aufzeichnung . . . Holstein," 23 December 1903, p. 74.
43  GP, XVII, No. 5186, Metternich to Foreign Office, 30 January 1902, p. 342. For the conclusion of the Entente Cordiale, see in particular also Dwight E. Lee, *Europe's*

*Crucial Years: The Diplomatic Background to World War I, 1902–1914* (Hanover, NH, 1974), pp. 50–74.

44  GP, XVII, No. 5188, Mentzingen, minister to Tangier, to Foreign Office, 14 September 1902, p. 344.

45  ibid., No. 5189, Richthofen to Eckhardstein, 25 September 1902, p. 345, and No. 5190, Eckhardstein's reply of 4 October 1903, p. 346. Also *Holstein Papers*, Vol. 4, No. 807, memorandum by Holstein, 1 October 1902, p. 264.

46  GP, XVII, No. 5193, Bülow to Metternich, 20 February 1903, p. 348; No. 5196, Richthofen to Mentzingen, 7 March 1903, pp. 351–2.

47  ibid., No. 5369, Eckhardstein to Bülow, 10 May 1903, pp. 567–70.

48  ibid., No. 5370, Bülow to Alvensleben, 13 May 1903, pp. 570–2; n.* on p. 572; *Holstein Papers*, Vol. 4, No. 815, Bülow to Holstein, 15 May 1903, p. 274.

49  GP, XVII, No. 5375, Bülow to Wilhelm, 20 May 1903, pp. 588–90.

50  PAAA, England 78, secr., Vol. 6, Bülow to Metternich, 13 March 1902.

51  See Jonathan Steinberg, "Germany and the Russo-Japanese War," *American Historical Review*, vol. 75, no. 7 (December 1970), p. 1967.

52  PAAA, England 83, Bd 7, Foreign Office to Metternich, 17 July 1902.

53  GP, XVIII, ii, No. 5911, Bülow to Foreign Office, 3 April 1903, pp. 839–40; Winzen, *Bülows Weltmachtkonzept*, p. 406.

54  PAAA, Russland 91, Bd 36, Alvensleben to Bülow, 9 July 1903, Wilhelm's comment "richtig" to a remark by Prince Merechevski.

55  *Spitzenberg*, p. 439; Winzen, *Bülows Weltmachtkonzept*, p. 407; Lee, *Europe's Crucial Years*, pp. 74–5.

56  GP, XX, i, No. 6388, "Aufzeichnung . . . Holstein," 3 March 1904, p. 37; *Holstein Papers*, Vol. 4, p. 297, n. 1; Winzen, *Bülows Weltmachtkonzept*, p. 408; Rich, *Holstein*, Vol. 2, pp. 681–5; H. Rogge, *Friedrich von Holstein, Lebensbekenntnis in Briefen an eine Frau* (Berlin, 1932), Holstein to Ida von Stüpnagel, 10 April 1904, p. 231.

57  GP, XX, i, No. 6378, Wilhelm to Bülow, 19 April 1904, pp. 22–3.

58  GP, XX, i, No. 6376, Bernstorff to Bülow, 16 April 1904, pp. 14–19.

59  ibid., p. 14, n.*.

60  ibid., No. 6379, Bülow to Wilhelm, 20 April 1904, pp. 23–4.

61  ibid., No. 6523, Bülow to Radolin, 21 July 1904, p. 211.

62  ibid., No. 6527, Metternich to Bülow, 15 August 1904, p. 221; Klehmet's interpretation of Metternich's comment in ibid., No. 6531, "Aufzeichnung . . . Klehmet," 6 September 1904, p. 225.

63  Winzen, *Bülows Weltmachtkonzept*, pp. 139–48, 177, 180, 182; Barbara Vogel, *Deutsche Russlandpolitik: Das Scheitern der deutschen Weltpolitik unter Bülow, 1900–1906* (Düsseldorf, 1973), pp. 9–10, 79–83, 87–103, 111.

64  Kennedy, *Samoan Tangle*, p. 187; also PAAA, Russland 131, Bd 8, Prussian minister in Stuttgart to Chancellor, 21 June 1899, Wilhelm's final comment. For his anti-Russian stance in the summer of 1899, see also Hatzfeldt, *Nachgelassene Papiere*, Vol. 2, No. 762, Holstein to Hatzfeldt, 8 June 1899, p. 1233.

65  PAAA, Orientalia Generalia 5, Bd 49, Richthofen to St Petersburg embassy, also initialed by Holstein, 19 December 1900.

66  ibid., Russland 99, Bd 3, Pückler to Bülow, 28 November 1901, Wilhelm's final comment.

67  GP, XVIII, i, No. 5381, "Aufzeichnung . . . Holstein," 4 December 1900, pp. 6–8.

68  PAAA, Russland 91, Bd 31, report of Lüttwitz, 1 March 1901.

69  ibid., Russland 72, Vol. 73, Schlieffen to Bülow, 19 and 22 March 1901; "Aufzeichnung," Foreign Office, 19 March 1901.

70  H St Ar Stuttgart, E73/73a, 12e, I, Varnbüler to Soden, 25 October 1901; also GP, XVIII, i, No. 5393, Bülow to Foreign Office, 12 September 1901; No. 5394, Bülow to Foreign Office, 14 September 1901, pp. 28–9; No. 5395, "Aufzeichnung . . . Bülow," 14 September 1901, pp. 29–31.

71  GP, XVIII, i, No. 5416, Bülow to Metternich, 8 August 1902, pp. 63–6.

72  BA, Bülow, *Nachlass*/22, Bülow's comments to Radolin to Bülow, 8 July 1900; PAAA, Deutschland 102, Geh., Bd 2, "Aufzeichnung Bülow," 15 February 1902, copy.

73  Winzen, *Bülows Weltmachtkonzept*, pp. 397–9; Vogel, *Deutsche Russlandpolitik*, pp. 108–12; Kennedy, *Antagonism*, 248–89.

74  Vogel, *Deutsche Russlandpolitik*, pp. 109–10; Vagts, *Deutschland*, Vol. 2, pp. 1173–4; GP XVII, No. 5055, "Aufzeichnung . . . Klehmet," 4 March 1902, and Bülow's comments to it, pp. 166–7.
75  GP, XIX, i, No. 5921, "Aufzeichnung . . . Holstein," 12 July 1902, p. 7.
76  GP, XVIII, i, No. 5421, Holstein to Bülow, 16 April 1903, p. 68.
77  loc. cit.
78  GP, XVIII, i, No. 5422, "Aufzeichnung . . . Bülow," 7 November 1903, pp. 75–6; BA, Bülow, *Nachlass*/97, "Aufzeichnung Richthofen," 12 November 1903; see also Pertti Luntinen, *The Baltic Question, 1903–1908* (Helsinki, 1975), pp. 19–26.
79  See below, pp. 210 ff.; Luntinen, *Baltic Question*, pp. 23–4.
80  PAAA, England 83, Bd 6, "Aufzeichnung . . . Lichnowsky," 9 March 1901. Bülow, in *Denkwürdigkeiten*, Bd II, p. 72, states, however, that Wilhelm counted on a Russian victory.
81  PAAA, Russland 72, Vol. 76, report of Lüttwitz, 17 April 1903.
82  GP, XIX, i, No. 5939, "Aufzeichnung . . . Lichnowsky," 15 January 1904, p. 29.
83  PAAA, Deutschland 129, Geh., Bd 13, Richthofen's *Promemoria* July 1904.
84  See above, p. 159.
85  PAAA, Oesterreich 95, Geh., Bd 1, Eckhardstein to Bülow, 14 September 1902, copy. Eckhardstein reported the Austro-Hungarian chargé d'affaires Mensdorff as telling him: "Should his government reach the conviction that there exists a truly insuperable difference [*Gegensatz*] which could in time lead to serious conflicts between England and Germany, then he feared that Austria would see herself being forced in time to allow a modification of her foreign policy to set in. His fears have been confirmed through conversations which he has had some time ago with Count Goluchowsky." For the dependence of Italy on Britain and the German awareness thereof, see p. 182.
86  PAAA, Deutschland 137, "Aufzeichnung Bülow," 14 March 1899, for the instruction of Prince Heinrich; ibid., Bd 3, "Aufzeichnung Bülow," 15 August 1899.
87  *Waldersee*, Vol. II, diary entry, 9 January 1900, p. 441.
88  PAAA, Oesterreich 88, Bd 5, Wedel to Bülow, 28 December 1904.
89  GP, XVIII, ii, No. 5704, Bülow to Wedel, Rome, 30 November 1900, p. 503. For Italy, see Lee, *Europe's Crucial Years*, pp. 19–48.
90  PAAA, Italien 72, Bd 17, Wedel to Hohenlohe, 22 February 1900, copy.
91  ibid., Italien 86, secr., Vol. 1, Wedel to Bülow, 6 July 1902, with Bülow's minute at the head of the report.
92  GP, XVIII, ii, Anlage zu No. 5818, Chelius to Wedel, 23 February 1901, pp. 689–90.
93  ibid., No. 5818, Wedel to Bülow, 24 February 1901, p. 687.
94  ibid., No. 5819, Schlieffen to Bülow, 12 March 1901, pp. 691–4.
95  ibid., No. 5712, Bülow to Wedel, 9 January 1902, pp. 515–18, and No. 5713, Bülow to Eulenburg, 9 January 1902, pp. 518–21; and No. 5715, "Aufzeichnung . . . Bülow," 12 January 1902, pp. 523–4.
96  PAAA, Deutschland 128, Geh., No. 1, Bd 15a, Wedel to Holstein, 15 January 1902.
97  GP, XVIII, ii, No. 5719, Wedel to Bülow, 19 January 1902, p. 532.
98  L. Albertini, *The Origins of the War of 1914*, Vol. 1 (London, 1952), p. 125; GP, XVIII, ii, No. 5774, Bülow to Wedel, 28 June 1902, p. 609.
99  GP, XVIII, ii, No. 5825, "Aufzeichnung . . . Klehmet," 7 September 1902, p. 703.
100  ibid., No. 5826, Wedel to Bülow, 18 November 1902, pp. 703–5.
101  Albertini, *Origins*, Vol. 1, pp. 129–30.
102  GP, XVIII, ii, No. 5776, Bülow to Monts, 9 June 1903, pp. 616–18.
103  PAAA, Italien 95, Bd 12, Monts to Bülow, 3 June 1903, copy.
104  ibid., Italien 70, Bd 14, Bülow to Wilhelm, 18 December 1903.
105  GP, XVIII, ii, No. 5827, Chelius to Schlieffen, 1 December 1903, pp. 705–7; No. 5828, Richthofen to Schlieffen, 11 December 1903, pp. 707–8; and No. 5829, Schlieffen to Richthofen, 14 December 1903, p. 708.
106  GP, XX, i, No. 6388, "Aufzeichnung . . . Holstein," 3 March 1904, pp. 37–9.
107  ibid., No. 6428, Bülow to Wilhelm, 5 March 1905, p. 95, enclosing Giolitti and Tittoni to Lanza, 25 February 1905, pp. 96–7.
108  ibid., No. 6429, Bülow to Wilhelm, 10 March 1905, pp. 97–8; and Wilhelm's marginal comment No. 2, p. 98.
109  See above, pp. 129–31.

110  Herwig, *Frustration*, pp. 30–2; Kennedy, *Samoan Tangle*, pp. 141 ff.; 263 ff.
111  A. Vagts, "Fears of an American-German war, 1870–1915, II," *Political Science Quarterly*, vol. 55, no. 1 (March 1940), p. 60.
112  Herwig, *Frustration*, pp. 22–4.
113  ibid., pp. 70–1; Vagts, *Deutschland*, Vol. 2, p. 1504.
114  GP, XVII, No. 5124, Holleben to Foreign Office, 16 December 1902, p. 264; No. 5127, Quadt, chargé d'affaires in Washington, to Foreign Office, 18 December 1902, p. 269.
115  Vagts, *Deutschland*, Vol. 2, p. 1604; GP, XVII, No. 5133, Quadt to Foreign Office, 23 January 1903, p. 274; No. 5144, Speck von Sternburg to Foreign Office, 31 January 1903, p. 285.
116  GP, XVII, No. 5151, Speck von Sternburg to Foreign Office, 19 February 1903, p. 291. For the impact of the Venezuelan episode, see Herwig, *Frustration*, pp. 79–80. For the hostility of the American navy toward Germany and frictions over Brazil late in 1903, see Vagts, *Deutschland*, Vol. 2, pp. 1604; 1758–61.

# 12 Naval Preparation for War, 1899–1905

## (1) Introduction

The break-up of the High Command separated tactical development from operational planning in so far as the former became the responsibility of the Command of the First Squadron and subsequently of the Command of the Fleet and the latter of the Admiralty Staff. Both tactics and operational planning would be affected by the growth of the fleet, new ship types, and changes in artillery, which were basically within the purview of the Imperial Naval Office, whose head, Tirpitz, had been the leader of the tactical and operational developments in the old High Command. From 1899 onward there was overlap in jurisdictions, conflict, and some cooperation. The Command of the First Squadron and of the Fleet developed their own operational notions and through war games and maneuvers cooperated with the Admiralty Staff as well as with the Commands of the Baltic and North Sea Stations in the area of tactics and operational planning. The Admiralty Staff commented on and made recommendations to Wilhelm regarding the tactical work of the First Squadron and Fleet.

The Admiralty Staff, which had the major responsibility for operational planning from 1899, was a much less powerful body than its predecessor, the High Command. According to Hopmann it was too far removed from practical military activity,[1] although it had an input into tactical development. Its planning for war in the near future was not coordinated with the long-term strategic concept and the building program of the Leipziger Platz. There were personality clashes between Tirpitz and several Chiefs of the Admiralty Staff as well as the inevitable disagreements arising from the Admiralty Staff's stress on quality and Tirpitz's emphasis on quantity. The first two Chiefs of the Admiralty Staff, both rather ineffective, Felix von Bendemann and Otto von Diederichs, held office relatively briefly, the former from March to December 1899 and the latter from December 1899 to August 1902. Diederichs was aggressive, wanting to extend the jurisdiction of his agency, and therefore soon clashed with the Secretary of State.

The operational work within the Admiralty Staff was divided as it had been in the staff section of the High Command. Department A was in charge of operations in Europe; section 1 of this department was in charge of Germany; section 2, Russia, Scandinavia, the Balkans, and Austria-Hungary; section 3, France; section 4, Great Britain, Holland, and Belgium; and section 5 handled strategy, tactics, maneuvers, and technical matters. Department B, also consisting of five sections, handled non-European areas.[2]

In January 1901, Diederichs expressed serious concern about the capability of his limited staff to prepare the mobilization and deployment plans for the different cases of war that were envisaged. He claimed that with a much larger staff the Great General Staff only had to work on one war plan, that against France and Russia.[3] He wanted to expand and to centralize the intelligence service, to subdivide the regional operations sections, A2, 3, and 4, and to subordinate the Naval Academy to the Admiralty Staff.[4] Initially, he obtained Wilhelm's approval for these proposals. Senden consented also, with the proviso that new personnel be acquired gradually. This approval was futile as there was no response from Tirpitz. Moreover, Diederichs had obtained Wilhelm's and Senden's consent to his proposals before he had heard the opinion of his own staff. Their opinion was expressed on 25 January 1901 by A2, Erwin Schäfer, A3, Dick, A4, Weber, and A5, Eckermann.[5] They saw the weakness of the existing system in the decentralization of operational work, maintaining that the autonomy of their sections could lead to oversights and gaps in the preparation of operations and allow insignificant detail to gain precedence over more important matters. In his comments on this submission, Diederichs declared his opposition to central prescription and his preference for allowing the uniqueness and initiative of individual sections. "Uniformity", he remarked, "is only necessary where the common work of several departments is involved." He was also concerned about tying the hands of the commanding admiral in wartime through excessive peacetime prescription by the Admiralty Staff.[6]

Diederichs' proposals appeared to serve two purposes: (1) increasing the war preparedness of the fleet through better operations plans, and (2) building up his own agency. On both counts he thus encountered Tirpitz's opposition. The State Secretary mobilized the "Front," the chiefs of the two naval stations, August von Thomsen and Koester, and the new Chief of the First Squadron, Hoffmann, against the Admiralty Staff.[7] Tirpitz's opposition was partly due to his hostility to the creation of a powerful naval agency at the expense of his own position as *primus inter pares*. It was also due to an even more basic disagreement between his long-term building plans and the immediate needs of the Admiralty Staff and the "Front." He needed time to build the fleet; the Admiralty Staff and the "Front" needed the fleet for immediate action. He looked to the future; the Admiralty Staff and the "Front" were by necessity concerned with the present. In the memorandum to Wilhelm of 13 February 1901,[8] Tirpitz maintained that Diederichs' plans for the increase of the Admiralty Staff were premature: there existed a general need for new officers on the part of the entire rapidly growing navy and there was no reason to provide the Admiralty Staff with preferential treatment. Rather, the development of the Admiralty Staff was to correspond to that of the rest of the navy. The current size of the Admiralty Staff was entirely suitable to the current size of the fleet. The time for it to expand was in 1904 when the entire fleet reached a new stage of development. Tirpitz, moreover, expressed his doubts about the use of the General Staff as the model for the Admiralty Staff. For the navy did not require a network of staff officers as did the army, and Admiralty Staff officers did not need specialized training to the same extent as did General Staff officers. Tirpitz thus rejected the proposal for the establishment of a naval academy.

Tirpitz succeeded in delaying the proposed expansion of the Admiralty Staff. Wilhelm's order of 16 March 1901 allowed only for the organization of the intelligence system, and on 24 June he ruled:

> much as I appreciate the efforts of the Admiralty Staff, in implementing the fleet law, to ensure the greatest possible efficiency for the navy, such endeavors must recede into the background before the necessity of the earliest achievement of the great aim itself.[9]

Tirpitz's supremacy was assured and most of the handicaps under which the Admiralty Staff worked were allowed to continue.

## (2) Planning for a War against the Dual Alliance

Under its first Chief, Bendemann, who had served in the High Command, the Admiralty Staff somewhat hesitantly began to pick up pieces of previous plans for new operations. Its first project for Continental war, the operational study of May 1899 for a war against France, adhered to notions dating back to Caprivi. The freedom of action of the German fleet was viewed as being dependent on the absence of the French Mediterranean forces from the northern theater at the outbreak of war. If the German forces were then inferior to the French northern squadron, they were to remain on the defensive, otherwise they could take the offensive. Therefore it was stressed that the power relationship between the German navy and the French northern squadron required close scrutiny. On certain days of the early mobilization the German side would have an advantage in ships of the line, but it would always be short of cruisers. This disadvantage rendered extensive operations against the French coast impossible. All that could be undertaken was an offensive between the sixth and tenth mobilization days—when the German navy enjoyed a superiority of 17,000 tons over the French northern fleet—against Dunkirk, and possibly against Calais and Boulogne.[10] This was a modest operational project.

The next operational study was entirely defensive. It assumed that France, like Britain, would launch an attack on Germany to destroy her fleet and to blockade her North Sea ports. This attack was not expected before the arrival of the Mediterranean squadron, after the fifteenth mobilization day. Once in the North Sea, the French were expected to try to secure a naval base. But their action in the Baltic was dependent on the favorable attitude of Denmark, whose position thus remained an important concern in German naval planning.[11] This reflected how German naval strategy against Britain was beginning to influence the operational planning against France.

It was not before 19 September 1899 that Bendemann himself issued the directives for the preparation of operations plans.[12] Drawing on the authority of Feldmarschall von Moltke, he maintained that no detailed operations could be planned in advance. Bendemann affirmed that the weaker side, when able to mobilize more quickly than the stronger side, can gain partial successes at the beginning of hostilities. The defensive role would be confined to the disturbance of the hostile deployment and the prevention of the blockade of its harbors so as to keep open its shipping lanes. In an offensive strategy, the fleet would be deployed partly along the hostile coast and partly at home, whereas in a defensive strategy the deployment would be confined to home waters.

In line with the above strategic notions, Bendemann requested that a clear statement be provided about whether war should be waged offensively or defensively and whether the deployment should be on the hostile coast or in home harbors.

On 25 November, Erwin Schäfer, who was in charge of section A3, provided the required answers regarding the operations plan against France. He maintained that in view of the excellent internal line of communication through the Kaiser Wilhelm Canal and of the weakness of the Russian naval forces in the Baltic Sea because of detachments to the Far East, it was possible for Germany to launch an attack against the French northern coast at the outset of hostilities.[13] But, because of the absence of a base near the French coast, the German navy would have to use British or Dutch waters for the replenishment of supplies and the disembarkation of the wounded. The operation thus depended on the benevolent neutrality of either Britain or Holland. And, if Britain's neutrality was not assured, the shelling of Calais and Boulogne was to be avoided since it was a threat to her interests and might be regarded as a provocation. Only Dunkirk should then be shelled. Thus Schäfer showed greater concern for Britain's attitude than had previous German planners of operations against the French coast. The fleet was to be deployed in the Elbe for both offensive and defensive purposes. Schäfer then proceeded to discuss the operations in considerable detail.

Probably encouraged by this study, Bendemann, on 10 December, reported to Wilhelm that the work on the offensive operations plan against France could be resumed and obtained his approval two days later. Bendemann gave as the reason for his report an inquiry on the part of the Chief of the General Staff as to whether "our navy was in condition, in compliance with the agreements with our partners of the Triple Alliance, to tie down the naval forces of the Dual Alliance located in the north and in particular to make Italy capable of honoring its alliance obligations in respect to the army." Italy's military assistance against France obviously became a special concern to the General Staff, which was in the next year to entertain doubts about her offensive operations in the west.[14]

The Chief of the Admiralty Staff was willing to have the navy do its share to encourage Italy to meet her obligations. He considered the resumption of the offensive operations plan against France feasible in view of the current naval power relationship of Germany and the Dual Alliance in northern waters: the German fleet, moreover, was increasing from year to year whereas there was no increase of any French forces because of lack in planning or of the Russian forces in the Baltic because of diversions to the Far East.[15] Wilhelm was not surprised by Bendemann's report, for he had already been apprised in April that the resumption of offensive operations against France was being considered in the Admiralty Staff.[16]

Bendemann reported again on 21 January 1900, when he informed

Wilhelm that, contrary to his previous report, the French navy, particularly its northern squadron, was being strengthened. The strengthening of her northern forces indicated that France was preparing for an encounter with Germany, not with Italy. This, of course, removed some of the urgency from the German strike for the purpose of encouraging the Italians, but at the same time made its execution more difficult. Bendemann, however, did not draw these implications for the offensive operations plan which had just received Wilhelm's approval.[17] He continued to work on this plan, stipulating in February 1900 that it be the subject of the *Admiralstabsübungsreise* of the North Sea station in 1900. By that time A3 had completed the preparations for the mobilization of the personnel and the *matériel* necessary for the offensive operations.[18]

Wilhelm's decision to revive the offensive operations plan against France led to a submission from the man who would have to execute it: Chief of the First Squadron, Admiral Koester. On 29 January 1900 he pointed out that the plan "required thorough study [*Durcharbeitung*] since the mutual relationship in ships of the line and particularly cruisers has shifted to our disfavor." As the chief spokesman of the "Front" he was more sensitive than the Admiralty Staff to the strengthening of the French northern forces. In addition, he expressed concern that no operations plan had been prepared against Russia.[19] The old sea dog was obviously questioning the wisdom of giving higher priority to a dangerous advance against a strengthened enemy for the purpose of encouraging a hesitant ally over the defense of one's own backwater against an inferior opponent.

Wilhelm's—and possibly Senden's—reaction to Koester's representation was surprising in view of the earlier decision of the High Command to desist from working on a plan against Russia alone, based on the conclusion of the General Staff that such a war was improbable. Was it because of doubts about offensive action against France at sea—voiced by Koester—or by land—voiced by Schlieffen himself?[20] With Russia distracted in the Far East there was no need of a preventive strike against her—unless there existed a desire for annexations of her territory, for which there is no evidence at this time. On 7 February, Senden informed the Chief of the Admiralty Staff of Wilhelm's decision to request him to report about Koester's submission and about the refusal to prepare an operations plan against Russia alone.[21]

The military and political situation led Diederichs to concur with Koester's doubts about the western offensive. But since the dispatch of Russian ships from the Baltic to the Far East made possible the concentration of German forces in the North Sea with less concern for the eastern theater of war Diederichs also rejected Koester's request for an operations plan against Russia. He fell back on a defensive strategy. The absence of a Russian threat and the availability of German torpedo-boats made a defensive stance in the North Sea against France a viable proposition.[22]

But, in spite of these doubts about the western offensive, A3 proposed that the strategic maneuvers of the next year continue to deal with the thrust against the French northern coast and obtained some support for this position in the Admiralty Staff.[23] Outside pressure, brought to bear by Schlieffen, also continued to work in favor of the offensive against the

French northern coast as part of the military cooperation of the Triple Alliance. The question of naval cooperation appears to have been raised by the Italian General Staff. The cue was taken up by Schlieffen, who first obtained the agreement of Diederichs and then of Wilhelm II to a conference of the representatives of the three navies.[24] The Italian program called for the designation of main operational areas for the three allies: the northern French coast for Germany; the Adriatic, including the defense of the Italian eastern coast, for Austria; and the western Mediterranean for Italy. Allied ships within the operational sphere of any one power at the outbreak of hostilities were to be subjected to its command for the course of the war. The Chief of the Admiralty Staff, however, viewed the Italian program as too ambitious and the Italians as too concerned about French attacks on those Italian eastern coastal railways used for mobilization and about a possible landing in Sicily.[25] With Diederichs' full approval A3 defined as the initial task of the Italian navy the pinning down and destruction of the French Mediterranean fleet, which would be the best means of defending the Italian coast, observing the Russian Black Sea fleet, and preventing its union with the French. He claimed that these aims could be best accomplished through an immediate offensive against the French southern coast. The smaller Austrian navy was, first, to defend the Adriatic and, second, to support the Italian operations. But A3 doubted if it was necessary to go along with the Italian wish of establishing permanent commands for the course of the war over the different spheres of operations except for the Adriatic. Nor did the Admiralty Staff want any rigid requirements for the subordination of the ships of one ally to the command of another at the beginning of the war. Diederichs' marginal comments expressed great concern about passing any information about German operations plans to Italy lest it leak to France or Britain. Schlieffen likewise thought that "different operational aims and objects of attack" of the allied fleets could only be determined at the time of the outbreak of war and wished to confine the discussion to general areas of operation. None the less, he defined the task of the German fleet as drawing "upon itself hostile forces in the Channel or on the west coast of France according to opportunity."[26]

As noted in the previous chapter, in February and March 1901 the German political leadership and the Chief of the General Staff, Schlieffen, concluded that Italy could not be expected to perform her obligation of sending five army corps to operate on the southern flank of the German army. Schlieffen's view was that only the British navy could effectively support the Italian war effort as a member of the Triple Alliance.[27] Wilhelm saw some of the correspondence. But it appears that the Admiralty Staff was not informed that political influence on Italy was no longer a rationale for German operational planning against France. In any case it continued with its offensive operations plan against France. This is yet another illustration of the poor coordination of the top echelons of the German leadership.

Adhering to his preference for the more ambitious strike against the French northern coast, Diederichs recommended to Wilhelm that it form the basis for next year's strategic maneuvers. At the same time Koester's eastern orientation was put to the test. In April 1901, Diederichs provided Wilhelm with information about a war game of the Admiralty Staff

involving a war between the Dual Alliance and the Triple Alliance in which
the German navy faced the French northern fleet and the Russian Baltic Sea
fleet. In attempting to prevent the union of the two hostile fleets, the German
navy was to seek to defeat them separately, turning first against the Russian
and then against the French fleet. But the outcome was unfavorable to the
German side. The main forces advancing into the northern Baltic failed to
bring the Russian fleet to battle and to prevent the break-out of some Russian
ships and were forced to return to Kiel as the Russian forces demonstratively
shelled the German Baltic Sea coast. The inferior German forces sent to
observe the advancing French northern fleet also fared badly. The conclusion
drawn from the war game served to confirm the western orientation in the
operational planning of the Admiralty Staff: France was to be attacked first.
As assumed for some time, the more excitable French could be brought to
battle more easily than the Russians. The Danish narrows could be blocked
more easily in the east against the Russians than in the north against the
French—another reason for knocking out the French forces first.[28]

As Chief of the Admiralty Staff, Diederichs had thus been unable to work
out a definite operations plan against the Dual Alliance. True enough, a
concentration in the Baltic had been rejected. The offensive against the
French northern coast was being worked on, but considerable doubt existed
about its viability. In view of the dismissal of Italy as a reliable ally by both
the German ambassador in Rome and the Chief of the Great General
Staff—a decision of which the Admiralty Staff was not informed—the major
reasons for the offensive had in fact been removed.

New life came into the Admiralty Staff when Wilhelm Büchsel replaced
Diederichs as its chief in August 1902. Diederichs and Tirpitz had been at
loggerheads but Büchsel was a crew comrade of the State Secretary, who had
supported his appointment as Diederichs' successor.[29] It could be expected
that Büchsel would prove more pliant and that the strategic thinking of the
Imperial Naval Office would come to have a greater influence over the
Admiralty Staff. As for planning for a Continental war, one of Büchsel's first
actions was to turn to one of the oldest and more obvious tasks of the planners
of German naval operations: how to support the operations of the army
against Russia. It is very possible that he did so after preliminary consultation
with Schlieffen. On 24 October 1902 he gave the following assignment to A2,
who appears at this time to be Hopmann, and A3 (Dick?):

> In the tense relations of Germany with the Dual Alliance, the navy is
> faced with the task of keeping open the connections at sea between the
> provinces to the east and to the west of the Vistula, of taking care of the
> First Army Corps located in Königsberg, and of preparing its transfer to
> Stettin.

He wanted to know how this task would affect the mobilization, deployment, and other war preparations of the German naval forces in 1903.[30]

This communication led to the finalization of the German naval
operations plan for a Continental war. In their reply of 26 November, A2
and A3 admitted that such a war would only be decided on land. Proceeding

to a more detailed discussion of the western operations, A2 and A3 estimated that the German First Squadron was superior to the French northern squadron. Moreover, the German side enjoyed superiority in torpedo-boats, training and gunnery practice, whereas the French were superior in cruisers.[31]

The defense of the Baltic, including the maintenance of connections with the First Army Corps, would be left essentially to the Second Squadron whereas the First Squadron would contribute to it by keeping the French out. Subsequently the memorandum listed a number of specific preparations that had to be made before the plan could be put into effect. On 12 December 1902, A3 dealt with the western operations in more detail. By Winkler's admission he did so in a great hurry and raised a number of questions which could not be answered at the time.[32]

There was no remedy for one of the major disadvantages of the German position in the English Channel: the absence of a base. It was impossible to seize one on the hostile coast unless the French naval forces were defeated and unless there was army support. The only suitable base in the Low Countries was the Scheldt estuary, but the German navy was not strong enough to maintain itself there. Thus Dutch and Belgian territory could only be temporarily used for tasks such as coaling "without consideration for their neutrality." English ports could be used to a very limited extent, as in 1870–71. The vulnerability of rear communications would have to be accounted for in allowing for extensive losses. Further, there was detailed discussion of the use of cables, the laying of mines, appropriate measures against French submarines, and the preparation of the Ems estuary as an alternative base for the returning First Squadron.

With the question of maintaining connections with the First Army Corps having thus led to the preliminary restructuring of German naval planning in a Continental war, Büchsel informed Schlieffen on 22 December that he expected to deal with this question in his next report to Wilhelm.[33] Schlieffen replied with unusual promptness on 26 December:

In a war with the Dual Alliance it would indeed be very desirable if the fleet ruled the Baltic Sea. Its task would then be:
(1)   To prevent the landing of hostile forces on the home coast.
(2)   To keep open the communications between the Baltic Sea ports, particularly the permanent connection between Königsberg in Prussia and the western harbor towns.
(3)   To disturb the Russian coast and thereby to arouse the belief among the Russians that German troop embarkations are intended for the Russian coast. Through these measures the Russians will consider themselves compelled to keep forces on their coast, something for which they already seem to have an inclination.

Having paid tribute to these traditional services expected from the navy by the army, Schlieffen turned to the western theater of operations:

But the destruction of the French fleet is much more important in a war against the Dual Alliance than this action in the Baltic Sea. If the navy declares itself strong enough to be able to engage in a struggle with the French fleet, then all forces ought to be used for this task. In this case any division of forces is to be avoided. The army would then naturally have to dispense with the cooperation of the fleet against Russia.[34]

A certain irony appears in Schlieffen's words: in view of the higher priority given to the navy, it should have been capable of dealing with its French rival in a Continental war.

On 2 January 1903, Büchsel provided Schlieffen with a negative answer: the German navy was not strong enough to destroy the French fleet and to control the French coast.

But if the army leadership, in view of the expected use of the fleet in the Baltic, places such a high value on the destruction of the French fleet, then it must be considered whether, even if complete success is not possible, the aim sought by the General Staff can none the less be achieved to a certain extent through the engagement of our fleet to the point of its destruction and whether the advantage that is thus gained for the conduct of war on land will balance the disadvantage.

Having thus considered the possible sacrifice of the German fleet for the aims of army strategy, Büchsel asked why its leadership viewed the destruction of the French fleet as so important. In particular, he asked:

whether the final aim is
(1)  to tie down as many French troops as possible to the north coast of France,
or
(2)  to make possible a transport of German troops over the North Sea and their landing on the French coast,
and
(3)  if the latter, which part of the French coast would come into question for such operations?[35]

Schlieffen again replied promptly. On 5 January he stated that since in a war against both France and Russia both powers could not be defeated simultaneously it was advisable to gain a victory first over the stronger and more dangerous opponent, namely France.[36] The result of the destruction of the French fleet would benefit the conduct of a war on land by securing the German and exposing the French communications by sea. None the less, the German navy should not be sacrificed: its destruction would lead to the disruption of Germany's overseas connections and the control over her coast by the French. The best course of action for the German fleet in a war against the Dual Alliance would be a defensive stance in the west and an offensive in the east leading to control of the Baltic Sea.

By 6 March 1903 the Admiralty Staff had prepared a draft of a memorandum which was to be submitted for Wilhelm's approval. This document constituted the end result of the operational planning that had been going on since May 1899, and met the recently expressed wishes of the General Staff. Entitled "War plan for the case of war Triple Alliance against the Dual Alliance," initialed by A, Winkler, A2, Hopmann, and A3, Dick, the document claimed that

> The growth of the fleet has in this year reached a point which makes possible the realization of the naval aims originally assigned by Your Majesty. It can oppose the French and the Russian northern fleets, for those parts of the German fleet which are not suitable for participation in the western theater of war are in a position to operate against the Russian Baltic fleet.[37]

The strategic purpose of the navy as defined by the High Command in 1895 had thus been fulfilled. This, however, was an overstatement, and Büchsel was to deny it.

It was stated that the traditional offensive plan for the German navy in a Continental war had been to defeat the French and Russian northern fleets before they had united for common operations or had been reinforced by turning first against the more formidable French fleet even if this meant temporarily relinquishing the Baltic Sea to the Russians. In recent years the naval forces of both the Dual Alliance and Germany had been strengthened, and so continued to balance one another. Although the French still followed the principle of relegating their older ships from the Mediterranean to the northern theater of operations, their strength in the north had none the less increased and the older German ships of the Siegfried and Baden class were no longer a match for them. The offensive thrust would thus have to be confined to the First Squadron, which in 1903 consisted exclusively of the Kaiser- and Wettin-class ships which were superior to the six older ships of the line and the four coastal armored ships of the French northern squadron: in battleworthiness the two forces were rated as 9·8 (German) and 9·3 (French). The first squadron would be accompanied by all available cruisers and torpedo-boats. The German side had a supremacy in torpedo-boats, while the French were superior in cruisers. French submarines and diving boats and their reorganized *défense mobile* increased the hazards for the German offensive force.

In view of the expectation that the French squadron would remain behind the strong fortifications of Cherbourg or Brest and could be lured to battle only by attacks against the French coast, the German side faced a dilemma: attacks against the strengthened coastal defenses would inflict such losses on the German force as to make it incapable of facing the French northern squadron, whereas action against weaker coastal places would not serve as an adequate lure. The authors of the memorandum therefore recommended that the German forces impose a blockade on Brest, the naval base to which the French northern squadron would probably withdraw. The effect of this blockade was to be reinforced by a bombardment of Dunkirk by the Siegfried ships. This was a more ambitious course than that considered in the earlier operational studies against France. The main thrust of the fleet was now extended to the Atlantic approaches, where, beside maintaining the blockade of the French fleet, the German navy could also damage French and protect German shipping entering the English Channel from the Atlantic. As yet, however, the German navy was viewed as inadequate for imposing a blockade on the entire French northern coast because of a shortage of cruisers and the vulnerability of its slow older ships to French torpedo-boats and submarines. The risk of exposing older ships was taken only in the action against the relatively close objective, Dunkirk.

In full realization that the chances of bringing the French northern squadron to battle were poor, the offensive was none the less justified on the grounds that otherwise the fleet would remain inactive against the French. For it was unlikely that the French would take the offensive themselves. If the German force returned from the west without having been able to bring the French to battle, it would still have gained a moral victory, for it would be the French who had refused its challenge. Moreover, the thrust was made necessary by the offensive spirit which had been instilled into the German navy, which "makes possible the greatest risks and successes. This navy can no longer tolerate waging a war like that of 1870–71." Also, in the eyes of the Admiralty Staff the obligations of the Triple Alliance were still binding in spite of the strong doubts of the Rome embassy and Schlieffen: the German navy was virtually obligated to take the offensive against the French northern squadron, which might otherwise head into the Mediterranean.

The advance of the German fleet would have to occur as soon after the outbreak of war as possible. It was expected to arrive on the seventh mobilization day before Brest where, in order to be more secure from French light forces and at the same time to provide maximum protection to German shipping, it was to stay a considerable distance from the coast but yet sufficiently close to Brest to present a threat to the French squadron. It could remain there for four days and would then have to return home for coaling. The author of the memorandum appropriately concluded that:

> In considering the war plan for the case of war Triple Alliance against Dual Alliance I had no doubts that the navy would most effectively contribute toward a German victory if it were to succeed in supporting either directly or indirectly the operations of the army. For the decision in this war would be reached on land.

Specific reference was made to the recent correspondence with Schlieffen. In contrast to the earlier plans to denude the Baltic of all naval forces for the purpose of executing the western advance and thus conceding naval control of it to the Russians, "The forces not needed in the western theater which are now freed for use in the Baltic Sea, i.e. essentially the Second and Third Squadrons, are seen as capable of maintaining control of the Baltic Sea." Thereby the expectations of the Chief of the General Staff were viewed as fulfilled: landings of Russian troops on the German coast were prevented, connections between German Baltic Sea ports were maintained, and landings on the Russian coast could be threatened to compel detachments of Russian troops for its defense. Moreover, there existed opportunities to defeat separately the Russian forces located in Libau and Kronstadt.

In view of Russia's involvement in the Far East it was not expected that her naval strength in the Baltic would increase in the foreseeable future. On the other hand, the French were steadily strengthening their coastal defenses and were expected to put in service in 1905 two new ships of the line and two new armored cruisers and in 1906 four new ships of the line and one new armored cruiser. But this increase in French naval power would be balanced by growing German strength. The proposed operational planning was thus not expected to be upset for some time by a change in the power relationship.

On 10 March 1903, Büchsel presented the finished version of the memorandum for Wilhelm's approval.[38] It did not differ from the draft in substance, but there were changes in wording and elaborations. The changes in the balance of naval power between France and Germany were elaborated on: in 1903 the German side was weakened through the rebuilding of all of the ships of the Brandenburg class and four ships of the Siegfried class which would thus be out of commission. There appeared a fuller explanation for the decision not to attack Le Havre: its strengthened fortifications reduced the chances of seriously damaging it and increased the threat of damage to the German forces; the German action against the city could be interrupted by the French northern squadron, which could force the Germans to give up the bombardment and then, without coming to battle, withdraw behind the fortifications of Cherbourg or Brest—an action which it could repeat several times and thus wear down the Germans. Moreover, coming at night close to the French coast would involve losses through submarine and torpedo-boat attacks. While a bombardment of Dunkirk presented less risk to the German side, it would also have less effect on the French naval leadership, which would probably ignore the bombardment and either concentrate on attacking German shipping entering the English Channel from the Atlantic or leave to reinforce the French Mediterranean forces. The chances of bringing the French fleet to battle through the double thrust against Brest and Dunkirk were regarded more favorably:

> Thus, our fleet will protect our merchant marine at the most dangerous time at the beginning of the war and prevent the loss of considerable wealth. The pressure on the hostile fleet will be no less: if, after the preparation of the Siegfried division, pressure is brought on French public opinion and military leadership through the shelling of Dunkirk, while *simultaneously* the first squadron is located within the sight of the French northern fleet, then it is to be hoped that the French admiral will not withstand this double pressure but will come to battle.

Whether this optimism reflected Büchsel's sincere opinion or was expressed for Wilhelm's personal benefit so as to obtain his approval for the operations plan cannot, of course, be determined.

The power relationship in the Baltic Sea was discussed somewhat more fully than in the previous memorandum. Its defense was left to four ships of the Baden class, six other older armored ships, five cruisers, two torpedo-boat flotillas and seven armored gunboats. This force would be confronted on the Russian side by five ships of the line, three coastal armored ships, thirteen cruisers, and fifty-nine torpedo-boats. Only from the beginning of June to the end of September could some of the Russian ships be expected to be ready for action before the German ships: only in this period was an early Russian offensive a possibility. Provision was also made for the use of the German Baltic Sea forces in case of Russian neutrality: they would then be deployed in the Elbe and their action would depend on the attitude of Denmark, the success of the German attack against the French coast, and the operations of the French Mediterranean fleet.

Wilhelm approved the new operations plan on the day that it was presented to him, and Büchsel immediately referred it, with some modification, to A, requesting him to undertake the mobilization preparations. Büchsel mentioned to A as a further specific task the maintenance by sea of connections with the First (East Prussian) Army Corps and its eventual evacuation to Stettin. He requested a progress report by 1 April. He further asked A5 to consider whether, and to what extent, the Chief of the General Staff and the Chief of the Fleet were to be immediately informed of the new basis for the operational work.[39]

In a memorandum drafted on 27 March 1903, Büchsel emphasized the limited capacity of the German fleet:[40]

The destruction of the enemy as expected from a superior or equal fleet—through the destruction of the hostile battle fleet and of the remaining sea forces of the enemy through the bombardment, destruction, and capture of his ports, the disruption of his trade, through the seizure of his colonies—is precluded for the German fleet in a war against France alone, as well as in the case of war Triple vs. Dual Alliance, in view of its own and its enemies' strength.

In this memorandum, unlike its predecessor, Büchsel stressed that the total strength of the French northern and Mediterranean squadrons, amounting to twenty-one ships of the line, was superior to the German strength of nine or twelve ships of the line and that the unification of the French forces would restrict Germany to defensive action. He also stated that the German navy would have to make preparations for the offensive before the outbreak of war by deploying the ships in Wilhelmshaven.

The operations plan was revised for the next year in October 1903.[41] In identical terms with the memorandum of 27 March 1903 this document mentioned the limitations of the German flcet. It also referred to the supremacy of the united French navy: twelve modern French ships of the line versus nine German equivalents; nine older French ships of the line versus four equivalent German Braunschweig-class ships; four French coastal armored ships which were superior to the German Baden-class equivalents, and ten older coastal armored ships which would face six equivalent Siegfried-class ships; twelve armored cruisers, compared to two or three German cruisers; and twenty-six protected cruisers, compared to thirteen German ships of the same type. But better battle readiness of the German forces made the previously proposed operations still viable in a war of the Triple Alliance against the Dual Alliance. Then came a reservation:

> We must reckon with the unification of the French forces if a period of tension precedes the outbreak of a war which would make such a unification possible and if we do not have an ally in the Mediterranean that is powerful at sea. For it would be incorrect militarily for France to weaken her offensive power against an available enemy in order to be armed against a possible enemy.

And then followed a correct assessment of the political situation:

> the existing alliances and groupings do not give any ground for the expectation that in a war against France alone we would find a Mediterranean power as an ally.

The caution expressed in the document produced a significant reaction from A3, Schäfer.[42] He wanted a clearer formulation of the offensive purpose of the plan. Realizing that the French northern squadron would not readily come to battle and would not be induced to do so by the bombardment of Dunkirk, A3 emphasized the need for various offensive actions, particularly against the most dangerous opponents, the heavy cruisers and torpedo-boats. He proposed attacking French rearward communications, the laying of mines, observing the bases of the *défense mobile*, undertaking *coups de mains* against possible ports of refuge, and launching torpedo-boat attacks against cruisers.

In order to prevent the unification of the French northern and Mediterranean squadrons A3 even proposed dividing the German fleet by leaving the weaker part to observe the northern squadron in Brest and proceeding with the stronger part to seek out and do battle with the Mediterranean squadron. This was the first suggestion that the German navy was capable of taking on the entire French fleet. Someone, however, raised the question in the margin whether this could be accomplished with the three first-class cruisers and the torpedo-boats available. A3 even asserted that the German navy was not to avoid battle against numerically superior, united French forces, for the morale and war readiness of the French northern squadron were low and would be reduced further as the Germans proceeded against it with vigor.

A3's offensive mentality led him to insist that the German western offensive be of longer duration. For this purpose better arrangements must be made for provisioning in the English Channel. Further instances of this mentality were proposals for the seizure of the Ile d'Ouessant as an advance observation-post before Brest, the destruction of the French submarines in Cherbourg through a coup before or at the time of the declaration of war, the sinking of a ship to block the entrance into the Brest harbor, and the making of detailed preparations for the passage of the fleet through the Channel.

On 10 October 1903, Büchsel expressed his agreement with A3's views.[43] He restricted his comments to the waging of war with France alone, remarking that the case of war of the Dual Alliance against the Triple Alliance would not come into consideration for some time. He concurred with the seizure of Ouessant, which he felt should be followed up by the blockade of Dunkirk and Le Havre and possibly of Brest, and the Gironde and the Loire estuaries. Cruisers and torpedo-boats mobilized later were to harass the French coastline east of Cherbourg. However, he thought the blockade of Brest would not lead to a decisive success. If the French refused to come out for battle, it was unlikely that Brest could be forced and, even if it could, the German fleet would be too weakened to challenge the French Mediterranean squadron and reserves which could now dominate the English Channel and cut off German imports by sea. What is more significant is Büchsel's current assertion:

. . . with our present means, namely with those available in the next budget year, we no longer need fear a battle with the united French northern and Mediterranean forces in case we should not succeed in defeating the French Mediterranean squadron before its entry into Brest.

According to it, parity in naval strength between Germany and France had been reached.

At the turn of the year arrangements were made between the Admiralty Staff and the Imperial Naval Office whereby the naval attaché in London would be responsible for gathering intelligence in a Franco-German war.[44]

On 26 March 1904, A3 drafted a report about a war game held in the Admiralty Staff which was to test the existing operations plan against France.[45] In the war game the two German squadrons operating in the west did not succeed in bringing the French northern fleet to battle through the actions envisaged in the operations plan for this purpose. The report stated that any action against Cherbourg was to be avoided even if the French fleet was located in its harbor, for this would expose the German fleet to torpedo-boat attacks and delay its advance to the west end of the English Channel. If the French northern fleet was concentrated in Brest, three courses of action were open to the German fleet: (1) observation and blockade of the port; (2) a stay in the Atlantic for the protection of German commerce; or (3) harassment of the French coast for the purpose of bringing the northern fleet to battle. The first two courses of action were dismissed—the former as too ambitious since it overtaxed the German forces and would entail great losses, and the latter as futile since it would fail to bring the French fleet to battle. The third course was correct but dangerous since the German side's lack of cruisers would expose it to attacks by French cruisers. A3 maintained: "The French superiority in armored cruisers makes the operations as envisaged by OP I [Operations Plan against France] difficult and dangerous." A marginal comment, apparently in Büchsel's hand, reads: "I agree throughout. The difficulty for us is that we must continuously use ships of the line for purposes for which they are suitable neither in numbers nor in type." Another serious difficulty was the absence of an operations base. A3 concluded:

The imponderables of such offensives cannot be represented in a war game, and therefore the war game—even if the German fleet leadership had been faultless—would have been unfavorable to the German party as little or nothing was attained and much was risked.

None the less, one must be clear that *at this time*, in consideration of the forces on both sides, in particular of armored cruisers, the offensive advance envisaged by OP I risks incomparably more than it can hope to gain. It is less suited for the present than for the near future when, with the help of a powerful first squadron and a larger number of armored cruisers, one part of the French forces can be pinned down and the other can be brought to battle and when conditions have become more favorable for us through careful preparations . . .

This denunciation of the existing operations plan led to a critical marginal comment:

I cannot concur with this conclusion. I think that at the time we cannot act otherwise, for if we give up the advance we probably give up the only opportunity that we could have for our navy to succeed . . . The French will not come to our coast. Once we are equal to the united French squadrons the plan would be more feasible since we would not be bound to a time schedule [*Zeit*] but could remain on the French northern and western coasts and could thus in any case be able to reckon with a battle.

This difference of opinion led to further discussions on 9 May from which Büchsel concluded:

The stronger we become—even next year—the less prospect we have that the French N. fleet will come to battle. As OP I now stands, we shall suffer heavy losses without substantially damaging the enemy. The inevitable losses have to occur where the enemy can also be damaged. How is this to come about? By forcing Brest? Or another place? By a torpedo attack against Brest? By going to meet the Mediterranean squadron?

He ruled that these questions were to be examined during the summer and that the operations plan was to be altered accordingly.[46] Büchsel's ruling led to a memorandum by A3 (Schäfer) of 18 October 1904, signed by A on 14 November.[47] This document purported to take account of the political changes that had occurred by 18 October. Russia was regarded as eliminated as a naval ally of France because of her "weakening . . . through the war in East Asia." Italy's rapprochement with France was taken into consideration by the Admiralty Staff, which regarded "it more probable that France would be able to free her Mediterranean squadron for use in the north." But, on 14 November, A neither responded to nor was aware of the impact of the Anglo-German war scare over the German fueling of the Russian "fleet that had to die" and the examination of Germany's position resulting from the Dogger Bank incident. The active German forces were regarded as equal to the united (northern and Mediterranean) French forces in terms of ships of the line: six ships of the French northern squadron and six or eight ships of the Mediterranean squadron facing twelve or thirteen (if *Schwaben* was included) of the German active squadrons. In terms of qualities of leadership, the officer corps, crews and training, the German forces would emerge still stronger, for the strategic training of French officers had suffered because of the absence of large-scale maneuvers since 1902 and the discipline of the crews had been weakened by the spread of socialism. Hence the German navy could take the offensive.

In spite of the Anglo-French entente and the Franco-Italian rapprochement, the French were expected to maintain their Mediterranean forces in the south at the beginning of the war. At that time the Germans would have to reckon only with the French northern squadron, located in Brest, and with the *défense mobile*. Despite strong doubts as to whether the inferior French northern squadron would under any circumstances come to battle with a now much stronger German fleet, and with due respect for the difficulties involved, an early German advance into the western entrance of the English Channel was urged. Considerations of internal politics made it impossible for a powerful German fleet not to take the offensive against an inferior opponent; military considerations favored an immediate offensive against an enemy whose morale and discipline were weak; and economic considerations demanded a speedy advance into the western entrance of the English Channel to protect German shipping and to send auxiliary cruisers into the Atlantic.

Older cruisers and torpedo-boats were now considered as adequate for protecting the rearward communications, and a special North Sea squadron consisting of Siegfried ships was to patrol the eastern Channel.

Experiences of German coaling of the Russian fleet, which had seriously jeopardized Anglo-German relations, were drawn upon to prove that the German fleet at the western end of the Channel could easily acquire coal in Britain, with whom the German leadership was to expect war in November and December![48] This was a highly ironical example of the lack of coordination of the top agencies of the German empire. That the document also considered operations against Russia, with whom an alliance was being seriously considered, was a further similar example.

As for operations in the English Channel, under the most favorable circumstances the possibility of a coup of the German North Sea squadron against Cherbourg was considered. Also planned was the observation of Brest, which came close to a blockade and was to be supported by the laying of mines. Büchsel, however, for the time being rejected the forcing of the Brest base and required further examination of this option. Arrangements were made to gather information through agents in Britain about the movement of the French Mediterranean fleet, which, if it were to steam north, the German fleet would try to intercept. If such an interception was not possible, the Chief of the German Fleet should decide under what circumstances he would fight against the numerically superior united French fleet. A proposed that the German fleet withdraw through the Channel and offer battle to the pursuing French forces once it was closer to its home bases and had been reinforced by the North Sea squadron—a course of action disapproved by Büchsel in his marginal comments—or that it head into the high seas where the French fleet would be deprived of the support of torpedo-boats and coastal armored ships. But if the French fleet failed to pursue the German fleet in either of the two courses of action the Chief of the German Fleet was free to seek battle wherever possible.

A number of enclosures to the memorandum dealt with matters such as commercial war, demonstrations against the French coast, mine war, the maintenance of rearward connections, and the use of bases in neutral waters. "Whether the Scheldt estuary could be utilized as a base will only be decided in the course of the war and will depend primarily on the successes and attitudes of the army and on a possible breach of Belgian and Dutch neutrality by France." Apparently, the Admiralty Staff had not been informed of the intention of the General Staff to violate Belgian neutrality.

In February 1905 an abbreviated version of this document was presented to Wilhelm and was approved by him.[49] There was also some change in content. It was based on the assumption that the plan corresponded "according to the current political situation to the direction and aims of Your Majesty's foreign policy." Unlike the previous document this plan no longer saw Russia as an opponent, since her entire fleet had been destroyed. The whole German navy was therefore to be used in the operations against France. But British neutrality was expected and regarded as essential for the success of the plan. It was made explicit that the German fleet was to be located at the western entrance of the English Channel for a long period since it was certain that the French northern squadron would not come to battle. The Chief of the German Fleet was to try to defeat the French northern and Mediterranean fleets separately but was not to shrink from battle with the united French navy.

A special memorandum was enclosed which incorporated the results of a study ordered by Büchsel about the forcing of the Brest fortifications. It concluded "that a modern squadron of ships, in so far as only artillery and coastal fortifications are concerned, would indeed be able to penetrate to the location of the French northern squadron and would be able to fight it with a prospect of success in spite of damages incurred. The question can also be solved without difficulty from the nautical point of view." This conclusion was a drastic departure from the previously established principle that battle with coastal fortifications was to be avoided. Assuming, however, that a German squadron that had forced its way into Brest and destroyed the French squadron would be so severely mauled as to be incapable of further fighting, the Admiralty Staff recommended to Wilhelm:

> to give the order to force Brest only if the Mediterranean squadron would be permanently and firmly pinned down by strong naval allies or if in one of the following years our naval supremacy over the French has become such as to be able to engage a squadron in the forcing of Brest without the loss of the supremacy of the rest of the German fleet over the remaining French naval forces.

There existed serious confusion in the planning of the Admiraly Staff against the Dual Alliance. Some of it resulted from poor communication with other agencies. The Admiralty Staff was left to make its own guesses about the military–political situation in the Mediterranean, particularly the position of Italy, by the Foreign Office and the General Staff; it was left in ignorance about the intended invasion of Belgium (as will be seen below, it first showed awareness of it on 1 January 1905); it was also allowed to disregard the rapprochement between Britain and France, planning operations against French Channel and Atlantic coasts without expecting to encounter British opposition, and, in fact, hoping to buy coal for its navy conducting these operations in Britain. Büchsel and his officers also contradicted each other in the spring of 1903 on the question whether the German navy was capable of taking on successfully the naval forces of the Dual Alliance.

## (3)   Operations Plans against Britain, 1899–1905

Before its dissolution, the High Command had dropped its offensive plans against Britain, including the fantastic notions of an invasion. It had not undertaken any work on defensive operational planning. The new Admiralty Staff therefore had to start from scratch. The decision on the part of Tirpitz and Bülow to avoid war with Britain at almost any cost until the German fleet construction had passed through the risk zone theoretically assigned naval planning against her the lowest priority. None the less, tension with Britain was a prerequisite for building a fleet against her and the "Copenhagen complex" gave rise to phobias about a British pre-emptive attack.

The first indication of operational work in the Admiralty Staff for a war against Britain is a conclusion reached in April 1899 and reported to Wilhelm about a maneuver held in 1898. According to it, a German fleet defeated in battle by a superior western fleet, presumably the British, was able through the use of torpedo-boats to inflict serious losses on the enemy if he decided to undertake a close blockade of the German coast. In the maneuver the enemy had seized Borkum as a base, whereas the Elbe estuary served as the place of deployment and retreat of the German navy.[50] By June 1899 the Admiralty Staff had become more explicitly concerned with planning against Britain. It then set the first stage for a war against Britain as the task for the strategic maneuvers of the year. In this war Germany was to be on the defensive. By the tenth mobilization day the British were expected to have ready for action fifteen ships of the line of the first and seven of the second class, four armored cruisers, twenty-eight cruisers, and thirty-nine torpedo-boat destroyers. They would have the choice of concentrating their bulk in the North Sea or in the Baltic Sea before Kiel. Because of the greater proximity and the importance of its ports, the British fleet was expected to choose the North Sea and send detachments into the Baltic. As previously established, the German fleet would be deployed in the Elbe estuary whence it could either directly proceed into the North Sea or go through the Kaiser Wilhelm Canal into the Baltic.[51]

A memorandum of November 1899, entitled "Preparatory work for an operations plan Germany alone against England alone,"[52] definitely opted for a defensive war: "As long as the building of our fleet has not proceeded any further, the war is to be waged in home and foreign waters defensively." For British supremacy was overwhelming and the better German mobilization measures would make little difference since

> numerous political circumstances of the last decades demonstrate that England will avoid neither inconvenience nor expense in preparing herself in terms of *matériel* and personnel for a naval war as soon as it is impending. As in most naval wars . . . England will not allow herself to be surprised by a declaration of war.

Hence a German offensive, launched however early, would be suicidal because of British preparedness. Such action would be justified only if followed by an invasion, but previous studies by the High Command had revealed that preparations for the transport of a large invasion force would not remain unnoticed and that the German merchant marine probably lacked sufficient capacity for transporting the troops which the General Staff considered necessary for a successful invasion. Germany could succeed in invading Britain only if allied with either France or Russia.

The British, while unassailable, were expected to launch a vigorous offensive against Germany to bring her to terms before she could cause much damage and prevent her from finding allies. Thus Germany could expect ruthless attacks on her shipping, a close blockade of her North Sea and Baltic Sea coasts, and control of the traffic through the Scheldt estuary. It was also probable that at the outset of war the British would threaten Copenhagen to force Denmark to become her ally. Then came an ominous statement: ". . . in the following considerations we have none the less assumed that this would be prevented by Germany through a naval invasion of the Danish islands." This was the first hint about the attitude of the Admiralty Staff toward Denmark within the context of operational planning against Britain. The assumption was that Denmark's strict neutrality or her alliance with Germany would result in the concentration of the British navy in the North Sea to blockade the German ports. It was expected to confine its activity in the Baltic to the observation of Kiel or its western sections. An attempt to block the Kaiser Wilhelm Canal and a seizure of bases for the support of the blockade of the North Sea ports—in order of probability, Borkum, Pellworm, and Sylt—were also to be expected.

Once the strategic defensive against Britain had been decided on, the Elbe was again chosen as the place of deployment for the German fleet. It is from there that thrusts against the blockading British forces and the defense of the German Bight and Kiel were to be undertaken.

At the time that the above considerations were put on paper, Bendemann in November 1899 personally prepared a memorandum "The defense against England"[53] in which he gave the strategic defensive against Britain a Baltic orientation. He opened this revolutionary document with an analysis of the political situation:

. . . as in the last decades other great civilized nations consciously and energetically began to emerge as competitors in world politics and world trade, Great Britain concentrated her strength and with great financial sacrifices created for herself a naval armament . . . which is equal to all occasions. Through this powerful effort she shows that she does not allow the extent of her development to be hindered by external powers; she shows that she is determined not to allow her overwhelming position in world politics and world trade to be limited without a struggle, not to speak of giving it up . . .

An alignment of all the great powers of the European continent against Britain, which would in the light of the situation be the only natural and correct course, can unfortunately for the time being be considered only a pious wish. Great Britain would act in her own well-understood interest only if she did not wait until this pious wish descended from the realm of phantasy and became a reality.

France, without drawing a sword, has already surrendered to Britain. Austria and Italy participate little or not at all in world politics. Russia, the most dangerous enemy of Britain, since she can attack her directly by land without being much damaged by reprisals [*Rückschlage*] at sea, apparently bides her time.

Germany, if she would by then have completed her naval armaments, could be a very welcome ally to Russia when she considered the time to be ripe.

The danger of the situation thus is that Britain could succumb to the temptation posed by Germany's impotence at sea and the neutrality of France to cripple Germany's capacity to pursue *Weltpolitik* . . . The task of diplomacy is thus *for so long as honor permits* to avoid armed conflict with Britain as long as Germany is weak at sea and unworthy of being an ally to Russia.

These observations fit in with the then current anglophobia, diplomatic speculations about a Continental bloc, Tirpitz's notions of the risk theory and of Germany becoming through her navy a worthy ally to other Continental powers, Bülow's hope of an eventual Russo-German alliance against Britain, and the attitude which Jonathan Steinberg has appropriately described as the "Copenhagen complex."[54]

In his ground-breaking memorandum Bendemann proceeded to discuss the military situation in an Anglo-German war from Germany's vantage-point. The division of Germany's coast by Denmark forced the attacker to wage war in two theaters whereas the German navy could switch from one theater to the other through the Kaiser Wilhelm Canal. To be successful the attacker's fleet must therefore be twice as strong as the German. This strength Britain possessed even without her Mediterranean or transoceanic forces. But Germany's chances of confronting Britain were better in the Baltic than in the North Sea. In the latter her battle fleet was outnumbered and in rough weather could not be supported in open water by torpedo-boats. In the Baltic, however, argued Bendemann,

. . . we can certainly operate all of our naval forces at any time. In addition we know these difficult waters thoroughly, whereas the enemy does not. The Belts and the western part of the Baltic Sea would therefore provide us with the best chances for a successful defensive. Moreover, the control of the Belts secures for us the freedom of movement in and the domination over the Baltic Sea without depriving us of the opportunity—thanks to the Kaiser Wilhelm Canal—of appearing in the Elbe and thus in the North Sea or when necessary responding to the forcing of the Elbe.

As long as the defender can move freely in the Baltic Sea and the Belts, the attacker may find it necessary occasionally to loosen the narrow blockade of the North Sea and thus give our commerce breathing-space and make possible the exit of our commerce raiders. For the attacker in the North Sea will always have to keep one eye on the Baltic Sea to secure himself against attacks from there.

Bendemann then drew on the authority of military history to prove that the British fleet would concentrate in the Danish Belts if the German fleet took action there. By diverting the British naval forces into the Danish straits, the German navy would prevent them from blockading the North Sea ports and retain an active role rather than being confined in harbors as it would in taking the defensive in the North Sea.

Success in the Danish straits against the British required a base. The autumn maneuvers of 1899 had demonstrated that Kiel was too distant to support torpedo-boats in the northern Belts.

For the control of the Belts it is therefore essential that their coasts are militarily in our hands. The conduct of a powerful defensive therefore requires that we bring Denmark to join us either voluntarily or forcibly . . .

It is . . . of the greatest importance that we establish in the first days of the war or, rather, before Denmark can carry out its mobilization our control over the coasts of the Belt.

Bendemann's eastern orientation was questioned by Grapow, head of section A4, which was responsible for the planning of operations against Britain. While agreeing that the occupation of the Danish islands would improve Germany's chances in a war with Britain, he did not think that it would prevent a blockade of the German North Sea coast. On the fourteenth mobilization day Britain's total European strength of thirty-six ships of the line, two armored cruisers, twenty-three large cruisers, forty-two small cruisers, twenty torpedo-gunboats, and seventy-four torpedo-boats would enable her both to establish a blockade of the North Sea and to launch an attack on the German forces in the Baltic. The German navy would probably be compelled to withdraw into the Elbe to prevent the British blockade fleet from forcing its way into it.[55] Bendemann responded to his subordinate's criticism by emphasizing that the action against Denmark must take place during the first ten days of mobilization and reiterating his conviction that the British would respond to a German attack on Denmark by coming to her defense. In case of a subsequent British attack on the Elbe estuary, the German fleet, having gained confidence, courage, and experience from the Danish operation, could easily return to its defense.[56] Grapow, however, remained unconvinced by the arguments of his chief. He replied:

> I have merely tried to draw attention to the fact that after fourteen days any terms of war can be imposed by England, even if we gain at first very great and later valuable advantages. The defensive war against England will in my opinion begin only after the English fleet has been mobilized. Therefore in my opinion the work on the old so-called "defensive O-Plan" must be continued.[57]

Specifically Bendemann called for the appearance of the fleet in the Belts at the outbreak of war to cut off connections between the Danish islands and the mainland and for the participation of army units in the occupation of Jutland, Fünen, and Zealand to establish control over the Belts for the duration of the war. He did not consider the occupation of Copenhagen essential, although he would welcome it if the army alone could take it. The execution of the plan required cooperation between the Admiralty Staff and the General Staff.

On 12 December 1899, Wilhelm declared himself in agreement with Bendemann's proposals and authorized that the Admiralty Staff consult with the General Staff about their detailed preparation.[58] Bendemann's planning was continued by Diederichs, although he thought that the numerous financial and economic ties between Germany and Britain made an attack by the latter on the former very improbable and did not share his predecessor's pessimism about Germany's disadvantages in an actual war with Britain. The army was thus expected to support the navy in a new theater of operations at a time that Schlieffen, prevented from increasing the size of the army, was beginning to have serious doubts about fighting a two-front war and had decided that the invasion of Belgium was essential for a successful outcome. Faced with the assignment of higher financial priority to the navy than to the army,[59] he was now expected to weaken the strength of the army in the main theater of war to support a privileged but as yet impotent navy. Ironically, while the decision to invade Belgium was the result of the weakness of the army, caused partly by the higher priority assigned to the navy, the decision to invade Denmark was the result of the youthful weakness of the navy. The concept of rape of small countries in German military and naval operations originated from weakness.

However reluctantly, Schlieffen entered into negotiations for the preparation of the plan for the invasion of Denmark.[60] He replied to Diederichs' formal request for cooperation of 20 December 1899[61] on 16 January 1900:

> The cooperation of the army in strategic defense of the German fleet in a war against England has as a necessary prerequisite that the war would be fought against England alone. If England has one or indeed two great Continental powers as allies, then those parts of the German army

capable of offensive undertakings are fully bound by operations on territorial boundaries.[62]

This prerequisite was very restrictive. For could one ever guarantee that both France and Russia would stay out of an Anglo-German war? Only from 1898 to 1905, with France rent by the Dreyfus case and its aftermath and her military discredited and with Russia committed to expansion in the Far East and as of February 1904 engaged in a disastrous war with Japan, was this eventuality even possible. Bülow had admitted half a year earlier that France made no attempt "to conceal her wish to attack Germany at the first given opportunity."[63]

In a war against only Britain—and Denmark—Schlieffen held that the army could provide the navy with effective support in a surprise occupation of the Danish islands. The capture of Fünen, the island closest to the mainland, presented no difficulty. The seizure of Zealand would only make sense if it occurred early enough to disrupt the Danish mobilization. But he doubted whether the troops required for the permanent occupation of Zealand would be available and in any case considered it unwise to commit them to the island where they could be cut off by the British through forcing the Great Belt and seizing its southern exit. He therefore recommended that the German amphibious operation plan be confined to the occupation of Fünen and the securing of the crossing over the Little Belt. "In secure possession of the coast and bays of Fünen, the defense of the narrows of the Great Belt by our torpedo-boats can be made possible." Fünen would be seized by the Eighteenth Division on the first and second days of mobilization.

In his response of 12 February Diederichs admitted that in case of energetic British action the navy would be unable to evacuate the German troops from Zealand. He agreed with Schlieffen to establish a joint committee to coordinate the actions of the navy and the army.[64] Within the Admiralty Staff the originally hesitant Grapow was put in charge of the details of the naval operations against Denmark,[65] and operations against Zealand and action against Copenhagen were made the subject of the imperial maneuvers of 1900.[66]

In a series of meetings in the spring of 1900 between Major von Zitzewitz and Major von Necker of the General Staff and Grapow and Kapitän-leutnant Erwin Schäfer of the Admiralty Staff tentative agreement was reached concerning the proposed operations.[67] The naval representatives several times assured their colleagues that the operations were only planned for a war against Britain alone.

In concluding the arrangements, the representatives of the Admiralty Staff argued that the navy would not restrict itself to a defensive stance south of the Danish islands. Rather, it would attempt an offensive which would have as its primary aim the seizure of the Little Belt. To obtain the necessary space for such an offensive, Samsö would have to be captured. They denied that the German position could be circumvented after the occupation of the Little Belt, for the Sound was too shallow for the passage of large ships and the Great Belt would be mined. The committee agreed that the Seventeenth

Division, consisting of three infantry brigades, and accompanied by the Fifteenth Hussar Regiment, would be used in Jutland. The Eighteenth Division, accompanied by the Sixteenth Hussar Regiment, would occupy Fünen and then proceed to take Samsö. Samsö and the east coast of Jutland to its latitude were to be occupied by the eighth mobilization day or whenever the establishment of British supremacy in Danish waters was to be expected. It was agreed that in the interest of speedy action the Ninth Army Corps was required to take some preparatory measures before the actual proclamation of mobilization. Arrangements were made for the distribution of troop-transports between railways and ships and for the setting up of army artillery for use against hostile ships and torpedo-boats. These discussions did not, however, lead to any binding decisions.

The eastern orientation of the Admiralty Staff was strengthened by a war game played aboard *Grille* from 30 May to 5 June 1900[68] dealing with the now rejected defensive operations against Britain in the North Sea. In the course of the game the British fleet, after first battering down the fortifications of Cuxhaven, proceeded to attack the German fleet, which had taken refuge in the Elbe. The German fleet was supported by mine-booms, torpedo-batteries, and torpedo-boats. A decisive battle severely damaged most ships of the line of both belligerents, but Britain, along with her older vessels, had enough seaworthy ships of the line and cruisers left for the establishment of control over the North and Baltic Seas and for imposing a blockade on the German coast. The explicit conclusion drawn from the war game was that the fortifications of Cuxhaven required strengthening and the implicit conclusion was that the recent Baltic orientation of the Admiralty Staff was correct.

On 12 April 1902, Kapitän-zur-See Heeringen, author of the first operations plan against Britain who in 1900 had been transferred from the headship of the information department of the Imperial Naval Office to the fleet, wrote a memorandum to Prince Heinrich, now Chief of the First Squadron, in which he also threw his weight behind the offensive in Danish waters,[69] arguing that other courses of action were futile. An immediate battle with the Royal Navy, for which there would be pressure from the German public and the army, would result in the destruction of the German fleet. And there existed few opportunities for wearing down the British blockade forces in the North Sea through defensive strategy. In such a case, the bulk of the British fleet would be located north-west of Heligoland and the German coasts and river estuaries would be closed completely by advancing torpedo-boats. Sorties against the bulk of the British fleet would be thwarted by cruisers. In the event of a German action against Denmark, however, the British would not be sufficiently strong to divide their forces into two so as to control both the Baltic and North Seas. They would have to choose between entry into the Baltic Sea where the German navy would be at an advantage or blockade of the German North Sea coast with detachments to the Skagerrak to prevent the exit of German ships from the Baltic. The obvious German response to the second course of action would be to attack the weaker British force in the Skagerrak.

Surprisingly Heeringen then raised the previously rejected notion of invading Britain: "A decisive success in the war can only be achieved through an invasion of England. The prerequisite of such an invasion must be the temporary possession of control of the North Sea." He further assumed that a permanent connection between the invasion forces and the homeland was unnecessary and that preparations for the invasion could be made in peacetime so that the invasion force could be launched at the earliest favorable occasion. Heeringen admitted: "It is immediately obvious that through such a course one departs from the general principles of war; nevertheless, the special case "Germany alone against England" justifies such extreme means." In discussing the course of action leading to the temporary attainment of domination in the North Sea, Heeringen contradicted his own arguments in favor of an offensive against Denmark and against deployment in the North Sea.

He advocated further extension of the German area of operations: "friendly invasion of Holland and Belgium," because of their proximity to England, would improve the chances of invasion, and their control by Germany would force the British naval leadership to divide its forces and to undertake the observation of the entire Continental coast from France's eastern border to Memel. And he suggested that the German expeditionary forces against Britain be embarked in the Elbe, the Danish harbors, the Scheldt estuary, and the Dutch ports. Lastly he recommended feint attacks against the west coast of Scotland.

Heeringen's long memorandum was riddled with contradictions and was subjected to serious criticisms by the officers of the Admiralty Staff, particularly Grapow, Winkler, and Wilhelm Souchon, the last of whom was currently in charge of section A2. Above all, the three men maintained that even the attainment of temporary control of the North Sea, which Heeringen viewed as the prerequisite of the invasion of Britain, was unattainable.[70] Heeringen, as a close associate of Tirpitz, must have been aware that his former chief opposed an invasion of Britain as long as the German troops that had landed there could be cut off by sea. It is most surprising that such a weak operational study had been prepared by so experienced an officer as Heeringen. A partial explanation is found in Heeringen's reply to a query on the part of the Admiralty Staff to the effect that he had not had time to study the matter.[71]

Souchon, however, soon came back to entertain doubts about the viability of the plan to attack Denmark.[72] He emphasized the need for the occupation of Zealand, without which it was impossible to obtain full control of the Belts and the Sound, to eliminate Copenhagen as a military factor, or to provide a favorable situation for Germany if Britain found an ally against her. On the strength of information from the General Staff, Souchon concluded that troops would be available for the occupation of the island and denied that there was any danger that they would be cut off as long as the German fleet was able to resist the British with success at the northern entrance into the Belts and at the southern exit from the Sound. Even if the resistance of the German fleet were broken, the advance of the enemy could still be delayed until the German troops were evacuated.

Winkler advocated the restriction of the activity of the army to Jutland

and Fünen, but Souchon prevailed. A, represented by Albedyll (?), and A5 agreed that the occupation of Zealand was essential for the success of the entire operation.[73] Subsequently a meeting of the section heads of the A department of the Admiralty Staff decided to clarify the issue in the *Grosse Admiralstabsreise* in June.[74] There is no evidence, however, of any such clarification.

This was the state of operational planning against Britain when Diederichs was replaced by Büchsel as Chief of the Admiralty Staff. As Tirpitz's close collaborator and nominee, he would be expected to subordinate the planning of the Admiralty Staff to the strategic thinking of the Imperial Naval Office: emphasis on battleships, deployment in the North Sea, and avoidance of any invasion plans of Britain. It is therefore ironic that Büchsel's work on the operations plans against Britain was started by a communication from the head of the European Department, A, Winkler, of 2 October 1902, to B, head of the Extra-European Department, asking to what extent cruiser warfare could facilitate German operations against Britain in European waters.[75] Reluctant to depart from Tirpitz's basic principle, "the decision lies with the battle fleet and not with cruiser warfare," Winkler proposed that the latter be conducted so as to weaken the British rather than the German battle fleet. He suggested that Germany's advantage over Britain lay in her more abundant trained personnel—an old argument of Tirpitz and Wilhelm II—which could be used to man auxiliary cruisers. Britain could thus be forced to detach precious manpower from her home fleet to man her cruisers and older battleships to patrol her more important shipping lanes. Provided that B went along with his suggestions, Winkler agreed to propose to Büchsel a meeting of all the involved section heads. On 8 October, B responded with an enthusiasm bordering on heresy: "St Mahan should not be viewed as infallible."[76] For Germany the preparation of cruiser warfare at the cost of "10 million marks or more" was a "burning issue."

Büchsel responded to Winkler's proposal on 21 October.[77] Aware of Tirpitz's emphasis on Britain's personnel problems and his aversion to the *jeune école,* he shifted the focus of the discussion; instead of limiting it to cruiser war, it dealt with a broader issue:

> what do we have that can force England to weaken her offensive naval strength by making her provide detachments for the protection of trade, her own coast, and for other tasks absorbing trained personnel? I am of the opinion that England has everything she needs and could need, except personnel. This is the most vulnerable spot and here we must kick.

Thus Büchsel reconciled potential heresy to Tirpitz orthodoxy.

On 10 November, Büchsel ruled that the following questions be answered at the next meeting:

(1) Can our fleet leadership bring the fleet in a battle of withdrawal as far as Kiel?

(2) Is it more correct to deploy our fleet north of Denmark or on the Elbe?

(3)    Is it at all necessary to occupy Denmark? Must Zealand be included [in the occupation]?[78]

These were searching questions regarding the whole area of operations against Britain.

By 24 November 1902, Büchsel had clarified his views in a memorandum which he circulated to A1, A2, A4, and A5 to serve as the basis for further discussions.[79] He stated that there was no way that Germany, through war, could impose her will on Britain. This could be achieved only by starving Britain into surrender by cutting off her imports or by invading her with at least six army corps. A prerequisite for either was naval domination, of which the German fleet was incapable. Thus, "it is the task of our diplomacy to avoid war with England as long as our honor permits [and], if that is impossible, to ensure that England's relationship to other states which are strong at sea will prevent her from turning her whole strength against us." This reasoning fell in line with the thinking of both Tirpitz and Bülow.

Should war break out anyway, Büchsel expected Britain to destroy Germany's trade, thus causing heavy damage to her industry and making difficult the feeding of her population, and to seek powerful Continental allies who, along with a British expeditionary force, would carry the war to Germany's soil. To attain these objectives Britain would impose a close blockade on the German North Sea coast, the exit into the Baltic Sea, and Dutch and Belgian harbors, and burn down the German maritime cities.

The German fleet could not do battle with the numerically superior British in the North Sea. Destruction of the German fleet would give the British undisputed naval mastery and thus the opportunity to attain all of their objectives. Having ruled out a naval battle, Büchsel also rejected the strategy of weakening the blockade fleet through offensive thrusts by light forces, for British cruisers were more than a match for German torpedo-boats. But Bendemann's original strategy to attack Denmark gave Germany a chance against her superior opponent. It would entice the British to divide their forces in order to fight in two theaters which would be joined for the German navy through the Kaiser Wilhelm Canal: "We thus want to gain the opportunity of being able to defeat one part of the English fleet with our united forces before the other part can come to its assistance." Büchsel was, however, more concerned about the defense of the Elbe. Its fortifications would have to be strengthened before the attack on Denmark could be launched and a part of the fleet would have to be held back to support Cuxhaven. Since Copenhagen would provide the British with a first-rate base for the struggle in Danish waters, Büchsel now adopted Souchon's position:

> If therefore in the struggle for Germany's existence we follow the plan to make the Baltic Sea a partial theater of war then, if this is politically at all possible and if Denmark does not become our ally, it is necessary that we come into the possession of the défilés and neutralize the Danish fleet before the arrival of the British, i.e. that we by surprise occupy Jutland up to the point that we dominate the Little and Great Belt, Fünen, Zealand,

and Copenhagen, and either seize or destroy the Danish fleet before the English arrive.

This was the most extreme position of the Admiralty Staff regarding Denmark. It made the navy entirely dependent on the army. Nor was the occupation of Zealand and Copenhagen covered by the preliminary arrangements made with the General Staff. But, claimed Büchsel, the army

> can for the time being be considered as permanently available, unless Britain gains a powerful Continental ally—besides Denmark, only Russia and France come into consideration—and the conditions at sea then become so unfavorable through the addition of their fleets to our enemy's that other considerations must prevail.

The operations against Denmark thus precluded any hostilities with France and Russia from the naval as well as from the military point of view.

In Büchsel's opinion the execution of the plan depended on a diplomatic situation which allowed pressure to be brought on Denmark. She was then to be served with an ultimatum offering her a choice of alliance or war. Its rejection would be immediately followed by a landing on Zealand, occupation of Copenhagen, the capture or destruction of the Danish fleet, and the seizure of Fünen along with the islands in the Belts. The same operations were to take place if Denmark were to become Britain's ally. If it was politically inadvisable to attack Denmark, then the German navy was to take the strategic defensive in the North Sea. But even in this case Büchsel adhered to his scheme of trying to divide the forces of his powerful opponent. He recommended that it be then considered

> whether it would be appropriate to attempt to draw on us a part of the English fleet through a strong presence in the Skagerrak, and thus possibly cause the English to put pressure on Denmark; this would also annoy Russia and provide us with an excuse for undertaking belligerent actions in the Belts without consideration for Denmark and for occupying Jutland and Fünen to secure the Little Belt.

The restricted action against Jutland and Fünen was also to be undertaken should Denmark join Britain later in the war.

Having thus provided for various diplomatic situations, Büchsel stipulated further preparations: discussions with the General Staff, the study of operational details such as the selection of a landing-site in Zealand; arranging for the occupation of Copenhagen, the invasion of Jutland and Fünen, the ships to be used for the transport of troops, and the measures for the defense of Cuxhaven; and determining the share of the army in the operations. The work on the operational planning against Britain was thus shifted into high gear.

Following the circulation of this memorandum, Souchon prepared an estimation of the probable action of the British in a war against Germany.[80]

and changed his mind completely. In fact, he now diametrically opposed
Büchsel on the importance of seizing Copenhagen. He expected the British
home fleet, Channel squadron, cruiser squadron, torpedo-boat flotillas and
their reinforcements to deploy before the Thames and then to proceed to the
Baltic and to arrive on the fourth mobilization day before Friedrichsort. The
British Mediterranean fleet would also be involved in the operations against
Germany. Assembling at Gibraltar, it would reach Cuxhaven on the fourth
mobilization day. Both fleets, each of them stronger than the German navy,
would have as their orders the destruction or enclosure of the German fleet
and the blockade of the German coast. In this gloomy situation a strategic
defense in the North Sea would mean the loss of the German commerce and
colonies, the end of neutral shipping to German harbors, and forgoing any
opportunity of damaging British trade. The only other course of action was
to attempt to retain control of the Baltic Sea by blocking the Great Belt, the
only entry for enemy battleships into the Baltic, at the very beginning of the
war at the Nyborg–Sprogö–Korsör line with the help of the army. This
would be the most useful position for the German fleet. It was also advisable
to occupy the coast along which the enemy would be advancing to this
position, the Kattegat and the Samsö Belt, and to secure the Small Belt and
the navigable waters between Zealand and Fälster. Copenhagen should not
be seized: it was of limited value to the enemy as a base and its capture would
cause too heavy losses to the German fleet, induce the Danes to resist with
greater vigor, and cause diplomatic reverberations. The man who had
earlier insisted on the seizure of all of Zealand now left the extent of its
occupation to the discretion of the army.

By maintaining control over the Baltic, Germany could damage British
trade, keep open German harbors from Hamburg to Memel, preserve the
German fleet and even inflict enough losses on the enemy to reduce his
relative superiority. German colonies and overseas commerce would, of
course, be lost.

On 22 December 1902 a conference was held between Büchsel,
Souchon, Hopmann and Winkler and Quartermaster-General Generalmajor Beseler and Oberst Deines of the General Staff.[81] In spite of the
serious reservations expressed by the representatives of the General Staff it
was agreed to continue the discussions concerning the cooperation of the
army and the navy. The Admiralty Staff proceeded with its own
preparations, and Büchsel drafted a report to Wilhelm about the
operations against Britain in 1903.[82] As established in the discussions with
the General Staff, the occupation of Zealand was not to include
Copenhagen, but the Danish navy was to be blockaded in its harbor.
Greater emphasis was placed on activity in the Skagerrak: if the British navy
did not enter the Danish waters, the German ships which were deployed
there were to attack its flank in the North Sea to relieve pressure on the
German coast and to escort German merchantmen to the ocean. Older
German ships were to safeguard the blockings in Danish waters. Büchsel
also mentioned the arrangements for attacks by the German warships
abroad on British trade and the sending out of auxiliary cruisers to prey on
British food imports. He made an ominous observation which threatened

the basis of all German operational planning: "We must keep in mind that the most dangerous tactic of the enemy is to blockade us from a distance and to avoid any offensive actions." This appears to be the first anticipation on the part of the German navy of a wide blockade on the part of Britain, as imposed during World War I.

There is no evidence that this report was ever presented to Wilhelm. Instead, a much shorter report of a general outline of the operational work, initialed in March 1903 by A, A1, A2, and A4, received his approval.[83] This approval did not finalize the plan but provided it with Imperial sanction and thus put some pressure on the General Staff to be more cooperative. But the plan received a blow from its examination within the Admiralty Staff. Both the autumn maneuvers[84] and the war game of the *Grosse Admiralstabreise* dealt with the operations against Britain. The latter, reported by A2 Hopmann on 30 September,[85] in fact tested the operations plan that was in preparation under conditions that were very favorable to Germany: the British Mediterranean squadron did not participate, although both Souchon and Büchsel in his report of March to Wilhelm assumed that it would do so. The German side followed the approved operations plan: the entire high-seas fleet concentrated in the Nyborg–Korsör position. Following an *ad hoc* plan of the General Staff, troops of the Ninth Army Corps were involved. The British obligingly divided their forces, leaving the "A" fleet of fifteen ships of the line, five armored cruisers, fourteen protected cruisers, and twenty-five torpedo-boats to blockade the Elbe, and sending their weaker "B" fleet of six ships of the line, eight armored cruisers, fifteen protected cruisers, nine torpedo command boats, and twenty-eight torpedo-boats to blockade Kiel and interrupt German commerce in Danish waters. A smaller detachment was to intercept shipping to Germany through Dutch and Belgian harbors. The war preparedness of the two sides was to correspond to actual conditions.

The game opened with the occupation of parts of Danish territory by German troops. On the second mobilization day the Nyborg–Korsör position was successfully occupied by a force of 5,600 men of the Seventeenth Division, the Eighteenth Division proceeded by land to occupy Fredericia, blockings had been set up in both Belts, and Denmark had responded with a declaration of war. On the third mobilization day Fünen was occupied and by the end of the fifth mobilization day the German position was substantially reinforced. German progress appeared to be satisfactory.

The British "B" fleet, however, having been unable to force the German Great Belt position by itself, was on the sixth mobilization day reinforced by the "A" fleet, which had initially been engaged in various inconclusive actions in the North Sea. The united British forces proceeded at once to force the German positions in the Great Belt. This occurred before the German preparations were fully completed: the Third Squadron and the Armored Boat Division were not yet mobilized and not all army reinforcements had arrived. Moreover, several German ships, including two ships of the line, had been detached to protect the German rear against some light British ships that had entered the Baltic through the Sound. Thereupon the war game was concluded.

In the opinion of Hopmann the outcome of the war game cast serious doubts on the practicability of the operations plan. If British naval leaders decided, as their German equivalents did in the game, to proceed immediately to assert naval domination at both ends of the Kaiser Wilhelm Canal, it was doubtful if the German side could ever establish a sufficiently strong position in the Belts. He expected that the forcing of the Great Belt would have led to the defeat of the German fleet. He concluded that at the very least the feasibility of the operations plan was dependent on accelerated occupation of Danish territory and establishment of the German defense positions. Winkler felt that Hopmann's conclusions were too extreme and thought that the German position would have improved considerably from better provisions for the early use of torpedo-boats.

As for details, Hopmann approved the choice of the defensive position in the Great Belt at the Nyborg–Korsör location, but recommended some changes in the laying of mine-booms. He also thought that it was a mistake not to block the Sound, allowing enemy units to proceed from there to the rear of the German position. In the future the Smeland Fairway was to be blockaded and Moen and the Gyden-Riff were to be occupied. He did not think that German torpedo-boats were able to stand up to the superior weapons of the British light forces. Hopmann also recommended that the intelligence service be improved; Winkler stated that this was already being done. In view of the danger of having the German forces on Zealand cut off by a rapid British advance, Hopmann backtracked from his original stand and questioned "whether it is not advisable to give up altogether the occupation of Zealand and to confine oneself to Jutland, Fünen, Samsö, and Sprogö." Thereby the German position would be so weakened, however, as to negate the need for the Danish operation. Hopmann thought that a possible substitute for the occupation of Zealand would be the seizure of the Halsbrö peninsula. His final comment was that if the army was unable to support the operations the Danish waters be given up unless forced by the British.

Souchon co-initialed Hopmann's report and remarked on 2 October that, while he entirely agreed with it, he thought that the existing plan would have to be worked on in default of a better one, particularly since in the following years Germany's chances would improve with her growing navy. By the time this conclusion had been reached by two of the major planners, further discouragement was provided by the General Staff. On 6 August 1903, Schlieffen wrote to Büchsel,[86] stating that the occupation of Danish territory to the extent intended by the Admiralty Staff would require two army corps. These troops would certainly be available as long as Britain was Germany's only enemy.

But this state of affairs will hardly last long. It is to be assumed with certainty that the unfavorable situation into which we shall be brought through a war against England and into which we shall place ourselves through a war against Denmark will be used against us by other powers. We shall then face a war for the waging of which we shall have to engage our last man and for which we can by no means dispense with those two army corps which occupy the Danish islands.

In view of these circumstances Schlieffen implored Büchsel "once more to consider whether the plan to occupy Danish territory could be dropped." These were powerful arguments against the plan. Büchsel, however, supported by Winkler and an officer representing both A2 and A4, was obstinate. In his reply of 13 August[87] he refused to consider the possibility that the war would not remain localized, insisted that in the preparation of the plan it had been constantly assumed that the political situation "left Germany a completely free hand against England," and drew on Wilhelm's authority for support: "Since His Majesty has ordered the working through of this plan, it must be expected that . . . [he] will order this plan to go into effect at the outbreak of war, the political situation permitting. I therefore consider it my duty, now as before, to promote as strongly as possible the preparation of this plan." It was not possible to dispense with the occupation of Danish territory by army troops, although the support of one army corps might suffice. Büchsel requested that the General Staff continue to cooperate on the preparation of the plan. Upon the receipt of the request, Schlieffen called on Büchsel and agreed to do so.[88]

Faced with doubts arising from a war game that was unfavorable to the German side and with serious misgivings on the part of the General Staff, the "A" Department decided in a conference of 17 October to restrict the extent of the operations in Danish territory.[89] The notion of occupying all of Zealand, Fünen, and Jutland was given up. Only if the British fleet was expected in Danish waters would mine-booms be laid in the Great Belt between Halsbro, Sprogö, and Knudshoved, which would be protected by army artillery and troops. The Little Belt would be blocked not at its northern entrance but along the line Arsens–Bagö–Arösund. In addition to the troops to be used on the Great Belt, a part of an army division was to be at the Jutland border to be used when and where necessary.

In May 1904, Lans, now in charge of Section 5, led the *Kleine Admiralstabsübungsreise* in which the possibility of enemy forces breaking through the Sound and arriving in the rear of the German navy in the Belts was examined.[90] The modified operations plan was tested in the war game of the *Grosse Admiralstabsreise* in June 1904.[91] Account was taken of the change in the diplomatic situation through the Anglo-French entente and the reluctance of the army to participate in the Danish operations. Thus at the hypothetical outbreak of the Anglo-German war France's attitude toward Germany was viewed as doubtful and the German army was not expected to be involved in the operations against Denmark. The British were to have sixteen ships of the line, ten armored cruisers, twenty-eight cruisers and torpedo-gunboats, and forty torpedo-boat destroyers operating in the Baltic with the main aim of destroying the German fleet. The German side set up a mine-boom in the Sprogö position in the Great Belt and left some light forces and four ships of the line to defend it, blocked the Little Belt with mines and ships sunk in the navigable passages, and left the defense of the Sound to the Siegfried ships, some cruisers, and a torpedo-boat flotilla. The German side further dispersed its forces by sending seven ships of the line and two armored gunboat divisions to the Elbe estuary when expecting that the British would force their way into it.

The British side tried to weaken the German defense by Sprogö and eventually managed to force the Little Belt with one ship of the line, four armored cruisers and two smaller cruisers which destroyed the German Siegfried ships which had been sent there. By thus threatening the rear of the German forces defending the mine-boom in the Great Belt, the British forced their withdrawal.

The conclusions that the participants drew from the war game were favorable to the continuation of the Danish operations plan. They recommended that it be carried out even without the involvement of the army, that the blocking of the Great Belt at the Sprogö position be continued, although in the Little Belt the blocking could be moved to the north. In any case both the Little Belt and the Flintrinne in the Sound, through which large ships could pass, ought to be blocked more effectively. A strong detachment would still have to be sent to the Elbe estuary before its defense works were fully mobilized. For the entire operations in Danish waters additional mine-ships and mines were considered necessary. Büchsel also responded favorably on 27 July to the outcome of the war game.[92] He stressed that the basic purpose of the Danish operations plan should not be forgotten:

We want to tie the enemy down in an area in which all of our torpedo-boats have a favorable opportunity for attack, and we further expect that through the forcing of the blockings on the part of the enemy his forces will be weakened to the point that our high-seas fleet has the opportunity to defeat it without being destroyed in turn.

Büchsel's major concern about the location of the blocking of the Great Belt was that it be at a sufficient distance from the Sound so that torpedo-boats entering the Baltic through it at night would not be able under the cover of darkness to reach the German bulk. The fleet should not commit too many ships to the defense of the blockings: it was sufficient to inflict losses on the enemy as he broke through, not to fight the decisive battle with him. If he broke through, the German ships could withdraw and when reinforced by the rest of the fleet come to battle with the enemy, if he was sufficiently weakened by forcing the blockings, or otherwise withdraw to Kiel. Büchsel also challenged the prevailing assumption that the high-seas fleet be from the outset located behind the blockings. He suggested as an alternative that it move at the beginning of war to Gniben (at the tip of the northwest corner of Zealand) to protect the entrances of both Belts until the arrival of a superior enemy, provide time for the blocking of the Belts and the Sound, and support the activity of torpedo-boats in the area south of Skagen. Only when a superior enemy bulk arrived was it to withdraw behind the blockings in the Great Belt. Büchsel attributed the British breakthrough in the Little Belt in the war game to the destruction of the Siegfried ships by enemy torpedo-boats and suggested that this could be prevented by surrounding those ships with small boats as protection. So favorable was the outcome of the war game in Büchsel's opinion that he ruled that in the winter an operations plan of the navy in Danish waters without army support be prepared and completed by March 1905.

On 3 October, Friedrich Boedicker demonstrated that he was the first officer of the Admiralty Staff to recognize that the rapprochement between Britain and France, the weakening of the Russian military power in Europe, and the rapprochement between her and Germany required a revision of operations planning. "The change in the political situation since last winter makes a war against the Dual Alliance less likely, in my opinion, than a war of Germany against England and a France allied to England." He queried whether the army which would now have to fight on only one front would continue to be unable to provide forces "for the coast against the united fleets of both strongest sea powers," and suggested further inquiries with the army authorities. This made necessary a joint OP I/OP II (Operations Plan against Britain), "i.e. we must then also prepare for the case of war Germany against England and France." It further required a change in the German naval mobilization: since the current mobilization arrangements of the German navy were primarily directed against France and the war against Britain was regarded as "a special case," "it is high time to prepare our mobilization the other way around. The war against England alone may be improbable and it may be probable that we will then simultaneously be involved with France: but I consider a war against France alone under current [*augenblicklichen*] political circumstances as entirely improbable."[93]

Büchsel, however, was more concerned about obtaining army support than about drafting a new mobilization plan against both Britain and France. He saw in the non-participation of Russia in a European war in the foreseeable future an opportunity for further negotiations with the army to achieve parallel preparations for "mobilization and provision of active troops" for a war of Germany against both France and Britain on the part of the navy and army. The urgency for this effort lay "in the conviction that a war with England would break out so quickly that operations which have not included the army would probably come too late to be implemented." Büchsel's comments were made on the day following the Dogger Bank incident. Earlier, Bülow had been impressed by the hostility of the British press to the coaling of the Russian Baltic Sea fleet heading for East Asia by the Hamburg–America Line, which it considered a breach of German neutrality, and both he and Holstein put out feelers for an alliance with Russia.[94] The Dogger Bank incident occurred on 22 October, but Büchsel was probably unaware of it (it was reported by Metternich to Bülow on 24 October) when he proposed a meeting on 26 October to deal with Boedicker's comments. By then the Dogger Bank incident was common knowledge, and on 27 October Wilhelm wired Nicholas proposing a defensive alliance to secure Russian support in case the coaling of the Russian fleet involved Germany in a war with Britain.[95] It was thus by no means surprising that, in the meeting with A, A1, A2, A4$_2$, and D on 26 October, Büchsel decided to take energetic action. Without referring to the political situation he insisted that the uncertainty about the operations plan be ended and a definite decision regarding the role of the army be sought from Wilhelm. He proposed that the Emperor require a joint report from himself and the Chief of the General Staff about the military aspects of the operation to be followed by a joint report of himself and the Chancellor "to establish the political bases for our military actions."[96] He hoped that these reports would lead to the formation of a committee of the agencies concerned which would be directly responsible to the Emperor to work out a new operations plan against Britain in consideration of the political and military factors concerned. His was thus one of the most serious efforts to coordinate political and military planning in Imperial Germany at a time when there was particular need for such coordination.

He himself got in touch with Schlieffen once more on 2 November, asking whether, in view of the changed political situation, troops could be more extensively relied upon in the operations against Denmark. Following Boedicker, he maintained:

> In so far as I comprehend the changed political situation, a war of Germany against France and Russia appears in the foreseeable future less probable, but the participation or involvement of France in a conflict of England with Germany has gained in probability.
>
> This situation means, in so far as I can judge, a relief for the army but a more difficult situation for the navy.

The army would no longer have to fight on two fronts; the navy, on the other hand, would have to take on both the French and British navies. He therefore wondered whether active troops could also be used in Denmark in case of a war against both Britain and France and whether in such a case provision for the participation of troops in naval operations could not be included in mobilization.[97] A copy of this letter was sent to the Imperial Naval Office.

## (4)  Operational Planning against the United States of America

Tirpitz's fleet was primarily built for use against Britain in the North Sea. Regular detachments for use abroad were minimal and confined to older ships, and irregular detachments abroad were made reluctantly. None the less, Tirpitz along with other naval leaders was interested in acquiring overseas bases and on 3 December 1899 requested the Admiralty Staff for a position-paper about what the German navy could accomplish against the United States as well as Britain. The paper was intended to help convince the Reichstag, whose members were bound to be influenced by prevailing anti-American sentiments, of the need for doubling the navy; none the less, he was more interested and more cooperative in the planning of the Admiralty Staff against the United States than against other powers.

On 20 January 1900, Diederichs responded that the strength provided by the Navy Law of 1898 did not make it possible to undertake an effective blockade of the American coast. What was possible was to defeat the American fleet and to seize, with army support, some cities on the coast of New England.

This is what Mantey had recommended in his two *Winterarbeiten*, which served as the basis of the *Marschplan* of the Admiralty Staff of March 1899—the official start of what later became Operations Plan III. The plan of March 1899 called for an advance of the German fleet against the United States as soon after the outbreak of war as possible. Because of the limited cruising range of the ships they would have to be recoaled in the western Azores. From there they would in the winter proceed to the American coast over the north-east Antilles and in the summer head there directly. Puerto Rico was dismissed as a base for operations against the American coast because of its distance from it. Instead a base on the American coast, Frenchman Bay, Maine, or Long Bay, South Carolina, would have to be seized. The Siegfried ships were to be taken along and would under certain circumstances be towed. Depending on the route, the decisive battle with the American fleet was to occur between the thirty-first and thirty-fourth or the thirty-ninth and forty-fourth mobilization days.[98] The man who had confronted Dewey at Manila Bay, Diederichs, developed the operations planning against his old enemies further. His work was supported by reports of the naval attaché in Washington, Rebeur-Paschwitz, who suggested Provincetown at the tip of Cape Cod as a base and recommended "unsparing, ruthless assaults against northeastern commercial and industrial centres," particularly Boston and New York. Tirpitz was unusually cooperative, not only making Rebeur-Paschwitz's report available to Diederichs but also allowing him to communicate directly with the Admiralty Staff.[99]

February 26, 1900, saw the first report to the Emperor regarding the operations plans against the United States. Diederichs did not substantially depart from the previous proposals except to include in the armada, against his better judgment, even older ships than the Siegfrieds so as to secure numerical superiority over the Americans: "To match these ships against modern vessels with rapid-fire cannon in battle more than three thousand miles from their home bases is more than risky." But as the strength of the German fleet improved by the fall of 1902 the proposed plan would become feasible.[100] As a concession to the cooperative Tirpitz, Diederichs desisted from preparing a formal operations plan until the approval of the Second Navy Bill, which, as he had stated in January, was necessary to provide the adequate means for operations against the United States.

The success of the operations against the United States, as with the earlier ones against Russia, for the invasion of Britain, or for the occupation of Holland and Belgium, and the subsequent ones to fight Britain in Danish waters, depended on army support. The key person was Schlieffen, prevented by naval expansion and the attitude of the Minister of War from effecting the increase in the army which he considered essential for victory over France and Russia. Wilhelm thus ordered in the margin of Rebeur-Paschwitz's telegram of 6 January 1900 a "joint report Admiralty Staff–General Staff."[101] But no such action was taken for almost a year. The Samoan crisis had blown over and there was no urgency about a war with the United States, the Second Navy Bill was being discussed, other operations plans had to be worked on, the Chinese expedition had to be prepared, and the Admiralstab had to do additional work on the plan against the United States. Diederichs requested Schlieffen's cooperation on 1 May, but received no reply.[102] He wrote again on 28 November and obtained Schlieffen's physical presence for a joint report to Wilhelm on 10 December 1900. There is no record that Schlieffen wrote or said anything. Diederichs, however, pointed out that by 1901 the German navy would have the necessary superiority over the Americans to undertake the projected expedition. This, however, was one of the few instances when Wilhelm disagreed with the naval planners. He was more cautious. Like Thomsen in regard to Mantey's *Winterarbeit*,[103] Wilhelm recommended the establishment of a base in the Caribbean instead of on the American coast: while Thomsen chose Puerto Rico, Wilhelm selected Cuba. He further instructed the Admiralty Staff to establish contact with the Foreign Office so as to be kept informed about the attitude of the Cubans toward the German invaders.[104] Diederichs accordingly approached the Foreign Office directly on 14 December, inquiring about the attitude of the population of Cuba and Puerto Rico and about the defenses, means of transportation, and war materials available on both islands. He was obviously influenced by Thomsen's recommendation that Puerto Rico should be considered as a base. Richthofen replied on 3 January 1901 stating that it would be difficult to gather such information through a circular dispatch to consular officials, but that an official, Lehmann, would visit the islands and make a special report.[105]

Diederichs—and probably Wilhelm—saw the seizure of Cuba as the first step in the campaign against the United States. He expected its seizure to result in a decisive naval battle fought where the American fleet would not enjoy the support offered by its coast or its auxiliary means. If the battle was favorable to the German side, additional troops could be transported to Cuba or directly to the American coast. On 25 February, Diederichs once more approached Schlieffen, asking him for two separate estimates: how many troops would be required (*a*) for the initial occupation of Cuba and Puerto Rico and (*b*) for the subsequent operations on the American mainland.[106] Schlieffen, who was obviously dragging his feet, answered on 13 March.[107] He admitted that the Cape Cod peninsula offered the great advantage that after the German side had gained control of the seas a landing by Provincetown could not be prevented and that the landed troops could very easily defend themselves against attacks from the mainland. But he pointed to the disadvantage that the troops could very easily be immobilized by being bottled up in the peninsula. This criticism annoyed the Admiralty Staff, who remarked in the margin: "military and naval attachés must determine this" and "This does not seem possible." Disregarding this major objection, Schlieffen then stated that "the peninsula is suitable as a base of operations against Boston as well as against New York," but that the number of troops necessary for securing the base and for advancing against Boston and New York depended on what troops the Americans were able to muster. This observation produced the ironical comment "This is very ingenious [*geistreich*]." For, argued Schlieffen, it was only possible to guess what would be the American strength since the regular army would in time of war only serve as a stem on which the volunteer corps would be grafted.

The regular army consisted of 100,000 men of whom 30,000–40,000 men were located in the northeast. Here the Admiralty Staff noted that the largest part of the regular army was currently tied down in the Philippines. According to Schlieffen, excepting the regular army, of the 11 million Americans capable of bearing arms only 106,000 had any military training. A larger proportion of those would volunteer in the event of a German invasion of the American mainland than did during the Spanish–American War. Schlieffen guessed that the German invading force would face at the outset 100,000 men of whom 30,000–40,000 would be regular troops. He therefore stated that, while one army corps would be adequate to seize and secure the Cape Cod peninsula, it was not strong enough to break out of it and would be bottled up. It would therefore almost immediately have to be augmented to 100,000 men—a number probably adequate for undertakings against Boston. A much larger number would be necessary for operations against New York because of longer lines of communications and increasing American forces.

Schlieffen devoted little attention to Cuba and Puerto Rico. He expected the Cubans to side with the Americans and therefore guessed in the light of previous Spanish experience that at least 50,000 men would be necessary just to hold Cuba. If its seizure were to lead to an invasion of the American mainland, 100,000 men would be needed to secure a base there and additional undetermined numbers for operations in the interior. Thirty thousand men had with some difficulty been sent to China;[108] Schlieffen was mentioning much greater numbers. Diederichs was most annoyed, remarking at the foot of the letter:

> Since in the view of the General Staff we are unable to accomplish anything on the mainland with the number of troops that we can transport there, we *must* advance *against the islands* [West Indies] or declare our military bankruptcy vis-à-vis the United States.

Actually Diederichs should now have suspended consideration of operations against the American coast. He refused to do so. He instructed Rebeur-Paschwitz to examine the coast in the Boston and New York areas for landing-sites. Jointly with Captain R. von Kap-herr he recommended Rockport and Gloucester. On 18 November, Diederichs forwarded the information assembled by the military attaché to Schlieffen. The Imperial Naval Office also maintained its interest in American naval developments. On 14 December the Chief of the General Staff raised new objections to the landing in Provincetown and rejected Rockport and Gloucester as landing-sites altogether. Subsequently Diederichs in consultation with Schröder, head of the "B" section, and B4 ruled that there be no further correspondence with Schlieffen regarding operations against the United States "because it is hopeless."[109] Since Schlieffen also pointed out that the Americans expected a German attack on Boston, Diederichs shifted his interest to New York as an object of attack and in January 1902 inquired of Rebeur-Paschwitz about landing-sites in its vicinity. New York was also chosen as the object of amphibious attack in an Admiralty Staff memorandum of January 1902.[110]

Büchsel took his time about the operations plan against the United States. He obviously assigned it a lower priority than the plans against the Dual Alliance and Britain and may well have been more aware than his predecessor of its fantastic nature. His first report to Wilhelm regarding this plan is dated 21 March 1903, after the shelling of Fort San Carlos had produced a crisis in German–American relations.

For the first time Büchsel placed the operations plan against the United States within the context of Germany's international position.

> *The necessary prerequisite* for a war of Germany against the United States is a *political situation in Europe* which leaves the German empire an entirely free hand abroad. Any uncertainty in Europe would preclude the successful execution of a war against the United States.

One might ask whether Germany could at all fight against the United States in view of her political situation. Büchsel may have been aware of this when he commented: "Such a war will therefore not be sought by us, but it can be forced on us." If this war had to be fought, it was to achieve definite aims. This is, indeed, the first time that precise war aims were formulated by German naval planners. They were to be the permanent acquisition of Culebra and Puerto Rico as "a wall against the effrontery of the Monroe Doctrine." Germany's aim was a "firm position in the West Indies. Free hand in South America. Revocation of the Monroe Doctrine." Germany would thus acquire important naval bases and be able with impunity to extend her economic and political influence on the American continent.

Since Germany could not afford a war of attrition and since she possessed numerical superiority over the American navy,

> There can only be *one* aim for Germany's strategy: direct pressure on the American east coast and its most populated parts, above all New York, i.e. also a ruthless offensive with the purpose of making the situation unbearable to the American people through the spread of terror and through damaging hostile trade and property.

Following the latest calculations of Diederichs, Puerto Rico and Culebra were to serve as bases for the operations and the special object of attack on the American coast was New York City. Dismissing a direct attack against New York as too risky, Büchsel viewed as feasible "a landing on and occupation of Long Island and a threatening of New York from the west end of this island." The American fleet was expected to come to battle in the Caribbean following the German seizure of Puerto Rico and Culebra. Its defeat and the acquisition of naval supremacy were prerequisites to the action against New York.

Wilhelm gave the project his approval, authorizing that detailed work be undertaken on it and that collaboration with the General Staff be established. Büchsel wrote to Schlieffen on 25 April 1903 stating that the navy could provide the units necessary for the occupation of Culebra but requesting estimates for the army troops for the occupation of Puerto Rico.

He stated that these would be transported by the ships of the North German Lloyd and the Hamburg–America Line after the American fleet had been defeated. This time Schlieffen raised no objections. According to his reply of 14 May, the occupation of Puerto Rico would require 12,000 men, 3,700 horses, and 671 mechanized vehicles. The Chinese expedition had proven that the German shipping lines could transport an expedition of this size a long distance. By November 1903 the war plan against the United States was officially known as Operations Plan III.

During the next two years the details of the plan were worked on. Fourteen special studies dealt with the supplying of the expedition. The Imperial Naval Office showed itself unusually helpful, assuring that it could provide the necessary coal for the expedition and find the thirty freighters with a totaling 100,000 tons in German harbors. Contact was maintained with the General Staff, which raised its estimates of required troops and provided information regarding most suitable landing-sites in Puerto Rico.[111] Like the operations plan against France or that against Britain, Operations Plan III was not modified by the changing political constellation, by the fear of war with Britain, particularly after the Dogger Bank incident, by the rapprochement between England and France, or by the Morocco crisis during which the German military probably advocated a preventive war against France.

Only in 1906 did Captain Georg Hebbinghaus bring about a major revision in the war plan against the United States. In his "March against the west" he stated: "A German declaration of war against the United States is only possible if we are allied with England and [if] our flank is protected against France by Austria, Italy, and possibly also Russia." In such a case German troops would be transported to Canada whence they would undertake land operations against the United States. Since Hebbinghaus realized that Britain and France would be hostile to Germany in the event of a war with the United States, all that Germany could do was to prey on the American shipping lanes and seize pawn objects outside the American mainland.[112] On 9 May 1906, Büchsel ruled that "the detailed preparatory works for a war against the United States not be continued."[113]

## (5) Planning for Naval Units Located Abroad

The Admiralty Staff continued the practice of issuing annual directives to the forces stationed abroad for possible cases of war that had been initiated by the High Command in 1896. In 1900, Bendemann drafted orders for five cases of war: (*a*) against the United States of America; (*b*) against France; (*c*) against France and Russia; (*d*) against Britain; (*e*) against Japan. The allocation of the first place to operations against the United States is a further indication that the Admiralty staff at this time viewed that country as its most important opponent outside of European waters. The case of war "Germany allied with Russia against England" was now dropped in spite of Germany's pro-Russian orientation and Bülow's calculation that Russia would be Germany's ally in an eventual war against Britain.

The major German naval force outside of Europe was the Cruiser Squadron, which now had a base in Tsing-tao in the Kiao-chow colony. In all of the five cases of war under consideration the forces of the Australian, West American and East African stations were to be subordinated to it. In all cases of war except that against Japan the ships of the West African station were to be stranded and the men shipped home or, if this was not possible, the ships were to conduct cruiser war. In a war against Japan they were to return home.[114] The activities of the Cruiser Squadron were by necessity predominantly restricted to East Asia. In 1900 Bendemann and in 1901–02 Diederichs correctly regarded the East Asian theater of war to be of secondary importance in all cases of war except that against Japan, for a decision against France, the Franco-Russian Alliance, or Britain would be reached in European waters and that against the United States in the Caribbean and on its east coast. In cases of war (b)–(d) the function of the Cruiser Squadron and the ships of other stations subordinated to it would be to relieve hostile pressure in the main theater of war and to cause maximum damage to the enemy.

It was entirely in accordance with Tirpitz's emphasis on building ships of the line for the North Sea that the defenses of Tsing-tao received an even lower priority than those of the German coast. Only in 1904 did this base acquire a battery of heavy guns and only in 1905 did the Admiralty Staff deem it capable of providing the cruiser squadron with adequate protection against a superior maritime opponent. Until then in a war against a superior enemy the squadron was required to leave its base to avoid being enclosed ignominiously, like the Russian Black Sea fleet in Sevastopol during the Crimean War.

The administration of Kiao-chow, the defense of Tsing-tao, and any arrangements for the coaling and provisioning of the Cruiser Squadron and any other ships abroad were the responsibility of the Imperial Naval Office. On the other hand, the operations overseas, like those in Europe, were handled by the Admiralty Staff. The two agencies appear to have cooperated fairly smoothly outside of Europe. By 1900 the Chief of the Cruiser Squadron had been provided with 5½ million marks in letters of credit and had recourse to funds deposited with German agents abroad to enable the squadron and other German ships abroad to purchase coal, other supplies, and transport-ships. During the first three months of war the Cruiser Squadron was expected to require fifteen transport-ships and each of the five stations one ship each. In 1900, however, arrangements remained to be made for the purchase of transport-ships and little had been done to acquire coaling stations. Diederichs stressed in February 1900 the need for such stations en route to Kiao-chow: some in German colonies in Africa, one on the coast of the Red Sea, another in Southeast Asia.[115] He proceeded to make arrangements through the Imperial Naval Office with the Hamburg–America Line and the North German Lloyd to establish a coaling station in Colombo.[116] In East Asia the Cruiser Squadron remained dependent in 1900 on the British coal supplies in Shanghai and ran the risk of being cut off from them in the event of war.[117] On 14 February 1903, Büchsel reported to Wilhelm about the situation in East Asia:

The execution of the operational orders issued by Your Majesty is secured in so far as the lack of a base permits. The operations plans are well thought through, the necessary measures well prepared. Only for a war with England does the acquisition of auxiliary ships, coal, provisions, and *matériel* require detailed examination and the opening up of new sources. The mobilization of supplies is estimated at six to nine days and can hardly be shortened. Here lies a serious danger as long as Tsing-tao is not fortified.[118]

In the course of 1903 the Imperial Naval Office regularized the arrangements for the acquisition of auxiliary steamers from German shipping lines and for the enlistment of sailors abroad.[119] On 12 February 1904, Büchsel was able to report to Wilhelm: "The work that was not yet completed last year concerning the acquisition of supplies, coal, and auxiliary ships for a war against England has been finished. The period necessary for the beginning of operations has been shortened."[120]

The power relationship of the Cruiser Squadron to all of its prospective opponents in East Asia remained unfavorable. In 1902 closest to its strength of 42,000 tons came the American forces with 51,400 tons and the French with 52,400 tons. The combined French and Russian forces amounted to 197,000 tons, the British strength was at 169,000 tons, and the Japanese navy at 245,000 tons.[121] By 1904 the power relationship deteriorated further.

Against the Americans the Cruiser Squadron at first seemed to have a chance. In the event of a war against them, the squadron was instructed in 1900 to remain in East Asia to seek out and tie down the American forces in the Philippines to prevent them from proceeding into the Atlantic or raiding German shipping. These instructions were changed in 1903 because of the expected increase of American forces in East Asia by five ships of the line. No longer a match against such strength, the Cruiser Squadron was now directed to attack the American west coast: this action was expected to compel the American Pacific forces to withdraw to defend their own coast and to prevent them from proceeding to the main theater of war in the Atlantic.[122] If hostile supremacy precluded success against America's Pacific coast, the Cruiser Squadron was either to return to East Asia or to proceed to the American west coast via Guam and Honolulu,[123] and in 1905 the question of attacking them was raised. But by February 1905 the Admiralty Staff had lost hope in relieving the situation in the Atlantic through raids against the American Pacific coast since the Cruiser Squadron had been weakened through withdrawals to Europe because of the political situation and since American forces on the Pacific coast had been further strengthened, precluding any chance of accomplishing anything through raids. In spite of these limits on the actions of the Cruiser Squadron, Büchsel refused to accede to the request of its chief to remain in Tsing-tao to ward off American forces with the help of its strengthened defenses. He remained in favor of offensive operations which could no longer be defined clearly.[124] In 1906 he suggested an initial attack on Guam whence further raids could be conducted against either the Philippines, America's Pacific coast, or against shipping. The foremost task of the Cruiser Squadron—to prevent the transfer of American men-of-war from the Pacific to the Atlantic—could no longer be accomplished because of its marked inferiority to the American Pacific forces.[125] German ancillary operations against the United States in the Pacific were thus proving to be as impracticable as those in the main theater of war in the Atlantic.

In a war against France the Cruiser Squadron and the ships subordinated to it were to remain in East Asia with the aim of attempting to defeat their slightly superior opponent and, if successful, raiding French shipping and colonies in the entire area of East Asia, the South Pacific, and the Indian Ocean. If France were allied with Russia, the German forces were to attempt to defeat the French before they joined the more powerful Russians, but to avoid battle with the latter and resort to cruiser warfare instead.[126] In 1906 the Cruiser Squadron was instructed in the event of a war against France or France allied with Russia to do battle with the French only if the power relationship offered a chance of success. It was to stay in the proximity of Tsing-tao at the beginning of hostilities to prevent the French from seizing it.[127] In 1904 operations against Russia as an ally of France were not considered.[128] Were Germany to be allied with Britain and Japan against France and Russia—an eventuality that the Admiralty Staff considered in February 1902, shortly after the conclusion of the Anglo-Japanese alliance—the German forces in East Asia were expected to join their allies in a common offensive. The ships of the East American station were expected in the event of a war against either France or the Dual Alliance to return home or, given a suitable opportunity, attack French shipping and fishing operations in the North Atlantic and destroy any French warships located there.

Were the much superior British forces to be the enemy, the instruction to the Cruiser Squadron and the forces attached to it from 1900 to 1902 was to fight cruiser warfare unless Germany had strong allies. In that case the German ships were to join those of their allies if this offered any prospect of success.[129] In February 1904, however, Büchsel reported to Wilhelm that British strength in the Pacific and Indian Oceans precluded any success from cruiser warfare. Nor did the fortifications of Tsing-tao, although now equipped with two 24 cm, four 21 cm and seven 15 cm guns, offer any prospect for a defensive stance. Büchsel instead discovered a suitable objective for the Cruiser Squadron in the shipping between Vancouver and East Asia and obtained Wilhelm's approval for the directive that in the event of war with Britain

The chief of the Cruiser Squadron immediately undertakes with all the ships that appear suitable to him and all the auxiliary ships an advance against the ports of the west coast of Canada in order to destroy the Canadian Pacific trade and, if possible, to defeat the English naval forces located on the Canadian coast. The remaining ships go as soon as possible to Tsing-tao where along with their crews they will be at the full disposal of the governor of Kiao-chow. Ships which for some reason cannot reach Tsing-tao will equip themselves as auxiliary cruisers.[130]

The attack on the Canadian west coast was, however, dropped in March 1906 on political grounds. The renewed Anglo-Japanese alliance was regarded as depriving the Cruiser Squadron of the opportunity of taking on supplies in Japanese ports. On the basis of further examination hostilities on the Canadian coast were expected to provoke the United States—something that had been surprisingly overlooked during the two previous years. Instead, Büchsel now recommended that the Cruiser Squadron take advantage of the overextension of British naval power in the Pacific and Indian Oceans. He obtained Wilhelm's approval for an extensive raid: the Cruiser Squadron was to attack British trade to Australia and Australian and Tasmanian ports. It was to steam via Yap and Matupi to Hobart and then head west along the southern coast of Australia. Büchsel was optimistic about the possibility of taking on coal in some Australian port. Heading west from Fremantle the squadron was to conduct cruiser war *en route* to Ceylon, take on coal near Sumatra, and eventually reach East Africa. The cruiser *Fürst Bismarck* was considered to be a match for the British Australian squadron.[131]

In the event of war against Japan, whose entire fleet would face the Cruiser Squadron, Bendemann in 1900 and Diederichs in 1901–02 instructed it to leave Tsing-tao, wage cruiser war, and then steam west to await reinforcements from Germany. For 1904 the orders to the squadron specifically included attacks on Japanese ports and the subordination of units unsuitable for cruiser war to the governor of Kiao-chow for the defense of Tsing-tao.[132] For 1905—in orders issued on 27 February, before the defeat of the Russian Baltic Sea fleet at Tshushima—the Cruiser Squadron and the ships subordinated to it were for the first time instructed to concentrate in Tsing-tao for the defense of Kiao-chow, aided by its now strengthened fortifications. Ships unable to reach Tsing-tao were to conduct cruiser war and "to join the advancing [*anmarschierende*] battle fleet from home."[133] Büchsel thus appeared ready to emulate the Russians, and Tsing-tao, if held until the arrival of the German battle fleet, could serve as the base for its operations against Japan. In 1906, with the Russo-Japanese War over and Germany no longer likely to get involved with Japan because of violations of her neutrality, Büchsel regarded a war with Japan as very improbable. Were it none the less to occur, Tsing-tao would have to be held until the arrival of the German home fleet. For that year the case of war of Germany against both Japan and Britain was also examined. It was to be governed by the same considerations as the case of war against Britain because of the strategic position of that power: the German fleet would have to face British forces in European waters.[134]

Although Tirpitz had consistently subordinated cruiser warfare to concentration in European waters, he was unwilling at the time of the Second Hague Conference to drop the sea-booty right, for threats to private property at sea, including grain imported in neutral bottoms, would damage Britain more than Germany by threatening her food-supplies, increase the risks of war for Britain and force Britain to detach her forces from the concentration against Germany.[135]

## Notes: Chapter 12

1  Hopmann, *Das Logbuch*, p. 272.
2  BA-MA, F 3302, PG 66704, Diederichs to Tirpitz, 29 March 1900; Hubatsch, *Der Admiralstab*, pp. 241–2.
3  BA-MA, F 3444, PG 67480, "Auszug aus der Denkschrift zum Immediat-Bericht des Admirals von Koester über seine Kentnissnahme in Admiralstabsarbeiten und Vorschläge über Entwickelung des Admiralstabes."
4  ibid., F 3302, PG 66704, Diederichs to Tirpitz, 29 March 1900; Diederichs to Wilhelm, 12 January 1901; for the following, see also Kelly, "Naval policy," fos 204–5.
5  BA-MA, F 7623, "Handaktenstücke für das Dezernat A I, 1902;" A3, Dick, A4, Weber, A5, Eckermann, and A2, Erwin Schäfer, to Diederichs, 25 January 1901.
6  Preparatory works in the widest sense were to include matters such as the establishment of a library, a map collection, information on the navies of the world, cruiser handbooks, military coast descriptions, and naval intelligence (*Kriegsnachrichtenwesen*). Preparatory works in the narrower sense included detailed tables of comparison for the various naval forces, with enclosed critical comments. In addition came preparatory studies from the different departments of the Admiralty Staff, including operations plans, war formation, mobilization arrangements, defense of the coast, deployment, and studies to facilitate the execution of the orders issued to the commanders at sea in the setting up of bases, execution of the blockade, and attacks or threats against coastal places.
7  Hubatsch, *Der Admiralstab*, pp. 96–7.
8  BA-MA, F 2044, PG 66075, "Immediatvortrag," 13 February 1901, typescript. On the first page there is a comment by Trotha: "This report must be presented in the period between April and June 1901." Hubatsch, however, states that this report was presented on 13 February, too: *Der Admiralstab*, p. 97.
9  ibid., pp. 99–100.
10  BA-MA, F 5596, III, 3.–1., Vol. 2, "Defensiver Operationsplan," initialed by A, A2, 17 May, A4, 12 May, A3, 9 May 1899. A3 appears to be the author. A4 can be identified as Grapow.
11  ibid., "Defensiver Operationsplan III, 2 (d), Kriegführung gegen Frankreich," initialed by A and A2 on 19 May, and by A3 and A4 on 12 May 1899.
12  ibid., F 5587, III, 1. N. 10., Vol. 1, Abschrift für die Akten, Bendemann, 19 September 1899, "Direktive für die Aufstellung der Operationspläne."
13  ibid., A3, "Disposition des Operationsplans für den Krieg gegen Frankreich," 25 November 1899.
14  See above, p. 183.
15  BA-MA, F 5596, III, 3.–1., Vol. 2, Chef des Admiralstabes, "Denkschrift zum Immediatvortrag über das Wiederinkrafttreten des offensiven Operationsplanes gegen Frankreich, 10 December 1899." At the head of the document appears a comment to the effect that Wilhelm approved the resumption of the offensive operations plan on 12 December. On 14 October, Bendemann had reported to Wilhelm on the strength of the Russian Baltic fleet, indicating that it possessed only three ships of the line of the first class, to which another such ship and one large cruiser would soon be added. Located in Libau, the Russian fleet was vulnerable to a superior enemy such as Britain. On 16 October he reported that there was no effective planning in the construction of the French navy. The northern squadron consisted of six ships of the line and the Mediterranean squadron had shrunk to the same number. Both *Denkschrifte zum Immediatvortrag* are located in BA-MA, F 2015, PG 65955. On 18 December he reported to Wilhelm that the French navy lacked firm leadership and standardized training: ibid. For French naval weakness in this period, see Samuel R. Williamson, *The Politics of Grand Strategy: Britain and France Prepare for War, 1904–14* (Cambridge, Mass., 1969), pp. 24–6.
16  In two memoranda "Zum Immediatvortrag," one dating 16 April and the other 29 April 1899, Bendemann dealt specifically with French naval strength in answer to the question whether a German thrust against the French northern coast immediately after the outbreak of war was feasible: BA-MA, F 2015, PG 65954.
17  ibid., PG 65956, "Denkschrift zum Immediatvortrag," 21 January 1900.
18  ibid., F 5596, III, 3.–1., Vol. 2, comment of A3, 9 February 1900; "Admiralstabsübungsreise der Nordsee 1900," February 1900.

19  ibid., F 3444, PG 67480, Koester to Wilhelm, 29 January 1900.

20  See above, pp. 162 ff.

21  BA-MA, F 3444, PG 67480, Senden to Diederichs, 7 February 1900.

22  BA-MA, F 5596, III, 3.–1., Vol. 2, Diederichs, 29 August 1900 (et correspondentia) to A3. On 21 January 1901 the naval attaché in St Petersburg reported that because of the strengthening of the Russian fleet in East Asia at the expense of the Baltic Sea fleet it "will and must remain for years without any noteworthy significance": BA-MA, F 7197, PG 68987, Schimmelmann to Tirpitz, 21 January 1901.

23  BA-MA, F 5596, III, 3.–1., Vol. 2, A and A6 agreed with A3. A3 to A and A4, 28 September 1900; A to A6, 28 September 1900; A6 to A3, 2 October 1900.

24  PAAA, Deutschland 143, Geh., Bd 1, Marine, Vol. 2, Schlieffen to the Foreign Office, 2 September 1900; Richthofen to Wilhelm, 7 September 1900, and to the Chief of the General Staff, 12 September 1900. BA-MA, F 5600, III, 3.–24., Vol. 1, Schlieffen to Chief of the Admiralty Staff, 17 September 1900.

25  BA-MA, F 5600, III, 3.–24., Vol. 1, "Ergebnis der vom III. hinsichtlich der Marinekonferenz unternommenen Schritte," initialed by A on 29 September and by A3, S[ouchon?], on 27 September 1900.

26  ibid., Schlieffen to Diederichs, 2 October 1900, and marginal comments to it.

27  See above, p. 196.

28  BA-MA, F 2016, PG 65958, Chief of the Admiralty Staff of the Navy, "Zum Immediatbericht, Kriegspiel des Admiralstabes im Winter 1901–02," 5 April 1901. On the first page there is the statement "Erledigt," initialed D[iederichs], 15 April.

29  ibid., F 2051, PG 66111, Tirpitz to Senden, 21 February 1902.

30  ibid., F 5586, III. 1. 0. 10., Vol. 3, Büchsel to A3 and A2, 24 October 1902.

31  ibid., A3 and A2, 26 November 1902, "Krieg gegen Zweibund. Deutsche Flotte soll Seeverbindungen in den Weichselprovinzen offen halten. I. A.C. in Königsberg verproviantieren und gebotenen Falls nach Stettin überführen."

32  ibid., A3, 12 December 1902, "Ms. Übung 1902. Denkschrift über den Vormarsch nach dem englischen Kanal im Kriege Zwei-Dreibund: Seeverbindung auf der Ostsee ist Aufrechtzuerhalten."

33  ibid., F 5598, Nebenakten zu III. 3.–1., Vol. 2, Büchsel to Schlieffen, 22 December 1902.

34  ibid., Schlieffen to Büchsel, 26 December 1902.

35  ibid., Büchsel to Schlieffen, 2 January 1903.

36  ibid., Schlieffen to Büchsel, 5 January 1903.

37  ibid., "Denkschrift. Kriegsplan für den Kriegsfall Dreibund wider Zweibund," initialed on 6 March 1903, by A, W, A2, and A3.

38  ibid., N 168/8, "Immediatvortrag über O-Pläne 1903," Berghahn has mistakenly given 10 February instead of 10 March as the date: *Tirpitz-Plan*, p. 332, n. 8. The "III" and "II" can be mistaken. In BA-MA, F 5596, III, 3.–1., Bd 3, Büchsel's instructions to A, 10 March 1903, give this as the date of the report to Wilhelm.

39  ibid., F 5996, III, 3.–1., Bd 3, Büchsel's instructions to A, 10 March 1903.

40  ibid., Bd 4, "Denkschrift über die Kriegführung zur See gegen Frankreich in den Kriegsfällen Deutschland wider Frankreich und Drei-wider Zweibund im Jahre 1903," Büchsel, 27 March 1903.

41  ibid., F 5597, III, 3.–1., Vol. 5, "Denkschrift über die Kriegführung zur See gegen Frankreich und Dreibund gegen Zweibund i. J. 1904," October 1903.

42  ibid., "Disposition und Gesichtspunkt für Umarbeitung der Denkschrift," n.d., initialed A3, Schäfer.

43  ibid., Büchsel's comment of 10 October 1903.

44  ibid., F 7183, PG 68922, Büchsel to Tirpitz, 7 December 1903; F 3443, PG 67478, Büchsel to Senden, 11 January 1904.

45  ibid., F 5598, III. 3.–1.A, Vol. 1.

46  ibid., "Aktenvermerk," of A2 or A3 (it is difficult to read the handwriting), 10 May 1904, on the first page of the memorandum.

47  ibid., F 5597, III, 3.–1., Vol. 5, "Denkschrift über die Kriegführung zur See gegen Frankreich in den Kriegsfällen: Dreibund gegen Zweibund und Deutschland gegen Frankreich im Jahre 1905."

48  J. Steinberg, "Germany and the Russo-Japanese War," *American Historical Review*, vol.

75, no. 7 (December 1970), esp. pp. 1976–9; L. Cecil, "Coal for the fleet that had to die," ibid., vol. 69, no. 4 (July 1964), pp. 990–1005.

49 BA-MA, F 5597, III, 3.–1., Vol. 5, "Zum Immediatvortrag," initialed by A3, 27.I, and by A2 on 3.II. Büchsel noted on either 15. or 18.II (it is difficult to figure out the exact date) that Wilhelm approved the plan and ordered that it be kept in greatest secrecy. No one outside of the Admiralty Staff was for the time being to be informed of it.

50 BA-MA, F 2015, PG 65954, "Zum Immediatvortrag," 16 (?) April 1899.

51 ibid., Bendemann's memorandum "Zum Immediatvortrag," 8 June 1899.

52 ibid., F 5587, III, 1. N. 10., Vol. 1, "Vorarbeit für einen O-Plan Deutschland allein gegen England," November 1899.

53 ibid., "Die Defensive gegen England," signed Bendemann, November 1899.

54 Jonathan Steinberg, "The Copenhagen complex," *Journal of Contemporary History*, vol. 1, no. 3 (July 1966), pp. 23–46.

55 BA-MA, F 5587, III, 1. N. 10., Vol. 1, Grapow's note of 19 December 1899.

56 ibid., Bendemann's note of 20 December 1899.

57 ibid., Grapow's marginal comment to the previous, 21 December 1899.

58 ibid., "Zum Immediatvortrag. Defensive gegen England," n.d. There is, however, a statement on the first page of the document that Wilhelm had approved the project on 12 December 1899.

59 See above, pp. 160 ff.

60 BA-MA, F 5587, III, 1. N. 10., Vol. 1, marginal comment to "Zum Immediatvortrag": approved . . . on 12 December 1899.

61 ibid., Diederichs to Schlieffen, 20 December 1899.

62 ibid., Schlieffen to Diederichs, 16 January 1900.

63 GP, XIV, ii, No. 4021, Bülow to Hatzfeldt, 6 May 1899, pp. 548–9.

64 BA-MA, F 5587, III, 1. N. 10., Vol. 1, Diederichs to Schlieffen, 12 February 1900; Schlieffen to Diederichs, 4 March 1900.

65 ibid., A IV, Grapow, "Disposition für einen O-Plan 'Deutschland allein gegen England.'"

66 BA-MA, F 2015, PG 65956, "Denkschrift zum Immediatvortrag," 17 February 1900.

67 ibid., F 5586, III, 1. 0. 10., Vol. 1, minutes of the meetings of 29 March 1900; n.d. April 1900; 10 May 1900; 19 May 1900.

68 ibid., F 2016, PG 65959, "Denkschrift zum Immediatvortrag," 19 June 1901.

69 ibid., F 5588, III, 1.–10a., Vol. 1, "Denkschrift Kapitän z.S.v. Heeringen betreffend den Krieg zwischen Deutschland und England," 12 April 1903.

70 Their marginal comments to ibid. In a report to Wilhelm of 31 May 1900 the Admiralty Staff had turned down a proposal of the Generalinspektor der Ingenieur und Pioniercorps to use barges to carry an invasion force to England. Specifically, preference was given to few large and fast steamships over numerous small and slow barges. More generally, it was stated that a force of four to six army corps, as viewed necessary by Schlieffen, could not be transported to England without possessing control of the sea: ibid., F 2015, PG 65957, "Denkschrift zum Immediatvortrag."

71 Souchon's comment of 15 November 1902 on the first page of ibid. reads: "Im Anschreiben vom 17.4.02 hierzu sagt Kapt. v. Heeringen, dass es ihm zu einer eingehenden Beschäftigung mit dieser Frage an Zeit gefehlt habe. Aus diesem Grunde habe er auch nicht näher auf die Details der gestellten Aufgabe eingehen können. Anschreiben vernichtet."

72 ibid., F 5586, III, 1.0.10., Vol. 1, A4, Souchon, to A, "Betrifft Besetzung dänischen Gebiets im Falle des Krieges gegen England," 17 May 1902.

73 ibid., "Vermerk," A i.v. Su., 17 May.

74 ibid., V. A2, Souchon, 30 May.

75 BA-MA, F 5588, III, 1.–10a., Vol. 1, Zu A 2533 IV, A, Winkler, to B, 2 October 1902.

76 ibid., statement of B, 8 October 1902.

77 ibid., Büchsel to A, 21 October 1902.

78 ibid., Souchon's "Aktenvermerk" for the meeting of 10 November and his "Aktenvermerk" for the meetings of 12 and 14 November. See also BA-MA, F 5586, III, 1.0.10., Vol. 1, for the meetings of 12 and 14 November.

79 BA-MA, F 5586, III, 1.0.10., Vol. 1, "Grundlage für Erwägungen, betreffend den Krieg zwischen Grossbrittanien und Deutschland," n.d., statement by Büchsel of 24 November 1902 at the end of the document.

80  BA-MA, F 5587, III, 1. N. 10., Vol. 1, "Voraussichtliches Vorgehen der Engländer im Kriege gegen Deutschland," Souchon, 19 December 1902.

81  ibid., F 5586, III. 1. 0. 10., Vol. 1, "Sitzung am 22. Dezember über Operationsplan gegen England," 23 December 1902, initialed by A, A2, and A4.

82  ibid., N 168/8, "Immediatvortrag Krieg England u. Deutschland." See also Berghahn, *Tirpitz-Plan*, pp. 335–8.

83  BA-MA, F 5587, III, 1. N. 10., Vol. 1, "Verwendung unserer Flotte zu Beginn eines Krieges mit England," March 1903. On the first page there is a comment by Büchsel, dated 14 April 1903: "S.M. haben die Grundlage für die Kriegführung der Flotte gegen England genehmigt."

84  ibid., N 168/8, n.d. "Herbstamanöver 1903" in Büchsel's handwriting.

85  ibid., F 5586, III, 1. 0. 10., Vol. 1, A4, "Betrifft-Kriegspiel der grossen Admiralstabreise 1903," 30 September 1903.

86  ibid., Schlieffen to Büchsel, 6 August 1903.

87  BA-MA, F 5587, III, 1. N. 10., Vol. 1, Büchsel to Schlieffen, 13 August 1903.

88  Souchon's "Notiz" of 15 October 1903 on the first page of ibid.

89  ibid., F 5586, III, 1. 0. 10., Vol. 1, "Sitzung über O.P. 2 vom 17. Oktober 03," 17 October 1903, initialed by A, Winkler, A1, von Rossing, A4, Souchon, and A2, Hopmann.

90  ibid., 8 May 1904.

91  ibid., 21 June 1904, "Leiter der grossen Admiralstabsreise 1904. Betrifft: Kriegsspiel auf der grossen Admiralstabsreise vom 14–22 Juni 1904."

92  ibid., Büchsel's minute of 27 July 1904 to letter from Dick to Büchsel, 3 July 1904, forwarding the war game to him.

93  ibid., F 5587, III, 1. N. 10., Vol. 2, Boedicker, 3 October 1904, "Übersicht über die Entwickelung des O.P. II."

94  Vogel, *Deutsche Russlandpolitik*, pp. 204–6; GP, XIX, i, No. 6084, Bülow to Romberg, 4 October 1905, pp. 257–9.

95  See Steinberg, "Germany," p. 1976; Cecil, "Coal," pp. 996–7.

96  BA-MA, F 5587, III, 1. N. 10., Vol. 2, "Aktenvermerk A IV, Boedicker," 26 October 1904.

97  ibid., F 5586, III, 1. 0. 10., Vol. 2, Büchsel to Schlieffen, 2 November 1904.

98  Herwig and Trask, "Naval operations," p. 13; Herwig, *Frustration*, p. 51.

99  Herwig and Trask, "Naval operations," pp. 15–16; Herwig, *Frustration*, pp. 52–3.

100  Herwig and Trask, "Naval operations," p. 16; Herwig, *Frustration*, p. 53.

101  ibid., p. 58; cf. Herwig and Trask, "Naval operations," p. 17, for a different date.

102  BA-MA, F 5174b, 1. 2–13.19a, Vol. 1, Diederichs to Schlieffen, 25 February 1901.

103  See above, p. 131.

104  Herwig and Trask, "Naval operations," pp. 17–18; Herwig, *Frustration*, pp. 58–9. BA-MA, F 2015, PG 65957, "Immediatvortrag," 9 December 1900.

105  PAAA, Deutschland 121, No. 12, Bd 9, Diederichs to Richthofen, 14 December 1900; Richthofen to Diederichs, 3 January 1901.

106  BA-MA, F 5174b, 1. 2–13.19a, Vol. 1, Diederichs to Schlieffen, 25 February 1901.

107  ibid., Schlieffen to Diederichs, 13 March 1901; also Herwig and Trask, "Naval operations," pp. 18–19; Herwig, *Frustration*, pp. 59–60. I use Herwig's translation of Diederich's final comment in *Frustration*, p. 60, with one minor modification.

108  Forstmeier, "Deutsche Invasionspläne," p. 351.

109  For the Imperial Naval Office, see Vagts, *Deutschland*, Vol. 2, p. 1395. BA-MA, F 5174b, 1. 2–13.19a, Vol. 1, Schlieffen to Diederichs, 14 December 1901, and comment at the foot of the letter.

110  Herwig and Trask, "Naval operations," p. 22; Herwig, *Frustration*, p. 65.

111  For the above, see Herwig and Trask, "Naval operations," pp. 24–6; Herwig, *Frustration*, pp. 85–8.

112  Herwig and Trask, "Naval operations," p. 27; Herwig, *Frustration*, p. 90.

113  Forstmeier, "Deutsche Invasionspläne," p. 349.

114  BA-MA, F 5170, III, 1.–9.b, Vol. 1, "Allerhöchste Befehle an S.M. Schiffe im Auslande," 1 February 1900; 26 February 1901; 8 February 1902.

115  ibid., F 2015, PG 65956, Diederichs, "Zum Immediatvortrag," 3 February 1900.

116   ibid., F 6158, XVII, I. 1.–28., Vol. 1, Diederichs to Tirpitz, 28 February 1900; Tirpitz to Directorates of the Hamburg–American Line and the North German Lloyd, 2 June 1900.
117   ibid., Tirpitz to Chief of the Cruiser Squadron, 15 March 1900.
118   ibid., F 2017, PG 65962, Büchsel, "Zum Immediatvortrag," 14 February 1903.
119   ibid., F 6158, XVII, 1. 1. 28., Vol. 2, "Mobilmachungs-Vorkehrungen des Staatssekretärs des Reichsmarineamts für Auslandschiffe," 17 March 1903.
120   ibid., F 2017, PG 65963, Büchsel, "Zum Immediatvortrag," 12 February 1904.
121   ibid., F 2016, PG 65960, Diederichs, "Zum Immediatvortrag," 8 February 1902.
122   ibid., F 2017, PG 65962, Büchsel, "Zum Immediatvortrag," 14 February 1903.
123   ibid., F 2017, PG 65963, Büchsel, "Zum Immediatvortrag," 12 February 1904.
124   ibid., F 2017, PG 65964, Büchsel, "Zum Immediatvortrag," 27 February 1905.
125   ibid., F 2017, PG 65965, Büchsel, "Denkschrift zu den Allerhöchsten Befehlen an S.M. Schiffe auf der ostasiatischen und der australischen Station," 6 March 1906.
126   ibid., F 2017, PG 65963, Büchsel, "Zum Immediatvortrag," 12 February 1904.
127   ibid., F 2017, PG 65965, Büchsel, "Denkschrift. . .," 6 March 1906.
128   ibid., F 2017, PG 65963, Büchsel, "Zum Immediatvortrag," 12 February 1904.
129   ibid., F 5170, III, 1.–9.b, Vol. 1, "Allerhöchste Befehle an S.M. Schiffe im Auslande," 1 February 1900; 16 February 1901; 8 February 1902.
130   ibid., F 2017, PG 65963, Büchsel, "Zum Immediatvortrag," 12 February 1904.
131   ibid., F 2017, PG 65965, Büchsel, "Denkschrift. . .," 6 March 1906.
132   ibid., F 2017, PG 65963, Büchsel, "Zum Immediatvortrag," 12 February 1904.
133   ibid., F 5170, III, 1.–9.b, Vol. 2, Büchsel, "Allerhöchste Befehle an S.M. Schiffe im Ausland für den Kriegsfall," 27 February 1905.
134   ibid., F 2017, PG 65965, Büchsel, "Denkschrift. . .," 6 March 1906.
135   PAAA, IAAa 37, No. 5, Bd 2, Aufzeichnung über den von der Russischer Regierung vorgeschlagene Programm der II. Haager Friedens Konferenz, am 21 April 27, 28, 29 Mai und 6 July Gehaltene Conferenz, and addition "Stellung der Marine zum Punkte III. 3 des russichen Entwurfs für das Programm der Zweiter Haager Friedenskonferenz." Also GP, 23, ii, No. 8003, Tirpitz to Bülow, 28 February 1907, pp. 350–3.

# 13 Diplomacy and Operational Planning in the Face of War, 1904–06

**I**

From the Dogger Bank incident on 22 October 1904 to the signing of the General Act of Algeciras on 7 April 1906, the possibility of war loomed large in the mind of the German leadership. Occasion for this concern was first provided by fear of British attack as the consequence of German coaling of the Russian "fleet that had to die," and by a contemplated Russo-German alliance, and later by the German Morocco policy. Debate over the motivation of the German leaders continues and will be touched on in the course of this chapter.

Barbara Vogel sees Bülow and Holstein using the coaling of Rozhdestvensky's fleet as a means of "forcing Russia to [undertake] extensive return services,"[1] and maintains that the Dogger Bank incident was "almost tailor-made for the Foreign Office in order again to activate the alliance feelers towards Russia since it increased the chance of forcing Russia to lean on Germany." Lamar J. Cecil concurs.[2] Bülow had, of course, long considered Russia as a possible ally. On the other hand, Holstein had repeatedly warned against a Russian alliance directed against Britain, since Germany was very vulnerable to a British attack for which Russia could provide few compensations. By October 1904 the Grey Eminence had changed his mind because he feared that France was trying to bring Russia and Britain together and thought that this coalition could only be prevented if Germany allied with Russia.[3] Bülow shared this view, defining the proposed Russo-German alliance as one "through which the possibility of a Russo-French–English alliance will be thwarted."[4] Both men may by now have had ulterior motives. In their assessment a controversial role is played by a memorandum which Holstein drafted in consultation with Bülow for the ambassador in Paris, Prince Radolin, the contents of which were expected to be leaked to the French government.[5] In this memorandum Holstein referred to the ease with which Germany could conclude a treaty with Russia if threatened by Britain or Japan. In such a case, Holstein warned, France would either have to opt for Russia and Germany or for Britain: she could not remain neutral. If she joined Britain, this was exactly what the German military party hoped for. But the military party, Holstein added, lacked influence.

What is one to make of this communication? If it was intended to prepare France for an alliance between Germany and Russia, it would make the conclusion of this alliance more difficult because of the obvious French remonstrances in St Petersburg unless Holstein and Bülow were absolutely certain that Russia would ally with Germany. And Bülow did not have this certainty, as he warned Wilhelm to play down France in his communications with Nicholas: "Everything is wrecked if Z[ar] thinks we baited France or wanted to attack her."[6] Was it intended to provoke the French government—one of the possibilities suggested by Barbara Vogel?[7]

An answer to this question requires at least a brief discussion of the controversial question whether in view of the weakened Russian military position in Europe during and after the Russo-Japanese War the German military leadership, in particular Schlieffen, wanted and pressed for a preventive war against France and whether the military influenced the political leadership. Answers range from Peter Rassow's, Gordon Craig's, Fritz Fischer's, and Barbara Vogel's to the effect that at least Schlieffen and Holstein—and, according to Fischer and Vogel, Bülow as well—sought to provoke a war with France to Gerhard Ritter's and Albrecht Moritz's to the effect that there is no evidence for such an interpretation.[8] The most recent and perceptive treatment is Heiner Raulff's.[9]

It cannot be denied that the German military leadership, including Schlieffen, accepted preventive war in principle. This is even conceded by Moritz, who disputes that Schlieffen urged it against France in 1905.[10] There is also incontestable evidence that both Schlieffen and Einem considered the occasion of the Russo-Japanese War as propitious for a preventive war against France. Thus, on 19 April 1904, Schlieffen told Lichnowsky, who had sought him out at Bülow's request, that Russia "currently found herself in a very unfavorable position for a western war" and that "if the necessity of a war with France should arise for us, the present moment would undoubtedly be favorable . . ." New evidence for Schlieffen's wish for a preventive war in 1904 is found in the unpublished memoirs of the German military attaché in London, Count von der Schulenburg-Tressow. He states in 1904: "Only Count Schlieffen remained calm. He did not understand the thoughts and ways of German diplomacy, but considered the inevitable war to be now most propitious for us, since Russia was put out of action."[11] As Raulff indicates, the favorable military situation created by the Russo-Japanese War influenced Schlieffen to draft his memorandum "Offensive war against France," which served as the basis for the General Staff journey of June 1904.[12] It was from the experience of this journey that Schlieffen concluded that the advancing German right wing which would undertake a much wider sweep through Belgium than previously considered would have to be reinforced considerably at the expense of the left wing.[13]

Schlieffen's estimate of the situation was, of course, taken into account by the Foreign Office and Bülow.[14] His above-cited statements to Lichnowsky led Holstein to observe, "If a German–French war broke out today, Russia's participation would be improbable, England's position incalculable,"[15] and induced Bülow to draw triple lines in the margin and to note "NB." It is significant that this estimate was provided by Schlieffen in response to Bülow's inquiries less than two weeks after the conclusion of the Entente Cordiale. Holstein, as is well known, was in close contact with

Schlieffen; they met regularly in Holstein's office, exchanged information, and dined together.[16]

Did the military have to use any real pressure to convince the political authorities of the desirability of a preventive war against France? Princess Marie Radziwill, not one of the most informed persons, wrote on 28–29 December 1905:

A year before talk of Morocco, I heard utterances from the Ministry of War, the Foreign Office, even the General Staff, that nothing was any longer to be feared from Russia and that the time had come for Germany to think of the boundary rectifications [*Grenzberichtigungen*] which appear necessary.[17]

While there is no evidence that the military pressed the political leadership, there existed a basic consensus about the opportunities available.

In one respect preventive war against France was entirely acceptable to the General Staff, the Ministry of War, Bülow, Holstein, the Kaiser, and even to some naval officers. This was in the context of the so-called "hostage theory." Heiner Raulff states: "The 'hostage theory' that was later formulated by Holstein was already in the fall of 1904 the common property of the political and military leadership."[18] The theory postulated a close relationship between France and Britain. It was based on the correct assumption that in a war against Britain the German navy would be ineffective, that Germany's shipping would be destroyed, her colonies seized, her overseas markets lost, and her coast blockaded. Therefore the best German strategy in the event of a war with Britain was to attack France—something that offered chances of success—exploit her resources during the course of the war, and hold her hostage at the time of peace negotiations.

Referred to by Schröder in the naval High Command in 1897, the "hostage theory" surfaced with Schlieffen in 1904. On 20 September 1904 the Imperial Naval Office had requested of the Prussian Ministry of War that the mobilization of the navy occur separately from that of the army. This request was referred to the General Staff and elicited a response from Schlieffen on 7 October which the Ministry of War forwarded to the Chancellor on 17 October.[19] Schlieffen's letter deserves being quoted at length:

A war of Germany against England alone is highly improbable. The German fleet cannot and will not take on the English fleet. The English army will not undertake to come to Germany, the German [army] will not be able [*vermag nicht*] to reach its opponent on the other side of the Channel. Only the English fleet is capable of action. It can virtually destroy German trade, with no great damage to its own. To give expression to the dislike [*Unbehagen*] which England feels toward Germany, she will, before proceeding to open war, use a number of other means . . . If she should none the less resolve on a course of open hostility, she will surely not stand alone.

In this case, France will surely be the ally of England. Were England to declare war on Germany, France would shortly follow the given example. *The first declaration must therefore be the signal for Germany to mobilize her entire army and if necessary to anticipate France [nöthigenfalls Frankreich gegenüber das Prävenire zu spielen].* To prejudice [*zu beeinträchtigen*] the course of this general mobilization through a preceding partial mobilization would be fatal [*im hohen Grade verderblich*].

This was Schlieffen's recipe for success in a war against Britain. It involved a preventive war against France which, of course, precluded the provision of troops to support naval operations in Danish waters. Einem did not question Schieffen's views, except to ask Bülow if they were appropriate. Bülow underlined the sentence advocating preventive war against France, adding his NB. In his reply to Einem, which was drafted by Holstein, who thus concurred with his chief,[20] Bülow admitted that in view of "the complexity of our present international relations it is erroneous to assert that any form of military action is out of the question" and that "I, too, share in principle the view that retarding mobilization of the land army, a necessary result of prior naval mobilization, could have a dire effect."

Bülow and Holstein were thus prepared to entertain the hostage theory and its implied concept of preventive war against France in the event of a war with Britain. Although Bülow writes in his memoirs that he opposed the hostage theory, which he says Holstein originated, it was he who brought it up for consideration prior to a discussion of the possible effects of a Russo-German treaty on Britain. On 15 December he wrote to Holstein that one of the questions requiring consideration was:

> In case of an English attack on us is France also to be drawn into the war? The argument against this is that the General Staff thinks France is a very serious adversary, more so than in 1870, that a move against France could bring in Russia against us unless we had previously come to some sort of agreement with her; that perhaps even Italy might side with England and France. The argument in favor is that if the war remained confined to ourselves and England we are practically powerless against England. By capturing our colonies and shipping, destroying our navy and trade, and paralyzing our industry, England could in a foreseeable time force us to a disadvantageous peace. But if France is involved, and particularly if we also bring in Belgium and Holland, we increase our risk, but we would at least have a chance of achieving military successes, obtaining guarantees, and exercising pressure . . .[21]

The inquiry shows that Bülow remained aware of the tenuous link of Italy to the Triple Alliance, that he was fully aware of the violation of the neutrality of Belgium and Holland by German military planning, and that, Raulff to the contrary, he was not a dogmatic adherent of the hostage theory. Holstein's reply to the Chancellor's inquiry is not extant.

The Kaiser also considered the hostage theory and for a while appeared to accept it uncritically. He mentioned it in the presence of several people sometime before 3 November 1904,[22] and to the Württemberg minister in Berlin, Axel von Varnbüler, on 4 November.[23]

## II

It is now necessary to return to the Russian alliance negotiations. Evidently in full agreement with the Foreign Office, Wilhelm wired Nicholas on 27 October. Without specifically mentioning an alliance, he told his *confrère* that if Britain demanded that Germany desist coaling the Russian fleet Russia and Germany would have to cooperate and remind France of her alliance obligations to Russia.[24] Nicholas replied positively, stating "Germany, Russia, and France should at once join in an arrangement to abolish Anglo-Japanese arrogance and insolence," asking that Wilhelm draft such a treaty.[25] The treaty was drafted by the German Foreign Office and its text communicated to Nicholas on the following day. It provided mutual support "by all land and sea forces" if "one of the two empires was attacked by another European power." France was included by the proviso of being called by both empires to perform her obligations to Russia.[26]

Once the initiative for the conclusion of the treaty with Russia was taken, Bülow called a meeting for 31 October of the German military and political leadership to assess its significance. This is one of the few instances in Imperial Germany when recorded formal meetings of political, military, and naval leaders occurred—but this time only after the basic decision had been made. Present were Bülow, the Secretary of State of the Foreign Office, Richthofen, Holstein, Tirpitz, and Schlieffen. It is curious that Büchsel, who would be responsible for planning the naval operations, was not present. His absence may be indicative of Tirpitz's continued precedence in the navy. If so, it was not conducive to efficiency. According to a copy of Tirpitz's notes drafted by Adolf von Trotha:

> Holstein pleads for attempt of an alliance with Russia: situation anyhow no longer intact; therefore conclusion [of treaty].
> Richthofen opposed.
> Chancellor agreed with Holstein.[27]

In his memoirs Tirpitz remarks:

> Count Schlieffen, speaking from a purely military standpoint, estimated that the Russians would indeed still be able to mobilize some army corps for a possible deployment against France. I noted . . . a certain neglect of non-military considerations in the dignified and taciturn [count], in his field so significant a strategist.[28]

It cannot therefore be maintained, as Steinberg does, that Schlieffen was opposed to the Russian alliance.[29] Both Schlieffen and Holstein were more concerned about pressure on and even action against France than with war against Britain. This suggests an interest in preventive war and the hostage theory. According to Tirpitz, Holstein's main argument for a treaty with Russia was that Germany and Russia could jointly bring military pressure to bear on France to secure her entry into a Continental League.

Tirpitz was the main opponent of the Russian treaty. Both in the meeting and in a letter which he sent on the following day to Richthofen,[30] he expressed his doubts as to whether joint Russo-German pressure on France would bring the latter into a Continental bloc, whether possible French influence in London would reduce British belligerence, or whether, in view of the Czar's personality, Russia would be capable of participating in a war against France. These appear to be objections to Holstein's plea for a treaty. Even without the treaty, Tirpitz considered the German eastern border secure for many years to come because of Russia's military impotence, and regarded the one or two hundred thousand men whom Russia would send to support Germany against France "in the most favorable case" as negligible in a contest that would involve millions. Tirpitz, like Holstein earlier, expected an alliance with Russia to increase the chances of a war with Britain without corresponding compensations. For in a war against Britain, as Russia's ally, "we would . . . with our as yet under-developed navy pay the price with our foreign trade and colonies."[31] Britain could, moreover, avoid war herself and incite Japan against Germany: "With a hostile England behind us we cannot fight such a war without friends who are powerful at sea."[32] And, taking into account the hostage theory, which was probably discussed at the meeting, Tirpitz argued that if Britain declared war on Germany alone and if Russia were obligated by treaty to come to Germany's help, "then the existing Dual Alliance of France and Russia which is directed against us paralyzes the freedom of our decisions in regard to France while Russian help plays no role for us." Tirpitz recommended that good relations with Russia be continued but no treaty with her be concluded. "On the whole the gaining of time and the construction of the fleet [are] our most important political task."[33] This was an old refrain.

Although Tirpitz and Richthofen were overruled, the Russo-German alliance failed to materialize. Bülow himself beat a retreat on 31 October, insisting that the Dogger Bank incident had to be settled before France was approached, for under existing circumstances

> the French will in no way go against England. The language of all French newspapers and information from Paris leave no doubt of it. The intended purpose of Your Majesty, namely to detach France from England and push her next to us and Russia would thus not only not be achieved, but probably the opposite [would be achieved].[34]

This communication indicates that it was not Bülow's intention, at least at this time, to confront France with a threat of war. On 7 November, Nicholas submitted to Wilhelm a revised text of the treaty which weakened the originally proposed pressure on France since it was now Russia, not Russia and Germany jointly, who made "the démarches necessary to initiate France into this accord and to engage to associate her as an ally." It also suggested changing the third article, possibly making it secret, by adding the clause: "The entente cordiale is equally to be in force in the face of difficulties which might arise in the period of the negotiations of peace between Russia and Japan."[35] Bülow opposed the extension of the alliance to the peace negotiations since this would extend Germany's obligations considerably and requested Wilhelm to inform Nicholas of his objections. On 23 November, however, Nicholas notified Wilhelm that he insisted on informing the French of the treaty before signing it, something that ran counter to German intentions and brought to an end the first stage of the Russo-German alliance negotiations.[36]

But the German fear of British attack continued. On 1 November, Wilhelm expected a British strike against the Russians; on the same day Metternich reported that Germany was viewed in Britain as the true enemy and, while the majority of the people and politicians did not want war with Germany,

England . . . would take less from Germany than from Russia. An incident like the one in the North Sea between Germany and England would provoke an insane excitement here and I could not answer positively the question whether an English government would then be capable of withstanding public passion.[37]

On 7 November he claimed that the well-known journalist Arnold White had published an article in the *Sunday Sun* stating that the destruction of the German fleet, modeled after Copenhagen if necessary, was a matter of life and death for Britain.[38] On 17 November the German naval attaché in London, Kapitän-zur-See Coerper, reported accelerated preparations of the British fleet, causing Wilhelm to comment, "Sheer preparations for indirect mobilization,"[39] and on 18 November he wrote that the view the German fleet would have to be destroyed had spread considerably.[40] The latter report impelled Bülow to note that he intended to discuss its contents with Tirpitz and that the power relationship between Britain and Germany at sea would not change within the next six years.[41] By 30 November, Wilhelm had ordered Büchsel to prepare for a British attack in the spring,[42] and on 5 December Holstein admitted that "I now believe—which I did not before—in the possibility of a war with England in which the attack would come from the English side."[43] In the first part of December, the British detention of the Hamburg–America Line collier *Kapitän W. Menzel*, taking on coal at Cardiff for the Russian fleet, led Wilhelm and Bülow to another unsuccessful attempt to seek an alliance with Russia.[44]

Under these circumstances the initiative that Büchsel and the Admiralty Staff had taken between 23 October and 2 November[45] secured strong support from above. This was obviously necessary for obtaining assistance from the army without which the planning against Britain remained theoretical. On the evening of 18 November, influenced by hostile articles in the *Naval Horizon* and the *Army and Navy Gazette*, the Kaiser in his usual impulsive manner summoned Büchsel to a meeting with Schlieffen and Bülow in Berlin to discuss the operations plan against Britain. Since Büchsel had already left for Kiel, he could not be reached and, as he somewhat peevishly remarked, "regrettably nobody got the idea of inviting my representative." So the basic decision to make the operations plan against Britain functional was made in the absence of the man responsible for it! Wilhelm, however, ordered Schlieffen, "who was very reticent and did not say a word," to provide the troops for the implementation of the operations plan in Danish waters. On the following morning in Kiel, Wilhelm ordered Büchsel to proceed with the operations. The "hostage theory" had thus been dropped. There is no evidence whether on 18 November Bülow defended this course of action or whether he questioned the wisdom of the violation of Danish neutrality on political grounds as he was to do later.

Büchsel, needless to say, was delighted with the outcome if not with the procedure. He was going to seek a Cabinet Order from the Kaiser which would place him in full charge of the planning:

All preparations are to be made in order to secure for my navy the execution of OP II. For the tasks that are hereby incumbent on my army, active troops are to be used and planned mobilization preparations are to be made for their use.

Under the chairmanship of the Chief of the Admiralty Staff, delegates of the Imperial Naval Office, the General Staff of the Army, the Ministry of War, and the Chancellor are to make the necessary preparations and the Chief of the Admiralty Staff is to report regarding the work of this committee.

Büchsel ordered the Admiralty Staff to give the work on Operations Plan II top priority, observe the movements of the British fleet, obtain better information than newspaper accounts (revealing thus the woeful inadequacy of German naval intelligence), and prepare the mine-ships for war.[46]

The Admiralty Staff proceeded with great speed. On 21 November, A, A1, A2, A4, A4₁, and N (Intelligence Department) jointly decided to complete the preparations for the plan by 1 March, 1905. Measures were to be taken to improve the intelligence service. N believed that it would be possible to get civilians and inactive German officers to observe movements of ships in Portsmouth, Chatham, and Plymouth. Spies were already available in Gibraltar and Malta. Since the British navy obtained its coal from Cardiff, agents familiar with the coal trade had to be found there to report on any major orders. It was further agreed to speed up all repairs and new constructions, and to order mines. These were indeed preparations for war.[47]

Büchsel and Tirpitz reached agreement on the increase of war preparedness of German ships abroad, and their representatives met to discuss details. Büchsel also persuaded Schlieffen, who was still dragging his feet, to resume discussions about operations in Danish waters.[48] Accordingly, on 25 November, Büchsel, A, A1, A2, and A4 met with Lieutenant-Colonel von Stein of the General Staff, who at once pointed out how inconvenient it would be for the army to have to participate in the operations against Denmark in the event of an attack on Germany by Britain, since it was impossible to foresee what other powers would be involved. Eventually he stated that one active division, reinforced by two Landwehr brigades, would suffice for the operations on land and that two batteries of 12 cm guns would be adequate to defend the mine blockings.[49] Büchsel reported to a very worried Kaiser on 3 December and stated that the troops offered by Stein would only be adequate if Denmark offered no resistance.[50] Otherwise two additional army corps would be necessary and those the General Staff refused to provide if the army were engaged elsewhere, i.e. against France, which it considered highly probable. Without saying whether in such a case the two army corps would be more useful against France than against Denmark, Büchsel argued that a considerable presence of the army in the north was essential. If the British fleet tried to force its way into the Baltic, Germany would have to take military action which could lead to hostilities with Denmark. Provision would have to be made for this eventuality as well as for the defense of the German coast and the Kaiser Wilhelm Canal in case of a British landing. Unless the two army corps were available, the entire operation in Danish waters was jeopardized. Büchsel won the day since Wilhelm ruled that the Ninth and Tenth Army Corps must remain in the north whatever the further ramifications of a British attack on Germany.

Büchsel's victory over Schlieffen was only temporary. His operational notions no longer enjoyed the full support of the navy. One of the dissidents was Bendemann, author of the operations plan in Danish waters, now in command of the North Sea station in Wilhelmshaven. In a memorandum of the same date as Büchsel's score over Schlieffen,[51] Bendemann expressed the widespread German suspicion of deep-seated British hostility on economic grounds and the temptation to launch a pre-emptive attack on the German fleet on political and military grounds: Russian naval power in Europe was nonexistent, France was friendly, Italy and Austria-Hungary did not count, and British naval supremacy over Germany was immense. In case of such an attack, Germany's position was next to hopeless. In weighing the advantages and disadvantages of the Baltic Sea strategy against the North Sea strategy, he opted for the latter. This change of mind is, perhaps, not altogether surprising since the role of the North Sea station would be minimized by the Baltic Sea strategy. A choice of the Baltic theater of war would throw the German fleet on the defensive since the British fleet would not enter the Baltic: the German fleet would indeed be preserved, but it would no longer be an instrument of war. Drawing on the lessons of the Russo-Japanese War, Bendemann argued that a fleet lying in a port would become incapable of further military action. Concentration in the Baltic would also allow the British navy to obtain its war aims without any effort: "The maritime trade of our North Sea ports is cut off from the beginning, and our shipping has been handed over to the English; the fleet has been paralyzed and blockaded." What Bendemann now recommended was bold and desperate action in the North Sea, as later advocated by Count Baudissin and allegedly favored by Tirpitz:

Encounter the English with everything we have in the North Sea in order to beat them. That would be a temporary tactical success . . . In view of the large English reserves the close blockade of our weakened fleet would follow sooner or later. But this course would have the great advantage of giving a break to our maritime trade and shipping, even for a short period of time, of enabling us to arm our fast steamers and send them out into the ocean where they would undoubtedly cause enormous damage before being caught; in short, regardless of points of honor, our fleet would have achieved what it could.

On 17 February 1905, shortly after Wilhelm reversed his decision on use of army troops against Denmark, the Chief of the Active Battle fleet, Admiral von Koester, who appears to have been unaware of this reversal, also expressed his disagreement with the strategy of the Admiralty Staff.[52] His first objection was that it entailed

. . . the total splitting of the high-seas forces at the beginning of war. A larger part of the fleet must go to the North Sea. Another must cover the transport of army troops and the blocking transports, the Sound must be guarded above and below, the rest must demonstrate in the Skagerrak. Indeed, the detachment sent to the Elbe is to return soon, but is this to be counted on? Probably before but certainly immediately after the declaration of war, hostile forces will appear in the German Bight, which makes questionable the return to the Baltic Sea of the detached ships.

Through these initial measures we cancel our great advantage of being able to concentrate our entire naval forces thanks to the favorable relation [*Lage*] of our war harbors to one another—an advantage which has influenced the current reorganization of the English fleet. The plan transfers the major operational area to the Great Belt, waters which are indeed known better to us than to English ships, but which will become a hostile area for us as a result of our measures against Denmark. We must count there on hostile undertakings of many kinds which could easily lead to heavier losses for us than those we can inflict on the English.

Moreover, he criticized the plan for relegating the fleet to the defensive. The concept that it was only to do battle once the supremacy of the enemy had been reduced was incorrect since the British would continue to be reinforced by their older ships. It was also contrary to the German tactical tradition which emphasized the offensive: "We see in [our] peacetime work directed toward the quickest possible, concentrated blow a compensation for the material superiority of our opponent." He was prepared to accept a brief demonstration on the part of one squadron in the Skagerrak to draw enemy forces into the Baltic, but once this squadron had fulfilled this task it was to join immediately the Second Squadron and other naval forces in the Elbe, which was to serve as the area of deployment. "Leaning on Heligoland, battle is then to be offered to the enemy as soon as possible . . . Delay of a day would bring us into a more unfavorable position."

Koester thus agreed with Bendemann's stand, revealing the opposition of at least two important representatives of the "Front" to the planning of the Admiralty Staff. Anachronistically, Koester still adhered to Tirpitz's risk theory: while he did not expect a victory for the German navy, he counted on sufficient weakening of the British fleet from the battle and subsequent nocturnal mine- and torpedo-boat actions as to end "the supremacy that Britain needs in the face of other maritime powers." This remark elicited the marginal comment from Büchsel: "But I doubt it." While Büchsel was criticized by the "Front," he was losing faith in Tirpitz. So were other naval leaders. There is some evidence that other naval men shared Bendemann's and Koester's objections to the operations in Danish waters. Gemzell cites Keyserlingk as stating that Georg Alexander von Müller, the future Chief of the Naval Cabinet, Prince Heinrich, and Tirpitz were also opposed to it.[53] As for Tirpitz, it ran counter to his entire North Sea strategy. And in the light of the in-fighting that was characteristic of the German navy the Danish operations plan would have enhanced the importance of the Admiralty Staff and thus led to reactions from other agencies.

Operations in the Baltic were ignored altogether in a memorandum of 27 November that was prepared by Waldemar Vollerthun, head of the N (Information) department of the Imperial Naval Office, and annotated by Tirpitz.[54] Was the intention of this memorandum to point out the futility of any current operational planning against Britain? If so, was it prepared with Tirpitz's approval or was it a criticism of his policy? Could one dare criticize Tirpitz from the Imperial Naval Office without risking one's career? Heeringen's statement, which will be discussed subsequently, seems to indicate that such criticism was still compatible with advancement.

Vollerthun frankly stated that, in a war with Britain, Germany's political and military position was untenable. Her rapprochement with Russia had only increased British and Japanese hostility; an alliance with Russia would be of little avail since it did not secure French support and Russia was incapable of providing direct assistance by attacking India. This was in line with Tirpitz's thoughts as expressed on 31 October–1 November 1904. More independently, Vollerthun argued that the British rapprochement with France had freed Germany from a threat of an attack by the latter country, who had thereby subordinated her policy to her Entente partner. "Only on the side of England will it become an opponent of Germany, but then defensively rather than offensively." Under these circumstances a war between Germany and Britain supported by France would be an utter disaster: a destruction of her entire maritime trade, a blockade of the German Bight and the Kattegat, and an escalation of internal conflicts. "The effect of such a war on our workers' conditions with a simultaneous increase of internal food-prices need not be more closely examined here. Its effects cannot be anticipated." The occupation of Holland or Denmark would not sufficiently extend the German-controlled coastline to make the blockade more difficult. Conceding some validity to the hostage theory, Vollerthun remarked: "A simultaneously conducted land war on French soil would make the conditions somewhat more favorable for us." There were no marginal comments from Tirpitz criticizing his subordinate.

According to Vollerthun, Germany's only succor against Britain and

France lay in a defensive alliance with the United States of America, less in an active military sense than as a deterrent to Britain, who because of her dependence on United States grain could not afford a war with her. The United States, in turn, would have an interest in avoiding destruction of her extensive trade with Germany by the British and could be offered concessions in the Pacific.

However unrealistic the proposal of an alliance with the Americans, Vollerthun showed an accurate appreciation of the political situation in Europe and of Germany's position in a war with Britain. Unlike the Admiralty Staff he appreciated the hostage theory and considered more seriously the consequences of the rapprochement between Britain and France. Lastly the Vollerthun memorandum implied the bankruptcy of the Tirpitz Plan: "Our Continental position, ground between the upper and the nether millstone, on the one hand, the need for overseas development on the other hand *have led to a politically untenable situation.*" Although underlined, this crucial sentence was not minuted by Tirpitz. Was this an admission of criticism?

A few days before Vollerthun had dated his memorandum, Tirpitz, in view of the danger of war, had formed a committee under the chairmanship of his trusted colleague Heeringen,[55] who presented his report on 14 December.[56] This report was fully annotated by Tirpitz. Heeringen stated that Tirpitz's assumption that peace could be preserved until the navy was completed, while correct initially because of the general reluctance to suffer economic damage through war, was no longer tenable.

> In the meantime, however, through the Russo-Japanese War, all powers have come somewhat closer to the idea of war. In England there exists an influential party which steadily becomes more accustomed to the belief that for her own security England is forced to defeat us before our fleet is ready. What deserves special attention here is that in the past years the influence of this party has increased considerably . . . It continues to grow rapidly.

Although he did not consider a British attack to be imminent, Heeringen challenged Tirpitz's doctrine that the German navy could not afford both quantity and quality and that therefore quantity had to be given priority over quality. He argued that quality had to be enhanced through improving the war readiness of the fleet to avoid a repetition of the Russian débâcle in the face of Japan. He recommended a number of measures that would remove funds from ship constructions, such as the maintenance of most ships in service throughout the year, avoidance of lengthy repair periods in the winter and precautions to prevent the ships located in Wilhelmshaven from being cut off from the fleet in Kiel.

Tirpitz, however, was unresponsive to his subordinate's criticism: above all, the construction of the battle fleet must remain the priority. "The danger zone for Germany is not only today but, with *greater* probability, tomorrow, and with this fact we must reckon in the development of the navy." The current threat of war was discarded.

With the naval leadership disunited about the priority accorded to construction and the directions of operations, Büchsel none the less proceeded with his preparations for the Danish operations, supported by Wilhelm's ruling regarding army support. On 20 December he obtained Schlieffen's promise to examine the support that the army would provide. But the Chief of the General Staff moved slowly. On 28 January 1905, Büchsel reminded him of his promise,[57] expecting him to participate in the presentation of a joint report by the middle of March. On 31 January, Büchsel presented to the Kaiser what appears to be a preliminary report in which he requested once more the participation of all the involved agencies to work on the operations in Danish waters. The Chancellor's responsibility would be the preparation of diplomatic notes to Denmark and other involved states at the outset of hostilities; he and the Secretary of State of the Imperial Naval Office would have to participate in the regulation of the sea-prize law, the embargo of all British ships in German waters, and the wartime use of the Kaiser Wilhelm Canal. All the army and navy agencies would be involved in the transport of necessary troops to Denmark.

In an attempt to coordinate naval and military planning with political action, Wilhelm ordered Büchsel to keep the Chancellor informed about naval operations[58] and, on 6 February, Senden provided Bülow with the information regarding Operations Plan II.[59] This is the first recorded communication of naval operations to the political leadership since Bismarck's time.[60] Bülow responded promptly on 9 February, and raised no objections on political grounds, except for insisting on absolute secrecy since, in view of British fears of German attack, leaks could lead to "incalculable catastrophes."[61] He objected no more to naval operations violating Danish neutrality than he had to the Schlieffen Plan violating Belgian and Dutch neutrality. More detailed discussions took place between the Undersecretary of State of the Foreign Office, Klehmet, Büchsel, and Captain Dick in which the representatives of the Admiralty Staff envisaged the violation of Swedish as well as Danish neutrality, for which "the Foreign Office was to give its approval and to keep on hand notes to the Danish as well as Swedish government to prevent both of these governments as long as possible from hostilities against us." Of these discussions, which also dealt with measures directed against the British coast and shipping and with privateering, no record was kept, presumably to maintain secrecy.[62] For a while Schlieffen appeared to be as cooperative as Bülow. On 4 February he provided estimates of Danish forces that would be facing the Germans, of transportation arrangements for German troops, and of guns necessary for the protection of the blockings.[63]

Büchsel prepared a report for Wilhelm on 3 February in the expectation of a parallel report from Schlieffen. He continued to argue that the navy would require army support both in a war against Britain and against Britain and France. In the former case the decision lay almost exclusively with the navy, for it alone could inflict damage on Britain. He questioned the hostage theory if France was Britain's ally because of the enormous setbacks to the German economy through British blockade:

Even if we succeed through the elimination of a Continental ally of England to feed ourselves for a while in the hostile country, the point in time when we must submit to the will of England can only be delayed. It cannot be avoided altogether.

Another Admiralty Staff memorandum, the draft of which was dated 1 January and a finished version of which eventually reached the Imperial Naval Office and was probably also available to Wilhelm, systematically defended the Danish operations plan. It dealt with many of the objections that had been raised, criticized the Schlieffen Plan, and took into account Germany's naval strategy against both Britain and France.[64]

Britain was described as "consciously arming politically and militarily for a war against Germany." She would probably launch a sudden attack. "We shall not fight the war against England alone; France will either be caused by England or by us to become involved." Russia was for the time being friendly toward Germany, but a rapprochement between her and Britain was possible in the future. For the first time the Admiralty Staff mentioned Russia's concern for Denmark: the extent of the occupation of Danish territory would depend on Russia's attitude. Sweden's response to the German violation of her neutrality through the closing of the Flintrinne was also expected to be governed by the Russian stand. Germany could expect the benevolent neutrality of Austria-Hungary; Italy would certainly not oppose Britain and might even join her. Unlike Vollerthun, the Admiralty Staff did not consider the United States a possible ally but conceded that because of her extensive trade with Germany she would have an interest in averting an Anglo-German war in which this trade would cease.

The views of the Admiralty Staff on Continental strategy were dominated by the disastrous effects of a British blockade on Germany: "a financial and social crisis . . . the consequences of which are entirely incalculable." It therefore categorically rejected the violation of Belgian and Dutch neutrality by the army in its advance on France, having obviously become aware of this aspect of the Schlieffen Plan:

The importance of Belgium and Holland for us in a war against England lies in the first instance in the fact that a large part of German trade, and namely that which supplies the important western and southern industrial regions of Germany, is permanently conducted through Belgian and Dutch ports.

The cutting off of the German North Sea coast through an effectively established British blockade will probably further direct the routes of German maritime trade to these ports. If England wants to destroy German maritime trade, and this is the aim of the war, then she must also cut off German imports and exports over Belgium and Holland, be it through a blockade of the ports concerned or through a strict observation of their trade.

In this war both states have nothing to hope from Germany and everything to fear from England: they will therefore have to accept any treatment accorded to them by England.

Thereby we have no cause to proceed militarily against both states. On the contrary, we have the greatest interest that both states remain neutral. For then we have the prospect that at least that trade which will know how to escape English observation would continue and, most significantly, that England must permanently use forces [*Mittel*] for this observation or a blockade.

While the Admiralty Staff was opposed to Schlieffen's insistence on the breach of Belgian and Dutch neutrality, it now accepted a modified form of the hostage theory, going further than did Büchsel in his report to Wilhelm on 3 February. In view of the catastrophic results of the blockade:

. . . we shall not only have to regret if, in a war of England against Germany, France places herself on the side of England, but we shall face France with the question whether it wants to go with us or against us, and then it will naturally resolve in favor of the latter.

Thereby we shall gain the opportunity to act on land, to occupy our numerous working-class population, unemployed and breadless through the cut-off of our entire maritime trade, and, we hope, to feed it on foreign soil at foreign expense.

By opposing the invasion of Holland and Belgium, however, the Admiralty Staff was proposing to tear up Schlieffen's formula for victory and thus preclude the possibility of a vanquished France solving the disastrous problems created for Germany by a British blockade. This was a major inconsistency.

Inconsistent also was the Admiralty Staff's continued adherence to Tirpitz's risk theory. Britain, the memorandum pointed out, would have to achieve her war aims:

I.   To destroy the German fleet
II.  To destroy German maritime trade
III. To protect her own coast and her own trade . . . without forfeiting her military supremacy over the other great neutral powers at sea, i.e. England cannot engage her naval power for their achievement without limitation, but must take care not to suffer excessive losses; for if these occurred, then England, even if she achieved her war aim, would be in a difficult position of facing neutrals who would then be superior to her at sea and might try to take advantage of it.

What neutrals? The Admiralty Staff just recognized France as a close friend and potential ally of Britain, the Russian naval power as almost broken, Japan as allied to Britain, and Italy as hardly mattering. That only left the United States, whom Vollerthun had unrealistically viewed as Germany's potential ally but against whom the Admiralty Staff continued to plan operations.

The Admiralty Staff now expected French and British navies to operate in separate theaters but none the less confined its deliberations to warfare with

Britain, who was expected to begin hostilities without a declaration of war. These would initially be directed toward capturing bases in the North Sea, possibly Heligoland, Sylt, Borkum, and Lister Tief, and toward the Elbe estuary and the western entrance of the Kaiser Wilhelm Canal, to deprive the German navy of its inner line of communications. There was some ambiguity as to whether Britain was expected to seek battle with the German fleet at the beginning of the war: while her war aims would be achieved through a victorious battle, she, more than Germany, could afford and would, in fact, benefit from a drawn-out war in so far as she would thereby establish a firmer hold on former German markets.

Rejecting both a strategic defensive and an immediate battle in the North Sea, the memorandum continued to plead for the offensive against Denmark as the only way of forcing the British to divide their naval forces and making it possible for the German navy to establish supremacy. Denmark was now definitely expected to offer resistance. As further measures, the Admiralty Staff advocated the strengthening of the coastal fortifications of the North Sea and the Elbe estuary and the removal of ships from Wilhelmshaven and Bremerhaven to prevent them from being cut off by early British action.

But these arguments of the Admiralty Staff were in vain. On 7 February, Senden informed Büchsel that on the basis of the report of 3 February the Kaiser had resolved "that, for the operations of the fleet in the case of war against England or England and France, the proposed occupation of a part of Zealand and Korsör cannot be reckoned with." He stated that the detachment of troops for the support of these operations would jeopardize the success of the advance against France. This was a victory for Schlieffen, who certainly did not underestimate his French opponent and who had steadily opposed the operations against Denmark, since he wanted every man available in the west. It may have been a victory for the hostage theory, although there is no evidence that it at this point entered Wilhelm's calculations. It was also a victory for Bülow, who, as Senden informed Büchsel, was now, for political reasons, opposed to the violation of Danish neutrality.[65] Although the Chancellor had not originally opposed the operations in Danish waters, he was having second thoughts about the violation of Danish neutrality by 15 December when he asked Holstein:

What about Denmark? Would the disadvantage of the move in that direction, the resulting irritation of the Russians, be greater than the advantage of at least being able to protect the Baltic coast and affording our navy a better chance?[66]

On 5 February 1905 he had written to the ambassador in Washington that Germany had to cultivate her relations with Russia because of the grave threat of an attack by Britain and France.[67] On the following day Holstein stated that he was opposed to the use of any pressure on Denmark to enter into an alliance with Germany since she was not ready for it and since such action would play into the hands of "the enemies of Germany and particularly those who are diplomatically working for a Franco-Russian–English

Triplice." Holstein's concern with encirclement continued. The minister in Copenhagen, Schoen, on 11 February entirely agreed with the Grey Eminence.[68] Bülow and the Foreign Office had thus come out against the Admiralty Staff.

Büchsel, realizing that without army support the operations in the Danish waters were unfeasible, cancelled preparations for them.[69] On 20 February the Admiralty Staff received the memorandum of Admiral Koester of 17 February, advocating deployment in the Elbe and an immediate battle with the British. It led A to comment:

> I am temporarily holding the view that we cannot set up a fixed plan for this case of war because the nature of the most suitable measures depends too much on the political situation at the outbreak of war. Thus, it may be as well that the participation of the army has been dropped. We would probably have tied ourselves down too much in this respect.

At least some officers in the Admiralty Staff were thus questioning the direction of previous planning and its disregard of political factors. A advocated greater flexibility.

The fact is that the German navy lacked an operations plan against Britain or against Britain and France at the time that Bülow and Holstein were about to challenge France's encroachment in Morocco, entailing the risk of war with France and possibly with France and Britain. Deliberate provocation of France cannot be precluded from German calculations. Success against France alone on land depended on the violation of Belgian and Dutch neutrality which Schlieffen expected in December 1905 to bring Britain into the war as well.[70] Maritime operations against France which followed from previous operational work were not coordinated with army planning and took no account of Britain's reaction to what was done to her Entente partner and potential ally. Moreover, a German offensive war against France was bound to provoke Russia, whose friendship Wilhelm, Holstein, and Bülow considered important in the event of an Anglo- German war.[71]

## III

"By the spring of 1905," writes Paul Kennedy, ". . . [the] uncoordinated German leadership had fastened upon a quite different issue with which to salvage some of its diplomatic prestige—Morocco."[72] By that time British hostility had become less acute and Russian military might had declined further. While German motivation continues to be disputed, it is clear that France was to be prevented from turning Morocco, in which Germany felt it had legitimate interests, into another Tunisia and that the French were to be shown that they were dependent on Germany and would be left in the lurch by their fair-weather British friends if challenged on the central issue of the Entente Cordiale: the establishment of French supremacy in Morocco.

Although Bülow had prevailed in 1898–1901 in scuttling the alliance negotiations with Britain, it was Holstein who largely directed the German

policy regarding Morocco. In the end, however, the hard line that he had
taken was repudiated and he himself was dismissed. Nor was he present
during the entire duration of the crisis; at the beginning of September 1905
his nerves gave out and he was on leave until the end of October; his health
also kept him at home in January 1906.[73] But as he described his role during
the first part of the crisis to his cousin Ida von Stüpnagel on 16 June 1905:

> During these eight months, as one difficult question followed another, I
> dealt with . . . [Bülow] alone, without disagreement. Richthofen is
> completely out of it . . . With the exception of Bülow, I discuss things
> with no one, but give orders what shall be done or do things myself. In the
> feeling of lonely responsibility I have many a sleepless night.[74]

Holstein was one of the first German leaders to realize the serious
limitations that the Entente Cordiale had imposed on German *Weltpolitik*.
As for Morocco specifically, early proposals for securing compensation in
the form of a port or some territory with the support of naval demonstrations
had been vetoed by Wilhelm, who was to be a restraining influence
throughout the Moroccan affair.[75] For a while the Foreign Office advocated
a dilatory stance, expecting Spain to lead the opposition to France's
unilateral action. In the discussion of the Russian alliance at the end of
October 1904, Holstein, as indicated above, took a primarily anti-French
stand in which he enjoyed Bülow's support. But when the Russians
declined the alliance, the French refused to offer concessions, and other
powers did not oppose French action, the German press began to protest a
do-nothing policy. Richard von Kühlmann, chargé d'affaires in Tangier,
proposed that Wilhelm land in that city during his Mediterranean cruise and
recognize the Sultan of Morocco as an independent sovereign.

"The origins of the Morocco action manifested in March 1905 by the
support of the Sultan (which Bülow approved) are to be found in the failure
of the first German alliance offer to Russia and in the Russian setbacks in
East Asia."[76] The immediate provocation was the dispatch of a French
military mission to Fez in January 1905, by which Delcassé showed that he
planned to bring Morocco under French control without bothering to consult
Germany.[77] Delcassé, who had for some time been regarded by the
German leadership as Germany's arch-enemy and the mastermind of her
encirclement, was now blamed by Wilhelm, Bülow, and Holstein alike for
Germany's failure to benefit from the Russo-Japanese War and to secure an
alliance with Russia.[78]

Was preventive war sought by any of the German leaders? Moritz has
argued that an important restraining factor was the re-equipment of
German infantry and artillery and in particular the considerable inferiority
of the German field-artillery to the French. This inferiority carried
particular weight with Wilhelm and Einem, and it appears that at one of the
several secret meetings, held in March 1905, between the Kaiser and the
political and military leaders during the Morocco crisis it was at Einem's
urging the reason not to provoke war with France.[79] Moritz cites as another
restraining factor the expectation on the part of Schlieffen early in 1905 that,

in a war against both France and Russia, Germany would confront 500,000 Russian soldiers. However, Moritz concedes that many Russian troops were moved to the Far East after the battle of Mukden of 23 February to 10 March. Schlieffen's confidant, Holstein, stated just after Mukden, when the German Morocco action was launched, that it was out of the question "that Russia could together with France and England attack Germany."[80] Schlieffen provided his own estimate of Russia's military position in Europe on 18 August in response to Bülow's inquiry:

> Russia has currently ten of her twenty-six European army corps, six of her thirty-eight reserve divisions, five of her eight rifle brigades in East Asia, *en route* there, or mobilized to be used there . . . as well as other personnel and *matériel* . . . Thereby the Russian forces have been greatly weakened not only in quantity and quality, but also in organization.[81]

And at the end of November Nicholas informed Wilhelm that two-thirds of his army was still in East Asia.[82] In short, the German leadership was well aware from March 1905 onward that Russian military power in Europe was negligible. Thus the incomplete re-equipment of the German army and the inadequacy of its field-artillery were more than balanced by the weakness of Russia, particularly as the re-equipment of the German army was speeded up in 1905.[83] Schlieffen, who, unlike Wilhelm and Bülow, never underestimated the quality of the French army and who was conscious of the inadequate size of the German army, may also have been encouraged to fight France by the decision regarding the naval operations plan in February which freed him of the obligation to detach two army corps against Denmark.

Recent evidence suggests that Schlieffen seriously considered preventive war against France and on at least one occasion suggested it to Wilhelm. According to Count von der Schulenburg-Tressow:

> During my holidays . . . I was each time received by Count Schlieffen for a report [*Vortrag*]. With open honesty he spoke of the military–political situation, saying that England would in the future be found on the side of our enemies. In 1905, therefore, it was necessary either to utilize the favorable military situation or to push through a complete understanding with France over Alsace-Lorraine.[84]

According to Wilhelm Groener's no less reliable testimony, Schlieffen used an article in the *Twentieth Century* in May 1905

> which called for the immediate conclusion of an alliance of England with France . . . as an occasion to urge the Kaiser and the government to go to war against France and thus destroy the net which he alone clearly recognized as tightly enveloping us. He recognized the unique advantage of the occasion [*Augenblicks*] which would never recur: that we could dispose of our French enemy . . . as long as Russia . . . would be entirely incapable of action and that at the same time, through the destruction of France, we would be able to strike a decisive blow against our British opponent.[85]

This statement is supported by other contemporary German assessments of Russian military strength and it includes the hostage theory. Subsequently Groener explains Schlieffen's position:

> His goal in 1905, when he counseled war, was neither Morocco, nor yet world-political ambition and sea power [Seegeltung]; his aim was apparently closer: he wanted nothing more than the security of the Continental power-base of the Reich, which was indeed most severely threatened by an English–French union [*Einigung*] with Russia in the background. This attitude represented a more realistic and healthy view of world politics than was common.

Schlieffen, however, failed to convince Wilhelm, who responded: "No! Never shall I be capable of such action!"[86] Einem also blames the Kaiser for "having in the years 1905–06—to our misfortune—prevented a collision with France."[87] There is no evidence that either Bülow or Holstein wanted a preventive war in the sense that it was advocated by Schlieffen, but they were certainly more prepared than the Kaiser to accept the risk of war. In his memoirs, Bülow explains the risk he was taking:

> I did not dread confronting France with the question of war because I knew I could keep it from coming to the extreme; I would cause Delcassé to fall, thus blunting the aggressive plans of French policy, knocking from the hand of Edward VII and the war group in England their Continental dagger, and thus simultaneously preserving peace and German honor and strengthening German prestige.[88]

He made several inquiries about the Russian and German military capacity, and the responses were such as not to discourage an aggressive course.[89] Holstein appeared to hold the view that if Germany backed down in the face of French intransigence war might indeed be avoided for the present but would be all the more certain in the future since giving in once would encourage future bullying. "The war which would be avoided by giving in now would certainly be forced upon us after a short interval, under some other pretext and worse conditions."[90] The last words indicate that Holstein viewed the situation as not unfavorable for war.

What should have discouraged the German leadership from risking war, however, was the attitude of Britain. Moritz had demonstrated that the German leadership was divided on the question of whether Britain would join France if the Morocco crisis escalated to war. Reports from London by Metternich, Bernstorff, Coerper and Schulenburg indicated that she would. Wilhelm was sure of it and dreaded a British attack on his fleet. Schlieffen allegedly first expected Britain to remain neutral, but changed his mind in the fall of 1905; in his December memorandum, he expected the British to be fighting on the side of the French. So did his successor Moltke, who stated in February 1906, at the time of the Algeciras Conference, that Britain had no other choice since a German victory over France would entirely upset the European balance of power. Bülow and Holstein lived under a delusion, however. While infinitely suspicious of Britain, the Chancellor did not think that she would support France militarily, and, except for one instance in June 1905, Holstein agreed.[91] This assumption was the basis for their calculation that pressure on France would break the Entente Cordiale. Both men did think, however, that there were elements in Britain that were encouraging a Franco-German war, Britain benefiting as *tertius gaundens*.

It took considerable pressure by Bülow to get the Kaiser to visit Tangier. Eventually he complied. It is difficult to estimate to what extent he may have been swayed by his recent pessimistic appraisal of the diplomatic situation: "The Triple Alliance loosened by the estrangement of Austria and Italy, Russia unchanged or indifferent [sic] toward us, England hostile, Gaul aiming at revanche."[92] He was instructed to speak in favor of the Sultan's independence and the principle of equal economic treatment of all nations. Bülow cautioned him, however, against promising the Sultan military aid against France: such extreme provocation was to be avoided.[93] The Kaiser's speech was intended to strengthen Moroccan resistance to France, make France uneasy and ready to negotiate, and to gain the support of nations interested in maintaining the "open door" in non-European areas, particularly the United States, whose role was to loom large in the calculations of German leaders.

Wilhelm's speech of 31 March in Tangier compelled Delcassé to offer to negotiate with Germany.[94] In response the German leadership first assumed a sphinx-like attitude, while Holstein forged a strategy according to which any bilateral negotiations with France would be refused and a conference of the signatories of the Madrid Conference of 1880 regarding Morocco would be required to regulate the future status of that country. While Holstein was opposed by the head of the Press Department, Hammann, Bülow accepted the proposal of the conference on 3 April.[95] Henceforth Holstein regarded any bilateral negotiations with France over Morocco as backing down from the Kaiser's public recognition of the Sultan of Morocco as an independent sovereign which "would stand at the same level as Olmütz and cause Fashoda to be forgotten." If France refused the conference, she would put herself in the wrong and be isolated; if she accepted it, Holstein was sure she would remain in the minority. Holstein adhered to this course until July with the full support of Bülow, who communicated his reasoning to Wilhelm.[96] The thrust was for France's isolation and the break-up of the Entente Cordiale.[97] More specifically it was directed against Delcassé. According to Bülow's comments of 8 April: "All criticism and attacks are to manifest the greatest possible respect for French national feeling against Delcassé's systematically anti-German, insolent, and clumsy policy." His fall was thus clearly one of Bülow's and Holstein's aims. Nor was war shunned at this point, as can be inferred from Holstein's comment about Olmütz and from Bülow's remark about the prospect of war: "Let no fear be shown of this! No cowardice [*Feigheit*]."[98] The hard line continued even after Delcassé was discredited, and the direction of French foreign policy was taken over by Rouvier on 19 April, and the Foreign Minister resigned on 6 June.

The Foreign Office continued to push for the conference in spite of British support for France and the unexpected lack of support for such a conference by other powers, although Wilhelm, who thought that peace had been saved by the fall of Delcassé, was beginning to show willingness to accommodate Rouvier.[99] The Foreign Office prevailed and an agreement to hold the conference was reached on 8 July but on terms that did not correspond to Holstein's and Bülow's original assumptions. France had not been isolated, the Entente Cordiale had been strengthened rather than weakened, and Germany had been compelled to accept France's special interests in Morocco. Within the German political leadership the usual disunity became henceforth more evident: only Holstein firmly adhered to the hard line.[100]

At this time the idea of an alliance with Russia re-emerged. Soon after the agreement on the conference, Wilhelm, with Bülow's concurrence, suggested to Nicholas that they meet during their summer cruises and the latter agreed. Wilhelm considered this an opportunity for attempting to commit Nicholas once more to the treaty that was under consideration the previous year. Both Bülow and Holstein were doubtful of the outcome and no longer held it possible to conclude a treaty with Russia behind France's back or to split the Dual Alliance. The only real advantage they saw in such a treaty was that it would prevent an Anglo-Russian rapprochement.[101] As is well known, contrary to Bülow's and Holstein's expectations, Wilhelm on 23 July obtained Nicholas's signature for the treaty; however, Bülow opposed freeing Russia from the obligation to support Germany in case of war outside of Europe, i.e. by advancing on India.[102]

Apparently the inclusion of the words "en Europe," which relieved Russia from this obligation, occurred at Wilhelm's initiative, following consultation with Moltke, the designated successor of Schlieffen as Chief of the General Staff. Wilhelm was reluctant to allow the Russian alliance to involve Germany in complications with Japan. He thus thought in European rather than in global terms. Wilhelm's thinking was governed by the hostage theory and the Schlieffen plan. In the event of a British attack on Germany two dispatches were to be sent, one to Brussels and the other to Paris

with the demand [*Sommation*] that they declare within six hours whether they are for or against us. We must immediately march into Belgium, however it may declare itself. If France should choose neutrality—which I do not consider entirely out of the question even though the probability is small—then the Russian *casus foederis* will not come into consideration. If she [France] mobilizes, then this is a threat of war against us in favor of England, and the Russian regiments must march with us.[103]

By October, Wilhelm had become more optimistic about detaching France from Britain once Russian neutrality in the Franco-German war was assured.[104]

Although fearful of how the British would react to the treaty and not entirely convinced of its benefits for Germany, Bülow eventually accepted it. Realizing its significance for Franco-German relations, he decided to reduce friction with France. For one thing, he envisaged the possibility of giving France a free hand in Morocco if she joined the Russo-German accord. He was becoming interested in extricating Germany from the Morocco affair.[105] Holstein did not entirely agree with his chief. For one, he considered the Björko Treaty to be more valuable. Not only would it prevent Russia from joining Britain, but it would also have a "crushing effect" on France by depriving her of Russian support and a cooling effect on Britain, who would know that a France deprived of a Continental ally would not be fighting her battles with Germany and that even with the "en Europe" restrictions the Russians might well attempt to establish a dominant position on the Persian Gulf during an Anglo-German war.[106] Nor was he prepared to be as conciliatory toward France as was Bülow. If Germany abandoned the position stated by the Kaiser on 31 March,

> the public, both German and non-German, would regard this as a humiliation of the German Emperor and the first great practical success of the Franco-English Entente Cordiale. It would put an end to any doubts as to the usefulness of the entente for France, and France would not be drawn closer to Germany but rather driven further away. In the foreseeable future she would stand steadfastly and firmly by England.[107]

Instead, because of the Björko Treaty, he expected Russian diplomacy to influence France to be more conciliatory toward Germany. But even the Grey Eminence softened. While visiting Bülow in Norderney, he did on 22 August 1905 pen a conciliatory letter to Radolin, instructing him to tell his French contacts that Germany sought no territorial gains in Morocco and that French policy must show consideration for Germany by not acting "*too fast* so that the Kaiser isn't forced to go back on his word."[108]

On 30 September, Bülow seemed to be asking the Foreign Office for advice about the line that should be taken toward France when requesting instructions for interviews with French journalists:

> But we must thereby be clear about what we want: whether we want to calm French public opinion and free for the future the road for Russo-German–French cooperation or whether we just want to act in a very plucky manner.[109]

Any need to consider Russo-German–French cooperation, leaving Morocco to France as a bribe, or to respect Russian sensitivities for her old ally ended when the Czar in his letter of 23 November virtually reneged on the obligations he had assumed at Björko.[110] By that time, with Holstein on holiday through most of September, the Kaiser and Bülow had made considerable concessions to France, particularly in regard to the agenda of the Algeciras Conference. These concessions were, however, inconsistently accompanied by threats. At the Algeciras Conference, which opened on 16 January 1906, Germany faced French intransigence, suspicion from other powers, and inadequate support from her own allies. The assumptions under which the German leadership had insisted on the conference had proven to be totally wrong. Although even Holstein had modified his hard line, Bülow and Wilhelm were not prepared to accept his policy of standing firm on key issues such as the police question and the internationalization of Casablanca.

In the spring of 1906 the Bavarian military attaché in Berlin, Gebsattel, reported that the military leadership, including Einem, regarded war with France as inevitable: "The war will and must come, and indeed hardly later than in twelve or eighteen months. The task of German diplomacy is to delay it until we are entirely prepared militarily."[111] Gebsattel's report dovetails with Moltke's assessment of Russia's military power. He reported to Bülow at about the same time that in terms of both numbers and quality of troops Russia was as weak as she had been reported to be by Schlieffen on 18 August 1905. While he expected Russia to be able to strengthen her position in the west in terms of numbers fairly soon, he did not expect her to improve the quality of her troops for a long time.[112] Thus, war should not be provoked immediately. The Kaiser decided on a retreat partly "because our artillery and navy were not in any condition to fight a war."[113]

The Morocco question thus resulted in a major diplomatic defeat for Germany. It greatly increased suspicions of German motives, particularly strengthening the hand of anti-German elements in Britain, and stimulated efforts toward military and naval co-operation between Britain and France. Misplaced, too, were German hopes that the incoming British liberal administration would be less aggressive and supportive of France and Russia. It was Edward Grey who made the informal military conversations between France and Britain official and provided firmer assurances of support to France than his predecessor Lansdowne. Grey, in addition, realized the desirability of an entente with Russia to check Germany.[114]

## Notes: Chapter 13

1   Vogel, *Deutsche Russlandpolitik*, p. 205.
2   ibid., p. 206; Cecil, "Coal," p. 997.
3   Rich, *Holstein*, Vol. 2, p. 688; GP XIX, i, No. 6148, p. 349.
4   GP, XIX, i, No. 6125, Bülow to Wilhelm, 16 November 1904, p. 312.
5   *Holstein Papers*, Vol. 4, No. 862, memorandum by Holstein, 22 October 1904, pp. 311–12.
6   Vogel, *Deutsche Russlandpolitik*, p. 204.
7   ibid., p. 205.
8   Peter Rassow, "Schlieffen und Holstein," *Historische Zeitschrift*, vol. 173, no. 2 (1952), pp. 297–313; Gordon A. Craig, *The Politics of the Prussian Army, 1640–1945* (New York, 1956), pp. 283–5; *From Bismarck to Adenauer: Aspects of German Statescraft*, revised edn (New York, 1965), pp. 31–2; Fischer, *Krieg*, pp. 98–101; Ritter, *Der Schlieffen-Plan*, pp. 102–38; Albrecht Moritz, *Das Problem des Präventivkrieges in der deutschen Politik während der ersten Marokkokrise* (Frankfurt, 1974), passim.
9   Heiner Raulff, *Zwischen Machtpolitik und Imperialismus: Die deutsche Frankreich-politik, 1904–05* (Düsseldorf, 1976).
10  GP, XIX, i, No. 6031, "Aufzeichnung . . . Lichnowsky," 19 April 1904, pp. 174–5; original in PAAA, Russland 72, Geh., Bd 14, in which a triple line and an NB appear in the margin next to the two passages. Such annotation is characteristic of Bülow. The original is addressed to Richthofen and Holstein. Schlieffen followed up on the conversation with a detailed exposé of the military situation in Russia: GP, XIX, i, No. 6032, 20 April 1904, pp. 175–7. Such immediate follow-up is in direct contrast to

Schlieffen's dilatory replies to proposals he disliked, as evidenced in his correspondence with naval authorities. For Einem's readiness to fight France in 1905, see *Erinnerungen*, pp. 111–13; Moritz, *Das Problem*, pp. 214–15; for the same in 1904, see Vogel, *Deutsche Russlandpolitik*, p. 165; Martin Kitchen, *The German Officer Corps, 1890–1914* (London, 1968), p. 99.

11 BA-MA, N 58, Graf v.d. Schulenburg-Tressow, *Nachlass*, 1. Erlebnisse, p. 34.
12 Raulff, *Zwischen Machtpolitik*, p. 72; Vogel, *Deutsche Russlandpolitik*, p. 167.
13 Ritter, *Der Schlieffen-Plan*, pp. 43–4.
14 Moritz, *Das Problem*, pp. 216–24.
15 GP, XIX, i, 6031, "Aufzeichnung . . . Lichnowsky," 19 April 1904, p. 175.
16 Raulff, *Zwischen Machtpolitik*, p. 89, esp. n. 54, *Holstein Papers*, Vol. 4, No. 865, Holstein to Schlieffen, 29 November 1904, p. 315; Helmuth Rogge (ed.), *Friedrich von Holstein: Lebensbekenntnis in Briefen an eine Frau* (Berlin, 1932), Holstein to Ida von Stüpnagel, 23 December 1897: "While I write, General Count Schlieffen sits in my room and reads documents, something that regularly happens once a week in turbulent times" (p. 187).
17 Marie Dorothea Elisabeth Fürstin Radziwill, *Briefe vom deutschen Kaiserhof, 1899–1915* (Berlin, 1936), pp. 273–4.
18 Raulff, *Zwischen Machtpolitik*, p. 77.
19 See above, PAAA, Deutschland 138, Geh., Bd 6, Einem to Bülow, 17 October 1904, enclosing Schlieffen to Königliche Allgemeine Kriegs-Department, 7 October 1904. The final paragraph of Schlieffen's letter was originally drawn to my attention by Professor Paul M. Kennedy. For Schlieffen's attitude to Britain, see Wallach, *Das Dogma*, pp. 113–14.
20 PAAA, Deutschland 138, Geh., Bd 6, Bülow to Einem, 25 October 1904.
21 Bülow, *Denkwürdigkeiten*, Bd II, pp. 80–1; *Holstein Papers*, Vol. 4, No. 869, Bülow to Holstein, 15 December 1904, pp. 318–19.
22 Robert Graf von Zedlitz-Trüzschler, *Twelve Years at the Imperial German Court* (London, 1951), diary entry for 3 November 1904, p. 91.
23 H St Ar Stuttgart, E 73/73a, 12e I.23, Varnbüler to Soden, 8 November 1904.
24 GP, XIX, i, No. 6118, Wilhelm to Nicholas II, 27 October 1904, pp. 303–4.
25 ibid., No. 6119, Nicholas II to Wilhelm, 29 October 1904, p. 305.
26 ibid., No. 6120, Bülow to Wilhelm II, 30 October 1904, and enclosures I and II, pp. 305–8.
27 BA-MA, F 2044, PG 66077. The copy is in Trotha's hand at the top of the first page of Trotha's copy of Tirpitz's letter to Richthofen of 1 November 1904. Since Tirpitz is not listed as one of the persons present, it is evident that the notes are Tirpitz's and not Trotha's as Steinberg, "Copenhagen complex," p. 33, "Germany," p. 1977, and Vogel, *Deutsche Russlandpolitik*, p. 207, state. Contrary to both, there is no evidence that Trotha was present at the meeting.
28 Tirpitz, *Erinnerungen*, p. 143. I am translating rather freely.
29 Steinberg, "Germany," p. 1977.
30 Tirpitz, *Erinnerungen*, pp. 143–6, fully quoting Tirpitz to Richthofen, 1 November 1904; a certified copy of the letter in Trotha's hand is in BA-MA, F 2044, PG 66077.
31 Tirpitz, *Erinnerungen*, p. 143.
32 ibid., p. 145.
33 ibid.
34 GP, XIX, i, No. 6123, Bülow to Wilhelm, 31 October 1904, pp. 309–10.
35 ibid., No. 6124, Nicholas II to Wilhelm, 25 October/7 November 1904, and enclosure, pp. 310–12.
36 Cecil, "Coal," pp. 997–8; GP, XIX, i, No. 6127, Bülow to Wilhelm, 24 November 1904, and enclosure of draft letter of Wilhelm to Nicholas II, pp. 318–19; H. Bernstein (ed.), *The Nicky–Willy Correspondence: Being the Secret and Intimate Telegrams Exchanged between the Kaiser and the Tsar* (New York, 1918), No. 21, Wilhelm II to Nicholas II, 26 November 1904, pp. 85–8.
37 GP, XIX, i, No. 6111, Metternich to Bülow, 1 November 1904, p. 292; Steinberg, "Germany," p. 1978.
38 PAAA, England 78, Bd 23, Metternich to Bülow, 7 November 1904.
39 BA-MA, F 2026, PG 65998, Coerper to Tirpitz, 17 November 1904.

40  GP, XIX, ii, No. 6149, Coerper to Tirpitz, 18 November 1904, p. 353.
41  PAAA, England 78, secr., Vol. 7, Bülow to Holstein and Richthofen, 3 December 1904.
42  GP, XIX, ii, No. 6150, "Aufzeichnung . . . Richthofen," 30 November 1904, p. 356.
43  ibid., No. 6153, "Aufzeichnung . . . Holstein," 5 December 1904, p. 359.
44  Cecil, "Coal," pp. 999–1001.
45  See above, pp. 225 ff.
46  BA-MA, N 168/8, "Aufzeichnung Büchsel," 20 November 1904, copy; the original appears in F 5586, III, 1, 0, 10., Vol. 2, where the document is dated in pencil 19 November 1904. A memorandum, "Spezial-Massnahmen zum O.P. II," in ibid., 24 November 1904, dates the evening meeting 18 November.
47  ibid., F 5586, III, 1, 0, 10., Vol. 2, memorandum of 21 November 1904, initialed by A, A1, A2, A4, A4₁, and N.
48  ibid., "Spezialmassnahmen zum O.P. II," 24 November 1904.
49  ibid., notes of meeting of 25 November 1904.
50  ibid., F 2017, PG 65964, Büchsel, "Zum Immediatvortrag," 2 December 1904.
51  BA-MA, F 2044, PG 66077, Bendemann, "Gedanken über die augenblickliche kritische Lage," 3 December 1904; also see Hubatsch, *Der Admiralstab*, pp. 117–18.
52  BA-MA, F 5587, III, 1, N, 10., Vol. 3, Koester to Büchsel, 17 February 1905.
53  Carl-Axel Gemzell, *Organisation, Conflict, and Innovation: A Study in German Naval Strategic Planning, 1888–1940* (Lund, 1973), p. 127, n. 69.
54  BA-MA, F 2044, PG 66077, Vollerthun, "Politische und militärische Betrachtungen über einen englisch-deutschen Krieg," 27 November 1904, copy.
55  ibid., F 2524, XVII, 1, 1, 21., Vol. 1, instruction of Tirpitz, 22 November 1904, copy.
56  ibid., F 2044, PG 66077, "Schlussvotum des Vorsitzenden der R-Kommission," 14 December 1904; see also Steinberg, "Germany," pp. 1979–81.
57  BA-MA, F 5586, III, 1, 0, 10., Vol. 2, Büchsel to Schlieffen, 28 January 1905.
58  ibid., F 2017, PG 65965, Büchsel, "Zum Immediatvortrag," 31 January 1905 and his comments on the margin of the document.
59  PAAA, Deutschland 138, Bd 6, Senden to Bülow, 6 February 1905.
60  See above, pp. 26 ff.
61  PAAA, Deutschland 138, Bd 6, Bülow to Senden, 9 February 1905.
62  ibid., "Aufzeichnung Klehmet," 14 November 1905.
63  BA-MA, F 5586, III, 1, 0, 10., Vol. 2, Schlieffen to Büchsel, 4 February 1905.
64  ibid., F 5587, III, 1, N, 10., Vol. 1, "Denkschrift über die Kriegführung gegen England 1905," thirty-two-page draft in longhand, dated in covering letter 1 January 1905, forwarded by A to Büchsel on 5 January 1905. There is a comment by Büchsel: "Zurück an A mit Beendung. Ich bitte jetzt Abschliessen." A few changes were made in the draft by other department heads and by Büchsel himself. A copy of the finished version, bearing a copy of Büchsel's signature, appears in F 2044, PG 66077, n.d. The first part of it is reprinted in Hubatsch, *Der Admiralstab*, No. 24, pp. 247–50, and is referred to on pp. 118–19. This document is one of several refutations of Wallach's contention that the navy was not informed of the projected violation of Belgian neutrality: *Das Dogma*, p. 161.
65  BA-MA, F 5586, III, 1, 0, 10., Vol. 2, Senden to Büchsel, 7 February 1905.
66  *Holstein Papers*, Vol. 4, No. 869, Bülow to Holstein, 15 December 1904, p. 319.
67  PAAA, England 78, secr., Vol. 7, Bülow to ambassador in Washington, 5 February 1905, copy.
68  *Holstein Papers*, Vol. 4, No. 876, memorandum by Holstein, 6 February 1904, p. 325; ibid., No. 877, Schoen to Holstein, 11 February 1905, p. 325.
69  BA-MA, F 5586, III, 1, 0, 10., Vol. 2, Büchsel, "Zum Immediatvortrag," 13 February 1905; drafts of Büchsel to Chief of the Fleet, Chief of the General Staff, Chief of the Naval Cabinet, Secretary of State of the Imperial Naval Office, Chief of the Baltic Sea Station, Chief of the North Sea Station.
70  Ritter, *Der Schlieffen-Plan*, pp. 148, 154.
71  See the excellent discussion in Kennedy, *Antagonism*, ch. XIV, passim. I have found no evidence of Admiralty Staff opposition to a Russian alliance: p. 274.
72  Kennedy, *Antagonism*, p. 275; Wallach demonstrates that the numbers of troops which Schlieffen expected to use in his December 1905 memorandum were exaggerated: *Das Dogma*, pp. 100, 138–9.

73 Moritz, *Das Problem*, pp. 17–18; Raulff, *Zwischen Machtpolitik*, pp. 104, 109.

74 Rogge, *Holstein*, p. 240; I have largely followed Rich's translation: *Holstein*, p. 707.

75 Pierre Guillen, *L'Allemagne et le Maroc de 1870 à 1905* (Paris, 1967), pp. 764–7; Raulff, *Zwischen Machtpolitik*, pp. 68–9.

76 ibid., pp. 84–5.

77 Eugene N. Anderson, *The First Moroccan Crisis, 1904–1906* (Hamden, Conn., 1966), p. 183.

78 Raulff, *Zwischen Machtpolitik*, pp. 85–6, 88.

79 Moritz, *Das Problem*, pp. 89–91; Raulff, *Zwischen Machtpolitik*, pp. 131–2; also Berndt F. Schulte, *Vor dem Kriegs-Ausbruch: Deutschland, die Türkei und der Balkan* (Düsseldorf, 1980), p. 31.

80 Moritz, *Das Problem*, pp. 95–6.

81 PAAA, Russland 72, Geh., Bd 14, Schlieffen to Bülow, 18 August 1905.

82 Raulff, *Zwischen Machtpolitik*, pp. 127–8; Moritz, *Das Problem*, p. 96.

83 Raulff, *Zwischen Machtpolitik*, p. 127.

84 BA-MA, N 58, Graf v.d. Schulenburg-Tressow, *Nachlass* 1. Erlebnisse, p. 18; Kennedy, *Antagonism*, p. 276.

85 ibid., N 46, Groener, *Nachlass* 1. Lebenserinnerungen. I. Ausfertigung, p. 87. Schulte, *Kriegsausbruch*, p. 66; Moritz, *Das Problem*, p. 115; Ritter, *Der Schlieffen-Plan*, pp. 114–15, esp. n. 17. There appears to be some confusion about the title of the journal: Raulff and Groener cite it as *Twentieth Century*; Moritz, following Ritter, refers to the *Nineteenth Century and After*. Actually the title of the journal changed: in 1901 the *Nineteenth Century and After* became the *Twentieth Century*. Ritter unconvincingly tries to discredit Groener as a source. See Craig, *From Bismarck to Adenauer*, pp. 31–2, esp. n. 37.

86 Raulff, *Zwischen Machtpolitik*, pp. 129–30.

87 Einem, *Erinnerungen*, p. 112; see Bay H St Ar, Abt IV Kriegsarchiv, M. Kr. 41, Gebsattel to Bavarian Minister of War, 30 March 1906.

88 Bülow, *Denkwürdigkeiten*, Bd II, p. 108.

89 See above, pp. 242; 259; also Einem, *Erinnerungen*, pp. 111–12.

90 *Holstein Papers*, Vol. 4, No. 888, Holstein to Radolin, 22 May 1905, p. 341.

91 Moritz, *Das Problem*, pp. 64–73; cf. Raulff, *Zwischen Machtpolitik*, p. 159.

92 GP, XX, i, No. 6429, Wilhelm's marginal comments to Bülow to Wilhelm, 10 March 1905, p. 98; Anderson, *First Moroccan Crisis*, p. 183.

93 GP, XX, i, No. 6576, Bülow to Wilhelm, 26 March 1905, pp. 273–7; Rich, *Holstein*, Vol. 2, pp. 694–5.

94 Anderson, *First Moroccan Crisis*, pp. 198–9; Christopher Andrew, *Théophile Delcassé and the Making of the Entente Cordiale: A Reappraisal of French Foreign Policy, 1898–1905* (London, 1968), p. 278.

95 Raulff, *Zwischen Machtpolitik*, pp. 97–9; GP, XX, ii, No. 6593, Bülow to Kühlmann, 3 April 1905, p. 295; No. 6594, Bülow to Monts, 3 April 1905, pp. 295–6, refusing to negotiate with France; No. 6596, Bülow to Radolin, 3 April 1905, instructing him to be evasive if Delcassé wanted to discuss Morocco, p. 297.

96 GP, XX, ii, No. 6601, "Aufzeichnung . . . Holstein," 4 April 1905, with Bülow's marginal comments, pp. 304–5; No. 6599, Bülow to Wilhelm, 4 April 1905, p. 303; *Holstein Papers*, Vol. 4, No. 882, Holstein to Bülow, 5 April 1905, p. 329; No. 883, Holstein to Radolin, 11 April 1905, pp. 330–1.

97 Anderson, *First Moroccan Crisis*, pp. 202, 206–8; Raulff, *Zwischen Machtpolitik*, p. 98.

98 Bülow's significant marginal comments appear in GP, XX, ii, No. 6609, "Aufzeichnung . . . Hammann," 7 April 1905, p. 313. See also the *Holstein Papers*, Vol. 4, No. 885, Holstein to Josef Neven-Dumont, 20 April 1905, pp. 336–7.

99 PAAA, Marokko 4, Bd 75, Wilhelm's marginal comment on Bülow to Wilhelm, 12 July 1905, suggesting a higher decoration to the banker Betzold, who had been instrumental in bringing about Delcassé's fall; Anderson, 239; PAAA, Frankreich 105, No. 1, Bd 22, Wilhelm's remark to Radolin to Bülow, 11 June 1905, regarding Rouvier's desire for an understanding: "Good all that we want [*sic*]." PAAA, Frankreich 102, Bd 31, Bülow to Sternburg, 13 June 1905, copy, for the Chancellor's expectation of the lesser likelihood of France going to war once Delcassé had fallen.

100 Anderson, *First Moroccan Crisis*, pp. 212–58; Raulff, *Zwischen Machtpolitik*, pp. 101–25; Andrew, *Delcassé*, pp. 274–302; Rich, *Holstein*, Vol. 2, pp. 691–713.

101  GP, XIX, ii, No. 6202, Bülow to the Foreign Office, 20 July 1905, pp. 435–6; No. 6203, Holstein to Bülow, 21 July 1905, pp. 436–8; No. 6204, Holstein to Bülow, 21 July 1905, p. 439; No. 6205, Holstein to Bülow, 22 July 1905, pp. 439–40; No. 6207, Holstein to Bülow, 22 July 1905, pp. 441–2; No. 6208, Bülow to the Foreign Office, 22 July 1905, pp. 442–5; also Rich, *Holstein*, Vol. 2, pp. 714–19.

102  GP, XIX, ii, No. 6222, Bülow to the Foreign Office, 26 July 1905, pp. 467–8; No. 6228, Bülow to the Foreign Office, 28 July 1905, pp. 476–7; No. 6229, Bülow to the Foreign Office, 30 July 1905, esp. pp. 480–1; and No. 6230, Bülow to the Foreign Office, 2 August 1905, p. 481.

103  ibid., No. 6229, Bülow to the Foreign Office, 30 July 1905, p. 479; Anderson, *First Moroccan Crisis*, p. 288; Kennedy, *Antagonism*, p. 281.

104  GP, XX, ii, No. 6871, Metternich to Bülow, 2 October 1905, p. 662.

105  ibid., No. 6782, Bülow to the Foreign Office, 31 July 1905, pp. 531–2; ibid., XIX, ii, No. 6230, Bülow to the Foreign Office, 2 August 1905, p. 481.

106  ibid., No. 6227, "Aufzeichnung . . . Holstein," 28 July 1905, pp. 474–6. No. 6236, Mühlberg to Bülow, 10 August 1905, initialed by Holstein, pp. 493–6; Rich, *Holstein*, Vol. 2, pp. 716–8.

107  *Holstein Papers*, Vol. 4, No. 904, memorandum by Holstein, 31 July 1905, pp. 356–7.

108  ibid., No. 907, Holstein to Radolin, 22 August 1905, p. 364; see also Rich, *Holstein*, Vol. 2, pp. 720–1.

109  PAAA, Marokko 4, Bd 96, Bülow to the Foreign Office, telegram, 30 September 1905.

110  Anderson, *First Moroccan Crisis*, pp. 303–4.

111  Bay H St Ar, Abt IV Kriegsarchiv, M. Kr. 41, Gebsattel to Minister of War, 30 March 1906.

112  PAAA, Russland 72, Geh., Bd 14, Moltke to Bülow, 7 March 1906.

113  *Holstein Papers*, Vol. 4, No. 948, memorandum by Holstein, 29 March 1906, n. 1, p. 405.

114  Kennedy, *Antagonism*, pp. 253–4; D. W. Sweet, "Great Britain and Germany, 1905–1911," in *British Foreign Policy under Sir Edward Grey*, ed. F. H. Hinsley (Cambridge, 1977); George Monger, *The End of Isolation: British Foreign Policy, 1900–1907* (London, 1963), pp. 281–3.

# 14 The Challenge to Britain: The Navy Laws of 1906 and 1908 and Increased War Preparedness

## I

Paul M. Kennedy maintains that the British made it clear to Germany after the Dogger Bank incident "that they regarded the ever-growing German fleet as the most serious obstacle to good relations between their two peoples and that, unless a change in Germany's naval policy occurred, countermeasures would be taken which would keep Tirpitz's creation permanently in the 'danger zone'."[1] The German leadership, however, decided to use the critical situation of 1904–05 for the introduction of yet another navy bill which was bound to lead to British countermeasures.

Tirpitz required a new navy law at the latest in 1906 when according to the law of 1900 only two keels would be laid down and thus the prospect of achieving a permanent building rate of three large ships per year would be jeopardized. He had already stated his intention of coming forward with a new bill as early as in 1901–02. On 6 January 1902 he contemplated maintaining the construction rate of three large ships per year between 1906 and 1910 by reintroducing the request for the six large cruisers for service abroad which had been struck from the Second Navy Bill—a request to which he was eventually forced to revert. Thus he expected to possess in 1910 thirty-eight ships of the line. He requested the Budget Department of the Imperial Naval Office to prepare estimates and arrangements for keeping ships in service. Construction was placed above war preparedness.

Several responses emerged from the Budget Department, headed by Eduard von Capelle. These were drafted by Harald Dähnhardt, according to Berghahn "a key figure," and initialed by Capelle, who appears to have had full confidence in his subordinate.[2]

Request 1 only entailed the increase of the fleet by five large cruisers and two ships of the line and was expected to create the least attention. Requests 2 and 3 involved the establishment of a second-line reserve fleet (*Seewehrschlachtflotte*) on the model of the Landwehr which would utilize the older ships and trained manpower consisting of older reservists—one of the main advantages that Germany had over Britain. To accomplish this, the replacement period for ships built after 1893 would be extended from twenty-five to thirty years. Ships would serve for their first ten years in the active fleet, the first double squadron, for the next ten years in the reserve, the second double squadron, and for the last ten years in the second-line reserve fleet consisting of the third double squadron. The second-line reserve fleet would not be fully established before 1928 and the fifty-seven or sixty ships of the line strength projected under requests 2 and 3 would not be available before 1930.[3] The second-line reserve fleet would be involved only in the later stages of war, after the first decisive battles and the destruction or damaging of the newer ships. Its establishment was represented as "the only security that we would have in case of a war against England,"[4] which was essential in view of increasing British hostility toward Germany, for which ample evidence was cited, and in view of the immense British naval supremacy, enhanced by recent construction.

In 1903, Britain was cited as having available or in construction 110 ships of the line and armored cruisers compared to Germany's thirty-nine. In answer to the question whether in view of this supremacy Germany could strengthen her fleet sufficiently to discourage an attack, Dähnhardt and Capelle referred to personnel shortage and financial shortfall as factors that would prevent Britain from maintaining the existing 3:1 (110:39) lead over the German navy. Assuming that Britain would continue the building rate of the last four years, namely replacing obsolete ships and adding three additional large ships annually, she would by 1930, when Germany would according to requests 2 and 3 possess fifty-seven or sixty ships of the line, have 109 ships of the line (fifty-seven ships available in 1903 plus fifty-two ships: two ships built in each of the next twenty-six years). This would, instead of the current Anglo-German ratio of fifty-seven to twenty ships of the line (about 3:1), establish a ratio of 109:60 (about 1.8:1) which would be further reduced (to 1.7:1) by Britain's need to keep ships of the line in East Asia. But, argued Dähnhardt and Capelle,

> This is not adequate superiority to deliver a successful blow against Germany and to set up an effective blockade, for if one assumes generally that for the execution of a successful blockade it is sufficient if the blockading power is one and a half times as strong as the blockaded power, then this assumption is incorrect in the face of an enemy, who, leaning on the Elbe, the Kaiser Wilhelm Canal, and Kiel would possess the advantage of an internal line. But regardless of this England can hardly think of concentrating her entire fleet in the German Bight of the North Sea without running the danger of risking her power position.

Belaboring this line of argument, Dähnhardt next examined the Anglo-German power relationship in both ships of the line and large cruisers: Germany would according to request 3 have eighty such vessels in 1929. If Britain continued to build three such ships every year in addition to replacements, she would confront Germany with 188 ships in that year (110 existing ships plus seventy-eight ships: three ships built in each of the next twenty-six years). Of the British ships thirty and of the German ten would be expected to be abroad. This would establish a ratio of 158:77 or 2:1 in Britain's favor in 1929. Britain would still possess a formidable advantage.

But this advantage could only be maintained if adequate manpower could be secured for British ships, which Dähnhardt and Capelle doubted since conscription was impracticable and the financial rewards offered by the navy were not comparable to the wages offered by the merchant marine or industry.

We are therefore well justified in assuming that if we adhere to our present annual building rate, leading in time to the establishment of the third double squadron, Germany would be sufficiently strong at sea so as no longer to fear an attack from England.

Berghahn remarks: "The draft of July 1903 in the meantime concealed what formidable power the German navy would constitute in 1928 . . . . Even if one accepts that no aggressive intentions in the military sense underlay the German fleet construction, for the English navy a confrontation with the completed *Seewehrschlachtflotte* could have catastrophic consequences."[5] The late date for the creation of this force would, however, prolong the danger zone during which the German fleet would be exposed to a British attack for more than a quarter of a century. Moreover, the reasons given for the inability of the British navy to maintain its established lead over the German were rather doubtful. Above all, the document provides the clearest evidence of plans for the long-term construction of Tirpitz's navy, which were difficult to reconcile with the activity of the German political leadership, the preparations of the "Front," or the planning of the Admiralty Staff.

Yet, in his subsequent memoranda of November 1903, Dähnhardt used the very magnitude of request 2 as the reason against making it. He stated that in 1905 Britain would have available or in construction sixty-two ships of the line whereas the long-term German strength would be fifty-seven ships of the line.[6] Dähnhardt and Capelle had in July expressed their preference for request 2, which had by October 1903 been further examined by the Budget Department.[7]

While these deliberations were being conducted in the Imperial Naval Office, Wilhelm pronounced himself in favor of promulgating a new navy law as soon as possible. He wanted this law to provide special ships of the line for service abroad, based on the Braunschweig type but having as secondary armament 21 cm instead of 17 cm guns, a speed of 23 knots, a displacement of 16,000 tons instead of 13,208–14,394 tons, and considerably more expensive.[8] This proposal was contrary to Tirpitz's North Sea strategy and his insistence on uniformity of types. It was rejected by Dähnhardt in his memorandum of 2 November 1903, on the ostensible grounds that the German people and the Reichstag would be suspicious of an adventurous overseas policy and that any larger German forces abroad would in wartime be hampered by the absence of bases and eventually be paralyzed by the British. In the memorandum of 11 November,[9] the Budget Department proposed instead that the first squadron of the *Seewehrschlachtflotte* consisting of eight ships of the line (plus one for the *matériel* reserve) and two reconnaissance groups of one large and two small cruisers each, as well as one large cruiser for East Asia and two torpedo-boat flotillas, be built in the years 1906–10. This was considered to be more practicable than a double squadron since it could be more convincingly related to the six cruisers rejected in 1900: it would merely request double that number of large ships. Unlike the demand for cruisers for service abroad this request would also be a definite step toward the establishment of the *Seewehrschlachtflotte* for which the second squadron could be added by a new bill in 1911. The replacement period for ships was to be extended to thirty years.

Tirpitz presented the final version of this memorandum to Wilhelm, arguing that "on grounds of foreign and internal policy I consider it out of the question that Your Majesty can obtain a considerable increase on the basis of a fleet abroad,"[10] and secured his oral agreement to the effect "that the further development of the fleet shall proceed along the line [*im Wege*] of strengthening the battlefield at home."[11] He had thus eliminated Wilhelm's potential disruption of his building program, but he himself remained dissatisfied with the limited extent of the request and made inquiries of the Budget Department whether more ships could be built.

Dähnhardt's nimble mind continued to work on other alternatives, and on 18 November he provided as many as seven different schedules, expressing his preference for the scheme which would by 1922 provide five full squadrons of ships of the line but retain the twenty-five-year replacement period.[12] By February 1904 it had become clear, however, that on financial grounds more ambitious plans had to be given up. On 21 December, during a meeting of Bülow, Richthofen, Metternich, Büchsel, Tirpitz, and Schlieffen, held to discuss the possibility of a war with Britain, the Secretary of State of the Imperial Naval Office served notice of his intention to introduce a new navy bill.[13] At this meeting Metternich warned that the introduction of a big navy bill (*stärkere Flottennovelle*) would serve as provocation for an attack on Germany by Britain, but other participants do not appear to have raised any objections to a new naval increase.

In February 1905 the Imperial Naval Office approved the minimal request of six large cruisers and groped toward an arrangement whereby the building rate would be stabilized at three large ships as long as possible and ships of the line would be replaced by new models before construction would be started on the new large cruisers. Thus the first step toward the construction of the third double squadron would be taken without running the risk of having the entire third double squadron rejected by the Reichstag on grounds of finance and fear of Britain. As Dähnhardt argued on 10 February 1905, in a presentation to Admiral von Müller: "Therefore it is better that we accept what we in all probability can get now and leave further decisions to the future. For the next four years (1906/7/8/9) one will thus achieve exactly what one would by an immediate demand for the third double squadron."[14]

Tirpitz's emphasis on quantity rather than on quality, and his careful consideration of costs and parliamentary circumstances, had until then resulted in the building of ships with lighter artillery and smaller displacement than those of other navies. The costs would escalate further if the increase in the displacement of ships should ever make necessary the widening of the Kaiser Wilhelm Canal and the locks of Wilhelmshaven. Large ships were also unsuitable for the shallow German coastal waters.[15]

There was constant pressure on Tirpitz from naval circles and the Kaiser for larger and faster ships and heavier artillery. In November 1899 both Max Fischel, head of the A Department of the Naval Office, and Bendemann urged that new ships of the line be armed with 28 cm instead of 24 cm heavy artillery because of thicker armor and larger guns of foreign ships and fighting at greater distances.[16] This time Tirpitz complied. In a meeting of the Imperial Naval Office in December 1899 he himself proposed that for ships built in 1901, i.e. the Braunschweig class, the caliber of the heavy artillery be increased to 28 cm and that of the middle artillery to 17 cm.[17] He managed to resist Wilhelm's pressure in 1903 for faster, heavier ships.[18]

In April 1904 the head of the Construction Department, Rudolf von Eickstedt, reported to Tirpitz about the new ship of the line type. The ship was to be equal to the strongest potential enemy ships "if not individually then in formation." It was to have as many 28 cm guns as possible, have strong armor, and possess adequate speed. The comparison group was not to be "the existing ships but those projected by the nation whom we have to fight," not the American Connecticut class or the British Edward VII class, but the British Nelson class and its successors. He expected that the British would eventually come up with a 16,000–18,000-ton ship with ten 30·5 cm guns. In short, Eickstedt was predicting the launching of *Dreadnought*. Yet he heeded Tirpitz's concerns, maintaining that because of shallow coastal waters and financial difficulties German ship types could not exceed the displacement of 14,000 tons. Only Heeringen was consistent in commenting that "in developing types we cannot take into account either coastal waters or finances."

Although Tirpitz's conservatism prevailed in the meetings of the Imperial Naval Office in April and May, in March 1905 he approved of the examination of the ship of the line with eight 28 cm guns and a displacement of 15,000–15,600 tons.[19] The capacity of the Kaiser Wilhelm Canal for larger ships was also to be studied.[20] Tirpitz's conservatism was thus not blocking further developments altogether. The determination of the type of the ship of the line was once more complicated by the interest of Wilhelm in increasing the size of the cruiser and developing fast ships of the line. On the cruiser question he was encouraged by Koester and Senden. Tirpitz was opposed to both of Wilhelm's projects because of costs and the resulting confusion of types. The new large cruisers, *Scharnhorst* and *Gneisenau*, that were built between 1904 and 1908 thus remained considerably smaller than the new ship of the line.

Tirpitz was clearly on the defensive. In reply to the Imperial remonstrance of July 1905 he defended the ship of the line of 16,000 tons, 24-meter beam, and 19-knot speed as the largest that could pass the Kaiser Wilhelm Canal. With its eight 45 caliber 28 cm guns and heavy armor it fully conformed to contemporary standards even if it did not establish a record. And he strongly recommended against building ships that would require the widening of the canal, for the costs would further compound the financial difficulties which the new navy bill would have to face. As for the armored cruiser proposed by

Wilhelm, Tirpitz stated that it was possible in the current budget to provide a ship of this type with even thicker armor but for some of the 21 cm guns those of 15 cm would have to be substituted.[21]

While Tirpitz had thus been able to scuttle the fast ship of the line and a proliferation of ship types, he was being compelled by Wilhelm and his own subordinates to build large, more heavily armed, and more expensive ships at a time when he was bringing in a new navy bill in the midst of financial difficulty. Escalation of costs continued. He was soon informed that Wilhelm and Bülow had decided to raise the question of widening the Kaiser Wilhelm Canal when the new navy bill was introduced and to justify it by the increase in the volume of commercial shipping. The canal need no longer be an obstacle to the increase of the displacement of ships. The head of the Central Department of the Imperial Naval Office, Reinhard Scheer, informed him: "I also believe, if I may say so, that we must go somewhat higher with displacements, for I fear that later—in history—Your Excellency could be blamed if our new construction were to remain in strength too far behind those of other maritime nations."[22]

Faced by these pressures and the agitation of the Navy League, Tirpitz remained hesitant and skeptical but kept an open mind. He warned Wilhelm and Bülow of the staggering costs if the rebuilding of the canal were brought in together with the new navy bill and doubted the credibility of the argument that the canal would be widened because of increased commercial shipping.[23] To Scheer he expressed his concern about jumping from a 13,000- to a 17,000–18,000-ton displacement and proposed to remain at a maximum of 17,000 tons so that in the face of the British and the French "we would not appear to be the drivers [*Treiber*] in displacement." He obviously feared the consequences that the appearance of escalating an armaments race would have for the reception of the navy bill in the Reichstag and for Anglo-German relations. It was, however, possible to construct a ship of 16,800-ton displacement with a maximum speed of 19 sea-miles, eight 28 cm and ten 17 cm guns, and outstanding armor and light armament, or for an additional 4 million marks an 18,000-ton ship with twelve 28 cm and eight 17 cm guns. The option of staying below 16,000 tons and avoiding the question of widening the canal was thus being eliminated on convincing technical grounds. Nor did Capelle think that the restriction to a displacement of 16,000 tons and the avoidance of the canal question would facilitate the passage of the new navy law.

By 10 September, Tirpitz realized that the displacement limit of 16,000 tons would have to be exceeded and that the canal question could no longer be avoided. "The only question is whether 16,800 tons or 18,000 tons or more."[24] At the meeting of 22 September 1905, chaired by Tirpitz, the Naval Office made its formal decision about ship types. The ship of the line was to have a displacement of 18,000 tons, and a maximum speed of 18·5 sea-miles, at a cost of 36·5 million marks. Its heavy armament was to consist of twelve 28 cm guns. "In consideration of the great penetration capacity of the new 28 cm guns, an escalation to 30·5 cm is in general not considered necessary." Heeringen was thus overruled. The middle armament was to consist of twelve 15 cm guns. The large cruiser was to have a displacement of

15,000 tons at a cost of 27·5 million marks, a speed of 23·5 sea-miles, but its heavy artillery was restricted to 21 cm guns since the 24 cm guns were not yet ready and the 21 cm caliber was considered adequate for fighting other large cruisers.[25] While anticipating the Dreadnought, Tirpitz thus avoided the appearance of advocating a new type of cruiser capable of fighting the ship of the line or serving in the line. Wilhelm approved the new ship of the line on 4 October[26] but remained dissatisfied with the new large cruiser, trying to modify it so that it could fight effectively in the line.[27] As Tirpitz wrote to Prince Heinrich on 25 December 1905: "The bill [*Novelle*] is deliberately set up so that it does not look like much, but requests more money than the fleet law of 1900."[28]

Parallel to the pressure of foreign naval construction and the intercession of the Kaiser and several naval officers ran the agitation of the Navy League (Flottenverein) for larger naval increases: first for the third double squadron which Dähnhardt and Capelle had seriously considered in July 1903, and later for the speedier replacement of obsolescent ships.[29] Unwilling to break with the Navy League entirely, since it was useful in keeping alive popular enthusiasm for the navy, particularly for the making of future demands, the Naval Office attempted to control its agitation. Although it was generally successful in keeping the extremists in check, criticism of Tirpitz's policy could not be prevented altogether. Although this enabled the Secretary of State to appear as a moderate in the Reichstag, it shook public confidence in his policy, increased British anxiety about German intentions, and contributed to Wilhelm's doubts about the agent of his naval ambitions.

Tirpitz's refusal to go along with the changing of the navy law brought about a further deterioration of relations between him and Wilhelm. The Kaiser's marginal comments to an article in the *Neue Politische Correspondenz* to the effect that not enough had been done for the navy led Tirpitz to tender his resignation.[30]

The desire of the Kaiser, of Bülow, and of the Navy League for a larger naval increase converged on 6 February when the Chancellor asked the Kaiser how the construction of the navy could be accelerated. Bülow had now taken the initiative in proposing to reduce substantially the age of ships so as to start the construction of more than three ships annually.[31] Tirpitz none the less prevailed. His reasons for refusing to budge are best summarized in his letter of 8 November 1905 to Bülow. In it he took into full account considerations of internal and external policy. The faster replacement of older ships of the line would create a construction bulge in the years 1906–09 but would leave a conspicuous gap in the period 1910–17, with no ship started until 1914 and only one ship put into construction annually from 1914 until 1917. A three-ship-per-year construction rate would make it possible to build an entire double squadron of eighteen ships of the line in this gap, which would give Germany in 1920 fifty-seven ships of the line, "more than Britain has now." In addition:

> The fact that Germany would in the next four years start building sixteen ships of 18,000 tons and, further, the realization that England would in the future have to reckon with the presence of 50–60 first-class German ships

of the line would effect such a shift in the actual power factors that even a calm and understanding English policy *must* come to the realization that such an opponent must be knocked down before he has achieved a military strength so dangerous for England as a world power. The prospect of war in the next four years before a single one of the new ships of the line is ready would be greatly increased.[32]

While the German public was prepared to accept a navy law that would defend Germany against Britain, at least the existing Reichstag would refuse to accept one that would seem to be aiming at parity with her. Nor did Tirpitz expect the dissolution of the Reichstag over the naval question to lead to favorable election results or the German Empire to be able to overcome an internal conflict similar to the one fought over the army increase in Prussia in the 1860s. But the current navy law did not preclude the construction of a fleet that would serve an offensive function against Britain. The new navy bill became a law on 26 May 1906.[33] The naval race with Britain had started through the acceptance, however reluctantly, by Tirpitz of the challenge presented by the Dreadnought-type construction. The first two German Dreadnought-type Nassau ships would not be launched until March 1908. The construction rate of three large ships per year was stabilized only until 1910.

Having convinced himself that a threat of war with Britain and France no longer existed, Wilhelm was reported in May 1906 as saying "that he counted on a new large navy law [*Novelle*] within a year which would bring a faster replacement of the old ships and the shortening of their lifespan, whereby within a year we could come to a four[-ship] tempo."[34] Tirpitz thought differently. While contemplating his resignation in June, he wrote that he had been advised to continue in office, for

I should lay the finishing stone of the Fleet Law—the perpetualization of the three-large-ship tempo. I, too, am concerned that my life work—if I may say so—is threatened when stupidities occur . . . A new bill cannot be introduced before the fall of 1909, and that is three years hence.[35]

However, the Imperial Naval Office had already started to work on a new bill. By May 1906, Tirpitz was able to provide directives for further preparations:

The next aim for further development should be the achievement of the twenty-year replacement period for ships of the line and the stabilization of the three[-ship] tempo, so that there would result a fleet of sixty large armored ships with a building rate of three ships per year. It cannot now be determined if and when we should shift to a four[-ship] tempo.[36]

Dähnhardt responded to Tirpitz's directives with the establishment of the *matériel* reserve squadron: by adding to the existing four ships of the *matériel* reserve both of the fleet flagships and the two newly requested ships of the line there would be besides the four squadrons of the active and reserve fleet of eight ships each, an additional eight-ship squadron of the *matériel* reserve—altogether forty ships of the line. Dähnhardt viewed 1910 as the date for the introduction of the new bill.[37]

## II

Tirpitz's principle of emphasizing quantity over quality was being challenged from several sides. He had just approved larger ship types than he would have liked because of Jackie Fisher's Dreadnought challenge—an approval that entailed the rebuilding of the Kaiser Wilhelm Canal. However much he had resisted the demands for strengthening coastal fortifications and increasing the war preparedness of the navy, the Dogger Bank incident compelled him to attend to them. On 22 November 1904 he had formed a committee under Heeringen's chairmanship to examine what measures were necessary.[38] He himself became particularly concerned with the need to defend Heligoland. As he instructed the Imperial Naval Office:

Heligoland in my opinion gains importance as a base with the growth of our fleet. The possibility of a battle before Heligoland should be considered in the budget, not just Heligoland's defence for its own sake as previously. First the landing-place is to be looked at, later more.

Heeringen's further instructions also called for the building of bridges, improvement of communications, and installation of light artillery on the island.[39] At the meeting of 20 December, Tirpitz also stressed the need to establish a protected position on Heligoland for torpedo-boats and submarines,[40] the latter being a new weapon as yet only considered for use jointly with the fleet.

Renewed operational planning in the North Sea also pointed to the need for strengthening the Heligoland position.[41] What appears to be a memorandum prepared for internal use in the Imperial Naval Office indicated that recent maneuvers had shown the increasing importance of Heligoland. Since a powerful and energetic opponent could impede the exit and deployment of the fleet from the Elbe estuary, it was recommended that it deploy outside the river and lean on Heligoland for support (Capelle inserted the words "before and after the battle"). Heligoland would thus serve as a base for the fleet both for attack and defense. Following the principle that one gun on land equals ten guns on board ship, the author thought that four heavy flat trajectory guns and some guns of middle caliber would be adequate as armament for the island. Provision should also be made for blockings in wartime.[42]

The strengthening of the defenses of the Elbe and Wilhelmshaven also came up. In the summer of 1906, Tirpitz sent Heeringen to discuss the question of fortifications of Heligoland and the German North Sea coast with Koester, Koester's designated successor Prince Heinrich, the Chief of the North Sea Station Bendemann, and other officers. His mission was to emphasize the importance of strengthening Heligoland and to play down the need of other coastal fortifications. As he reported, Prince Heinrich "was quite convinced that a strongly fortified Heligoland would gain much more importance for the use of the fleet in the German Bight than the fortification of the coast itself." Koester immediately recognized the importance of Heligoland as a torpedo-boat base, but failed to realize its significance for a naval battle. While Koester was convinced of its latter purpose by Heeringen and Hopmann, "probably the brightest member of the Fleet staff," he still held it essential to build Cuxhaven into a first-rate base. Heeringen also persuaded the representative of Bendemann, Captain Kalau, to accept the fortification of Heligoland and put off the question of fortifying Wilhelmshaven. Kalau even assured Heeringen that his superior, Bendemann, would create no further difficulties for the Imperial Naval Office.[43]

In considering the new navy bill, however, Dähnhardt still proposed in July 1906 to adhere to the previously valid principle of turning the funds toward shipbuilding and delaying the larger coastal defense projects, including the fortifications and harbor of Heligoland, until 1910,[44] and at a meeting of the Imperial Naval Office in October 1906 Tirpitz proposed to use discarded ship-guns for coastal fortifications as soon as possible "thus to weaken the pressure for coastal fortifications [Küstenwerke]."[45] Capelle questioned whether the Heligoland project, the fortifications of Borkum and the Elbe, and the construction of dockyards could be separated from the bill.[46]

In 1908, Tirpitz, however, continued to consider the defenses of Heligoland to be important. Both the Imperial Naval Office and the North Sea Station recommended in 1908 that its garrison be increased.[47] Soon thereafter Tirpitz urged that its fortifications and harbor construction be promoted as much as possible.[48] On the eve of the Agadir crisis, the Imperial Naval Office also concerned itself with improved security measures against a surprise attack, similar to those proposed by the Admiralty Staff in 1906.[49]

There was continued pressure after the Dogger Bank incident to improve other aspects of war preparedness. On 7 January 1905 the Kaiser ordered that in the coming year ship repairs be arranged so as to have at all times eight ships of the line ready for action and that by 1 March all ships of the line be ready for war.[50] A few days later Koester stated that the fleet was ready for war, but complained that torpedo-boats lacked practice in operating together with the fleet. While Tirpitz agreed to strengthen the High Seas Fleet by bringing back ships serving abroad, he refused to keep additional ships in service or to activate two reserve squadrons for the autumn tactical maneuvers.[51] Between 1906 and 1908, Prince Heinrich complained officially to his brother about the inadequate war preparedness of the High Seas Fleet: it was fully prepared for war only four months of the year. The situation was further compounded by the practice of having new ships entering the fleet take over the crews of the ships relegated to the reserve and doing their trial runs independently of the rest of the fleet. Thus at the beginning of the training year 1909–10 the first squadron would be reduced to only six ships. The situation would become worse still in the years when four large ships would be joining the fleet annually. Heinrich further complained about the low value of the reserve divisions, claiming that his subordinates and the Chief of the North Sea Station agreed with him. His sharpest protest was made on 21 December 1908, when he asked his brother to settle the differences between himself and Tirpitz.[52] Upon being approached, Tirpitz promised to re-examine the situation. As a result he and Wilhelm agreed to drop the practice of weakening the fleet for the trial runs of the Nassau-class ships and to accede to most of Heinrich's wishes. The draft of the letter which the Imperial Naval Office prepared for Wilhelm to be sent to his brother stated, however, that he

> had confidence that the Secretary of State of the Imperial Naval Office always puts military interests first and that only because of the inexorable pressure of the shortage of money or of the political situation does he ever leave unfulfilled justified wishes of the Front. The only agency from which all pertinent circumstances can be viewed is the Imperial Naval Office. This can never be forgotten when the wishes or requests of the front are not followed.[53]

The submissions of Prince Heinrich gave rise to an intemperate attack on Tirpitz by the chief of the Admiralty Staff, Count Friedrich von Baudissin, on 5 January 1909, in which he charged the Secretary of State with damaging the effectiveness of the fleet by squandering money on dockyards. Müller, Chief of the Naval Cabinet, claims to have supported Tirpitz against Heinrich and Baudissin, who were eventually dismissed.[54] Tirpitz prevailed once more but soon came to clash with Wilhelm himself for refusing to accede to the Kaiser's demand for retroactive requests to the Reichstag to activate cruisers of the reserve for the preservation of fleet effectiveness during the absence of active cruisers in the Mediterranean.[55]

If Prince Heinrich and Baudissin had briefly allied themselves against Tirpitz on the question of war preparedness, Tirpitz was to ally himself subsequently with the Admiralty Staff against the new Chief of the High Seas Fleet, Henning von Holtzendorff, who wished to deploy the fleet in the Baltic rather than in the North Sea.[56] At the beginning of 1911, Tirpitz and Holtzendorff also clashed over the arrangements for keeping ships in service in 1911. Holtzendorff protested on 14 January over not having been consulted and complained that the reduction of the cruiser unit by one ship, *Blücher*, which was to be used as an artillery-training ship, weakened the military effectiveness of the fleet.[57] Family connections made both Prince Heinrich and Holtzendorff uncomfortable enemies for Tirpitz: while the former was the Kaiser's brother, the latter was related to Müller, the power-broker in much of the in-fighting between the different naval agencies.[58] The Secretary of State responded by conceding an additional cruiser but stated that financial constraints would then compel the reduction of the number of active ships of the line from seventeen to sixteen. He also insisted that they be used for artillery practice.[59] The last provision impelled Holtzendorff to complain to Wilhelm, who, however, once more backed his Secretary of State.[60]

On the whole, Tirpitz managed to hold his own against the Kaiser and the Front between 1905 and 1911. His major concessions had been for larger ships and the fortification of Heligoland, which fitted in with his North Sea strategy. His "quantity versus quality" argument, however, no longer prevailed. The results were escalation of costs and the weakening of his own position. In addition came the challenge presented by retired Vice-Admiral Karl Galster between October 1907 and January 1910, who criticized the ship-of-the-line school, advocating the concentration on *Kleinkrieg*, chiefly submarines, in case of a war against Britain. Tirpitz obtained the support of Müller and Koester to organize the social ostracism of Galster, whose views Bülow had wanted discussed in public by the naval officer corps. In January 1910, Galster agreed to fall in line.[61]

## III

More expensive than the need to improve war preparedness was the further escalation in ship types. In the early summer of 1906, Carl Coerper, the naval attaché in London, reported that the British Admiralty had placed orders for a 34·3 cm cannon and was considering going up to a 40·6 cm caliber. The new ships of the line would be armed with a heavy artillery of the former caliber and would have a displacement of more than 20,000 tons. What is more, wrote Coerper, the armored cruiser of the Invincible class would have as heavy armament 30·5 cm guns—an even greater challenge to Tirpitz in view of his refusal to increase the caliber of the heavy artillery of the large cruisers above 21 cm and to go along with the Kaiser's fast-ship-of-the-line project.[62]

This time Tirpitz made a quick decision. From his retreat in St Blasien he instructed his subordinates on 18 July 1906:

> If the plans of the English to enlarge the displacement and armaments of their 1906 battleships and cruisers, which have recently come to my attention, should be confirmed, it would become necessary to go ahead with further enlargements of our designs even for the estimates for 1907.[63]

The final decision about ship types was reached at the meeting of the Imperial Naval Office of 19 September 1906, when, against the advice of Eickstedt, who considered the 21 cm or 24 cm caliber adequate, and at the prompting of Heeringen, Capelle, and Ahlefeld, Tirpitz decided to start building large cruisers with 28 cm guns which would come close to the Invincible class.[64] On 28 September, Tirpitz reported the decision to Wilhelm without having discussed it with Bülow, predicting that it would lead to strong agitation by British Conservatives against the Liberal administration:

> The English have seen that with their action with the Dreadnought in the previous spring they made a mistake in the face of Germany and are angry about it. This annoyance will increase as they see that we follow them

immediately with large cruisers, all the more so, as ours will be somewhat larger than *Invincible*.[65]

Tirpitz thus definitely anticipated a deterioration in Anglo-German relations as a result of the decision to match Britain in ship types. He also warned Wilhelm that for the next two or three years, before a new navy bill was introduced, it would be necessary to keep down other naval expenditures. The Kaiser concurred with his State Secretary. The two men further agreed that the Foreign Office was to be informed. This decision is an astounding revelation of the weakness of the political leadership in Wilhelmian Germany. On the previous day Bülow had written Tirpitz that, in view of the expected deficit in the 1907 budget, expenditures would have to be kept down until new sources of revenue could be found![66] As seen in the next chapter, Tirpitz's prediction about an unfavorable British reaction soon came true. His expectation of having to wait two or three years for another navy bill proved wrong, however. The elections following Bülow's dissolution of the Reichstag in December 1906, undertaken with Tirpitz's approval, produced the most pro-governmental body since the existence of the Bismarckian *Kartell*. The so-called Bülow bloc of Conservatives, Free Conservatives, National Liberals, and Progressives formed a pro-governmental majority; the Social Democrats were decimated, and the Centre, although slightly strengthened, was now more docile as it tried to escape the recently attached *Reichsfeindlich* label.[67]

In spite of Dähnhardt's caution Capelle insisted on the introduction in 1908 of both the tax and navy bills. The core of the new navy bill was to be the reduction of the active life of the ships of the line and cruisers from twenty-five to twenty years. In addition were to come the increased costs for the larger 30·5 cm ships of the line, improved torpedo-boats, and submarines which Tirpitz had reluctantly agreed to construct in 1904. The total amount requested for the period 1908–17 was roughly estimated at 700–800 million marks, but: "The *Novelle* must accordingly appear meager and small."[68]

Tirpitz was prepared to go along with the head of his Budget Department. On 7 March he reported the proposed procedure to the new Chief of the Naval Cabinet, Müller,[69] and on 9 March he obtained Wilhelm's approval, having once again bypassed Bülow. He explained to the Kaiser that the bill would "perpetuate the three-ship tempo with a cosmetic flaw, which, however, would not be without benefit as a new point of attack."[70] This cosmetic flaw was that either in the years 1913–15 or in the years 1916–17 the building rate would drop to two large ships per year.

The Imperial Naval Office now proceeded with the paperwork; various drafts of the new law were prepared, with Tirpitz communicating them to different department heads for comment and arranging conferences with his associates. Negotiations were also conducted with politicians, particularly members of the Progressive, Centre, and National Liberal parties. Difficulties were raised by Hermann von Stengel, Secretary of the Imperial Treasury, who continued to stress economy,[71] and by Bülow. Although a letter to the Chancellor had been drafted on 25 February 1907, it had not been sent by 9 March.[72] The formal letter informing him of the proposed navy bill and enclosing its third draft dates 17 May—the same date as the communication to Stengel.[73]

On 27 May, Tirpitz noted in his report to the Kaiser that Bülow approved the introduction of the bill in 1907 but requested that it be made to appear moderate and indicated that its costs would create difficulty. Tirpitz must have felt uneasy about the Chancellor's response since he also jotted down that "HM [must] if necessary be firmly [hart] for the bill."[74] According to Tirpitz's dictation in November 1912, Bülow had either in May or June 1907 succumbed to Metternich's influence and wanted to advise the Kaiser to reduce the building rate for ships, but had been turned down.[75] Although Tirpitz may have confused 1907 with 1908, when there is corroborative evidence of Bülow's changed stance, Holstein's influence also came to bear on the Chancellor in 1906–07. After his dismissal Holstein resumed social relations with the Bülows by agreeing to dine with them on 17 May 1906. On the same day he drafted a memorandum, possibly for use with Bülow, stating his objections to the German naval policy.

> (1) Can we ever, no matter how great our efforts, achieve naval parity with the combined fleets of England and France? In our own right? By alliance? (2) Will the sum total of German military strength be augmented or relatively diminished by an extreme program of fleet building? A restriction of our land forces, a cause for war . . . We cannot conduct a war against England without allies. No allies in sight. Against Japan we might perhaps proceed with America. Our conflicts with all other Great Powers will be decided on land.[76]

By November he was viewing the navy as the main factor in the deterioration of Anglo-German relations and as a cause of the Anglo-French rapprochement.[77] It is possible that Bülow, who was regularly consulting Holstein after his retirement, was receptive to his influence. In response to Holstein's letter of 29 August, he defended Tirpitz as one who two years earlier had resisted "fantastic fleet plans," without mentioning that he himself had been prepared to go along with them, and assured his former subordinate that he would now confine himself to the absolute essentials. He added further:

> The idea that we can ever come close to matching the English fleet—much less the united fleets of the western powers—is of course sheer madness. But there can be no doubt that in the Reichstag and in the country the great majority want a gradual construction of a fleet which is strong enough to ensure the safety of our coasts and our coastal cities so that our fleet in the event of an attack will at least not represent a *quantité absolument négligeable*.[78]

This letter may well be an indication of Bülow's basic misunderstanding of the Tirpitz Plan.[79] It may also be an attempt by the Chancellor to defend himself against his former mentor and subordinate. It does not support the view that Bülow had dissociated himself from Tirpitz. But would he at this time have dared to admit his break with Tirpitz to Holstein? Nevertheless, the possible effect of German naval increases on Britain concerned Bülow, as is shown by his instructions in October 1907 to play down in the press the autumn maneuvers and other naval matters.[80] The financial consequences of the bill for the future of the Bülow Bloc and for Bülow himself were undoubtedly further, probably more serious, considerations in the Chancellor's mind about the Fourth Navy Bill.[81] So was his concern about strengthening the German position on land, as seen in the next chapter.

In February 1907, Dähnhardt had optimistically assumed that in view of the British building rate of four large ships per year a German construction rate of three large ships annually would by 1917 transform the power relationship in such ships from the current 1:3 to a 1:2 ratio. The situation would be further improved if, as seemed likely, the British construction rate dropped to three large ships per year.

> But if we should . . . for no obvious reason, switch to a four-ship rate, then not only will we bear the stigma of starting a fruitless armament race and draw even more hostility against a German Empire already denounced as a peace disturber but, what is much worse, the Liberal ministry in Britain will be swept away and a Conservative one take its place which will, through enormous naval appropriations, completely remove our prospect of approaching Britain as a naval power in the foreseeable future.[82]

Apparent moderation was the way to improve Germany's power relationship with Britain.

In the late summer the situation faced by the Imperial Naval Office changed. In spite of sedulously cultivating the National Liberal and Progressive members of the Bülow Bloc, it was unable to secure the Progressive approval for the age of the ships, particularly since it would not take effect before 1912 and therefore did not require a change in the law in 1908. On the other hand, just as in 1905–06, the Navy League continued its independent agitation for a larger bill. Under these circumstances a new opportunity was presented by the speech of the Centre Party leader Peter Spahn on 11 August 1907, offering his party's support for further fleet increases. Acceptance of the Centre's cooperation presented Tirpitz, who had dissociated the navy from the electoral campaign against the Catholic party at the risk of being labeled as a "Centre man," with a way out of his difficulty. Moreover, the successful interview between Edward VII and the Kaiser on 12 August and the favorable British response to the latter's proposed visit may have encouraged Tirpitz to disregard Dähnhardt's warnings of February concerning the introduction of a four-large-ship building rate. He thus decided to start the construction of four large ships in each of the years 1908–11.[83]

As he told Bülow on 21 September, the international situation was not unfavorable for the introduction of such a request, which presented the military advantage that Germany would by the fall of 1913 possess a double squadron of Dreadnought-type ships of the line and four battle cruisers. The disadvantage was that as of 1912 the building rate would drop to two ships per year until 1917 when it would again rise to three large ships. Thus another bill would have to be introduced by 1912 to stabilize the rate. Bülow approved the new bill on 21 September, and Wilhelm on 29 September 1907.[84] Tirpitz was depressed, however, about the ease with which the Kaiser was willing to give up the perpetuation of the building rate of three large ships annually, "which aim [I] incessantly followed for ten years."[85] On 27 March 1908 a large majority of the Reichstag approved the bill at the first reading.

According to the Navy Law of 1908, there would have been built in the period 1898–1920 forty-five ships of the line and twenty-two large cruisers.[86] According to Tirpitz, Germany would have had ready for action by 1920 thirty-three capital ships, i.e. Dreadnought-type ships of the line and battle cruisers.[87] Reluctant as he had been to allow the large cruiser to escalate to the size of a ship of the line, this development provided him with the opportunity of increasing the number of ships capable of fighting in the line.

## Notes: Chapter 14

1   Kennedy, *Antagonism*, p. 272.
2   Berghahn, *Tirpitz-Plan*, p. 309, n. 14.
3   BA-MA, F 2037, PG 66046, "Zur E-Denkschrift No. 4, Vorlage II."
4   ibid., "Sonder-Begründung der Vorlage II"—exclusively for members of the Reichstag Budget Committee.
5   Berghahn, *Tirpitz-Plan*, p. 315.
6   Quoted in ibid., pp. 322–3; the identical wording also appears in the finished version in BA-MA, F 2037, PG 66046, "Denkschrift zum Immediatvortrag über die Weiterentwicklung der Flotte nach dem Jahre 1906, Ganz Geheim. E-Denkschrift No. 5," 11 November 1903.
7   BA-MA, F 2037, PG 66046, "Vorarbeit zur E-Denkschrift No. 5," October 1903.
8   BA-MA, N 253/20, Notizen Tirpitz, 17 October 1903.
9   BA-MA, F 2037, PG 66046, "Denkschrift zum Immediatvortrag über die Weiterentwicklung der Flotte nach dem Jahre 1906, Ganz Geheim. E-Denkschrift No. 5," 11 November 1903.
10  ibid., F 2044, PG 66076, "Immediatvortrag," 14 November 1903, copy, initialed by Trotha. The original in Tirpitz's own hand appears in ibid., N 253/20.
11  ibid., F 2037, PG 66046, "Denkschrift zum Immediatvortrag über die Weiterentwicklung der Flotte nach dem Jahre 1906, Ganz Geheim. E-Denkschrift No. 5," 11 November 1903.
12  ibid., "Nachtrag zur E-Denkschrift No. 5," 18 November 1903.
13  Tirpitz, *Aufbau*, pp. 13–14.
14  BA-MA, F 2044, PG 66077, Dähnhardt to Müller, 10 February 1905.
15  See the extremely useful tables in Herwig's *"Luxury" Fleet*, particularly tables 2 and 6; also pp. 43–4; S. Breyer, *Schlachtschiffe und Schlachtkreuzer, 1905–1970* (Munich, 1970), p. 50; Marder, *Anatomy*, p. 548.
16  BA-MA, F 4142, VI, 1. 1.–23., Vol. 1, Fischel to Tirpitz, 21 November 1899; Bendemann to Tirpitz, 25 November 1899.
17  ibid., F 2046, PG 66084, "Protokoll über die Sitzung vom 21 December, 1899."
18  ibid., F 2044, PG 66076, Wilhelm to Tirpitz, 11 September 1903, and Wilhelm's comments in pencil to an American report for Tirpitz's benefit, n.d.; also N 253/20, Wilhelm to Tirpitz, 8 November 1903, and Tirpitz's "Notiz zum Immediatvortrag," 14 November 1903, copy. The undated original is in N 253/20.
19  ibid., F 4142, VI, 1. 1.–23., Vol. 4, Eickstedt to Tirpitz, 2 April 1904; Vol. 5, "Protokoll

über die Sitzung vom 25 April, 1904;" Eickstedt, 4 March 1905; Bürkner's memorandum regarding the meeting on 13 March 1905; F 2038, PG 66048, Dähnhardt's estimate of 6 May 1905 of the costs of such a ship.

20 ibid., F 2046, PG 66086, "Protokoll, Sitzung vom 4 November, 1904."
21 ibid., F 2044, PG 66078, Tirpitz to Wilhelm, 30 July 1905, copy certified by Trotha.
22 ibid., Scheer to Tirpitz, 1 September 1905.
23 ibid., Tirpitz to Senden, 6 September 1905, copy.
24 ibid., Tirpitz to Scheer, 10 September 1905.
25 ibid., F 4143, VI, 1. 1.–23., Heft 1, "Protokoll über die Sitzung vom 22 September 1905."
26 ibid., F 2044, PG 66078, "Denkschrift zum Immediatvortrag," 16 June 1906, signed Trotha.
27 ibid., N 253/23, Müller to Tirpitz, 6 March 1906; Lans to Scheer, 17 April 1906; N 253/16, Ahlefeldt to Tirpitz, 22 April 1906.
28 BA-MA, F 2044, PG 66079, Tirpitz to Prince Heinrich, 25 December 1905.
29 Berghahn, *Tirpitz-Plan*, pp. 483–93; Deist, *Flottenpolitik*, esp. pp 172–94.
30 Tirpitz, *Aufbau*, pp. 30–2; for the Kaiser see also Berghahn, *Tirpitz-Plan*, pp. 500–4; Deist, *Flottenpolitik*, pp. 184–91; Kelly, "Naval policy," fos 269–70.
31 Berghahn, *Tirpitz-Plan*, pp. 499–502; Deist, *Flottenpolitik*, pp. 186, 188.
32 Quoted in Berghahn, *Tirpitz-Plan*, p. 494. I have used the version in BA-MA, F 2044, PG 66079.
33 For its passage through the Reichstag, see Hansgeorg Fernis, *Die Flottennovellen im Reichstag, 1906–12* (Stuttgart, 1934), pp. 21–54.
34 Tirpitz, *Aufbau*, p. 34.
35 Hassell, *Tirpitz*, p. 173.
36 BA-MA, N 253/9, "Denkschrift über die weitere Entwickelung der Marine," May 1906, drafted by Dähnhardt, corrected by Capelle; Berghahn, *Tirpitz-Plan*, p. 508.
37 BA-MA, N 253/23, "Warum kann in den nächsten Jahren keine Novelle eingebracht werden?" no signature, on the first page there is a note May/June 1906.
38 BA-MA, F 2524, XVII, 1. 1. 21., Vol. 1, Tirpitz's instructions of 22 November 1904.
39 ibid., F 2525, XVII, 1. 1.–23., Heft 2, Tirpitz to A, W, and C, 14 December 1904, copy; Heeringen to A and C, 17 December 1904.
40 ibid., Scheer to A and Bb, 20 December 1904; also F 2287, PG 66291, "Protokoll über die Sitzung am 20. Dezember, 1904."
41 See below, pp. 334 ff.
42 BA-MA, N 253/6, typescript memorandum, n.d., no signature.
43 ibid., Heeringen to Tirpitz, 25 June 1906.
44 ibid., F 2040, PG 66060, Dähnhardt's memorandum of 17 July 1906, presented to Tirpitz and Capelle.
45 ibid., F 2046, PG 66087, "Protokoll über die Sitzung vom Oktober, 1906."
46 ibid., N 253/23, Capelle to Tirpitz, 12 and 16 August 1906.
47 ibid., F 2525, XVII, 1. 1.–23., Heft 2, memorandum of the Chief of the North Sea Naval Station, February 1908.
48 ibid., F 2316, PG 94453, "Protokoll über die Etatsitzungen—einmalige Ausgaben—am 10. und 11. März 1908," 11 April 1908.
49 ibid., F 2525, XVII, 1. 1.–21., Vol. 3, copy of memorandum, no signature, 6 February 1911; see below, p. 334.
50 ibid., N 253/21, Wilhelm to Chancellor (Imperial Naval Office), 7 January 1905, copy.
51 ibid., F 3303, PG 66708, Schmidt on behalf of Tirpitz to Baudissin, 30 March 1908.
52 ibid., Prince Heinrich to Wilhelm, 21 December 1908.
53 ibid., Wilhelm to Command of High Seas Fleet, 9 January 1909.
54 ibid., N 159/3, p. 408; Müller, *Der Kaiser*, p. 73; Hubatsch, *Der Admiralstab*, pp. 140–1.
55 PAAA, Deutschland 138, Bd 39, Jenisch, Corfu, to the Foreign Office, 18 April 1909, telegram; Krocker, Imperial Naval Office to the Foreign Office, 19 April 1909; Wilhelm to Bülow, 21 April 1909, telegram; Bülow to Wilhelm, 22 April 1909, copy.
56 See below, pp. 352; 391.
57 BA-MA, F 3303, PG 66708, Holtzendorff to Tirpitz, 14 January 1911.
58 Müller's father-in-law and Holtzendorff had the same grandmother.
59 BA-MA, F 3303, PG 66708, Tirpitz to Holtzendorff, 1 February 1911.
60 ibid., Holtzendorff to Wilhelm, 4 February 1911; Müller to Tirpitz, 4 March 1911.

61  *Deutsche Marinegeschichte der Neuzeit,* p. 258; Herwig, "*Luxury*" *Fleet,* p. 39; Tirpitz, *Aufbau,* p. 51.

62  See above, pp. 273 ff.; Berghahn, *Tirpitz-Plan,* pp. 511–12.

63  BA-MA, N 253/23, Tirpitz, St Blasien, to Trotha, 18 July 1906, copy; original in F 4140, VI, 1. 1.–21a., Heft 1; Jonathan Steinberg, "The Novelle of 1908: necessities and choices in the Anglo-German arms race," *Transactions of the Royal Historical Society,* 1970, p. 35 (read 13 February). I am using Steinberg's translation.

64  BA-MA, F 4140, VI, 1. 1.–21a., Heft 1, "Protokoll über die Sitzung vom 19. September, 1906, betr. Projekt des grossen Kreuzers 1907," 1 October 1906.

65  ibid., F 2045, PG 66080, document initialed by Tirpitz on 28 September 1906; Berghahn, *Tirpitz-Plan,* pp. 522–3.

66  BA-MA, F 2316, PG 66453, Bülow to Tirpitz, 27 September 1906; Berghahn, *Tirpitz-Plan,* pp. 527–8.

67  ibid., pp. 529, 556–7; Steinberg "Novelle," pp. 29–30.

68  BA-MA, N 253/9, Capelle to Tirpitz, 17 (18) February 1907; Berghahn, *Tirpitz-Plan,* pp. 559–60; Steinberg, "Novelle," p. 33.

69  BA-MA, N 159/3: Müller states that Tirpitz proposed the fleet law for 1909.

70  ibid., according to Müller's entry for 9 March 1907 "Damit 3$^{\text{er}}$ Tempo eternisiert;" N 253/9, Tirpitz's notes in pencil for report to Wilhelm, 8 March 1907; and F 2045, PG 66080, Tirpitz's memorandum for report to Wilhelm, 9 March 1907; Berghahn, *Tirpitz-Plan,* p. 561.

71  BA-MA, F 2316, PG 66453, Stengel to Tirpitz, 13 May 1907, copy.

72  ibid., N 253/9, Tirpitz to Bülow, 25 February 1907.

73  ibid., F 2040, PG 66058, Tirpitz to Bülow, 17 May 1907; Tirpitz to Stengel, 17 May 1907.

74  ibid., N 253/9, Tirpitz's note, 27 May 1907.

75  ibid., "Im November 1912 diktierte Notiz."

76  *Holstein Papers,* Vol. 4, No. 982, Marie von Bülow to Holstein, 14 May 1906; and No. 983, memorandum by Holstein, 17 May 1906, pp. 427–8.

77  ibid., No. 1006, Holstein to Brandt, 20 November 1906, pp. 449–50.

78  Rich, *Holstein,* Vol. 2, p. 806.

79  Fernis, *Flottennovellen,* p. 60.

80  Berghahn, *Tirpitz-Plan,* p. 568.

81  ibid., pp. 561–3, 565.

82  ibid., p. 569.

83  ibid., pp. 570–83; Deist, *Flottenpolitik,* pp. 212–13; Steinberg, "Novelle," pp. 38–9.

84  BA-MA, N 253/9, typescript, n.d., no signature, "Vortrag beim Kanzler, Norderney;" in Tirpitz's hand "Rominten, 29.9 [1907];" and F 2040, PG 66058, "Denkschrift zum Immediatvortrage über die Marinevorlage, Winter 1907/08," 24 September 1907, initialed by Dähnhardt and Capelle.

85  ibid., N 253/9, "Rominten 29.9. [1907];" Berghahn, *Tirpitz-Plan,* p. 588.

86  BA-MA, F 2040, PG 66059, "Denkschrift zum Immediatvortrag," 19 February 1908, signed Capelle.

87  Tirpitz, *Aufbau,* table on last unnumbered page.

# 15 Foreign Policy from Algeciras to Agadir, 1906–11

## I

As shown in the previous chapter, late in 1905 and early in 1906, Bülow and Wilhelm, unlike Tirpitz, had been prepared to go ahead with a large expansion of the navy. By May 1906, however, Tirpitz had come to consider a building rate of four large ships per year and by December 1906 he had definitely decided to increase the size of German battleships to match those of the British in spite of his anticipation of a resulting deterioration of Anglo-German relations. He was thus consciously engaging in a naval race with Britain. By then, however, the German political leadership had begun to waver.

Germany's isolation had become evident at Algeciras where only Austria-Hungary had supported her. Britain had drawn closer to France, and subsequently sought an agreement with Russia whose military strength was slowly recuperating. The theme of encirclement soon came to dominate the thinking of German diplomacy. As previously, between 1906 and 1908 the Dual Monarchy was not viewed as a strong ally. Yet, on 31 May 1906, Bülow, when providing Wilhelm with instructions for his impending trip to Vienna, admitted "that our relations with Austria are now more important than ever since the *Kaiserreich* is our only reliable ally."[1]

In May 1907, Bülow and Tschirschky, in conversations with the new Austro-Hungarian Foreign Minister, Alois von Aehrenthal, agreed to provide the Dual Monarchy with fuller support against possible Russian ambitions in the Balkans[2] where Bülow also wanted Austro-Hungarian and German interests to be more closely coordinated.[3] In the concluding report on his diplomatic career, Wedel on 23 October 1907 stated that although Francis Joseph presented a guarantee of Austria-Hungary's loyalty to Germany "we count more opponents than supporters in the Dual Monarchy, particularly as the now ruling Independence Party in Hungary has partly turned against us."[4] Both he and his successor Tschirschky viewed Aehrenthal as a supporter of the German alliance.[5] On 7 February 1908, Tschirschky reported that, with the loss of influence of the German alliance and the emergence of the federalist anti-German Slav-feudal bloc in Cisleithania, Germany would in the future have to cultivate the Magyars more carefully.[6] This report was extensively annotated by Wilhelm, who approved the suggestion that attacks on the Hungarians by the German press should cease. Bülow instructed that the expulsion of Austro-

Hungarian workers be henceforth handled more humanely.[7] German diplomats were also aware of Austro-Hungarian concern about deteriorating German relations with Britain with whom Vienna had no quarrel.[8] On 15 July 1908, Bülow directed Schoen to instruct the embassy in Vienna "to observe carefully signs which indicate that forces are at work in Austria which seek to bring this empire into the Anglo-French current."[9]

What were Germany's relations with her other ally? On the eve of the Algeciras Conference, Monts reported from Rome that the Italian government was aware that Italy could play the role of a great power only within the framework of the Triplice.[10] He expected Italo-German relations to improve with the solution of the Morocco question and recommended the renewal of the alliance.[11] He also reported assurances received from Italian leaders[12] and a statement by the Chief of the Italian General Staff, Saletta, "that Italy took her duties as an ally very seriously."[13] Moltke claimed that as a soldier he honored the military obligations to Italy, hoped to maintain good relations with the Italian General Staff, and continued working on the transportation of Italian troops to Germany.[14] Late in February, Monts remarked that in spite of growing sympathy for France "Italians would be unpleasantly surprised if the Triple Alliance were to suddenly collapse over their heads,"[15] but also reported the former Italian Prime Minister, Antonio Rudini, as saying that in a war between Germany and France Italy might still side with the former, but if Britain were the ally of the latter "no government would be strong enough to carry out an organized mobilization."[16] And to a report of Monts of 8 March Wilhelm remarked: "It will end in Italy's standing with the Anglo-Gallic group. We shall do well to take this into account and to write off this ally . . ."[17] The Kaiser clearly realized that Italy would desert the Triplice if there was no improvement in Anglo-German relations and was impulsively inclined in April to join Austria-Hungary in teaching Italy a lesson.[18] By that time he may have read the report of the military attaché in Rome, Hammerstein-Equord, stating that "one hardly counts on the possibility of a war against France but wants to take all measures for the eventually expected and popular war against Austria."[19] Bülow, however, advised in May that German press attacks against Italy be called off.[20] At the same time he considered Italy "as a militarily never fully calculable factor."[21]

At the beginning of June, Monts submitted to the Foreign Office two memoranda as the basis for the renewal of the Triplice.[22] The first indicated that some of the original assumptions of the alliance had changed: the attack by France alone against Germany, which would bind Italy to assist her, was no longer probable and close Anglo-German relations which might bring Britain into the Triple Alliance were nonexistent. Yet the alliance would still provide a guarantee for European peace and monarchical solidarity, protect Austria against an Italian stab in the back, restrain Italy's advance into the Orient, and prevent "a further isolation of Germany through hindering Italy from joining a possible anti-German coalition advanced by France and England." Within the Foreign Office, Counselor Klehmet stated that, although the existing terms of the Triple Alliance were unsatisfactory, any attempt to change them would lead to the dissolution of the alliance, which would "be viewed as our enemies' success."[23] These calculations were accompanied by Hammerstein-Equord's reports of Italian military concentrations against Austria-Hungary, described as being of a more offensive nature than the previous ones against France.[24] By the end of October, Monts commented about increasing Italian friendship for Germany but attributed it to the desire to have Germany restrain Austria-Hungary from attacking Italy in response to her irredentism.[25] Wedel reported from Vienna that, while Italy was useless as an ally in war, her membership in the Triplice would be a partial deterrent to a war between her and Austria.[26] Monts further stated that in view of the combined Franco-British naval power in the Mediterranean "A stand against both these states who are powerful at sea would in fact be stark lunacy for a navally weak Italy with her long and open coast."[27]

Thus the German leadership drifted toward the renewal of the Triple Alliance in full realization of Italy's unreliability, her confused internal circumstances, dire need for reform, and corrupt government.[28] It did so with the approval of Aehrenthal, who thought that Italy's secession from the Triplice would strengthen her irredentism as well as warlike tendencies in France and Britain.[29] Adhering to Monts', Klehmet's, Wedel's, and Aehrenthal's arguments and rejecting the contrary advice of the retired Holstein,[30] Bülow ruled on 16 November 1906 that Germany renew the Triplice.[31] In the spring of 1907, Moltke, in agreement with the Austro-Hungarian General Staff, agreed to continue to work on the arrangements to transport Italian troops to Germany,[32] and on 7 July 1907 the Triple Alliance was automatically renewed on its old terms.

Almost a year later, on 19 April 1908, Bülow reported to Wilhelm from Venice that "the foreign policy of the Italian government is as before determined by fear for the safety of the mainland from navally dominant England and by the wish not to part ways with Germany."

In the event of a Franco-German war, Italy would most likely remain neutral. Realization of her military weakness had, however, caused Italy's relations with Austria to improve during the last two years. Monts essentially concurred with his chief's estimate.[33] It is thus evident that German leadership realized that relations with Austria-Hungary and Italy were affected by Anglo-German hostility and the Anglo-French rapprochement.

## II

A significant German perception of British concern about German naval armaments first appeared in a report of 16 April 1904 by chargé d'affaires Bernstorff.[34] In November 1906, Coerper, the naval attaché in London, referred to the dissatisfaction of Britain's naval enthusiasts with her limited naval program in view of the German decision to build ships of the same strength as the Dreadnought.[35] In January 1907 the British naval attaché in Berlin expressed to Tirpitz British concerns about a German attack, which led Bülow to advise Tirpitz to undertake discussions with the British naval leadership.[36] Metternich, Coerper, and the chargé d'affaires, Wilhelm vom Stumm, concurred that Germany's growing naval power was the main cause for the deterioration of Anglo-German relations.[37] Although the German military attaché in London, Captain Ostertag, denied that Britain was preparing for an offensive war against Germany, Monts reported from Rome that an active minority in the Admiralty pressed for the destruction of the German navy before it grew any larger.[38]

In November 1907, Britain reacted to the publication of Germany's Fourth Navy Bill. The new naval attaché, Wilhelm Widenmann, reported that it was viewed as an enormous threat, and Stumm wrote in January 1908 that the prevailing view was that the German threat presented Britain with the greatest crisis since the Napoleonic wars.[39] In February 1908, Metternich, whose initial reaction had been restrained, wrote that German naval construction had given the upper hand to the supporters of Sir John Fisher, who advocated an escalation of naval armaments.[40]

Wilhelm was sufficiently impressed by the reports to resort to the unconventional tactic of writing to the First Lord of the Admiralty, Lord Tweedmouth, denying that the new navy bill was a challenge to Britain. In doing so he consulted neither Bülow nor Metternich.[41] His brother Heinrich wrote directly to Fisher to disclaim any German threat.[42] In the spring and summer of 1908, Metternich's and Stumm's reports about British concerns regarding German construction became more numerous and intense,[43] but succeeded only in arousing the Kaiser's ire against both Metternich and the British. He considered the British concern not as the result of German construction, but as the backfiring of the "entirely *crazy Dreadnought policy* of Sir J. Fisher and His Majesty" which instead of checkmating Germany had destroyed British naval supremacy.[44] He thought that British fears could be best allayed by the conclusion of an entente or agreement with Germany, but was at the same time outraged at Metternich's willingness to consider the reduction of German naval building subject to an improvement of Anglo-German relations,[45] and viewed any British requests for German fleet reductions as tantamount to a declaration of war. Both Schoen and Bülow, however, insisted that British fears about the German superiority in Dreadnoughts by the end of 1911 be allayed.[46]

## III

German fears of encirclement had greatly increased. The main focus of this phobia was Britain. As for France, reports from Paris were ambivalent: most Frenchmen were regarded as pacific, but in the aftermath of the Morocco crisis viewed war with Germany as inevitable.[47] Georges Clemenceau, Premier as of October 1906, was represented as a firebrand. France's military preparations in particular, as well as her continued revanchism, desire to regain Alsace-Lorraine, and aspirations to hegemony, caused Bülow to insist on the best preparations on land and to ask Einem on 1 June 1906, without the knowledge of the Kaiser, what military measures Germany should take:

Do we need more machine-guns? Is a faster rearmament of artillery not necessary? What is the state of affairs with the transportation troops? With the transport [*Bespannung*] of the heavy artillery of the field-army? With the dirigibles? With a practical uniforming of the army, directed more than now toward actual conditions . . .[48]

Einem replied in some detail, indicating that the army was in the process of modernization, re-equipment, and reorganization. None the less, he would be prepared to proceed more rapidly and even break with the Quinquennate, "if the political situation makes an imminent war a probability." To the last clause Bülow added an n.b. In his notes on reports from Paris in October he credited the French with aggressive intentions. Moltke, too, commented on Einem's reply. His chief concern related to the inadequate utilization of machine-guns in the German army.[49] At this point Bülow drew a double line in the margin of the document. Bülow also appears to have harbored some expansionist designs. As he stated in a memorandum of 30 May 1906:

The progress of the German Empire in world policy naturally arouses the jealousy of those European great powers who are fed up with the competition and the development of German power from political and commercial grounds. Therefore, more than ever, it is the duty of the German Empire to rely on herself and to strengthen her own arms.

This brings up the question whether it is not important for the security of Germany, united under the Prussian flag, to cultivate, beside her ally Austria, the friendship of the United States as well as of the neighboring . . . states of The Netherlands, Belgium, Denmark and Switzerland . . . since the Reformation, the common Protestant confession has united Brandenburg-Prussia not only with The Netherlands but also with Denmark and the Protestant parts of Switzerland.[50]

Concern continued about the Anglo-French rapprochement. On 19 September 1906, Flotow reported from Paris that during the Morocco conflict wide-reaching military agreements had been concluded between the two countries.[51] An excerpt from this report was forwarded to the General Staff. In another report Wilhelm minuted: "The Gauls have resigned themselves to the role of lackeys and mercenaries for England's Continental interests and we must reckon with it. A strong army and a strong fleet are more necessary than ever."[52] Toward the end of January 1907, Metternich reported a conversation with Haldane in which the latter denied the existence of an Anglo-French military convention but admitted that there may have been conversations between military men of which he disclaimed any knowledge: something which Wilhelm rightly refused to believe.[53] Both he and Tschirschky discounted British denials about a military convention with France.[54] And, at the end of May 1907, Metternich reminded Bülow that, if Germany were to attack France over Morocco, Britain would come to the assistance of the latter.[55]

There were also unjustified suspicions of an Anglo-French naval convention whereby the French would concentrate their naval power in the Mediterranean and limit themselves to the defensive in the Channel and the Atlantic where they were assured of British support. Italy could be forced to join the Anglo-French combination.[56] These suspicions were shared by German military and naval leadership. In June 1908, shortly after the French president Armand Fallières' visit to London, Metternich expected an Anglo-French alliance to be concluded "*as soon as we are involved in a war with France*. For it has gradually become a political axiom of both parties in England *that France should not again* emerge weakened from a war with Germany." The italics appear to be Bülow's. The Chancellor thus seems to have realized that Britain would take France's side in a war with Germany.[57]

In view of the improved Anglo-French relations, the hostage theory surfaced again. The Kaiser had been discouraged from using it as a threat against the French in 1906.[58] However, he commented on an article in *Le Soleil* of 23 May 1908 that "France is my hostage for the good conduct of England. As soon as the latter seriously attacks the interests of Germany, I shall invade Champagne."[59] What might have been construed as an erratic emperor's comments appeared in a statement from the chargé d'affaires in Paris, von der Lancken, and the minister in Tangier, Wangenheim, as a threat of an attack on France if she were to remain neutral in an Anglo-German war.[60] While entertaining the hostage theory, Kaiser Wilhelm also appears to have harbored plans for an understanding with France which would have involved a large-scale reorganization of Europe. In a memorandum from Wilhelm to Bülow of 20 April 1907 it was queried:

Is an understanding with France perhaps possible on the following basis? For France: Influence on Italy and Spain toward a Latin union and republican constitution. Domination over the Mediterranean. Morocco French and one harbor on the Mediterranean and one on the Atlantic coast German. Germany dissolves the alliance with Italy.
For Germany: Influence on Switzerland, German Austria, Sweden, Norway, Denmark and Holland up to a defensive and offensive alliance and customs union. The Belgian miscarriage will be removed through the cession of the Walloon provinces to France and the Flemish to Holland. North and Baltic Sea German. France dissolves her alliance with Russia or (resp.) Germany joins it as the third partner.[61]

The reference to a Continental bloc relates to Wilhelm's previous thinking.

There was also serious concern about an Anglo-Russian rapprochement. In view of Russian revolutionary developments Bülow had in July 1906 warned about the collapse of Czarist autocracy.[62] Just previously Wilhelm had, according to Bülow, considered the possibility of the dissolution of the Russian Empire into a federation of republics, in which case he was prepared to incorporate the Baltic provinces into Germany and establish an independent Poland.[63] On 9 August 1906, however, Moltke reported to Bülow that the Russian forces to be used against Germany and Austria-Hungary were considerable in spite of the need to retain troops at home for the maintenance of order: twenty-five infantry divisions and two rifle brigades would be used against Germany and twenty-two infantry divisions and two rifle brigades against Austria. The mobilization of these forces would be slow, their training inferior, but their battle efficiency would be improved.[64] Russia was ceasing to be a negligible military factor. On 31 July 1906, Metternich reported that reconciliation with her was a very important part of Edward Grey's policy.[65] Wilhelm commented on a report of September 1906 from St Petersburg about negotiations for an Anglo-Russian entente: "Nice prospects! In the future one can count on an Alliance Franco-Russe, a Franco-Anglaise Entente Cordiale and an Anglo-Russe Entente, with Spain, Italy, Portugal as additional dependents . . ."[66]

To the announcement of 31 August that the Anglo-Russian accord had been signed, Bülow commented that it should be discussed calmly by the German press and not be built up as an alliance or a threat to German interests.[67] Wilhelm, however, noted that as a result of the agreement "Europe will become even more disagreeable for us than before."[68] Yet he and Tschirschky had previously been impressed by good relations with Russia because of his interview with Nicholas at Swinemünde in early August. Wilhelm had remarked: "Yet the Russians will not march against us."[69] By the end of May and in June 1908 the German phobia about encirclement had been increased by the visit of President Fallières to London and the meeting of Edward VII and Nicholas II in Reval. In response to Bülow's inquiry, Metternich denied that Fallières' visit created a new situation, but repeated his earlier observation that it was almost certain that Britain would side with France in a war with Germany and that Britain, France, and Russia had come together as a counterweight to the Triple Alliance without, however, having any offensive intentions.[70] To Pourtalès' report about a Russian newspaper article stating that the visits of the heads of state of the Triple Entente powers might incline Germany "to draw the sword immediately and not to wait until Russia and England had completed the reorganization of their armies" Wilhelm minuted: "would be the only correct action militarily. Frederick the Great would have done it and he would have been right."[71] Pourtalès' report that the Reval meeting had brought Britain and Russia more closely together led Wilhelm to conclude: "Therefore Imperial finance reform! Many indirect taxes, strong fleet, strong army!"[72] Wilhelm's indiscreet comments that Germany was ready to fight if encircled,[73] which he subsequently denied, led Bülow to provide him with his assessment of the diplomatic situation. He did so also for the Prussian ministers in Munich, Dresden, Stuttgart, and Karlsruhe. To Wilhelm he wrote:

It is obvious everywhere that there are intrigues and plots against us. As before I believe that England, on economic and military grounds, would be very reluctant to decide on war. I believe that Russia needs and wants peace. I also believe that even France, although she still feels pain over the loss of her 250-year *prépondérance légitime* on the Continent and has not given up the idea of revanche, has doubts about risking the incalculable chances of war. But I also believe that it lies in the interest of these powers to make us appear nervous and restless. This is therefore the tactic of our enemies, since every actual or apparent threat on our part will cause the French to fortify more strongly their eastern border, the English to build more Dreadnoughts, and the Russians to place more troops on their western boundary . . . We must as quickly as possible work on the striking readiness and war effectiveness of the army, but avoid drawing unnecessary attention to our work and to us and arousing new suspicions.[74]

Although stress was placed on the preparation of the army, no mention was made of the navy. Bülow thus appeared to have switched from *Weltpolitik* back to *Kontinentalpolitik*. In his circular to the Prussian ministers to the German courts, he provided additional reasons for this. While accepting the assurances that the Reval meeting had no offensive edge against Germany or Austria-Hungary, he recognized that it limited Germany's freedom of action.

We have to reckon that if we or Austria-Hungary should come into a serious conflict of interest with one of the Entente powers the hitherto loose and vague ententes and understandings would tighten into concrete alliances, so that we, along with Austria-Hungary, could see ourselves confronting a strong coalition.[75]

However, he viewed Russia as incapable of military action for a long time because of her débâcle in the war with Japan, and France as a gradually declining military power owing to a static birth rate.

The further we delay an armed conflict with our western neighbor, the less will he be capable of taking up the struggle which is becoming [to him] unequal in numerical terms even with support from another party.[76]

Bülow's arguments had been used before by the Foreign Office in the spring and summer of 1907. On 22 April, Lerchenfeld had reported Tschirschky as saying:[77]

. . . we must above all avoid playing the steward of the world. He further stated that time was running in favor of Germany. In ten years the Reich will have a population of 70 million and ten Dreadnoughts. Germany could therefore face the future calmly and could keep her policy on a steady course.

In July the Deputy State Secretary of the Foreign Office, Mühlberg, wrote Bülow: "As Your Highness has said, time is on our side, and on the firm block which we together with Austria form in Central Europe the paper missiles of the nations that are unfriendly to us will fall impotently."[78]

## IV

British concern about German naval construction was represented by Trotha to Tirpitz in March 1908 as meaning: "a faster increase [of the navy] was hardly possible without overstraining the bow. The steady development is the greatest [part] in it and provides the most secure guarantee for the future."[79] What to the Imperial Naval Office appeared as justification for not going ahead with the extremists of the Navy League was an element of concern to the Admiralty Staff. On 29 June 1908, Admiral Müller reported in his diary: "Report of . . . [Count] Baudissin: Worries of war."[80] The warnings issued by Metternich in the spring and summer of 1908 and Hardinge's interview in August failed to sway the Kaiser to slow down German naval construction. Instead Wilhelm came to view any attempts to interfere with it as tantamount to a declaration of war.[81] At the same time, according to Bülow, he sought some sort of understanding with Russia "in order to find a secure military basis, [for] otherwise we are in the most miserable military situation" and erratically demanded "an understanding with America and China! which would not fail to make an impression on England. Also the Mohammedans can be had; one must only proceed skillfully and have the will."[82] These were bizarre proposals which probably reflected Wilhelm's excitement and despair. Bülow also reported that British proposals for a fleet limitation were "From the standpoint of the All Highest War Lord treason toward his armed forces and his people in arms, a humiliation *à la* Olmütz and Fashoda."[83] Wilhelm's most notorious response to the difficult situation was the interview with Colonel Stuart Wortley published in the *Daily Telegraph* which produced a major constitutional crisis in Germany and "amused contempt" in Britain.[84] In his memoirs Bülow remarks that he stated to Wilhelm in July 1908, "if we could achieve through the slowing down of the fleet-building tempo a promise from England to us that she would not stand by France if she attacked us, we would strike a good deal," but encountered strong opposition.[85]

At the same time Tirpitz became suspicious that Metternich's reports were contributing to "a decline of sentiment for the fleet."[86] On 5 August, Bülow advised Metternich to avoid discussing any British disarmament proposals, stating that future bilateral agreements were as yet an open question. For them a more friendly British policy toward Germany would be a prerequisite.[87] Under pressure from Holstein to improve relations with Britain through a naval agreement, the Chancellor on 16 August made his first authentic statement to his unofficial adviser about slowing down the naval race, but only after the completion of the German financial reform:

> If I am still Chancellor then, I will not permit any such Icarus flight. Not only for reasons of foreign policy, but for domestic policy as well. We cannot have both the largest army and biggest navy. We cannot weaken the army, for our destiny will be decided on land.[88]

A week later he informed his confidant that he had told Wilhelm that, although four years earlier he had rejected the danger of a war with Britain, he "now regarded the situation as serious" and accepted his advice to ship off Tirpitz to justify his ways to Englishmen.[89] By that time Bülow had also reacted to Stumm's report of 8 September 1908 suggesting that the British naval panic demonstrated how powerful a lever the German navy was to extract concessions from Britain in other areas. The negotiations might, however, lead to the defeat of the Liberal administration by a much less conciliatory Unionist Imperialist–Protectionist government. Bülow's marginal comments indicated full appreciation of Stumm's proposals for British concessions in return for German naval reductions.[90] In a meeting of the Eighth Committee of the Bundesrat on 15 November, Bülow stated that Britain had for several years worked on the isolation of Germany because of the expansion of Germany's overseas trade and navy and the activity of the press. He, Bülow, however, had always restrained excessive naval demands. "The future of Germany lay in the strength of the army. It must, above all, be kept strong."[91]

Pressed by Metternich's reports and Holstein's admonitions, Bülow on 30 November 1908 at last told Tirpitz that there existed serious fear of the German navy and talk of a preventive attack on it in Britain, and requested his opinion "whether Germany and the German people could calmly and with confidence envisage an English attack?"[92] Tirpitz's answer of 17 December was negative, since British superiority was too great.[93] He then asserted that the danger of war with Britain had decreased rather than increased with the growth of the German fleet and that "in a few years our fleet would be so strong that an attack on it even by Britain would mean a great military risk." He attributed British hostility to general Anglo-German competition rather than to naval rivalry and mendaciously referred to the reduction of the German building rate after 1911 to two large ships per year (which the Naval Office intended to raise) as having a calming effect. Bülow informed Holstein of his correspondence with Tirpitz and in his minutes subjected Tirpitz's reply to close scrutiny.[94] He juxtaposed Kleinkrieg as an alternative to the battleship school, queried how one could decrease the risk of war in the next few years when, according to Tirpitz, the German navy was still vulnerable, and suggested the stabilization of the building rate of large ships to three from 1909 to 1917 rather than building four such ships from 1909 to 1911 and two from 1912 to 1917. He remarked finally that Tirpitz had not answered the question what the German fleet could currently accomplish in a war against Britain. "On the answer to this question depended the further question whether we would be better protected through coastal forts, mines, submarines, etc., than through the exclusive building of battleships."[95] At last Bülow, who had in 1906 vaguely supported Galster's Kleinkrieg proposals, was seriously questioning the Tirpitz Plan. On 25 December he elaborated on his objections.[96] In particular he pointed to the British concern that through the construction of four large German ships in 1909, 1910, and 1911 Germany would by the end of the last year confront twelve British Dreadnoughts with thirteen. In defense of his proposal to stabilize the building rate he remarked: "Were war to break out none the less in the so-called transition period, two ships of the line would not make much difference."

In his marginal comments Tirpitz denied that the British could any longer retain the two-power standard. More realistically their power ratio against the German fleet would be 3:2 or 16:10. If Germany now gave in to the British, she could never get out of the "danger zone." In his reply to Bülow he accordingly rejected any concessions as an indication of capitulation before British threats and of German humiliation.[97] Like Holstein, who entirely disagreed with him about the navy, he viewed a humiliation as an invitation to further threats, which, when coming from Britain, would further escalate the risk of war. He was now more concerned with prestige and national pride than ever before and used the navy law as a shield against reducing the current tempo of four large ships per year rather than as a means for stabilizing the rate at three such ships per year which he had done earlier. Was he concerned about his position with Wilhelm, responding to the Navy League's anticipated attacks, or just refusing to make any concessions? Or was he really hoping to gain an edge on the British? Admitting that "our situation in the face of England was very serious . . . as [he] had stated for twelve years," he adhered to the view "that the lesser danger of war for us existed in perseverance and that giving in would in spite of the connected humiliation of Germany only increase the danger." Under attack, Tirpitz was now becoming the supporter of an armaments race rather than being the long-term systematic builder. Continuing to stress the importance of battleships, he described the proposed preparations for *Kleinkrieg* as inadequate:

> We can double and triple our torpedo-boat system and submarines, we can spike our entire coast with cannon, but this part of our naval power can in no way have a pacific influence. Without a battle fleet we would be exposed to every insolence [*Unbillness*] on the part of England.

Bülow's response denied that he was prepared to suffer a humiliation through accepting a reduced building rate; it also conceded on the basis of Metternich's report of 29 December that the redistribution of the German naval construction would have little effect on the British attitude toward Germany.[98] Metternich, who was increasingly viewed by Tirpitz as his foe, thus strengthened his case against Bülow. None the less, the latter continued to press the case for *Kleinkrieg*, particularly submarines, and coastal defense to which he thought the Reichstag would gladly divert money from Dreadnoughts. He also wondered if Germany should be receptive to possible proposals for a naval agreement from King Edward and Hardinge during their impending visit to Germany, in view of the concern now expressed in Britain that through accelerated construction Germany would have seventeen instead of the stipulated nine Dreadnoughts in service by 1912. Tirpitz was amenable, provided that the agreement would be mutually advantageous.[99] As for Dreadnoughts, Tirpitz claimed that Germany would at the most have nine in service in the fall of 1911 and thirteen in the fall of 1912. As for the details of an agreement, he proposed that Germany bind herself not to start the construction of more than three capital ships per year, if Britain obligated herself to build no more than four such ships annually over the next ten years. This rate, he claimed, would absolutely deny Germany the 33·3 per cent superiority which would be necessary for a successful naval offensive: this was roughly the superiority which current strategic thinking also expected a successful attacking force to possess.[100] Tirpitz expected that this formula would be acceptable to Britain since in her constructions she had reached the limits of her financial capabilities.

Bülow's minutes to this letter and his response of 27 January 1909 indicated a complete parting of ways with Tirpitz.[101] He considered the 4:3 construction rate as unacceptable to the British since it would not allay their fears. Nor did he think that their economic and financial resources would force them to adhere to such a formula.[102] In his minutes he stated: "If Tirpitz considers this route to be correct, he should go to England to negotiate it."[103] In its place he proposed a naval agreement that might incline Britain to pursue a more friendly policy toward Germany.[104] Expressing his exasperation in the final comment on Tirpitz's letter of 20 January he stated:[105]

> The point of my question to Tirpitz was whether Germany could calmly and securely face an English attack which, indeed, is not probable, but under the circumstances not out of the question. After Tirpitz answered this question outright negatively we had to consider how we could anticipate such a threatening possibility.

In his reply to the State Secretary of the Naval Office, the Chancellor remarked that Metternich and almost everyone with any knowledge about Anglo-German relations regarded German naval armaments as the reason for British hostility. "This is all the less desirable since our western neighbor's desire for revanche has not disappeared altogether and pan-Slav tendencies have continued in Russia."[106] Tirpitz's response of 4 February was blunt: all that Germany could do in a situation as described by Bülow and in face of "the concentration of a much superior English force against our coast" was "to arm according to all our strength."[107] He denied that reductions in German building would wring political concessions from Britain and regarded any British promises of neutrality as meaningless since France and Russia were certain to join Britain if she were to declare war on Germany—the most likely scenario.[108] Tirpitz thus admitted the inaccuracy of his original assumption that the strengthening of Germany's fleet would enhance her alliance value with other powers. According to E. L. Woodward, "Bülow's exasperation with Tirpitz was at its height."[109]

The Foreign Office, rallying behind Bülow, expressed its view that any mention to the British of the 3:4 building ratio would be a provocation of war.[110] It also expected a failed attempt at a naval agreement to lead to a deterioration of Anglo-German relations, which had briefly improved with King Edward's state visit in February.[111] On 3 March, Metternich reported at length about British fears of the German navy:[112]

> For one who, like myself, stands in the middle of the course of events here

[*hiesigen Getriebe*] and maintains relations on all sides, there can be no doubt that the conviction gains more and more ground that Germany intends to challenge the English domination of the sea.

This comment elicited Wilhelm's minute "Madhouse idea . . . Pathological condition." Metternich maintained that, while the British accepted the German navy law they were concerned about accelerated German building which could provide Germany with twenty-one Dreadnoughts in April 1912 instead of the officially scheduled thirteen in February of that year. If authorized to emphasize "that on our side no speeding up of the publicly proclaimed building rate was taking place or was being intended, I shall be able to scatter the fears which have arisen here." He also wanted a specific response from Tirpitz to British estimates of German acceleration. Wilhelm's final comment on the report was: "Poor Metternich! he can neither understand nor stand the fleet!"

On 8 March, Tirpitz communicated his response to this report directly to the Kaiser.[113] He claimed that the ambassador had exaggerated the alarm about the allegedly accelerated German building rate in British political circles, inclusive of the government, although conceding that naval and conservative manipulators had succeeded in creating a panic among the public. His denial that there was any acceleration in German building was communicated to Metternich by Bülow on the following day,[114] but subsequently Tirpitz did admit that contracts for two ships of the 1909 budget were, in fact, issued before they were due.[115] This belated admission, communicated with Bülow's approval to Grey on 19 March, did not contribute to British faith that Germany was adhering to her official building schedule; neither did statements in the German press at the time of the Reichstag debate over German naval appropriations.[116] Tirpitz's and Wilhelm's refusal of mutual inspection of ship constructions, recommended by Metternich and Bülow,[117] did not diminish British suspicions of German intentions. On 29 March the House of Commons, although defeating a Conservative motion of censure, accepted a naval program consisting of four Dreadnoughts to be put into construction immediately and a further four "contingent" capital ships. Widenmann considered this debate to be the apex of the British naval panic.[118]

On 3 April, Tirpitz reported to Wilhelm in the presence of Müller and his General-Adjutant, Hans von Plessen. While calumniating Metternich, he once again suggested a 3:4 ratio in capital ships as a basis for an agreement between Germany and Britain. The Kaiser showed some reluctance to enter into any agreement, partly in view of the building programs of Russia and France. Tirpitz replied "that the lead which our fleet has gained over both these other fleets . . . was already so great that we could never be caught up by these navies, and our fleet could hold its own against the Russo-French coalition plus Italy."[119] Subsequently Tirpitz had a hostile interview with Bülow.[120] After some mutual recrimination concerning Tirpitz's intransigence and Metternich's incompetence, Bülow turned to what he considered the central issue:

that the Germans were building for themselves a large fleet and from this resulted a conflict with England. He could no longer take the responsibility . . . we would now throughout the world have England as an enemy . . . [who] would use the first opportunity to attack us with other powers. It could be after two years, as soon as the reorganization of the Russian army was completed.

The Secretary of State countered with his old arguments. Wilhelm supported his naval architect and linked the 3:4 ratio to the withdrawal of Metternich's alleged promise that there would be no new German navy law in 1912.[121]

Bülow, who had departed for Venice, rejected Tirpitz's formula, as modified by the Kaiser;[122] he may have been in possession of the note that Holstein had scribbled on his deathbed, pointing out that his success in the Bosnian question was "a trifle compared to what you will gain for His Majesty if you will simultaneously obtain for the German people the security of property at sea and a détente with England, that is, a firm peace."[123] By 17 April, Tirpitz himself had come to doubt whether the 3:4 ratio, which was a possibility in the fall and early winter, was any longer appropriate.[124] But he denied that there was much risk of a British preventive attack and claimed that during the four years required to build the eight recently approved British Dreadnoughts "our total war capacity increases greatly. We shall then have what we now lack: reserve in *matériel* which will for the first time put to full use our reserve in manpower."[125] While in Venice, Bülow on 14 April discussed his concerns about the consequences of an Anglo-German naval race with Müller, Plessen, and the Chief of the Emperor's Civil Cabinet, Rudolf von Valentini. He was particularly worried that annoyance with Germany might bring the Conservatives to power in Britain, who would be more likely than the Liberals to go to war with Germany. This concern was shared by Valentini. Germany should therefore make concessions to the Liberals to keep them in power. Assuring Tirpitz that he had defended his position, Müller informed the Secretary of State that the Chancellor repeatedly expressed his fear to the Emperor about being able to preserve the peace and raised the question: "When shall we be at the point when we can beat the English?" Müller viewed Wilhelm as under-estimating the dangers of war with the island state just as much as Bülow overestimated them. Perhaps privately alluding to Tirpitz's misrepresenta-tions of the danger zone, he remarked that the Kaiser "believes, for instance, that the strength of the existing fleet already prevents the British from taking decisive steps and that we would be much closer to a war if we did not have the fleet." To provide the Kaiser with a more realistic assessment of the risks of war, he had arranged that the Admiralty Staff provide him with a memorandum concerning the expected situation in a war of Germany allied with Austria-Hungary against Britain, which the Chancellor considered probable.[126] The various influences brought to bear on the Kaiser in Venice appear to have had a moderating effect. Bülow noted on 17 April that Wilhelm had no wish to rival or surpass the British navy, expected the relationship between the two navies to remain what it currently was, did not regard Britain as Germany's major naval opponent, and considered a naval agreement with her possible within a context involving promises of neutrality and colonial understandings.[127] Several texts of a broader agreement were subsequently drafted.

On 3 June 1909 a high-level meeting took place in the Chancellor's residence to discuss an agreement with Britain. Bülow presided; present were Theobald von Bethmann-Hollweg, Vice-Chancellor and State Secretary for the Interior, Tirpitz, Moltke, Müller, Metternich and Schoen.[128] Bülow voiced all of his previously expressed concerns. Diplomatic means were no longer adequate to calm down Britain. The question of naval rivalry could perhaps be resolved through the mutual reduction of the construction rate, best linked, as Wilhelm was earlier reported as saying, to other issues. "Our relations with England were the only dark cloud on the horizon." Metternich attributed British hostility solely to the German fleet policy. Moltke pointed out "that we had no chance whatsoever of fighting a war with Britain with any success. An honorable understanding, perhaps on the basis of a slowing down of the building tempo, also appeared desirable to him. Thereby one should not conceal that the failure of attempts to seek an understanding could mean war." He is also reported to have remarked that in order to use the army in a war against England he would have to request the Kaiser to start a war with France.[129] The hostage theory thus continued to be upheld by the General Staff. Metternich and Bethmann-Hollweg also supported the slowing down of the building rate. Tirpitz, backed by Müller, agreed to sign the protocol only if his version of his comments was included, according to which he was obviously and obstinately on the defensive. He denied that he opposed a naval agreement with Britain. He refused to extend the terminal date of the navy law from 1920 to 1925, as allegedly advocated by Metternich: the extension would cost Germany fifteen capital ships and scuttle the entire fleet program. On the other hand, a reduction of the building rate from four to three capital ships was possible for the next two years. All participants agreed that such an agreement would have to involve concessions on Britain's part. Tirpitz assured:

*In his opinion the danger zone in our relationship with England would be overcome in five to six years, thus approximately by 1915, after the enlargement of the Kaiser Wilhelm Canal and the preparation of the Heligoland position.* Already in two years they [sic!] will be considerably less.

To Bülow's question, "This is very nice. But the question is once again: how do we get over the current danger?", he replied that this was possible through an agreement on the basis of a 3:4 ratio. To Bülow's request that he draft a formula for the agreement Tirpitz responded with a refusal: it could lead to misunderstandings and should only follow British initiatives. Soon after this discussion Bülow was forced to resign, having failed to disentangle himself from the Tirpitz Plan which had brought him to power.[130]

**V**

The Tirpitz–Bülow rift coincided with the Bosnian crisis. Moltke,
Holstein, Bülow, and Wilhelm had recognized the need to support
Austria-Hungary as Germany's only reliable ally. Holstein had perhaps
most clearly realized the need to slap Russia on the wrist and to use naval
concessions to buy off the British who were pushing Russia forward and
sought to complete the encirclement of Germany.[131] When, without prior
consultation with Germany, Austria-Hungary concluded the Buchlau
Bargain with Russia which involved her annexation of Bosnia-Herzegovina,
Wilhelm and Marschall, the ambassador in Constantinople, were greatly
annoyed by the adverse effect this action would have on Germany's
influence in Turkey.[132] Bülow, however, was relieved "that the clouds that
had gathered over the [English] Channel had been swept east . . . We would
then not have to worry that all powers would turn against us."[133] He did not
think that the annexation would have serious consequences: after her defeat
by Japan and domestic revolts, Russia did not want war; France did not want
to fight, either, especially because of the Balkans; and Britain "would be
little inclined to fire a cannon shot, particularly over oriental questions."[134]
What was probably Bülow's and the German leadership's most important
motive:[135]

> In the existing world situation we must preserve a loyal ally in
> Austria-Hungary, all the more so as the Viennese Cabinet has in recent
> years repeatedly demonstrated its loyalty as an ally, partly without
> consideration for its own interests.

The internal conditions of this ally, however, were described by Tschirschky
on 1 December 1908 as "wretched" (*trostlos*).[136]

The German leadership maintained its stance throughout the Bosnian
crisis with fair consistency.[137] Only on 30 November 1908 did Bülow
suggest that Austria-Hungary establish closer contact with Bulgaria since,
contrary to rational assumptions, the Russian government might because of
its weakness, pan-Slav agitation, and British intrigues become militarily
involved on behalf of the Balkan Slavs.[138]

As of February 1908 the Prussian General Staff had started providing the
Chancellor with periodic assessments of the military strength of the
European powers.[139] In its first assessment it stated that the imminence of
war with Germany during the Morocco crisis had caused the French to
extend universal military service to the utmost on the basis of the two-year
service period through the law of 1907. This, however, had reduced the
strength of the French standing army by 35,000 men. Because of the low
French birth rate 39 million French people confronted 60 million Germans.

> That the French have nevertheless succeeded in keeping up with
> Germany in the strength of the standing army is explained through their
> drafting of approximately 80 per cent (as compared to Germany's 54
> per cent) of their annual levies of men liable for military service.

Bülow commented that this should be emphasized in the German press to counter the charge of militarism that was more often levelled against Germany than against France. The memorandum further pointed out that France could also draw on her North African troops, which would in the next years make her standing army almost equal to the German. Nor were French reserves inferior to the German in numbers. If German troops would have to be used against Russia and French troops would not have to be used against Italy, French forces on their eastern front would be stronger than the German. Also the current German superiority in artillery would be cancelled out by the French reforms of this year. Neither was Germany superior to France in war preparedness and mobilization arrangements. "Thus [France] made enormous efforts and readily assumed the greatest sacrifices in order not to remain behind Germany in her military capacity." In line with his interest in strengthening the German army, Bülow at this point commented: "Also this must penetrate German consciousness more deeply." As for France, the General Staff memorandum concluded that the state of her army would discourage her leadership from seeking war with Germany at this time. In view of the utmost strain on her military resources, a quick defeat would, unlike 1870–71, preclude France from continuing the war. This statement earned a marginal line from Bülow and the comments "NB" and "if Germany knows how to utilize this superiority."

The General Staff overestimated the strength of the British Expeditionary Force as consisting of 160,000 officers and men, as being better equipped with technical auxiliary means than any Continental army, and as capable of appearing in Dunkirk, Calais, or Antwerp on the thirteenth mobilization day. In addition several divisions of the 300,000-man territorial army could be used on the Continent. "During the entire course of her history, England has never been as strong militarily as now." The General Staff expected that in case of a Franco-German conflict "the English army would stand in the field against us on the side of the French." With reference to the hostage theory, a British presence on the Continent was welcomed as offering Germany the only opportunity of settling accounts with the island state. A struggle with France allied to Britain was not to be feared. "The situation would only become difficult if Russia would also join our enemies." (Bülow added his NB) For Russia was now capable of deploying fifty-six infantry divisions against Germany and Austria-Hungary, as compared to forty-eight in the summer of 1906; her military efficiency had improved and new strategic railways would speed up her deployment by three days. Although it would be in Russia's interest to avoid war until her army was completely reorganized, it was difficult to estimate how internal developments, particularly revolutionary forces, would affect her decision to become involved in a war earlier. According to a paragraph which Bülow marked with three lines in the margin:

> Considered from a purely military viewpoint, the state of her army, though still unprepared, does not compel Russia to remain inactive in a war of the Western Powers against Germany.

The Austro-Hungarian army was not underestimated; its numbers were considerable and its morale was as yet unaffected by national strife. Since the Mürzsteg Agreement, however, the Austro-Hungarian war plans were directed against Italy rather than against Russia.

In spite of Austria-Hungary's undoubted loyalty to the alliance, it therefore appears questionable whether Germany could in all circumstances count on the active support of the Austro-Hungarian army. The military measures of the allied *Kaiserstaat* will basically be determined by Italy's stance.

This comment elicited another of Bülow's NBs. On the other hand, Italy's military efficiency was rated considerably below Austria-Hungary's. Bülow gave his now common annotation to a paragraph stating:

Understandably Italy, aware of her military weakness, is concerned about her stronger neighbors and allies, and apprehensive concerning her long unprotected coast before which waves the flag of a navally superior England.

A further report about the capacity of European powers was forwarded to Bülow by Moltke on 29 January 1909.[140] Unlike its predecessor it dealt first with the military capacity of Austria-Hungary, undoubtedly because of the Bosnian crisis and the support that Moltke, with the approval of Wilhelm and Bülow, had agreed to provide if Russia should intervene in a struggle between her and Serbia.[141]

On 14 December 1908, Bülow had insisted that Germany must support the Dual Monarchy if it were to hold through the existing crisis; she was to be encouraged to concentrate her entire army against Russia rather than diverting it against Italy. He claimed to have the support of Holstein, Kiderlen, Jagow, and Moltke. The Chief of Staff was encouraged to establish contact with his Austro-Hungarian counterpart. In the course of the ensuing discussions it was agreed to view Italy as a neutral, not as an ally,[142] to assure Austria-Hungary of German support against Russia in the event of her action against Serbia, although Moltke warned Franz Conrad von Hötzendorf on 21 January 1909 that the bulk of German forces would have to be concentrated against France, who would not remain neutral in a war involving Russia. Confident of victory against France, Moltke basically stated that the war would be decided on the western front. Like Bülow, Moltke did not believe that the current crisis would lead to war.[143]

In his report to Bülow,[144] Moltke expressed dissatisfaction with the military preparations of the Dual Monarchy. He welcomed the improved relations with Italy, stressed the tension with Russia, and pointed to the preparations undertaken against Serbia and Montenegro. In a war against the latter states he expected Austria-Hungary to reserve troops for possible action against Russia and for the maintenance of order in Czech-inhabited territories. But "*if it avoided the splitting of its forces simultaneously against Italy and Russia the Kaiserstaat would have enough troops available if it* engaged four army corps against Serbia in order successfully to counter a Russian attack. But this [was the case] only under the assumption of simultaneously effective German help." Bülow remarked to the underlined part of the report: "It therefore comes to it that Austria does not commit the stupidity of setting up more than the minimal forces [*Allernothwendigste*] against Italy . . ." He further minuted: "Also against Serbia and Montenegro Austria would do well not to engage too many troops. Russia is the decisive point." Both Moltke and Bülow expressed concern that Austria-Hungary avoid guerilla warfare in Serbian territory that might spread to Bosnia and Herzegovina.

Italy's military capacity received no higher estimate than in the previous year. The assessment of French military power was less favorable. The numerical strength of the standing army would be maintained by drawing increasingly on inferior manpower and the staffs of individual units were too small to provide recruits with adequate training. "Gradually . . . the decrease of the annual levies [now involving 90 percent of eligible manpower] will bring about a shift in favor of Germany. Above all, to achieve her military strength France has placed the last man who could be found in the field . . ." Bülow remarked "NB" and expressed his regret at France's lead over Germany in machine-guns, noted in the report. Mention was also made of the introduction of a new rifle in three years and of improvements in field-artillery. Prevailing anti-militaristic sentiments were expected to be overcome by patriotism in wartime and—Bülow agreed—inferior training and discipline could be surpassed by good leadership, which, however, was held to be inferior to the German. The conclusion drawn about French military strength was the following: "The advantages of the army are countered by considerable weaknesses. War against it can be waged with full confidence." It elicited three lines in the margin and another NB from Bülow.

As for Britain, the Haldane reforms were considered to be incomplete regarding the reserves. As before, the BEF was regarded as ready for action. Britain's real strength lay in the navy, which was concentrated in the North Sea to the neglect of her world interests. "In England it has surely been realized that the current situation cannot continue for long if British prestige is not to suffer heavy damage in remote regions." To this passage Bülow commented: "In this lies the danger of an English preventive war. *Vide* my correspondence with Tirpitz." The General Staff memorandum continued:

> Without question it must be most desirable for England if a feared Germany would be weakened in a general European war or thrown to the ground without the involvement of English armed forces.

Bülow minuted: "Very correct."

Russia was considered to be militarily weaker than in the previous year's assessment. Her army was still in the process of reorganization and she could send only fifty-four divisions against Germany and Austria-Hungary as compared to fifty-six in 1908: "the great burdens which Russia has to bear to secure the regions held by her in East Asia . . . are a further reason for her effort to maintain peace." A lengthy military–political report about Russia was penned by the military plenipotentiary in St Petersburg, Kapitän-zur-See Paul von Hintze, on 9 December 1908.[145] It gave high ratings to the stolidity of the Russian common soldier; both the army and navy had recently experienced war, which provided them with initial advantages. The military wanted no war, concentrated on reforms, but now expected hostilities to break out in February.

> Is war probable? According to considerations based on reason, no. But reason does frequently not have the last word. Temporarily it prevails; passions of so-called public opinion have calmed down considerably.
> Should Austria and Germany be fearful of war? If the interests of both states must lead to a war with Russia, then war is to be *better waged today* than later since Russia is completing her armaments.

Hintze could thus be identified as a member of the German war party mentioned by Fritz Fischer.

In his memorandum of 29 January 1909, Moltke deemed the capacity of the Belgian and Dutch forces inferior to that of the German reserve troops. The two memoranda from Moltke to Bülow indicate a much closer cooperation between the political and army leadership than had existed before. Bülow considered the information provided by Moltke's latest memorandum as "very important and valuable."[146]

With tension mounting in the east, the German leadership avoided using the Casablanca incident, involving conflict between German and French officials over the desertion of some German and Austro-Hungarian nationals from the French Foreign Legion, to confront France or to test the Entente Cordiale; rather, both Bülow and Wilhelm wished to extricate Germany from the affair.[147] It was the Bosnian crisis which was to be used to break the "ring of encirclement" around Germany. On 1 January 1909, Wilhelm, in delivering an address to the German generals, subscribed to Schlieffen's recently expressed views according to which Franco-German, Slavo-German, and Austro-Italian tensions contributed to the danger of a concentric attack on Germany and Austria-Hungary at a time that the former power had concentrated in the west and the latter in the Balkans.[148] In refusing to go along with French and Italian mediation proposals, Bülow, as he stated on 6 February 1909, intended not only to stand by Austria-Hungary, but also to force the French to counsel moderation in St Petersburg. "If we wait calmly, France must act on her own and thus the ring of encirclement, which has for some time become brittle, will be broken."[149] It was the Franco-Russian alliance which was to be broken. Wilhelm saw French counsels of moderation in St Petersburg as angering Izwolsky and cooling the friendship of the two powers.[150]

On 24 February, Hintze sent a lengthy dispatch to Wilhelm in which he refuted all reports that Russia would at this time go to war even if Serbia were invaded by Austria-Hungary, provided that it was clear that this war would also involve Germany. None the less, Russia had resumed her traditional European policy: control over the Straits, rule over the Balkan peninsula, and domination over the Slav world. For the implementation of this policy she expected to be militarily prepared in three to five years. The report caused Wilhelm to comment: "therefore in the future, collision with European culture and the Germanic world. Therefore union [*Zusammenschluss*] of the Teutons and Anglo-Saxons, and possibly the Gauls;" and "by then we must come to a trustworthy, clear relationship with France."[151] Bülow must have been impressed by the report, for on 2 March he instructed that an excerpt be taken from it.[152]

Whether or not Wilhelm had read Hintze's report by the time he commented on Tschirschky's report of 24 February 1909, in clear contradiction to his above views, is not certain. He now stated that "in view of the seriousness of the situation" Germany must request France to join her in making Russia understand that a Russo-Austrian war would involve Germany, and lead to her mobilization. In addition France must issue a binding promise to refrain from entering this war on Russia's side: a refusal to make such a declaration was to be regarded as a *casus belli*. He maintained that this action was necessary "so that we first utilize our mobilization against France and finish her off . . . We must engage everything toward the west or toward the east . . ." Wilhelm added that Moltke was in agreement with him.[153]

It is significant that in these calculations involving a Continental war Britain, with whom German relations had reached an all-time low, was hardly considered.

With the strong encouragement of Kiderlen and Holstein, Bülow on 14 March, issued his warning to St Petersburg according to which Germany would allow matters to take their course unless Russia restrained Serbian hostility toward Austria-Hungary.[154] On the previous day Hintze had reported from the Russian capital that Russia had definitely decided against going to war for the time being.[155] This report was probably not yet available to Bülow. The Russian reply was unsatisfactory to the Wilhelmstrasse and led it, provided with further evidence that Russia would not interfere in an Austro-Serbian war,[156] to the dispatch of the so-called "German ultimatum," forwarded by Bülow to Pourtalès on 21 March 1909.[157] There is variation of opinion about how close this action came to the issue of an ultimatum. Agreement exists only on the fact that in the opinion of the German decisionmakers the Russians were expected to give in. Fritz Fischer, not unexpectedly, considers it to be an ultimatum and refers to a German war party favoring the crushing of France and Russia.[158] Bernadotte Schmitt views the action as just falling "short of a definite ultimatum."[159] Luigi Albertini regards it as an ultimatum in a substantive if not in a literal sense.[160] Dwight Lee is cautious about making a pronouncement, but regards the Bosnian crisis as "a dress rehearsal for that of July 1914" and claims that the "resulting rift between Russia and the Central Powers remained unclosed."[161] According to him, it also "confirmed and deepened British conviction that Germany was pursuing an aggressive policy," particularly as it coincided with a more intense naval rivalry.[162] Paul Kennedy views it as "sabre-rattling with a vengeance."[163]

Russia backed down. The German government tried to follow up on its apparent victory. The press was instructed not to humiliate Russia and efforts were made to enter into an alliance with her as long as its obligations did not conflict with those to Austria: in short, an attempt was made to reconstruct the old Three Emperors' League.[164] Information about changes in Russian military planning also reduced its threat for a while and could have given the German military leadership cause to act more provocatively toward France so as to implement the Schlieffen Plan.

Notice of changing Russian deployment was first served by the German military attaché in St Petersburg, Count Posadowsky-Wehner, on 6 May 1909, when he reported the prospective withdrawal of Russian troops from Poland to avoid being trapped by an Austro-German pincer movement from Galicia and East Prussia. This action, in his opinion, would greatly lessen Russia's value as France's ally.[165] Following a preliminary discussion, on 29 May, Moltke provided Bülow with a detailed report about the eastward deployment of the Russian forces.[166] He pointed out that the Russian units located in Poland were too distant from their reserve districts and that the terrible living conditions in Polish villages served as a deterrent to the recruitment of officers. Concurring with Posadowsky-Wehner's assessment of the risks of deployment in Poland in the event of a war against Germany and Austria-Hungary, he considered that it constituted an offensive deployment against Germany which was only tenable if the German forces in the east were too weak to launch an offensive, i.e. that the German bulk would be engaged against France. But the Bosnian crisis had just shown that France might well leave Russia in the lurch. The possibility of British noninvolvement in an eastern war would also enable the German navy to undertake landing operations in the Gulfs of Finland and Riga. Being partly the result of the weakening of the Franco-Russian alliance, the withdrawal of the Russian troops from Poland would also cause its further disintegration. Moltke expected the new Russian deployment to occur along the Kovno–Grodno–Bialistok–Brest–Litovsk–Dubno–Proskurov line and to be of a defensive nature. If the Russians proceeded from it to the offensive, "then there must be intimidation [*abschrecken*] against both Prussia and Galicia, and thus a separation of the central army group. Once arranged, this deployment could not be changed if war breaks out, even if the political situation were more favorable to Russia," i.e. Germany deployed her main forces against France and left a minimum strength to face Russia. Both Wilhelm and Bülow instructed that the Russian dislocations not be discussed in the German press and Wilhelm remarked on Posadowsky-Wehner's report that the Russians must always be told:

(1) that we want nothing from them; and (2) that we have an interest in the preservation of Czardom; also (3) [we] skillfully hint at the military weakness and social break-up of France.[167]

Germany's thrust to break the Dual Alliance obviously continued. The expected Russian redeployment would have offered Germany the opportunity for the execution of the Schlieffen Plan in the west.

As for Italy, the Germans realized that the Bosnian crisis had brought about a further deterioration of her relations with Austria-Hungary.[168]

## VI

Having permitted Germany's relations with Britain to reach an all-time low, having allowed the tightening of the Entente Cordiale, having failed to gain Russia as an ally, having witnessed her conclude an entente with Britain, having issued her with a quasi-ultimatum, and having tied Germany more closely to the faltering Habsburg Empire, Bülow tendered his resignation in Kiel on 26 June 1909. He claims at this time to have provided Wilhelm with two pieces of advice: obtaining a naval agreement with Britain and avoiding repetition of "the Bosnian action" since future dangers lay in the Balkans.[169] On 14 July he was succeeded by Bethmann-Hollweg, a highly educated and successful bureaucrat,[170] who, however, knew little about foreign policy.[171] In his initial briefing by the Foreign Office, British policy was described as "unfriendly toward us and opposing us everywhere in the world," because of the construction of the German fleet.[172] With the later support of Alfred von Kiderlen-Wächter, whom in spite of Wilhelm's hostility he managed to appoint Secretary of State of the Foreign Office in June 1910, he attempted to seek the naval–political understanding with Britain that had eluded his predecessor. He very soon formalized the unofficial conversations between the Director of the Hamburg–America Line, Albert Ballin, and the British banker Sir Ernest Cassell.[173] Not wanting to complicate the naval agreement through any colonial understandings, Bethmann more importantly wanted to link it to "an explicit assurance . . . that the alliances and ententes concluded by England would not be directed against us." As interpreted by Schoen: "Thereby we in no way request from England a renunciation of her friends."[174] This formula was subsequently defined by the Chancellor as a British assurance of neutrality if Germany were attacked by France and/or Russia or if she supported Austria-Hungary if attacked by Russia.[175]

Tirpitz wrote to his friend Eisendecher that "We shall do everything to come to a tolerable relationship with [the British] and I believe that it will go better with Bethmann than with Bülow."[176] His formula for an agreement was now a construction ratio of 1:1·45 in capital ships from 1910 to 1914, involving the reduction of the German rate for 1910 from four to three and that for 1911 from four to two capital ships. Schoen thought that this formula might be acceptable to the British.[177] Tirpitz expected the British, in turn, to postpone the four "contingent Dreadnoughts" of 1909 to 1910. When he subsequently tried to improve the construction rate in Germany's favor, Bethmann objected.[178] In view of the impending British elections, the German political leadership decided against pushing the agreement too hard.[179] As during the later Haldane mission, British reservations concerned chiefly the neutrality agreement.[180]

At the end of September 1909, Kiderlen worked out an alternative strategy for the conclusion of a naval agreement.[181] Just as had Holstein, with whom he had collaborated during the Bosnian crisis, he considered the improvement of relations with Britain as the key to strengthening Germany's Continental position: it would be attractive to Austria-Hungary and Italy, and force Russia to draw closer to her. A hostile Britain, on the other hand, would oppose Germany anywhere and join her enemies in any future war. Contrary to Bethmann, Kiderlen advocated a gradual and cautious approach to the island state, generating friendly exchanges, welcoming initiatives rather than making specific proposals, and informing it at an appropriate time that "we would not link an arms understanding with a political agreement, but that the more comprehensive the political agreement, the more cooperative we should be in the arms question."[182] Kiderlen's ideas influenced the conversation which Bethmann and Schoen had with the British ambassador, Sir Edward Goschen, on 14 October.[183] Metternich, none the less, expressed doubts whether German naval concessions, which he considered crucial to any understanding with Britain, were sufficient to secure a neutrality agreement with her.[184] He did, however, agree that such an agreement was the minimum that Germany should gain in return for the reduction of her naval armaments.[185]

The outcome of the British elections in January 1910 caused Bethmann to doubt whether in view of "the need of an overwhelming British naval power, emphasized on all sides," the precarious position of the Liberal administration, and the attitude of the Conservative leadership a naval agreement was attainable, and, as before the elections, advised Metternich to take a delaying stance.[186] The ambassador concurred, denying that either the shortage of manpower, which was merely a financial matter that would now be solved, or the capacity of British shipyards would serve as limits to British ship construction. Psychologically the British were not in the least prepared to give in to the Germans on the naval issue. An agreement on the basis of a 4:3 ratio, as earlier suggested by Tirpitz, would be totally unacceptable.[187] On 11 March he informed Bethmann that the British fleet program for 1910 comprised the construction of five new capital ships: the four "contingent ships" were built under the 1909 program.[188] This cancelled Tirpitz's formula for an agreement. There was a lull in Anglo-German negotiations until August when Bethmann interpreted various British actions as indicating

> The English place no value on an agreement with us, adhere to the entente policy which allegedly serves to maintain the balance of power but actually amounts to a limitation of German power. This is so basic to their foreign policy that the English government cannot be induced to give it up even by the most extensive concessions in the area of our maritime armaments.[189]

A few days after this skeptical assessment of the situation, Bethmann was presented with a memorandum by Goschen which suggested various parts of a naval agreement.[190] The part that was successfully negotiated before the Agadir crisis dealt with the exchange of information regarding constructions.

Wilhelm now welcomed an agreement, insisting, however, that its political part be concluded first.

Tirpitz's attitude toward Britain improved when Arthur Wilson replaced Fisher as First Sea Lord and with the activity of John Jellicoe. According to him: "The salutary tone of the new gentlemen in the Admiralty extended to the new naval attaché in Berlin, Captain Watson."[191] As for Goschen's proposals, he favored dockyard visits by the naval attachés of the two countries and was prepared to bind Germany to start the construction of no more than two capital ships per year from 1912 to 1917 if Britain limited herself to three.[192] On 24 October he proposed a 2:3 ratio in capital ships between Germany and Britain as appropriate; the ratio of 3:4 was unattainable and that of 1:2 would negate the entire German shipbuilding program by not presenting a sufficient risk to Britain in a war against Germany.

> Not now, but when implemented, our current fleet law with sixty capital ships of 25,000 tons probably corresponds to the 2:3 relationship. England will hardly be able to afford more than ninety capital ships.[193]

At the end of July, the Württemberg representative in Berlin wondered if the increase of the German navy might incline Wilhelm to use it to solve internal difficulties by resorting to war:

> In the years 1912–15—so someone . . . who to a great degree knows the ideas of Admiral Tirpitz told me—the power relationship of our navy to the British will be more favorable than ever before, and more favorable than in the foreseeable future. Our fleet will then amount to two-thirds of the British. Thus the moment will have come in which an active foreign policy is again possible and therefore appropriate. The re-established [*neugefestigte*] Secretary of State of the RMA [Imperial Naval Office] considers the next years as plainly decisive, as "historical." The leader of fate of the Empire will now have, beside the always well-ordered army, at last a second sword—one that is somewhat short but sharp—the Dreadnoughts.[194]

This statement about the fleet may be taken as its justification to German governments and politicians; on the other hand, it also fits in with Tirpitz's apparent effort to benefit in the short run from the Dreadnought race.

By the time that the Agadir crisis had led to a further deterioration of Anglo-German relations, both Tirpitz and Wilhelm were having second thoughts about a 3:2 building rate, fearful that it would bind Germany after 1911 to the construction of two capital ships per year, which would preclude the introduction of another navy bill, stabilizing the building rate at three capital ships per year.[195] For, as P. Kelly states, "It was clear that Tirpitz had in mind a novelle as early as 1908."[196] As he told Bethmann on 4 May 1911, the 2:3 rate would not only prevent the escalation of the building rate of capital ships in the period 1912–17, but also make difficult its rise after 1917: thus the navy law would be changed by the reduction of the final size of the German fleet from sixty to forty capital ships. According to Tirpitz's notes, Bethmann concurred.[197] Müller also insisted that Germany not be bound to the construction of two capital ships per year beyond 1917, but advised that the Kaiser not turn down British proposals for an agreement altogether.[198]

At this time Bethmann found it difficult to understand why Britain could not enter into a neutrality agreement with Germany. He envisaged Anglo-German hostilities only if Germany "should become involved in a war with Russia and France and England would actively take the side of our enemy." He pointed out that the possibility of war with Russia had been postponed indefinitely since the Potsdam Agreement, and that France, even if certain of Russian support, would only attack Germany if assured of British assistance.[199] Britain was obviously the key to Bethmann's foreign policy until the Agadir crisis—and perhaps beyond.


## VII

As for Russia, there were reports in the fall of 1909 about lack of hostility toward Germany which were not taken very seriously by the German leadership, particularly Wilhelm.[200] Alarm was expressed about the agreement between her and Italy at Racconigi on 24 October 1909, the first clause of which stipulated the preservation of the *status quo* in the Balkans and the second assured support for the national development of the states in the area. The second article, Wilhelm noted, presupposed the destruction of the first.[201] He envisaged the agreement as aiming at the formation of a Balkan alliance, the liquidation of Turkey in Europe, and the containment of Austria-Hungary.[202]. There was additional concern about an article by Prince Sviatopolsk-Mirski, published in the otherwise not anti-German *St Peterburskaia Viedomost*, about an inevitable war between Russia and Germany.[203]

The Dual Alliance, however, continued to be regarded as weakened by Russian troop dislocations and by the dissatisfaction of the military establishments of the two countries with each other's preparations.[204] Hintze pointed to the magnitude of the reorganization of the Russian army, including the removal of the troops from Poland, which was bound to paralyze its mobilization. He wrote on 19 January 1910 that "for the foreseeable period one must still count on the old deployment and the old mobilization of the Russian army, both slowed down and impaired through transitionary measures."[205] The military attaché in Paris commented soon thereafter that he had reported several times that the new dislocation of Russian troops reduced their offensive capacity and thus diminished the value of the alliance,[206] and subsequently reported French press comments on the subject.[207] And Posadowsky-Wehner reported a few days later that, in spite of French pressure to prevent Russian troop withdrawals, "I do not believe that the Russians will yield in principle. But perhaps some compromise can be found."[208] In an exchange of opinions resulting from Hintze's report about his conversations with the Russian commander in the Japanese war, Kuropatkin, according to which Russia, with Britain's aid, was suspected of seeking an understanding with Austria-Hungary in disregard of Germany, the military plenipotentiary suggested that Germany should be made to appear as Russia's most dangerous enemy.[209] Obviously, it was better to be feared than loved. Hintze's stand was supported by Wilhelm[210] and criticized by Pourtalès, Stumm, Tschirschky, and Bethmann.[211] Although Hintze followed Kuropatkin's view that Russia was militarily weak, he maintained that the Russian population was psychologically prepared for a war with Germany. The troop dislocations were undertaken for this eventuality: troops were removed from Poland so as to avoid a Sedan-type defeat and two army corps were established in Finland to prevent German landings on the Russian coast. Russia was thus fearful of German naval might. The Russians, however, envisaged war with Germany for the future, not for the present.[212] In August 1910, Berlin received a report of Posadowsky-Wehner about Russian maneuvers for the publicly announced case "Germany and Sweden are in a war against Russia."[213] This announcement was regarded as an indication of growing Russian hostility toward Germany. Wilhelm commented: "Will my ministers at last believe that Russia is up to something and we must build up our armaments!!?" and that "Political entente with England is therefore the correct political answer"[214]—an amazing statement in view of his often-voiced objections to such an agreement.

On 19 August, Hintze used these explicitly anti-German maneuvers as further evidence for his thesis that Russia was arming against Germany, driven by the French alliance and the British entente, with her public opinion stirred up by the government and the army prepared by its leadership. Wilhelm's excitement mounted further. In a rare disagreement with Hintze, he also considered Nicholas an enemy. His final comment was: "I think that this material will suffice for the Chancellor and the Minister of War"[215]—possibly to increase German armaments, possibly to undertake a preventive war against Russia. Wilhelm's general-adjutant, Plessen, however, considered Hintze's report as too alarmist and warned him to change his tone.[216] On 15 September, Bethmann reported to the Emperor that Izvolsky's impending exchange of the Foreign Ministry for an embassy would improve Austro-Russian relations; whether it would also lead to better Russo-German relations was questionable. If it failed to do so, Austria-Hungary might take a more independent line from Germany.[217] Soon afterwards Pourtalès reported a conversation with Izwolsky's successor, Sergei Sazonov, describing him as motivated "by ardent patriotism, bordering on chauvinism." Wilhelm minuted this report by expressing his doubts about the success of a visit with Nicholas and complaining of massive Russian agitation against Germany. Referring to Hintze's report of 19 August as hitting the nail on the head, he remarked: "Those fellows only want to calm us since they *are* not yet ready, *voilà tout*."[218] In October, Moltke expressed the view to an Austrian Captain Putz that the Balkans would be the starting-point for a war; the question was whether it would be started by Russia or Britain. He also assured the Austrian that Germany was prepared for a great offensive against Russia, although it was unlikely that France would remain uninvolved in a war with her and the deployment of the Russian forces further in the interior presented difficulties for an Austro-German offensive which did not appear in the case of France or Italy.[219]

In spite of all apprehensions, Germany welcomed Sazonov's initiatives for political discussions during the Czar's visit to Potsdam.[220] In the discussions the Germans agreed to mediate between Russia and Austria-Hungary, not to support Austrian expansion into the Balkans or Turkish aggression, and to recognize the Russian sphere of influence in Persia as defined by the Anglo-Russian entente. Sazonov agreed to uphold "the sick man of Europe" and not to oppose the extension of the Berlin-to-Bagdad railway.[221] Subsequently Bethmann submitted the written text of the agreement to Pourtalès, including also a declaration on the part of the Russian government refusing to support a British policy hostile to Germany.[222] He described as the essence of the Potsdam interview: "it was again confirmed that both governments will not enter into any agreements which have an aggressive aim against the other."[223] While the Russians refused to publish the agreement, thus diminishing its value and causing Kiderlen to remark that it was tantamount to a customer requesting a prostitute not to greet him in public, Bethmann none the less declared in the Reichstag that the two governments "would not enter into any combinations which could have an aggressive aim against the other."[224] Hintze's alarmist reports from St Petersburg ceased, as he was removed from his position because of them,[225] but Pourtalès remarked in February 1911 that Germany was not gaining friends among the Russians, who saw an improved relationship with her as a necessity and not a choice.[226]

One of the reasons for the attempt of the German leadership to improve relations with Russia had been to avoid excessive dependence on Austria-Hungary. Both Wilhelm and Bethmann-Hollweg were afraid that, if Germany's relations with Russia were worse than Austria-Hungary's, the latter might aspire to the leadership of the Triple Alliance or remain neutral if the first Russian attack were directed against Germany.[227] Aehrenthal realized that the Potsdam agreement had ended Germany's *Niebelungstreue*.[228] Since Bülow's resignation, German reporting about the internal conditions of the Dual Monarchy had become somewhat less negative.[229] There was some concern about the political decline of the German element in the face of the Slavs.[230] Tschirschky expected, however, that the Slavs and Hungarians could be persuaded to support the German alliance.[231] Late in 1910 he, in fact, stated that this alliance was accepted by all parties, including the Slavic, in Cisleithania.[232] But there was some concern about Anglo-French activity to detach Austria-Hungary from Germany.[233]

There were also indications of greater Italian loyalty to the Triple Alliance. True, at the end of 1909 Wilhelm wrote "lies . . . words"[234] on Bethmann's report of the Italian ambassador's comment that his government sought closer relations with Germany and Austria-Hungary, but the Germans saw some improvement in Italy's attitude toward her allies when Antonino Marquis di San Giuliano became Foreign Minister.[235] Bethmann welcomed and encouraged improved communications between the Italian and Austro-Hungarian leaders.[236] According to the new ambassador to Italy, Gottlieb von Jagow, it was the backing down of the Entente powers during the Bosnian crisis that made the impression "that Italy's interest requires also further membership in the strong Triple Alliance group." Yet lack of friction with France had turned the belligerent elements to view Austria-Hungary, with whom Italy was engaged in an armaments race, with greater hostility. But he concluded: "The country wants no war."[237] And on the eve of the Agadir crisis Jagow reported that owing to the policy of San Giuliano and his predecessors Italy's relationship with the Dual Monarchy had substantially improved. Her military strength appeared as more impressive than France's. "With the fading of the Franco-Russian star, the value of the Triple Alliance, above all respect for Austria, has increased. In politics respect is often more effective than love."[238] The Bavarian representative in Berlin, Lerchenfeld, reported that the Wilhelmstrasse was very pleased with the pro-Triplice program of San Giuliano and the improvement of Austro-Italian relations.[239]

## VIII

Franco-German relations continued to be specifically affected by Morocco. From the February Accord of 1909 until the end of the year the two powers regulated their relations there amicably. The German leadership was fully aware that an improvement of Anglo-German relations depended on the settlement of the Franco-German differences over Morocco.[240] Subsequently mutual distrust increased because of economic rivalry, particularly relating to railway construction and mining claims. In 1910–11, with the enthusiastic support of the Pan-German League, the Mannesmann concern launched a public campaign largely directed against the German Foreign Office in favor of its mining interests in Morocco.[241] German leadership proved quite sensitive to the reaction of the public to the extension of French influence in the Sherifian Empire.[242] This was the immediate background to the German reaction to the French expedition requested by Mulay Hafid to relieve the Europeans besieged in the capital of Fez by his insubordinate subjects.

During the first months of Bethmann's chancellorship the French government was not viewed as hostile to Germany; in January 1910, Germany joined the Czar, the King of the Belgians, and the Pope in providing relief for French flood victims.[243] Schoen reported from his new posting in Paris on 6 April 1911:

If the Potsdam interviews have aroused French concern that a new shift has occurred in the political situation to the disadvantage of France, then this feeling has deepened through indications of our closer relations with England as well as through our successes in matters of the Bagdad railway.[244]

He also referred to a general feeling of weakness vis-à-vis Germany and remarked that it was significant that the Foreign Minister, Stephen Pichon, openly spoke of the desire to maintain good relations with Germany.[245]

At the beginning of April, Kiderlen warned the French against the occupation of Fez or Rabat: it would tear up the Algeciras Acts, excite German public opinion, and raise demands for compensation, possibly the port of Mogador on the Atlantic coast of Morocco.[246] Bethmann advised the French to proceed cautiously and, like Kiderlen, expressed the fear that once they occupied Fez they would never leave.[247] Wilhelm's first reaction, on 22 April, to the possibility of a major French expedition to Fez was one of noncommitment.[248] In partial agreement with some previous military estimates, he welcomed French military involvement in Morocco which would divert troops from the German border.[249] On 2 March 1910, Moltke did not expect that the conquest of Morocco, like that of Algeria, would involve 80,000–100,000 French troops annually over a period of thirty years. Nor did he think that a subdued Morocco would in the foreseeable future provide France with many native troops against Germany.[250] Another estimate of the General Staff indicated that an interchange of Moroccan and Algerian troops between the two territories would free French troops, although not all of them could be removed from North Africa. But "If we allow this process to mature whereby 40 million North Africans capable of military service become a source of recruits for France, this would cost us an extensive army increase to maintain its present peace-securing strength."[251] It therefore appears that Wilhelm's estimate about the liabilities of French military involvement in Morocco was more extreme than that of the General Staff. He also wanted Germany to stay in the background and to leave the protests against the French violation of the Algeciras Acts to other powers, particularly Spain. He specifically rejected the use of warships in Moroccan harbors as a protest against the French action[252]—something with which Bethmann concurred.[253]

On 28 April, Kiderlen announced to the French ambassador, "If French troops remained in Fez, so that the Sultan would only govern with the assistance of French bayonets, we could no longer regard him as the Sultan confirmed by the Algeciras Acts. We would then regard the Acts as dissolved *and* fully resume our freedom of action."[254] The course taken by Kiderlen involved the risk of war; however, it had the approval of neither the Chancellor nor the Kaiser:[255] the latter denied wanting war over Morocco.[256] A position-paper of 3 May, attempting to explain Kiderlen's actions, described at some length the anarchy in the Sherifian Empire and questioned the ability of the French to evacuate their troops from the interior once they invaded Fez. The Algeciras Acts would thus lose their validity. The French were then to be asked politely how long they expected to remain in Fez. Until their departure Germany would station ships in the harbors of Mogador and Agadir as pledges for compensation.[257] While there was "no mention of partitioning Morocco or of a German retention of a port,"[258] the memorandum referred to the rich hinterland of these ports. Possessing them, Germany could calmly await the course of events in Morocco, including the deeper involvement of the French, as stressed by Wilhelm. No mention was made of Britain—a significant omission—except to note that Mogador and Agadir were too remote from the Mediterranean to excite her. France was expected to offer appropriate compensation for the removal of German warships from the two ports. The program was approved by a reluctant Wilhelm on 5 May.[259] On 7 May, Schoen reported from Paris that there existed a genuine desire to find a lasting understanding with Germany over Morocco through colonial or economic compensations. He mentioned specifically the exchange of the French Congo for Togoland.[260] German plans for intervention were further encouraged by the Spanish action in Larash.[261] The course of action was elaborated on by a memorandum of the Deputy Secretary of State, Arthur Zimmermann, of 12 June, fully approved by Kiderlen.[262] According to it, other than the areas occupied by Spain, northern Morocco was assumed as being henceforth under French control from which other powers were largely excluded economically. "Once it is clear to the world that France has succeeded, under the protection of the Algeciras Acts, in realizing her old plans, it would become evident that we have suffered a diplomatic setback whose effect should not be under-estimated, not to mention the storm of indignation that would sweep through Germany." French offers of compensation were not considered promising since German requests would raise outcries in the French press and be opposed by Britain, so that Germany, blamed as a disturber of the peace, would be left with empty hands. Under these circumstances the German government would declare that it was no longer bound by the Algeciras Acts and dispatch two cruisers each to Agadir and Mogador to protect German interests: thus France would be compelled to offer compensations.

In June, Kiderlen held the first serious discussions with the French ambassador, Jules Cambon, in Bad Kissingen about compensations,[263] and on 1 July, instead of the four cruisers to be used against two Moroccan Atlantic ports, only the gunboat *Panther* limped into Agadir. This action none the less created great excitement both in Germany and abroad.[264] Wilhelm sought a quick deal; Kiderlen and the Foreign Office expected the French in due time to make suitable offers. On 6 July, Bethmann reported that

> until now all governments, particularly the French and the English, seek to impose on the press and public opinion a calm approach to the Morocco question. In the meantime England, Russia, and France negotiate about a common stand on the matter . . .

Wilhelm requested bilateral negotiations with France, pointing out that Russia was not at all involved in Morocco.[265] On 15 July, Bethmann reported to Wilhelm, who was on his annual Norwegian cruise, that Kiderlen had shocked Cambon by requesting the entire French Congo as compensation for Morocco; judging by the ambassador's reaction, Kiderlen had concluded that Germany "must make a very strong appearance." Wilhelm realistically noted that such a request would greatly annoy London and he must return home. "*Le roi s'amuse*. And during it we steer towards mobilization! *without me* this cannot happen. About this our allies must be informed. For this can arouse sympathy among them!"[266] Indeed, the German policy had failed to secure substantial support from Austria-Hungary and had suffered a rebuff from Italy.[267] The Kaiser concluded that the lengthy German action had made it possible for the French to seek advice in London and St Petersburg. He for one caught a glimpse of the specter of war. His comments were relayed to both Bethmann and the Foreign Office. On 17 July, Kiderlen reacted to them in a letter to Bethmann. "We must obtain the entire French Congo." Otherwise the French were to be told to evacuate the whole of Morocco. "I do not believe that the French would pick up the gauntlet, but they must feel that we are prepared to go to the extreme. Conceding Morocco for colonial border rectifications would make our enemies so insolent that we would sooner or later have to face them again." Unless his position was accepted, Kiderlen was prepared to resign.[268] Although he had been inadequately consulted, the Chancellor agreed to stand by his Secretary of State.[269] Kiderlen's second offer to resign was made on 19 July and led to Wilhelm's response of 21 July that negotiations be conducted as previously. The German missions abroad, particularly the embassies in Paris and London, were not informed about the intentions of the Foreign Office; nor did they provide any input into the decisionmaking process. The Colonial Office and the Imperial Naval Office had not been consulted at all.[270] Ima Barlow rightly concluded that Kiderlen was practicing brinkmanship. The Kaiser, for one, realized this.

Ima Barlow states: "The ultimate success of Kiderlen's plan depended to a large degree upon the skilful use of tactics to keep England aloof."[271] Already before the "Panther leap" Grey had told Metternich that Britain "was bound in the Morocco question by the agreement with France and obligated to support her."[272] The impact of this report may have been canceled, however, by Wilhelm's impression during his visit to Britain that the French expedition to Fez was regarded as "highly undesirable."[273] On 3 July, Grey told Metternich that in view of the *Panther* action Britain would have to protect her own interests in Morocco[274] and on the next day also referred to the "treaty obligations with France."[275] On 21 July, Metternich reported Grey as expressing his concern about the German demands for compensation and the presence of *Panther* in Agadir. The failure of Germany to reach an understanding with France, he said, must lead to discussions between Germany and Britain.[276] On the next day David Lloyd George delivered his Mansion House speech,[277] and on 26 July Metternich telegraphed that the British Atlantic fleet was ordered to give up its cruise to Norway and to proceed to Portsmouth. According to Emily Oncken, the British involvement bankrupted Kiderlen's wait-and-see policy. "From the stronger position of one applying pressure, Berlin had unexpectedly come into the weaker position of one placed under pressure."[278]

Although Wilhelm's immediate reaction to the Mansion House speech was to fight rather than to allow Germany "to be overwhelmed for the second time,"[279] neither he nor Bethmann considered it necessary to respond by changing the Norwegian journey of the German navy.[280] By the end of July both men were still not informed about Kiderlen's motives. Continuing to demand the entire French Congo in compensation for Morocco, he was prepared at this time to go to war to achieve his aim.[281] Wilhelm, however, was described as being "fearful of war, not happy about war."[282]

The German navy was none the less partially prepared for a possible war. The third squadron was activated "according to plan" on 31 July. In a response to a telegram from Wilhelm and an inquiry from the navy, Kiderlen, Capelle, Hans von Seebohm, and the Acting Chief of the Admiralty Staff, Rieve, met on the afternoon of 8 August. Kiderlen remarked that Wilhelm thought the German fleet, dispersed along the Norwegian coast, should unite itself. Rieve stated that the fleet would according to plan unite on 10 August, then proceed rapidly in a simulated withdrawal battle to Skagen, and continue its exercises in the northern Kattegat, where it would be in contact with Germany.[283] On 10 August the Third Squadron also joined the fleet. The trials of the Dreadnought *Helgoland* were speeded up to enable it to enter service on 23 August and a number of other measures were taken in August and the first part of September to increase the war preparedness of the navy. As Emily Oncken states: "The precautionary measures of the naval authorities lacked aggressive tendencies."[284] As will be seen in the next chapter, the Admiralty Staff at the time lacked a viable operations plan against Britain.

Kiderlen had obviously decided to back down by 8 August, perhaps as a result of a conference with the Kaiser and Bethmann in Swinemünde on 29 July.[285] While he was concerned whether Britain was bellicose or would remain neutral in a Franco-German war and was interested in the situation arising from a naval war with Britain and France, he maintained that Germany could not fight a war over Morocco.[286] On 10 August, Seebohm wired Tirpitz that Kiderlen "did not consider the political situation dangerous" and several times stated

that we cannot start a war because the French do not want to give us enough of the Congo. It would be somewhat different if we came back to the Algeciras Acts; but then we should give the French a limited period for the evacuation of Morocco. Only after the expiry of this period could a possible *casus belli* arise. In the course of the conversation Kiderlen said that if the situation became more acute we should declare war on England in the assumption that France would then declare war on us. Then our allies would have a *casus belli*; otherwise—so far as is known—a *casus belli* is not present for the Triple Entente if we declare war on England.[287]

Bethmann appears to have accepted part of Kiderlen's reasoning. As he told his friend Wolfgang von Oettingen on 14 November 1911, the "Panther leap" was a risky trick. "It should have served as an object of attack in case it came to complications with England and France, so that

Germany, as the attacked party, would be sure of the support of Austria and Italy."[288] This scenario was strongly criticized by Tirpitz. He doubted if a German declaration of war on Britain would be countered by a declaration of war on Germany by France. Instead, Germany might have to declare war on her as well, in which case Italy would certainly not join and Austria-Hungary would support her most reluctantly. "As for naval war, the time is as unfavorable as possible. Each subsequent year brings a much more favorable situation. Heligoland, Canal, Dreadnoughts, U-boats, etc."[289] On 12 August, Kiderlen noted the increasing belligerence of German public opinion, claiming that he could make himself popular by steering toward war, "which would be easy. But I do not have this ambition."[290] Two days later Capelle reported to Tirpitz that the Morocco question appeared settled.[291] At the end of August, Walther Rathenau reported Bethmann as saying:

> Precisely because of England, Agadir was necessary. The Morocco question welds England to France and had therefore to be "liquidated." [He] condemns the incitement to war because we [are] in the least favorable instant [*Moment*] concerning alliances.[292]

Although the German leadership was slowly backing down in its negotiations with France, the specter of war was not altogether banished. There was the possibility that the French might initiate war.

On 7 August, Detlow von Winterfeldt reported from Paris that, although the possibility of war with Germany was being widely discussed in the French press, this did not mean that the majority of the French population wanted war: the press campaign was probably intended to impress on Germany that France preferred war to a humiliation. "In any case it must be counted on that the French government has in the course of the last weeks considered the possibility of war." Should the crisis continue, he advised the General Staff to use its intelligence to observe possible mobilization preparations in the departments adjacent to Germany. He thought, however, that the French army had a number of weaknesses which should detract from its confidence in arms.[293] A few days later Schoen reported that national pride and confidence had replaced earlier French excitement and concern. If the negotiations for German compensations were to have results favorable to France, Germany's position toward her would be weakened for a long time to come.[294] On 19 August, Winterfeldt repeated that the French Ministry of War and General Staff were preparing for a possible war with Germany. Although the French leadership, army, and public did not consider such a war as imminent, they viewed it as inevitable in the long run.[295] On 24 August he informed Berlin that the French had canceled their great northern maneuvers on the pretext of an outbreak of foot and mouth disease but possibly as a preparation for war.[296] This report alarmed Wilhelm, since the cancellation of the great French maneuvers would give the French army a definite advantage in accelerating its mobilization unless the impending German maneuvers were canceled as well and the troops returned to their regular locations.[297] The Prussian Minister of War, Josias von Heeringen, admitted that the German maneuvers, already begun, would delay mobilization by at least forty-eight hours until their completion at the end of September; their cancellation would, however, sharpen the political situation, and possibly provoke war. In response to his query, he was assured by Bethmann and Kiderlen that the German maneuvers presented no risk, for during the negotiations that were being resumed with France "a serious crisis" could be avoided to give the troops time to mobilize. In their opinion the cancellation of the maneuvers "would be viewed as a direct preparation for German mobilization. This might frighten the French. Much more unpleasant would be the effect on the German people if a mobilization order did not follow such a measure."[298] It is significant that both men were more concerned about the reaction of a bellicose German public than about the escalation of the crisis by a threat to France.

On 3 September the Bavarian military attaché, Gebsattel, reported from Berlin that the Foreign Office "neither denied nor necessarily expected the development of serious difficulties" but that in military circles "the mood was belligerent, more belligerent than I believed a few days ago."

From many sides—also exalted ones—it is stressed that we should use the situation that is relatively favorable for us to strike [*zum Losschlagen*]. Russia has not yet completed the reorganization of her army, England is concerned with labor unrest, the French army permeated with anti-militaristic propaganda while the German army is not touched by it.[299]

Gebsattel deliberately excluded Moltke and Heeringen from the military war party. As for the exclusion of the former, he may have been too generous, for the Chief of the General Staff had written to his wife on 19 August that if Germany suffered a setback in "this wretched Morocco affair" he would "despair of the future of the German Empire. Then I shall quit. But before that I shall propose that we do away with the army and place ourselves under the protection of Japan; then we can concentrate on making money and become country bumpkins."[300] As for the Kaiser, Gebsattel continued, "as reluctantly and painfully [*schwer*] as he would decide for war, if a foreign power or coalition should attempt to force Germany to her knees, he would be obligated to do so." But all who were knowledgeable of the situation "are agreed that even in the worst case our diplomacy must see to it that we are not the aggressors in world opinion. For only then could the very unwarlike [*kriegsunlustige*] Czar feel himself free of the obligation to help France, whereas Austria and Italy would be forced to come to our side." On the following day Gebsattel reported that the influence of the warlike military elements had diminished,[301] but qualified his view two days later by stating that the intention of both the French and German governments to continue the negotiations could be upset at any time by various incidents or outbursts of popular passions.[302] On the same day, the Bavarian legation in Berlin reported that many influential people regarded war as inevitable.[303]

On 7 September, Moltke produced a report about the military situation in Europe.[304] It dealt with French preparations, but represented them as only aiding a later mobilization.

> Whether in the now pending negotiations France is firmly determined on war because of confidence in her army is difficult to say, [but should be doubted] . . . on the whole, the feeling seems to prevail in France that her army is fully equal to the German army in terms of strength, discipline, and leadership.

Neither the British army nor navy was considered to be engaged in any preparations for war, except, perhaps, by sending an armored cruiser of the Mediterranean fleet to Port Said for the possible blocking of the Suez Canal. "In a Franco-German war England would come to the side of the French, but in so far as possible shift the burden of war to the ally." The small but well-trained BEF, which also served as the reserve for the colonial army, would, "if at all, be used on the Continent very carefully." Its possible tasks were:

> Joining the French army, diversions in Belgium or Jutland, occupation of parts of the Dutch–Belgian coast (possibly the Scheldt estuary) to prevent its falling into Germany's hands or becoming a pawn for the conclusion of peace. A speedy mobilization would be necessary only for the first-named possibility. In all other cases, England would probably take time and be more concerned about her own interest than that of her allies.

On 9 September, Kiderlen told the Bavarian minister Lerchenfeld that he was determined to avoid war because of Germany's weakness at sea in the face of Britain; the French, in turn, would avoid war because of their fear of it.[305] On 12 September he told the Baden minister

> he believed that the English would *now* be as averse to war as were the Russians; at the moment the latter played the same role as the French had two years ago in the Bosnian–Serbian question: they indeed pledged the *nation amie et alliée* their firm loyalty as an ally, but most urgently advised an understanding in Paris; the English, on the other hand, played a doubly crooked game since they wanted only to assure themselves . . . of the support of the French in case of later conflict.[306]

Baroness von Spitzenberg reported on 25 September that "Morocco appears finally settled,"[307] and on 4 November the Franco-German accords were signed, granting what appeared to much of the German public inadequate compensations for the German claims to Morocco in the French Congo and options for the purchase of Spanish Guinea.[308] At a considerable risk of war Germany achieved little; left were a great deal of bitterness about a "second Olmütz" in Germany, much increased hostility between Germany and France, and further deterioration of the Anglo-German relationship. According to Paul Kennedy: "While the details [of the Agadir crisis] may be left unrecounted, the grave consequences cannot."[309]

# Notes: Chapter 15

1 GP, XXI, ii, No. 7154, Bülow to Wilhelm, 31 May 1906, pp. 360–1.
2 PAAA, Österreich 92, No. 4, Bd 2, "Aufzeichnung . . . Tschirschky," 7 May 1907.
3 ibid., Österreich 95, Vol. 12, Bülow to Kiderlen-Wächter, 23 May 1907.
4 ibid., Vol. 14, Wedel to Bülow, 23 October 1907, copy.
5 ibid., Österreich 91, No. 2, Bd 10, Tschirschky to Bülow, 8 December 1907.
6 ibid., Vol. 11, Tschirschky to Bülow, 7 February 1908.
7 ibid., Österreich 95, Vol. 15, Bülow to the Ministry of the Interior, 18 March 1908.
8 ibid., Deutschland 128, Vol. 5, Tschirschky to Bülow, 23 June 1908; ibid., Österreich 95, Geh., Bd 2, Schoen to Foreign Office, telegram, 5 September 1908.
9 ibid., Österreich 95, Bd 15, Bülow to Schoen, 15 July 1908; an almost verbatim dispatch was sent by Schoen to the Vienna embassy on the following day.
10 ibid., Marocco 4, Bd 114, Monts to Bülow, 10 January 1906.
11 ibid., Deutschland 128, No. 1, Bd 25, Monts to Bülow, 13 January 1906.
12 ibid., Italien 82, Bd 7, Nos 60 and 62, Monts to Bülow, 10 February 1906.
13 GP, XXI, ii, No. 7174, report of the military attaché in Rome, Hammerstein-Equord, 2 February 1906, pp. 411–12.
14 ibid., No. 7173, Moltke to Hammerstein-Equord, 2 February 1906, pp. 410–11.
15 PAAA, Italien 88, Bd 23, Monts to Bülow, 25 February 1906, copy.
16 GP, XXI, i, No. 7050, Monts to Bülow, 27 February 1906, pp. 231–2.
17 ibid., XXI, ii, No. 7150, Monts to Bülow, 8 March 1906, p. 353; also Albertini, *Origins*, Vol. 1, p. 175. I am using Isabella Massey's translation.
18 Albertini, *Origins,* Vol. 1, p. 175.
19 PAAA, Deutschland 143, Geh., Bd 9, Hammerstein-Equord to the Minister of War, 20 March 1906.
20 ibid., Österreich 92, No. 10, Bd 3, Bülow to Tschirschky and Hammann, 14 May 1906.
21 ibid., Deutschland 121, No. 3, secr., Bd 1, Bülow to Einem, 1 June 1906; also see Bülow, *Denkwürdigkeiten,* Bd II, p. 226.
22 GP, XXI, ii, No. 5156, Monts to Tschirschky, 8 June 1906, pp. 364–70.
23 ibid., No. 7159, "Aufzeichnung . . . Klehmet," 9 July 1906, pp. 374–6.
24 ibid., No. 7176, report of Hammerstein-Equord, 26 July 1906, pp. 414–17.
25 PAAA, Italien 82, Geh., Bd 1, Monts to Bülow, 21 October 1906; Tittoni's friendship is also attested to in GP XXI, ii, No. 7161, "Aufzeichnung . . . Tschirschky," 20 October 1906, pp. 377–9.
26 ibid., No. 7162, Monts to Bülow, 21 October 1906, pp. 380–1.
27 ibid., No. 7163, Monts to Bülow, 10 November 1906, p. 383.
28 PAAA, Italien 68, Bd 49, Monts to Bülow, 29 October 1906.
29 GP, XXI, ii, No. 7164, "Aufzeichnung . . . Bülow," 16 November 1906, p. 386.
30 *Holstein Papers,* Vol. 4, No. 999. Holstein to Bülow, 25 October 1906, copy, p. 442, and No. 1000, memorandum by Holstein, 27 October 1906, pp. 442–3.
31 GP, XXI, ii, No. 7165, Bülow to Monts, 16 November 1906, pp. 387–8.
32 ibid., No. 7178, Moltke to Bülow, 15 May 1907, p. 419.
33 PAAA, Deutschland 128, No. 2, Bd 27, Bülow to Wilhelm, 19 April 1908, copy; Italien 95, Bd 14, Monts to Bülow, 21 May 1908.
34 GP, XX, i, No. 6376, Bernstorff to Bülow, 16 April 1904, p. 18. E. L. Woodward, *Great Britain and the German Navy* (Hamden, Conn., 1964), p. 86.
35 GP, XXIII, i, No. 7777, Coerper to Tirpitz, 19 November 1906, p. 36.
36 ibid., No. 7779, Tirpitz to Bülow, 12 January 1907, pp. 39–42.
37 ibid., XXI, ii, No. 7204, Metternich to Bülow, 30 January 1907, p. 566; No. 7205, Metternich to Bülow, 31 January 1907, p. 468; No. 7206, Metternich to Bülow, 21 January 1907, pp. 471–2; XXIII, i, No. 7785, "Aufzeichnung . . . Coerper," 14 March 1907, pp. 48–51.
38 ibid., XXI, ii, No. 7214, Stumm to Bülow, 9 April 1907, p. 492, and enclosure, report of military attaché Ostertag, 9 April 1907, pp. 494–5; No. 7215, Monts to Bülow, 18 April 1907, pp. 496–7.
39 GP, XXIV, No. 8176, Stumm to Bülow, 4 January 1908, p. 27; BA-MA, F 2040, PG 66059, Widenmann to Tirpitz, 23 November 1907.

40  GP, XXIV, No. 8179, Metternich to Bülow, 3 February 1908, pp. 30–1; Woodward, *German Navy*, pp. 157–8.
41  GP, XXIV, No. 8181, pp. 32–5; Tirpitz, *Aufbau*, pp. 58–61; Peter Padfield, *The Great Naval Race: The Anglo-German Naval Rivalry, 1900–1914* (London, 1974), pp. 181–2; Volker R. Berghahn, *Germany and the Approach to War in 1914* (London, 1973), p. 67.
42  Padfield, *Great Naval Race*, p. 186.
43  Woodward, *German Navy*, pp. 168–74.
44  GP, XXIV, No. 8193, Metternich to Bülow, 8 March 1908, Wilhelm's final comment, p. 46; No. 8196, Schoen to Metternich, 14 March 1908, p. 50.
45  ibid., No. 8212, Metternich to Bülow, 30 June 1908, Wilhelm's final comment, p. 88; No. 8217, Metternich to Bülow, 16 July 1908, marginal and final comments, pp. 103–4.
46  ibid., No. 8195, Metternich to Bülow, 10 March 1908, p. 48; No. 8196, Schoen to Metternich, 12 March 1908, pp. 49–50; No. 8197, Bülow to Metternich, 17 March 1908, pp. 50–1.
47  ibid., XXI, ii, No. 7237, Flotow to Bülow, 18 October 1906, pp. 545–6; also No. 7249, Radolin to Bülow, 22 February 1907, p. 559.
48  PAAA, Deutschland 121, No. 3, secr., Bd 1, Bülow to Einem, 1 June 1906. Bülow quotes the letter in his *Denkwürdigkeiten*, Bd II, but misdates it 1 July 1906. Also see Schulte, *Deutsche Armee*, pp. 387–90.
49  PAAA Deutschland 121, No. 3, secr., Bd 1, Einem to Bülow, 18 June 1906; Moltke to Tschirschky, 9 October 1906.
50  BA, Bülow, *Nachlass*, No. 22, Pro-Memoria, 30 May 1906.
51  PAAA, Frankreich 116, Geh., Bd 1, Flotow to Pourtalès, 19 September 1906. An excerpt appears in GP, XXI, ii, No. 7229, pp. 529–30.
52  ibid., Frankreich 116, Bd 20, Flotow to Bülow, 18 October 1906, Wilhelm's final comment.
53  GP, XXI, ii, No. 7205, Metternich to Bülow, 31 January 1907, and Wilhelm's marginal comments to it, pp. 468–70. See Samuel R. Williamson, *The Politics of Grand Strategy: Britain and France Prepare for War, 1904–1914* (Cambridge, Mass., 1969), pp. 59–88.
54  GP, XXI, ii, No. 7211, Tschirschky to Metternich, 9 February 1907, p. 481.
55  ibid., No. 7219, Metternich to Bülow, 31 May 1907, pp. 507–9.
56  ibid., No. 7234, Stumm to Bülow, 2 March 1907, pp. 534–5; No. 7235, Tschirschky to Monts, 8 March 1907, p. 536, No. 7236, Monts to Bülow, 18 March 1907, pp. 536–7, and enclosure, "Aufzeichnung . . . Rampold," 18 March 1907, pp. 538–9. Fisher merely wanted the French to provide a submarine-destroyer cordon across the Channel. Williamson, *Politics*, pp. 68–70, 78–9.
57  PAAA, Frankreich 116, Geh., Bd 1, Metternich to the Foreign Office, telegram, 1 June 1908.
58  Giessler, *Die Institution*, p. 77.
59  PAAA, Frankreich 116, Geh., Bd 1.
60  GP, XXIV, No. 8350, von der Lancken to Flotow, 6 July 1908, pp. 305–6. The comment of the editors of the *Grosse Politik* that these statements "were in no way approved by the Foreign Office," p. 305, n. **, are unsubstantiated.
61  PAAA, Frankreich 103, Bd 39, initialed L, Wilhelmshaven to Bülow, 20 April 1907. The tone is unmistakably Wilhelm's.
62  Bülow, *Denkwürdigkeiten*, Bd II, p. 239.
63  ibid., Bd II, p. 243; Fischer, *Krieg*, p. 81.
64  PAAA, Russland 72, Geh., Bd 14, Moltke to Bülow, 9 August 1906; also see Risto Ropponen, *Die Kraft Russlands: Wie beurteilte die politische und militärische Führung der europäischen Grossmächte in der Zeit von 1905 bis 1914 die Kraft Russlands* (Helsinki, 1968), p. 219.
65  GP, XXI, ii, No. 7181, Metternich to Bülow, 31 July 1906, p. 441.
66  ibid., XXV, i, No. 8518, Miquel to Bülow, 19 September 1906, p. 23.
67  ibid., No. 8534, Miquel to the Foreign Office, 31 August 1907, Bülow's marginal comment 1 September, p. 40.
68  ibid., No. 8536, Miquel to Bülow, 25 September 1907, Wilhelm's marginal comment on p. 45.
69  PAAA, Russland 91, Bd 41, Wilhelm's comment to article "Retour de Russie," in *Le Galois*, 8 August 1907; also Bay H St Ar Abt II, Geh St Ar, MA III, 2685, Lerchenfeld to Prince Regent, 6 August 1907.

70  GP, XXIV, No. 8206, Bülow to Metternich, 1 June 1908, p. 64; No. 8209, Metternich to Bülow, 5 June 1908. pp. 68–76.

71  PAAA, Frankreich 116, Bd 22, Pourtalès to Bülow, 3 June 1908.

72  GP, XXV, ii, No. 8807, Pourtalès to Bülow, 12 June 1908, p. 454.

73  GP, XXV, ii, No. 8812, Metternich to the Foreign Office, 15 June 1908, p. 463.

74  ibid., No. 8815, Bülow to Wilhelm, 17 June 1908, pp. 466–7.

75  ibid., No. 8820, Bülow to Schlözer, 25 June 1908, pp. 474–9.

76  ibid., p. 477.

77  Bay H St Ar, Abt II, Geh St Ar, Bay Ges Berlin, No. 1079, Lerchenfeld's report, 22 April 1907.

78  GP, XXI, ii, No. 7270, Mühlberg to Bülow, 14 July 1907, p. 591.

79  BA-MA, N 253/16, Trotha to Tirpitz, 18 March 1908.

80  ibid., N 159/3, p. 380. Baudissin was the new Chief of the Admiralty Staff. See below, p. 338 ff.

81  Woodward, *German Navy*, pp. 168–78; Padfield, *Great Naval Race*, pp. 188–91.

82  BA, Bülow, *Nachlass*, No. 154, 3 October 1908.

83  loc. cit.

84  The most recent account is Terence F. Cole, "The *Daily Telegraph* affair and its aftermath: Bülow and the Reichstag, 1908–1909," in Röhl and Sombart, *Wilhelm II*, esp. pp. 253–66; also Craig, *Germany*, pp. 283–5; the most detailed account of the incident is Wilhelm Schüssler, *Die Daily-Telegraf-Affaire: Fürst Bülow, Kaiser Wilhelm und die Krise des zweiten Reiches 1908* (Göttingen, 1952). Bülow's account appears in BA, Bülow, *Nachlass* 34, Aufzeichnung Bülow, n.d.

85  Bülow, *Denkwürdigkeiten*, Bd II, p. 319.

86  Tirpitz, *Aufbau*, p. 84.

87  GP, XXIV, No. 8220, Bülow to Metternich, 5 August 1908, pp. 117–19.

88  *Holstein Papers*, Vol. 4, No. 1117, Bülow to Holstein, 16 August 1908, p. 551.

89  ibid., No. 1120, Bülow to Holstein, 23 August 1908, pp. 553–5.

90  GP, XXIV, No. 8244, Stumm to Bülow, 8 September 1908, pp. 156–8; Woodward, *German Navy*, pp. 179–81.

91  Bay H St Ar, Abt II, Geh St Ar, MA III, 2686, report of the Bavarian minister to Berlin, 15 November 1908; this is similar to GLA, Karlsruhe, 49/2041, Berckheim to Brauer, 13 November 1908.

92  Tirpitz, *Aufbau*, p. 96; also GP, XXVIII, No. 10235, pp. 21–3; Woodward, *German Navy*, pp. 197 ff.

93  Tirpitz, *Aufbau*, pp. 97–9; GP, XXVIII, No. 10238, pp. 26–30.

94  *Holstein Papers*, Vol. 4, No. 1161, Bülow to Holstein, 4 December 1908, p. 600.

95  The minutes are printed in GP, XXVIII, No. 10238, p. 30.

96  ibid., No. 10242, Bülow to Tirpitz, 25 December 1908, pp. 38–40.

97  ibid., No. 10247, Tirpitz to Bülow, 4 January 1909, 51–5; Tirpitz, *Aufbau*, pp. 104–9.

98  GP, XXVIII, No. 10251, Bülow to Tirpitz, 11 January 1909, pp. 60–4; No. 10243, Metternich to Bülow, 29 December 1908, pp. 40–5; Tirpitz, *Aufbau*, pp. 112–15.

99  GP, XXVIII, No. 10254, Tirpitz to Bülow, 20 January 1909, pp. 67–70. He charged Bülow with having failed to obtain reciprocity from Britain for the promise to refrain from introducing a new naval bill in 1912.

100  See Kennedy, "Tirpitz, England," p. 46.

101  GP, XXVIII, No. 10256, Bülow to Tirpitz, 27 January 1909, pp. 75–8; Tirpitz, *Aufbau*, pp. 117–20, dates this document 29 January. According to PAAA, England, 78, secr., Vol. 17, it is dated 27 January.

102  GP, XXVIII, No. 10256, p. 76.

103  ibid., No. 10254, p. 70.

104  ibid., No. 10256, p. 77.

105  ibid., No. 10254, p. 70.

106  ibid., No. 10256, p. 77.

107  ibid., No. 10257, Tirpitz to Bülow, 4 February 1909, p. 78.

108  ibid., p. 79.

109  Woodward, *German Navy*, p. 200.

110  GP, XXVIII, No. 10258, "Aufzeichnung . . . Metternich," 8 February 1909, p. 80; No. 20359, "Aufzeichnung . . . Schoen," 12 February 1909, p. 81.

111  ibid., No. 10263, "Aufzeichnung . . . Bussche-Haddenhausen," 19 February 1909, pp. 91–2.

112  ibid., No. 10266, Metternich to Bülow, 3 March 1909, pp. 93–9; Tirpitz, *Aufbau*, pp. 125–8, reproduces most of this report. As background for British suspicions and fears, see Woodward, *German Navy*, pp. 203–15; Padfield, *Great Naval Race*, pp. 198–214; A. J. Marder, *From Dreadnought to Scapa Flow*, Vol. 1, *The Road to War, 1904–1914* (London, 1961), pp. 151–62; Kennedy, *Antagonism*, pp. 443–4.

113  GP, XXVIII, No. 10267, Tirpitz to Wilhelm, 8 March 1909, pp. 101–2; Tirpitz, *Aufbau*, pp. 128–9.

114  GP, XXVIII, No. 10168, Bülow to Metternich, 9 March 1909, pp. 102–3.

115  ibid., No. 10272, Tirpitz to Bülow, 17 March 1909, p. 107; Woodward, *German Navy*, pp. 228–9.

116  ibid., pp. 229–30.

117  GP, XXVIII, No. 10287, Metternich to Bülow, 23 March 1909, pp. 123–6; No. 10288, Bülow to Wilhelm II, 27 March 1909, p. 127; No. 10289, Tirpitz to Bülow, 28 March 1909, p. 129.

118  ibid., No. 10293, Widenmann to Tirpitz, 30 March 1909, p. 142.

119  Tirpitz, *Aufbau*, pp. 145–6; a fuller, somewhat different version appears in typescript in BA-MA, F 3446, PG 67489, which includes the reference to Germany's lead over France, Russia, and Italy.

120  There are references to it in Tirpitz, *Aufbau*, pp. 147, 149; a full account appears in BA-MA, F 3446, PG 67489, "Aufzeichnung des Staatssekretärs des RMA," 3 April 1909.

121  GP, XXVIII, No. 10294, Wilhelm to Bülow, 3 April 1909, pp. 145–7.

122  ibid., No. 10295, Bülow to Schoen, 9 April 1909, pp. 148–9.

123  BA, Bülow, *Nachlass*/97, Holstein to Bülow, 6 April 1909.

124  BA-MA, F 3446, PG 67489, Tirpitz to Müller, 17 April 1909.

125  Tirpitz, *Aufbau*, Tirpitz to Müller, 6 May 1909, pp. 150–2.

126  BA-MA, F 3446, PG 67489, Müller to Tirpitz, 17 April 1909; copy in ibid., N 253/46.

127  GP, XXVIII, No. 10297, "Aufzeichnung . . . Bülow," 17 April 1909, p. 150.

128  ibid., No. 10306, "Protokoll einer Besprechung . . . am 3 Juni 1909 über die Frage einer Verständigung mit England," pp. 168–78.

129  This is according to Müller's version: Tirpitz, *Aufbau*, p. 160.

130  For other statements of Tirpitz, I am following his version as printed in the right-hand column of GP, XXVIII, No. 10306, pp. 170–7.

131  *Holstein Papers*, Vol. 4, No. 1158, Holstein to Bülow, 26 November 1908, p. 598; No. 1159, Holstein to Bülow, 28 November 1908, pp. 598–9; and No. 1185, Holstein to Bülow, 12 March 1909, pp. 620–1; Rich, *Holstein*, Vol. 2, pp. 814–33. The fullest account of the Bosnian crisis is still Bernadotte E. Schmitt, *The Annexation of Bosnia, 1908–1909* (Cambridge, 1937).

132  For the initial German reaction, see ibid., pp. 40–3.

133  Bay H St Ar, Abt II, Geh St Ar, MA III, 2686, report of the Bavarian minister in Berlin, 15 November 1908.

134  GP, XXVI, i, No. 9033, Bülow to Tschirschky, 13 October 1908, p. 161. See an almost identical analysis of the situation in Bülow's circular to the ministers at the German courts, also presented to Wilhelm on 20 October 1908. PAAA, Orientalia Generalia 5, Bd 65.

135  PAAA, Deutschland 128, Geh., Bd 5, Bülow to Foreign Office, 5 October 1908, copy.

136  ibid., Österreich 70, Bd 46, Tschirschky to Bülow, 1 December 1908.

137  Schmitt, *Annexation*, pp. 58–9; 69, 76, 83, 147–8, 153–4, 178–80, 183.

138  GP, XXVI, ii, No. 9292, Bülow to Tschirschky, 30 November 1908, p. 513.

139  PAAA, Deutschland 121, No. 31, Geh., Bd 1, "Ganz Geheim. Zu Nr. 1260. 08 Chef des Generalstabes d. A.A.S. pr. 23 February 1908 p.m.;" for Russia, see Ropponen, *Die Kraft*, p. 220.

140  PAAA, Deutschland 121, No. 31, Geh., Bd 1, Moltke to Bülow, 29 January 1909, "Militärische Leistungsfähigkeit der wichtigsten Staaten Europas zu Beginn dieses Jahres."

141  Albertini, *Origins*, Vol. 1, pp. 268–73; Schmitt, *Annexation*, pp. 94–6.

142  GP, XXVI, i, Bülow to Monts, 14 December 1908, pp. 336–8; GP, XXVI, ii, No. 9259, Aehrenthal to Szögyenyi, 7 January 1909, pp. 479–81; for Italy see ibid., No. 9302, Bülow to Aehrenthal, 8 January 1909, p. 528.

143  F. Conrad von Hötzendorf, *Aus meiner Dienstzeit, 1906–1918*, Vol. 1 (Vienna, 1921), pp. 379–84; above all, see Norman Stone's important article, "Moltke and Conrad: relations between Austro-Hungarian and German General Staffs, 1909–1914," *Historical Journal*, vol. 9, no. 2 (1966), pp. 201–28; reprinted in Kennedy, *War Plans*, pp. 222–51.

144  See above, n. 140.

145  PAAA, Orientalia Generalia 5, Geh., Bd 17, Hintze to Wilhelm II, 9 December 1908; Ropponen, *Die Kraft*, pp. 221–2.

146  PAAA, Deutschland 121, No. 31, Geh., Bd 1, Bülow to Moltke, 9 February 1909.

147  Gerald E. Silberstein, "Germany, France and the Casablanca incident, 1908–1909: an investigation of a forgotten crisis," *Canadian Journal of History*, vol. 11, no. 3 (December 1976), pp. 331–54; see also GP, XXIV, No. 8364, "Aufzeichnung . . . Bülow," 28 September 1908, p. 332.

148  Ernst Jäckh, *Kiderlen-Wächter: der Staatsmann und Mensch*, 2 vols (Berlin, 1924), Vol. 2, pp. 20–1, n. 1.

149  GP, XXVI, ii, No. 9372, Bülow to Tschirschky, 6 February 1909, pp. 596–7.

150  ibid., No. 9388, Bülow to Wilhelm, 22 February 1909, Wilhelm's final comment of 23 February, p. 620.

151  PAAA, Russland 98, Geh., Bd 1, Hintze to Wilhelm, 24 February 1909. An excerpt from this document (without Wilhelm's comments) appears as n. ** in GP, XXVI, ii, to No. 9390, pp. 621–2.

152  PAAA, Orientalia Generalia 5, Geh., Bd 15. It is this excerpt that is reproduced in the GP.

153  GP, XXVI, ii, No. 9391, Tschirschky to Foreign Office, 24 February 1909; Wilhelm's final comment, pp. 623–4; Schmitt, *Annexation*, p. 158, n. 7.

154  ibid., pp. 187–8; GP, XXVI, ii, No. 9437, Bülow to Pourtalès, 14 March 1909, pp. 669–70.

155  GP, XXVI, ii, No. 9428, pp. 655–7; Ropponen, *Die Kraft*, p. 223.

156  GP, XXVI, ii, No. 9451, Pourtalès to Foreign Office, 17 March 1909, p. 683.

157  ibid., No. 9460, Bülow to Pourtalès, 21 March 1909, pp. 693–5. Quoted in Schmitt, *Annexation*, p. 194.

158  Fischer, *Krieg*, pp. 105–6.

159  Schmitt, *Annexation*, p. 196.

160  Albertini, *Origins*, Vol. 1, p. 286.

161  Lee, *Europe's Crucial Years*, pp. 203–4.

162  ibid., p. 206.

163  Kennedy, *Antagonism*, p. 445.

164  For the latter, see GP, XXVI, ii, No. 9540, Bülow to Pourtalès, 25 May 1909, pp. 797–8; No. 9549, Bülow to Wilhelm, 10 June 1908, p. 818.

165  PAAA, Russland 72, Vol. 89, Posadowsky-Wehner to the Minister of War, 6 May 1909.

166  ibid., Russland 72, Geh., Bd 15, Moltke to Bülow, 29 May 1909.

167  See above, n. 165.

168  GP, XXVI, ii, No. 9538, Jagow to Bülow, 20 May 1909, pp. 793–5; No. 9550, Jagow to Bülow, 10 June 1909, pp. 819–20; and PAAA, Italien 72, Bd 23, Jagow to Bülow, 15 June 1909.

169  Bülow, *Denkwürdigkeiten*, Bd II, pp. 512–13.

170  See, above all, Konrad H. Jarausch, *The Enigmatic Chancellor: Bethmann-Hollweg and the Hubris of Imperial Germany* (New Haven, Conn., 1973), pp. 9–66; Eberhard von Vietsch, *Bethmann-Hollweg: Staatsmann zwischen Macht und Ethos* (Boppard, 1969), pp. 30–91; Fritz Stern, "Bethmann-Hollweg and the war: the limits of responsibility," in *The Responsibility of Power: Historical Essays in Honor of Hajo Holborn*, ed. Leonard Krieger and Fritz Stern (New York, 1967), pp. 254–5.

171  Bülow, *Denkwürdigkeiten*, Bd II, p. 512; Jäckh, *Kiderlen-Wächter*, Vol. 2, pp. 32–3; GP, XXVII, ii, No. 10169, Bethmann-Hollweg to Wilhelm, 11 December 1910, Wilhelm's marginal comment, pp. 867–8; also H. Henning, *Deutschlands Verhältnis zu England in Bethmann-Hollwegs Aussenpolitik, 1909–1914* (Cologne, 1962), p. 42.

172  GP, XXVIII, No. 10320, "Aufzeichnung . . . Bussche-Haddenhausen," 15 July 1909, p. 201.

173  ibid., No. 10323, "Aufzeichnung . . . Ballin," 15 July 1909, pp. 205–10; No. 10325,

"Aufzeichnung . . . Bethmann-Hollweg," 13 August 1909, pp. 211–17; No. 10326, Bethmann-Hollweg to Schoen, 14 August 1909, pp. 217–18; No. 10327, Schoen to Bethmann-Hollweg, 19 August 1909, p. 219; Tirpitz, *Aufbau*, pp. 163–5; Jarausch, *Enigmatic Chancellor*, p. 113; Lamar Cecil, *Albert Ballin: Business and Politics in Imperial Germany, 1888–1918* (Princeton, NJ, 1967), pp. 171–4.

174   GP, No. 10325, pp. 214, 216.
175   ibid., No. 10326, Bethmann-Hollweg to Schoen, 14 August 1909, pp. 217–18.
176   AHA, II, 8, Nachlass Eisendecher, Tirpitz to Eisendecher, 23 August 1909.
177   GP, XXVIII, No. 10327, Schoen to Bethmann-Hollweg, 16 August 1909, pp. 218–19.
178   ibid., No. 10339, Tirpitz to Bethmann-Hollweg, 1 September 1909, pp. 227–30; No. 10340, Bethmann-Hollweg to Tirpitz, 16 September 1909, pp. 230–2.
179   See ibid., Nos 10343–6, pp. 234–8.
180   Woodward, *German Navy*, pp. 269–70.
181   Jäckh, *Kiderlen-Wächter*, Vol. 2, "Denkschrift des Gesandten von Kiderlen für den Reichskanzler von Bethmann-Hollweg über eine deutsch-englische Verständigung," pp. 48–59.
182   ibid., p. 58.
183   GP, XXVIII, No. 10347, "Aufzeichnung pr. 15 Oktober 1909," pp. 239–43. For Kiderlen's role in the negotiations, see C. Waldron Bolen, "Kiderlen's role in Anglo-German conversations, 1909–12," *Journal of Central European Affairs*, vol. 9, no. 2 (July 1949), esp. pp. 136–49.
184   GP, XXVIII, No. 10352, Metternich to Bethmann-Hollweg, 29 October 1909, p. 252; No. 10360, Metternich to Bethmann-Hollweg, 5 November 1909, p. 267.
185   ibid., No. 10362, Metternich to Foreign Office, 15 November 1909, p. 270.
186   ibid., No. 10369, Bethmann-Hollweg to Metternich, 1 February 1910, pp. 282–3.
187   ibid., No. 10370, Metternich to Bethmann-Hollweg, 3 February 1910, pp. 284–90.
188   ibid., No. 10375, Metternich to Bethmann-Hollweg, 11 March 1910, p. 301.
189   ibid., No. 10400, Bethmann-Hollweg to Metternich, 8 August 1910, p. 349.
190   ibid., No. 10401, memorandum dated 26 July 1910, presented by Goschen to Bethmann-Hollweg on 14 August 1910, pp. 351–4.
191   Tirpitz, *Aufbau*, p. 179.
192   GP, XXVIII, 10408, "Aufzeichnung . . . Tirpitz, Gesichtspunkte für Agreement," 23 September 1910, p. 360. It also appears in BA-MA, N 253/24.
193   Tirpitz, *Aufbau*, pp. 184–5; the notes for the report, corrected by Capelle, appear with some differences in BA-MA, N 253/24, n.d.
194   H St Ar, Stuttgart, E73/73a 12e, Verz. 61, signature illegible, to Weizsäcker, 28 July 1910.
195   GP, XXVIII, No. 10444, Wilhelm to Tirpitz, 14 May 1911, p. 415; Tirpitz, *Aufbau*, pp. 195–6.
196   Kelly, "Naval Policy," fo. 415.
197   BA-MA, N 253/8 and F 3443, PG 67473 both have copies of "Aufzeichnungen über die Unterredung S.E. des Herrn Staatssekretärs des RMA mit dem Reichskanzler über die Agreement-Angelegenheit am 4. Mai 1911."
198   ibid., F 3443, PG 67473, Müller, "Persönliche Auffassung der Agreementsfrage," 15 May 1911.
199   GP, XXVIII, No. 10441, "Aufzeichnung . . . Bethmann-Hollweg, 5 April 1911; Anlage," p. 409; No. 10443, Bethmann-Hollweg to Metternich, 9 May 1911, p. 414.
200   PAAA, Russland 131, Geh., Bd 14, Bethmann-Hollweg to Wilhelm, 15 September 1909; ibid., Russland 131, Bd 31, Pourtalès to Bethmann-Hollweg, 21 September 1909.
201   Albertini, *Origins*, Vol. 1, pp. 306–10.
202   GP, XXVII, No. 9888, Bethmann-Hollweg to Wilhelm, 9 November 1909; Wilhelm's comments on p. 423.
203   PAAA, Russland 72, Vol. 89, Posadowsky-Wehner to the Minister of War, 30 April 1910.
204   ibid., Vol. 90, Posadowsky-Wehner to Minister of War, 8 August 1910; military attaché in Paris, Winterfeldt, to Minister of War, 21 May 1910.
205   ibid., Russland 98, Bd 5, Hintze to Wilhelm, 19 January 1910.
206   ibid., Russland 91, Bd 42, Winterfeldt to Minister of War, 3 February 1911.
207   ibid., Frankreich 116, Bd 25, Winterfeldt to Minister of War, 7 February 1911.

208 ibid., Russland 91, Bd 42, Posadowsky-Wehner to Minister of War, 10 February 1911.

209 GP, XXVII, ii, No. 9945, Hintze to Wilhelm, 24 March 1910, pp. 521–9.

210 Marginalia to ibid., p. 529.

211 ibid., Nos 9946, 9947, 9949, 9948, pp. 530–7.

212 PAAA, Russland 98, Geh., Bd 1, Hintze to Wilhelm, 10 August 1910.

213 GP, XXVII, ii, No. 9950, Posadowsky-Wehner to the Minister of War, 12 August 1910, p. 541; Ropponen, *Die Kraft*, pp. 246–7.

214 GP, XXVII, ii, No. 9951, Pourtalès to Bethmann-Hollweg, 12 August 1910, pp. 542–3.

215 ibid., No. 9956, Hintze to Wilhelm, 19 August 1910, pp. 548–53.

216 ibid., No. 9957, Plessen to Bethmann-Hollweg, 17 September 1910, pp. 554–5.

217 PAAA, Russland 131, Geh., Vol. 14, Bethmann-Hollweg to Wilhelm, 15 September 1910, draft Kiderlen.

218 ibid., Pourtalès to Bethmann-Hollweg, 22 August 1910.

219 Kriegsarchiv, Vienna, Conrad Archiv, B I, "Unterredung Hptm. Putz mit Exz. v. Moltke, 1.10.1910."

220 For Wilhelm's doubts, see GP, XXVII, ii, No. 10148, Jenisch to Bethmann-Hollweg, 13 October 1910, p. 830.

221 ibid., No. 10155, Bethmann-Hollweg to Pourtalès, 8 November 1910, pp. 840–2.

222 ibid., No. 10159, Bethmann-Hollweg to Pourtalès, 15 November 1910, Anlage I "Projet," p. 847.

223 ibid., "Anlage II," p. 849.

224 ibid., No. 10166, Pourtalès to Kiderlen, 2 December 1910, pp. 858–60; No. 10167, Kiderlen to Pourtalès, 4 December 1910, pp. 861–2; No. 10169, Bethmann-Hollweg to Wilhelm, 11 December 1910, pp. 866–8, PAAA, Russland 131, Geh., Bd 16, Kiderlen to Pourtalès, 20 December 1910: "nur grüss mich nicht unter den Linden."

225 Kriegsarchiv, Vienna, Mil. Att. Berlin, Vol. XI, Bienerth to Chief of the General Staff, 17 January 1911.

226 PAAA, Russland 131, Geh., Bd 16, Pourtalès to Bethmann-Hollweg, 16 February 1911.

227 ibid., Bd 18, Bethmann-Hollweg to Wilhelm, 15 September 1910, and Wilhelm's marginalia.

228 Lee, *Europe's Crucial Years*, p. 220.

229 See in particular PAAA, Österreich 70, Bd 47, Tschirschky to Bethmann-Hollweg, 26 December 1910.

230 e.g. ibid., Österreich 91, Bd 16, Tschirschky to Bethmann-Hollweg, 22 December 1909.

231 ibid., Österreich 95, Bd 18, Tschirschky to Bethmann-Hollweg, 3 January 1910.

232 ibid., Bd 19, Tschirschky to Bethmann-Hollweg, 20 October 1910, copy; ibid., Österreich 91, No. 2, Bd 11, Tschirschky to Bethmann-Hollweg, 12 and 16 November 1910.

233 ibid., Österreich 95, Geh., Bd 3, Tschirschky to Bethmann-Hollweg, 27 and 28 January 1910; ibid., Österreich 95, Bd 18, Tschirschky to Bethmann-Hollweg, 1 February 1910.

234 ibid., Deutschland 128, No. 2, Bd 29, "Aufzeichnung . . . Bethmann-Hollweg," 14 December 1909.

235 See Michael Palumbo, "German-Italian military relations on the eve of World War I," *Central European History*, vol. 12, no. 4 (December 1979), p. 346; GP XXVII, i, No. 9861, Bethmann-Hollweg to Tschirschky, 1 June 1910, p. 359; PAAA, Deutschland 128, No. 2, Bd 29, Oberndorff to Bethmann-Hollweg, 4 September 1910, regarding the favorable impression made by San Giuliano on Aehrenthal.

236 GP, XXVII, i, No. 9865, Bethmann-Hollweg to Aehrenthal, 19 September 1910, p. 369.

237 PAAA, Italien 72a, Bd 19, Jagow to Bethmann-Hollweg, 13 January 1911.

238 GP, XXVII, i, No. 9876, Jagow to Bethmann-Hollweg, 30 May 1911, pp. 392–3.

239 Bay H St Ar, Abt II, Geh St Ar, MA III, 2688, Lerchenfeld to Prince Regent, 31 May 1911.

240 Lee, *Europe's Crucial Years*, pp. 241–2. The fullest account of the Agadir crisis involving all powers is still Ima Christina Barlow, *The Agadir Crisis* (Chapel Hill, NC, 1940); pp. 46–206 deal with the developments from Algeciras to the "Panther leap." The February Accord is discussed on pp. 76–7. An excellent recent treatment of German policy is Emily Oncken, *Panthersprung nach Agadir: Die deutsche Politik während der Zweiten Marokkokrise 1911* (Düsseldorf, 1981). She covers the developments from the February Accord to 1911 on pp. 22–45.

241 Barlow, *Agadir*, pp. 133–43; George W. R. Hallgarten, *Imperialismus vor 1914: Die soziologischen Grundlagen der Aussenpolitik der europäischen Grossmächte vor dem Ersten Weltkrieg* (Munich, 1963), Vol. 2, pp. 219–32; Oncken, *Panthersprung*, p. 31.

242 GP, XXIX, No. 10493, Schoen to Radolin, 25 January 1910, p. 41; No. 10499, Lancken to Foreign Office, 17 February 1910: Schoen's final comment of 18 February, p. 45. Oncken argues that there existed no strong internal reasons for the German Morocco action; *Panthersprung*, pp. 64–95 passim, esp. pp. 94–5.

243 PAAA, Frankreich 102, Bd 48, Lancken to Foreign Office, 24 July 1909, telegram, copy; Frankreich 87, Bd 89, Bethmann-Hollweg to Wilhelm, 20 January 1910.

244 ibid., Frankreich 118, Bd 3, Schoen to Bethmann-Hollweg, 6 April 1911.

245 ibid., Frankreich 102, Bd 52, Schoen to Bethmann-Hollweg, 8 April 1911, copy. For the German view of France before 1911, see Oncken, *Panthersprung*, pp. 51–2.

246 Lee, *Europe's Crucial Years*, p. 248; Barlow, *Agadir*, pp. 183–4.

247 ibid., pp. 187, 191.

248 GP, XXIX, No. 10538, Wilhelm to Bethmann-Hollweg, 22 April 1911, p. 89.

249 PAAA, Frankreich 95, Bd 61, Moltke to Schoen, 25 January 1910, "Afrikanische Truppen als Verstärkung der französischen Wehrmacht."

250 ibid., Moltke to Schoen, 2 March 1910.

251 ibid., memorandum of the General Staff "Die militärische Bedeutung der Marocco-frage," n.d., no signature, for the estimates of the military significance of Morocco, see also Oncken, *Panthersprung*, pp. 208–12.

252 See above, n. 248.

253 GP, XXIX, No. 10539, Bethmann-Hollweg to Wilhelm, 22 April 1911, pp. 89–90.

254 ibid., No. 10545, "Aufzeichnung . . . Kiderlen," 28 April 1911, p. 97; Barlow, *Agadir*, pp. 194–5; Oncken, *Panthersprung*, p. 113.

255 Albertini, *Origins*, Vol. 1, p. 328; Jarausch, *Enigmatic Chancellor*, pp. 120–1.

256 GP, XXIX, No. 10548, Jenisch to Kiderlen, 30 April 1911, p. 101.

257 ibid., No. 10549, "Aufzeichnung . . . Kiderlen," 3 May 1911, pp. 101–8; Lee, *Europe's Crucial Years*, pp. 249–50; Fischer, *Krieg*, p. 122; Barlow, *Agadir*, pp. 220–2. Oncken points out the numerous inaccuracies in the memorandum and concludes that it was less a statement of Kiderlen's program than an attempt to sway the Kaiser; *Panthersprung*, pp. 113–19.

258 Lee, *Europe's Crucial Years*, p. 249.

259 Jäckh, *Kiderlen-Wächter*, Vol. 2, p. 122; Fischer, *Krieg*, p. 199; Lee, *Europe's Crucial Years*, pp. 149–50; for Wilhelm's reluctance, see Barlow, *Agadir*, pp. 225–6.

260 GP, XXIX, No. 10555, Schoen to Bethmann-Hollweg, 7 May 1911, p. 115; Barlow, *Agadir*, p. 227.

261 GP, XXIX, No. 10571, Schoen to Bethmann-Hollweg, 10 June 1911, pp. 140–1, and n. *; Oncken, *Panthersprung*, pp. 131–2.

262 ibid., No. 10572, "Aufzeichnung . . . Zimmermann," 12 June 1911, pp. 142–9, incl. n. *; Fischer, *Krieg*, pp. 119–20; Lee, *Europe's Crucial Years*, pp. 250–1; Barlow, *Agadir*, pp. 228–9; Oncken, *Panthersprung*, p. 131.

263 GP, XXIX, No. 10572, n. *, pp. 142–3.

264 Fischer, *Krieg*, pp. 120–3; Jarausch, *Enigmatic Chancellor*, p. 122.

265 PAAA, Frankreich 102, No. 8, Bd 1, Bethmann-Hollweg to Wilhelm, 6 July 1911, and Wilhelm's marginalium. Oncken, *Panthersprung*, pp. 142 ff.

266 GP, XXIX, No. 10607, Bethmann-Hollweg to Wilhelm, 15 July 1911, p. 185; Wilhelm's marginalia on p. 186.

267 GP, XXIX, No. 10583, Tschirschky to Foreign Office, 1 July 1911, p. 158; No. 10582, Jagow to Foreign Office, 1 July 1911, p. 157; Fischer, *Krieg*, pp. 132–5. See Oncken, *Panthersprung*, pp. 59–63, 287–9.

268 Jäckh, *Kiderlen-Wächter*, Vol. 2, Kiderlen-Wächter to Bethmann-Hollweg, 17 July 1911, pp. 128–30; Barlow, *Agadir*, pp. 264–5.

269 Jäckh, *Kiderlen-Wächter*, Vol. 2, Bethmann-Hollweg to Kiderlen-Wächter, 18 July 1911, p. 131; for Wilhelm's and Bethmann-Hollweg's doubts about Kiderlen's policy, see Oncken, *Panthersprung*, pp. 167–73.

270 Jäckh, *Kiderlen-Wächter*, Vol. 2, pp. 132–4; Oncken, *Panthersprung*, pp. 144, 151, 153, 163–4, 174–86.

271 Barlow, *Agadir*, p. 267.

272 GP, XXIX, No. 10561, Metternich to Bethmann-Hollweg, 22 May 1911, p. 119.
273 ibid., No. 10562, "Aufzeichnung . . . Bethmann-Hollweg," 23 May 1911, p. 120.
274 ibid., No. 10588, Metternich to Foreign Office, 3 July 1911, pp. 164–5.
275 ibid., No. 10592, Metternich to Foreign Office, 4 July 1911, p. 167.
276 ibid., No. 10617, Metternich to Bethmann-Hollweg, 21 July 1911, pp. 199–203.
277 See M. L. Dockrill, "British policy during the Agadir crisis of 1911," in F. H. Hinsley (ed.), *British Foreign Policy under Sir Edward Grey* (Cambridge, 1977), esp. pp. 273–8; M. G. Fry, *Lloyd George and Foreign Policy,* Vol. 1, *The Education of a Statesman: 1890–1916* (Montreal, 1977), pp. 131–9.
278 GP, XXIX, No. 10629, Kiderlen to Treutler, 26 July 1911, p. 219; Oncken, *Panthersprung,* p. 291.
279 GP, XXIX, No. 10628, Kiderlen to Treutler, 26 July 1911, p. 217, Wilhelm's marginalium on p. 218.
280 ibid., No. 10630, Wilhelm to Bethmann-Hollweg, 27 July 1911; No. 10631, Bethmann-Hollweg to Wilhelm, 27 July 1911, p. 220.
281 K. D. Erdmann (ed.), *Kurt Riezler: Tagebücher, Aufsätze, Dokumente* (Göttingen 1972), nos. 511–13, 177–81; Jäckh, *Kiderlen-Wächter,* Vol. 2, p. 83; Jarausch, *Enigmatic Chancellor,* pp. 122–3.
282 Tirpitz, *Aufbau,* p. 200.
283 ibid., 201; Oncken, *Panthersprung,* pp. 202–7.
284 BA-MA, F 2041, PG 66061, Scheer, "Denkschrift zum Immediatvortrag über Hebung der Bereitschaft unserer Seestreitkräfte im August-September 1911," obviously misdated 8 August 1911; Oncken, *Panthersprung,* p. 205.
285 Barlow, *Agadir,* pp. 338–9.
286 Tirpitz, *Aufbau,* p. 202.
287 BA-MA, F 2051, Tagesmeldungen VI-IX, 1911, Tagesmeldung No. 35, Seebohm, 10 August 1911; Oncken, *Panthersprung,* p. 307.
288 BA, Kleine Erwerbungen (see p. 435 for holdings of Bundesarchiv Koblenz) 517–2, Tagebuch W. v. Oettingen, 14 November 1911.
289 Tirpitz, *Aufbau,* Tirpitz to Capelle, 12 August 1911, p. 205.
290 Jäckh, *Kiderlen-Wächter,* Vol. 2, p. 138.
291 BA-MA, N 253/25, Capelle to Tirpitz, 14 August 1911.
292 Walter Rathenau, *Tagebuch 1907–1922,* ed. H. Pogge von Strandmann (Düsseldorf, 1967), p. 294.
293 GP, XXIX, No. 10705, "Bericht . . . Winterfeldt," 7 August 1911, pp. 323–5.
294 ibid., No. 10706, Schoen to Bethmann-Hollweg, 10 August 1911, p. 326.
295 ibid., No. 10715, "Bericht . . . Winterfeldt," 19 August 1911, pp. 332–5.
296 ibid., No. 10723, "Bericht . . . Winterfeldt," 24 August 1911, pp. 344–5.
297 ibid., No. 10724, Wilhelm to Bethmann-Hollweg, 28 August 1911, p. 345.
298 ibid., No. 10726, "Aufzeichnung . . . Heeringen," 31 August 1911, pp. 346–8.
299 Bay H St Ar, Abt IV, M.Kr. 41, Gebsattel to [Bavarian] Minister of War, 3 September 1911. For the German reaction to the cancellation of the French maneuvers and the estimates of the German military about the possibility of war, see also Oncken, *Panthersprung,* pp. 215–17. She also claims that the cancellation of the French maneuvers limited the German range of options; p. 297.
300 Fischer, *Krieg,* p. 137. I am following Marion Jackson's translation in the 1975 English edition, p. 88. Oncken plays down the significance of this statement: *Panthersprung,* p. 217, n. 26.
301 Bay H St Ar, Abt IV, M.Kr. 41, Gebsattel to Minister of War, 4 September 1911.
302 ibid., Gebsattel to Minister of War, 6 September 1911.
303 ibid., Abt II, Geh St Ar, B. Ges, Berlin, 1083, Sch(?) to Hockwohlgeb. H. (?), 6 September 1911.
304 PAAA, Deutschland 121, No. 31, Geh., Bd 1, "Chef des Generalstabes der Armee, Berlin, September 7, 1911, Zu Nr. 11352, Die Militärpolitische Lage."
305 Bay H St Ar, Abt II, Geh St Ar, MA III, 2689, Lerchenfeld to "Lieber Freund," 9 September 1911.
306 GLA, Karlsruhe, 49/2044, Berchheim to Dusch, 12 September 1911.
307 *Spitzenberg,* p. 533.
308 Fischer, *Krieg,* p. 137.
309 Kennedy, *Antagonism,* p. 447.

# 16 Groping for Viable Naval Operations Plans in European Waters, 1905–11

As the operations plan in Danish waters was scuttled, work on the new plans against Britain and France had to start from the very beginning at a time that war against these powers was a distinct possibility. The Morocco policy entailed a risk of war; the Kaiser on several occasions expressed fear of a British attack and emphasized the need for increasing the war preparedness of the fleet. Tirpitz had noted on 22 February 1905 that the next five years would constitute the greatest danger zone for Germany.[1] There was thus the utmost urgency in preparing the new plans.

As for France, the Kaiser had in February 1905 approved a new version of the old offensive plan against the French northern coast. Late in 1905, A3 revised the plan for the following year by making provisions for laying mines along the French coast.[2] The *raison d'être* for the plan was questioned by A2, who suggested that the role of Britain in a war between Germany and the Dual Alliance could no longer be ignored in view of diplomatic developments of the previous year. A3 dismissed this criticism, however, by remarking that the document confined itself to the war with the Dual Alliance. Thus he separated naval planning from political realities. On 3 March, 1906, A3 laconically noted that "His Excellency [Büchsel] has not been able to look through OP I again because of lack of time. He has none the less decided that it should be copied and duplicated."[3] Büchsel thus either considered the operations plan for a Continental war as unimportant or possessed unbounded confidence in his staff. Nor did he think that this operations plan required any revision in July when he reported to Wilhelm the French decision to concentrate all the newest ships of the line and armored cruisers in the Mediterranean and to leave in Brest only a squadron of six older armored cruisers and in Cherbourg a reserve division of coastal armored ships. He concluded: "Through the new distribution of the French naval forces the situation has thus changed only in so far as we must from the outset expect a battle with the united French forces since it is to be assumed with certainty that the united French fleet will as soon as possible speed from the Mediterranean to help the threatened north." Büchsel based this assumption on recent statements in the French press and parliament. "Everyone presses for a naval offensive against Germany, since French conceit cannot as yet admit that the German fleet has become at least equal if not superior to theirs." But if the French were, in any case, to advance with their united forces against Germany what need was there for the offensive against their coast? Büchsel's answer was not entirely convincing. He claimed that an offensive would have a great impact on an enemy lacking firm discipline, provide maximum relief for German shipping, and encourage German allies. At the same time he doubted whether the Italian navy "would under present conditions be a willing and energetic opponent of France."[4]

As for operations against Britain, the Chief of the Fleet, Koester, had criticized the Baltic concentration of the old plan and urged an immediate battle by Heligoland in the North Sea as soon as the Siegfried ships had reached the Elbe from Danzig.[5] He did not, however, expect the battle to have a favorable outcome. The Admiralty Staff instead opted for a strategic defensive in the North Sea which would for some time retain a "fleet in being." Rather unrealistically, it at first planned for a war against Britain alone.[6] On 21 March 1905, Büchsel reported to Wilhelm and obtained his approval for the concentration of the fleet in the Elbe for the conduct of a strategic defensive.

The first battle line of the British and German naval forces was estimated for July 1905 as shown in Table 16.1.

**Table 16.1**

|  | *Britain* | *Germany* |
|---|---|---|
| Ships of the Line | | |
| Available immediately | 20 (292,000 tons) | 14 (160,000 tons) |
| Available later | 6 (82,000 tons) | 8 coastal armored ships (33,000 tons) |
| Armored cruisers | 12 (126,200 tons) | 3 (27,000 tons) |
| Torpedo-vehicles | 72 destroyers | 18 large torpedo-boats |
| | 36 torpedo-boats | 4 D Boats |
| | | 35 small boats |

No battle was to be sought until the German naval forces, including the Third Squadron of Siegfried ships located in Danzig, were united and the supremacy of the British had eroded. Rather unrealistically Büchsel expected Germany's alliance value to increase in the eyes of other powers through the tying down of British forces on the German coast. He insisted that preparations be made to fortify the Frisian islands to prevent the British from establishing a base there, for which he recommended discussions of the representatives of the Admiralty Staff, the Imperial Naval Office, the Fleet Command, and the General Staff. For the balance of the year the preparations at sea were to be placed in the hands of the Chief of the Fleet and autumn maneuvers were to test the new strategy.[7] Büchsel did not, however, inform Tirpitz, Koester, and Schlieffen about the new plan and the need for consultation before 15 April. The last was warned that if the Frisian islands were well fortified the British might violate Danish neutrality by seizing Esbjerg on the western coast of Jutland as a base. In such a case the German army would again be involved in operations on Danish soil.[8]

Late in 1905 and early in 1906 the Admiralty Staff prepared the operations plan against Britain for 1906. The plan was presented to and approved by Wilhelm on 3 April 1906.[9] The document opened with a depressing statement about British superiority in *matériel*, in war preparedness, and in the training of personnel. There followed a discussion of British war aims—the destruction of the German fleet, the interruption of maritime trade, and bombardment and burning of coastal cities—and strategy. The memorandum favored the deployment of the active German forces in the Elbe estuary as soon as war appeared imminent.

The tying down of the British fleet was expected to relieve its pressure on the powers friendly to Germany, presumably Austria-Hungary and Italy, and thus improve her diplomatic position. In his observations on the memorandum Büchsel commented that actions by neutrals could cause the British to detach forces from the blockade fleet and thus enhance Germany's chances of success.[10] Unlike in March 1905, the possibility of France and Russia being allies of Britain was taken into consideration. It was taken for granted that if France was Britain's ally the two fleets would operate separately and that the French fleet would select the Baltic Sea as its operational theater. Such action on the part of the French fleet should not cause the German fleet to give up its concentration in the Elbe or to divert forces to the Baltic. The principle of concentrating in the North Sea against the main enemy was thus adhered to. Because of the destruction of her fleet the effects of Russia's involvement as Britain's ally were dismissed as negligible.

It is significant, however, that A3 raised the possibility of a wide blockade of the North Sea from Dover and the Shetland Islands.[11] Such a blockade had been mentioned by Büchsel himself in 1903 as "for us the most dangerous tactics of the enemy"[12] and was referred to and dismissed in the memorandum of March 1905.

In a report to Wilhelm on 27 March 1906,[13] Büchsel stressed the need to improve German coastal defenses, intelligence, and security to meet a surprise attack which the Royal Navy could successfully launch because of its high degree of preparedness. Lastly, the Third Squadron of the Siegfried ships was to be located in the Kiel–Elbe position instead of Danzig. Following this report even Tirpitz, who had consistently opposed the strengthening of coastal defences at the expense of the battle fleet, concurred and there followed a steady improvement of German coastal fortifications and other precautionary measures which soon caused the British to realize that an assault on the German coast would prove to be difficult.[14]

German concern about a British landing in Esbjerg, mentioned by Büchsel in March 1905, or in Schleswig-Holstein had been increased by the so-called Delcassé revelations in *Le Matin* on 7 October, according to which he had received oral promises of British support against Germany, including the landing of 100,000 men in Schleswig-Holstein and the seizure of the Kaiser Wilhelm Canal.[15] In November 1905, Schlieffen wrote to Büchsel, inquiring whether British landings were possible in locations in Jutland and Schleswig-Holstein other than Esbjerg and whether the navy could provide for troop movements on the eastern coast of Schleswig-Holstein—questions which Büchsel answered negatively.[16] At the end of February 1906, Schlieffen's successor Moltke, who was at the time concerned about the imminent outbreak of war, provided Büchsel with information about probable British action against Germany in case of a Franco-German war which he alleged to have obtained from a reliable source. The British navy would be mobilized in four days and ready in the Thames estuary for action against Germany. In the course of hostilities the British expected the German navy to offer battle and be destroyed. In spite of its losses the Royal Navy, even without French support, would be able to establish a blockade of the German North Sea coast and the Baltic and to seize Borkum as a base. British forces, consisting of three army corps and three cavalry brigades, would land either in Esbjerg, whence, with the support of three French corps, they would advance on Berlin; or, if the German fleet were not entirely destroyed, in Antwerp. The reaction of the Admiralty Staff to this communication was the comment by one officer that the British only handled common operations with the French as a contingency and as yet appeared to have no firm commitments to them, and the forwarding of copies of the communication to the Naval Office and the Chief of the Active Battle Fleet.[17]

At about the same time the Admiralty Staff studied another, possibly internally prepared memorandum concerning the use of the British army on the Continent.[18] Its author considered as prerequisites for such action the availability of a Continental ally and the security of Britain's colonial possessions. Although 116,000 men could be transported to the Continent, their location on the left wing of the French army was dismissed as being contrary to British self-esteem. The alternatives were a landing in Antwerp or in Esbjerg, with the latter more probable because it offered the opportunity to attack the Kaiser Wilhelm Canal and Kiel and because of the evidence provided by the Delcassé revelations.

The strategic defensive in the North Sea was examined in the Admiralty Staff voyage of July 1905,[19] and in the autumn maneuvers of 1906 during which, partly because the action of the leader of the Yellow (British) party was limited by rigid instructions, the Blue (German) party was successful. But Büchsel warned Wilhelm that this success should not be viewed as indicative of what would happen in an actual war.[20] On the basis of these and other studies the Chief of the Active Battle Fleet reasserted his offensive stance, recommending that the fleet should no longer be restricted to the Elbe, where it could be easily shut in, but should be allowed to extend its operations to the whole of the Heligoland Bight so as to be able "at any time to utilize the mistakes and disturbances in the advance of hostile forces and weather conditions for energetic counterattacks and partial successes." Büchsel, however, remained more cautious. Could the German fleet fully control the Bight? It would certainly have to return to the Elbe at night to avoid exposure to torpedo-boat attacks. And when returning to the Bight the next morning it would have to proceed with extreme caution since the enemy could have infested the waters with mines during the night. While the fortifications of Heligoland might protect the northern flank of the German fleet against encirclement, the danger of a superior enemy getting behind it and preventing its return to the Elbe could not be disregarded.[21]

The Great Admiralty Staff voyage of 1906 dealt with the deployment of the British naval forces against the German coast under conditions most favorable to them. This was admittedly a worst-case analysis, which was regarded as necessary.[22] By that time the Admiralty Staff had found out that in addition to the British Channel and Atlantic fleets the Home Fleet would be set up to which ships would be detached from the other two fleets. The British Mediterranean fleet was also expected to arrive in the north within five days and the total British strength as augmented by the entire Home Fleet and reserve was estimated at thirty-nine ships of the line of the first class, thirteen ships of the line of the second class, thirty-two armored cruisers, thirty-seven large protected cruisers, and thirty-seven small protected cruisers.

In the autumn maneuvers of 1906 the Fleet Command concluded that the defense of the Elbe required immediate improvement, that the British light forces were inadequate to impose a close blockade on German river estuaries, and that torpedo-boats could be used effectively in the rear of the blockading British forces.[23]

By the end of 1905 the Admiralty Staff had considered France's alliance with Britain a distinct possibility and made some provisions for it; by 1907 it had come to regard it as certain that any war against Britain would also involve France. In March 1907 the aim of a war game of the Admiralty Staff, led by Büchsel himself, was:

> Obtaining a view of the formation of the general situation in a war of Germany against England and France and, in particular, of our action against the French fleet if it proceeds shortly after the outbreak of war into the Baltic Sea.

From this game A concluded that the operations plan should be revised to give the Chief of the Active Battle Fleet greater freedom than allowed by the prescription to concentrate in the Elbe estuary. The offensive mentality of the Fleet Command was thus extending to the Admiralty Staff. Büchsel, however, did not entirely concur with A. While agreeing that a French attack on Kiel was improbable, he was opposed to keeping the fleet in the Baltic under any circumstances since it would give the British full opportunity to control the North Sea and wreak whatever havoc they could and would force the German fleet to come to the North Sea but under more difficult circumstances.[24]

In the spring of 1907 the Admiralty Staff drafted a revised plan. By that time the Foreign Office on political grounds and the General Staff on military grounds had expressed their approval of defensive operational planning. Büchsel had reported on 19 March.

> The State Secretary of the Foreign Office held it to be very necessary with regard to neutral powers in a German–French–English conflict to prevent our opponents from having successes at sea at the outbreak of war. Every

naval victory of Germany, especially near the enemy coast, however small, would work extraordinarily favorably. The Chief of the General Staff expressed the opinion that it would be unwelcome for the army if the English achieved unrestricted mastery in the North Sea soon after the start of the war and therewith the opportunity of transporting troops in chosen directions.[25]

Current planning thus enjoyed broad approval. The revised plan assessed the political situation as follows:

If Germany in 1907 is involved in a European war, the expected enemies will be France and England. If a quarrel with France is the cause of the war, England will intervene; if England starts the war, it will have been with assurances of French support.

The attitude of the other powers will probably not improve our position. The present view is that one cannot at first count on the Mediterranean powers; Denmark will try to remain neutral and will probably limit herself to protests if her neutrality is violated; the attitude of Russia will not have any influence on the course of a naval war in 1907.[26]

Except, possibly, for the assumption that Britain would join France in a war against Germany over any issue, the political assessment was realistic.

The French navy was not expected to play a major role in the north at the outset of hostilities. The real naval opponent was Britain. Her Mediterranean forces would move north and would definitely attack the German fleet if located in the North Sea. If it was in Kiel, a British attack against the Elbe position and the western locks of the Kaiser Wilhelm Canal was to be expected. If the French fleet arrived in German waters, either the Elbe or Kiel could be attacked unless supported by the German fleet, which would thus be pressed to divide its forces.

In view of the probable British intentions the Elbe concentration was upheld but the fighting was to occur before rather than in the river estuary so as to inflict maximum losses on the enemy. If the French were to attack Kiel at the beginning of the war, the fleet was also to deploy in the Elbe and only units unsuitable for action in the North Sea were to be sent for its defense. Only later in the course of the war could the fleet be shuttled through the canal for the purpose of gaining partial successes in the Baltic. It was not denied that such a defensive war might lead to greater losses on the German than on the British side, but if this was likely to be the case the strategy could be changed. The warfare in the main theater was to be reinforced by attacks on Britain's coast, war harbors, communication lines, and trade to weaken her and to draw her naval forces away from the German coast. A surprise torpedo-boat attack at the beginning of war against ships in the harbors on the eastern British coast—Sheerness–Chatham, the Humber estuary, the Firth of Forth, and the Medway—was closely examined but it was ruled that the decision was to be made only once war had broken out. As for commerce raiding, the fast ships of the Hamburg–America Line and the North German Lloyd were to be armed and used as auxiliary cruisers.

German naval planning against Britain came to be seriously affected by intelligence about probable British strategy as revealed in the fleet maneuvers held in October 1907. It was learned through the indiscretion of a local British newspaper that the purpose of the maneuvers was to determine "whether the blockading English fleet would be so weakened by German torpedo-boat attacks that the German battle fleet could accept battle with any prospects of success." From the maneuvers, which came to be known in detail, it was concluded that the bulk of the British fleet would remain at considerable distance from the German coast and use torpedo-nets for protection at night. It would thus be difficult for the German torpedo-boats to reach and attack it with success. Nor would the British bulk force the Elbe but wait for the German fleet to come out and offer battle. Until then the armored cruisers and light forces would from their closer blockade positions have on their own to contend with the German forces. Under these circumstances, concluded the Admiralty Staff: "It must therefore be the task of our fleet to force the bulk of the blockade fleet to come closer through energetic daytime attacks on the blockade forces."[27]

## II

It was this conclusion—that the British were not going to accommodate themselves to the wishful thinking of the Admiralty Staff—and the replacement of Büchsel by Friedrich Count von Baudissin in January 1908 that for a while ended the defensive mentality of the Admiralty Staff. A clever and experienced man, Baudissin had served as the captain of the Kaiser's yacht *Hohenzollern* and proven himself as Chief of the First Squadron. He was a representative of the "Front" and shared Koester's offensive mentality. A bluntly arrogant aristocrat, he utterly lacked tact and soon fell victim to the power struggle between the Admiralty Staff and the Imperial Naval Office which had victimized his predecessor.[28] On the day that Baudissin assumed office A4, Wilhelm Taegert, completed the first draft of the defensive operations plan for 1908.[29]

On 1 February, Baudissin stated his fundamental disagreement with the draft:

(1)  The memorandum must be structured differently. It must originate from an *offensive* intention [*Charakter*] and must distinguish between our offensive action before the battle itself and what follows.
(2)  There appears a fundamental error in the memorandum; namely this: that we leave coasts, etc., undefended if no ships are located there. One defends Swinemünde, for instance, if one fights a battle in the middle of the ocean, and this indeed is the only possible and correct defense by a fleet.
(3)  I personally entirely fail to understand how a battle *in* the Elbe is being envisaged. The utilization of the coast, shallows, etc., is something very good; but a hundred times higher stands the question of the inner value of the ships which I can only bring fully to bear in the high seas.[30]

Baudissin had thus broken both with the defensive mentality and with the preference for fighting in narrow coastal waters more familiar to oneself than to the enemy with the support of coastal guns, mines, and other blockings, and favored battle in the open sea where the qualities of seaworthiness and seamanship would be the decisive factors.

Following Baudissin's instructions Grapow and Taegert started to work on the revisions. The latter was to cooperate with the Chief of the High Seas Fleet, Prince Heinrich, on tactics during and after the decisive battle.[31] At the same time A3 prepared a study of the role of France as Britain's ally in a war against Germany.[32] This appears to have been the first detailed examination by the Admiralty Staff of France's role since it came to regard her as a certain British ally. The role of Italy was considered to be the main influence on French action: were she on the German side or assuming a waiting stance, substantial allied forces would have to be kept in the Mediterranean; were she to provide assurances of her neutrality, France would still have to keep watch on Austria-Hungary but could place the modern ships of her First and Second Mediterranean Squadrons at Britain's disposal in the north; or, were she to join the allies, it would be her task to watch Austria-Hungary, and France could send her entire forces to the north. The major French task in the Mediterranean was to assure the transport of the Nineteenth Army Corps from Algeria to Europe and for this she would need her entire naval forces which would not be available in the north regardless of Italy's stance until the Nineteenth Corps had been moved to France. Italy's stance would not affect France's use of her northern naval forces. Their coastal armored units would at first defend the French coast, and the northern squadron would be mainly engaged in cruiser warfare. Only later would the major French naval forces in the Mediterranean affect the power relationship in the north to Germany's disadvantage.

In his change in strategy Baudissin established contact with the General Staff. That agency had been more cooperative with the Admiralty Staff since Schlieffen's departure, particularly as naval operations plans no longer conflicted with its operations plans. Discussions had taken place for the improvement of North Sea defenses—a more congenial subject for cooperation than the attack on Denmark. Moreover, since February 1905 they had also discussed the blocking of the Scheldt against British reinforcements from the sea during the siege of Antwerp by the army, which also came to involve the Imperial Naval Office. This time it was the General Staff that had called for navy support to facilitate its operations. The correspondence was friendly, the Admiralty Staff was informative, and made many helpful suggestions for action, most of which were accepted by the General Staff.

By September 1908 the army had made preparations to counter a British landing in Antwerp or Vlissingen. In the opinion of A2, Schwenger, the General Staff was also interested in undertaking combined offensive operations with the navy in the Rhein, Maas, and Scheldt estuaries.[33] This impression impelled Schwenger to undertake a study of limited joint army–navy operations against Holland in the event of a war against Britain which could be grafted on to existing army preparations.[34] Schwenger's study was criticized by A4, Taegert, who proposed a much more extensive army–navy action against the Low Countries in an Anglo-German war. Taegert justified the proposed action as follows:

> Holland and Belgium must be occupied. The war England–Germany cannot end in the sacrifice of our fleet and the starvation of the country while the army looks on inactively . . .
>
>   In our possession, Holland is a permanent threat to England even after the conclusion of peace. Therefore the occupation of Holland in peacetime is under given circumstances a valuable, perhaps the only, compensation object which we can offer in a desperate situation.

This was a new version of the hostage theory, now involving Holland rather than France. Taegert expected that the British would dispatch troops to defend Holland, thus involving the German army.

> Finally, through the invasion of Holland and Belgium, we achieve a favorable starting position for a war against France which will, indeed, be inevitable.

The assumption was that the war with Britain would start first. British army landings in the Low Countries would involve the German army in support of the navy, which would find itself in a more favorable position for the subsequent operations against the French. Thus the Tirpitz Plan dovetailed with the Schlieffen Plan. Taegert admitted that the action could not occur by surprise, as Schröder had speculated in 1897.[35] The document was annotated by A, Grapow, who authorized Taegert to conduct the necessary correspondence with the General Staff with the aim "that the question of a war with England would at last receive a full discussion between both agencies."[36] This correspondence did not produce any results, however. On 8 February 1910, with the support of Rieve, who had assumed the position of A, Taegert sought clarification regarding Germany's attitude toward Holland and Belgium if Germany were at war with Britain or Britain allied with France.[37] Conceding that the final decision about the action lay with the army, Taegert none the less had changed his mind, reverting to Büchsel's criticism of the Schlieffen Plan in 1905.[38] He and Rieve requested the new chief of the Admiralty Staff, Fischel, to seek a decision from Wilhelm. Their concern lay chiefly with the question of Dutch neutrality. As for Belgium, it was admitted that her "occupation . . . will probably occur automatically in the course of the land war."

At Fischel's request Rieve conferred with Oberst Stein of the General Staff on 23 February with the result that:

> Concerning Holland, the army will observe the strictest neutrality as long as possible, difficult as it may be to avoid our advance over Maastricht. His Majesty has agreed. If the other side makes it impossible for Holland to maintain her neutrality, then Germany would naturally act accordingly.

Regarding Belgium, Rieve reported that Stein, though reticent, admitted that the General Staff must have a free hand.[39] Since the General Staff had since 1908 planned an attack on the railway junction of Lüttich which would make a violation of Dutch neutrality unnecessary by avoiding a congestion of German troop movements against France, it agreed to respect Dutch neutrality. Moltke remained consistently opposed to the violation of Dutch neutrality. Although probably out of touch with these developments, the retired Schlieffen still planned for the movement of troops through Holland in his memorandum of 28 December 1912.[40] The possible violation of Dutch and Belgian neutrality on the part of Britain also continued to occupy the Admiralty Staff toward the end of 1910 and at the beginning of 1911. Direct British action against Holland was considered unlikely, since the Dutch would resist it.

Baudissin maintained contact with the General Staff about operations plans in general, writing to Moltke on 21 February 1908 to inform him of the British maneuvers of the previous October and to request information about army operations plans against Britain and other powers outside Europe. On 29 February he contacted Moltke again, this time to enlist his support for the change in naval strategy against Britain. Referring to the interest expressed by him in the previous spring in preventing the British from establishing mastery in the North Sea at the beginning of hostilities, and stating that naval operations plans must fit into the overall strategy, he requested answers to several questions:

I.  In a war against France and England simultaneously:

   (*a*)  Is it probable that the allied opponents will undertake a landing operation of a large scale on our or the Danish coast as soon as they adequately dominate the seas?
   (*b*)  Is there a danger that such a landing can influence the waging of war in the main theater of war considerably or even decisively?
   (*c*)  Is it desired that the fleet would first have to be preserved [*erhalten*] for the prevention of this danger even if the resulting defensive attitude would later unfavorably influence the leadership in France?
   (*d*)  How long would the limitation of the freedom of operation imposed on the fleet probably last?
   (*e*)  What influence can the fleet bring to bear on land war if it must limit itself to the domination of the Baltic Sea?

II.  In a war against England alone:

   (*a*)  Do the army leaders wish that the fleet not be initially involved in a decisive battle?
   (*b*)  How long will this limitation on the freedom of action of the fleet last?[41]

Moltke replied promptly, on 2 March, expressing appreciation for Baudissin's concern and providing precise answers to all of his questions:

I.   (*a*)   I consider large-scale landing operations on our or the Danish coast probable.

    (*b*)   I do not attribute to such a landing a considerable or decisive influence on the waging of war in the main theater of war.

    (*c*)   I do not consider it desirable to preserve the fleet only for the purpose of defense against such a landing if thereby the waging of naval war would be immediately or later influenced unfavorably.

        Particularly I would consider it regrettable if it should cost the fleet the chance for success through offensive action against hostile naval forces.

    (*d*)   Has been answered by (*c*).

    (*e*)   If the fleet must limit itself to the domination of the Baltic Sea, it can have no influence on the waging of war on land.

II.  (*a*)   The military leadership has no objections to the full involvement of the fleet in a decisive battle at the beginning. The military leadership would happily greet any tactical success that the fleet would have.

    (*b*)   Answered by (*a*).[42]

This was one of the closest contacts between the Admiralty Staff and the General Staff regarding common planning. The General Staff continued to concern itself with the prospect of a British landing on the German or Danish coast, although it did not greatly fear it, and did not insist that the German navy be preserved as a "fleet in being" to prevent it. Nor did it then have any interest in naval control of the Baltic Sea. Russia was militarily and navally impotent and the army would according to the Schlieffen Plan push west. No objections were raised to the proposed offensive strategy of the navy in the North Sea.

By 12 March, Baudissin had prepared a report initialed by A, Grapow, A4, Taegert, and D, to inform Wilhelm of the change in operational planning.[43] Probable change in British strategy, as shown in the maneuvers of last October, was cited as the reason for the change: the British bulk could no longer be damaged by a German fleet restricted to strategic defensive. The new strategy envisaged in the first stage of the war a series of battles between the German light forces and the British blockade line: here existed the first prospect for damaging the British. In the second stage, the entire German strength was to be used energetically against the enemy bulk even if there was no chance of total success but only the prospect of destroying parts of the hostile fleet. The entire plan was to be rebuilt within an offensive framework. It also envisaged a surprise torpedo-boat attack against the Royal Navy at the outbreak of war, and attacks against Britain's coast, trade, and cable connections during the war to force the detachment of her forces from the main theater of war in the North Sea. Baudissin proposed re-examination of the major questions involved in the operations plan—(1) is the fleet secure in the Elbe, (2) how can it return from the sea, and (3) how can it establish a favorable power relationship with the enemy in the course of hostilities? Summer maneuvers were to investigate German operations in the light of the further development of British submarines and torpedoes.

Wilhelm approved of the changes in operational planning, and Baudissin proceeded with the preparation for: (*a*) a strict defensive and (*b*) a ruthless offensive in both the North Sea and the Baltic. On 13 April, A4, Taegert, completed a memorandum dealing with possible British action.[44] He expected Britain to act immediately, weighed the previously considered advantages and disadvantages of her various courses of action, and provided the closest consideration to date of the possibility of a wide blockade of the North Sea. While Taegert considered such action as contrary to British offensive naval traditions, he admitted that there was evidence that it had been considered:

> This manner of waging of war would have the advantage of keeping one's own naval forces relatively intact while bringing heavy pressure to bear on Germany. German maritime trade ceases. Eventually the German fleet, if it does not want idly to await the ruin of the country, must engage in battle, whatever the circumstances.

It is significant that Tirpitz himself had seriously considered the possibility of a wide blockade a year earlier. In considering the attitude to be taken by the German representatives at The Hague Conference regarding the sea-prize law, he observed that in a few years Britain would no longer be able to enforce a close blockade on the German coast:

> She would limit herself then to the closing to us of the passage north and south of England and stand with her bulk in the North Sea, leaning on England. Such an extended blockade would have pretty much the effect of a narrow coastal blockade. In the long run we would not be able to survive it economically.[45]

Germany would, however, have the military opportunity to attack the British coastline. In January 1909, Tirpitz expected that the close blockade of the German coast would be carried out by light forces and that the British bulk would be located "behind the Dogger Bank in the proximity of England."[46]

On 24 October, Baudissin presented to the Kaiser a detailed report in support of an offensive strategy against Britain.[47] In a war against Germany British action would be limited by two extremes: (1) an immediate ruthless attack on the German fleet and (2) a wide blockade of the North Sea. Either would fulfill the British aim of cutting Germany off from the sea. Baudissin's logic became rather confused subsequently, but essentially he argued that in any blockade-type situation Germany would suffer more than Britain and that a vigorous offensive would be more important than the maintenance of a "fleet in being" in enhancing her alliance value: German successes would provide encouragement for Austria-Hungary and Italy, who could provide military and economic support, and for the rivals of Britain, who would benefit from her setbacks. Ultimately, however, the military rather than the political situation must determine German action. Since the German naval development had concentrated on ships of the line rather than on light forces, the latter must by necessity be subordinated to the former. Since ships of the line are built for battle, the decisive battle must remain the aim of German naval strategy. The question was when and where the battle was to be fought. In answering this double question Baudissin considered three possible areas: (1) the Elbe, (2) the Baltic, and (3) the open sea. In the Elbe, he argued, the fleet could not choose the time for battle. Although this had to some extent been ignored, every maneuver had produced evidence that the river estuary could be strewn with enemy mines which would deter a later exit of the fleet, since enemy superiority would make mine clearance very difficult. The Elbe, moreover, offered no protection against attacks by torpedo-boats and the new submarine weapon unless the fleet withdrew upstream or into the Kaiser Wilhelm Canal. The advantages that superior knowledge of the waters provided for the German forces in the Elbe would be offset by the confidence the British gained from their numerical superiority. Concentrated in Kiel, the fleet could attack the enemy only if the Danish islands were seized and fortified. Otherwise it would be a purely defensive position. There remained the open North Sea. There, however, neither Heligoland nor mine blockings offered the fleet any protection against torpedo-boat attacks and mobility was its main defense. Unlike the British, German ships were not equipped with torpedo-nets. From this situation Baudissin concluded:

> The significant question—what do we want in war?—is answered in view of our location, our development, and our capacity in favor of an offensive against a hostile fleet wherever and whenever we find it.

He therefore recommended an immediate offensive against the Royal Navy and prepared the following instructions for the Chief of the High Seas Fleet:

> Your task is to do the greatest damage to the enemy, risking all the forces at your disposal. To that end you should attack the enemy with all available high-seas forces. If the foe is not encountered during the first sortie, then some of his coastal areas listed . . . are to be infested with mines and hostile shipping is also to be destroyed by other means as far as possible.[48]

Wilhelm approved the new operations with enthusiasm. In a series of separate meetings held subsequently between the representatives of the Admiralty Staff, the Command of the Baltic Sea Station, the Command of the North Sea Station, and the Command of the High Seas Fleet unanimous agreement was reached about the desirability of the offensive.

The Admiralty Staff pushed ahead with its preparations. The separate meetings with representatives of other naval agencies are indicative of Baudissin's earlier stress on confidentiality. Although the heads of the agencies were thus involved, Baudissin realized that further detailed work would include other higher officers from whom operational intentions could not be concealed. He therefore recommended that directives be issued to the effect that operational planning ranged from a strict defensive to a ruthlessly offensive action so as to make the offensive plan appear as just one of several.[49]

In the spring of 1909 an examination of the advance of the High Seas Fleet against the British coast was referred to the Chief of the High Seas Fleet, Prince Heinrich.[50] He was to answer the following questions: (1) Where could the High Seas Fleet be most securely and inconspicuously prepared for the sortie? Should it, regardless of where it was located at the proclamation of mobilization, proceed for provisioning to the Elbe? Preference was expressed for the final preparations occurring in Kiel and Wilhelmshaven. (2) What was to be done if upon arriving in the Elbe the fleet were to find the river estuary blocked by the enemy? (3) Which ships should participate in the sortie? (4) What course was the fleet to take if it was not informed of the location of the Royal Navy? The Admiralty Staff expressed its preference for approaching the British coast under the cover of night when mine-ships could best dispense with the protection of the fleet. (5) Since mine-laying was one of the most important actions in the proposed sortie, which ships of the High Seas Fleet were to be equipped with mines? (6) How was information to be made available to different units of the attacking High Seas Fleet? (7) How were torpedo-boats to be supplied with coal on the high seas? And (8) what was to be done to provide coal and protect the returning High Seas Fleet if the Elbe estuary was blocked and it had to proceed to the Baltic through Skagen?

Prince Heinrich responded on 31 July 1909.[51] In reply to question 1, he favored equipping and provisioning the ships in the two war-harbors before they proceeded to the Elbe. But he saw a problem arising in the autumn: the Nassau-class ships joining the fleet could not pass the Kaiser Wilhelm Canal. If they were in the Baltic at the beginning of mobilization or hostilities and were to deploy in the Elbe, they would require forty hours to circumnavigate Denmark during which they would be so vulnerable as to have to be excluded from the sortie. Instead of dispensing with these ships he raised the question whether they should instead be permanently located in Wilhelmshaven:

> The importance of Wilhelmshaven, which already emerges through the completion of the third causeway, will thereby be pushed even further into the foreground. The value of its flank position to the Heligoland Bight and the increasing value of Heligoland as support through the submarines based there will considerably increase our security in the Heligoland Bight and thus make us more independent of the Elbe.

Prince Heinrich thus considered extending the German defensive position into the entire German Bight.

As to action if the Elbe was blocked by the enemy, Heinrich advised against the return of the fleet into the Baltic and its subsequent advance against the British coast from Skagen: instead he recommended an immediate attack against the blockings. If they could not be forced, the fleet would have to retreat into the Baltic and advance from Skagen, with the decisive battle to be expected in the North Sea. In response to the third question he proposed that all ships which would not slow down the sortie take part in it. As for the direction of the sortie, Heinrich agreed that use be made of night cover, that the mine-layers be taken along, and suggested that the objective be the Thames and Humber estuaries. He emphasized that the major aim of the sortie was battle with the Royal Navy or parts thereof; the secondary purpose, disturbance of the British economy and public opinion, would also improve German chances in battle by diverting British forces. Regarding offensive mine warfare, he agreed that it was "one of the main instruments of battle," but insisted that mines carried on board destroyers and cruisers be secured against exploding under enemy fire. He did not consider the exchange of information during the sortie as presenting a major problem. For coaling torpedo-boats he proposed locating coalers in prearranged locations in the North Sea; and for coaling the fleet along the longer return route around Denmark setting up depots on the Norwegian coast and locating coalers in Danish waters. Reserve formations were to secure the passage through the Danish Belts. There thus existed good communications and substantial agreement between the Admiralty Staff and the High Seas Fleet.

In its work on the offensive operations plan against Britain the Admiralty Staff also examined the role of France as Britain's ally. In response to questions from A in 1908, A3 stated a month later that no French Mediterranean forces would be available for immediate use against the German coast, but that eight armored ships and twenty-four torpedo-boat destroyers located on the French northern coast could appear there. He thought it unlikely that French forces would be used in the Baltic, as suspected previously, and instead expected them to protect the flank of the British forces by guarding the Baltic exits and blocking the entry into the English Channel with torpedo-boats and submarines. Within the Mediterranean he anticipated that the French forces would safeguard the transport of the Nineteenth Army Corps from Algeria to France, observe Italy, and try to destroy the Austrian Navy.[52]

At Wilhelm's request the Admiralty Staff reported to him in April 1909 on a case of war in which Germany allied with Austria-Hungary would be at war with Britain, with all other powers being neutral.[53] This case of war was rather hypothetical in spite of Germany's close support of her ally during the Bosnian crisis. Why should Austria wish to support Germany against Britain if Russia remained neutral? She was certainly under no obligation to do so. The memorandum indicated the obvious: that the two fleets would have to operate separately. It also noted that Britain had an interest in paralyzing the Austrian navy since it constituted a threat to her Suez route from Asia; she would therefore in addition to her Mediterranean forces have to detach ships from her Atlantic squadron against the Austrians. None the less, superior British forces would still be left to confront the High Seas Fleet in the north. This slight advantage provided by Austria-Hungary as an ally would be more than offset, however, by her being less able to supply Germany with her own produce and imports across her boundaries than if she were a neutral. The only real advantage gained from the Austrian alliance for the German navy was if it were located in the Atlantic or the Mediterranean at the outbreak of war and could more easily enter the Austrian harbors than return home. The conclusion was that in a war against Britain the German navy would benefit more from Austria-Hungary as a neutral than as an ally.

# III

From 1906 to 1909 the operational planning of the Admiralty Staff involved France only as an ally of Britain and disregarded a war against France alone, against France allied with Russia, or against Russia alone. Sometime before January 1909, probably prompted by the Bosnian crisis and the Casablanca incident, Wilhelm ordered a report about the state of operational planning against France, Russia, and the Dual Alliance. A draft was prepared by the Admiralty Staff in January 1909,[54] followed by a fuller report of 9 March.[55] This included a long statement of Britain's inexorable hostility toward Germany, described as being grounded in her historical opposition to the strongest Continental power with maritime ambitions. Hence "one has to reckon that if Germany becomes involved in any war the English fleet will join the enemy either immediately or at the appropriate opportunity." Therefore in a war with either France or the Dual Alliance Germany would have to reserve strong forces against Britain: she was the main enemy at sea. A war against Russia alone was improbable. While the statement about operations against France remained vague—it was not at all clear which French forces would be attacked in which location by which German forces—operations against Russia were elaborated. They were to open with the destruction of the Russian torpedo-boats in Libau. Subsequently the navy was to keep open the connection between Königsberg and the western Baltic and to assist the army by demonstrations against the Russian coast. Some cruisers might appear as far north as the Bay of Narva and possibly support troop landings there to tie down the St Petersburg garrison. The navy thus expected to perform in the Baltic its traditional role of supporting army operations, and Baudissin appropriately suggested closer cooperation with the General Staff.

Wilhelm approved the guidelines as reported to him and ordered that they be followed in the preparation of further operations.[56] On 17 March, Baudissin contacted Moltke, requesting a meeting to discuss the revision of the plans.[57] The latter was obviously interested and on the next day the two men met accompanied by Oberst Stein of the General Staff and A1 of the Admiralty Staff, Kapitän-zur-See Rieve. Baudissin explained the position of his agency and found Moltke in full agreement, stressing that in a war with France and Russia Germany "would always have to count England as an enemy." Moltke did not consider naval support against Russia essential, for he did not expect Russian troop-transport by sea or Russian landings on the German coast; a feint attack by the navy on Libau would, however, be desirable to tie down the Russian Twentieth Army Corps. Moltke was more interested in naval support in the west. Although the German military attaché in London, Major Ostertag, had still reported in June 1908 that in a war of Germany against France and Britain the British army would be landed in Esbjerg or in Antwerp,[58] the Chief of the General Staff now thought that Britain had bound herself to send troops to assist French operations on land and hoped that the navy could delay their transport. Apparently uninformed since 2 March 1908 of the changes in naval planning, he still expected the navy to take a defensive position in the Elbe. He was therefore very pleased to learn that the navy would proceed to an immediate offensive which he described as "valuable support for the army."[59]

More precise details for cooperation between the army and the navy were settled through a questionnaire sent by the Admiralty Staff to the General Staff and returned on 2 April.[60]

(1) The question whether the army expected East Prussia to be cut off was answered with some ambiguity: by the time the Russians could accomplish it, German operations would cancel it. Were the encirclement to occur anyway, Königsberg as well as Pillau could hold out without naval sea connections.

(2) As at the meeting, the question about possible Russian landings was answered in the negative. Should they occur anyway, the army was prepared.

(3) Likewise the question about possible Russian troop movements at sea was answered in the negative.

(4) In response to the question whether it intended to cooperate in landings on the Russian coast, the General Staff replied that they would be useful but of only secondary importance. None the less, feint or actual operations of the navy against Libau, Riga, or even St Petersburg would be appreciated to pin down Russian forces. These operations were not to detract from the main tasks of the navy, however.

(5) As to whether the army wanted the navy to keep open a supply port in the Baltic to support its operations, the General Staff stated that the coast was not sufficiently close to them.

(6) The answer to the question "What demands does the army make on the navy in the event of an outbreak of war against France?" was that the General Staff would want the navy to cause greatest damage to the enemy "without dividing itself for subsidiary tasks in support of secondary concerns of the army."

(7) The General Staff further agreed to accede to its best ability to the request of the Admiralty Staff for information about the movement of French and Russian naval forces.

In short, Moltke was not tempted by Baudissin's inviting questions to have the navy serve in a subsidiary role in a war against the Dual Alliance. Convinced that Britain would join the Dual Alliance, he was appreciative of the willingness of the Admiralty Staff to undertake an immediate offensive against Britain and thus delay the arrival of her land forces in France. Russia was not a serious opponent because she was recuperating from the wounds inflicted by the Japanese. Thus the Chief of the General Staff was happy to have the navy conduct its own independent strategy as an equal partner in Germany's defense.

Following the discussions with the General Staff, the Admiralty Staff drafted a memorandum which was to serve as a basis for talks with the Chief of the High Seas Fleet.[61] In it the political situation was more clearly outlined than previously: perhaps information had been supplied in the audience with Wilhelm, in the discussions with the General Staff, or from other sources.

At present it is Serbia which may lead Russia into a war with Austria. Germany must then help the latter whereas France will support Russia and England will never permit France, for a second time, to be humiliated by Germany. The course of events will always be the same when conflict occurs between two powers, whatever the cause.

The main enemy for the navy was Britain, against whom its main strength must be united. Therefore Baudissin proposed that in future operations only those naval forces support the army which were nonessential in the offensive against Britain:

The navy supports the army against Russia in so far as it would have forces available to tie down Russian troops and to create in the rear of the advancing Russian armies military and political confusion through direct or feint attacks against the Russian coast. The support against France consists of offensive action against the transports of the supporting English army and thus corresponds to the aims of the war against England.

What emerges from these discussions is that whatever conflicts we have on the Continent, we, the navy, always view England as our main enemy.

Baudissin further proposed to prepare an operations plan against Russia alone since "it is possible, although extremely improbable, that we could be involved in a war against Russia alone, if England were tied down elsewhere and France had no desire to carry out the obligations of the Entente Cordiale" (toward Russia). In such a case a most vigorous offensive should be undertaken against the vastly inferior Russian naval forces to establish full control over the Baltic and provide support for the army beyond the requirements of the General Staff.

Parallel to the cooperation between the Admiralty Staff and the General Staff, contact was also established between the Imperial Naval Office and the Prussian Ministry of War, apparently at the instigation of the former. Periodic meetings were agreed upon to avoid conflicts in the acquisition of war supplies.[62]

IV

The difficulty presented to German naval operations by the inability of the increasing number of Dreadnoughts to pass the Kaiser Wilhelm Canal, first mentioned by Prince Heinrich, was also recognized by the Imperial Naval Office, which had been so concerned about the financial side of the problem. In May 1909 the Naval Office therefore became involved in one of its few exercises in operational planning. A, Paschen, submitted to Tirpitz a document drafted by Fregattenkapitän von Usslar, Korvettenkapitän von Bülow and Korvettenkapitän Vollerthun which examined the case of war "Germany and Austria-Hungary against France and England" in the years 1910–13 when they expected the canal to remain closed to Dreadnoughts. The authors expected Britain's aim to be the destruction of the German fleet before Germany could defeat France and the support of France in a land war. The expectation that a British landing would occur in Jutland indicated that the Naval Office was unaware of the recent planning of the Admiralty Staff and of its contacts with the General Staff. The option for a defensive over an offensive strategy, since the latter would lead to an immediate destruction of the German fleet, showed either a total ignorance or a callous disregard of the preference of the Admiralty Staff, the High Seas Fleet, the Baltic and North Sea stations, and the General Staff. The authors continued to favor the deployment of the fleet in the Elbe at the outbreak of war. For later operations they weighed the advantages and disadvantages of concentration near Heligoland or in the Kattegat. If the former location was chosen, the fleet was to be protected by mines south of the island. This concentration offered the advantages of presenting a greater threat to Britain, including the possibility of raids against her coast, offensive mine war and commerce raiding, good opportunities for the use of light forces, pinning down more enemy ships, and making difficult the landing of hostile troops on the coast of Jutland—something that the General Staff no longer expected. The "fleet in being" could be maintained for a long time and immediate battle was to be offered to the British only if they threatened to enclose the High Seas Fleet with mines. The main disadvantages of the Heligoland position were that the enemy could freely operate in the Baltic and bring pressure on Denmark to join him.

The advantages of deployment in the Kattegat—more favorable climatic conditions for the use of older German *matériel*, more space for the movements of the High Seas Fleet, and better intelligence about what the enemy was doing—were more than offset by the disadvantages: the position in the Kattegat became untenable if Denmark joined Britain; the fleet had no real strategic role since it posed no threat to the enemy and allowed him full scope for action in the North Sea, the opportunity to seize bases in Holland or on the west coast of Jutland, or bring his numerical superiority to bear in the Kattegat itself. In comparing the conditions under which a decisive battle would be fought in the two locations, the authors pointed out that, although in the Kattegat the German side would have the advantage of being better acquainted with the area and being in a very favorable defensive position against the enemy entering through the northern défilés, the opponent would be able to choose the time for battle and be able to force it on the High Seas Fleet earlier than in the North Sea. The authors therefore opted in favor of deployment by Heligoland.

In an enclosure the strength of the two sides in ships of the line was compared as follows: excluding the Siegfried- and Sachsen-class ships, which were viewed as incapable of participating in battle either in the Kattegat or in the North Sea, Germany would have twenty-eight ships, including four of the Nassau class, whereas Britain and France would have fifty-two ships, including eight Dreadnoughts.

Tirpitz minuted the memorandum on 22 June:

Taken notice of with interest.
The preceding standpoint assumes
(1)  that one should operate with the fleet in the direction *in being*
(2)  that mines are already now directly available in mass.
Both do not hold true at the time for actual preparations.

This cryptic comment confirms Tirpitz's knowledge of the offensive operations plan but, contrary to his memoirs, may imply that he disapproved of it.[63]

In the fall of 1909, Baudissin exchanged posts with Fischel. He had come into conflicts with Tirpitz which were more violent than those that had led to his predecessor's departure and had also annoyed Wilhelm and Müller, both of whom had come to realize that he and Tirpitz could no longer work together. He was already informed on 27 March 1909 that "since HM would count for years on the present Secretary of State," he would be transferred to the less sensitive post of the Chief of the North Sea Station.[64] Fischel had fully approved Baudissin's offensive strategy and continued to adhere to it.

On 5 October the new Chief of the High Seas Fleet, Henning von Holtzendorff, questioned the offensive strategy. He wrote to the Admiralty Staff to inquire whether he was correct in his assumption that the offensive operations plan was valid only in the summer and that the offensive action of the fleet was subject to the degree to which units were trained for warfare, particularly during the winter. On behalf of the Admiralty Staff, A, Rieve, gave an affirmative answer.[65] In late October, Fischel was presented by his staff with a report concerning preparations for operations in the coming winter. In view of Germany's naval weakness they maintained that she would never start a war with Britain; it must originate with the latter power. They revived the hostage theory: once Britain attacked, Germany must start a war on land, presumably against France, "if we do not want to end up in a position of dependency on our unweakened neighbors through economic exhaustion resulting from a long naval war." While the offensive strategy was described as theoretically correct, it was stressed that much work remained to be done in preparing for enemy attack against coastal defenses and river estuaries, securing intelligence about the movements of the British fleet, and arranging for the decisive battle in the North Sea. The problem of the Nassau ships was brought up. They should be removed from the Baltic in times of political tension, but if caught there at the outbreak of war they should under no circumstances be allowed to proceed alone to the North Sea through the Danish waters. Were the High Seas Fleet, including the Nassau ships and *Blücher*, in the Baltic when war broke out it would remain dependent on the Danish Belts for its exit. "We must therefore make provision for securing the Belt against the entry of hostile forces and for keeping it open for offensive purposes." It was recommended that the Admiralty Staff provide guidelines and the Fleet work on appropriate tactics for such an eventuality and that both collaborate closely. The possibility of a decisive battle resulting from the struggle for the Belts was to receive further examination. It was recognized that the entire question of deployment was further complicated by the stationing of the First Squadron of the High Seas Fleet in Wilhelmshaven: it could be cut off by the British soon after the outbreak of war if the High Seas Fleet was forced to concentrate in the Baltic.

Another major complication for German operations, according to the report, was shown by the maneuvers in the fall of 1908 in which the Blue or German side lost all of its light forces in the fight for the control of river estuaries without being able to inflict any losses on the enemy. Because of this experience it was assumed that British mine-layers would enter the river estuaries in daytime under the protection of more numerous, faster, and larger armored cruisers than possessed by Germany to strew mines. The long-range fire of the armored cruisers would make mine clearance very difficult and the German fleet would risk being enclosed. Hence the report recommended as a partial remedy the strengthening of the Heligoland position by locating there submarines and torpedo-boats during periods of political tension that might lead to war and as a more effective remedy providing the Chief of the High Seas Fleet at the very beginning of hostilities with ships of the line to fight off enemy armored cruisers that would be supporting mine-strewing in the Elbe estuary. The Chief of the High Seas Fleet should be prepared for the possibility that the struggle for the estuary might lead to a major sortie and decisive battle. The report also echoed Holtzendorff's concern for the low state of preparedness during the winter months which made an offensive impossible: at that time whatever ships were ready for action should concentrate in the Elbe, attempt to keep the connection with Wilhelmshaven open, and await reinforcements.[66]

Thus Baudissin's doctrine of an immediate offensive in the North Sea was losing its force: lack of preparedness, particularly in the winter, and the difficulty of controlling the river estuaries undermined the possibility of an offensive; the possible location of the new large ships in the Baltic made impossible the deployment in the Elbe under all circumstances.

In view of the reopening of the question of operations in Danish waters, Fischel inquired whether there was any possibility of army support, and upon receiving what must have been the expected negative reply drafted guidelines for the Chief of the High Seas Fleet to respect Danish neutrality. For these he obtained Wilhelm's approval.[67]

Fischel invited Holtzendorff to a meeting which extended over two days, 19–20 December, and temporarily convinced him that the Admiralty Staff was right. It was agreed that the solution to the problem posed by the inability of the new ships to pass the canal lay in the transfer of all fleet training to the North Sea until the canal had been rebuilt. At first the First Squadron of the High Seas Fleet and the cruisers would be transferred to the North Sea; the Second Squadron would follow once adequate berthing facilities were available.[68] On 21 December, Fischel obtained Wilhelm's renewed approval for deployment in the North Sea and for an offensive strategy. The Kaiser, whether from overconfidence, naïveté, or willingness to deliver the first blow, affirmed that it would be possible to bring the Nassau ships and *Blücher* from the Baltic to the North Sea before the outbreak of war.[69]

Within the Admiralty Staff several memoranda drafted early in 1910 continued to justify an offensive North Sea strategy. A memorandum entitled "Ostsee oder Nordsee als Kriegsschauplatz," summarizing the arguments in favor of the offensive North Sea strategy, was enclosed for Wilhelm's approval and for subsequent distribution to the commanding admirals. A copy of the memorandum was sent by Fischel to Tirpitz on 12 August 1910 and received his approval. Tirpitz had thus sided with Fischel against Holtzendorff's defensive Baltic Sea strategy. But he agreed that it was a good idea to test both the North Sea and Baltic Sea strategy through war games: the latter might be necessary because of "special conditions . . . Besides, the situation is becoming more favorable from year to year. Let our enemies build as much as they want."[70]

In the winter of 1910–11 the operational planning against Britain was tested in several war games: the Imperial War Game of the High Seas Fleet for which general instructions were issued by the Admiralty Staff, the War Game of the North Sea Station, the War Game of the Baltic Sea Station, and the War Game of the Admiralty Staff.

The Imperial War Game was played on 23 February 1911, and Holtzendorff wrote a report of its outcome on the same day. According to his report, the head of the German party decided to choose the Elbe as the place of deployment and launched the attack a day before the declaration of war, the hypothetical 11 September. But the mine-laying cruisers and torpedo forces which had preceded the sortie of the High Seas Fleet accomplished nothing: those approaching British harbors were driven back by destroyers which were ready for action when political tension broke out. The Royal Navy had united its forces on the same day as the German advance was launched and was advancing toward the German Bight behind a strong protective screen of light forces; on the night of 11–12 September, the British destroyer vanguard encountered the German fleet which was advancing without a protective screen of which it had been deprived by the detachments for torpedo and mine action against the British coast. The High Seas Fleet was severely damaged by repeated mass attacks of British destroyers and was compelled to withdraw to the German Bight where in the morning of 12 September it was forced to come to battle, without support from the detached cruisers and torpedo-boats, with an undamaged and now considerably superior British force.

Holtzendorff considered the fatal flaw in the German advance to have been the separation of the light forces from the main fleet action which, he claimed, was justified by the leader of the German party on the grounds of a consensus in past years to launch an immediate attack against the British coast by torpedo-boats and mine-ships. He now stated that such an attack was only permissible before political tension had set in, i.e. if it was part of an offensive war undertaken by Germany, and enjoyed an element of complete surprise. For this to occur the Chief of the High Seas Fleet must already in peacetime have full control over the forces to be used for the torpedo and mine-laying operations. Holtzendorff was obviously trying to extend his bailiwick. He further criticized the war game for being based on a best-case analysis of the power relationship and war preparedness of the two sides, and referred to the British maneuvers of 1909 according to which in case of "war imminent" all British forces intended for immediate action would go to sea and the German Bight between Sylt and Borkum be effectively blockaded.

The Admiralty Staff, particularly Taegert, extensively annotated Holtzendorff's memorandum. The annotations reflected the disagreements between the Admiralty Staff and the Command of the High Seas Fleet over operational planning. Taegert denied that the Admiralty Staff was in favor of an immediate attack of the German light forces against the British coast; it had only made preparations for it in response to the proposals of the High Seas Fleet. Both Taegert and Fischel now expressed their disapproval of this separate strike. To Holtzendorff's claim that a surprise attack of light forces against the British coast could be launched under special circumstances, Taegert responded that these could only be assessed by the Admiralty Staff and must even be concealed from the High Seas Fleet.

Holtzendorff had not condemned the offensive strategy against Britain outright; he had only strongly criticized the advance strike of the torpedo and mine-laying forces and indicated that the instructions of the Admiralty Staff for the Imperial War Game in which the German side failed was based on a best-case analysis. That, perhaps, was the most politic case to be made for his Baltic Sea strategy.

In June 1911 the Admiralty Staff completed a report to the Kaiser about all the war games played in the winter of 1910–11, which, however, was not submitted to Wilhelm until October 1911.[71] It admitted the failure of the German side in the Imperial War Game of the High Seas Fleet. Further, it reported on the war games of the North Sea station, the Baltic Sea station, and the Admiralty Staff itself. The first involved the union of the High Seas Fleet near Heligoland and its advance against the British coast without the torpedo-boat flotillas. The fleet advanced to Scotland, stood for six hours before Aberdeen, and then swept the North Sea to find the enemy. During this operation the defense of the North Sea was left to the Third Squadron and the torpedo-boat flotillas and submarines. Meanwhile the British side had united its forces, occupied Sylt, blocked the German Bight, and infested the Ems with mines, while suffering some losses from German torpedo-boats. The German High Seas Fleet none the less managed to re-enter the Heligoland Bay intact. Both sides were judged as having made mistakes. The war game of the Baltic Sea station involved the advance of the High Seas Fleet and torpedo-boat flotillas against the British coast and the British advance for the purpose of blockading the German Bight and the Baltic Sea. Upon learning of the exit of the German Second Squadron from the Baltic through Danish waters, the British detached a cruiser squadron and torpedo-boat destroyer flotilla to observe its movements. Although the German Second Squadron managed to unite with the units deploying in the North Sea, the united German forces gave up the advance against the British coast because of their observation by the pursuing British cruisers and destroyers. They were brought to battle by the superior British force at Hornsriffe where (and in subsequent torpedo-boat attacks) two-thirds of the ships of both sides were put out of action. The rest of the German fleet withdrew into the Elbe and the British forces which were being reinforced occupied Sylt and imposed a blockade on the German coast. There was a further battle when the High Seas Fleet came out of the Elbe to challenge the British upon their entry into the Heligoland Bight in which the German losses were heavier and the British retained naval supremacy and were able to continue with the blockade. According to the Admiralty Staff, the maneuver leadership concluded that, although an early battle was advantageous to the German side, it should not be fought far from the German coast and that the High Seas Fleet should not attempt to unite its forces in the Skagerrak.

In the war game of the Admiralty Staff, the advancing High Seas Fleet managed to come between the two parts of the Royal Navy which in their advance against the German Bight had arranged their junction further east. The southern British force, however, managed to avoid battle until the northern force was sufficiently close to be involved. When it came to battle near the Dutch coast the British won because of the engagement of their united force, although they, too, suffered serious losses.

The Admiralty Staff, which in March 1911 came to be headed by Tirpitz's disciple Heeringen, concluded from all these games that it was improbable that the German forces could in their advance against the British coast defeat parts of the Royal Navy separately; all the games had shown that the British would be able to unite their forces before the arrival of the High Seas Fleet, even when war broke out under conditions unusually favorable to the German side. Therefore "an offensive thrust so far from our coast is not to be recommended. A defeat at the hands of superior forces must become all the more fateful to us the further we are from our coast." Under normal conditions for the outbreak of war in which the British would be fully prepared, the High Seas Fleet must instead seek battle at the earliest opportunity in German waters through short thrusts of the entire fleet and other ruthless actions against blockading forces. In the light of the outcome of the war game of the High Seas Fleet, the Admiralty Staff recommended that because of the current power relationship the bulk of the fleet could not be separated from the light forces: the two must support one another in any aggressive action against the enemy in German waters. It surmised that the view of all of the naval agencies participating in the war games was that an immediate battle with the Royal Navy was to be sought, but only in German waters, and that the mine- and torpedo-boat attacks against the British coast were unfeasible unless war broke out as a complete surprise to the British, i.e. if it was an unexpected pre-emptive strike on the part of Germany.

The Admiralty Staff requested Wilhelm to approve the distribution of its report that was prepared in June 1911 to the officers of the different agencies that would be involved in naval operations against Britain. The Emperor granted this approval only on 17 October 1911. This schedule shows that during the second Morocco crisis, which involved an acute threat of war with Britain, the German navy, just as during the first Morocco crisis, was in the midst of indecision regarding its operations against her, of which Wilhelm was made aware by Holtzendorff's report of 23 February.[72] This is a further serious example of the poor coordination of the German leadership.

## V

It may not be a coincidence that on 3 May 1911, the same day as Kiderlen-Wächter developed his Morocco program that culminated in the "Panther leap," Holtzendorff addressed a letter to Heeringen pointing out that according to his information the case of war against France had not been worked on for several years and remarking that "the possibilities of a conflict which would occur only between Germany and France are not out of the question."[73] While Heeringen replied on 10 May that it had been decided in the event of such a war to keep most of the naval forces ready against Britain,[74] by the previous day A3 and A4 had prepared a lengthy study of such a war.[75] Why this speed? It may have been an attempt to coordinate political and naval action. The study opened by repeating that a war against France alone was improbable and could start only with a French attack on Germany; whether or not Britain had pledged herself to support France militarily and navally, Germany would have to expect that she would not miss any favorable opportunity to destroy the German fleet. It was then stated that the destruction of either the German or French fleet would only benefit Britain and then inconsistently pointed out that a German naval victory over France would be a step toward using the High Seas Fleet for world policy whereas a French naval victory would provide respite for Germany by leading to Anglo-French rivalry. Subsequently the authors of the document examined operations against France along traditional lines: they dismissed the advance against Brest, considered an advance into the Mediterranean as necessary for bringing the French fleet to battle but argued that for operations there an enormous amount of supplies was necessary and a base was lacking which could at best be established in Corsica. But such an operation would expose German trade in the North Sea to French depredations and the German coast to possible British attack, and arouse in Britain fears of a German invasion. The launching of a Mediterranean armada was therefore not considered worth the risks it entailed. An enclosed memorandum by A3 dealt with the history of German operational planning against France since 1897 and asserted that Britain could now be expected to join any power with which Germany was at war. A further enclosure dealt with the military reasons behind the decision in 1909 to give up the attack against the French northern coast: the threat of a British surprise attack, absence of an objective in view of the increasing concentration of French naval power in the Mediterranean, and the delay in the arrival of the German forces in the Atlantic to protect German shipping by the circumnavigation of the British Isles because of the presence of French submarines in the English Channel. According to the author these reasons had since then become even more convincing:

If Germany mobilizes, England will certainly draw her forces together at home. The warnings of German danger in the North Sea will become more strident. A departure of the German fleet from the North Sea will give grounds for wild rumors of an attack against England. In spite of all friendly assurances, England as well as Germany would in the case of an advance of our fleet no longer remain master of the situation; from various issues a conflagration can develop. The situation is precarious [*bedenklich*], even if we trust England's assurance of neutrality. For this we have no grounds . . . on the contrary, England would probably use the favorable opportunity of perhaps defeating the German fleet outside the North Sea by a surprise attack. A strong concentration of power in the North Sea is the best way to make it difficult for England to join France.

France was expected to continue to concentrate her naval power in the Mediterranean, particularly so as to assure the passage of the Nineteenth Army Corps from Algeria to France. The stationing of the French Second Squadron in the Atlantic was considered to be temporary. The last point in favor of concentrating the German naval forces at home was that Russia was no longer a navally negligible quantity.

Beside being divided about the operations against Britain and the Entente Cordiale, the Admiralty Staff did not possess an offensive operations plan against France during the Agadir crisis. She could thus proceed to use her naval forces with impunity against Germany's allies in the Mediterranean.

## Notes: Chapter 16

1 Tirpitz, *Aufbau,* p. 17.
2 See above, p. 208; BA-MA, F 5598, Nebenakten zu A. d. M, III, 3.–1., Vol. 1, Entwurf, "Denkschrift über die Kriegführung zur See gegen Frankreich in den Kriegsfällen Dreibund gegen Zweibund und Deutschland gegen Frankreich im Jahre 1906" and for covering letter by A3 of December 1905 requesting permission to submit the revised operations plan to Büchsel.
3 ibid., A2 weiter an A4, 11 January 1906; A4 to D, 11 January; D to A2, 24 January; A3's reply to comments of A2 and D, 30 January; finally Aktenvermerk A3, 3 March 1906.
4 BA-MA, F 5597, III, 3.–1., Vol. 6, "Immediatvortrag," July 1906, "Einfluss der Neuverteilung der französischen Seestreitkräfte auf den Operationsplan gegen Frankreich," initialed by Büchsel and by A3, Schäfer (?), A4, and A5. On 1 October, Rampold, military attaché in Rome, reported to Tirpitz that the Italian navy was weakened by the spread of democratic and anti-militaristic tendencies: PAAA, Italien 72a, Bd 18.
5 See above, pp. 250 ff.
6 BA-MA, F 5589, III, 1.–10b., Vol. 1. "Disposition für eine Denkschrift über die Kriegführung gegen England 1905," A, 5 March 1905.
7 ibid., F 5587, III, 1. N. 10., Vol. 2, "Denkschrift zum Immediatvortrag über den

Aufmarsch und die Verwendung Eurer Majestät Flotte im Kriege gegen England im Ms-Jahre 1905," 20 March 1905.

8 ibid., Bd 3, Büchsel to Schlieffen and Koester, 15 April 1905; F 2044, PG 66077, Büchsel to Tirpitz, 15 April 1905.

9 ibid, F 5587, III, 1. N. 10., Vol. 2, "Denkschrift über die Kriegführung gegen England in 1906," March 1906.

10 BA-MA, F 5589, III. 1.–10b., Vol. 1, memorandum by Büchsel, n.d.

11 ibid., A3 to A2, 7 December 1905.

12 Kennedy, "Development of German operations plans," p. 64, n. 5.

13 BA-MA, F 2018, PG 65966, "Immediatvortrag über OP II," 27 March 1906.

14 Kennedy, "Development of German operations plans," p. 64.

15 Oron J. Hale, *Germany and the Diplomatic Revolution: A Study in Diplomacy and the Press, 1904–06* (Philadelphia, Pa, 1931), pp. 196–9.

16 BA-MA, F 5587, III, 1. N. 10., Vol. 3, Schlieffen to Büchsel, 3 November 1905; Büchsel to Schlieffen, 13 November 1905.

17 ibid., Moltke to Büchsel, 24 February 1906. For the views of the General Staff about possible British action, see Wallach, *Das Dogma*, pp. 203 ff. At this time Anglo-French discussions were concerned with British landings in France. Williamson, *Politics*, pp. 85–8.

18 BA-MA, F 5587, III, 1. N. 10., Vol. 3, "Unternehmung Englands gegen Deutschland zu Lande," n.d., no signature.

19 ibid., F 5590, III, 1. N. 10., Bd 2/05, "Admiralstabsreise 1905," July 1905.

20 ibid., F 2018, PG 65967, Büchsel's "Notizen zum Immediatvortrag," 22 September 1906; the report was made on 11 October 1906.

21 ibid., enclosure dated 8 October 1906.

22 ibid., F 5590, III, 1. N. 10., Vol. 3/06, A4 (initial illegible), "Zur Ausarbeitung der Grossen Admiralstabsreise 1906: Betrachtungen über Einrichtung und Handhabung einer Blockade der deutschen Nordseeküste im Kriege England-Deutschland," 24 January 1907.

23 ibid., F 2018, PG 65968, "Zum Immediatvortrag," 23 February 1907.

24 ibid., F 5589, III, 1.–10b., Vol. 1, "Bemerkungen zum Kriegsspiel No. 2" of A3 (initial N), 22 April, Z, 22 April, and Büchsel, 4 May 1907.

25 Quoted in Weniger, "Die Entwicklung des Operationsplanes der deutschen Schlacht-flotte," *Marine-Rundschau* (1930), p. 3. With a few changes I am using Kennedy's translation: "Development of German operations plans," p. 63. Also see Hubatsch, *Der Admiralstab*, p. 122. Moltke's statement is quoted in BA-MA, F 5587, III, 1. N. 10., Vol. 4, Baudissin to Moltke, 29 February 1908.

26 BA-MA, F 5587, III, 1. N. 10., Vol. 3, "Denkschrift zum O.P. 1907," approved by Wilhelm on 21 May 1907 according to Büchsel's remark of the same date.

27 ibid., F 2019, PG 65970, "Zum Immediatvortrag. Die englischen Flottenmanöver Oktober, 1907," 12 December 1907. Reported to Wilhelm on 7 January 1908.

28 ibid., N 159/3, pp. 407–9; Müller, *Der Kaiser*, pp. 73–4; Hubatsch, *Der Admiralstab*, pp. 130–44.

29 BA-MA, F 5589, III, 1.–10b., Vol. 2, "I. Entwurf einer Denkschrift zum O.P. 1908."

30 ibid., Baudissin, "Vorläufige Bemerkungen zum Entwurf der Denkschrift zum O.P. 1907," 1 February 1908.

31 ibid., A. Grapow to Baudissin, 10 February 1908.

32 ibid., A3, "Welche Rolle wird Frankreich in einem Kriege England-Frankreich gegen Deutschland zur See zufallen?," 10 February 1908.

33 ibid., F 5600, III, 3.–18., Vol. 2, Schwenger to A2, 13 June 1908.

34 See ibid., "Geeigenheit des Rhein-Maas-und-Scheldte Mündungsgebiets für kriegerische Unternehmungen unserer Armee und Flotte," A2, Schwenger, 18 September 1908.

35 See above, p. 126.

36 BA-MA, F 5600, III. 3.–18., Vol. 2, "Kritik zu der angefassten Arbeit: Teil IV Holland u. Belgien," A4, Taegert, 2 October 1908; Grapow's marginal note is dated 14 October.

37 ibid., F 5587, III, 1. N.. 10., Vol. 5, "Seiner Exzellenz vorzulegen. Unser Verhalten gegenüber Holland und Belgien in einem Kriege gegen England allein und gegen England-Frankreich," 8 February 1910, initialed by A4, Taegert, and A, Rieve.

38 See above, pp. 254–5.

39  BA-MA, F 5587, III, 1. N. 10., Vol. 5, "Aktenvermerk," A, Rieve, 24 February 1910.
40  Ritter, *Schlieffen-Plan*, p. 188; Schulte, *Kriegsausbruch*, p. 39; Wallach, *Das Dogma*, pp. 140 ff.
41  BA-MA, F 5587, III, 1. N. 10., Vol. 4, Baudissin to Moltke, 29 February 1908.
42  ibid., Moltke to Baudissin, 2 March 1908.
43  ibid., F 5589, III, 1.–10b., Vol. 2, "Immediatvortrag zur A.O. an den Chef der Hochseeverbände gegen England," 12 March 1908.
44  ibid., A4, Taegert, "Denkschrift zum OP/08: Wie wird der Feind voraussichtlich handeln?"
45  GP, XXIII, ii, No. 8006, Tirpitz to Bülow, 20 April 1907, enclosure: "Über die Bedeutung des Seebeuterechts," 20 April 1905, pp. 364–5.
46  GP, XXVIII, No. 10247, Tirpitz to Bülow, 4 January 1909, p. 54; also Tirpitz, *Aufbau*, p. 108.
47  BA-MA, F 5587, III, 1. N. 10., Vol. 5, "Denkschrift zum Immediatvortrag," 24 October 1908.
48  Quoted also by Kennedy "Development of German naval operations plans," p. 66, from Weniger.
49  BA-MA, F 5589, III, 1.–10b., Vol. 2, "Immediatvortrag: Operations-befehle für den Krieg gegen England," finished version dispatched on 29 March 1908.
50  ibid., F 5587, III, 1. N. 10., Vol. 4, "Entwurf. Reinschrift ab 21. Mai 1909."
51  ibid., Prince Heinrich to Baudissin, 31 July 1909.
52  ibid., A to A3, 5 September 1908; A3, 9 October 1908.
53  ibid., "Denkschrift über Verlauf und Folgen eines Krieges: England allein gegen Deutschland und Österreich," Baudissin, 20 April 1909. See above, p. 300.
54  ibid., F 5597, III, 3.–1., Vol. 6, no signature.
55  ibid., F 2018, PG 65972, Baudissin, "Zum Immediatvortrag," 9 March 1909.
56  ibid., Baudissin's marginal comment of 9 March on the first page of the report.
57  ibid., F 5593, III, 2.–2., Vol. 3, Baudissin to Moltke, 17 March 1909.
58  PAAA, Frankreich 116, Bd 23, Ostertag to Minister of War, 4 June 1908.
59  BA-MA, F 5593, III, 2.–2., Vol. 3, minutes of the meeting in the General Staff on 18 March 1909, drafted by Rieve on 19 March 1909.
60  The questionnaire is enclosed to ibid.; the reply, Moltke to Baudissin, 2 April 1909, is in BA-MA, F 5593, III, 2.–2., Vol. 3.
61  ibid., F 5592, III, 2.–1., Vol. 3., "For discussion in Kiel with the Chief of the Fleet in March 1909," 19 March 1909.
62  ibid., K 10–4/2525, Tirpitz to Einem, 23 February 1909; Einem to Tirpitz, 8 March 1909.
63  ibid., F 2045, PG 66081, "Dem Herrn Staatssekretär vorzulegen," 17 May 1909, signed by Paschen, 17 June 1909.
64  BA-MA, F 3302, PG 66705, Müller to Baudissin, 27 March 1909. See also ibid., N 159/3, Müller's diary entries for 1, 5, 7 January 1909; also Müller, *Der Kaiser*, pp. 73–4, 93.
65  ibid., F 5587, III, 1. N. 10., Vol. 4, Holtzendorff to Chief of the Admiralty Staff, 5 October 1909; Rieve to Chief of the High Seas Fleet, 8 October 1909.
66  ibid., F 5589, III, 1.–10b., Vol. 3, "Denkschrift über die Operationsvorarbeiten im Winter 1909–10," initialed by A4, A1, and A. There is a comment on the first page by A: "Hat S. E. vorgelegen."
67  ibid., F 5587, III, 1. N. 10., Vol. 5, Fischel, "Zum Immediatvortrag. Operationsbefehle für 1910," 4 November 1909.
68  ibid., A, Rieve, "Die Entwickelung der Operationsdirektiven für 1910," 23 December 1909.
69  ibid., draft of "Zum Immediatvortrag," Rieve, 18 August 1910.
70  ibid., F 5589, III, 1.–10b., Vol. 3, "Ostsee oder Nordsee als Kriegsschauplatz," 18 August 1910, with comments by A4, 19 October 1910. ibid., N 253/24, Tirpitz to Fischel, 16 August 1910. For Fischel's memorandum see also Gemzell, *Organisation*, pp. 79–80.
71  A comprehensive survey of all the games appears in BA-MA, F 2020, PG 65974, June 1911, "Zum Immediatvortrag, Strategische Kriegsspiele Winter 1910–11;" the instructions of the Admiralty Staff to the High Command appear in ibid., F 6471, Kommando der Hochseeflotte, "Kaiserkriegsspiel 1910/11, Anlage 4," Fischel to Holtzendorff, 12 October 1910; instructions of Holtzendorff and his Chief of Staff Scheer, 9 November 1910, to Heeringen who was in charge of the war game appear in ibid., Anlage

4; Holtzendorff's report to Wilhelm, 23 February 1911, about the war game appears in ibid., F 5663, I, 1.–5., Vol. 1; the information about the war game of the Baltic Sea naval station appears in ibid., F 7643, Bd 1, Kriegsspiel der Marinestation der Ostsee, 1910–11, and that about the war game of the North Sea station in ibid., F 7642, Bd 6, Kriegsspiel der Stabsoffiziere der Nordseestation, 1910–11.

72    ibid., F 2020, PG 65974, "Zum Immediatvortrag. Strategische Kriegsspiele Winter 1911," June 1911, with the comment by Heeringen, 17 October 1911, that Wilhelm approved the circulation of the document among the officers concerned.

73    ibid., F 5597, III, 3.–1., Vol. 7, Holtzendorff to Heeringen, 3 May 1911.

74    ibid., Heeringen to Holtzendorff, 10 May 1911.

75    ibid., "Erwägungen über den O-Plan im Kriege mit Frankreich."

# 17 The Eclipse of the Tirpitz Plan, 1911–14

## I

Whatever the specific conclusions and contentions, the Fischer controversy has demonstrated that the period from the Agadir crisis to the outbreak of World War I was marked by increasing risks of war and a willingness on the part of the German leadership to take them. Within Germany the phobia of encirclement intensified. Wide circles of the public came to regard war as inevitable and many saw it as a solution to the problems arising from the internal socio-political deadlock.[1]

As already apparent after 1908, the army was regaining its privileged status in German armament policy. After the acrimonious debate in the Reichstag and the press[2] over the Franco-German accords of November 1911, the Director of the War Department of the Prussian Ministry of War, Generalmajor Franz von Wandel, drafted a memorandum stating that an increase in Germany's army was necessary because of the growing number of her enemies and the weakness of her friends. Britain would in all circumstances side militarily with France in a war with Germany. Russia was energetically enlarging her army and was growing more anti-German. France could add Moroccan troops to her armed forces, and her military leaders now favored an offensive strategy. Germany would also require troops against Belgium and Holland. Italy was paralyzed because of the war with Turkey. The excitement created by the Moroccan crisis had prepared the German public to expect a military increase.[3] A few days later, Moltke sent Bethmann-Hollweg another of the General Staff memoranda, analyzing the military–political situation and stressing in his covering letter the need for cooperation between the military and political leadership.[4] France, the key to the calculations of the General Staff, was not viewed as wanting a war with Germany but as more confident and as preparing more actively for such a war; the nationalist elements, hopeful of support from friends and allies, inspired by notions of revanche, and desirous of regaining Alsace-Lorraine, could easily plunge the country into a war with Germany. Against France on the Continent Germany's stance was defensive. Accepting the demands of *Weltpolitik*, the General Staff claimed that "Germany must follow offensive aims. Her ever-growing population points to colonial expansion, along a way that will certainly intersect England's path of world domination." A Franco-German war could no longer be localized. Nor was it likely that either Russia or Britain would refrain from supporting France. The involvement of England would prevent Italy from fulfilling her alliance obligations to Germany because of the vulnerability of her coastline to the Royal Navy. France could thus use the troops intended for a war with her against Germany.

In a war against France and Britain, Germany's chances would be favorable if Russia remained neutral. Although her involvement would bring Austria-Hungary into the war as Germany's ally, "the moment that Italy swerved toward the Entente powers, the effectiveness of Austria against Russia would be paralyzed." She might then launch an offensive against Italy—and for this Conrad's statements offered ample evidence—and remain on the defensive against Russia. Whatever the military–political constellation, it would be in Germany's best interests to open the campaign with an offensive against France and to destroy her.

> If France is defeated in the first great battles, a country which does not have at its disposal large reserves of manpower would hardly be capable of waging a lengthy war, whereas Russia can [continue war] after a lost battle in the interior of her immeasurable territory and prolong it indefinitely.

The Italo-Turkish War, which had broken out on 29 September, was deplored by Moltke, as it had been by the Kaiser.[5] The General Staff maintained that it could cost Germany an ally, Italy, or a friend, Turkey. The latter was now regarded as an important potential ally since after the Anglo-Russian rapprochement she was the only power that could threaten Britain on land. A Turkish offensive could threaten the Suez Canal and Egypt and deter Britain from using the entire BEF on the Continent. Turkey could also tie down Russian troops in the Caucasus and prevent Bulgaria from attacking Romania. "The weight that Turkey can throw into the scales in favor of Germany and Austria in a European war is thus very considerable." This was the first time that Turkey and the military situation in the entire Near and Middle East had figured in the communications between the General Staff and the German political leadership.

In considering the military power that Germany and Austria-Hungary would have to face if they alone confronted the powers of the Triple Entente, Moltke stated that in the past years "the conditions have very much shifted to the disadvantage of the allied monarchies." Particularly impressive were Russia's preparations: the improvement of her mobilization, the reorganization of her reserves, the construction of new strategic railways toward the west and the southwest, and the rejuvenation of her officer corps would enable her to take the offensive. As in his previous estimates, Moltke expected France to use her entire manpower. The Agadir crisis had provided additional impetus for the improvement of her military forces: the increase of the field-artillery to 150 batteries had canceled out previous German superiority in that area, the army was equipped with machine-guns, airplanes were being used for military purposes, and the eastern border was more strongly fortified against an invasion. Belgium, Holland, and Switzerland were also increasing their military preparations.

As for Britain, her standing army could, by drawing on colonial troops, be increased to 150,000 men. Summarizing the situation:

> It is evident that the tension between Germany and France which has existed for years and which has periodically sharpened has called forth an increased military activity in almost all European states. All prepare themselves for the great war which all expect sooner or later.

Britain was viewed as welcoming a war between Germany and France in which she would support the latter with all her might and destroy the German fleet. She was, however, unlikely to go to war with Germany without being certain of French support. If she none the less did so, she would fight a naval and commercial war and retain control of the seas regardless of the losses she might suffer from the German navy. Because of her naval supremacy, an invasion of Britain by Germany was impossible; an invasion of Belgium and the Scheldt estuary would inflict some losses on her, but such action would also involve France. In the case of an Anglo-German war the General Staff fell back on the hostage theory: "the mobilization of the entire army and war with France." For France would become involved in the war anyway and immediate action against her would give Germany "a head start in mobilization." While stating in respect to the hostage theory, "The power position of Germany rests now as before on the strength of her army," the report none the less concluded that the increases of the German navy and army "must go hand in hand." While attributing infinitely greater importance to the army than to the navy in the German armament policy, particularly in once more subscribing to the hostage theory, Moltke refrained—perhaps, as Fischer suggests, as a concession to the Kaiser[6]— from suggesting that the increase of the army should occur at the expense of the navy.

## II

By this time the Tirpitz Plan was getting into deeper trouble. The Secretary of State had seen the indignation stirred up over Agadir as a means of pushing through another navy bill. Capelle briefly suggested the continuation of a four-ship building rate, but maintained that strong nerves were required for it.[7] Tirpitz thought that a three-ship rate was preferable on financial, diplomatic, and technical grounds.[8] By the end of August, Tirpitz made this request to Bethmann, asking for an additional six large ships for the purpose of forming a third active squadron, but the Chancellor expressed a fear that even this increase might mean a war with Britain. To his question, which had several times been posed by Bülow, whether Tirpitz could guarantee a successful outcome of such a war, the Secretary of State replied in the negative, adding "but we must run the risk or abdicate politically."[9] Tirpitz's next chance came in his audience with Wilhelm on 26 September. Capelle urged him to do his best as the father of the Navy Law to prevent the perpetual decline of the building rate to two large ships per year, for it would reduce the German navy to a permanent strength of forty capital ships. He also drew to his chief's attention the reservations of the "Front," particularly Holtzendorff, about further fleet increases because of its inadequate preparedness and manpower.

Holtzendorff had taken advantage of the state of the fleet during the Moroccan crisis to point out its weaknesses. He referred to the shortage of small and large cruisers. More men and officers were necessary, the reserve divisions had to be placed into service more quickly, there was need for more torpedo-boats, both the laying of mines and their clearance had to be improved, the submarines were inadequate, and the fleet had to be rendered capable of much more effective action after 1 October.[10] While Tirpitz would have been unable to deal with most of Holtzendorff's grievances, he did consult with Heeringen after he had taken over the Admiralty Staff. Theirs was a frank exchange over questions of long-term naval development, the reserve fleet, the keeping of ships in service, and the reconnaissance forces. Tirpitz was, however, considerably annoyed by Heeringen's opinion concerning triple gun-turrets in response to an inquiry from the Kaiser, which led Heeringen to request an intermediary to mend his relations with the Secretary of State.[11] Tirpitz had previously expressed his annoyance about a submission from Heeringen criticizing fleet excursions into the Mediterranean, which "is filled with French torpedo-boats and submarines and can possibly be a mousetrap for our fleet."[12]

Tirpitz was thus squeezed, on the one hand, between the diplomatic and financial problems which a new navy law would raise and the demands of the army and, on the other, the continued interference with his work by the other naval agencies.[13] In his confidential correspondence with Capelle, Tirpitz raised the question whether in view of the objections that had been raised to a new navy bill it might be postponed until 1915 since "we would then stand at the height of our naval power" and the risks of a war with Britain would be minimized. He agreed that after the reduction of the building rate to two large ships per year it would be very difficult to return to the three-ship rate and labeled the "Front" and its main spokesman Holtzendorff as stupid.[14] Capelle informed his chief that his previous slogan "alliance capability," involving the possibility of a Continental alliance against Britain, had failed because of the British entente policy, culminating in the Agadir crisis; so had the formula of a 3:4 and a 2:3 ratio.

> Now there only remained the third possibility, to come militarily so close to Britain that she would recognize Germany as an equal factor, which would justify the previous fleet policy. If this did not succeed, history would pass its judgment: *pro nihilo*.[15]

Capelle claimed to have told Müller that the navy law required regular modifications and that a "*Novelle* for 1912 had been planned for some time, aiming to restore a three-ship building rate." He did not think that he had been able to win over Müller, who thought that if he were in the position of the British he would respond to such a bill with a declaration of war. Bethmann was reported by Capelle as also having stated that a bill as envisaged by Tirpitz would mean war with Britain. Müller, however, was willing to provide full support for a new navy bill if Tirpitz would postpone it until the fall of 1912; he also mentioned the possibility of postponing the bill until 1915 since by then the British threat would be considerably diminished: "4 × 4 = 16 modern ships would be in front of us, the canal, Heligoland [would be] ready, and [the number of] torpedo- and U-boats increased."

With the usual assistance of Dähnhardt and Capelle, Tirpitz presented the plans for a new navy bill to Wilhelm on 26 September 1911. He proposed a power relationship of 2:3 between Germany and Britain, claiming that it would offer Germany an adequate defensive chance without threatening Britain. He further maintained that Britain's recent threat of war to Germany provided an ideal opportunity for the introduction of a navy bill after the impending elections. The major issue was a long-term one: if the three-ship rate were not introduced before 1918 the two-ship rate would become a habit and the navy would eventually be reduced to forty large ships. Through the construction of three additional ships of the line a fifth (or third active) squadron of battleships could be formed and through the building of three battle cruisers there would be established two squadrons of six such ships each. The third active squadron of battleships would be formed through the addition of both fleet flagships and four ships of the material reserve to the new ships.[16] An earlier memorandum had set 1920 as the target date for the establishment of the active part of the High Seas Fleet and of the most important forces abroad consisting of modern ships through a construction of three large ships annually in the period 1912–17. Germany would have twenty-five Dreadnought-type battleships—a fleet flagship and three squadrons of eight ships each—and fourteen battle cruisers, of which eight would serve with the High Seas Fleet, four as a flying squadron for service abroad, and two as the core of the Cruiser Squadron. Sixteen pre-Dreadnought battleships would constitute the reserve and another six would perform sundry duties. In all there would be twenty-five Dreadnoughts and twenty-two pre-Dreadnoughts—forty-seven battleships plus fourteen Dreadnought battle cruisers: in short a force of sixty-one ships capable of serving in the line.[17]

Wilhelm thought that the financial situation would compel Britain to accept a 3:2 power relationship with Germany in capital ships.[18] Müller reported that the Kaiser was "obviously relieved that such a minimally aggressive way had been found."[19] But a few days later he had to report to Wilhelm that Tirpitz had "encountered the opposition of the Fleet [Command] and the Admiralty Staff, and that I personally did not find it easy to preserve peace."[20] Wilhelm accepted Tirpitz's proposals. To Bethmann he promised the postponement of a navy bill for a year, but also spoke of its introduction in the current year![21] He proposed to announce the 3:2 power relationship in the Reichstag and, out of courtesy, to the British government.[22] On 3 October there was a meeting between Bethmann and Tirpitz in the presence of Müller in which the Chancellor strongly objected to the bill and Müller sided with the Secretary of State. Bethmann expressed his concern about a bill that was specifically directed against Britain, doubted if a 3:2 ratio would appeal to the Reichstag, but finally authorized Tirpitz to get in touch with the Secretary of State of the Imperial Treasury, Adolf Wermuth, about the fiscal implications.[23] He subsequently objected to the proposed justification of a new naval increase because of the deterioration of Germany's international position through the Agadir crisis and the Italo-Turkish War. He stated that in his impending report to the Kaiser about Germany's diplomatic position he would also have to deal with the possibility of a war with Britain. Touching on a sore spot, he inquired to what extent Germany's chances in such a war would be improved by the completion of the Kaiser Wilhelm Canal and the Heligoland fortifications.[24]

The Chancellor posed the same questions to Heeringen, who played down the significance of the completion of the Heligoland fortifications and the canal. On the island the submarine pens were already completed and sixteen submarines ready to be stationed there: "they would secure not only the German Bight against a close blockade, but also the harbor and island against shelling." But what was really significant in the chances of the German navy against the British was *"the excessive superiority of the English fleet."* The German fleet therefore had to be increased regardless of the risk of war it entailed.

> It is impossible in the long run for our fleet to live with the concept that it is only a risk to England in the sense that its defeat could perhaps shift [her] maritime power position in face of the neutrals.
>
> For the preservation of its internal morale as well as for external success our fleet requires a *militarily useful chance* against England.

Referring to an earlier discussion with Tirpitz, Heeringen reasserted his belief that Britain alone would never threaten Germany with war, but would "become our enemy if we went to war with another power." Therefore the German navy would have to be capable of taking on the British. They were only impressed by might, which, if available to Germany, would increase her chances "for political success and the preservation of peace."[25] Heeringen had responded as a true disciple and loyal colleague of Tirpitz.

In his reply Tirpitz likewise argued that the improvement of Germany's chances against the British through the completion of the canal and the fortifications of Heligoland should not be exaggerated; he played down the risk of war that a new navy bill would present and emphasized the need of the bill because of the drop in the building rate in 1912 from four to two large ships: it would be difficult to raise the rate to three ships subsequently. If it was not possible to reduce the gap in naval power between Britain and Germany, the naval policy of the past fourteen years would have been in vain.

> The events of the past summer have in my opinion indeed shown clearly that the danger of war has come closer if Germany is still to conduct an active world policy, all the more so as England has clearly shown that she would actively participate in a Franco-German war.[26]

Müller also supported the 3:2 ratio as the minimum if the German navy was to be "a weighty political factor," as a numerical expression of the navy law of 1898, as a guarantee against a close blockade, and as not constituting a threat to Britain.[27] In spite of doubts about a new navy bill from the "Front," particularly Holtzendorff, the three major naval agencies had thus joined ranks against the Chancellor in defense of the 2:3 German–British power relationship in capital ships.

By the end of October, however, Holtzendorff had voiced his reservations regarding the demands of his colleagues. He attributed greater importance to the completion of the canal and the risk of war entailed in another navy bill, and suggested that the most propitious time for a war would be "(*a*) when our High Seas Fleet consists exclusively of modern ships of the line and cruisers; (*b*) when the canal is ready for the passage of these ships." The time would be the fall of 1914. Until then the emphasis should be placed on the increase of the war preparedness of the fleet.[28]

On 15 October, Wilhelm decided in favor of proclaiming the 2:3 German–British power relationship in the Reichstag immediately and introducing a new navy bill in the spring of 1912 "if possible." This compromise satisfied neither Bethmann-Hollweg nor Tirpitz.[29] On 23 October, Capelle drafted a memorandum about the Anglo-German relationship for Wilhelm's use in which he viewed an understanding between the two countries as the ultimate aim of the German naval policy. The alternatives were war or an armaments race. War would serve the interests of neither Germany nor Britain: Germany was navally weaker than Britain and the island state could only gain a pyrrhic victory since, in a much weakened condition, it would be faced by the United States and Japan, the increased aspirations of its dominions for independence, a strengthened trade union movement, democratization, the Irish problem, and a divided government. An armaments race would be too expensive for Britain and could only be sustained through naval concentration in the North Sea which would force her to relinquish her interests in the rest of the world. Rather than risk these sacrifices "England must and will in the near future choose Germany instead of France as her ally, for the French alliance only imposed on her the task of defending France and tied down her entire naval strength to the North Sea." On the other hand, an alliance with Germany would immediately restore the British position as a world power. The British must come to Germany for an agreement consisting of a political alliance and a German fleet limitation.[30] Although there were lines drawn in the margin of this naïve although in the long run not entirely unrealistic document, there is no evidence that it ever left the Imperial Naval Office. In his report of 27 October to Wilhelm, Tirpitz also attempted to satisfy the needs of the "Front" for greater war preparedness by pointing out that the proposed bill would fill the gaps in manpower, increase the number of submarines, improve coastal defense, provide for more torpedoes and mines, and speed up the construction of a battleship, a battle cruiser, and some torpedo-boats.[31]

By the end of November, Heeringen had approved the proposed navy bill in so far as the measures directed toward war preparedness were concerned, but questioned whether the 2:3 building rate might not restrict the total German strength in large ships to forty, or whether such a rate could retain its validity in view of the recently started reconstruction of the Russian Baltic Sea fleet.[32] On 6 December, Heeringen responded to the second draft of the proposed bill. He questioned the use of new recruits but credited the bill for strengthening the fleet against Britain. Further, he disputed the arguments that Germany should concentrate on land warfare at the expense of her naval armaments, thus questioning the hostage theory:

> Even if . . . we should be entirely victorious in a land war, a Continental war could never compensate for the damage which a long-term naval domination by the British would cause us . . .
>
> Even if we should occupy as much of Holland, Belgium, and France as possible, England could with impunity gain advantage from continuing the war as long as she is able to protect her shipping and blockade our coasts and [those] . . . of the territories we occupy.
>
> She would gain control of our colonies, her shipping would extend over all areas which in peacetime have been exploited by us, [and] her industry would not only be rid of a powerful competitor, but take its place in many parts of the world.

The only German course of action would be a further navy bill, for without it the strength of the Royal Navy would proportionally exceed that of the German.[33]

While Wilhelm showed interest in the *Novelle* at the beginning of November,[34] it ran into opposition from Bethmann and Wermuth. On 11 November, Capelle expressed doubts about its passage before 1913.[35] Late in November, Bethmann asked Josias von Heeringen if there was need for army expansion;[36] Josias von Heeringen told his brother August that it was essential because of the inadequacy of the previous quinquinnate and the shift of the military–political situation to Germany's disadvantage because of the defection of Italy and Britain's guardianship of Holland and Belgium: the former development had freed three French army corps for use against Germany.[37] On the same day Bethmann-Hollweg expressed his, Josias von Heeringen's and Moltke's agreement with Wilhelm "that the strengthening of the navy must go hand in hand with the strengthening of the army" and soon thereafter Wilhelm commented on a newspaper article stating that Britain would side with France in a war against Germany: "We must now certainly *always* have to count on both, even in an attack against us! This requires an entirely unusual increase of the *army* and navy in the form of a defense bill."[38] On 9 December he strongly supported a new navy bill in the presence of Tirpitz, August von Heeringen, and Müller as a means of cutting the Gordian knot.[39] Müller was requested to inform Bethmann of this decision. On the same evening the Chancellor called on the Kaiser, raising his objections to the navy bill, which would involve financial difficulties and trouble with Britain:

> If England would not directly make war because of the *Novelle,* she would

none the less cause us trouble until we would find it necessary to prepare an Ems dispatch and thus an aggressive war.

He also preferred the request for personnel for the Third Squadron, which would have immediate military significance, to the construction of new ships, which would not be ready for three years, a period during which Britain might not wait.[40]

The discussion about the new navy bill at the top levels of German leadership was accompanied by conflicting reports from London between the diplomats Metternich and Kühlmann on the one hand and the naval attaché Widenmann on the other. Widenmann was very much an agent of Tirpitz and was taken seriously by Wilhelm; the professional diplomats had the ear of the Foreign Office and the Chancellor and were generally disregarded by Wilhelm: Metternich was eventually dismissed.[41] Widenmann favored the promulgation of a naval law as formulated by the Imperial Naval Office, arguing that Britain was only impressed by the power of her opponents.[42]

On 3 December the Württemberg minister in Berlin, Axel von Varnbüler, reported that, if Britain did not bluff with her military preparations of the previous summer, the introduction of a new navy bill would mean war: "for many fear that the Morocco business, however peacefully it is now settled, has brought us closer to war—the great conflict has become inevitable."[43] A few days later, Friedrich August, the King of Saxony, informed the Grand Duke of Oldenburg on the basis of the report of his minister in Berlin that a navy bill escalating the naval race with Britain would immediately be met with a British attack. Since many important people in Berlin were aware that the real decision in war would be reached on land and great increases were being requested for the army, he would personally oppose any fleet increases not covered by taxes.[44] On 11 December, Bethmann told Lerchenfeld that he hoped to reach an agreement with Britain, in spite of her attitude during the Morocco crisis and poor communications:

> . . . England would come to us in three months. None the less, on the assumption that we make no mistakes; the I[mperial] Chancellor counts a large navy bill as such a mistake . . . no navy bill could be introduced without an army bill. For if it came to war because of the fleet increase the decision would be reached on land. But we must not forget that France, in spite of a much smaller population, has almost the same military strength as Germany. We are surely in many respects superior to the French. Only in one point, the development of air power, which appears destined to play a role in a future war, does a great supremacy exist on the French side. Thus, no increase of the fleet without [an] increase of the army.

Bethmann claimed to have the full support of Josias von Heeringen and Moltke, but little support from the Kaiser and none from Tirpitz, "who could not be relied upon, [for] one never knew what he wanted." But he himself still admitted that something had to be done for the navy, which was defenseless from October to February because of the breaking in of new recruits and engagement of new officers.[45] Two days later Bethmann was informed that Britain was prepared to help Germany increase her colonial empire,[46] which inclined Valentini to persuade the Kaiser for the time being to reduce the naval requests to an increase in personnel. Through Müller's mediation it was agreed on 23 December by Tirpitz, Bethmann, and Valentini to introduce a new navy bill in the spring of 1912, but to reduce it from four cruiser replacements and three new ships of the line to one cruiser replacement and three ships of the line.[47] On 1 January 1912 the Kaiser declared in his New Year's message to the commanding generals: "The navy leaves the major part of the financial means available to the army."[48] Subsequently Bethmann, Moltke, the Secretary of State of the Imperial Colonial Office, Wilhelm Solf, Arthur Zimmerman and Wilhelm von Stumm of the Foreign Office, Professor Theodor Schiemann, and the bankers Ludwig Delbrück and Arthur Gwinner continued to press for the reduction of the navy bill to a personnel increase.[49] By 12 January a temporary compromise was reached: the building of the third active squadron was slowed down through an alternating rate of three and two large ships per year, and no mention was to be made of a 3:2 ratio in Anglo-German naval strength.[50] On the same day the Reichstag elections produced a defeat of the pro-government parties,[51] thus reducing the chances of obtaining support for a large navy bill, and subsequently the Ballin mission offered the German political leadership further opportunities for an agreement with Britain in return for naval concessions.[52]

As opposition to substantial naval increases was mounting, the Imperial Naval Office worked out various internal drafts of arguments justifying the third active squadron and the cruiser replacements to the Budget Committee and *plenum* of the Reichstag. The Agadir crisis was mentioned as proof that a war could break out suddenly. The formation of a new active squadron, rather than the activation of one of the two reserve squadrons, was claimed to be necessary so as to leave Germany with a secondary fighting force utilizing reserve manpower—one of the advantages that she possessed. Such a force would have particular value since the impending war would be a long one. The new cruisers were necessary to form a cruiser squadron to deal with the great British supremacy of cruisers, to protect the flanks of the High Seas Fleet against envelopment, and to support the submarines and torpedo-boats in their sorties against a British wide blockade. Three active squadrons and the new cruisers would more easily absorb the recruits who would every year replace one-third of the discharged veterans than would the previously existing two active squadrons and four large cruisers.[53] Another document pointed to the advantage gained by Germany from the "Dreadnought leap," presenting her with the opportunity of establishing a 2:3 ratio with Britain in capital ships, which, however, could only be utilized by having a larger proportion of the German fleet in active service: hence the need for a fifth (or third active) squadron of ships of the line. By 1928—and this is indicative of the long-term planning of Tirpitz—Germany would have launched sixty-one capital ships; a recent speech of Churchill was cited in arguing that the British could not maintain 122 capital ships by that time. "If the English cannot build us to death because it would be too expensive for them and cannot beat us to death because that would be too expensive for them after the approval of the *Novelle*," then they would probably change their policy toward Germany, "and from the present armed encounter a really friendly relationship of Germany and England would develop." Thus "the aim of German naval policy would be reached."[54] For the Budget Committee of the Reichstag, the Imperial Naval office pointed out that in the summer and fall of 1911 there had existed a real danger of a British naval attack on Germany.[55] It was also argued that, since the value of the older ships of the reserve was reduced by the Dreadnoughts, the third active squadron would have to consist of the latter.[56]

## III

The Haldane Mission of February 1912, aimed at an agreement for British neutrality in a Continental war in return for the limitation of the German fleet, was doomed to failure by the announcement of the new navy bill just before Haldane's arrival in Berlin, the German insistence that the establishment of the third active squadron be included in the agreement, and the British refusal to accept the German demand for British unconditional neutrality in a war between Germany and the Dual Alliance.[57] At the time that the agreement floundered, fears were expressed by Wilhelm,[58] Bethmann-Hollweg, and Zimmerman that failure to conclude it would lead to war. The last two expected the war to start with France;[59] the Chancellor thought that she, being already in the throes of chauvinism, would become so arrogant "that we would be forced to attack her. In such a war France would automatically have the help of Russia and undoubtedly that of England, while the *casus foederis* would not set in for our allies and we would rather be forced to request their neutrality or help." He appears to have regarded an agreement with Britain as a panacea. As he told the Badenese minister in Berlin, it "would with one blow change the political situation in Europe in our favor." French chauvinism would collapse.[60] The agreement was the key to the dissolution of the Triple Entente.[61] Tirpitz and Wilhelm, on the other hand, firmly held on to the *Novelle,* opposed linking it to the finding of adequate revenue, whereas the British refused to accept the neutrality agreement on which Bethmann, the German Foreign Office, and Wilhelm insisted.[62] On 26 February, Tirpitz concluded that the discussions had become a vicious circle, making a mutually acceptable agreement impossible.[63] On the next day Wilhelm wrote Bethmann that he shared Müller's view that the new bill would have to include the first building estimates for two of the new battleships, fill the gaps that had occurred because of previous parsimony, and meet the needs for new manpower, although he was prepared to leave the date for the construction of the third new ship of the line open. He wanted the increases for both the army and navy to be determined as soon as possible.[64] Bethmann still hesitated about the bringing in of the new navy bill, causing Wilhelm to remark: "He cannot be cured! he is hopeless."[65] Yet on the next day the Chancellor conceded that both the army and navy bills had to be brought in.[66]

Capelle marshaled the arguments for the navy bill. For the statement in the Prussian State Ministry he stressed first the need to use recruits: with a third active squadron, the crews of only one squadron would be replaced, leaving the other two fully battleworthy. Second, the bill would considerably raise the number of ships available for a decisive battle, which would probably occur soon after the outbreak of war. Currently only twenty-one of the fifty-eight large ships could be ranged for battle, but with the third active squadron and the new armored cruisers their number would increase to thirty-seven: by 76 percent. There would also be the increase in the number of submarines—something that Bülow had emphasized—to seventy-two.[67] He reported a very cool reception of the navy bill in the Ministry of State by Bethmann, who was much more favorable to the proposals to increase the army, mentioned that there existed the choice between the navy bill or an agreement with Britain, and conjured up the specter of a war with France, which Capelle observed, "is obviously the argument with which all opponents try to kill the navy bill."[68] Capelle insisted that the date for the construction of the new ships of the line not be left open as a concession to the British. At issue was not the making of concessions but the strengthening of the German active fleet through the establishment of its third squadron. Leaving the construction dates open could reduce the originally requested six large ships to zero: this would wreck the quest of naval equality with the British as expressed in the 3:2 formula. "If we now remain for six years at a two-ship tempo, we provide England with the opportunity to regain what she had lost" when Germany built four Dreadnoughts per year and reached a 2:3 rate in them.[69]

On 5 March, Bethmann wrote to Tirpitz, forwarding to him a draft of the army and navy bills as a basis for discussions on 10 March.[70] According to it: "In the first line stands the need of the army which exceeds that of the navy by many times whereas the expenditure of the navy will become relatively larger in the course of later years." The memorandum concentrated on the financial aspects of the two bills. What was intended for the army was the establishment of the skeleton staffs of the Twentieth and Twenty-First Army Corps through the setting up of their staffs and special units, the formation of the third battalions for small infantry regiments, and new machine-gun companies.[71] According to the Bavarian military attaché in Berlin, Generalmajor Karl Wenninger, the Foreign Office had been convinced by the end of the year that further naval increases would have threatened a war with Britain, who would at least have been joined by France.

> Particularly in a land war against France the saving that had been forced on the military administration in the recent period would have taken its revenge. So it seemed to be better tactics to concentrate at first on the improvement of the shortcomings and gaps of the army, while temporarily reducing the naval requests. Through the German army increase the desire of the French to take the English chestnuts out of the fire would

perhaps disappear altogether. Then it would be time to speed up the completion of the navy to one's heart's content without any danger of war.[72]

At this time there was bitter conflict between Wilhelm and Bethmann as to whether the projected navy bill should be published. Following Bethmann's threat to resign on 6 March,[73] Wilhelm agreed to leave open the dates for the commencement of the three ships of the line,[74] but Bethmann gave in[75]—something that Wilhelm considered a victory for himself and the navy[76]—and only the date for the start of the construction of the third ship was left open. Concurrently Wilhelm, in agreement with Widenmann, continued to maintain the long-held view that the British would be unable to man the ships built in competition with Germany.[77] He also thought that Britain would be unable to bear the costs of the naval race.[78] The Imperial Naval Office confirmed this opinion by maintaining that Britain would be financially unable by 1928 to uphold the 2:1 standard against the sixty-one German Dreadnoughts which the new navy bill would make available.[79]

On 22 May 1912, Capelle prepared a report on the *Novelle,* as accepted in the Reichstag. He stated that the work on the Third Active Squadron would start in October; by the winter of 1913 it would consist of seven ships and in the fall of 1914 there would be three active squadrons of eight battleships each, two of the Dreadnought class and one of the Deutschland class. In addition, the increase in the number of the large cruisers to twelve, six for the home fleet and six as a flying squadron whose deployment would be shifted from abroad into home waters, would create an active fleet of thirty-seven large ships. Its small cruisers would be increased from twelve to eighteen. At a building rate of six per year, there would exist seventy-two submarines in 1925; in addition two dirigibles would be constructed annually. But Capelle warned that the financial constraints of this navy law would make further requests for naval increases impossible.[80]

Capelle's last comments, emphasized by Tirpitz, were significant. The Secretary of State had been under pressure from his staff to make innovations and to increase the caliber of the heavy artillery. In May 1910 he had been in favor of developing oil engines—an area in which Germany had a lead over other nations. At the same time he was reluctant to increase the caliber of the heavy guns of the large cruisers to that of the ships of the line. He also opposed changes in the types of the ships of the line started in 1911, preferring that they remain uniform with their predecessors. Dislike of experimentation, of larger ship sizes, and the consequent higher prices was the reason for his reticence.[81] In September, however, Tirpitz was prepared to increase the heavy artillery of the large cruiser K to 30.5 cm[82] and to change, at greater cost, the location of the artillery of 1911 ships of the line to a midship position.[83]

In June 1911 the Admiralty Staff joined those clamoring for a caliber increase. Heeringen stated that since 1909 Britain had gone up to a 34 cm caliber, since 1910 the United States had switched to a 34·5 cm caliber, and that both Italy and France were planning to exceed the 30·5 cm caliber. He maintained that the heavier calibers had greater accuracy and range as well as greater power of penetration and explosion. Lower calibers could be effective against heavier ones only at shorter ranges, but in reaching them one was thus vulnerable to longer-range enemy artillery. It was also possible that Germany's potential enemies would increase the armor of their battleships.

> In view of our inferiority in the number of ships and our manifold difficulties with training and personnel there should be no other point of view determining the development of our weapons than equality with our enemies.[84]

Perhaps spurred on by his former disciple, Tirpitz ruled on 4 August that battleship types with a heavy artillery of 35 cm, 38 cm, and 40 cm caliber should be considered.[85] At the meeting of 1 September of the Imperial Naval Office, Tirpitz acted as an energetic chairman. He insisted on the construction of a gun which would secure the greatest percentage of hits and cause the greatest damage to the vital parts of enemy ships.[86] In subsequent discussions, following what was first the minority view of his subordinates, Tirpitz ruled in favor of the 40 cm gun. However, as of 1913, *Ersatz Wörth*, the first of a series of eight ships of the Bayern class, was to be equipped with 38·1 cm guns.[87]

In July 1912, Wilhelm returned to his old complaints about Germany having fallen behind other states in the quality of naval construction. He complained that the new German small cruisers had guns of inadequate caliber and an insufficient number of torpedo-tubes. In respect to the heavy artillery of the capital ships he complained that Germany had been a follower and not a leader and claimed that it was only at his request that the newest ships had been armed with 38 cm guns. The development of the triple turret had been neglected and the range of German torpedoes had dropped to less than half of other navies. In spite of her excellent engineers, technicians, and officers, Germany had fallen behind "because the administrative agency adheres to a one-sided departmental point of view, without having vital and fruitful communications with the active front." The Kaiser requested that Tirpitz provide him with a new shipbuilding program.[88] Tirpitz responded at the beginning of August from St Blasien.[89] He blamed Wilhelm's complaints about the heavy artillery of the Dreadnoughts on the "screaming" of the "Front," stating that: "Our principle should be—here is the weapon, make the most of it. Thus we proceeded in 1870 with the needle-gun, which was dangerously inferior to the *chassepot*." This comment absolutely infuriated Wilhelm: if the German ships were as inferior to the British as the needle-gun to the *chassepot*, the principles involved were totally wrong and would lead to a catastrophe like that of St Privat. "As Supreme War Lord I shall never tolerate such a point of view! The best and the newest weapon is exactly right for my fleet."[90]

Müller managed to persuade Wilhelm not to convey his comments to Tirpitz in writing lest they lead to a "personnel catastrophe," but to have them communicated orally, and invited Tirpitz to report to Wilhelm on the contentious issues.[91] The Kaiser remained outraged, but was somewhat calmed down by his brother Heinrich, who remarked that if Tirpitz resigned he would be replaced by Holtzendorff—"although Heinrich could only warn me against him . . ." Both Wilhelm and Heinrich now came up with a project of a torpedo-battleship which "could take on a division of Dreadnoughts" and would be a substitute for the "incredibly increasing Dreadnoughts for which no one could any longer pay."[92] Müller subsequently defended Tirpitz, agreed with Heinrich that Holtzendorff would be unsuitable as his successor, and remarked that he had mentioned only Heeringen as his possible replacement.[93] Subsequently, however, Wilhelm was further annoyed with Tirpitz by accidents with guns in *Oldenburg* and *Helgoland* which had claimed the lives of a number of men.[94]

At the end of September 1912, Wilhelm approved a design for a new battle cruiser of 29,000 tons at a cost of 52.4 million marks. The Imperial Naval Office had some difficulty with it. Was it to have guns of the same caliber as the new ships of the line or was it to be restricted to 34 cm guns? If it was to have the heavier cannon, their number would either have to be reduced or the displacement of the ship would have to be increased. Rollmann asked Tirpitz for a decision.[95] The report of the Secretary of State to Wilhelm of the end of April, drafted by one of his subordinates, opposed the merger of the large cruiser and the ship of the line on grounds of cost, at least until the annual three-ship building rate was restored. He opposed guns of a caliber smaller than those on ships of the line in the interests of standardization, but also objected to the reduction of speed or armor protection of the battle cruisers. Therefore he proposed that the armored cruisers started in 1914 carry only six guns of 38 cm caliber. In June 1913 the Imperial Naval Office agreed with his decision.[96]

## IV

The Agadir crisis, which had influenced the Imperial Naval Office to introduce a bill to improve long-term war preparedness, also impelled other German naval agencies faced with the problems of immediate war to improve their readiness. On 27 May 1911, Heeringen complained to Wilhelm that inadequate emphasis was placed on the deployment of naval forces against Britain and that confusion had resulted from the detachment of forces for the eastern Baltic; he agreed with Holtzendorff's dissatisfaction about the situation, suggesting that very special provisions be made for the use of naval forces against a power other than Britain and that the rest be firmly subordinated to the Chief of the Fleet.[97] In November he urged on Tirpitz the need, which he claimed to have explained to him orally, that in case of an impending threat from Britain the German Baltic Sea forces be sent to the North Sea as soon as possible.[98] This was part of the ongoing debate about deployment in the North Sea as opposed to the Baltic, but indicates fuller understanding by Heeringen for Holtzendorff's responsibilities. Heeringen further pressed the Foreign Office to inform him, particularly because of the split of the fleet, "if through incidents, political actions, sharpest exchanges of notes or similar [events] a crisis may arise so that . . . the success of a surprise action can be prevented."[99] In January 1912, Heeringen, in contrast to Tirpitz and the Kaiser, opposed a major visit of German naval forces to the United States so as not to weaken the strength of the fleet at home.[100] But Tirpitz was also concerned about the danger of war. In June 1912 he wrote to the Foreign Office that he assumed that in case of a threat of war or mobilization naval attachés would be immediately informed by ambassadors so that countermeasures could be taken immediately.[101]

Disagreement existed between the Imperial Naval Office and the Command of the High Seas Fleet about the engagement of new recruits in the fall: the former rejected the recommendations of the latter that the crews of one of the three proposed active squadrons be replaced entirely so as to keep the two others entirely battleworthy. The Command of the High Seas Fleet and the Admiralty Staff both came to favor the view that recruits be engaged twice a year, in October and April, rather than just in October, to avoid any great weakening of the battle readiness. On 12 November 1912, Heeringen sent Tirpitz a list of measures to improve the war preparedness of the navy, including immediate trials of the recently completed Dreadnoughts, *Kaiser* and *Friedrich der Grosse,* the transfer of the submarines to Heligoland, and the acceleration of repairs on the other ships.[102]

On 25 November, Tirpitz presided over a meeting of the Imperial Naval Office, stating that the political situation had become more serious (presumably because of the perceived Russian willingness to go to war as noted in Müller's diary for 23 November),[103] and asking what could be done for the preparation of mobilization. The Head of the General Naval Department suggested that the trials of *Kaiser* and *Friedrich der Grosse* be broken off altogether and that they join the active fleet at once, while another officer mentioned that those of *Kaiser* would be completed by the end of November anyway. Tirpitz ordered *Friedrich der Grosse* to Kiel and to prepare for war as soon as possible. The repairs of the other ships were to be speeded up. Without creating any undue attention, the chiefs of the Baltic and North Sea stations were to be informed orally of the danger and they were to communicate this to the directors of the docks. Tirpitz expressed concern about the concentration of Russian torpedo-boats in Neunkirchen and Libau and the ships that would be most slowly manned with reservists, particularly *Braunschweig* and *Elsass*. The mineship *Arcona* was to go to the Ems and serve as the mother ship to submarines. Tirpitz further ordered the preparation of a firm plan for the establishment of a submarine base in Emden. The newer cruisers in Danzig were to be exchanged for older ones in Kiel and Wilhelmshaven. Since there was no danger that the Siegfried ships would be cut off in Danzig in the winter, they were to be left there, but a special mine-sweeping division was established for the Baltic. Questions by Tirpitz about the availability of gunpowder and ammunition received satisfactory answers.[104]

But then, probably influenced by Müller's calmer assessment of the situation on the basis of information provided by Kiderlen,[105] Tirpitz wrote to Heeringen on 30 November, that, while most of the proposals he was making to improve the war preparedness of the German navy had either been carried out or were being carried out, he did not think that the political situation was so dangerous as to necessitate preparatory measures of only temporary significance.[106] On 28 November, Heeringen had himself reported to Kiderlen that, while the Royal Navy possessed a high degree of war preparedness, "For the time being they do not show any aggressive intentions toward us, particularly not in the deployment of the fleet." The Russian Baltic Sea fleet was only involved in regular peacetime activity, although the Black Sea fleet was very active.[107] These discussions within the Imperial Naval Office and the exchanges between it and the Admiralty Staff were the fullest to date in respect to war preparedness in the face of an immediate crisis.

The question of engaging recruits without substantially reducing the effectiveness of the fleet remained a serious issue of contention and contributed to the weakening of Tirpitz's position. His proposals to experiment with a new system on two ships led to bitter remonstrances from Holtzendorff on 30 July 1912,[108] and caused Capelle to advise his chief not to push ahead with the matter, but to allow him to carry on preliminary discussions with the Command of the High Seas Fleet, which was becoming an ever stronger centre of opposition to him.[109] By the end of August the tension between Tirpitz and Holtzendorff had eased somewhat, but Tirpitz considered that his position was shaken because of the loss of Wilhelm's confidence, hostility from Bethmann, lack of support from Müller, and systematic opposition from Holtzendorff.[110] Capelle assured Tirpitz that he continued to enjoy Wilhelm's confidence, doubted if Bethmann wanted to burden himself with the responsibility of his dismissal, but otherwise shared his chief's suspicions.[111] Capelle was not entirely correct. On 31 August, Trotha, who reported to Wilhelm on behalf of the Imperial Naval Office, heard the Kaiser's complaints about the isolation of the Imperial Naval Office from the other naval agencies and Tirpitz's unfortunate reference to the needle-gun in 1870, and informed Capelle that Wilhelm definitely expected closer cooperation between Tirpitz and the "Front."[112]

On 14 December, Holtzendorff made another complaint to Wilhelm about Tirpitz's lack of efficiency and cooperation. He argued that German torpedoes were generally inferior in range and speed to the British and that contrary to demonstrated tactical needs Tirpitz had ordered that the German torpedoes that had the greatest range be assigned to battleships and large cruisers instead of to the fastest torpedo-boats and large cruisers. Tirpitz, moreover, had refused to hold discussions on this vital matter.[113] Following as it did the so-called "war council" of 8 December 1912, this report must have damaged Tirpitz's position.

Indicative of some greater preparation for war after the "war council" of 8 December were more serious efforts by Tirpitz to settle the recruit question. On 18 and 19 December meetings of the representatives of the various naval agencies were held in the Imperial Naval Office. In a speech drafted by Scheer, Tirpitz maintained on 14 December that the settlement of the question was essential "if we do not want to reckon with great setbacks . . . The political situation is not such as to allow an immediate change of system." The aim of the discussions was essentially to exchange opinions. Tirpitz referred to the objections that the army had raised to some of the proposed solutions, particularly to an increase of the length of enlistment which would keep in service the men about to be discharged along with the raw recruits. He also stressed that it was necessary for entire squadrons of the High Seas Fleet to make appearances abroad in order to impress on Britain the need of a naval agreement. "Either it comes to war in the foreseeable future, or we make an arrangement with England." This was an astounding statement from the man who had most strenuously objected to such an arrangement at the time that the Kaiser expected Britain to be involved in a war of the Dual Alliance against Germany. In the same document Tirpitz justified himself against the "Front," which wanted to utilize the new manpower to consolidate the First Squadron rather than develop the Second.[114] He further referred to a number of other possible solutions to the recruiting issue other than the lengthening of the period of service, which was impossible.[115] Subsequently, discussions took place between the Imperial Naval Office, represented at first by Tirpitz and later by Scheer, Kontre-Admiral Christian Schutz of the High Seas Fleet, Paul Behncke of the Admiralty Staff, Georg Hebbinghaus of the Baltic Sea station, Stosch of the North Sea station, and Trotha, now representing the Naval Cabinet. In those Schutz proposed to keep the reservists with the active crews for three months so as to break them in and delay the decline of battle readiness of the fleet from October to December—a month in which the outbreak of war would be less likely. Tirpitz responded that this involved the lengthening of the period of military service, which was impossible according to the army. In turn Schutz objected to the Naval Office's suggestion of a modification of the system of changing recruits on the torpedo-boats according to which some ships would change their crews entirely and thus be useless for a lengthy period of time. The Baltic Sea station basically supported the position of the fleet. The Admiralty Staff proposed a system of clandestine mobilization whereby reservists would be summoned to serve on their old ships with which they were acquainted. April was the best time for this subterfuge, but it could only work at a time of political tension. Tirpitz retorted that it was better to have a part of the fleet rather than the entire fleet in a state of limited battle readiness and then stated what Scheer had mentioned in the draft of his speech: "that we would in the foreseeable future come to war or an arrangement with England." In both cases it was correct to concentrate all means on the fleet. Obviously briefed by Heeringen, who had participated in the 8 December meeting, Behncke "pushes the case of war to the forefront; currently we [are] still under pressure." Trotha stated as his personal opinion that changes could not be made on paper, but must be worked through in trials. The representative of the North Sea station sided with Tirpitz, agreeing that the period of military service could not be lengthened. Schutz refused to be party to a consensus sought by Scheer that it was the responsibility of the Imperial Naval Office to improve the war preparedness of the navy.[116] There followed an altercation between the two men, with Schutz claiming that there was no reason to invite him to the meeting if the final decision was to be left with the Imperial Naval office. A partial agreement was finally found in raising the recruit quota and calling up reservists to serve on individual ships with which Schutz refused to associate himself.[117] This was far from being a definite solution. Prior to submitting his resignation Holtzendorff complained about the lack of manpower—"We cannot properly use the excellent *matériel* that is put in our hands"—a complaint for which Müller had no sympathy.[118]

The mobilization arrangements for the summer of 1913, presented to Wilhelm by the Chief of the Admiralty Staff in January 1913, only added the Third Mine Search Division to the High Seas Fleet. The active formations consisted as yet of two squadrons of ships of the line, the first with nine and the second with eight ships, and twelve cruisers. The reserve and new formations comprised two squadrons, the third with seven, and the fourth with eight ships, and twelve cruisers. The mobilization arrangements for the entire term 1913–14, however, included three ships of the Third Active squadron in the High Seas Fleet. They were transferred to Kiel in the fall of 1913,[119] and by the summer of 1914 the Third Active Squadron comprised a full contingent of eight ships.

## V

On 4 January 1913, Wilhelm took the initiative for introducing yet another navy bill, stipulating for the coming year the first rates for a ship of the line and two large cruisers as a step toward stabilizing an annual three-ship building ratio.

Tirpitz was requested to establish contact with the Chancellor and the Minister of War about the general armaments policy.[120] The Secretary of State reacted by pointing out that such a piecemeal procedure would make mockery of the Navy Law. If one wanted to return to a three-ship building tempo, rates for three large cruisers would have to be spread over several years.[121] Dähnhardt elaborated on Tirpitz's reactions while warning that such an increase would lead to a deterioration of Anglo-German relations, and further proposed requesting additional money for torpedo-boats, submarines, and airships.[122] On 5 January Bethmann informed a very pleased Kaiser of his intention to introduce a very large army bill at the cost of 300–400 million marks, but insisted that because of the currently improving relations with Britain the stabilization of the three-ship building rate would have to wait until next year. Wilhelm concurred.[123]

Unable to obtain a new navy bill because of the priority given to the army, the Imperial Naval Office none the less managed successfully to oppose Churchill's proposals for a "naval holiday," which, it argued, were one-sided since Britain could build the ships designated for the Mediterranean or ordered by her dominions or foreign countries which she could subsequently commandeer.[124] In the summer of 1913, Capelle prepared a set of notes for an unofficial report that Tirpitz was to present to Wilhelm. They opened with the astounding statement: "In respect to naval policy, the English are at the limit of their strength in terms of finances, politics, and naval technology." Financially there were the needs of social policy and the question whether the wealthy or the masses would pay the taxes. The radical group of the Liberal Party, particularly Lloyd George, hated the diversion of funds from the welfare program to the navy. As for considerations of foreign policy, "the opening of the Panama Canal, the Mediterranean issues, and the Chinese–Japanese policy made it impossible for Britain to continue to concentrate her navy in home waters in order to blockade one corner of the North Sea." As for naval and technical issues, there existed great difficulties with the construction of the 38 cm guns and a serious shortage of personnel. The only way for Britain to get out of her naval bankruptcy was to wreck the German navy law which she had earlier attempted to do by the threat of the stick, but was now, under Churchill's leadership, trying to accomplish by intrigue and promises, such as the offer of a naval holiday, a limitation of armaments, and the freezing of type increases. The next step would be to tie the German navy by treaty to the present building rate of two large ships per year.[125] In early 1914 the Imperial Naval Office opposed Wilhelm's request to introduce a supplementary budget for four small cruisers for abroad as undermining the confidence of the Reichstag in the naval program.[126] Tirpitz's requests for the 1915 budget did not include any new ships and involved largely the increase of ship types.[127] He refrained from including the third large ship stipulated by the *Novelle* of 1912 into this budget as not being sufficiently important to create "a new unavoidable naval scare."[128]

## VI

The Agadir crisis had stimulated concern to increase both the army and the navy. For some time there had existed an inclination to give priority to the army over the navy, expressed among others by Bülow and Bethmann-Hollweg. Wermuth had argued that the financial situation did not permit equal treatment of both. The initiative for another, more substantial army increase came from Wilhelm at the Hubertusstock meeting on 13 October 1912, and was first opposed by Josias von Heeringen, who considered it impracticable after the previous one.[129] On the same day, independently of the Kaiser, Erich Ludendorff, Chief of the Deployment Department of the Great General Staff, forwarded a memorandum requesting a major army increase, convincing Moltke, who had agreed at Hubertusstock that the preceding bill would fill the gaps in the army, that such an increase was indeed necessary.[130] Although the Ministry of War was not as easily convinced as the Chief of the General Staff, the defeat of Turkey by the Balkan League at the end of the month and in November changed the situation. Turkey lost her position as a potentially powerful German ally, as Moltke had considered her on 3 December 1911, and compelled Austria-Hungary to concentrate more troops against Serbia and have Germany shoulder more of the burden of the war against Russia.[131]

In spite of his reticence in October, Heeringen had told the Reichstag Budget Committee at the beginning of 1912 of formidable Russian preparations: the establishment of six new army corps, of peacetime cadres for thirty-three reserve divisions, and of a much faster movement of Russian troops to the front. "Therefore in a two-front war Germany could no longer count on beating the French before having to face the Russians." Austria-Hungary was not in a strong position to attack the Russians from the flank since they would be protected by swampy ground. Besides, six Austrian corps would have to be used against the Balkan states and other troops would have to be detached against Italy. In the west both Belgium and Holland had strengthened their military forces, and the landing of the BEF in Dunkirk would force Germany to concentrate her western forces on her right flank. Germany was basically left to her own resources to fight the powers of the Triple Entente. In agreement with Kiderlen, the Bavarian minister Lerchenfeld thought that Heeringen had painted too glum a picture of the situation.[132] He was none the less concerned. On 12 November, Moltke reported to Kiderlen that Russia was preparing to speed up mobilization in her western military districts.[133] She had also refrained from discharging her reservists and thus increased her peacetime military strength by 400,000 men.[134] Other measures could also be viewed as the beginning of mobilization.[135] Referring to the tense political situation in 1912–13, Groener wrote that

> the utility of our allies was also weighed in the circles of the General Staff. I believe that many others, if not most, thought as I did that the Italians would be of little if any help. Nor did they think the Austrian ally would provide much help.[136]

Wilhelm commented on a report of Kiderlen of 19 November 1912, which mentioned unobtrusive Austrian countermeasures to the Russian deployment on the Galician border, that France was probably making secret preparations for war as well: "We must present the Reichstag with requests for better training of the 100,000 men of our replacement reserve. About time."[137] On the following day Bethmann discovered that Josias von Heeringen was not opposed to extensive army increases.[138]

On the basis of a report from Paris of November 1912, according to which the French were prepared to support Russia with a bold offensive, the General Staff decided to make a push for a major military increase along the lines proposed by Wilhelm and found Bethmann receptive. Discussions were held between the Ministry of War and the General Staff. In a letter to Heeringen of 25 November, Moltke stated his reasons for a major army increase:

> We must, in my opinion, go even further and give our entire army the strength which alone guarantees final success in the next war, which we shall indeed fight with allies, but essentially with our own strength, for Germany's greatness. We must decide to use our manpower. We must again become a nation in arms . . .

He requested the introduction of universal military service in so far as it was possible.[139] On 2 December, Heeringen approached Bethmann, admitting Germany's military weakness in face of the threat of war in the past weeks, and providing the financial estimates of an army increase. He suggested 1 October 1913 as the date for the introduction of the new bill.[140] Bethmann had become convinced that Germany had to support Austria-Hungary with her entire strength if in the defense of her "vital interests which she could not give up without her reduction as a great power, she would be attacked by Russia . . . The purpose of our alliance is to keep the Great Central European monarchy beside us inviolable as a great power, so that we would one day not, as Prince Bismarck put it, find ourselves *nez-à-nez* with Russia, with France at our back."[141]

On the basis of a report of Prince Karl von Lichnowsky, the new ambassador in London, of 3 December, according to which Haldane told him that Britain would not remain neutral if Germany attacked France, Wilhelm on 8 December called a meeting of Müller, Tirpitz, August von Heeringen, and Moltke. There are several contemporary reports of the meeting giving minor variations of what was said as well as recent accounts attributing to it varying degrees of importance. Wilhelm considered Haldane's statement as one that clarified the military–political situation. Austria-Hungary should henceforth take a strong stand against the Slavs; were Russia to help the Serbs, war would be inevitable for Germany as well. But perhaps Bulgaria, Romania, Albania, and Turkey could be won over to the side of the Central Powers so as to free the armies of Austria-Hungary for use against Russia and allow the German land forces to concentrate against France. The High Seas Fleet was to deploy against Britain rather than engaging in operations against Russia, as Heeringen had recently proposed;[142] it was also to attack British troop transports to the Continent. Moltke strongly supported the Kaiser. He stated that war was inevitable and wanted it to occur as soon as possible. Shortly after the meeting he remarked that the Triple Entente would solidly oppose Germany and Austria-Hungary. Italy would be an unreliable ally and the entire strength of the Dual Monarchy would be engaged against the Balkan states and Russia. He attributed greater strength to the Triple Entente than to the Triple Alliance because of its offensive aims. The German army had to be concentrated in an attack on France through Belgium and could not be used for offensive undertakings elsewhere. It still had an advantage against France in artillery, infantry weapons, tents and field-kitchens which, however, might not last for long. While Russia enjoyed a superiority of numbers over Germany, she was still at a disadvantage because of "the reorganization, equipment, and armament of her army." Therefore the "Triple Alliance would not even here have to fear a war for the time being." The German army would, however, have to be substantially strengthened for the future.[143] On 8 December, Moltke is also alleged to have stated that the prospects for a successful war had never been so favorable since the conclusion of the Triple Alliance.[144]

According to different accounts, Tirpitz wanted the conflict to be postponed by either a year or a year and a half until the Heligoland fortifications and the Kaiser Wilhelm Canal were completed, causing Moltke to remark that the navy would never be ready and that any postponement of war would place the army in a more unfavorable situation. Müller appears to have agreed with Moltke but regretted that the Chief of the General Staff did not draw the consequence from his advocacy of an immediate war that "Russia or France or both would have to be faced with an ultimatum which would open the war with right on our side."[145] Moltke also recommended that the press be utilized to popularize a war against Russia. Wilhelm is supposed to have accepted the delay in the outbreak of war for either twelve or eighteen months with some reluctance.[146]

What was the outcome of the meeting? Fritz Fischer regards it as the war council for 1914; its most thorough investigator John Röhl comes close to the same conclusion. Mommsen and Erwin Höltzle play down its importance altogether, while Kennedy sees it as an indication of psychological preparedness for war.[147] There is a temptation to disregard the importance of the meeting altogether because of Müller's statement "The result was approximately zero." Yet something occurred. Definite orders were issued during and after the meeting: Tirpitz was instructed to speed up the construction of submarines and to confer with other naval agencies; on the following day Wilhelm ordered Tirpitz and Josias von Heeringen to make preparations for big navy and army bills. When finally passed, the new army bill was the largest since 1893, providing an addition of 117,000 men and almost 19,000 officers and noncommissioned officers.[148] As seen above, however, the initiative for the new army bill had been taken earlier and the Kaiser's orders after the meeting of 8 December could only have accelerated the pressure for its passage; no large navy bill followed. The Kaiser ordered Tirpitz at the meeting and Müller instructed Bethmann-Hollweg soon afterward to direct the press to prepare the country for a war arising from a Serbo-Austrian conflict. As John Röhl has demonstrated, the press was appropriately instructed, preparations were made for a while to strengthen the diplomatic position of the Central Powers in the Balkans, measures were taken for an economic mobilization, and some military preparations were considered.[149] So the result was more than zero.

But was the meeting of 8 December a war council for 1914? It is tempting to provide an affirmative answer to the question since the obvious German willingness to risk a general war in 1914 followed the opening of the Kaiser Wilhelm Canal to capital ships; it also coincided with the alleged eighteen-month postponement of the conflict as requested by Tirpitz according to Müller. Yet what had the navy done to prepare itself for war? Tirpitz himself had not asserted that the political situation was more serious after the meeting of 8 December than he had described it on 25 November. But, as instructed on 8 December, he did (as seen above) initiate more serious discussions with other naval agencies than before to solve the question of recruitment; no definite solution to that question was found and no substantial changes were made in the arrangements for mobilization. As will be seen below, attention was given to submarine, mine, and air attacks against British troop-transports to the Continent, but, contrary to the instructions of Wilhelm on 8 December, they were assigned a relatively low priority. In contrast to Wilhelm's instructions of 8 December that naval operations against France and Russia be suspended, the Admiralty Staff, with the Kaiser's own later approval, continued to work on them. But what is the most telling argument from naval sources against a continuity of German strategic and foreign policy from 8 December 1912 to 30 July 1914 is that the Admiralty Staff failed to work out an operations plan against an expected wide blockade—a fact of which Wilhelm himself became aware on 26 May 1914. This removed the element of rationality that appeared to be present on 8 December 1912 from the considerations of July 1914. And, lastly, would any instruction provided by Wilhelm be consistently adhered to by either himself or his subordinates? Fritz Fischer himself admits that "he allowed himself to be driven by occasional moods and influenced by irresponsible advisers without considering the consequences of his policy."[150] Although his annoyance with Britain's stance of December 1912 lasted for some time, in July 1914 he was prepared to back down when Serbia accepted most of the terms of the Austro-Hungarian ultimatum, attempted to seek until the end a compromise on the basis of the "halt in Belgrade" proposal, and tried to achieve an agreement with Britain. This is hardly continuity in the action of the chairman of an alleged war council; nor in that of a Chancellor who did not participate in it and subsequently at least sometimes rejected the assumption that Britain would become involved in a European war; nor in that of the *primus inter pares* of the Imperial Navy. Except for Moltke's persistent advocacy of a preventive war against the Dual Alliance, it is difficult to accept the meeting of 8 December 1912 as leading to the war of 1914.

## Notes: Chapter 17

1   Above all, Fischer, *Krieg,* passim; Volker R. Berghahn, *Germany and the Approach to War in 1914* (London, 1973), esp. pp. 145–210. Dirk Stegmann, *Die Erben Bismarcks: Parteien und Verbände in der Spätphase des Wilhelminischen Deutschlands. Sammlungspolitik, 1897–1918* (Cologne/Berlin, 1970), esp. pp. 257–448, passim; Klaus-Dieter Wernecke, *Der Wille zur Weltgeltung: Aussenpolitik und Öffentlichkeit in Deutschland am Vorabend des Ersten Weltkriegs* (Düsseldorf, 1969), passim; for more qualified interpretations, see Wolfgang J. Mommsen, "Domestic factors in German foreign policy before 1914," *Central European History,* vol. 6, no. 1 (March 1973); Geoff Eley, *Reshaping the German Right: Radical Nationalism and Political Change after Bismarck* (New Haven, Conn., 1980), pp. 316–34.
2   Berghahn, *Germany,* p. 114; Fischer, *Krieg,* pp. 138–44; Jarausch, *Enigmatic Chancellor,* pp. 124–6.
3   Reichsarchiv, *Kriegsrüstung,* Vol. 1, Anlage Band, No. 41, "Denkschrift des Direktors des Allgemeinen Kriegsdepartments Generalmajors Wandel vom 29 November 1911," pp. 132–35; Fischer, *Krieg,* p. 175.
4   PAAA, Deutschland 121, Geh., Bd 1, Moltke to Bethmann-Hollweg, 2 December 1911, enclosing "Geheim. Die militärpolitische Lage Deutschlands," signed by Moltke. It is also printed in Reichsarchiv, *Kriegsrüstung,* Vol. 1, pp. 126–35; a brief summary of it appears in Fischer, *Krieg,* pp. 176–7.
5   Albertini, *Origins,* Vol. 1, p. 343.
6   Fischer, *Krieg,* p. 177.
7   Tirpitz, *Aufbau,* p. 203; Berghahn, *Germany,* p. 101.
8   Tirpitz, *Aufbau,* p. 206.

9  ibid., p. 209.
10  BA-MA, F 3303, PG 66708, Holtzendorff to Tirpitz, 16 September 1911.
11  ibid., N 253/24, Heeringen to "Edn" (Capelle?), 10 August 1911.
12  ibid., Heeringen to Tirpitz, 8 July 1911.
13  Tirpitz, *Aufbau*, Capelle to Tirpitz, 11 September 1911, pp. 209–11.
14  ibid., Tirpitz to Capelle, 13 September 1911, pp. 211–12.
15  BA-MA, N 253/25, Capelle to Tirpitz, 14 September 1911.
16  ibid., Capelle, "Begründung. Skizze zu einer Novelle," n.d.
17  ibid., Schrader, "Seiner Exzellenz dem Herrn Staatssekretär vorzulegen," 9 September 1911.
18  ibid., "Vortrag am 26 September 1911," in Dähnhardt's handwriting, corrected by Tirpitz; for a résumé, see Tirpitz's *Aufbau*, pp. 213–15. See also BA-MA, F 3443, PG 67474, Müller, "Leitsätze aus dem Imm.-Vortrag St. Sek. RMA betr. Flottenentwickelung," Rominten, 26 September 1911.
19  Müller, *Der Kaiser*, p. 93; BA-MA, N 159/4, p. 82.
20  Müller, *Der Kaiser*, p. 93; BA-MA, N 159/4, p. 83.
21  BA-MA, F 3443, PG 67474, Wilhelm to Bethmann-Hollweg, 26 September 1911; also PAAA, Orientalia Generalia No. 5, Geh., Bd 17, Jenisch to Kiderlen, 28 September 1911.
22  BA-MA, F 2041, PG 66061, Wilhelm to Bethmann-Hollweg, 30 September 1911; dispatched 2 October 1911, copy.
23  Müller, *Der Kaiser*, pp. 93–4; BA-MA, F 3443, PG 67473, Müller, "Notitzen aus Besprechung beim Reichskanzler an 3.10.1911;" N 159/4, p. 84.
24  BA-MA, F 2041, PG 66061; reprinted in Tirpitz, *Aufbau*, pp. 218–20, Bethmann-Hollweg to Tirpitz, 4 October 1911.
25  BA-MA, F 3343, PG 67474, Heeringen to Bethmann-Hollweg, 7 October 1911, reprinted in Tirpitz, *Aufbau*, pp. 220–1.
26  BA-MA, F 3443, PG 67474, "Antwort des Staatssekretärs auf die Anfragen des Reichskanzlers," n.d. Abbreviated in Tirpitz's *Aufbau*, with the date of 7 October 1911, pp. 222–4.
27  BA-MA, F 3443, PG 67474, Müller to Bethmann-Hollweg, 4 October 1911.
28  BA-MA, 2045, PG 66082, Holtzendorff's memorandum of 25 October 1911.
29  Müller, *Der Kaiser*, pp. 97–8; BA-MA, F 2045, PG 66082, Müller to Tirpitz, 15 October 1911; N 159/4, pp. 91–3.
30  BA-MA, N 253/24, memorandum by Capelle, 23 October 1911.
31  ibid., F 2045, PG 66082, "Notiz zum Immediatvortrag, 27 October 1911, im Auftrag von Müller," copy.
32  ibid., F 2041, PG 66061, Heeringen to Tirpitz, 24 November 1911.
33  ibid., Heeringen to Tirpitz, 6 December 1911.
34  Müller, *Der Kaiser*, p. 100; BA-MA, N 159/4, p. 96.
35  BA-MA, N 253/35, Capelle to Tirpitz, 11 November 1911.
36  Berghahn, *Germany*, p. 115; BA-MA, N 253/25, "Material-Notizen zum Immediatvortrag," in Dähnhardt's handwriting, covering events from 14 November 1911 to 6 December 1912; ibid., F 3443, PG 67474, Müller to Chief of the Civil Cabinet, 16 November 1911; ibid., F 2041, PG 66061, Bethmann-Hollweg to Josias von Heeringen, 28 November 1911.
37  BA-MA, F 2045, PG 66082, "Mitteilung des Chefs des Admiralstabes über seine Unterredung mit dem Kriegsminister," 30 November 1911.
38  PAAA, England 78, secr., Bd 28, Bethmann-Hollweg to Wilhelm, 30 November 1911; BA-MA, F 2027, PG 66003.
39  Müller, *Der Kaiser*, p. 101; BA-MA, N 159/4, p. 100.
40  BA-MA, F 2045, PG 66082; also Tirpitz, *Aufbau*, Wilhelm to Müller, 9 December 1911, pp. 264–5.
41  Wilhelm Widenmann, *Marine-Attaché an der kaiserlich-deutschen Botschaft in London, 1907–1912* (Göttingen, 1952), pp. 212–74, passim; Giessler, *Die Institution*, pp. 70–3, 158–69; Gerhard Ritter, *Staatskunst und Kriegshandwerk*, Vol. 2 (Munich, 1960), pp. 213–38, passim.
42  GP, XXXI, No. 11313, Widenmann to Tirpitz, 28 October 1911, pp. 11–15; and No. 11317, Widenmann to Tirpitz, 10 November 1911, pp. 25–6.

43  H St Ar Stuttgart, E73/73a, 12e II, Varnbüler to Weizsäcker, 3 December 1911.
44  BA-MA, N 253/25, King of Saxony to Grand Duke of Oldenburg, 7 December 1911, copy.
45  Bay H St Ar, Abt II, Geh St Ar, Bay. Ges. Berlin, 1083, report of Bavarian minister in Berlin, 11 December 1911.
46  John C. G. Röhl, "Admiral von Müller and the approach to war, 1911–1914," *Historical Journal*, Vol. 12, no. 4 (1968), p. 656; Müller, *Der Kaiser*, p. 103.
47  Müller, *Der Kaiser*, p. 104; BA-MA, F 2041, PG 66061, "Vortrag des Kabinettchefs bei S.M. am Sonnabend den 23. Dez;" ibid., Müller to Tirpitz, 23 December 1911; N 159/4, p. 104; Berghahn, *Germany*, p. 117.
48  Müller, *Der Kaiser*, p. 105; BA-MA, N 159/4, p. 105.
49  ibid., pp. 106–9; Röhl, "Müller," pp. 656–7; BA-MA, F 3443, PG 67474, "Aktennotiz Müller," n.d.
50  BA-MA, F 3443, PG 67474, Müller to Bethmann-Hollweg; Bethmann-Hollweg to Müller, 12 January 1912.
51  Fischer, *Krieg*, pp. 148–9.
52  Jarausch, *Enigmatic Chancellor*, pp. 127–8; Röhl, "Müller," pp. 657–8; Cecil, *Albert Ballin*, pp. 181–4; Woodward, *German Navy*, pp. 323–9. Tirpitz continued to grumble about the changes requested by Bethmann, e.g. BA-MA, N 253/26, Tirpitz's comment to Dähnhardt's handwritten memorandum of 13 January 1912.
53  BA-MA, F 2041, PG 66062, "Novellen-Rede," draft. There is a comment in the margin: the "Reinkonzept" has been given to C, E, and D1.
54  ibid., "Material für Begründung der Novelle. I. Begründung der Novelle im Plenum," n.d., drafted by Dähnhardt; approved by Capelle.
55  BA-MA, F 7633, Budgetcommission 1912, "Ganz Geheim," 8 February 1912.
56  ibid., "In Verteidigung der Novelle," n.d., no signature.
57  See above all Jonathan Steinberg, "Diplomatie als Wille und Vorstellung: Die Berliner Mission Lord Haldanes in February 1912," in Schottelius and Deist, *Marine*, pp. 263–95; Kennedy, *Antagonism*, pp. 451–2; Berghahn, *Germany*, pp. 121–3; Jarausch, *Enigmatic Chancellor*, pp. 126–8; Fischer, *Krieg*, pp. 188–92; Woodward, *German Navy*, pp. 323–65, passim; Padfield, *Great Naval Race*, pp. 277–85.
58  Müller, *Der Kaiser*, p. 111; BA-MA, N 159/4, entry for 4 February 1912, p. 114.
59  BA-MA, N 253/26, Korvettenkapitän Müller of the Central Department of the Imperial Naval Office to Widenmann, 4 March 1912, reprinted in Tirpitz, *Aufbau*, pp. 314–15; Jäckh, *Kiderlen-Wächter*, Vol. 2, Bethmann-Hollweg to Wilhelm, 6 March 1912, p. 160.
60  GLA, Karlsruhe, 233/34815, Berckheim's report of 15 March 1912.
61  Bay H St Ar, Abt II, Geh St Ar, Bay Ges Berlin, 1084, Lerchenfeld's report of 15 March 1912.
62  See in particular GP, XXXI, No. 11374, Metternich to Bethmann-Hollweg, 24 February 1912, and Wilhelm's marginalia, pp. 135–7; also in Tirpitz, *Aufbau*, pp. 302–3.
63  BA-MA, F 3443, PG 67475; also in N 253/26 as a rough draft; reprinted in Tirpitz, *Aufbau*, pp. 298–301, Tirpitz to Müller, 26 February 1912.
64  BA-MA, F 3443, PG 67475; reprinted in Tirpitz, *Aufbau*, pp. 306–8, Wilhelm to Bethmann-Hollweg, 27 February 1912.
65  BA-MA, F 3443, PG 67475, Müller to Wilhelm, 27 February 1912.
66  Tirpitz, *Aufbau*, "Meldung des Reichskanzlers an den Kaiser," 28 February 1912, p. 308.
67  BA-MA, N 253/26, Capelle, "Skizze des Vortrages im Staatsministerium am 4. März der eventuell vor den leitenden Ministern der Bundesstaaten zu wiederholen war," 4 March 1912.
68  ibid., Capelle to Tirpitz, 4 March 1912.
69  ibid., "Aufzeichnung Capelle," n.d., as basis for discussions with the prime and finance ministers of the Empire on 10 March 1912.
70  ibid., F 2041, PG 66062, Bethmann-Hollweg to Tirpitz, 5 March 1912.
71  Berghahn, *Germany*, p. 130; Hans Herzfeld, *Die deutsche Rüstungspolitik vor dem Weltkriege* (Bonn, 1923), p. 13.
72  Bay H St Ar, Kriegsarchiv, Abt IV, M Kr 42, Wenninger to the Minister of War, 24 February 1912.
73  Müller, *Der Kaiser*, p. 116; Jarausch, *Enigmatic Chancellor*, p. 129; Vietsch,

*Bethmann-Hollweg*, pp. 138–40; Jäckh, *Kiderlen-Wächter*, Vol. 2, pp. 159–61; BA-MA, N 159/4, p. 124.

74  BA-MA, N 253/26, Tirpitz, "Gespräch mit Admiral v. Müller" (in Trotha's hand); N 159/4, p. 124; Müller, *Der Kaiser*, p. 117; Tirpitz, *Aufbau*, pp. 322–3.
75  BA-MA, F 3443, PG 67475, Bethmann-Hollweg to Wilhelm, 11 March 1912.
76  ibid., N 253/26, Trotha, "Notiz über die Mitteilungen Sr. Majestät am 11. 3. 1912;" also in Tirpitz, *Aufbau*, pp. 324–5.
77  BA-MA, F 3443, PG 67475, marginal comment on Widenmann to Tirpitz, 7 March 1912.
78  ibid., Bethmann-Hollweg to Wilhelm, 14 March 1912; enclosure: Widenmann to Tirpitz, 11 March 1912.
79  See ibid., F 7633, Budgetcommission 1912, "Aufrechterhaltung des 2:1 Standards durch England," n.d., no signature; and "2:3 Standard," n.d., no signature. For the treatment of the fifth naval bill in the public and the Reichstag, see Fernis, *Flottennovellen*, pp. 94–154, passim.
80  BA-MA, F 2041, PG 66063, Capelle, "Reinkonzept. Denkschrift zum Immediatvortrag. Flottengesetznovelle 1912," 22 May 1912.
81  ibid., F 2046, PG 66088, "Protokoll. Sitzungen über Linienschiffe und grosse Kreuzer 1911," on 6, 8, 11, and 17 May 1910.
82  ibid., F 2287, PG 94292, "Entscheidungen . . . des . . . Staatssekretärs in der Sitzung am 1 September 1910 über den grossen Kreuzer 'K,'" 2 September 1910.
83  ibid., F 2046, PG 66088, "Protokoll über die Sitzung am 24 September 1910. Linienschiffstyp und grosser Kreuzertyp 1911."
84  ibid., N 253/24, Heeringen to Tirpitz, 22 June 1911.
85  ibid., F 2051, Tagesmeldungen, RMA Central Department, Tirpitz, 4 August 1911, to W. K. and A.
86  ibid., F 2046, PG 66088, "Protokoll der Sitzung am 1 September 1911, betr. Kalibersteigerung der schweren Artillerie."
87  ibid., "Kalibersteigerung der schweren Artillerie," n.d.; "Protokoll über die am 24 September 1911 gehaltene Sitzung über die Kalibervergrösserung."
88  ibid., F 3502, PG 67858, Müller to Tirpitz, 17 July 1912; F 2045, PG 66082, Wilhelm's memorandum, 29 July 1912, communicated to Tirpitz by Müller on the same day.
89  ibid., F 3502, PG 67858, Tirpitz to Müller, 2 and 5 August 1912.
90  ibid., "Bemerkungen zu dem Schreiben RMA vom 5 VIII 1912," 12–15 August 1912.
91  ibid., Müller to Tirpitz and to Wilhelm, 20 August 1912.
92  ibid., Wilhelm to Müller, 24 August 1912.
93  ibid., Müller to Wilhelm, 28 August 1912.
94  ibid., N 253/27, Plessen to Tirpitz, 26 August 1912; Tirpitz to Plessen, 28 August 1912, telegram.
95  ibid., F 4141, VI, 1. 1. 21a., Heft 3, Rollmann to Tirpitz, 3 April 1913.
96  ibid., N 253/28, "Notiz zum Immediatvortrag, grosser Kreuzer 1914," 29 April 1913, no signature. The handwriting is unrecognizable. The document appears to be a dictation of Tirpitz; F 2046, PG 66087, "Sitzung bei dem Herrn Staatssekretär am 17. 6. 1913, betreffend grossen Kreuzer. 1914."
97  ibid., F 3444, PG 67478, Heeringen to Wilhelm, 27 May 1911.
98  ibid., F 3443, PG 67472, Heeringen to Tirpitz, 23 November 1911, copy.
99  ibid., Heeringen to Kiderlen-Wächter, 25 December 1911.
100 Müller, *Der Kaiser*, pp. 109–10.
101 PAAA, Deutschland 121, No. 12, Bd 13, Tirpitz to the Foreign Office, 12 June 1912.
102 BA-MA, F 787, PG 77646, Heeringen to Tirpitz, 12 November 1912.
103 Müller, *Der Kaiser*, pp. 123; BA-MA, N 159/4, pp. 167–8.
104 BA-MA, F 2046, PG 66088, "Sitzung am 25 11 1912 bei Sr Exz dem Herrn Staatssekretär."
105 Müller, *Der Kaiser*, diary entry for 26 November, pp. 123–4; BA-MA, N 159/4, p. 168.
106 BA-MA, F 787, PG 77646, Tirpitz to Heeringen, 30 November 1912.
107 PAAA, England 71b, Geh., Vol. 1, Heeringen to Kiderlen, 28 November 1912, enclosing "Zusammenstellung über die militärische Lage zur See in England, Frankreich und Russland."
108 BA-MA, F 3303, PG 66709, Holtzendorff to Tirpitz, 30 July 1912, copy.
109 ibid., N 253/27, Capelle to Tirpitz, 3 and 10 August 1912.

110   ibid., Tirpitz to Hopmann, n.d.
111   ibid., Capelle to Tirpitz, 29 August 1912.
112   ibid., F 3502, PG 67858, note by Trotha, 1 September 1912.
113   ibid., N 253/28, Holtzendorff to Wilhelm, 14 December 1912, copy to the Chancellor (Imperial Naval Office) "zum Bericht, 21 Dezember 1912."
114   ibid., N 253/27, Scheer, "Gesichtspunkte für die Besprechung am 18 Dezember 1912 über Besetzung der Geschwader mit Rekruten," 14 December 1912; N 253/28, "Sitzung im Reichs-Marine-Amt über Besetzung der Marine mit Rekruten."
115   ibid., N 253/28, "Notizen für die Besprechung am 18 Dezember 1912 über Besetzung der Geschwader mit Rekruten."
116   ibid., "Diskussion am 18 Dezember 1912."
117   ibid., "Sitzung am 19 Dezember 1912."
118   ibid., F 3303, PG 66710, Holtzendorff to Wilhelm, 14 January 1913; Müller, "Allerunterthänigste Meldung," 16 January 1913.
119   BA-MA, F 2020, PG 65976, Heeringen, "Zum Immediatvortrag," 17 January 1913; Tirpitz reported the next month about mobilization arrangements with no real changes; ibid., F 6372, XVII, 1. 1. 6., B 21, Bei-Heft 1, approved by Tirpitz, 4 February 1913.
120   ibid., 2045, PG 66083, Müller to Tirpitz, 4 January 1913, copy; N 159/4, p. 175; also Müller, Der Kaiser, p. 127.
121   BA-MA, F 2045, PG 66083, "Notiz Tirpitz," 5 January 1913.
122   ibid., "Ausarbeitung des Kontre-Admirals Dähnhardt für C. Novelle 1913," n.d.; also "Notizen für den von S.E. den Staatssekretär auf Allerh. Befehl dem Herrn Reichskanzler zu erstatteten Vortrag," n.d.
123   ibid., Müller to Tirpitz, 6 January 1913; Müller, Der Kaiser, pp. 127–8.
124   BA-MA, F 2045, PG 66083, F 2039, PG 66057, Dähnhardt's memoranda, 7 May 1913, 25 October 1913.
125   ibid., N 253/28, Capelle, "Notizen für die Kieler Reise (aber nicht für einen amtlichen Vortrag)," n.d.
126   ibid., N 253/29, initialed by Capelle and Dähnhardt on 9 February 1914, "Seiner Exz. nebenstehende Skizze für den Sonnabendvortrag vorzeigen;" objections accepted by Wilhelm on 17 February 1914, GP, XXXIX, No. 15594, Müller to Bethmann-Hollweg, 18 February 1914, p. 82.
127   BA-MA, F 2045, PG 66083, Tirpitz to Bethmann-Hollweg, 22 May 1914.
128   ibid., F 3443, PG 67475, "Aufzeichnung Müller," 19 May 1914. Reported to Wilhelm on the same day.
129   Reichsarchiv, Kriegsrüstung, Vol. I, p. 120.
130   ibid., pp. 154–7.
131   ibid., pp. 157–9; Schulte, Kriegsausbruch, esp. pp. 13–15, 17, 26–7, 44–5, 64; the Kaiser was at first unperturbed by Turkey's collapse; John C. G. Röhl, "An der Schwelle zum Weltkrieg: Eine Dokumentation über den Kriegsrat vom 8 Dezember 1912," Militärgeschichtliche Mitteilungen, no. 1 (1977), pp. 79–80.
132   Bay H St Ar, Abt II, Geh St Ar Bay Ges, Berlin, 1084, report of Lerchenfeld, 5 May 1912.
133   PAAA, Russland 72, Vol. 93, Moltke to Kiderlen-Wächter, 12 November 1912.
134   ibid., Moltke to Kiderlen, 12 November 1912, amplifying the previous report, initialed by Bethmann-Hollweg on 20 November.
135   GP, XXXIII, No. 12412, Moltke to the Foreign Office, 21 November 1912, and its enclosures indicated considerable concern about Russian, but little about French and British preparations for war, pp. 381–2; ibid., No. 12462, Moltke to the Foreign Office, 29 November 1912, enclosure 1, reported trial mobilization measures in France, pp. 435–6.
136   BA-MA, N 46/1, Groener, Nachlass, 171.
137   GP, XXXIII, No. 12395, Kiderlen-Wächter to Wilhelm, 19 November 1912, pp. 359–60; Reichsarchiv, Kriegsrüstung, Vol. I, p. 161.
138   ibid., pp. 161–2.
139   ibid., pp. 163–4; quotation from p. 164.
140   ibid., pp. 166–7.
141   GLA Karlsruhe, 49/2045, report of Dusch, 29 November 1912.
142   The fullest account of this meeting is in BA-MA, N 159/4, pp. 169-71.

143   Reichsarchiv, *Kriegsrüstung*, Vol. I, *Anglageband*, pp. 158 ff.; most of the document is published in Röhl, "An der Schwelle," No. 27, pp. 116–19.

144   Fischer, *Krieg*, p. 234.

145   ibid., pp. 233–4; Röhl, "An der Schwelle," p. 88.

146   ibid., No. 22, p. 113.

147   Fischer, *Krieg*, pp. 232–4; Röhl, "Admiral Müller," pp. 661–73; "An der Schwelle," passim; and most recently "Die Generalprobe. Zur Geschichte und Bedeutung des "Kriegsrates" vom 8. Dezember 1912," in Dirk Stegmann, Bernd Jürgen Wendt, Peter-Christian Witt (eds), *Industrielle Gesellschaft und politisches System: Beiträge zur politischen Sozialgeschichte. Festschrift für Fritz Fischer zum siebzigsten Geburtstag* (Bonn, 1978), pp. 357–73, with a good summary of the controversy on pp. 357–8, n. 3; Mommsen, "Domestic factors," esp. pp. 12 ff; Erwin Hölzle, *Die Selbstentmachtung Europas: Das Experiment des Friedens vor und im Ersten Weltkrieg* (Göttingen, 1975), p. 180; Kennedy, *Antagonism*, p. 456.

148   Ritter, *Staatskunst*, Vol. II, p. 279.

149   Röhl, "An der Schwelle," pp. 89–91; No. 5, p. 100; No. 6, p. 101; No. 14, pp. 106–7; No. 29, pp. 121–2; No. 38, pp. 125–6.

150   Fischer, *Krieg*, p. 429.

# 18 Naval Operational Planning from Agadir to the July Crisis, 1914

## I

The Agadir crisis had caught the German naval leadership with the question of the deployment of its fleet unsettled. The First Squadron had been transferred to Wilhelmshaven and the number of large cruisers incapable of passing the canal had increased. The Admiralty Staff, allegedly in consultation with the Fleet, therefore drafted new directives for a war with Britain which Heeringen on 24 October 1911 presented for Wilhelm's approval.

(1) The task of the High Seas Fleet is to come to battle with the enemy as soon as possible, even involving all the forces at its disposal.
(2) The North Sea, including the Skagerrak, is the operation area under normal conditions.
(3) If the war is not to be fought offensively, His Majesty will provide special directives.[1]

In their justification Heeringen argued that war games and deliberations supported an immediate battle with the enemy, but that an advance against the British coast could only be considered if the High Seas Fleet was able to fight separate battles against parts of the Royal Navy. Therefore these would preferably have to be fought in German waters, the North Sea and the Skagerrak. The deployment of major parts of the High Seas Fleet in the Baltic was rejected since it would free the British of the threat of an immediate battle. This was obviously a concession by Holtzendorff to Heeringen. In turn Heeringen made the concession of including the Skagerrak within the German area of operations. His reasons for this were: (a) should the High Seas Fleet be in the Baltic at the outbreak of war, it would because of the inability of the newest ships to pass through the canal have to circumnavigate Denmark to reach the North Sea; (b) if the fleet was split between the Baltic and the North Sea and an increasing number of new ships remained in Kiel, they, along with the older ships located there, would have to circumnavigate Denmark, and it would then depend on the circumstances if they would be joined by the First Squadron of the Dreadnoughts in the Skagerrak or in the German Bight. The memorandum then used the old arguments against the Skagerrak deployment. The special directives that were mentioned, dealing presumably with a war that was entirely defensive, were to prevail in the period from October to December when the fleet was in a poor shape to fight because of the engagement of new recruits and officers and repairs.

Wilhelm approved the new directives and left it to the Admiralty Staff to decide when the unification of the fleet should be sought. The Chancellor was to be informed where the fleet was to unite, but his opinion on the matter was not to be solicited. A truly militaristic stance! He was, however, to keep the Admiralty Staff constantly informed about the political relationship with Britain. To avert suspicion, there should be an annual exercise to unify the fleet.[2]

This apparent compromise between the Admiralty Staff and the Fleet was broken by a tentative decision to transfer all the newest ships of the line and large cruisers to Wilhelmshaven, opening a vigorous round of debate, Tirpitz and Heeringen against Holtzendorff, in which Müller eventually sided with the former. On 2 and 11 December, Holtzendorff protested against this decision. It would, he claimed, disturb the training of the Cruiser Squadron by splitting it; the fortifications of Heligoland were as yet unable to provide an adequate defensive for the North Sea; furthermore, the canal did not offer adequate passage for the older ships. He therefore supported the journey of all the ships located in the Baltic around Skagen to surprise the British from there.[3] The Admiralty Staff denied that the passage through the canal would present the pre-Dreadnoughts with any difficulty and that the appearance of the High Seas Fleet at Skagen would surprise the British: their expectation of it was attested by the construction of the base at Rosyth in the Firth of Forth and by maneuvers; if a battle was to be fought near Skagen, the German crews would already be weary, some of the coal would be burned up, and, depending on weather conditions, the torpedo-boats could be useless; moreover, for actions against the British coast, shipping, and landing forces the Skagerrak was further than the German Bight.[4]

On 17 January 1912, Holtzendorff threatened to resign in protest against the transfer of all ships incapable of passing the canal to Wilhelmshaven. In view of Wilhelm's decision of the previous day to effect the transfer, Müller advised him against doing so.[5] On 30 January an audience of Heeringen, Holtzendorff, Tirpitz, and Prince Heinrich occurred with Wilhelm in Müller's presence.[6] Müller had earlier provided Wilhelm with a draft of an order to concentrate in the North Sea and the advice that it go into effect unless Holtzendorff provided any new objections to it.[7] During the audience, however, it was Heeringen who made a new point in favor of the concentration in the North Sea: that the Chief of the General Staff wanted the navy at the outset of hostilities to attack the transports of British troops to France. The very presence of the High Seas Fleet in the German Bight and its attacks against the blockading British forces would deter these transports; a more direct threat would be energetic submarine attacks against the Thames estuary and Dover.[8] No decision was reached on that day. On 2 February, Tirpitz drafted a report to Wilhelm, strongly supporting the concentration in the North Sea. He reiterated most of the arguments of the Admiralty Staff, pointing out further that deployment in Kiel would disappoint the German public, which would view the German navy as bankrupt. He claimed that there were no military arguments, only considerations of training, against the deployment in the North Sea; moreover, a retreat could be more easily undertaken in the German Bight, where the fleet could withdraw under the guns of Heligoland and the river estuaries, than from Skagen.[9] A definite decision was made on 3 February.[10] The fleet was to concentrate in the North Sea, but in the summer months of 1912 the reconnaissance forces were still to be located in the Baltic. This was the only concession to Holtzendorff. Wilhelm also requested Heeringen to provide him with specific information regarding the dates for the completion of the canal, of the fortifications and submarine bases of Heligoland, the effectiveness of submarines, the availability of mine blockings, and other details.[11] This information was provided on 22 March by Tirpitz: the canal would be passable for Dreadnoughts only in April 1914; the fortifications of Heligoland were well under way and its harbor could already accommodate submarines and have eventually a capacity for thirty-six; the action radius of submarines U5–22 was 200 sea miles and their number would be fourteen in the fall of 1912, twenty-two in the fall of 1913, and thirty-one in the fall of 1914. By the fall of 1912, Wilhelmshaven would be able to accommodate seventeen large ships.[12]

Holtzendorff was to show considerable annoyance with the decision of 3 February as well as with the decision reached in the summer to relocate all ships incapable of passing the canal in Wilhelmshaven, which would in effect split the reconnaissance forces. Holtzendorff's complaints were to turn Müller, who had earlier attempted to placate the Chief of the High Seas Fleet, against him.[13] In April 1913 he was replaced by Vice-Admiral Friedrich von Ingenohl.

## II

As Heeringen had informed Wilhelm, the Admiralty Staff was in January 1912 cooperating with the Great General Staff for action against the transportation of the BEF to the Continent. In a memorandum of 23 January, which was to serve as a basis for further discussions,[14] the Admiralty Staff stated that 200 steamers of approximately 3,000 tons, which would be necessary to transport the 170,000 men of the BEF, would at any time be available in British ports. The embarkation could begin on the tenth mobilization day from several British harbors. According to the experience of the Agadir crisis, preparations would already be undertaken at the time of tension so that embarkation could start at the very outbreak of war. There was some doubt, however, whether the British would dare to undertake the transport of their troops while Germany had a "fleet in being" or whether the German Bight would be blockaded and the transports, for greater security, would be sent west of the Strait of Dover to Cherbourg, Le Havre, Boulogne, and Calais. The Admiralty Staff thus appears to have realistically rejected the possibility of a British landing in the Netherlands or in Esbjerg. In the margin of the document the following typewritten comments appear:

Which views does the Great General Staff have on these matters, particularly on the expected disembarkation points? How does the Great General Staff estimate the effectiveness of the English Expeditionary Corps for the French war effort?

Is it from the standpoint of fighting a land war necessary to cut off the transports at all in the first days after the outbreak of war?

To hinder the transports the High Seas Fleet was to break through the British blockade line to enable its submarines and torpedo-boats to attack the British naval forces and coastline and to lay mines. This action would probably prevent the BEF from embarking. If a delay of the transports was of particular urgency, the entire High Seas Fleet could attack them. In a fuller report prepared for Heeringen's orientation on 1 February somewhat different figures and timetables were given. Fewer British troops were expected to be involved because of the needs of home defense and the suppression of possible colonial uprisings.[15] Nor were landings in Holland and Belgium ruled out entirely. The measures against the transports remained unchanged. On 8 February, Wilhelm agreed with these views and ordered that trials be conducted for the use of submarines against the transports and that mines be made available for use against them.

On 2 February, Moltke informed Heeringen that the General Staff was also studying the use of the BEF against Germany and raised two questions on which its destination would depend:

whether the English fleet is able beside its main task to undertake the local protection of the transport fleet during its journey and landing, and in which destination of the transports could this be most easily undertaken?[16]

Heeringen replied that the Royal Navy could carry out this additional task, which would be most effectively accomplished west of the Calais–Dover line with the support of the French *défense mobile* and six armored cruisers of the Channel force. Transports to Belgian ports would also be possible, but those to Denmark were too risky to be likely.[17] The view that the BEF would be disembarked in France was confirmed by the reports of the German military and naval attachés in London, Ostertag and Widenmann. The latter stressed the importance of the German concentration in the North Sea as a deterrent to the transport of the BEF and advised: "The decisive battle should be postponed . . . lest a possible English victory at once relieve the Admiralty of the fear of the 'fleet in being.'" He concluded: "Only if our fleet lengthens and strengthens the right wing of the German army in the North Sea will it fulfill its true task, which in my opinion consists in the support of the work of the army on the Continent."[18] It is interesting that Widenmann, who was obviously close to Tirpitz, now saw the primary task of the navy as supporting the army on the Continent. Were he and Tirpitz prepared to render lip-service to the Continental orientation of German defense policy?

The General Staff prepared a memorandum on the BEF which it forwarded to the Foreign Office and the Admiralty Staff on 30 May 1912.[19]

It took for granted that, in spite of the absence of a definite military convention with France, Britain would fight on her side in a war with Germany. The main asset of her support was her naval power, which would secure France's imports from overseas, her troop-transports from North Africa, free her of any concerns about coastal defense, and restrain Italy from attacking her, thus releasing French Alpine forces for use against Germany. In addition France would have the support of the 131,000-man BEF (a lower estimate than that of the Admiralty Staff), which in spite of the inexperience of its leaders would constitute "an equal [*ebenbürtiger*] opponent" to German troops. Fear of native uprisings in the colonies rather than considerations of home defense, however, might inhibit its use on the Continent. In spite of the reluctance to subordinate British forces to the French, increasing evidence pointed to their disembarkation in Dunkirk, Calais, and Boulogne on grounds of greater safety. From there they could also move into Belgium. Zeebrugge and Ostend would be possible landing-places in Belgium, but landings in Holland and Esbjerg were most improbable. Yet Moltke also suggested that the British might occupy the coast of Belgium and Holland if they placed their own interests above those of the Entente.

> For the English are convinced that either during the war or at the conclusion of peace Germany would intend to come into the possession of the Rhein–Maas–Scheldt estuaries, which England could not tolerate on strategic or economic grounds. It is therefore not precluded that England will engage her expeditionary corps for [this purpose] and not primarily for the ally.

Not neglecting the calculations of the General Staff, the Admiralty Staff on 24 August drafted directives for the stance toward Belgium and Holland in a war of Germany against France and Britain.[20] In the event of enemy landings on their coasts they would be requested to relinquish their neutrality and declare themselves for or against Germany, should the army consider it necessary to use "the territory of one or both states." If on the other hand the leadership of the army wanted to preserve the neutrality of Belgium, or Holland, or both, a statement of their intentions would be requested with the proviso that their neutrality could only be honored if they were able and willing to honor it themselves. Were there no question of hostile landings it would be in German naval interests to honor the neutrality of both states, but particularly of Holland since her belligerence would create difficulties for fighting on the Ems. Moltke was in full agreement with these directives.[21]

In November 1913 the Quartermaster-General, Count Georg von Waldersee, expected the BEF to land in Dunkirk, Calais, and Boulogne, expressing his view, which, he claimed, was shared by Bethmann-Hollweg, "that for the time being one still had to count on British hostility."[22] A year earlier the Admiralty Staff had mentioned in its report to Wilhelm special orders for action against the BEF to be brought up only "If HM approaches the transport question more closely." Apparently there was reluctance to subordinate naval warfare to land war too much. Recommended were the use of submarines and the infestation of the ports of embarkation and disembarkation and the transport routes with mines, rather than the use of the bulk of the High Seas Fleet. The laying of mines in Dutch and Belgian ports was to depend on circumstances.[23] In October 1913 the Admiralty Staff ordered a war game to study actions along these lines in case of a close British blockade.[24]

## III

In partial subordination to land warfare, the Admiralty Staff continued to examine operations against Russia, whose naval power in the Baltic Sea was being rebuilt, and departed from its plans of 1909. In October 1911 an operations plan was devised against her if Germany was at war with the Triple Entente.[25] Russian naval strength was estimated to consist of twenty-eight large torpedo-boats in Libau, two divisions of submarines in Reval, eighteen torpedo-boats in Helsingfors, and two ships of the line, five armored cruisers, and one cruiser in Kronstadt. A expected an offensive against the German coast only from the torpedo-boats in Libau and Helsingfors, with the rest of the Russian fleet being on the defensive with the support of coastal fortifications. A2, however, anticipated that during the summer season the rest of the Russian fleet would take the offensive as well.[26] Both officers advocated an attack on the part of the Siegfried ships, which were located in Danzig, against Libau for the purpose of blockading the torpedo-boats and supporting the operations of the army if they could be ready for action at the outbreak of war. Indicating contact with the General Staff, the document stated that in its opinion such action would tie down the Russian Twentieth Army Corps near Riga because of the fear of landings by German troops. Consideration was given to the traditional scheme of blockading the Gulf of Finland, but it was admitted that the means were inadequate to execute it. A1 concurred with the plan, provided that the Imperial Naval Office would keep the Siegfried ships in the Baltic.[27] On 16 December another document was submitted to Wilhelm.[28] According to it, two ships of the line, four armored cruisers, forty-nine large torpedo-boats, and thirteen submarines had been added to the Russian Baltic Sea Fleet since the preparation of the previous report, raising its total strength to five ships of the line, six armored cruisers, fifty-five large torpedo-boats, and thirteen submarines. This was impressive strength. In construction were four Dreadnought-type ships, one large torpedo-boat, one submarine, and one mine-ship for the Baltic, and two ships of the line, thirteen large torpedo-boats, and four submarines for the Black Sea. By 1930 the Russian Baltic Sea fleet would consist of an active fleet of sixteen ships of the line, of which eight would be ready in 1918, eight armored cruisers, six cruisers, sixty-four large torpedo-boats, and twenty submarines. If Germany then still counted Britain as her main naval enemy, the Russian navy would constitute a substantial threat. Russia's increasing naval strength, which coincided with the build-up of her army, may well have reinforced the wishes of the General Staff for a preventive war.

But even the revised German operations plan in the Baltic, initialed by A2 on 21 February 1912, definitely expected a Russian offensive, led by torpedo-boats and supported by four ships of the line, six armored cruisers, and four cruisers, with the blockade of Danzig as its first probable objective and subsequent actions against Swinemünde and the island of Rügen.[29] As long as Germany would simultaneously have to fight Britain and France and most of her strength would be deployed in the North Sea, she would be unable to counter the Russians with equal forces. The eight Siegfried ships and two cruisers located in Danzig would not be ready for action before the eighth mobilization day when the Russian blockade was expected to have started. Incapable of either offensive or defensive action, the German navy would have to relinquish the defense of the coast of the eastern Baltic to the army. Were the Russians to enter the western Baltic, the naval defensive position would be the Fehmarn Belt, and if they none the less managed to enter the Kiel Bay ships would have to be withdrawn from the North Sea for its defense. If the German forces in the Baltic could be adequately reinforced, the Russian coast, particularly Libau, should be attacked so as to relieve the army, and cruiser raids might extend up the Gulf of Finland. The revised draft of the operations plan against Russia was thus much more modest because of greater Russian strength.

On 30 April, A, Paul Behncke, drafted the final version of the operations plan against Russia for the summer of 1912.[30] He took into consideration various cases of war. If Russia was Germany's only opponent, the High Seas Fleet would have an immense superiority making possible a blockade of and landing operations on the Russian coast. If Germany faced Russia and France, her offensive operations against France were precluded; with Austria-Hungary as Germany's ally in such a war French forces would be tied down in the Mediterranean. If Germany alone faced the Dual Alliance, France might launch an offensive against the German North Sea coast and shipping. In this case the aims of the German navy would be the defense of the German North Sea coast, the protection of shipping, and the establishment of domination over the Baltic; it would probably be unable, however, to blockade and support landings on the Russian coast. In a war against the Triple Entente, the German navy had to deploy against its major enemy, Britain. The same estimate was made of the Russian naval strength as in the February memorandum, but the war preparedness of the Russian navy was rated lower. Although the large ships located in Kronstadt were icebound from the end of November to the end of April, the completion of Reval as the main naval base by 1918 and the location there of eight ships of the line, four armored cruisers, four cruisers, thirty-six large torpedo-boats, and twelve submarines would make these forces much more mobile since with the help of icebreakers they could steam west in the winter. Also the Russian fleet had steadily improved since 1911 and was more likely to take the offensive. Its leaders possessed above-average ability. But until the completion of the Reval base only Kronstadt was an effective base for large ships, and being frozen in during the winter and too far from the German coast in the summer they could not launch an immediate offensive against Germany. Only the torpedo-boats in Libau were capable of such action. The coastal fortifications of the Baltic were considered as adequate against a Russian offensive. The narrow part of the Baltic Sea west of Bornholm offered a suitable position for the defense of the western Baltic; further west the défilés of the Gjedser-Riff and the Fehmarn Belt could serve as defenses of the Kiel Bay. The first Russian attack would probably be directed against Neufahrwasser followed by an attempt to establish a blockade of the Bay of Danzig, supported by extensive mine-laying. A German offensive against Libau was rejected, just as in the February version of the plan. Only rapid sorties could be directed against the Russian offensive, and more ambitious operations would have to depend on the union of the Danzig and Kiel forces later on in the war.

Although in the event of a war against the Triple Entente the deployment against Britain would make a permanent strengthening of the German forces in the Baltic impossible, favorable circumstances in the west might make their temporary reinforcement possible; it might be made necessary if the Russians proceeded to an effective blockade of the Kiel Bay or an attack on Kiel itself. It was suggested that the Siegfried ships be removed from Danzig to serve the harbor defense of Wilhelmshaven and Kiel or as coastal defense forces in the western Baltic and be replaced with more mobile ships, something that the Imperial Naval Office had allegedly promised to do after the summer of 1912.

At about the same time Keyserlingk, the naval attaché to the Northern States, reported to Tirpitz that the Russian navy, although prepared to defend the Baltic provinces and Finland against Germany, would not take the offensive against her navy even if most of it was engaged elsewhere.[31] To this report A2 and B5 commented: "If Germany is not only 'overwhelmingly' but with *all* forces capable of battle involved in the North Sea, the Russian navy will also probably give up its waiting stance and proceed to offensive undertakings against the eastern part of the Baltic Sea coast."

There was no real change in the operations plan against Russia for the winter of 1912–13, other than the removal of the Siegfried ships from Danzig.[32] Heeringen appraised Moltke of the change of the situation in the Baltic, also pointing out the danger of dividing the forces through operations against the Russian coastal towns, and obtained his approval.[33] Wilhelm consented to the new plan on 5 November.[34] Heeringen had already informed Tirpitz on 17 February 1912 of the changing power relationship in the Baltic; on 12 November he did so in greater detail: with the removal of the Siegfried ships Germany confronted the increasing Russian strength in the Baltic with six small cruisers, three large and five small torpedo-boats, four submarines, and three auxiliary mine-steamers, of which only one small cruiser and the submarines were in active service. Although claiming to be basically unable to change the situation, he requested Tirpitz to refuse requests for more ships from overseas stations.[35] On 14 November, Behncke informed the Baltic Sea station of the changed operational conditions against Russia in a war against the Triple Entente.[36]

Warfare against British and Russian commerce in the Baltic Sea was also examined. According to a document dated 28 November,[37] attacks against British shipping, which was considerable, were to occur in Danish waters. The forces used would be older cruisers, torpedo-boats, and auxiliary ships equipped in the Baltic. Ideally, the most effective action would be the blockade of the Gulf of Finland, but for this the German forces were inadequate. Since only a small proportion of Russian imports and exports through the Baltic was carried in Russian bottoms (8 percent in 1909), attacks on them promised little success. More successful would be an offensive against Russian coastal shipping, in which the participation of Russian vessels was 50–60 percent, but it could not be undertaken because of the supremacy of the Russian navy. Were Germany at war with both Britain and Russia, actions against Russian long-range shipping would be worthwhile since they could be carried out with the same forces as used against the British. Before 1914 the effectiveness of the Russian fleet could be impaired by the cutting off of the British coal supplies on which it depended. The four ships of the line of the Gangut class, entering service in 1914, could, however, use a combination of coal and naphtha; since Russia could provide enough of the latter, her navy would thereafter be more independent of British coal.[38]

The Admiralty Staff also completed a study of possible Russian landings on the German coast in the event of a war against Russia and Britain.[39] France was excluded from consideration, as she had been in the examination of commercial warfare in the Baltic, probably because of her limited involvement in the area. The Russians were expected to be able to transport 20,000 men, inclusive of the required artillery and cavalry, from Libau and Riga to the Pomeranian coast. The undertaking could, however, be imperiled by the light German forces in the Baltic and even more so by a possible transfer of forces from the North Sea. The British were not expected to send major naval forces into the Baltic before a decision in their favor had been reached in the North Sea. This memorandum was forwarded to Moltke, who replied that the contemplated Russian action was improbable but not altogether impossible, and advised that the navy keep Russian harbors and coastal forces under permanent observation.[40]

On 29 November 1912 the Admiralty Staff completed a report for the Kaiser, dealing with a case of war against France and Russia with Britain assuming a neutral or waiting stance. Wilhelm approved it on 3 December.[41] Unlike the plan that had been approved by him on 5 November 1912, the new document assumed that

the newly arisen situation brings us to a case of war in which England would at first assume a waiting stance. We would then at first, and perhaps for the duration of war, only have Russia and France as opponents.

But since we cannot be certain of England's posture we shall always have to count on the possibility of her switching [to the side of our enemies].

This assumption still required that the High Seas Fleet—at least, those ships unable to pass the Kaiser Wilhelm Canal—be kept in the North Sea, but allowed a part of the fleet to secure the control of the Baltic by delivering several strong blows against the Russian naval forces and bases immediately after the outbreak of war. Such action would also help the army. If sufficient forces could be spared in the North Sea, a blockade of the Gulf of Finland could also be attempted. The command in the Baltic was initially to be left to the Chief of the Second Squadron, Vice-Admiral Ingenohl. The first offensive actions against Russia were to include the blocking of the harbor of Libau and the destruction of its submarines, the elimination of the torpedo-boats and submarines in Reval, and the infestation of Helsingfors with mines. Detailed plans were to be worked out for these operations to be conducted by light forces. These were to be backed by the Second Squadron which, because of its vulnerability to mines, torpedo-boats, and submarines should not participate in them, but be ready to fight the Russian fleet, to which it was still superior, in open waters. All German forces should avoid action in the eastern part of the Gulf of Finland because of a great risk of losses.

On the other hand, any attacks against France were to be avoided. The North Sea forces, however, had as their responsibility to keep the French away and to protect German shipping. Limited actions against the eastern entrance of the English Channel could be ventured. If British neutrality was absolutely certain, special orders could be issued to allow German cruisers to steam into the Atlantic to protect German shipping and to engage in commerce raiding.

## IV

On the same day as Wilhelm approved the operations plan against Russia and France, he consented to a draft of an operations order against Britain, dated 28 November.[42] It was partly based on recent maneuvers and war games.

In the spring of 1912 it had been decided to hold three partial maneuvers. The first involved war in the North Sea if the Blue (German) party were divided at the time of the threat of war and had, without the use of the canal, to deploy in the German Bight at the time that the Yellow (British) party had made preparations for war. The second maneuver would deal with Blue action against a Yellow blockade when its bulk was at a considerable distance from the German coast. The Blue force was to attack the Yellow bulk in daytime with submarines and through sorties of its fleet and at night with submarines and small cruisers. The third action would deal with a battle situation between a weakened Yellow blockade force and a Blue fleet strengthened by the mobilization of its reserves at a time that the Yellow force still maintained its northern blockade line to prevent the exit of the Blue commerce raiders. The last exercise was intended to provide experience for the leadership of the prospective Third Active Squadron.[43] In the second partial maneuver the leadership of the Blue party was given to Holtzendorff and that of the Yellow party to Karl Paschen.[44] The Blue side managed to inflict sufficient losses on the Yellow blockade forces and to bring out its submarines so as to prevent the Yellow side from maintaining the blockade at night. While listing mistakes on both sides, the Admiralty Staff considered the outcome of the maneuver to be favorable to the Blue party. The third maneuver indicated the importance of submarines, mine, and the battle cruisers in generally damaging the enemy blockade forces, since neither the small cruisers nor the older armored cruisers could stand up to them. On the other hand, Blue torpedo-boats were proven to be vulnerable to rough seas and limited in range for long-distance action. On 26 October, Heeringen reported to Wilhelm about the war game of the "Front,"[45] pointing out that only the North Sea Station had submitted a war game involving the use of airships in an offensive against British forces.

The report of the Admiralty Staff of 28 November, which Wilhelm approved as an operations order on 3 December, assumed that an Anglo-German war would be preceded by a period of political tension. During it, as demonstrated by the British maneuvers of 1909 and 1910 and actions of 1911 during the Agadir crisis, the Royal Navy would proceed in a high state of war preparedness to its positions of deployment. Light units would take advance positions along the German North Sea coast and coastal defenses would be ready for war. Under these conditions, a long-range offensive against the British coast, as contemplated by Baudissin and Fischel, would have no prospects of success and the best prospects would be offered by energetic daytime attacks against the forces blockading the German Bight. In this report, a wide blockade of the North Sea was not considered.

The first document that Heeringen prepared, after the 8 December 1912 meeting, for the waging of war against Britain included the guidelines sent on 18 February 1913 to the Chiefs of the High Seas Fleet and the North Sea and Baltic Sea stations.[46] They were allegedly based on the Imperial Maneuvers of 1912. As in the report of 28 November, a large-scale offensive for the domination of the sea was regarded as impossible; none the less, the offensive spirit of the navy must be maintained. As had older operations plans, the guidelines favored repeated advances against enemy blockade forces rather than a thrust against his bulk, which was expected to be further removed from the German coast but to become involved in supporting the light blockade forces. The enemy bulk was to be engaged no further than fifty sea miles from Heligoland—a range within which German torpedo-boats and submarines could still be used. Also, more remote offensive action would leave the High Seas Fleet vulnerable to harassment by the light British blockade forces. In daytime the light blockade forces should be attacked by the bulk and at night by small cruisers, torpedo-boats, and submarines. The bulk should return to the Elbe estuary at night. A close blockade of the German North Sea coast was still being assumed, although only on the part of light forces, whereas Britain's bulk could be located as far back as in her coastal waters. It was recommended that submarines should already be stationed in the North Sea in peacetime to attack the British coast. If the British bulk came sufficiently close to the German coast, it was to be attacked even if it was superior to the High Seas Fleet because of the advantage that the latter would enjoy from the presence of its torpedo-boats. Wilhelm agreed with the guidelines, but wanted greater emphasis to be placed on the long-range offensive of the submarines. He also wished that the guidelines be extended to the rest of the North Sea and Danish and Baltic waters—a wish that appears contradictory to the decision to concentrate in the North Sea against Britain.

The Admiralty Staff, on 13 December, had prepared a paper on long-distance use of submarines.[47] Initially, they were to attack hostile forces in the open sea, preferably the British bulk, which was expected to be located on the northeast coast of Scotland, although parts of it might be further south. The second line of attack would be against the British bases, and the third would be against the transports and escorts of the BEF. The submarines were viewed as being most effective if launched at the immediate outbreak of war. Probably in response to Wilhelm's comments, the Admiralty Staff provided specific tasks for study in the use of submarines.[48] These included the need of reconnaissance, its cooperation with the U-boats, the way they were to approach hostile targets, and the time they required for operation against fleets of different sizes, the transports of the BEF, and British bases and ports. Heeringen also forwarded a list of these tasks to the Imperial Naval Office for study by the Torpedo Inspectorate. Another document dealt with the use of the air force in a war against Britain and France.[49] It was to be used both for reconnaissance and attacks to be directed against enemy blockade forces, bulk, the transports of the BEF, French and British ports, and the Admiralty Building in London! These working-papers appear to bear a relationship to the instructions of 8 December.

The war game of the North Sea station, reported to Wilhelm on 27 March 1913,[50] demonstrated the difficulties that the British would encounter in maintaining a close blockade of the German Bight. An energetic defense could loosen or break it altogether. The Yellow (British) party managed to convoy 150,000 men to the Scheldt, and the Blue (German) operations against its transports were unsuccessful, but it was speculated that fuller use of mines and submarines could have endangered them more. An indecisive battle occurred with the Yellow forces blockading the German Bight, which lifted the blockade for several days, enabling the Blue party to undertake several unsuccessful and costly attacks against the Yellow coast. Although the conclusion was that the British blockade of the German Bight could not be maintained, the Chief of the North Sea Station, Fischel, raised serious objections to sorties against the British coast. On 2 May 1913 the new Chief of the Admiralty Staff, Hugo von Pohl, also reported that operations against the British coast by German submarines could not be undertaken because of their inadequate range.[51]

In the fall of 1913 the Admiralty Staff concerned itself seriously with the wide blockade of the North Sea. French maneuvers in the summer of 1913 had indicated that in a war against Germany the French forces would close the Dover–Calais strait.[52] On 17 October, Pohl had obtained Wilhelm's approval for a war game dealing with Anglo-German hostilities during which Britain limited herself to a blockade of the entrances into the North Sea and advanced against the German North Sea coast with only light forces.[53] Her aim would be to bring the High Seas Fleet to action as far as possible from the German coast. The German side was to study the direction and prospect of offensive undertakings. This war game was to be played by the Admiralty Staff in the winter of 1913–14.[54] The rules for the game were provided by Pohl on 29 October. It was assumed that war would break out on 1 April 1914, after four days of political tension in which Germany, supported by Italy and Austria-Hungary, would find herself opposed by Britain and France. Russia's position would still be uncertain and the other powers would be neutral. The constellation under consideration was unrealistic. On 8 December 1912, Wilhelm had expected a war to emerge from an Austro-Russian quarrel over Serbia; Moltke was pushing for a preventive war against Russia; and Austria-Hungary was under no obligation to support Germany in a war not involving Russia. The French would impose a blockade line across the English Channel, and the Kaiser Wilhelm Canal would be passable for large ships. The Blue (German) party was to be led by A, Kapitän-zur-See Behncke, and the Yellow (British and French) party by Kapitän-zur-See Kurt Grasshoff. The Blue side had to count on both a close and a wide blockade. Although politically unrealistic, this was obviously a war game for the future.

The planning of the war game of the Admiralty Staff coincided with intelligence reports about British maneuvers which took place between 15 July and 2 August.[55] According to them, the British side established a wide blockade of the North Sea. The Firth of Forth and the Moray Firth served as bases for the Yellow (British) bulk in the north. Nine cruisers and twenty destroyers held a line of 340 sea miles. To Pohl this line appeared too long since it utilized too many cruisers that were needed elsewhere; he rather expected the shorter but more northerly blockade line from the Shetland Islands to Norway to be chosen. Pohl stated that since the previous year's British maneuvers also represented a wide blockade of the North Sea it appeared that Britain was giving up the notion of a close blockade, and long-distance operations by the High Seas Fleet would have to be undertaken to do battle with the Royal Navy. There would exist opportunities for surprise attacks against British forces; detachments and temporary withdrawals would offer opportunities for either attacking inferior forces or for mine-laying and submarine attacks along and bombardment of the British coast. To accomplish these purposes the German navy must at all times be informed of the location of the British bulk, which Pohl hoped to accomplish with the help of aerial reconnaissance. After his audience with Wilhelm, Pohl noted on 13 January 1914: "His Majesty has learned with great interest of the English maneuvers and approved the conclusions drawn from them, particularly regarding our action in a wide blockade." Pohl knew, however, that Fischel had raised objections to sorties against the British coast.[56] Moreover, the war game of the Admiralty Staff was to show how difficult such actions would be.

The actual power relationship between the Entente Cordiale and Germany was to serve as the basis of the game. Heydel, the Chief of Staff for Grasshoff, ruled on 13 November that in case of a wide blockade four British squadrons with twenty-nine ships of the line be concentrated in the Firth of Forth. Two squadrons were left in the Thames and two in Dover to guard the Dover–Calais strait. The narrower of the northern entrances into the North Sea—Norway–the Shetlands–the Orkneys–the northeastern tip of Scotland—rather than the wider one from Battray Head to Norway was chosen for sealing off the North Sea from the north. The observation of the German Bight, the Ems, and the Skagerrak was left for light forces.[57] Behncke's instructions of 15 November provided for the offensive, including energetic fighting against the blockade. In an offensive, favorable circumstances for battle should be sought but could not be guaranteed. To prepare his party for all eventualities his instructions left open the question whether the Yellow side would engage in a close or a wide blockade. He correctly assumed that Yellow's First Fleet would be located in the Firth of Forth and that its Second and Third Fleets would be defending the Thames and the Channel. He expected that the First Fleet would be kept together to maintain numerical superiority over the three active squadrons of the Blue fleet and that the Second and Third Fleets could also be used to block the return of the Blue forces from a distant sortie. Behncke did not provide the Blue party with the best opportunities; but he did permit the Yellow to divide the forces of the First Fleet so as to guard his long coast against offensives that could either come from the German Bight or the Skagerrak. In case of a wide blockade, Blue was to advance against the Firth of Forth, locating submarines and laying mines inside and outside the Firth to damage the Yellow fleet as it came out to do battle with the Blue fleet. It would be much more disadvantageous to Blue if the Yellow fleet were already at sea. In any case a lengthy presence of the Blue fleet in Yellow waters was dangerous: its advance should occur soon and be swift. Good weather, essential for the use of torpedo-boats and coalers, and efficient reconnaissance were considered necessary for a potentially successful advance. The auxiliary cruisers which were to prey on Yellow shipping in the Atlantic were to be sent out as soon as possible and the cables leading through the North Sea to Yellow territory were to be cut.

What happened in the war game which was played at the beginning of March was that the departure of the Blue force was delayed by poor weather conditions by a day and a half. It was also discovered that in the meantime the Yellow force had left the Firth of Forth. None the less, the Blue advance was continued to escort the mine-ships and submarines toward the Firth of Forth where they had some success. The advance of the Blue High Seas Fleet was then interrupted and it returned toward Heligoland but was brought to battle by the Yellow bulk, which had interposed itself between it and the island. Since the defeat of Blue was inevitable because of Yellow superiority, the war game was interrupted. Behncke, however, was given a second chance. This time he managed to defeat two squadrons of the advancing Yellow bulk through a torpedo-boat attack whereupon a battle resulted between approximately equal Blue and Yellow forces.[58] Grasshoff considered the battle fought during the second retreat to have led to a serious mauling of the Yellow bulk, breaking Britain's overwhelming supremacy at sea; however, the Yellow blockade of the German Bight was still possible since Blue had lost most of its light forces and could confront the fourteen battleships of the Third Fleet with only four.

In the light of the war game Grasshoff considered a close British blockade of the German Bight very improbable, thought that Rosyth in the Firth of Forth would lose its value as a naval base because of its vulnerability to submarine attacks, and that the best position of the British bulk would be further north in the proximity of Scapa Flow. He expected the greatest success in a German advance if it were undertaken before or at the outbreak of war, ahead of the establishment of British observation positions. Blue's ability in the war game to exit belatedly was an accident on which one should not count in a war: he would probably be subjected to torpedo-boat attacks during the first two nights of his advance. Another fortunate accident was the absence of Yellow submarines before the Elbe at the time of the exit of the Yellow forces.[59] The maneuver leadership criticized the Blue party for not returning immediately upon discovering that the Yellow bulk had left the Firth of Forth and confining further attack to its light forces.[60] It did not consider the battle fought in the replaying of the withdrawal of Blue to be decisive.

In the abbreviated report of the war game to Wilhelm of 5 May 1914, over which an audience was held on 26 May—a rather long interval if war was still as imminent as it seemed in the "war council" of 8 December 1912—Pohl drew the conclusion that it demonstrated that the existing power relationship did not allow the High Seas Fleet to undertake offensive thrusts so far to the north.[61] Such action might be possible if aerial reconnaissance, which Germany as yet lacked, provided continuous information about the British to gauge the right time and place for an attack. But if Germany had this advantage so, most likely, would Britain. Pohl's response to a wide blockade was to dispatch only the submarines and mine-ships for a long-range offensive and to retain the bulk of the fleet "for an energetic ceaseless struggle against the forces guarding the German Bight," thus forcing the British to augment them and make possible the erosion of their strength to the point that the High Seas Fleet could confront the Grand Fleet on equal terms. But there was no certainty— something that Pohl overlooked—that Britain would leave any forces to guard the German Bight. The Admiralty Staff thus failed to respond to the obvious challenge of a wide blockade, which it considered more than probable because of the British maneuvers of 1912 and 1913 and the French maneuvers of 1913. It had also learned that a close blockade would be extremely dangerous even to a superior force and could assume that the British had learned the same lesson. Pohl noted that the Kaiser "thoroughly agreed with the execution of the game and the conclusions drawn from it." Yet he is reported to have added "'In all defensive plans . . . the offensive idea is not to be dropped' . . . and attributed great value to the cooperation of the submarines with the High Seas Fleet and [their] use . . . before battle." Germany thus approached World War I with no definite plans for naval operations against Britain and the Triple Entente.

## V

Although, according to Admiral Müller, Wilhelm stated in the "war council" of 8 December 1912 that naval operations against France and Russia, which he had approved on 3 December, should no longer be considered,[62] they continued to be examined. On 23 January 1913, Heeringen wrote to Tirpitz about a conference concerning the removal of warships from Danzig.[63] He pointed out that the Russian naval leadership had during the last two years considered offensive operations against Germany and that in the exercises of December 1912 Russian torpedo-boats had approached Rügen. In the current winter Russian ships of the line, armored cruisers, and mine-ships were no longer located in Kronstadt but in Helsingfors and Reval, whence they could, with the assistance of icebreakers, proceed south. He complained that, in spite of his earlier remonstrances, the Siegfried ships were still in Danzig, along with several small cruisers. The former ships could still do useful service in the river estuaries of the North Sea. Instead of maintaining ships in Danzig, which could be blockaded by the Russians, he proposed that the fortifications to the Kiel Bay be strengthened by mines, torpedo-boats and submarines. Kiel was to serve as the centre of defense for the ports of the western Baltic and the protection of trade with Sweden. These were strictly defensive proposals. Although Tirpitz appeared to agree with them, Wilhelm indicated some objections in his marginal comments. A more offensive mentality appeared in the considerations of the Admiralty Staff for the acquisition of Swedish and Finnish pilots who were familiar with Finnish waters,[64] of ships to be sunk for the blocking of Russian harbors,[65] and of a surprise attack on the Russian fleet in a war also involving Britain.[66] The last proposal, involving an attack on Libau, Helsingfors, and Reval by the Second Squadron of the Deutschland and Brandenburg ships, supported by light forces, originated with A2. It was supported by the Department for Tactics and Admiralty Staff Training (D), for "we must in my opinion use the time which England leaves us to make Russia harmless at sea,"[67] but was criticized by A, who minuted that a guarantee of success against the Russians would require more forces than proposed, thus weakening Germany's position against Britain. A requested that the operations against Russia be examined in the Admiralty Staff voyage of July 1913.[68]

In 1912–13 and 1913–14 the staff officers of the Baltic Sea station were involved in war games against Russia. The game of 1912–13 concerned a Russian offensive against the German coast and resulted in a complete Russian success, including the enclosure of the Bay of Danzig. This game led to a comment, apparently from Pohl, that such "rapid and decisive action" as taken by the Russian side in the war game "does not generally suit the Russian national character."[69] The game of 1913–14 dealt with offensive operations on the part of the German navy which, according to the Chief of the Baltic Sea Station, Coerper, were unsuccessful because Germany's forces were inadequate and previous information of her actions was available to the Russians. The war game even drew on the old notion of using the Moon Sound as a base against the Gulf of Finland. The game was, however, handicapped by ignorance of the operational plans of the army, which led Coerper to suggest a joint army–navy war game. Pohl considered such a game to be impossible since it would make public the operations plans of the Great General Staff.[70] These war games indicated that, contrary to Wilhelm's instructions of 8 December 1912, the navy was not prepared to concentrate against Britain to the point of excluding offensive operations against Russia. Moreover, Pohl minuted on 10 June 1914 that Wilhelm himself had shown great interest in a war game of the Baltic Sea station and "ordered that we should be more than ever concerned with the waging of war in the Baltic Sea."[71]

On 17 February 1914, A2 prepared a memorandum dealing with operations in the Baltic.[72] He favored a major attack against Russia which, in addition to light forces, would involve the Second Squadron, consisting of ten ships of the line, one large cruiser, and two small cruisers, aimed at the destruction of the Russian naval forces. The attack was to be directed against Libau and Reval. The major attack by the Second Squadron was to be delivered against Reval where, according to the available intelligence, were located four armored cruisers, two mine-ships, six submarines and an unknown number of torpedo-boats. A2 considered the attack against Libau as feasible but that against Reval as questionable. Marginal comments on the document questioned the use of the Second Squadron against Reval on the grounds that it would contravene the principle of not exposing ships of the line to the danger posed by torpedo-boats, submarines, and mines. The very assumption that the Russian navy could be destroyed was challenged by the marginal comment: "Of no avail. The decision is made in the North Sea. There we must be as strong as possible."

It appears that in the summer and fall of 1913 the certainty of Britain being involved in a Continental war waned in the making of naval preparations. On 9 June 1913, Pohl wrote to Tirpitz about the possibility rather than certainty of British hostility in a war between Germany and the Dual Alliance.[73] In October he obtained Wilhelm's approval for two war games involving the Dual and the Triple Alliance in which Britain remained neutral.[74] In both the greater part of the High Seas Fleet was deployed in the Baltic for strong offensive operations against Russia, although the Dreadnoughts remained in the North Sea. The first game was to be played by the North Sea station to examine the defense of German trade, action against French shipping, and operations against the French northern coast on the assumption that most French forces had remained in the Mediterranean. The second game, played by the Baltic Sea station, was to study powerful surprise attacks against Russian naval forces with the aim of "rendering them harmless," the blockade of the Russian coast, and warfare against Russian commerce.

Although these games reflected consideration of more active warfare in the Baltic than would have been warranted by the Kaiser's instructions of 8 December 1912, the General Staff was informed by the Admiralty Staff in November 1913 not to expect much help in that theater of war. On 5 November a discussion was held between the representatives of the Admiralty Staff and the Quartermaster-General Waldersee.[75] The General Staff recognized that the deployment of the German naval forces in the North Sea would render the navy relatively inactive in the Baltic. It continued to hope that the navy would observe possible Russian preparations for a landing on the German Baltic Sea coast. Such landings were not expected in a war in which Britain remained neutral but were regarded as probable in case of British belligerence and a successful Russian offensive on land. The increase in Russian strength was obviously a concern for the Great General Staff. Waldersee consented to have the General Staff examine the possible location and significance of Russian landings and provide the relevant information to the Admiralty Staff. The representatives of the latter agency pointed out that, if Königsberg and Danzig were cut off by Russian troops, communications with them by sea might be maintained but could not be guaranteed. Waldersee stated that because of coordinated Austro-German operations there would be no German advance against St Petersburg but that a strong naval attack in its direction "could under given circumstances be of decisive importance." Although he denied that the General Staff had made any preparations for such an action, he maintained that it would be more effective if undertaken in the interior of the Gulf of Finland. Pohl replied that such an action would be very difficult to undertake.

It is known that from the beginning of 1913 the General Staff no longer planned for a mobilization against Russia alone. Adolf Gasser and Fritz Fischer argue that it was a decision for a preventive war.[76] Although underestimating the quality of the Russian troops, the army was fully aware of how thin was the line with which it could confront their mass.[77]

## VI

As of January 1913 the Admiralty Staff became involved in German–Italian military discussions which had started in December and would involve the possibility of Italian attacks on the French coast, transport of Italian troops to Germany, and negotiations of an Italo-German–Austrian naval convention. These had been made possible by the pro-Triplice policies of the Italian Foreign Minister San Giuliano and the Chief of the General Staff Alberto Pollio.[78] The German army, needless to say, was interested in the elimination of Austro-Italian hostility and in any Italian assistance against France; for Italy a naval convention with Austria and Germany would provide security against the Anglo-French naval forces. Such a convention would provide assistance for Germany in impeding the transport of the French Nineteenth Army Corps from North Africa to the European continent. Going along with the interests of the General Staff, the Admiralty Staff acceded to the Italian wish for joint operations of the Austro-Italian naval forces which would enable the Austro-Hungarian navy to exit from the Adriatic for operations against the French. But it placed little confidence in such collaboration.[79] Neither did the representative of the General Staff, Oberst Erich Ludendorff. But, as he admitted, the General Staff had a great interest in attacks on the French troop-transports.[80] Heeringen had further doubts about the superiority of the joint Austro-Italian force in the Mediterranean if British forces there were at the expected strength, including the four Invincibles reinforced by the Fourth Battleship Squadron. Wilhelm acceded to the wishes of the General Staff, ordering the Admiralty Staff to establish contact with the Austro-Hungarian military attaché for the purpose of concluding a naval agreement between Austria-Hungary and Italy for joint operations against French troop-transports from Africa.[81]

The naval convention was negotiated in Vienna and signed on 23 June 1913.[82] Its purpose was to secure "the naval control of the Mediterranean through the swiftest possible defeat of the enemy fleets."[83] German ships in the Mediterranean were to be subordinated to the Mediterranean Command, under either Austro-Hungarian or Italian seniority, and information was to be provided by the Admiralty Staff regarding those German ships in the area which the Italians would consider suitable as mine-layers.[84] Considerable information about British and French navies was exchanged between the Admiralty Staff and the Italian naval leadership. The Chief of the German Mediterranean Division, Souchon, was informed in January 1914 that his squadron, with *Goeben* as flagship, together with light Italian forces, was to attack French troop-transports from Africa. Its main base was to be Maddalena, in Sardinia.[85]

Early in July 1914 the Admiralty Staff envisaged Gaeta as the base for the German forces in the Mediterranean.[86] It had been assured by the Italian Admiralty that provision had already been made for their use of that harbor. From there they would conduct reconnaissance and subsequently operate against the French troop-transports, using Messina as a base—a port where the Italian and Austro-Hungarian navies were to deploy as soon after the outbreak of war as possible. Their aim was to be the defeat of the British naval forces in the Mediterranean before their union with the French navy. An offensive action against the French fleet in Toulon was not considered: its defeat was envisaged only if it advanced against the Ligurian peninsula at the outbreak of war. Because of Italian neutrality and the subsequent hostilities in World War I, all these preparations were doomed to futility.

## VII

As for ships located outside Europe, the period 1907–14 showed little change. The most important unit, the Cruiser Squadron, was strengthened in 1910 through the exchange of *Scharnhorst* for *Bismarck* and the increase in the number of small cruisers.[87] In 1907 it had been instructed in the event of a war against the United States (which was no longer considered in the Atlantic) to attack shipping en route to Shanghai and Hong Kong to prevent American ships from going to the main theater of war. Attacks on American shipping near the Philippines were at this point not considered because of the comparative weakness of the German force.[88] In January 1909 the more aggressive Baudissin again ordered the Cruiser Squadron along with the ships of the Australian station to attack American communications with the Philippines.[89] Subsequent orders were that the Cruiser Squadron cause maximum damage in wartime to all enemy shipping, including the American.[90] Attack on American trade with the Philippines surfaced in Pohl's operational orders of 24 April 1913, approved by Wilhelm on 29 April.[91]

In a war against France or France and Russia the Cruiser Squadron was after 1907 expected to take the offensive because of its superiority against the forces of both powers in East Asia.[92] The operational orders issued in January 1909 made no reference to Russia but provided for the destruction of recently weakened French forces; were this not possible in the open sea, French ships in Saigon were to be blockaded.[93] The operational orders of April 1913 essentially repeated the same order for the purpose of relieving German trade and, if the French naval forces could not otherwise be defeated, prescribed action against the coast of Indo-China to draw them back for its defense and to attempt to destroy them there. No mention was made of any action against Russian naval units.[94]

The war against Japan alone came to be regarded as unlikely. The orders of 1907 provided that Tsing-tao be held against her as long as possible. The instructions of 1909 stated that in this war the relief of the Cruiser Squadron by the High Seas Fleet could not be undertaken because of the attitude of other powers, particularly Britain. The squadron was not unconditionally bound to defend Tsing-tao; while encouraged to attack Japanese supply-lines and troop-transports, it was discouraged from fighting superior Japanese forces.[95]

Most important, of course, was warfare against Great Britain. The cruiser squadron was instructed in 1907, as it had been in the previous year, to attack Australia; it was to conduct cruiser warfare on her northwestern coast, then in the Colombo–Aden or the Colombo–Sabang areas, and lastly in the China Sea.[96] It was instructed to change its areas of operation quickly to retain an element of surprise. Its orders for 1909, however, were restricted to action in Australian waters, and it was forbidden to engage a superior British force.[97] According to the mobilization orders issued by Fischel at the end of 1910, it was to proceed more aggressively by attacking the shipping lanes of its strongest enemy and while battle with superior enemy forces "was to be avoided as far as possible [it was not to be shunned] in principle."[98] In April 1911 it was stressed that the recently established favorable power relationship between the Cruiser Squadron and the British East Asian forces should be maintained. The squadron could only be removed from East Asia in the event of war if provision was made for coaling it for that purpose.[99] Similar orders were issued in 1912.[100] On 30 December, Graf Maximilian Spee, the

Chief of the Cruiser Squadron, ordered a war game for its southward journey in the case of war of Germany and Austria-Hungary (and possibly Italy) against the Triple Entente, with Japan neutral but sympathetic to the latter.[101] The instructions of the Admiralty Staff of April 1913 established as the foremost task of the Cruiser Squadron the damaging of British shipping and, second, the attempt to divide and defeat separately the British East Asian forces. The continued existence of the squadron was regarded as the best defense of Tsing-tao: it was not to be tied down in its immediate defense.[102] The orders issued on 12 March and approved by Wilhelm on 17 March amplified the previous ones by recommending an attack on the British forces immediately after the war "if circumstances for the Cruiser Squadron . . . are particularly favorable."[103]

As for instructions to other German warships abroad, in 1907 the ships of the East African station were to assemble in a war against the United States or Japan in a German colony for the purpose of accompanying coalers; in other cases of war they were to conduct cruiser warfare. The ships of the East American and West African stations were in all cases of war other than that against Japan to conduct cruiser warfare in the South Atlantic. In a war involving Britain they were specifically ordered to intercept her food-imports from Argentina.[104] In 1909 the ships of the East African station were instructed in a war against France in the Indian Ocean where her forces were weak to cause maximum damage and in a war against Britain to avoid being blocked in and to conduct cruiser warfare. The East American station was to undertake sorties in the Caribbean in a war against the United States, wage cruiser warfare against France and Britain, and in particular raid the food-imports of the last power from South America, the Caribbean, and Asia. The ships of the West African station were to maintain order in the German colonies in cases of war not involving Britain or France; in the latter cases the two ships of the station, *Panther* and *Sperber*, were to proceed to the Brazilian coast to be stranded and to give up their armaments and crews to auxiliary cruisers.[105] According to the orders of April 1913, the ships of the East American and West African stations were in a war against the United States only to undertake brief attacks against her trade in the Caribbean because of the expected arrival of her superior forces; in a war against France they were to operate against troop-transports from the Moroccan west coast to France. The most effective action against Britain would be attacks on the shipments of food and raw materials from the United States, Canada, Spain, and Portugal. Since those shipping routes would be well protected, they could best be raided by fast passenger-ships converted into auxiliary cruisers. The West American and Australian stations were to be subordinated to the cruiser squadron.[106] The same orders were repeated in March 1914.[107]

What was new about the operational directives for German warships in non-European waters after 1906 were better arrangements for providing them with cash and coal.[108] What was also new after 1908 was the equipment of passenger-ships as auxiliary cruisers to augment and replace some of the antiquated German *matériel* abroad. The ships to be used for this purpose had to be able to maintain a certain speed, have two propellers, a double bottom, a submerged rudder, engines and munition chambers that lay below the water level, coal chambers that would serve as protection for engines and boilers, and arrangements to set up cannon and convey ammunition to them. A number of ships of the East Africa Line, the North German Lloyd, and the Hamburg–America Line were reported as meeting these requirements.[109] The operational orders of February 1909 stressed in particular the use of auxiliary cruisers in the Atlantic against Britain; suitable ships located in New York were to depart during the impending threat of war to be converted on the Brazilian coast into auxiliary cruisers, and two or three suitable ships located at home were to be re-equipped and escorted into the Atlantic.[110] These arrangements became somewhat more systematic by January 1911. The activity of the auxiliary cruisers was then considered to be limited in terms of time because of their shortage of coal. They were to "do and die." Another of their purposes was to detach British cruisers from Europe and thus improve the fighting chances of the High Seas Fleet.[111] A memorandum of April 1911 suggested that attack on British shipping in the South Atlantic and through the Suez Canal was a particularly suitable objective of these auxiliary cruisers. In April 1913, however, the best transoceanic passenger-ships were excluded from the duty of serving as auxiliary cruisers on grounds of being too expensive to be sacrificed. Otherwise, however, all the weaker and slower German ships abroad were to be stranded and to give up their armaments and crews to the faster auxiliary cruisers. Specific provisions were also made for escorting four fast steamers of the North German Lloyd into the Atlantic north of Scotland, with three other steamers to be considered as a reserve force. Further ships were to be requisitioned from the Hamburg–South American Steamship Company. Provisions were made to acquire other fast commercial ships at sea. The most important operational area in the Atlantic was divided into five zones along the most important shipping routes, and the decision to dispatch the auxiliary cruisers into the different zones was to be left to the senior officer of the West American station.[112]

## Notes: Chapter 18

1 BA-MA, F 5587, III, 1. N. 10., Vol. 5, Heeringen to Holtzendorff, 24 October 1911.
2 ibid., "Zum Immediatvortrag," 24 October 1911. Originally drafted in June 1911.
3 ibid., F 3443, PG 67472, Holtzendorff to Tirpitz, 2 and 11 December 1911.
4 ibid., F 5587, III, 1. N. 10., Vol. 5, initialed by D, 18 December 1911. "Stellungnahme zu Flotte . . . vom 11. 12. 1911," B to A, "Bemerkungen zur Verlegung von Streitkräften nach der Nordsee," 21 December 1911, F 3343, PG 67472, Heeringen to Holtzendorff, 28 December 1911, copy.
5 ibid., F 3443, PG 67472, Müller to Holtzendorff, 18 January 1912.
6 Müller, *Der Kaiser*, p. 110.
7 BA-MA, F 3443, PG 67472, Müller to Wilhelm, 26 January 1912.
8 ibid., F 5601, III, 3.–25a., Bd 1, "Zum Immediatvortrag," 28 January 1912.
9 ibid., F 3443, PG 67472, Tirpitz to Wilhelm, 2 February 1912.
10 Müller, *Der Kaiser*, p. 111; BA-MA, N 159/4, p. 114.

11  BA-MA, F 5587, III, 1. N. 10., Vol. 5, Müller to Heeringen, 3 February 1912.
12  ibid., F 3303, PG 66709, Tirpitz to Wilhelm, 22 March 1912.
13  ibid., F 3443, PG 67472, Holtzendorff to Müller, n.d.; Müller to Holtzendorff, 12 June 1912, copy; Heeringen to Holtzendorff, 4 June 1912; F 3303, PG 66709, Tirpitz to Müller, 16 June 1912.
14  ibid., F 5589, III, 1.–10b., Vol. 3, initialed by A, Behncke, 23 January 1912, "Zur Besprechung mit dem Grossen Generalstabe. Englische Landung in einem englisch-französisch-deutschen Kriege."
15  ibid., initialed by A, Behncke, 6 February 1912, "Zur Orientierung für Seine Excellenz," 1 February 1912. For the British decision to ship troops to Calais in January 1908 and the spring of 1911, as well as John Fisher's objections to a Continental strategy, see Williamson, *Politics,* pp. 107–8, 173–6.
16  BA-MA, F 5589, III, 1.–10b., Vol. 3, Moltke to Heeringen, 2 February 1912.
17  ibid., Heeringen to Moltke, 23 February 1912.
18  PAAA, Frankreich 116, Geh., Bd 1, Ostertag to the Minister of War, 15 February 1912; Widenmann to the Secretary of State of the RMA, 16 February 1912.
19  See ibid., Deutschland 121, No. 31, Geh., Bd 1.
20  BA-MA, F 5587, III, 1. N. 10., Vol. 6, initialed by A, Behncke, A4, initials H and D, "Direktiven für unser Verhalten gegenüber Holland und Belgien in einem Kriege Deutschlands mit England und Frankreich," 24 August 1912.
21  ibid., marginal comment of A2 on Heeringen to Moltke, 24 October 1912, draft of an unsent letter.
22  ibid., F 5589, III, 1.–10b., Vol. 3, "Besprechung über die Überführung des englischen Expeditionskorps mit dem O. I des Gr. Gs. Gen Mj. Graf Waldersee 6. 11. 1913," initialed by A, Behncke.
23  ibid., F 2020, PG 65975, initialed by A4, 28 November 1912, "Entwurf zum Operationsbefehl für den Krieg gegen England." The section dealing with action against the BEF was crossed out in pencil.
24  ibid., Pohl, "Zum Immediatvortrag," 17 October 1913; F 7644, II. 1. 5b., Vol. 5, "A-Kriegsspiel 1913–14," initialed by A, Behncke, and A4, 15 October 1913.
25  ibid., F 5593, III, 2.–2., Vol. 3, initialed by A and A4, 4 October 1911, "Unterlagen für einen Operationsplan gegen Russland für das Winterhalbjahr 1911/12 in der Ostsee."
26  ibid., marginal comment dated either 28 or 29 January 1912.
27  ibid., A1 to A5, October 1911.
28  ibid., BA-MA, F 2020, PG 65974, Heeringen, "Zum Immediatvortrag," 7 December 1911.
29  ibid., F 5593, III, 2.–2., Vol. 3, initialed by A2, "II Entwurf eines Operationsplans gegen Russland in der Ostsee für das Sommerhalbjahr 1912."
30  ibid., F 5592, III, 2.–1., Vol. 3, "Operationsplan gegen Russland in der Ostsee für das Sommerhalbjahr 1912."
31  ibid., F 5594, II.–R. 3, Bd 6, Keyserlingk to Tirpitz, 26 April 1912.
32  ibid., F 5592, III, 2.–1., Vol. 3, "O-Plan gegen Russland Winter 1912–13," signed by A, Behncke, 22 October 1912, presented to Wilhelm on 24 October 1912.
33  ibid., F 5593, III, 2.–2., Vol. 3, Heeringen to Moltke, 7 October 1912; Moltke to Heeringen, 9 October 1912.
34  ibid., F 2020, PG 65975, "Denkschrift zum Immediatvortrag über die Operationslage in der Ostsee," 24 October 1912; Müller, *Der Kaiser,* p. 122.
35  ibid., F 5593, III, 2.–2., Vol. 3, Heeringen to Tirpitz, 12 November 1912.
36  ibid., F 5592, III, 2.–1., Vol. 3, A, Behncke, to Chief of the Baltic Sea Station, 14 November 1912, enclosing document of the same date, "Operationslage Ostsee."
37  ibid., F 5593, III, 2.–16b., Vol. 1, "Aussichten eines Handelskrieges in der Ostsee," 28 November 1912, no signature.
38  Enclosure to ibid., "Kohlenversorgung der russischen Ostsee-flotte im Kriege," 28 November 1912, no signature.
39  ibid., Heeringen, "Erwägungen über die Durchführbarkeit einer russischen Landung an der deutschen Ostseeküste in einem Kriege Deutschland gegen Russland und England," 29 November 1912.
40  ibid., F 5593, III, 2.–2., Vol. 3, Moltke to Heeringen, 13 December 1912.

41  ibid., F 2020, PG 65975, "Denkschrift zum Immediatvortrag betr. Kriegführung gegen Russland und Frankreich bei abwartenden oder neutralen Haltung Englands," 29 November 1912.

42  ibid., "Zum Immediatvortrag. Entwurf zum Operationsbefehl für den Krieg gegen England," 28 November 1912, initialed A4, approved by Wilhelm on 3 December 1912.

43  ibid., Heeringen, "Zum Immediatvortrag. Strategisches Kaisermanöver 1912," 22 May 1912, approved by Wilhelm on 6 June 1912.

44  ibid., "Das Kaisermanöver im Jahre 1912."

45  ibid., Heeringen, "Zum Immediatvortrag betreffend Kriegsspiele der Front," 26 October 1912.

46  ibid., "Gesichtspunkte für eine Kriegführung aus der Deutschen Bucht der Nordsee gegen eine überlegene Seemacht."

47  ibid., F 5589, III, 1.–10b., Vol. 4, 13 December 1912, initialed by D, A, and A4.

48  ibid., 22 February 1913, initialed by D, A, and A4.

49  ibid., Vol. 3, "Verwendung der Luftwaffe im Kriege gegen England-Frankreich," initialed by D2 and A on 23 January 1913.

50  ibid., F 2020, PG 65976, "Zum Immediatvortrag," 6 March 1913; reported to Wilhelm on 27 March 1913.

51  ibid., Pohl to Tirpitz, 2 May 1913.

52  ibid., Pohl, "Zum Immediatvortrag: Die französischen Flottenmanöver im Sommer 1913," 30 September 1913.

53  ibid., Pohl, "Zum Immediatvortrag, 17 October 1913."

54  ibid., F 7644, II, 1.–5., Bd 4, "Kriegsspiel des Admiralstabes, Winter 1913–14," 29 October 1913.

55  ibid., F 2021, PG 65977, "Zum Immediatvortrag. Englische Flottenmanöver 1913," 17 December 1913, presented to Wilhelm on 13 January 1914.

56  See above, p. 401.

57  ibid., F 5644, II, 1.–5., Bd 4, "A-Kriegsspiel 1913–14;" Heydel's considerations for the British deployment, 13 November 1913; on 26 November, Grasshoff essentially elaborated on Heydel's thoughts.

58  ibid., "Schlussbesprechung des Blauen Parteiführers, Paul Behncke," 11 March 1914.

59  ibid., "Schlussbericht des Parteiführers zur Kritik," Grasshoff, 14 March 1914.

60  ibid., "Kriegstagebuch. Leitung," 1 April 1914.

61  ibid., F 2021, PG 65977, Pohl, "Denkschrift zum Immediatvortrag über das strategische Kriegsspiel des Admiralstabes Winter 1913/14," 5 May 1914.

62  Röhl, "An der Schwelle," No. 4, p. 100.

63  BA-MA, F 6371, XVIII, 1.–1., B 21, Vol. 10, Heeringen to Tirpitz, 23 January 1913.

64  ibid., F 5592, III, 2.–1., Vol. 3, A2, Z, A2$_2$, G, 30 January 1913, initialed by A, Behncke, 26 April 1913, "Verwendung von finnischen und schwedischen Lotsen auf dem Ostkriegsschauplatz."

65  ibid., F 5593, III, 2.–2., Vol. 3, Heeringen to Tirpitz, 13 February 1913.

66  ibid., F 5592, III, 2.–1., Vol. 3, initialed by A2 on 18 March 1913, "Ausarbeitung zu A 3222/18 vom 29. 11. 1912."

67  ibid., D to A, 9 May 1913.

68  ibid., F 5563, III, 1.–5., Vol. 1, "Kriegsspiel-Aufgabe No. 3., östliches Kriegstheater," initialed P[ohl], 3 November 1913. It dealt with the German offensive against Russia in which the Second Squadron served as the main force.

69  ibid., P[ohl], "Zum Immediatvortrag. Stabsoffizier-Kriegsspiel der Ostseestation 1912–13," 5 June 1913.

70  ibid., Coerper, "Stabsoffizier-Kriegsspiel der Ostseestation 1913," n.d.

71  ibid., "Zu Kriegsspiel Ostseestation," 23 May 1914, with Pohl's minute of 10 June.

72  ibid., F 5592, III, 2.–1., Vol. 4, initialed by A2, 17 February 1914, "Denkschrift zu A 3223/12 über die geplante Kriegführung in der Ostsee im Kriegsfall B."

73  ibid., F 5587, 1. N. 10., Vol. 6, Pohl to Tirpitz, 9 June 1912.

74  ibid., F 2020, PG 65976, "Zum Immediatvortrag," 17 October 1913.

75  ibid., 5592, III, 2.–1., Vol. 4, initialed by P[ohl] (?) with comment "Einverstanden" and by A, A1, and A2, "Besprechung betr. Ostseekriegsschauplatz," 5 November 1913.

76  Schulte, *Kriegsausbruch*, pp. 72, 74; Adolf Gasser, "Deutschlands Entschluss zum Präventivkrieg," in Marc Sieber (ed.), *Discordia Concors: Festgabe für Edgar*

*Bonjour zu seinem siebzigsten Geburtstag am 21, August* (Basle, 1968), Vol. 1, pp. 173–221, passim, esp. pp. 177–82, 185–7, 207–8; and Fischer, *Krieg* (following Gasser), p. 565.

77   Schulte, *Kriegsausbruch*, p. 70.
78   For background information, see in particular Paul G. Halpern, *The Mediterranean Naval Situation, 1908–14* (Cambridge, Mass., 1971), esp. pp. 222–79; and Michael Palumbo, "German–Italian military relations on the eve of World War I," *Central European History*, vol. 12, no. 4 (December 1979), pp. 343–71.
79   BA-MA, F 5600, III, 3.–24., Vol. 2, discussions of A 3 with Oberst Erich Ludendorff on 3 January 1913, initialed by A3, Erich Köhler.
80   For Moltke's interest, see ibid., Moltke to Kleist (in Rome), January 1913, copy of draft.
81   BA-MA, F 2020, PG 65976, "Zum Immediatvortrag," 8 January 1913.
82   ibid., F 5601, III, 3.–24., Nebenakten Vol. 3, 23 June 1913, signed by Köhler, Cicoli, Conz.
83   Halpern, *Mediterranean*, p. 254.
84   ibid., pp. 258–60.
85   BA-MA, F 5600, III, 3.–24., Vol. 3, Pohl to Souchon, January 1914.
86   ibid., "Denkschrift über die Kriegführung des Dreibunds gegen Frankreich und England im Mittelmeer," with covering letter of 3 July 1914, no signature.
87   ibid., F 2019, PG 65972, Fischel, "Zum Immediatvortrag," approved by Wilhelm on 23 November 1910.
88   ibid., F 5171, III, 1.–9b., Bd 3., Büchsel, "Immediatvortrag über O-Angelegenheite," 9 March 1907, approved by Wilhelm.
89   ibid., Bd 4, Baudissin, "Denkschrift zu den Allerhöchsten Befehlen an S.M. Schiffe im Auslande für den Kriegsfall," 31 January 1909; approved by Wilhelm on 2 February 1909.
90   ibid., F 5172, III, 1.–9b., Bd. 8, Heeringen, "O-Befehle fur Auslandschiffe," 3 April 1912.
91   ibid., F 2020, PG 65975, Pohl, "Zum Immediatvortrag," 24 April 1913.
92   ibid., F 5171, III, 1.–9b., Bd 3, Büchsel, "Immediatvortrag über O-Angelegenheiten," 9 March 1907.
93   ibid., Bd 4, Baudissin, "Denkschrift zu den Allerhöchsten Befehlen an S.M. Schiffe im Auslande für den Kriegsfall," 31 January 1909.
94   ibid., F 2020, PG 65975, Pohl, "Zum Immediatvortrag," 24 April 1913.
95   ibid., F 2019, PG 65972, Baudissin, "Zum Immediatvortrag," 2 February 1909; F 5171, III, 1.–9b., Bd 4, Baudissin, "Denkschrift zu den Allerhöchsten Befehlen an S.M. Schiffe im Auslande für den Kriegsfall," 31 January 1909.
96   ibid., F 5171, III, 1.–9b., Bd 3, Büchsel, "Immediatvortrag über O-Angelegenheiten," 9 March 1907.
97   ibid., F 5171, III, 1.–9b., Bd 4, Baudissin, "Denkschrift zu den Allerhöchsten Befehlen an S.M. Schiffe im Auslande für den Kriegsfall," 31 January 1909.
98   ibid., F 2019, PG 65972, Fischel, "Immediatvortrag," held on 23 November 1910.
99   ibid., F 5167, III, 1.–5a., Bd 1, B "Denkschrift über den Kreuzerkrieg gegen England," 27 April 1911.
100  ibid., F 5172, III, 1.–9b., Bd 8, Heeringen, "O-Befehle für Auslandschiffe," 3 April 1912.
101  ibid., F 7643, "Kriegsspiel 1912–14. Kreuzergeschwader. Spee "Strategisches Kriegsspiel. Südreise 1912," 30 December 1912.
102  ibid., F 2020, PG 65975, Pohl, "Zum Immediatvortrag," 24 April 1913.
103  ibid., F 2021, PG 65977, Pohl, "Zum Immediatvortrag," 12 March 1914.
104  ibid., F 5171, III, 1.–9b., Bd 3, Büchsel, "Immediatvortrag über O-Angelegenheiten," 9 March 1907.
105  ibid., Bd 4, Baudissin, "Denkschrift zu den Allerhöchsten Befehlen an S.M. Schiffe im Auslande für den Kriegsfall," 2 February 1909.
106  ibid., F 2020, PG 65976, Pohl, "Zum Immediatvortrag," 24 April 1913.
107  ibid., F 2021, PG 65977, Pohl, "Zum Immediatvortrag," 12 March 1914.
108  ibid., F 6158, XVII, 1. 1. 28., Vol. 2, Tirpitz to Büchsel, 20 November 1906; Büchsel to Tirpitz, 18 February and 15 March 1907; Vol. 3, Tirpitz, "Mobilmachungs-Vorkehrungen des Staatssekretärs des Reichs-Marine-Amts für Auslandschiffe," 30 September 1908.

109   ibid., Vol. 3, Tirpitz, "Mobilmachungs-Vorkehrungen . . .," 30 September 1908.
110   ibid., F 5171, III, 1.–9b., Bd 4, Baudissin, "Denkschrift zu den Allerhöchsten Befehlen an S.M. Schiffe im Auslande für den Kriegsfall," 31 January 1909.
111   ibid., F 2020, PG 65974, Fischel, "Zum Immediatvortrag," 24 January 1911.
112   ibid., PG 65976, Pohl, "Zum Immediatvortrag," 24 April 1913.

# 19 Epilogue and Conclusions

Very soon after the assassination of Franz Ferdinand the German leadership insisted that Austria-Hungary crush Serbia.[1] The Kaiser criticized Tschirschky for having counseled moderation in Vienna and remarked: "One must make a clean sweep of the Serbs, and very soon."[2] On 1 July the well-known German journalist Victor Naumann[3] and on 4 July Jagow urged that Austria-Hungary take strong action against the Serbs.[4] Official German support for Austria-Hungary, regardless of consequences, was promised on 5–6 July. Although there were differences between the German leaders' estimates of the consequences of the promise, there exists no doubt now that it involved the risk of a general war. Appropriate military and naval preparations were made very soon.[5]

For the army it was the opportunity for the preventive war which it had advocated since 1912. The Prussian General Staff and Ministry of War seemed to agree that the timing was opportune. German artillery was considered as being superior to the Russian and the French, particularly in respect to howitzers; so was the German infantry rifle. The Russian army was estimated as lacking confidence and the French army as being weakened by poor morale and weak training because of the transition from a two- to a three-year term of military service.[6] Moltke himself and his deputy Waldersee were absent from Berlin on 5–6 July. But the Minister of War, Erich von Falkenhayn, and the Chief of the Military Cabinet, Moritz von Lyncker, were consulted, as was Waldersee upon his return. Falkenhayn assured that the army was ready for anything.[7] Waldersee departed once more, to Ivenach, not far from Berlin, but from there undertook several visits to the capital.[8]

Fritz Klein describes one of the illusions of the German leaders in July:

> Again and again there emerges the hope in German documents that Russia was not ready for war and would not support Serbia, so that France and England could even more easily stay out of consideration.[9]

This hope was expressed by Wilhelm on 5[10] and 6 July. He did not think that Russia would support regicides, and considered both her and France unprepared for war.[11] It was also voiced by Bethmann on 8 and 16 July, and by Jagow on 18 July. It became the basis of the policy of localization, i.e. confining the war to Austria-Hungary and Serbia. But the crushing of Serbia none the less involved a change of the European balance in favor of the Central Powers. As Bethmann remarked to Riezler on 8 July: "If the war does not come or if the Czar does not want it, or if a dismayed France counsels peace, we would still have the prospect of splitting the Entente over this action."[12] If Britain and France failed to support Russia, she might break her ties with them and, perhaps, even enter the German orbit.[13] In any case, the crushing of Serbia, while Russia stood by, would strengthen Austria-Hungary in the Balkans at the expense of the Czarist Empire, and contribute to her internal consolidation. As Jagow was also aware, successful action against Serbia would again re-establish the faltering Dual Monarchy as a great power.[14] In the words of Wilhelm: "Austria must become preponderant in the Balkans in the face of other small [powers] at the cost of Russia. Through an Austrian victory over Serbia in a localized war Germany had nothing to lose and much to gain." According to Klein: "Lastly it was not an action against Serbia; it was an attack of the German–Austro-Hungarian bloc on the imperialist positions of Czarist Russia."[15]

On 18 December 1912, however, Bethmann-Hollweg had written to Wilhelm: "That a war with Russia involves a war with France is certain."[16] While hoping for the localization of the conflict with all of the advantages that it offered, Bethmann was also aware that "An action against Serbia can lead to a world war."[17] Crucial in this calculation was the position of Britain. In the so-called "war council" of 8 December 1912 it was assumed that she would take the side of France and Russia. This assumption was not shared by the absent Chancellor, however, who remarked on 18 December that it was "doubtful if England would become actively involved if Russia and France were to appear as the direct instigators."[18] On 10 February 1913 he explained to the Austro-Hungarian Foreign Minister, Leopold Graf von Berchtold, that he had not offered fuller support against Serbia because it would have given the upper hand to the Russian war party, and that war with Russia would have involved war with France and Britain as well. But he added that Britain's position was changing.[19] According to Paul M. Kennedy, he "continued to hope that Britain's links with her *entente* partners might slowly dissolve."[20] Yet at the beginning of June 1914 he expected that in a war between Germany and the Dual Alliance the island state would oppose her,[21] and along with Jagow became concerned about the negotiations of an Anglo-Russian naval convention, which appeared as the final link in Germany's encirclement.[22] Wolfgang J. Mommsen has effectively argued that during the July crisis Bethmann-Hollweg placed less hope in Britain's neutrality than in her restraint on France and Russia, which would have contributed to the localization of the conflict.[23] Yet in opposing Wilhelm's proposal to recall the fleet from its Norwegian journey Bethmann stated on 25 July that Edward Grey was not interested in participating in a Continental war and would act toward the localization of the conflict between Austria-Hungary and Serbia.[24] When informed by Lichnowsky's telegram of 29 July that Britain would be involved on the side of France and Russia against Germany,[25] Bethmann for the first time seriously attempted to restrain Austria-Hungary by advocating that her troops stop for purposes of negotiation after occupying

Belgrade—a proposal made by Britain and supported by the Kaiser.[26] The evidence that is available does not make it possible to provide a definite answer to the question whether in July 1914 Bethmann-Hollweg counted on Britain's neutrality or on her restraint of her Entente partners. Perhaps he confused the two issues. In any case, his statement to the Prussian Ministry of State on 30 July made it clear that he expected Britain to be involved in a Continental war.[27]

Wilhelm II least expected a general war in 1914. Subsequently he took seriously Heinrich's report of George V's statement "we shall try all we can to stay out of this and shall remain neutral."[28] He was therefore particularly infuriated by Grey's communication to Lichnowsky that Britain would enter a war against Germany. None the less, he made an attempt to appeal through his brother to George V to keep Russia and France out of the war,[29] advocated restraint in Vienna, and continued to attempt to mediate between Austria-Hungary and Russia. In spite of the risk of war that the German leadership had taken in supporting Austria-Hungary, on 30 July Wilhelm viewed the outbreak of war as an Entente conspiracy:

> The whole war is plainly arranged between England, France and Russia for the annihilation of Germany . . . and the Austro-Serbian strife is only an excuse to fall on us! God help us in this fight for our existence, brought about by falseness, lies and poisonous envy.[30]

The Kaiser's attitude in July 1914 makes it particularly difficult to establish a link between the so-called "war council" of 8 December 1912, over which he presided, and the outbreak of World War I.

Unlike the Kaiser and the political leaders, Tirpitz, his deputy Hopmann, and the acting chief of the Admiralty Staff Behncke were convinced in July 1914 that Britain would fight against Germany. Tirpitz did not want a war in 1914: the sixty-one capital ships would not be available before 1928 and Britain might still falter in the naval race or reach an agreement with Germany. On 31 July he advocated a last-minute arrangement with Russia.[31]

As for the Continental power relationship, Bethmann-Hollweg and Jagow shared Moltke's concern about the growth of Russian power and came close to accepting Moltke's arguments for a preventive war. "I want no preventive war," wrote Jagow on 18 July, "but if the struggle appears we must not flinch."[32] He feared that without German support Austria-Hungary might defect to the Western Powers; like Kiderlen-Wächter in 1911 he also realized that Austro-Hungarian support was only certain if war broke out in the east: "then we have a chance to win."[33] For it was unlikely that Austria-Hungary would support Germany against Britain over naval rivalry or against France and Britain over colonial issues or over a German preventive war against France.

In order to calm world opinion after the deliberations of 5–6 July, Bethmann-Hollweg encouraged the Kaiser to undertake his habitual Norwegian cruise, departed himself for his estate in Hohenfinow, and urged the leading military or naval figures either to go or to stay away. Pressure continued to be exerted on Vienna to proceed with its action against Serbia; it was instrumental in overcoming the objections of the Hungarian Prime Minister, Count Stephen Tisza, to war. Unlike the German leadership, that of Austria-Hungary had no doubt that action against Serbia would lead to a European war. The text of the Austro-Hungarian ultimatum to Serbia, which was expected to be rejected, was drafted on 14 July. It was presented to Serbia only on 23 July, so that its terms would not become known in St Petersburg during the state visit of the French President, Raymond Poincaré. Germany was informed of its contents on the evening of 22 July. Throughout the planning of the Austro-Hungarian action, the German government disclaimed any knowledge of it.

Although originally little apprehensive that the blank check to Austria-Hungary would lead to a general war, in view of the possibly rapid developments after the expected Austro-Hungarian ultimatum to Serbia on 23 July, during his Norwegian cruise Wilhelm became concerned about the state of German commercial shipping, its involvement as an auxiliary for German cruiser warfare overseas, and about the High Seas Fleet which, as in 1911, was cruising along the Norwegian coast, this time under the command of Holtzendorff's successor (since April 1913) Admiral von Ingenohl. He issued orders on 19 July that the directors of the Hamburg–America Line and the North German Lloyd be prepared to observe the orders issued to ships abroad.[34] Appropriate action was subsequently undertaken. The German political leadership was more reluctant to follow Wilhelm's wishes regarding the High Seas Fleet. His instructions of 19 July that it be united until 25 July, the date of the expiry of the Austro-Hungarian ultimatum to Serbia, and avoid entry into Norwegian ports "so that it could quickly follow the order to complete the voyage,"[35] worried Bethmann-Hollweg since in the event of the rejection of the ultimatum, on the one hand, any conspicuous movements of the fleet could escalate the crisis and, on the other, "a wrong location of the fleet could become fatal." Disclaiming expertise in naval matters, he therefore proposed that the Admiralty Staff be consulted.[36] On 22 July, Behncke informed the Foreign Office that an impending British declaration of war would also involve an attack on the High Seas Fleet by the Royal Navy:

> In its numerical inferiority our fleet can under no circumstances be subjected to this eventuality.
> As soon as the possibility of war with England within a six-day period is to be counted on, the fleet is to be recalled.[37]

According to the information provided by the Admiralty Staff, the Foreign Office and the Chancellor expected that the Royal Navy would return to its home ports on 27 July, after the completion of its maneuvers. Jagow responded to the communication of Behncke:

> It is very improbable that England would decide on an immediate attack

on us and that the question of a European war would at all be resolved so soon . . . If our fleet were recalled prematurely, England would keep hers together.[38]

Bethmann-Hollweg fully agreed with his Secretary of State.[39] Presumably the recall of the German navy would escalate the crisis and through the continued concentration of the Royal Navy provide it with a military advantage over the High Seas Fleet once war broke out. On 24 July, Wilhelm renewed the pressure for the return of the High Seas Fleet.[40] Beside the Royal Navy, which he considered as prepared for war, "we must have to reckon with the Russian fleet which, in case Russia mobilizes against Austria, can appear within the shortest time with its ships which are now in service before our Baltic Sea ports." In spite of all objections, he ordered the return of the fleet on 26 July.[41] On the following day the Admiralty Staff reported that Russia was mobilizing secretly— information that dovetailed with that from other sources—but it now also maintained that measures were being taken by the Royal Navy in Hull and the Medway area that indicated greater war preparedness.[42] On the morning of 25 July, Müller reported Wilhelm as giving Ingenohl "a type of OP order against Russia, involving the destruction of Libau and Reval."[43] The Admiralty Staff had, in fact, completed an operations plan against the Dual Alliance which was approved by Wilhelm on 30 July, when Britain's involvement in a Continental war appeared certain.[44] It indicated the expectation that Britain would remain neutral, which was not shared by Tirpitz, his deputy Hopmann, or by Behncke, and certainly not by Bethmann-Hollweg on that day: it was thus proof of the failure of the German leadership to coordinate its views. Expressis verbis, however, the plan was prepared on the assumption that Britain would none the less interfere in the war, particularly if land warfare was favorable to Germany. As long as Britain's neutrality was not certain, battleworthy ships were not to be risked against torpedo-boats, mines, submarines, and coastal fortifications; in any case, the western theater of war was to be considered as more important because of its significance for Germany's overseas commerce. Since France's naval forces in the English Channel were weak and unlikely to offer battle, and her overseas trade through the northern and western ports was limited, German measures in the west were to be restricted to repelling attacks of French light forces from the eastern estuary of the English Channel, escorting home of German shipping north of Britain, and mine operations against Dunkirk, Calais, Le Havre, and Cherbourg. The effect of the last operations on Britain was not considered. Were British neutrality assured, the High Seas Fleet could proceed to blockade French Channel and Atlantic ports, although a legally binding blockade was considered unfeasible because of the risks it entailed. Even a loose blockade was expected to require an entire squadron of ships of the line and all the light forces of the High Seas Fleet. The provisioning of this force was not easy: coal would have to be purchased from Britain and the other supplies would have to be brought from home, circumnavigating the British Isles. The German fleet would be divided: a squadron would be involved in safeguarding the shipping north of the British Isles and another would have to defend the North Sea along with whatever auxiliary forces were available. It was also suggested that a squadron or even all ships available in the western theater of war be sent to the Mediterranean to establish firm control over it. Pohl rightly vetoed this suggestion for the time being.

As for the eastern theater of war, "the Russian Baltic Sea fleet must be made so harmless as to make its offensive capacity impossible," so as to allow German forces control over the Baltic Sea. Operations in the Baltic were to start as soon as possible, spearheaded by the naval units located furthest to the east; the most important Russian harbors were to be blocked by sunken ships and mines, and torpedo-boats and submarines were to be dispatched against the strongest Russian naval units in the Gulf of Finland. Next the Libau base was to be destroyed and surprise attacks were to be undertaken against Helsingfors and Reval. Eventually the destruction of Helsingfors and Kronstadt might be undertaken, although it would entail considerable losses. With Britain neutral, a Russian attack against the German coast was no longer expected. The units to be used for the Baltic offensive were to consist of the Second Squadron of the Deutschland ships, another active ship of the line, two ships of the line of the reserve, one armored cruiser, four small cruisers, two torpedo-boat divisions, each accompanied by a cruiser, one mine-searching division, and two mine-layers. The new Russian Dreadnoughts, *Gangut* and *Sebastopol,* were not expected to be ready for service before September. Were the Russian fleet, contrary to expectations, to offer battle in the open sea, it was to be accepted.

Conceived explicitly for the purpose of assisting the army, the plan was politically unrealistic. German operations against the French coast would, according to the Anglo-French naval convention of 1912, have involved the Royal Navy on the side of France. In July, German naval officers expressed concern about the reappearance of the hostage theory, this time in the Foreign Office. On 20 July, Jagow told Behncke that he considered threatening Britain with the occupation of Holland if she declared herself to be Germany's enemy. Behncke replied:

> that the occupation of Holland would make the British operations during a war difficult and that the occupation of Holland after a successful war, if utilized by us militarily and economically, would mean an effective threat to England. I therefore believe that a threat to occupy Holland could influence England's decisions in the desired sense. But maybe it could also provide cause for her siding against us at once, if she were prepared to fight.[45]

Hopmann was more exercised about the proposal. He stated that it was made to Behncke both by Zimmermann and Wilhelm von Stumm, Political Director in the Foreign Office.

> According to His Excellency Capelle and also according to my views, we cannot do the English a greater favor. They would then have in black

and white the best means of agitation to draw all the smaller states, Belgium, Holland, Denmark, etc., to their side, they could speak of brutal violation of international law, and, what is even worse, immediately close the Belgian and Dutch ports to us, land troops as their defenders, etc.

This criticism recalls the Admiralty Staff's serious doubts about the Schlieffen Plan in 1905. Hopmann now also argued that "it is very questionable to me whether our General Staff would have even one transport soldier [*Trainsoldaten*] for such amateur waging of war."[46] Behncke, whom Hopmann regarded as too soft over the proposal, agreed to protest against it after discussions with Capelle.[47]

During the July crisis the navy undertook various preparations for war and sided with the Kaiser against the objections to the coaling of the High Seas Fleet in Norwegian waters and to its return to Germany.[48] Hugo von Pohl, who returned to Berlin on 25 July, wrote to Jagow about possible cooperation between Germany and Sweden for a war against Russia in the Baltic Sea.[49] On 27 July the Austro-Hungarian military attaché reported that he had recently obtained the impression that the Imperial Naval Office and the Admiralty Staff envisaged "all possible complications with the greatest calmness" and viewed "the time very favorable for a great reckoning." He added that this view was due to the very low opinion held of the French and Russian navies.[50] But what about Britain?

As for the most critical operations of the German navy, those directed against Britain, the final order was drafted by Behncke, who had lost the war game for the German side against a wide British blockade. Amazingly, his draft was for operations against a close blockade which the Admiralty Staff had recognized as being too costly to the blockading party and as not being imposed by Britain because of her naval maneuvers of 1912 and 1913. Behncke wrote:

I.   The aim of the oper[ations] should first be:
   (1)   To damage the Engl[ish] through the guard a[nd] blockade forces in the German Bight by a mine and U-boat offensive extending to the British coast.
   (2)   After the power relationship has been evened through such waging of war and the English forces have been weakened through mines, destroyers and submarines, it is to be attempted under favorable circumstances to engage our fleet in battle through the preparation and involvement of all its strength.

Behncke stated further: "On the basis of this note which Exc[ellency] v. Pohl took along to the Im[mediate] Audience, the operations order was approved on 1 (?) August 1914."[51] Actually it was approved on 30 July. This order may have been precipitated by the report of the naval attaché in London which reached the Kaiser on 30 July to the effect that in a Franco-German war Britain would take immediate action against the

German navy.[52] On 31 July, however, Pohl decided to provide a negative answer to the question by the Foreign Office whether an attack on the British fleet was possible.[53]

Tirpitz, who had built the navy to do battle against Britain, criticized the defensive stance against a close blockade. Allegedly, when asked in May 1914 what was to be done with the fleet "if the English altogether failed to appear in the German Bight, the Chief of the Fleet and his staff failed to provide him with an answer."[54] Tirpitz was also opposed to the final operational order of the Admiralty Staff against Britain.[55] Later he objected to the failure to use the fleet in an offensive against Britain immediately after the outbreak of war and deplored that naval operations had not been discussed with the army.

The navy had thus been assigned a passive role when following the proclamation of the Russian partial mobilization on 29 July the timetable for the action of the army became particularly urgent. As Jagow was to state later:

> Our operations plan and our chances of victory rested on the speed of action. If we could have waited until the state of war developed through military actions and declarations of war by the enemy, our policy would have found itself in a much more favorable situation.[56]

To support Austria-Hungary against Russia in the east, Germany would have to attack France through Belgium and would thus provide the war party in Britain with an upper hand. With the slowness of the mobilization of the Dual Monarchy and its decision to concentrate a large part of its forces against Serbia, the Schlieffen Plan could only succeed because of the slowness of Russian mobilization. This was the reason why the German army preferred a war in 1912 or in 1914 rather than in 1916 or 1917 when the Russian military preparations were expected to be completed and a rapid Russian mobilization was regarded as feasible. Information about Russian military preparations in July 1914 alarmed the German leadership and caused it to resort to threats.[57] On 29 July 1914 a memorandum of the Great General Staff indicated the inexorable way in which mobilizations would lead to war. The partial Austro-Hungarian mobilization against Serbia was leading to a Russian mobilization against the Dual Monarchy which would make necessary a complete Austro-Hungarian mobilization. Once this occurred, an Austro-Russian war would be inevitable. According to her alliance obligations, Germany would then have to mobilize against Russia—an action which would lead to Russia's total mobilization and enable her to claim French support on grounds of being attacked by Germany.

> For the military measures intended on our part in such a case, it is of the greatest importance as soon as possible to secure clarification whether Russia and France are willing to let it come to a war with Germany. The further the preparations of our neighbors proceed, the faster will they be able to complete their mobilization. The military situation will therefore

become from day to day less favorable to us and can lead to fateful results if our enemies can calmly prepare themselves further.[58]

Moltke was also concerned that, if Austro-Russian hostilities broke out before Germany mobilized, her ally would be crushed and Germany would have to fight Russia single-handed.[59]

Although Bethmann-Hollweg was able on the evening of 29 July to overrule the request for a German mobilization in response to the Russian mobilization against Austria-Hungary,[60] Wilhelm's response to the Russian partial mobilization was "Thereupon I must also mobilize,"[61] and Moltke's reaction was to overrule Bethmann-Hollweg's serious advocacy of the "halt in Belgrade" proposal of 30 July, encouraging the Dual Monarchy to mobilize fully[62] and causing Berchtold to remark: "who governs: Moltke or Bethmann?"[63] The full Russian mobilization of 30 July led the German leadership to declare the "state of imminent war" on the following day and mobilization on the day thereafter. The military plans involved an attack on Luxemburg on 2 August and one on Belgium on 4 August. The German declaration of war on Russia occurred on 1 August and that on France on 3 August. As of midnight on 4 August, Britain was also in a state of war with Germany. The definite declaration of Italian neutrality on 3 August, which Germany had attempted to avoid, was a disappointment to both the German navy and army because of the closer relationship of the previous year.[64]

## II

It is now necessary to attempt a verdict about the operational planning of the German navy before 1914. There existed several basic problems. The first was the failure to coordinate the different agencies of the German leadership. The Chancellor, even Bismarck, could not do it. The army was continuously subject to the jealously preserved prerogative of the King and Kaiser. From the foundation of the Empire the navy was an agency of the Empire and theoretically subject to the Chancellor, but it, too, came under the close control of the Kaiser, first with the break-up of the Admiralty in 1889 and then with the destruction of the High Command in 1899: this control he failed to exercise effectively. Not only did Wilhelm have to coordinate the civilian administration, including the Foreign Office, with the military authorities, but he also had to referee between the army and the navy as well as between the multiplying naval agencies struggling against each other—a task which was probably beyond anyone, but certainly beyond an impulsive and erratic man, incapable of hard or systematic work.

Compared to the army the navy was a junior service. Its personnel remained much smaller and the level of training of its officers stayed lower. There was no equivalent to the General Staff Officers. Until the appointment of Tirpitz as Secretary of State in 1897 there existed no clear concept of naval strategy. Ideas of the *jeune école* continued to challenge

Tirpitz's battleship school even afterward and enjoyed some support from the Kaiser. As of the 1860s it was the task of the navy to show the flag and protect German interests abroad and to defend the German coast. The latter task came to involve operations plans against France and Russia which, in view of the weakness of the Imperial Navy, often assumed an adventurous form. These plans entailed the support of the operations of the army—in spite of inadequate consultation with the General Staff—and the encouragement of the operations of the military and naval operations of Germany's allies by putting pressure on France. Only in 1903 was it admitted in the Admiralty Staff that the navy was capable of taking on the forces of the Dual Alliance. By then, however, the German navy was faced with more formidable tasks: war against Britain which from 1896 to 1914 was its chief preoccupation, war against the United States of America from 1899 to 1906, and the rather vague task of prying open the doors to world power in agreement with or in opposition to Britain. From 1900 to 1912 the navy was assigned priority over the army particularly because of the support of the Kaiser and Chancellor Bülow. There were statements and building projects dealing with catching up with Britain; some calculations made until 1914 assumed that she would allow the German building plans to catch up with her because of shortfalls in manpower and finances. Until 1904–05, when he was proven wrong, Tirpitz also thought that because of her imperial commitments Britain would be unable to concentrate her entire fleet against the growing German strength in the North Sea and that Germany's value as an ally of other powers would be enhanced. In 1904–05 the Tirpitz Plan came to be questioned both in naval and political circles and subsequently the debate over "quantity versus quality" of the navy was to become particularly acute. With the erratic support of Wilhelm II, who, like Tirpitz, realized that it would take a generation to build the fleet, the Secretary of State was able to stress quantity as opposed to quality against the demands of the Admiralty Staff and the "Front," for both quality and quantity the German finances did not allow. By the end of 1908, Bülow, who had been Tirpitz's supporter since 1897, came to question his building program, which remained under fire until 1914.

Tirpitz, the man responsible for the building and the general strategy of the German navy, was not in charge of its day-to-day use as an instrument of war, although he had in his capacity as Chief of Staff in the High Command from 1892 to 1895 been responsible for this task. The navy might be successful as an instrument against the Dual Alliance; it was not and probably could never be strong enough against the Dual Alliance and Britain once Tirpitz's building plans had largely contributed to their consolidation as the Triple Entente. This was beyond Germany's means. The operations plan in Danish waters which would have provided the navy with army support if the British had complied by responding to the German violation of Denmark through sending their fleet into Danish waters was not feasible once the strength of the German army was required against the entire Triple Entente, as was the case in 1914. Besides, there had existed substantial opposition to the Admiralty Staff's Danish operations plan earlier. A defensive concentration in the Baltic against the west ran counter to the basic assumptions of the Tirpitz Plan. Tirpitz himself had rejected an invasion of Britain as long as the German navy could not maintain a permanent control of the sea—as had Schlieffen—and appears to have been opposed to Baudissin's offensive strategy against her. The war games against a wide blockade of the North Sea by Britain in March 1914 had failed. The concentration on *Kleinkrieg,* which had gained Bülow's support, was contrary to Tirpitz's emphasis on battleship construction. The Admiralty Staff and the so-called "Front," who were responsible for "quality" in a war against the Triple Entente, were doomed to confront it with both inferior quality and quantity. In 1914 the naval power relationship stood as set out in Table 19.1.[65]

Table 19·1

| | Capital ships | Older ships of the line | Older large cruisers | Small cruisers | Destroyers and torpedo-boats New | Old | Submarines offensive | defensive |
|---|---|---|---|---|---|---|---|---|
| Germany | 16 | 22 | 5 | 14 | 42 | 46 | 10 | 18 |
| Britain | 24 | 36 | 20 | 35 | 78 | 77 | 7 | 51 |

Arthur Mahan, however, had estimated that in order to be successful in a naval war Germany would, because of her geographic location, require a considerable superiority over her opponents. The power relationship between the Central and the Entente Powers, as shown in Table 19·2, did not improve the situation (the number of capital ships appears in brackets and includes battle cruisers in the ship-of-the-line column).[66]

Table 19·2

| | Ships of the line | Cruisers | Torpedo-boats and destroyers | Submarines |
|---|---|---|---|---|
| Central Powers | 59 [17] | 62 | 322 | 34 |
| Entente Powers | 91 [26] | 326 | 666 | 154 |

Since Britain's strength in capital ships improved after July 1914, because of her recently accelerated building program and the confiscation of foreign ships under construction in her dockyards, the outbreak of war might have been the most opportune time for Germany to seek a naval battle with her. But the outcome would hardly have been different from that described by Moltke (who was either unaware of recent developments in naval planning or unwilling to represent them) to the Belgian military attaché at the end of 1913:

In the event of war our fleet will be ordered to attack the British fleet. It will be defeated—that is very possible, even probable, because the English have numerical superiority. But what will the English fleet have after the destruction of the last German armored cruiser? Certainly we shall lose our ships; England, however, will lose her control of the seas, which will for ever pass on to the Americans.[67]

This was a belated expression of the risk theory which even Tirpitz expressed on 1 August. But as Admiral von Müller observed in respect to the July crisis: "Surely in view of the general political situation England had no reason to fear the risk that her fleet encountered in a war against us. Rather the contrary."[68] The construction of the German fleet had failed to provide Germany with the opportunity of becoming a major world power and had substantially contributed to her so-called "encirclement."

## Notes: Chapter 19

1 I shall not refer to the immense literature concerning the outbreak of World War I. See, however, n. 1 to Chapter 17 on p. 384.

2 *Die Deutschen Dokumente zum Kriegsausbruch: Vollständige Sammlung der von Karl Kautsky zusammengestellten amtlichen Aktenstücke mit einigen Ergänzungen. Im Auftrage des Auswärtigen Amtes nach gemeinsamer Durchsicht mit Karl Kautsky herausgegeben von Graf Max Montgelas und Prof. Walter Schücking,* 4 vols (Berlin, 1927) (henceforth abbreviated as DD), Vol. I, No. 7, Tschirschky to Bethmann-Hollweg, 30 June 1914, p. 13.

3 *Österreich-Ungarns Aussenpolitik von der bosnischen Krise 1908 bis zum Kriegsausbruch 1914: Diplomatische Aktenstücke des Österreich-Ungarischen Ministeriums des Äussern. Ausgewählt von Ludwig Bittner, Alfred Francis Pribram, Heinrich Srbik und Hans Uebelsberger. Bearbeitet von Ludwig Bittner und Hans Uebelsberger,* 8 vols (Vienna/Leipzig, 1930) (henceforth abbreviated as Ö-UA), Vol. VIII, No. 9966, "Aufzeichnung . . . Hoyos," 1 July 1914, p. 235.

4 ibid., No. 10,038, telegram to Berlin, 4 July 1914, p. 295.

5 For naval preparations, see Volker R. Berghahn and Wilhelm Deist, "Kaiserliche Marine und Kriegsausbruch 1914: Neue Dokumente zur Juli-Krise," *Militärgeschichtliche Mitteilungen,* Issue 1 (1970), nos 1 and 3, Hopmann to Tirpitz, 6 and 7 July 1914, pp. 45–7.

6 See Imanuel Geiss, *Julikrise und Kriegsausbruch 1914* (Hanover, 1964), Vol. 2, No. 704, Wenninger to Kress, 29 July 1914, pp. 297–8; No. 916, Lerchenfeld to Hertling, telephone call, 31 July 1914, p. 481; and Lerchenfeld to Hertling, 31 July 1914, p. 483.

7 Fischer, *Krieg,* p. 492.

8 Fritz Klein and others, *Deutschland im Ersten Weltkrieg,* Vol. I (Berlin, 1970), pp. 221–2; Albertini, *Origins,* Vol. 2, p. 143, n. 2. For the view that the army was not fully prepared for war in 1914, see Ulrich Trumpener, "War premeditated? German intelligence operations 1914," *Central European History,* vol. 9, no. 1 (March 1976), esp. pp. 63–5, 83–5.

9 Klein, *Deutschland,* p. 223.

10 Ö-UA, VIII, telegram from Berlin, 5 July 1914, pp. 306–7.

11 Berghahn and Deist, "Dokumente," No. 1, p. 45.

12 Kurt Riezler, *Tagebücher, Aufsätze, Dokumente,* ed. K. D. Erdmann (Göttingen, 1972), diary entry for 7 July 1914, p. 182; DD, I, No. 58, Bethmann-Hollweg to Roedern, 16 July 1914, p. 79; ibid., No. 72, Jagow to Lichnowsky, 18 July 1914, p. 93.

13 See Riezler, *Tagebücher,* diary entry for 20 July 1914, p. 187.

14 DD, I, No. 48, Jagow to Lichnowsky, 15 July 1914, p. 69, and No. 72, Jagow to Lichnowsky, 18 July 1914, p. 92.

15 ibid., Wilhelm's marginal comment to No. 155, Tschirschky to the Foreign Office, 24 July 1914, p. 152; Klein, *Deutschland,* p. 233.

16 GP, XIL, No. 15560, Bethmann-Hollweg to Wilhelm, 18 December 1912, pp. 9 ff.; also Röhl, "An der Schwelle," No. 31, pp. 122–3.

17   Riezler, *Tagebücher*, diary entry for 7 July 1914, p. 183.
18   See above, n. 16.
19   GP, XXXIV, No. 12818, Bethmann-Hollweg to Berchtold, 10 February 1913, pp. 346 ff.
20   Kennedy, *Antagonism*, p. 452.
21   Jarausch, *Enigmatic Chancellor*, p. 151.
22   E. Zechlin, "Deutschland zwischen Kabinettkrieg und Wirtschaftskrieg: Politik und Kriegführung in den ersten Monaten des Weltkrieges 1914," *Historische Zeitschrift*, Bd 199 (1964), Heft 2, pp. 348–51; Riezler, *Tagebücher*, diary entry for 7 July 1914, p. 182.
23   Mommsen, "Domestic factors," pp. 38–9.
24   DD, I, No. 182, Bethmann-Hollweg to Wilhelm, 25 July 1914, p. 175.
25   ibid., II, No. 368, Lichnowsky to the Foreign Office, 29 July 1914, pp. 78–80.
26   ibid., No. 395, Bethmann-Hollweg to Tschirschky, 30 July 1914, pp. 113–14.
27   ibid., No. 456, "Protokoll der Sitzung des K. preussischen Staatsministeriums," 30 July 1914, p. 164.
28   ibid., No. 374, Heinrich to Wilhelm, 28 July 1914, p. 88.
29   ibid., No. 417, Heinrich to George V, 30 July 1914, p. 131; No. 474, Wilhelm to Reichsmarineamt and Admiralstab, 31 July 1914, pp. 177–9.
30   ibid., No. 402, "Randbemerkungen des Kaisers vom 30. Juli vorm. zum Artikel der "Morning Post" vom 28. Juli, 1914," p. 121.
31   Berghahn and Deist, "Dokumente," No. 10, "Aufzeichnung . . . Behncke," 20 July 1914, p. 54, and No. 12, Hopmann to Tirpitz, 22 July 1914, pp. 56–7; BA-MA, N 253/202, Tirpitz to Lichnowsky, 30 December 1912; Tirpitz, *Erinnerungen*, pp. 231, 238, 242, and *Politische Dokumente. Deutsche Ohnmachtspolitik im Weltkriege* (Hamburg, 1926), pp. 10 ff.
32   DD, I, No. 72, Jagow to Lichnowsky, 18 July 1914, p. 93; Klein, Mommsen, *Deutschland*, p. 144; "Domestic factors," pp. 39–40.
33   Riezler, *Tagebücher*, diary entry for 8 July 1914, p. 184; Fischer, *Krieg*, p. 693.
34   DD, I, No. 80, Wedel, Gesandte im Kaiserlichen Gefolge, to the Foreign Office, 19 July 1914, pp. 97–8.
35   ibid., No. 82, Chief of the Admiralty Staff of the Navy to the Secretary of State of the Foreign Office, 20 July 1914, p. 99.
36   ibid., No. 101, Bethmann-Hollweg to the Foreign Office, 21 July 1914, p. 115.
37   ibid., No. 111, Behncke to the Foreign Office, 22 July 1914, p. 120.
38   ibid., No. 115, Jagow to Bethmann-Hollweg, 22 July 1914, p. 121.
39   ibid., No. 116, Bethmann-Hollweg to the Foreign Office, 22 July 1914, p. 122.
40   ibid., No. 174 "Aufzeichnung . . . Zimmermann," 25 July 1914, p. 169, and No. 175, Admiralty Staff to Jagow, 24 July 1914, p. 170.
41   ibid., No. 231, Wilhelm to the Foreign Office, 26 July 1914, pp. 204–5.
42   ibid., No. 255, Admiralty Staff to the Secretary of State of the Foreign Office, 27 July 1914, p. 222.
43   Walter Görlitz (ed.), *Regierte der Kaiser? Kriegstagebücher, Aufzeichnungen und Briefe des Chefs des Marinekabinetts Admiral Georg Alexander von Müller, 1914–18* (Göttingen, 1965), p. 33. BA-MA, N 159/4, p. 253.
44   BA-MA, F 2041, PG 65977, Pohl, "Denkschrift über den O-Plan bei einem Krieg Dreibund gegen Zweibund," 24 July 1914. See also Conrad, *Aus meiner Dienstzeit*, Vol. 4, for the report of the Austro-Hungarian naval attaché in Berlin, pp. 277 ff.
45   Berghahn and Deist, "Dokumente," No. 10, "Aufzeichnung . . . Behncke," 20 July 1914. I have used the original in BA-MA, F 7583/12, Nachlass Behncke.
46   Berghahn and Deist, "Dokumente," No. 11, Hopmann to Tirpitz, 21 July 1914, p. 56.
47   ibid., No. 12, Hopmann to Tirpitz, 22 July 1914, p. 57.
48   ibid., pp. 57–8.
49   Geiss, *Julikrise*, Vol. II, No. 1015 (*b*) Pohl to Jagow, 1 August 1914, p. 572.
50   Conrad, *Aus meiner Dienstzeit*, Vol. 4, pp. 277 ff.
51   BA-MA, F 7585/12, n.d.
52   Müller, *Regierte der Kaiser?*, p. 37, and DD, II, No. 407, Wilhelm's final comment to Bethmann-Hollweg to Wilhelm, 30 July 1914, p. 125; BA-MA, N 159/4, p. 256.
53   Tirpitz, *Ohnmachtspolitik*, pp. 5, 8.
54   Hopmann, *Das Logbuch*, p. 393.
55   Tirpitz, *Erinnerungen*, p. 129.

56  Quoted in Klein, *Deutschland*, p. 278.
57  DD, II, No. 342, Bethmann-Hollweg to Pourtalès, 29 July 1914, p. 55.
58  ibid., II, No. 349, Moltke to Bethmann-Hollweg, 29 July 1914, "Zur Beurteilung der politischen Lage," pp. 60–2. According to Albertini, *Origins*, Vol. 2, p. 488, the memorandum was drafted on the previous day.
59  Geiss, *Julikrise*, No. 512, p. 118.
60  Klein, *Deutschland*, p. 253.
61  DD, II, No. 399, Wilhelm's marginal comment to Bethmann-Hollweg to Wilhelm, 29 July 1914, pp. 116–17.
62  ibid., No. 395, Bethmann-Hollweg to Tschirschky, 30 July 1914, pp. 113–14.
63  Conrad, *Aus meiner Dienstzeit*, Vol. 4, p. 152–3.
64  Müller, *Regierte der Kaiser?*, p. 40; BA-MA, 159/4, p. 265.
65  Klein, *Deutschland*, p. 303.
66  ibid.
67  Fischer, *Krieg*, pp. 319–20.
68  Müller, *Regierte der Kaiser?*, p. 39.

# Bibliographical Note

I have decided not to provide a full bibliography. My sources should be obvious from the notes at the end of each chapter. I have none the less provided fuller information about archival sources, but have refrained from mentioning every file that I consulted. The archives of the German Democratic Republic have not been used since I have twice been refused access to them. As for published sources and secondary literature, I have listed only those works that were most important and most relevant to my central theme. I have, however, referred readers to the bibliographies of two excellent recent books for older literature.

My most important sources have been the holdings of the Bundesarchiv-Militärarchiv in Freiburg/Breisgau. Principal sources for naval operational planning were the files of the Admiralität (until 1889), the Oberkommando (until 1899), and the Admiralstab der Marine (from 1899 to 1914).

A summary of the work of the Oberkommando and Admiralstab appears in the reports that these agencies rendered to the Emperor:

Oberkommando   Acta betreffend Immediatvorträge, F 2023–24, PG 65986–92

Admiralstab      Acta betreffend Immediatvorträge, F 2015–2021, PG 65954–73, covering the period March 1899 to December 1910; I.3–8, Vols 21 and 22, covering the material from January 1911 to December 1912, and PG 65976–77, extending to December 1914.

For the detailed planning of operations, the following files of the Admiralität, Oberkommando, and Admiralstab have been particularly useful:

F 5244     Oberkommando der Marine, Acta betr. Kriegführung in der Ostsee, III, 2.–7., Vol. 1.

F 5551     Admiralstab der Marine, Acta betr. England. Flottenmanöver 1907–13, II–E7, Bd 1–6.

F 5563     Oberkommando der Marine—Admiralstab der Marine—II, 1.–5., Bd 1, Friedensakten betr. See-Kriegsspiele.

F 5586     Admiralstab der Marine, Acta betr. Operationspläne gegen England, Ostsee, III, 1. 0. 10., Bd 1–2.

F 5587     Oberkommando der Marine (Admiralstab der Marine), Acta betr. Operationspläne gegen England, III, 1.–10., Vol. 1; Acta betr. Operationspläne gegen England-Nordsee, III, 1. N. 10., Bd 1–6.

F 5588     Admiralstab der Marine, Acta betr. Operations-Arbeiten gegen England. Vorarbeiten und veraltete Ausarbeitungen pp. III, 1.–10a., Bd 1–2.

F 5589     Admiralstab der Marine, Acta betr. Material zum O.P., III, 1.–10b., Bd 1–4.

F 5592     Oberkommando der Marine (Admiralstab der Marine), Friedensakten
           betr. Operationspläne gegen Russland, III, 2.–1., Vols 1–4.
F 5593     Acta A.S. Dec. II. Betreffend Russland III, 2.–2., Bd. 1–3.
F 5595     Admiralstab der Marine, Acta betr. den Mobilmachungsfall, III,
           2.–16b., Bd 1.
F 5596–7   Oberkommando der Marine (Admiralstab der Marine), Operations-
           pläne gegen Frankreich, III, 3.–1., Vols 1–7.
F 5598     Nebenakten zu Oberkommando der Marine (Admiralstab der
           Marine), Operationspläne gegen Frankreich (in Europa), III, 3.–1.,
           Bd 1–3; III, 3.–1a., Bd 1.
F 5599     Admiralstab der Marine, Acta betr. Admiralstabsreisen in westl.
           Kriegsschauplatz, III, 3.–4., Bd 1; III, 3.–5., Bd 1.
F 5600     Oberkommando der Marine (Admiralstab der Marine), Angriffspläne
           gegen Holland und Belgien, III, 3.–18., Vols 1–2.
           Acta betreffend Nebenoperationen. Westlicher Kriegsschauplatz, III,
           3.–20., Vol. 1.
           Acta betreffend Allgemeine Operationen, Dreibundmächte, III,
           3.–24., Vols 1–3.
F 5601     Admiralstab der Marine, Acta betr. Handakten des Dez. A IV für
           den Krieg gegen England, III, 3–25a., Bd 1.
F 5666     Admiralstab der Marine, Acta betreffend Admiralstabreisen
           (Allgemeines)
           III, 1.–1., Bd 4.
           III, 1.–2., Bd 3.
           III, 1.–3., Bd 3.
           III, 1.–4., Bd 2.
           III, 1.–1., z. Acta betr. Admiralstabsreisen, Bd 1.
F 5171–72  Admiralstab der Marine. O-Angelegenheiten. Allgemeines, III,
           1.–9b., Bd 3–9.
F 5174b    Oberkommando der Marine (Admiralstab der Marine), Acta betr.
           Vorarbeiten zu den Operationsplänen gegen die Vereinigten Staaten
           von Nordamerika, III, 1.–16., Vols 1–4.

This is difficult material to use; most of it is handwritten, often corrected by
someone else who in many cases cannot be identified. The authorship of documents
and comments is at times impossible to determine as is the identity of the heads of
individual sections (*Dezernate*) involved in operational planning.

    Although operations outside of European waters, other than the United States
of America from 1899 to 1906, served only a secondary purpose for the German
navy and have, correspondingly, been handled briefly in this book, scholars wishing
to examine them further should study in greater detail the following files:

Oberkommando-Admiralstab:
F 5161–5   III, 1.–3b., Vols 1–6.
           III, 1.–3c., Vols 1–7.
           III, 1.–3d., Vols 1–3.
           III, 1.–3e., Vols 1–2.
           III, 1.–3f., Vols 1–5.
           III, 1.–3h., Vol. 1.
F 5167     III, 1.–5a., Vol. 1.
F 5170–2   III, 1.–9b., Vols 1–9.
F 5491     I, 3.–20., Vols 1–4.

For operations abroad, the following files of the Imperial Naval Office are also useful:

F 6158    Reichsmarine-Amt, Acta betr. Mobilmachung der Auslands-Schiffe, XVII, 1. 1. 28, Vols 1–4.
F 6159    Reichsmarine-Amt. Allgemeines Marinedepartment. Mobilmachung der Auslandsschiffe, Hierzu ganz geheime Akten, XVII, 1. 1. 28, Heft 1–3.

For the building program of the Imperial Naval Office, I have used most of the naval files utilized by Volker R. Berghahn's important book *Der Tirpitz-Plan: Genesis und Verfall einer innenpolitischen Krisenstrategie unter Wilhelm II* (Düsseldorf, 1971). Into particular consideration would come:

F 2026    Kaiserliche Admiralität, Acta betreffend Correspondenzen allgemeien politischen Inhalts, PG 65998–9.
F 2026–8    Reichsmarine-Amt, Zentralabteilung Akten: Politische Angelegenheiten. Beiakten Archiv der Marine, PG 66000–7.
F 2031–46    Reichsmarine-Amt, PG 66016–88, are of particular importance for the building program.
F 2050    Reichsmarine-Amt, PG 66102–7 are also important for naval construction.

Other particularly important files of the Imperial Naval Office are:

F 2051    PG 61108–13.
F 2235–6    PG 94606–10 include newspaper clippings with Wilhelm II's marginal comments.
F 2316    PG 64453–4 concern themselves specifically with budgetary considerations of the Naval Office.
F 2321    PG 64471–3 deal with the naval bills of 1905–6, 1907–8, and 1912.
F 2338    PG 64535–6 concern themselves with naval attachés.
F 2339    PG 64542–3 concern the Russian navy.
F 2340    PG 64545–6 concern the British navy.
F 2347    PG 64590 and
F 2378    PG 64737 deal with the immediate origins of the war of 1914.
F 3131    I, 1. 1.–5., Vols 4–10, include the reports of the Central Department to the Emperor (*Immediatvorträge*).
F 3159    II, 1. 1.–1b., Vols 1–5, contain the correspondence of the Central Department of the Naval Office with the Secretary of State.
F 3181–3    III, 1. 2.–24., Vols 22–38, include the documents of the Central Department of the Naval Office concerning naval budgets from 1897 to 1914, as do
F 3185–7    III, 1. 2.–27., Vols 1–14, and III, 1. 2.–28., Vols 1–3.
F 3187    Adhib. 1 zu III, 1. 5.–1.RM/1/1846
    Adhib. 2 zu III, 1. 5.–1.RM/1/1847
    Adhib. 3 zu III, 1. 5.–1.RM/1/1848 and
    Adhib. 18, III, 1. 5.–1, Vol. 1, also include material about fleet construction.

The most valuable documents of the Imperial Naval Cabinet (Kaiserliches Marinekabinett) involving various policy and personnel issues appear in

F 3301–4    PG 66700–18 and
F 3443–46   PG 67468–94

Its documents concerning military–political matters and foreign fleets appear in

F 3450–1    PG 67517–21

The following private papers in the Bundesarchiv-Militärarchiv have been used. They are listed in descending order of importance:

N 253       Nachlass Tirpitz
N 168       Nachlass Büchsel
N 170       Nachlass Senden-Bibran
N 255       Nachlass Diederichs
F 7621–3    Nachlass Heeringen
N 170       Nachlass Capelle
N 159       Nachlass Müller
F 7580–5    Nachlass Behncke
F 7630–1    Nachlass Dähnhardt
N 58        Nachlass Schulenburg-Tressow
N 43        Nachlass Schlieffen
N 46        Nachlass Groener
N 78        Nachlass Moltke the Younger
N 30        Nachlass Beseler
N 32        Nachlass Deines
N 284       Nachlass Taegert
N 239       Nachlass Levetzow
N 584       Nachlass Knorr

As indicated in the preface and evident in the notes, I have made extensive use of the holdings of the German Foreign Office (Politisches Archiv des Auswärtigen Amts) in Bonn. Some of its holdings have been used in the microfilm projects U.C.I, U.C.II, and U.M. The following files have been of particular value:

Deutschland    102, Geh.
               121, No. 3.
               121, No. 3., Geh.
               121, No. 12.
               121, No. 31., Geh.
               127.
               128.
               128, Geh.
               128, No. 2.
               129, Geh.
               137.
               138.
               143, Geh.
               143, No. 1.
Bulgarien      20.
England        71b.
               71b, Geh.
               78.
               78, Secr.

| | |
|---|---|
| | 78, Secretissima. |
| | 83. |
| | 92, No. 3. |
| Frankreich | 87. |
| | 95. |
| | 102. |
| | 103. |
| | 105, No. 1. |
| | 116. |
| | 116, Geh. |
| | 116, No. 1. |
| | 118. |
| Italien | 68. |
| | 70. |
| | 72. |
| | 72a. |
| | 82, Geh. |
| | 86, Secr. |
| | 88. |
| | 95. |
| Marocco | 4. |
| Österreich | 70. |
| | 73. |
| | 88. |
| | 91. |
| | 91, No. 2. |
| | 92, No. 4. |
| | 95. |
| | 95, Geh. |
| Orientalia | |
| Generalia | 5. |
| | 5, Geh. |
| Russland | 72. |
| | 72, Geh. |
| | 72b. |
| | 91. |
| | 93. |
| | 98. |
| | 99. |
| | 131. |
| | 131, Geh. |

For both naval and foreign policy, the reports of the Bavarian, Baden and Württemberg ministers and of the Bavarian military attaché in Berlin have been of some use. The Bavarian ministerial reports are located in two series in the Bayerisches Hauptstaatsarchiv, Abteilung II, Geheimes Staatsarchiv:

MA (Ministerialabgabe) III, which includes the reports received in Munich, and the
Bayerische Gesandschaft Berlin, which includes the original drafts of the reports.

The reports of the Bavarian military attaché are in Bayerisches Hauptstaatsarchiv, Abteilung IV, Kriegsarchiv,

M.Kr. 41–3.

The reports of the Badenese ministers appear in the Badisches Generallandes-archiv, Karlsruhe, in two series as well:

Abteilung 49, Haus-und Staatsarchiv, Gesandschaftsakten, which includes the originals, and
Abteilung 233, Staatsministerium: Gesandschaftsberichte aus Berlin, the reports that reached Karlsruhe.

The Hauptarchiv, Stuttgart

Württembergisches Ministerium der Auswärtigen Angelegenheiten, Gesandschaft Berlin, has only one set of reports.

The Bundesarchiv, Koblenz, was utilized largely for several private papers. In descending order of importance, the following were most useful

Nachlass Fürst von Bülow
Nachlass Hohenlohe
Nachlass Oswald von Richthofen
Nachlass (Correspondez) Eulenburg
Kleine Erwerbungen 517.–/: Nachlass Oettingen
Nachlass Boetticher
Nachlass Thimme

The Bismarck-Archiv in Friedrichsruh was of considerable use for the first part of the book.

The American Historical Association Microfilm Project II includes

Nachlass Eisendecher.

Several published papers and documentary collections have been used. Alfred von Tirpitz's *Erinnerungen* (Leipzig, 1919) and his *Politische Dokumente, Der Aufbau der deutschen Weltmacht* (Stuttgart, 1924) have much information even if they fall short of telling "the whole truth and nothing but the truth." Georg Alexander von Müller's *Der Kaiser,* ed. Walter Görlitz (Göttingen, 1965), falls somewhat short of his *Nachlass* in Freiburg, but is still a basically reliable source. Bernhard von Bülow's *Denkwürdigkeiten,* especially Volumes 1 and 2 (Berlin, 1930), and his *Deutsche Politik* (Berlin, 1917) provide more accurate information than was earlier assumed. *The Grosse Politik der Europäischen Kabinette, 1871–1914: Sammlung der Diplomatischen Akten des Auswärtigen Amtes.* Im Auftrage des Auswärtigen Amtes herausgegeben von Johannes Lepsius, Albrecht Mendelssohn-Bartholdy und Friedrich Thimme, 40 volumes in 54 (Berlin, 1924–7), has been invaluable for the treatment of foreign policy and, although obviously intended to serve a political purpose, has struck me as less tendentious than other recent historians. Although some material incriminating Germany is omitted, much equally damaging material is included. For the immediate origins of the war, the so-called Kautsky Documents and Imanuel Geiss's documentary collections are indispensable. The documentary publications of John C. G. Röhl about the "war council" of 8 December 1912 and Volker R. Berghahn and Wilhelm Deist's "Kaiserliche Marine und Kriegsausbruch 1914: Neue Dokumente zur Juli-Krise,"

*Militärgeschichtliche Mitteilungen,* no. 1 (1970), have been utilized more fully because of their fuller inclusion of the navy. *The Holstein Papers,* ed. Norman Rich and M. H. Fisher, particularly Volumes 3 and 4 (Cambridge, 1961, 1963), are invaluable both for diplomacy and the debate about the navy. They are complemented by *Botschafter Paul von Hatzfeldt: Nachgelassene Papiere, 1832–1901,* ed. G. Ebel (Boppard, 1976). *Kiderlen-Wächter der Staatsmann und Mensch: Briefwechsel und Nachlass,* ed. Ernst Jäckh (Stuttgart, 1925), particularly Volume 2, casts light on criticism of the navy by the German political leadership and on diplomacy in general, but is not entirely reliable. Chlodwig zu Hohenlohe's *Denkwürdigkeiten der Reichskanzlerzeit* (the third volume of his memoirs), ed. Karl-Alexander von Müller (Stuttgart, 1931), contains the most important parts of his *Nachlass* in Koblenz for the period of his chancellorship. In addition to Tirpitz's and Müller's publications, there are several published memoirs of German naval officers. For my purposes the most important are Albert Hopmann, *Das Logbuch eines deutschen Seeoffiziers* (Berlin, 1924), and Reinhard Scheer, *Vom Segelschiff zum U-Boot* (Leipzig, 1925). Wilhelm Widenmann's *Marine-Attaché an der kaiserlich-deutschen Botschaft in London, 1907–1912* (Göttingen, 1952) is a biased but still useful account of the Anglo-German naval race.

As for secondary materials, my comments will be few. For German naval and socio-political history before *c.*1970, I refer the reader to the full bibliography of Volker R. Berghahn's *Der Tirpitz-Plan: Genesis und Verfall einer innenpolitischen Krisenstrategie unter Wilhelm II* (Düsseldorf, 1971), an important book about which more will be said later. As for material on German foreign policy, particularly relations with Britain, as well as internal developments in the broadest sense before *c.*1979, I invite the reader to consult the first-rate bibliography of Paul M. Kennedy's brilliant book, *The Rise of Anglo-German Antagonism, 1860–1914* (London, 1980). As for the secondary studies that have been most useful to me, I impose on him the task of consulting my notes.

Works involving the operational planning of the German navy are limited. Only two books deal with the subject: Walther Hubatsch's *Der Admiralstab und die obersten Marinebehörden in Deutschland, 1848–1945* (Frankfurt, 1958) and Carl-Axel Gemzell's *Organization, Conflict, and Innovation: A Study in German Naval Strategic Planning, 1888–1940* (Lund, 1973). Both devote only limited space to the period I am considering; the former has taken a rather narrow approach, is very selective in the use of his sources, and rather uncritical; the latter complicates his treatment through the use of sociological concepts. The best work has been done by Paul M. Kennedy in three articles: "The development of German naval operations plans against England, 1896–1914," *English Historical Review,* vol. 89, no. 350 (January 1974); "Tirpitz, England, and the Second Navy Law of 1900: a strategical critique," *Militärgeschichtliche Mitteilungen,* no. 2 (1970); and "Maritime Strategieprobleme der deutsch-englischen Flottenrivalität," in H. Schottelius and W. Deist (eds), *Marine und Marinepolitik im kaiserlichen Deutschland, 1871–1914* (Düsseldorf, 1972), itself a useful collection of papers on the Imperial German Navy. Kennedy's concern is, however, almost entirely with German operational and strategic planning against Britain; the last two articles are more concerned with Tirpitz in the Reichsmarineamt than with the Oberkommando or Admiralstab, with whom lay the responsibility for actual planning. Three articles by Jonathan Steinberg also involve German naval operational planning: "A German plan for the invasion of Holland and Belgium, 1897," in *Historical Journal,* vol. 6, no. 1 (1963); "The Copenhagen complex," in *Journal of Contemporary History,* vol. 1, no. 3 (1966); and "Germany and the Russo-Japanese War," *American Historical Review,* vol. 75, no. 7 (December 1970). They are very good but, of necessity, fragmentary. Holger H. Herwig and David F. Trask in their

"Naval operations plans between Germany and the United States of America, 1898–1913: a study of strategic planning in the Age of Imperialism," first published in the *Militärgeschichtliche Mitteilungen,* no. 2 (1970), have an article which I have followed very closely. Several of these papers have been republished in Paul M. Kennedy's valuable anthology on operational planning, *The War Plans of the Great Powers, 1880–1914* (London, 1979), the bibliography of which I also draw to the reader's attention. Army–navy relations are discussed in Friedrich-Christian Stahl's work, mentioned in the bibliography of Kennedy's anthology. For the relationship between the military and the civilian leadership, Gerhardt Ritter's *Staatskunst und Kriegshandwerk,* Vols 1–2 (2nd edn, Munich, 1959–60), and *Der Schlieffen-Plan* (Munich, 1956), now also available in English, are indispensable. Recent works on the army and army planning are Berndt F. Schulte's *Die deutsche Armee, 1900–1914: Zwischen Beharren und Verändern* (Düsseldorf, 1977) and *Vor dem Kriegsausbruch 1914: Deutschland, die Türkei und der Balkan* (Düsseldorf, 1980). Both use new source materials, although the former lacks focus and the latter suffers from poor organization. Dennis E. Showalter's "The eastern front and German military planning, 1871–1914: some observations," in *East European Quarterly,* vol. 15, no. 2 (June 1981), is a perceptive synthesis of army planning against Russia. Regarding the Prusso-German army the old Reichsarchiv publication *Kriegsrüstung und Kriegswirtschaft,* Vol. 1, *Die militärische, wirtschaftliche und finanzielle Rüstung Deutschlands von der Reichsgründung bis zum Ausbruch des Weltkrieges* and *Anlageband* (Berlin, 1930), are still a mine of information.

As for naval construction, Berghahn's *Der Tirpitz-Plan* constitutes a milestone, although it does not extend beyond 1908 and is subject to criticism because of its "Kehrite" interpretation. It is based on accurate use of excellent sources. Berghahn's other work in this area, mentioned in my notes and in the bibliography of Kennedy's *Antagonism,* also deserves serious attention. Geoff Eley in his *Reshaping of the German Right: Radical Nationalism and Political Change after Bismarck* (New Haven, Conn., 1980), as well as in his other publications, has challenged the whole "Kehrite" interpretation of German history, as have a number of other British historians: see Wolfgang Mock's review article in *Historische Zeitschrift,* Bd 232, Heft 2 (April 1981). Wilhelm Deist's *Flottenpolitik und Flottenpropaganda* (Stuttgart, 1976) extends beyond the study of propaganda and is also based on excellent sources. Holger H. Herwig has provided a very useful book, *The German Naval Officer Corps: A Social and Political History, 1890–1918* (London, 1973), on a theme which he has also developed in other publications, and a work on selected aspects of the Kaiser's navy, *"Luxury" Fleet: The Imperial Germany Navy, 1888–1918* (London, 1980), which is particularly useful for its tables. P. Kelly's unpublished doctoral dissertation, "The naval policy of Imperial Germany, 1900–1914", Georgetown University, 1970, is a straightforward account, based on new material, and partly fills the gap between 1908 and the outbreak of World War I. Of the older works Hans Hallmann's *Der Weg zum deutschen Schlachtflottenbau* (Stuttgart, 1933) is still very useful in spite of being somewhat of an apology for Tirpitz. Jonathan Steinberg's *Yesterday's Deterrent* (London, 1965) was the first account to use critically the mass of new material that became available after World War II. The publication of the *Militärgeschichtliches Forschungsamt* by Wolfgang Petter and others, *Handbuch zur deutschen Militärgeschichte,* Bd 7, *Deutsche Marinegeschichte der Neuzeit* (Munich, 1977), is a very good general survey. Tirpitz still lacks a good biography. Michael Salwski's recent *Tirpitz: Aufstieg—Macht—Scheitern* (Göttingen, 1979) is general, uncritical, and does not use significant unpublished material. Perhaps Tirpitz must remain a nonperson: in spite of excellent documentation, I would hesitate to attempt his biography.

There are two fine works in diplomatic history relevant to this topic which have appeared since the appearance of Kennedy's *Antagonism* which I want to draw to the reader's attention: Emily Oncken's *Panthersprung nach Agadir: Die deutsche Politik während der Zweiten Marokkokrise 1911* (Düsseldorf, 1981), and Konrad Canis's *Bismarck und Waldersee. Die aussenpolitischen Krisenerscheinungen und das Verhalten des Generalstabes 1882 bis 1890* (Berlin, 1980). I also want to remind the reader of the appearance of two new relevant biographical works: Lothar Gall's *Bismarck: der weisse Revolutionär* (Frankfurt, 1980), the most perceptive study of the Iron Chancellor available, and John C. G. Röhl and Nicolaus Sombart (eds), *Kaiser Wilhelm II: New Interpretations* (Cambridge, 1982), which opens new vistas to the understanding of that complicated monarch.

# Index

Prepared by Margaret MacVean